Cracking the AP:
Physics Exam

1999-2000 Edition

THE PRINCETON REVIEW

Cracking the AP:
Physics Exam

BY STEVEN A. LEDUC

1999-2000 EDITION
RANDOM HOUSE, INC.
NEW YORK

Princeton Review Publishing, L.L.C.
2315 Broadway
New York, NY 10024
E-mail: info@review.com

ISBN: 0-375-75289-7
ISSN: 1521-9453

AP is a registered trademark of Educational Testing Service.

Editor: Rachel Warren
Production Editor: Kristen Azzara
Production Coordinator: Robert McCormack

Manufactured in the United States of America on partially recycled paper.

9 8 7 6 5 4 3 2

ACKNOWLEDGMENTS

My thanks and appreciation to Evan Schnittman, John Katzman, Steve Quattrociocchi, Paul Maniscalco, Ian Stewart, and Suellen Glasser for making me feel at home, Rachel Warren for her support and fantastic editing, and to Greta Englert, Scott Harris, Neil McMahon, Robert McCormack, Evelin Sanchez O'Hara, and Chris Thomas for their beautiful production work.

Special thanks to Paul Kanarek for his friendship, counsel, and encouragement.

DEDICATION

This work is dedicated to my great aunt,
Norma Perron Lamb Piette.

CONTENTS

Topics that appear only on the B exam are denoted by [B].
Topics that appear only on the C exam are denoted by [C].
All other topics are on both exams.

INTRODUCTION

The AP (Advanced Placement) Examinations are given in May of each year and offer students the opportunity to earn advanced placement or college credit for work they've done in high school or independently. Exams are available in a variety of subjects, but since you picked up this book, you're interested in the AP Physics Exam.

There are two versions of the AP Physics Exam; they're called Physics B and Physics C. The Physics B Exam covers a wide range of topics, but the questions are not too mathematically sophisticated. The Physics C Exam covers a smaller range of topics, but the questions are more challenging and calculus is used widely. The Physics C Exam is actually composed of two separate exams: one in Mechanics and one in Electricity and Magnetism (E & M). You can take just the Mechanics, just the E & M, or both. Separate scores are reported for the Mechanics and E & M sections.

Whether you decide to take Physics B or Physics C, the exam will contain two sections, a multiple-choice section and a free response section. Questions in the multiple-choice section are each followed by five possible responses (only one of which is correct), and your job, of course, is to choose the right answer. Each right answer is worth 1 point, but 1/4 of a point is subtracted for each wrong answer. Therefore, there's little to be gained by randomly guessing on a question you know nothing about, but if you're able to eliminate one or more answer choices, then it's a good strategy to guess among the remaining choices. There are 70 multiple-choice questions on Physics B and the same total number on the full Physics C exam, and the time limit is 90 minutes. You may *not* use a calculator on the multiple-choice section.

The free response section consists of about 6 multi-part questions, which require you to actually write out your solutions, showing your work. The total amount of time for this section is 90 minutes, so you have an average of 15 minutes per question. Unlike the multiple-choice section, which is scored by computer, the free response section is graded by hand by high school and college teachers. They have guidelines for awarding partial credit, so you don't need to correctly answer every part to get points. You are allowed to use a calculator (programmable or graphing calculators are OK, but ones with a typewriter-style keyboard are not) on the free-response section, and a table of equations is provided for your use on this section. The two sections—multiple-choice and free response—are weighed equally, so each is worth 50% of your grade.

Grades on the AP Exam are reported as a number: either 1, 2, 3, 4, or 5. The descriptions for each of these five numerical scores are as follows:

AP Exam Grade	Description
5	Extremely well qualified
4	Well qualified
3	Qualified
2	Possibly qualified
1	No recommendation

Colleges are generally looking for a 4 or 5, but some may grant credit for a 3. How well do you have to do to earn such a grade? Each test is curved, and specific cut-offs for each grade vary a little from year to year, but here's a rough idea of how many points you must earn—as a percentage of the maximum possible raw score—to achieve each of the grades 2 through 5:

AP Exam Grade	Percentage Needed
5	≥ 75%
4	≥ 60%
3	≥ 45%
2	≥ 35%

So, what's on the exams and how do you prepare for them? Here's a listing of the major topics covered on the Physics B and C Exams, along with an approximate percentage of the questions in each topic (what the College Board calls the *percentage goal*):

Topic	Physics B	Physics C
Mechanics	35%	50%
Kinematics	7%	9%
Newton's Laws	9%	10%
Work, Energy, and Power	5%	7%
Linear Momentum	4%	6%
Circular Motion and Rotation	4%	9%
Oscillations and Gravitation	6%	9%
Thermal Physics	10%	
Temperature and Heat	3%	
Kinetic theory and Thermodynamics	7%	
Electricity and Magnetism	25%	50%
Electrostatics	5%	15%
Conductors and Capacitors	4%	7%
Electric Circuits	7%	10%
Magnetostatics	4%	10%
Electromagnetism	5%	8%
Waves	5%	
Optics	10%	
Atomic and Nuclear Physics	15%	

Naturally, it's important to be familiar with the topics—to understand the basics of the theory, to know the definitions of the fundamental quantities, and to recognize and be able to use the equations. Then, you must acquire practice at applying what you've learned to answering questions like you'll see on the Exam. This book is designed to review all of the content areas covered on the Exam, illustrated by hundreds of examples. Also, each chapter (except the first) is followed by sample multiple-choice and free-response questions, and perhaps even more importantly, *answers and explanations are provided for every example and question in this book.* You'll learn as much—if not more—from actively reading the solutions as you will from reading the text and examples. Also, a full-length practice test is provided for Physics B and another one for Physics C. Again, a solution is provided for every question in both of these sample exams. The difficulty level of the examples and questions in this book is at or slightly above AP level, so if you have the time and motivation to attack these questions and learn from the solutions, you should feel confident that you can do your very best on the real thing.

Here are a few simple strategies: On the multiple-choice section, do not linger over any one question. Go through the exam and answer the questions on the topics you know well, leaving the tough ones for later when you make another pass through the section. All the questions are worth the same amount, so you don't want to run out of time and not get to questions you could have answered because you spent too much time agonizing over a few complex questions. No one is expected to answer all of them, so maximize the number you get right.

On the free-response section, be sure to show the graders what you're thinking. Write clearly—that is *so* important—and show your steps. If you make a mistake in one part and carry an incorrect result to a later part of the question, you can still earn valuable points if your method is correct. But the graders can't give you credit for work they can't follow or can't read. And, where appropriate, be sure to include units on your final answers.

Sample test questions are also available directly from The College Board. You can request information about ordering such materials by contacting them by mail, phone, or on the web:

Advanced Placement Program
PO Box 6670
Princeton, NJ 08541-6670
(609) 771-7243
http://www.collegeboard.org/ap/html/indx001.html

You can also shop in the College Board's online store at

http://cbweb2.collegeboard.org/shopping

I wish you all the best as you study for the AP Physics Exam. Good luck!

1
VECTORS

INTRODUCTION

Vectors will show up all over the place in our study of physics. Some physical quantities that are represented as vectors are displacement, velocity, acceleration, force, momentum, and electric and magnetic fields. Since vectors play such a recurring role, it's important to become comfortable working with them; the purpose of this chapter is to provide you with a mastery of the fundamental vector algebra we'll use in subsequent chapters. For now, we'll restrict our study to two-dimensional vectors (that is, ones that lie flat in a plane).

DEFINITION

A **vector** is a quantity that involves both magnitude and direction and obeys the **commutative law for addition,** which we'll explain in a moment. A quantity that does not involve direction is a **scalar**. For example, the quantity *55 miles per hour* is a scalar, while the quantity *55 miles per hour, to the north* is a vector. Other examples of scalars include mass, work, energy, power, temperature, and electric charge.

Vectors can be denoted in several ways, including:

$$\mathbf{A}, \mathit{A}, \vec{A}, \bar{A}$$

In textbooks, you'll usually see one of the first two, but when it's handwritten, you'll see one of the last two.

Displacement (which is net distance traveled plus direction) is the prototypical example of a vector:

$$\underbrace{\mathbf{A}}_{\text{displacement}} = \underbrace{4 \text{ miles}}_{\text{magnitude}} \underbrace{\text{to the north}}_{\text{direction}}$$

When we say that vectors obey the commutative law for addition, we mean that if we have two vectors of the same type, for example, another displacement,

$$\mathbf{B} = \underbrace{3 \text{ miles}}_{\text{magnitude}} \underbrace{\text{to the east}}_{\text{direction}}$$

then $\mathbf{A} + \mathbf{B}$ must equal $\mathbf{B} + \mathbf{A}$. The vector sum $\mathbf{A} + \mathbf{B}$ means *the vector A followed by B*, while the vector sum $\mathbf{B} + \mathbf{A}$ means *the vector B followed by A*. That these two sums are indeed identical is shown in the following figure:

Two vectors are equal if they have the same magnitude and the same direction.

VECTOR ADDITION (GEOMETRIC)

The figure above illustrates how vectors are added to each other geometrically. Place the tail (the initial point) of one vector at the tip of the other vector, then connect the exposed tail to the exposed tip. The vector formed is the sum of the first two. This is called the "tip-to-tail" method of vector addition.

Example 1.1   Add the following two vectors:

Solution. Place the tail of **B** at the tip of **A** and connect them:

SCALAR MULTIPLICATION

A vector can be multiplied by a scalar (that is, by a number), and the result is a vector. If the original vector is **A** and the scalar is k, then the scalar multiple $k\mathbf{A}$ is as follows:

$$\text{magnitude of } k\mathbf{A} = |k| \times (\text{magnitude of } \mathbf{A})$$

$$\text{direction of } k\mathbf{A} = \begin{cases} \text{the same as } \mathbf{A} \text{ if } k \text{ is positive} \\ \text{the opposite of } \mathbf{A} \text{ if } k \text{ is negative} \end{cases}$$

Example 1.2 Sketch the scalar multiples $2\mathbf{A}$, $\frac{1}{2}\mathbf{A}$, $-\mathbf{A}$, and $-3\mathbf{A}$ of the vector **A**:

Solution.

VECTOR SUBTRACTION (GEOMETRIC)

To subtract one vector from another, for example, to get **A** – **B**, simply form the vector –**B**, which is the scalar multiple (–1)**B**, and add it to **A**:

$$\mathbf{A} - \mathbf{B} = \mathbf{A} + (-\mathbf{B})$$

Example 1.3 For the two vectors **A** and **B**, find the vector **A** – **B**.

Solution. Flip **B** around—thereby forming –**B**—and add that vector to **A**:

STANDARD BASIS VECTORS

Two-dimensional vectors, that is, vectors that lie flat in a plane, can be written as the sum of a horizontal vector and a vertical vector. For example, in the following diagram, the vector **A** is equal to the horizontal vector **B** plus the vertical vector **C**:

The horizontal vector is always considered a scalar multiple of what's called the **horizontal basis vector**, **i**, and the vertical vector is a scalar multiple of the **vertical basis vector**, **j**. Both of these special vectors have a magnitude of 1, and for this reason, they're called **unit** vectors. Unit vectors are often represented by placing a hat (caret) over the vector; for example, the unit vectors **i** and **j** are sometimes denoted $\hat{\imath}$ and $\hat{\jmath}$.

For instance, the vector **A** in the figure below is the sum of the horizontal vector **B** = $3\hat{i}$ and the vertical vector **C** = $4\hat{j}$.

The vectors **B** and **C** are called the **vector components** of **A**, and the scalar multiples of $\hat{i}$ and $\hat{j}$ which give **A**—in this case, 3 and 4—are called the **scalar components** of **A**. So vector **A** can be written as the sum $A_x\hat{i} + A_y\hat{j}$, where A_x and A_y are the scalar components of **A**. The component A_x is called the **horizontal** scalar component of **A**, and A_y is called the **vertical** scalar component of **A**.

VECTOR OPERATIONS USING COMPONENTS

The use of components makes the vector operations of addition, subtraction, and scalar multiplication pretty straightforward:

Vector addition: *Add the respective components*
$$\mathbf{A} + \mathbf{B} = (A_x + B_x)\hat{i} + (A_y + B_y)\hat{j}$$

Vector subtraction: *Subtract the respective components*
$$\mathbf{A} - \mathbf{B} = (A_x - B_x)\hat{i} + (A_y - B_y)\hat{j}$$

Scalar multiplication: *Multiply each component by k*
$$k\mathbf{A} = (kA_x)\hat{i} + (kA_y)\hat{j}$$

Example 1.4 If **A** = $2\hat{i} - 3\hat{j}$ and **B** = $-4\hat{i} + 2\hat{j}$, compute each of the following vectors: **A** + **B**, **A** − **B**, 2**A**, and **A** + 3**B**.

Solution. It's very helpful that the given vectors **A** and **B** are written explicitly in terms of the standard basis vectors $\hat{i}$ and $\hat{j}$:

$$\mathbf{A} + \mathbf{B} = (2 - 4)\hat{i} + (-3 + 2)\hat{j} = -2\hat{i} - \hat{j}$$

$$\mathbf{A} - \mathbf{B} = [2 - (-4)]\hat{i} + (-3 - 2)\hat{j} = 6\hat{i} - 5\hat{j}$$

$$2\mathbf{A} = 2(2)\hat{i} + 2(-3)\hat{j} = 4\hat{i} - 6\hat{j}$$

$$\mathbf{A} + 3\mathbf{B} = [2 + 3(-4)]\hat{i} + [-3 + 3(2)]\hat{j} = -10\hat{i} + 3\hat{j}$$

MAGNITUDE OF A VECTOR

The magnitude of a vector can be computed with the Pythagorean Theorem. The magnitude of vector **A** can be denoted in several ways: A or $|\mathbf{A}|$ or $\|\mathbf{A}\|$. In terms of its components, the magnitude of $\mathbf{A} = A_x\hat{\mathbf{i}} + A_y\hat{\mathbf{j}}$ is given by the equation

$$A = \sqrt{\left(A_x\right)^2 + \left(A_y\right)^2}$$

which is the formula for the length of the hypotenuse of a right triangle with sides of lengths A_x and A_y.

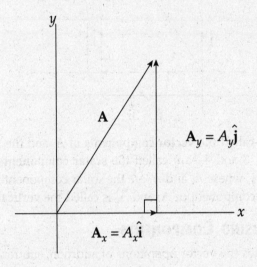

DIRECTION OF A VECTOR

The direction of a vector can be specified by the angle it makes with the positive x axis. You can sketch the vector and use its components (and an inverse trig function) to determine the angle. For example, if θ denotes the angle that the vector $\mathbf{A} = 3\hat{\mathbf{i}} + 4\hat{\mathbf{j}}$ makes with the $+x$ axis, then $\tan\theta = 4/3$, so $\theta = \tan^{-1}(4/3) = 53.1°$.

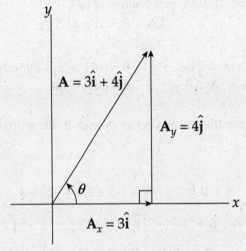

If **A** makes the angle θ with the +x axis, then its x- and y-components are $A \cos \theta$ and $A \sin \theta$, respectively (where A is the magnitude of **A**).

$$\mathbf{A} = \underbrace{\left(A\cos\theta\right)\hat{\mathbf{i}}}_{A_x} + \underbrace{\left(A\sin\theta\right)\hat{\mathbf{j}}}_{A_y}$$

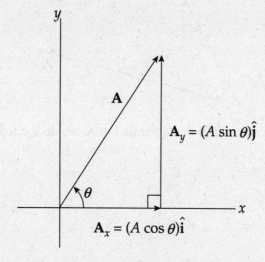

In general, any vector in the plane can be written in terms of two perpendicular component vectors. For example, vector **W** (shown below) is the sum of two component vectors whose magnitudes are $W \cos \theta$ and $W \sin \theta$:

THE DOT PRODUCT

A vector can be multiplied by a scalar to yield another vector, as you saw in Example 1.2. For instance, we can multiply the vector **A** by the scalar 2 to get the scalar multiple 2**A**. The product is a vector that has twice the magnitude and, since the scalar is positive, the same direction as **A**.

Additionally, we can form a scalar by multiplying two vectors. The product of the vectors in this case is called the **dot product** or the **scalar product**, since the result is a scalar. Several physical concepts (work, electric and magnetic flux) require that we multiply the magnitude of one vector by the magnitude of the component of the other vector that's parallel to the first. The dot product was invented specifically for this purpose.

Consider these two vectors, **A** and **B**:

In order to find the component of **B** that's parallel to **A**, we do the following:

As this figure shows, the component of **B** that's parallel to **A** has the magnitude $B \cos \theta$. So if we multiply the magnitude of **A** by the magnitude of the component of **B** that's parallel to **A**, we would form the product $A(B \cos \theta)$. This is the definition of the dot product of the vectors **A** and **B**:

$$\mathbf{A} \cdot \mathbf{B} = AB \cos \theta$$

where θ is the angle between **A** and **B**. Notice that the dot product of two vectors is a scalar.

The angle between the vectors is crucial to the value of the dot product. If $\theta = 0$, then the vectors are already parallel to each other, so we can simply multiply their magnitudes: $\mathbf{A} \cdot \mathbf{B} = AB$. If **A** and **B** are perpendicular, then there is no component of **B** that's parallel to **A** (or vice versa), so the dot product should be zero. And if θ is greater than 90°,

then the component of one that's *parallel* to the other is actually *antiparallel* (backwards), and this will give the dot product a negative value (because $\cos \theta < 0$ for $90° < \theta \leq 180°$).

The value of the dot product can, of course, also be figured out using the definition above ($AB \cos \theta$) if θ is known. If θ is not known, the dot product can be calculated from the components of **A** and **B** in this way:

$$\mathbf{A} \cdot \mathbf{B} = (A_x \hat{\mathbf{i}} + A_y \hat{\mathbf{j}}) \cdot (B_x \hat{\mathbf{i}} + B_y \hat{\mathbf{j}}) = A_x B_x + A_y B_y$$

This means that, to form the dot product, simply add the product of the scalar x components and the product of the scalar y components.

Example 1.5

(a) What is the dot product of the vectors $\hat{\mathbf{i}}$ and $\hat{\mathbf{j}}$?

(b) of $\hat{\mathbf{i}}$ and $\hat{\mathbf{i}}$?

Solution.

(a) Since $\hat{\mathbf{i}}$ and $\hat{\mathbf{j}}$ are perpendicular to each other ($\theta = 90°$), their dot product must be zero, because $\cos 90° = 0$. (In fact, unless **A** or **B** is already zero, it's also true that two vectors are perpendicular to each other when their dot product is zero.)

(b) Because $\hat{\mathbf{i}}$ and $\hat{\mathbf{i}}$ are parallel to each other, their dot product is just the product of the magnitudes, which is $1 \cdot 1 = 1$.

Example 1.6 If $\mathbf{A} = -2\hat{\mathbf{i}} + 4\hat{\mathbf{j}}$ and $\mathbf{B} = 6\hat{\mathbf{i}} + B_y \hat{\mathbf{j}}$, find the value of B_y such that the vectors **A** and **B** will be perpendicular to each other.

Solution. Two vectors are perpendicular to each other if their dot product is zero. The dot product of **A** and **B** can be determined as follows: Multiply the scalar x components, $(-2)(6) = -12$, multiply the scalar y comonents, $(4)(B_y)$, and add them: $-12 + 4B_y$. Setting this equal to 0, we see that B_y must equal 3.

THE CROSS PRODUCT

Some physical concepts (torque, angular momentum, magnetic force) require that we multiply the magnitude of one vector by the magnitude of the component of the other vector that's *perpendicular* to the first. The cross product was invented for this specific purpose.

Consider these two vectors, **A** and **B**:

In order to find the component of one of these vectors that's perpendicular to the other one, we do the following:

As this figure shows, the component of **B** that's perpendicular to **A** has magnitude $B \sin \theta$. Therefore, if we multiply the magnitude of **A** by the magnitude of the component of **B** that's perpendicular to **A**, we form the product $A(B \sin \theta)$. This is the definition for the magnitude of what's called the **cross product** of the vectors **A** and **B**, denoted $\mathbf{A} \times \mathbf{B}$:

$$|\mathbf{A} \times \mathbf{B}| = AB \sin \theta$$

where θ is the angle between **A** and **B** (such that $0° \leq \theta \leq 180°$).

The equation above gives the magnitude of the cross product. The cross product of two vectors is another vector that's always perpendicular to both **A** and **B**, with its direction determined by a procedure known as the right-hand rule. The direction of $\mathbf{A} \times \mathbf{B}$ is perpendicular to the plane that contains **A** and **B**, but this leads to an ambiguity, since there are two directions perpendicular to a plane (one on either side; they point in opposite directions). The following description resolves this ambiguity. Place the wrist of your right hand at the common initial point of **A** and **B**, with your fingers pointing along **A** in such a way that your palm faces **B** (so you can curl your fingers inward, toward **B**). Now your thumb points in the direction of $\mathbf{A} \times \mathbf{B}$. This is called the **right-hand rule**.

You know that the standard basis vectors $\hat{\mathbf{i}}$ and $\hat{\mathbf{j}}$ can be used to write any two-dimensional vector, but now that we have introduced the cross product, we need a third basis unit vector, to write three-dimensional vectors. This third unit vector is denoted $\hat{\mathbf{k}}$ and, like $\hat{\mathbf{i}}$ and $\hat{\mathbf{j}}$, it points along the direction of a coordinate axis. The vector $\hat{\mathbf{i}}$ is the unit vector that points along the x axis, $\hat{\mathbf{j}}$ along the y, and now $\hat{\mathbf{k}}$ along the z. The three basis vectors are mutually perpendicular:

The coordinate axes shown define a *right-handed* coordinate system, because the directions of the x, y, and z axes obey the right-hand rule. That is, $\hat{\mathbf{i}} \times \hat{\mathbf{j}}$ points in the direction of $\hat{\mathbf{k}}$. In fact, $\hat{\mathbf{i}} \times \hat{\mathbf{j}}$ actually equals $\hat{\mathbf{k}}$, since the magnitude of $\hat{\mathbf{i}} \times \hat{\mathbf{j}}$ is 1.

Unlike the dot product, the cross product is not commutative; $\mathbf{A} \times \mathbf{B}$ is not equal to $\mathbf{B} \times \mathbf{A}$. This is because applying the right-hand rule to determine the direction of $\mathbf{B} \times \mathbf{A}$ would give a vector that points in the direction opposite to that of $\mathbf{A} \times \mathbf{B}$. Therefore, $\mathbf{B} \times \mathbf{A} = -(\mathbf{A} \times \mathbf{B})$.

The cross product can be computed directly from the scalar components of $\mathbf{A}$ and $\mathbf{B}$ without first determining the angle θ, as follows: If $\mathbf{A} = A_x\hat{\mathbf{i}} + A_y\hat{\mathbf{j}} + A_z\hat{\mathbf{k}}$ and $\mathbf{B} = B_x\hat{\mathbf{i}} + B_y\hat{\mathbf{j}} + B_z\hat{\mathbf{k}}$, then the cross product (magnitude and direction) of $\mathbf{A}$ and $\mathbf{B}$ is

$$\mathbf{A} \times \mathbf{B} = (A_yB_z - A_zB_y)\hat{\mathbf{i}} + (A_zB_x - A_xB_z)\hat{\mathbf{j}} + (A_xB_y - A_yB_x)\hat{\mathbf{k}}$$

Example 1.7 Calculate the cross product of the vectors $\mathbf{A} = 2\hat{\mathbf{i}} + 3\hat{\mathbf{j}}$ and $\mathbf{B} = -\hat{\mathbf{i}} + \hat{\mathbf{j}} + 4\hat{\mathbf{k}}$, and verify that it's perpendicular to both $\mathbf{A}$ and $\mathbf{B}$.

Solution. First we figure out the cross product:

$$\mathbf{A} \times \mathbf{B} = [(3)(4) - (0)(1)\hat{\mathbf{i}}] - [(2)(4) - (0)(-1)]\hat{\mathbf{j}} + [(2)(1) - (3)(-1)]\hat{\mathbf{k}} = 12\hat{\mathbf{i}} - 8\hat{\mathbf{j}} + 5\hat{\mathbf{k}}$$

Now, to verify that this vector is perpendicular to both $\mathbf{A}$ and $\mathbf{B}$, we use the property of the dot product: Two vectors are perpendicular to each other if their dot product is zero. Extending the computation of the dot product in terms of the scalar components to three dimensions, we get:

$$(\mathbf{A} \times \mathbf{B}) \cdot \mathbf{A} = (12\hat{\mathbf{i}} - 8\hat{\mathbf{j}} + 5\hat{\mathbf{k}}) \cdot (2\hat{\mathbf{i}} + 3\hat{\mathbf{j}}) = (12)(2) + (-8)(3) + (5)(0) = 0$$

$$(\mathbf{A} \times \mathbf{B}) \cdot \mathbf{B} = (12\hat{\mathbf{i}} - 8\hat{\mathbf{j}} + 5\hat{\mathbf{k}}) \cdot (-\hat{\mathbf{i}} + \hat{\mathbf{j}} + 4\hat{\mathbf{k}}) = (12)(-1) + (-8)(1) + (5)(4) = 0$$

2

KINEMATICS

INTRODUCTION

Kinematics is the study of an object's motion in terms of its displacement, velocity, and acceleration. Questions such as *How far does this object travel?* or *How fast and in what direction does it move?* or *At what rate does its speed change?* all properly belong to kinematics. In the next chapter, we will study **dynamics**, which delves more deeply into *why* objects move the way they do.

DISPLACEMENT

Displacement is an object's change in position. It's the vector that points from the object's initial position to its final position, regardless of the path actually taken. Since displacement means *change in position*, it is generically denoted $\Delta\mathbf{s}$, where Δ denotes *change in* and $\mathbf{s}$ means spatial location. (The letter $\mathbf{p}$ is not used for position because it's reserved for another quantity; momentum.) If it's known that the displacement is horizontal, then it can be called $\Delta\mathbf{x}$; if the displacement is vertical, then it's $\Delta\mathbf{y}$. The magnitude of this vector is the *net* distance traveled and, sometimes, the word *displacement* refers just to this scalar quantity. Since a distance is being measured, the SI unit for displacement is the meter: $[\Delta s] = \text{m}$.

> **Example 2.1** A rock is thrown straight upward from the edge of a 30 m
> cliff, rising 10 m then falling all the way down to the base of the cliff. Find
> the rock's displacement.

Solution. Displacement only refers to the object's initial position and final position, not the details of its journey. Since the rock started on the edge of the cliff and ended up on the ground 30 m below, its displacement is 30 m, downward.

> **Example 2.2** An infant crawls 5 m east, then 3 m north, then 1 m east.
> Find the magnitude of the infant's displacement.

Solution. Although the infant crawled a *total* distance of 5 + 3 + 1 = 9 m, this is not the displacement, which is merely the *net* distance traveled.

Using the Pythagorean Theorem, we can calculate that the magnitude of the displacement is

$$\Delta s = \sqrt{(\Delta x)^2 + (\Delta y)^2} = \sqrt{(6 \text{ m})^2 + (3 \text{ m})^2} = \sqrt{45 \text{ m}^2} = 6.7 \text{ m}$$

> **Example 2.3** In a track-and-field event, an athlete runs exactly once
> around an oval track, a total distance of 500 m. Find the runner's dis-
> placement for the race.

Solution. If the runner returns to the same position from which she left, then her displacement is zero.

The *total* distance covered is 500 m, but the net distance—the displacement—is 0.

SPEED AND VELOCITY

When we're in a moving car, the speedometer tells us how fast we're going; it gives us our speed. But what does it mean to have a speed of say, 10 m/s? It means that we're covering a distance of 10 meters every second. By definition, **average speed** is the ratio of the total distance traveled to the time required to cover that distance:

$$\text{average speed} = \frac{\text{total distance}}{\text{time}}$$

The car's speedometer doesn't care in what direction the car is moving (as long as the wheels are moving forward). You could be driving north, south, east, west, whatever; the speedometer would make no distinction. *55 miles per hour, north* and *55 miles per hour, east* register the same on the speedometer: 55 miles per hour. Speed is a scalar.

However, we will also need to include *direction* in our descriptions of motion. We just learned about displacement, which takes both distance (net distance) and direction into account. The single concept that embodies both speed and direction is called **velocity**, and the definition of average velocity is:

$$\text{average velocity} = \frac{\text{displacement}}{\text{time}}$$

$$\bar{\mathbf{v}} = \frac{\Delta \mathbf{s}}{\Delta t}$$

(The bar over the **v** means *average*.) Because $\Delta \mathbf{s}$ is a vector, $\bar{\mathbf{v}}$ is also a vector, and because Δt is a *positive* scalar, the direction of $\bar{\mathbf{v}}$ is the same as the direction of $\Delta \mathbf{s}$. The magnitude of the velocity vector is called the object's **speed**, and is expressed in units of meters per second (m/s).

Notice the distinction between speed and velocity. In everyday language, they're often used interchangeably. However, in physics, *speed* and *velocity* are technical terms whose definitions are not the same. *Velocity is speed plus direction.*[1]

> **Example 2.4** If the infant in Example 2.2 completes his journey in 20 sec, find the magnitude of his average velocity.

Solution. Since the displacement is 6.7 m, the magnitude of his average velocity is

$$\bar{v} = \Delta s / \Delta t = (6.7 \text{ m})/(20 \text{ s}) = 0.34 \text{ m/s}$$

> **Example 2.5** Assume that the runner in Example 2.3 completes the race in 1 minute and 18 seconds. Find her average speed and the magnitude of her average velocity.

Solution. *Average speed is total distance divided by elapsed time.* Since the length of the track is 500 m, the runner's average speed was (500 m)/(78 s) = 6.4 m/s. However, since her displacement was zero, her average velocity was zero also: $\bar{v} = \Delta s / \Delta t = (0 \text{ m})/(78 \text{ s}) = 0 \text{ m/s}$.

---

[1] Technical note: The magnitude of the velocity is the speed. However (and this is perhaps a bit unfortunate and can be confusing), the magnitude of the average velocity is *not* called the average speed. Average speed is defined as the *total* distance traveled divided by the elapsed time. On the other hand, the magnitude of the average velocity is the *net* distance traveled divided by the elapsed time.

Solution. The answer to the first question is *yes*. For example, if you set your car's cruise control at 55 miles per hour but turn the steering wheel to follow a curved section of road, then the direction of your velocity changes (which means your velocity is not constant), even though your speed doesn't change.

The answer to the second question is *no*. Velocity means speed and direction; if the velocity is constant, then that means both speed and direction are constant. If speed were to change, then the velocity vector's magnitude would change (by definition), which immediately implies that the vector changes.

ACCELERATION

When you step on the gas pedal in your car, the car's speed increases; step on the brake and the car's speed decreases. Turn the wheel, and the car's direction of motion changes. In all of these cases, the velocity changes. To describe this change in velocity, we need a new term: **acceleration**. In the same way that velocity measures the rate-of-change of an object's position, acceleration measures the rate-of-change of an object's velocity. An object's average acceleration is defined as follows:

$$\text{average acceleration} = \frac{\text{change in velocity}}{\text{time}}$$

$$\bar{\mathbf{a}} = \frac{\Delta \mathbf{v}}{\Delta t}$$

The units of acceleration are meters per second, per second: $[a] = \text{m/s}^2$. Because $\Delta\mathbf{v}$ is a vector, $\bar{\mathbf{a}}$ is also a vector; and because Δt is a *positive* scalar, the direction of $\bar{\mathbf{a}}$ is the same as the direction of $\Delta\mathbf{v}$.

Furthermore, if we take an object's original direction of motion to be positive, then an increase in speed corresponds to a positive acceleration, while a decrease in speed corresponds to a negative acceleration (deceleration).

Notice that an object can accelerate even if its speed doesn't change. (Again, it's a matter of not allowing the everyday usage of the word *accelerate* to interfere with its technical, physics usage.) This is because acceleration depends on $\Delta\mathbf{v}$, and the velocity vector $\mathbf{v}$ changes if (1) speed changes, or (2) direction changes, or (3) both speed and direction change. For instance, a car traveling around a circular racetrack is constantly accelerating even if the car's *speed* is constant, because the direction of the car's velocity vector is constantly changing.

Solution. Since the car is traveling at a constant velocity, its acceleration is zero. If there's no change in velocity, then there's no acceleration.

Solution. Assuming that the direction of the velocity doesn't change, it's simply a matter of dividing the change in velocity, 32 m/s − 20 m/s = 12 m/s, by the time interval during which the change occurred: $\bar{a} = \Delta v / \Delta t = (12 \text{ m/s}) / (3 \text{ s}) = 4 \text{ m/s}^2$.

> **Example 2.9** Spotting a police car ahead, the driver of the car in the previous example slows from 32 m/s to 20 m/s in 2 sec. Find the car's average acceleration.

Solution. Dividing the change in velocity, 20 m/s − 32 m/s = −12 m/s, by the time interval during which the change occurred, 2 s, gives us $\bar{\mathbf{a}} = \Delta \mathbf{v} / \Delta t = (-12 \text{ m/s}) / (2 \text{ s}) = -6 \text{ m/s}^2$. The negative sign here means that the direction of the acceleration is opposite the direction of the velocity, which describes slowing down.

UNIFORMLY-ACCELERATED MOTION AND THE BIG FIVE

The simplest type of motion to analyze is motion in which the acceleration is *constant* (possibly equal to zero). Although true uniform acceleration is rarely achieved in the real world, many common motions are governed by approximately constant acceleration and, in these cases, the kinematics of uniformly accelerated motion provide a pretty good description of what's happening. Notice that if the acceleration is constant, then taking an average yields nothing new, so $\bar{a} = a$.

Another restriction that will make our analysis easier is to only consider motion that takes place along a straight line. In these cases, there are only two possible directions of motion. One is positive, and the opposite direction is negative. Most of the quantities we've been dealing with—displacement, velocity, and acceleration—are vectors, which means that they include both a magnitude and a direction. With straight-line motion, direction can be specified simply by attaching a + or − sign to the magnitude of the quantity. Therefore, although we will often abandon the use of bold letters to denote the vector quantities of displacement, velocity, and acceleration, the fact that these quantities include direction will still be indicated by a positive or negative sign.

Let's review the quantities we've seen so far. The fundamental quantities are displacement (Δs), velocity (v), and acceleration (a). Acceleration is a change in velocity, from an initial velocity (v_i or v_0) to a final velocity (v_f or simply v—with no subscript). And, finally, the motion takes place during some elapsed time interval, Δt. Therefore, we have five kinematics quantities: Δs, v_0, v, a, and Δt.

These five quantities are related by a group of five equations that we call *The Big Five*. They work in cases where acceleration is uniform, which are the cases we're considering.

		Variable that's missing
Big Five #1:	$\Delta s = \bar{v}\,\Delta t$	a
Big Five #2:	$\Delta v = a\,\Delta t$	Δs
Big Five #3:	$\Delta s = v_0 \Delta t + \dfrac{1}{2} a (\Delta t)^2$	v
Big Five #4:	$\Delta s = v\Delta t - \dfrac{1}{2} a (\Delta t)^2$	v_0
Big Five #5:	$v^2 = v_0^2 + 2a\,\Delta s$	Δt

Some of these equations will be provided on the non-multiple-choice section of the AP Physics exam, but they will not be provided in the multiple-choice section. In Big Five #1, the average velocity is simply the average of the initial velocity and the final velocity: $\bar{v} = \frac{1}{2}(v_0 + v)$. (This is a consequence of the fact that the acceleration is constant.) Also, if we agree to start our clocks at time $t_i = 0$, then $\Delta t = t_f - t_i = t - 0 = t$, so we can just write t instead of Δt in the first four equations. This simplification in notation makes these equations a little easier to write down.

Each of the Big Five equations is missing one of the five kinematic quantities. The way you decide which equation to use when solving a problem is to determine which of the kinematic quantities is missing from the problem—that is, which quantity is neither given nor asked for—and then use the equation that doesn't contain that variable. For example, if the problem never mentions the final velocity—v is neither given nor asked for—the equation that will work is the one that's missing v. That's Big Five #3.

Big Five #1 and #2 are simply the definitions of $\bar{v}$ and $\bar{a}$ written in forms that don't involve fractions. The other Big Five equations can be derived from these two definitions and the equation

$\bar{v} = \frac{1}{2}(v_0 + v)$, using a bit of algebra.

> **Example 2.10** An object with an initial velocity of 4 m/s moves along a straight axis under constant acceleration. Three seconds later, its velocity is 14 m/s. How far did it travel during this time?

Solution. We're given v_0, Δt, and v, and we're asked for Δs. So a is missing; it isn't given and it isn't asked for, and we use Big Five #1:

$$\Delta s = \bar{v}\Delta t = \frac{1}{2}(v_0 + v)t = \frac{1}{2}(4 \text{ m/s} + 14 \text{ m/s})(3 \text{ s}) = 27 \text{ m}$$

Note: This last equation could also have been written as

$$\Delta s = \bar{v}\Delta t = \frac{1}{2}(v_0 + v)t = \frac{1}{2}(4 + 14)(3) = 27 \text{ m}$$

That is, it's OK to leave off the units in the middle of the calculation *as long as you remember to include them in your final answer.* Leaving units off of your final answer will cost you points on the AP exam.

> **Example 2.11** A car that's initially traveling at 10 m/s accelerates uniformly for 4 seconds at a rate of 2 m/s², in a straight line. How far does the car travel during this time?

Solution. We're given v_0, t, and a, and we're asked for Δs. So v is missing; it isn't given and it isn't asked for, and we use Big Five #3:

$$\Delta s = v_0 \Delta t + \frac{1}{2}a(\Delta t)^2 = (10 \text{ m/s})(4 \text{ s}) + \frac{1}{2}(2 \text{ m/s}^2)(4 \text{ s})^2 = 56 \text{ m}$$

Example 2.12 A rock is dropped off a cliff that's 80 m high. If it strikes the ground with an impact velocity of 40 m/s, what acceleration did it experience during its descent?

Solution. If something is *dropped*, then that means it has no initial velocity: $v_0 = 0$. So, we're given v_0, Δs, and v, and we're asked for a. Since t is missing, we use Big Five #5:

$$v^2 = v_0^2 + 2a\Delta s \Rightarrow v^2 = 2a\Delta s \quad (\text{since } v_0 = 0)$$

$$a = \frac{v^2}{2\Delta s} = \frac{(40 \text{ m/s})^2}{2(80 \text{ m})} = 10 \text{ m/s}^2$$

Notice that since a had the same sign as Δs, the acceleration vector points in the same direction as the displacement vector. This makes sense here, since the object moves downward and the acceleration it experiences is due to gravity, which also points downward.

KINEMATICS WITH GRAPHS

So far, we have dealt with kinematics problems algebraically, but you should also be able to handle kinematics questions in which information is given graphically. The two most popular graphs in kinematics are position-vs.-time graphs and velocity-vs.-time graphs. For example, consider an object that's moving along an axis in such a way that its position x as a function of time t is given by the following position-vs.-time graph:

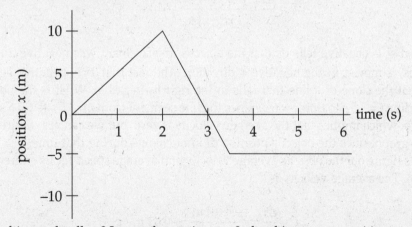

What does this graph tell us? It says that at time $t = 0$, the object was at position $x = 0$. Then, in the next two seconds, its position changed from $x = 0$ to $x = 10$ m.

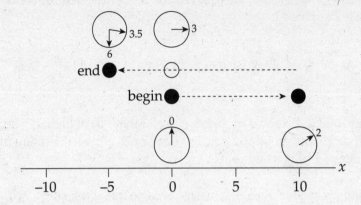

Then, at time $t = 2$ s, it reversed direction and headed back toward its starting point, reaching $x = 0$ at time $t = 3$ s, and continued, reaching position $x = -5$ m at time $t = 3.5$ s. Then the object remained at this position, $x = -5$ m, at least through time $t = 6$ s. Notice how economically the graph embodies all this information!

We can also determine the object's average velocity (and average speed) during particular time intervals. For example, its average velocity from time $t = 0$ to time $t = 2$ s is equal to the distance traveled, $10 - 0 = 10$ m, divided by the elapsed time, 2 s:

$$\bar{v} = \frac{\Delta x}{\Delta t} = \frac{(10-0)\text{ m}}{(2-0)\text{ s}} = 5 \text{ m/s}$$

Notice, however, that the ratio that defines the average velocity, $\Delta x / \Delta t$, also defines the slope of the x vs. t graph. Therefore, we know the following important fact:

The slope of a position-vs.-time graph gives the velocity.

What was the average velocity from time $t = 2$ s to time $t = 3.5$ s? The slope of the line segment joining the point $(t, x) = (2\text{ s}, 10\text{ m})$ to the point $(t, x) = (3.5\text{ s}, -5\text{ m})$ is

$$\bar{v} = \frac{\Delta x}{\Delta t} = \frac{(-5-10)\text{ m}}{(3.5-2)\text{ s}} = -10 \text{ m/s}$$

The fact that $\bar{v}$ is negative tells us that the object's displacement was negative during this time interval; that is, it moved in the negative x direction. The fact that $\bar{v}$ is negative agrees with the observation that the slope of a line that falls to the right is negative. What is the object's average velocity from time $t = 3.5$ s to time $t = 6$ s? Since the line segment from $t = 3.5$ s to $t = 6$ s is horizontal, its slope is zero, which implies that the average velocity is zero, but we can also figure this out from looking at the graph, since the object's position did not change during that time.

Finally, let's figure out the object's average velocity and average speed for its entire journey (from $t = 0$ to $t = 6$ s). The average velocity is

$$\bar{v} = \frac{\Delta x}{\Delta t} = \frac{(-5-0)\text{ m}}{(6-0)\text{ s}} = -0.83 \text{ m/s}$$

This is the slope of the imagined line segment that joins the point $(t, x) = (0 \text{ s}, 0 \text{ m})$ to the point $(t, x) = (6 \text{ s}, -5 \text{ m})$. The average speed is the total distance traveled by the object divided by the elapsed time. In this case, notice that the object traveled 10 m in the first 2 s, then 15 m (albeit backwards) in the next 1.5 s; it covered no additional distance from $t = 3.5$ s to $t = 6$ s. Therefore, the total distance traveled by the object is $d = 10 + 15 = 25$ m, which took 6 s, so

$$\text{average speed} = \frac{d}{\Delta t} = \frac{25 \text{ m}}{6 \text{ s}} = 4.2 \text{ m/s}$$

Let's next consider an object moving along a straight axis in such a way that its velocity, v, as a function of time, t, is given by the following velocity-vs.-time graph:

What does this graph tell us? It says that, at time $t = 0$, the object's velocity was $v = 0$. Over the first two seconds, its velocity increased steadily to 10 m/s. At time $t = 2$ s, the velocity then began to decrease (eventually becoming $v = 0$, at time $t = 3$ s). The velocity then became negative after $t = 3$ s, reaching $v = -5$ m/s at time $t = 3.5$ s. From $t = 3.5$ s on, the velocity remained a steady -5 m/s.

What can we ask about this motion? First, the fact that the velocity changed from $t = 0$ to $t = 2$ s tells us that the object accelerated. The acceleration during this time was

$$a = \frac{\Delta v}{\Delta t} = \frac{(10-0) \text{ m/s}}{(2-0) \text{ s}} = 5 \text{ m/s}^2$$

Notice, however, that the ratio that defines the acceleration, $\Delta v / \Delta t$, also defines the slope of the v vs. t graph. Therefore,

The slope of a velocity-vs.-time graph gives the acceleration.

What was the acceleration from time $t = 2$ s to time $t = 3.5$ s? The slope of the line segment joining the point $(t, v) = (2 \text{ s}, 10 \text{ m/s})$ to the point $(t, v) = (3.5 \text{ s}, -5 \text{ m/s})$ is

$$a = \frac{\Delta v}{\Delta t} = \frac{(-5-10) \text{ m/s}}{(3.5-2) \text{ s}} = -10 \text{ m/s}^2$$

The fact that a is negative tells us that the object's velocity change was negative during this time interval; that is, the object accelerated in the negative direction. In fact, after time $t = 3$ s, the velocity became more negative, indicating that the direction of motion was negative at increasing speed. What is the object's acceleration from time $t = 3.5$ s to time $t = 6$ s? Since the line segment from $t = 3.5$ s to $t = 6$ s is horizontal, its slope is zero, which implies that the acceleration is zero, but you can also see this from looking at the graph; the object's velocity did not change during this time interval.

Another question can be asked when a velocity-vs.-time graph is given: How far did the object travel during a particular time interval? For example, let's figure out the displacement of the object from time $t = 4$ s to time $t = 6$ s. During this time interval, the velocity was a constant -5 m/s, so the displacement was $\Delta x = v\Delta t = (-5 \text{ m/s})(2 \text{ s}) = -10 \text{ m}$.

Geometrically, we've determined the area between the graph and the horizontal axis. After all, the area of a rectangle is *base* × *height* and, for the shaded rectangle shown below, the *base* is Δt, and the *height* is v. So, *base* × *height* equals $\Delta t \times v$, which is displacement.

Signed area = displacement

We say *signed area* because regions below the horizontal axis are negative quantities (since the object's velocity is negative, its displacement is negative). Therefore, counting areas above the horizontal axis as positive and areas below the horizontal axis as negative, we can make the following claim:

Given a velocity-vs-time graph, the area between the graph and the t axis equals the object's displacement.

What is the object's displacement from time $t = 0$ to $t = 3$ s? Using the fact that displacement is the area bounded by the velocity graph, we figure out the area of the triangle shown below:

Since the area of a triangle is $(1/2)$ × base × height, we find that $\Delta x = \frac{1}{2}(3 \text{ s})(10 \text{ m/s}) = 15 \text{ m}$.

A NOTE ABOUT CALCULUS

The use of graphs for solving kinematics questions provides a link to some basic definitions in calculus. The slope of a curve is the geometric definition of the **derivative** of a function. Since the slope of a position-vs.-time graph gives the velocity, the derivative of a position function gives the velocity. That is, given an equation of the form $x = x(t)$ for the position x of an object as a function of time t, the derivative of $x(t)$—with respect to t—gives the object's velocity, $v(t)$:

$$v(t) = \frac{dx}{dt}$$

Often, a derivative with respect to time is denoted by a dot above the quantity, so an alternative notation for the equation above is $v(t) = \dot{x}(t)$.

Next, since the slope of a velocity-vs.-time graph gives the acceleration, the derivative of a velocity function gives the acceleration. That is, given an equation of the form $v = v(t)$ for the velocity v of an object as a function of time t, the derivative of $v(t)$—with respect to t—gives the object's acceleration, $a(t)$:

$$a(t) = \frac{dv}{dt}$$

Combining this equation with the previous one, we see that the acceleration is the second derivative of the position:

$$a(t) = \frac{dv}{dt} = \frac{d}{dt}\left(\frac{dx}{dt}\right) = \frac{d^2x}{dt^2}$$

Using the dot notation, these last two equations may be written as $a(t) = \dot{v}(t)$ and $a(t) = \ddot{x}(t)$, respectively.

The area bounded by a curve and the horizontal axis is the geometric definition of the **definite integral** of a function. Since the area bounded by a velocity-vs.-time graph gives the displacement, the definite integral of a velocity function gives the displacement. That is, given the equation $v = v(t)$ for the velocity v of an object as a function of time t, the integral of $v(t)$ from time $t = t_1$ to time $t = t_2$ equals the displacement during this time interval:

$$\text{displacement} = \int_{t_1}^{t_2} v(t)\,dt$$

For the velocity-vs.-time graph examined above, the slope of the imaginary line segment from $(t, v) = (0, 0)$ to $(t, v) = (2, 10)$ can be described by the equation $v(t) = 5t$, and the line segment from $(t, v) = (2, 10)$ to $(t, v) = (3, 0)$ can be described by the equation $v(t) = -10t + 30$ (with t in seconds and v in m/s in both equations). Therefore, the acceleration of the object from time $t = 0$ to $t = 2$ s is

$$a = \frac{dv}{dt} = \frac{d}{dt}(5t) = 5 \text{ m/s}^2$$

as we found above.

Also, the displacement of the object from time $t = 0$ to $t = 3$ s is the value of the integral from $t = 0$ to $t = 3$ s, which we can get by adding the integral of $v(t) = 5t$ from $t = 0$ to $t = 2$ s to the integral of $v(t) = -10t + 30$ from $t = 2$ s to $t = 3$ s:

$$\text{displacement} = \int_0^2 5t\,dt + \int_2^3 \left(-10t + 30\right)dt$$

$$= \left[\frac{5}{2}t^2\right]_0^2 + \left[-5t^2 + 30t\right]_2^3$$

$$= \frac{5}{2}\left(2^2 - 0^2\right) + \left[\left(-5 \cdot 3^2 + 30 \cdot 3\right) - \left(-5 \cdot 2^2 + 30 \cdot 2\right)\right]$$

$$= 10 + \left[45 - 40\right]$$

$$= 15 \text{ m}$$

which also agrees with the value computed above.

Example 2.13 The velocity of an object as a function of time is given by the following graph:

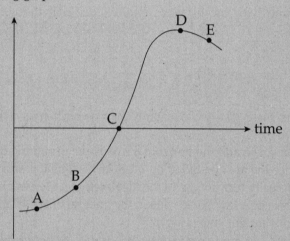

At which point (A, B, C, D, or E) is the magnitude of the acceleration the greatest? How would you answer this same question if the graph shown were a position-vs.-time graph?

Solution. The acceleration is the slope of the velocity-vs.-time graph. Although this graph is not composed of straight lines, the concept of slope still applies; at each point, the slope of the curve is the slope of the tangent line to the curve. The slope is essentially zero at Points A and D (where the curve is flat), small and positive at B, and small and negative at E. The slope at Point C is large and positive, so this is where the object's acceleration is the greatest.

If the graph shown were a position-vs.-time graph, then the slope would be the velocity. The slope of the given graph starts at zero (around Point A), slowly increases to a small positive value at B, continues to slowly increase to a large positive value at C, then, at around Point D, this large positive slope decreases quickly to zero. Of the points designated on the graph, Point D is the location of the greatest slope change, which means that this is the point of the greatest velocity change. Therefore, this is the point at which the magnitude of the acceleration is greatest.

FREE FALL

The simplest real-life example of motion under pretty constant acceleration is the motion of objects in the earth's gravitational field, near the surface of the earth and ignoring any effects due to the air (mainly air resistance). With these effects ignored, an object can fall *freely*, that is, it can fall experiencing only acceleration due to gravity. Near the surface of the earth, the gravitational acceleration has a constant magnitude of about 9.8 m/s²; this quantity is denoted g (for *gravitational acceleration*).[2] And, of course, the gravitational acceleration vector, **g**, points *downward*.

Since the acceleration is constant, we can use the Big Five with a replaced by $+g$ or $-g$. To decide which of these two values to use for a, make a decision at the beginning of your calculations whether to call "down" the positive direction or the negative direction. If you call "down" the positive direction, then $a = +g$. If you call "down" the negative direction, then $a = -g$. It might make things easier if you always take the direction of the object's displacement as positive.

In each of the following examples, we'll ignore effects due to the air.

> **Example 2.14** A rock is dropped from an 80-meter cliff. How long does it take to reach the ground?

Solution. Since the rock's displacement is *down*, we call *down* the positive direction, so $a = +g$. We're given v_0, Δs, and a, and asked for t. So v is missing; it isn't given and it isn't asked for, and we use Big Five #3:

$$\Delta s = v_0 t + \frac{1}{2}at^2 \Rightarrow \Delta s = \frac{1}{2}at^2 \ \left(\text{since } v_0 = 0\right)$$

$$t = \sqrt{\frac{2\Delta s}{a}}$$

$$= \sqrt{\frac{2\Delta s}{+g}} = \sqrt{\frac{2(+80\text{ m})}{+9.8\text{ m}/\text{s}^2}} = 4.0\text{ s}$$

> **Example 2.15** A baseball is thrown straight upward with an initial speed of 25 m/s. How high will it go?

Solution. Since here we are concerned only with the baseball's upward motion, the baseball's displacement is *up*, so we call *up* the positive direction. Therefore, *down* is the negative direction, so $a = -g$. The ball's velocity drops to zero at the instant the ball reaches its highest point, so we're given a, v_0, and v, and asked for Δs. Since t is missing, we use Big Five #5:

$$v^2 = v_0^2 + 2a\Delta s \Rightarrow 2a\Delta s = -v_0^2 \ \left(\text{because } v = 0\right)$$

$$\Delta s = -\frac{v_0^2}{2a}$$

$$= -\frac{v_0^2}{2(-g)} = -\frac{\left(+25\text{ m}/\text{s}\right)^2}{2\left(-9.8\text{ m}/\text{s}^2\right)} = 32\text{ m}$$

---

[2] On the AP Exam, you may use $g = 10$ m/s² as a simple approximation to $g = 9.8$ m/s².

> **Example 2.16** One second after being thrown straight down, an object is falling with a speed of 20 m/s. How fast will it be falling 2 seconds later?

Solution. Call *down* the positive direction, so $a = +g$ and $v_0 = +20$ m/s. We're given v_0, a, and t, and asked for v. Since Δs is missing, we use Big Five #2:

$$\Delta v = at$$
$$v - v_0 = at$$
$$v = v_0 + at = (+20 \text{ m/s}) + (+9.8 \text{ m/s}^2)(2 \text{ s}) = 40 \text{ m/s}$$

> **Example 2.17** If an object is thrown straight upward with an initial speed of 8 m/s and takes 3 seconds to strike the ground, from what height was the object thrown?

Solution. The figure below shows that the displacement is *down*, so we call *down* the positive direction. Therefore, $a = +g$ and $v_0 = -8$ m/s (because *up* is the negative direction). We're given a, v_0, and t, and we need to find Δs. Since v is missing, we use Big Five #3:

In this example, the magnitude of the displacement equals the height from which the object was thrown.

$$\Delta s = v_0 t + \frac{1}{2} a t^2$$
$$= (-8)(3) + \frac{1}{2}(+9.8)(3^2)$$
$$= 20 \text{ m}$$

PROJECTILE MOTION

In general, an object that moves near the surface of the earth will not follow a straight-line path (for example, a baseball hit by a bat, a golf ball struck by a club, or a tennis ball hit from the baseline). If we launch an object at an angle other than straight upward and consider only the effect of acceleration due to gravity, then the object will travel along a parabolic trajectory.

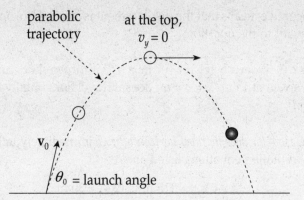

parabolic trajectory

at the top, $v_y = 0$

$\mathbf{v}_0$

θ_0 = launch angle

To simplify the analysis of parabolic motion, *we analyze the horizontal and vertical motions separately*, using The Big Five. This is the key to doing projectile motion problems. Calling *down* the negative direction, we have

Horizontal motion:

$$\Delta x = v_{0x}t$$

$$v_x = v_{0x} \text{ (constant!)}$$

$$a_x = 0$$

Vertical motion:

$$\Delta y = v_{0y}t + \frac{1}{2}(-g)t^2$$

$$v_y = v_{0y} + (-g)t$$

$$a_y = -g$$

The quantity v_{0x}, which is the horizontal (or x) component of the initial velocity, is equal to $v_0 \cos \theta_0$, where θ_0 is the **launch angle**, the angle that the initial velocity vector, $\mathbf{v}_0$, makes with the horizontal. Similarly, the quantity v_{0y}, the vertical (or y) component of the initial velocity, is equal to $v_0 \sin \theta_0$.

$\mathbf{v}_0$

$\mathbf{v}_{0y}$

θ_0

$\mathbf{v}_{0x}$

Example 2.18 An object is thrown horizontally with an initial speed of 10 m/s. How far will it drop in 4 seconds?

Solution. The first step is to decide whether this is a *horizontal* question or a *vertical* question, since you must consider these motions separately. The question *How far will it drop?* is a *vertical* question, so the set of equations we will consider are those listed above under *vertical motion*. Next, *How far...?* implies that we will use the first of the vertical-motion equations, the one that gives vertical displacement, Δy.

Now, since the object is thrown horizontally, there is no vertical component to its initial velocity vector $\mathbf{v}_0$; that is, $v_{0y} = 0$. Therefore,

$\mathbf{v}_0 = \mathbf{v}_{0x}$

Δy

$$\Delta y = v_{0y}t + \frac{1}{2}(-g)t^2 \rightarrow \Delta y = \frac{1}{2}(-g)t^2 \left(\text{because } v_{0y} = 0\right)$$

$$= \frac{1}{2}(-9.8)(4^2)$$

$$= -78 \text{ m}$$

The fact that Δy is negative means that the displacement is *down*. Also, notice that the information given about v_{0x} is irrelevant to the question.

> **Example 2.19** From a height of 100 m, a ball is thrown horizontally with an initial speed of 15 m/s. How far does it travel horizontally in the first 2 seconds?

Solution. The question, *How far does it travel horizontally...?* immediately tells us that we should use the first of the horizontal-motion equations listed above:

$$\Delta x = v_{0x}t = (15 \text{ m/s})(2 \text{ s}) = 30 \text{ m}$$

The information that the initial vertical position is 100 m above the ground is irrelevant (except for the fact that it's high enough that the ball doesn't strike the ground before the two seconds have elapsed).

> **Example 2.20** A projectile is traveling in a parabolic path for a total of 6 seconds. How does its horizontal velocity 1 s after launch compare to its horizontal velocity 4 s after launch?

Solution. The only acceleration experienced by the projectile is due to gravity, which is purely vertical, so that there is no horizontal acceleration. If there's no horizontal acceleration, then the horizontal velocity cannot change during flight, and the projectile's horizontal velocity 1 s after it's launched is the same as its horizontal velocity 3 s later.

> **Example 2.21** An object is projected upward with a 30° launch angle and an initial speed of 39 m/s. How long will it take for the object to reach the top of its trajectory? How high is this?

Solution. When the projectile reaches the top of its trajectory, its velocity vector is momentarily horizontal; that is, $v_y = 0$. Using the vertical-motion equation for v_y, we can set it equal to 0 and solve for t:

$$v_y \overset{\text{set}}{=} 0 \Rightarrow v_{0y} + (-g)t = 0$$

$$t = \frac{v_{0y}}{g} = \frac{v_0 \sin\theta_0}{g} = \frac{(39 \text{ m/s})\sin 30^\circ}{9.8 \text{ m/s}^2} = 2 \text{ s}$$

At this time, the projectile's vertical displacement is

$$\Delta y = v_{0y}t + \frac{1}{2}(-g)t^2 = (v_0\sin\theta_0)t + \frac{1}{2}(-g)t^2$$

$$= \left[(39 \text{ m/s})\sin 30^\circ\right](2\text{s}) + \frac{1}{2}(-9.8 \text{ m/s}^2)(2 \text{ s})^2$$

$$= 19 \text{ m}$$

> **Example 2.22** An object is projected upward with a 30° launch angle and an initial speed of 59 m/s. For how many seconds will it be in the air? How far will it travel horizontally?

Solution. The total time the object spends in the air is equal to twice the time required to reach the top of the trajectory (because the parabola is symmetrical). So, as we did in the previous example, we find the time required to reach the top by setting v_y equal to 0, and now double that amount of time:

$$v_y \overset{\text{set}}{=} 0 \Rightarrow v_{0y} + (-g)t = 0$$

$$t = \frac{v_{0y}}{g} = \frac{v_0 \sin\theta_0}{g} = \frac{(59 \text{ m/s})\sin 30^\circ}{9.8 \text{ m/s}^2} = 3 \text{ s}$$

Therefore, the *total* flight time (that is, up and down) is $T = 2t = 2 \times (3 \text{ s}) = 6 \text{ s}$.

Now, using the first horizontal-motion equation, we can calculate the horizontal displacement after 6 seconds:

$$\Delta x = v_{0x}T = (v_0 \cos\theta_0)T = [(59 \text{ m/s})\cos 30^\circ](6 \text{ s}) = 310 \text{ m}$$

By the way, the full horizontal displacement of a projectile is called the projectile's **range**.

[C] KINEMATICS WITH CALCULUS

As we mentioned earlier, velocity is the time derivative of position, and acceleration is the time derivative of velocity. Equivalently, the integral of acceleration is velocity, and the integral of velocity is position. These relationships can be summarized in the following diagram:

$$\text{position} \xrightarrow{\text{differentiate}} \text{velocity} \xrightarrow{\text{differentiate}} \text{acceleration}$$
$$x(t) \xleftarrow{\text{integrate}} v(t) \xleftarrow{\text{integrate}} a(t)$$

> **Example 2.23** The position of an object (measured in meters from the origin, where $x = 0$) moving along a straight line is given as a function of time t (measured in seconds) by the equation $x(t) = 4t^2 - 6t + 40$. Find
> (a) its velocity at time t,
> (b) its acceleration at time t,
> (c) the time at which the object is at the origin, and
> (d) the object's velocity and acceleration at the time calculated in (c).

Solution.

(a) The velocity as a function of t is the derivative of the position function:

$$v(t) = \dot{x}(t) = \frac{d}{dt}(4t^2 - 6t + 40) = 8t - 6 \text{ (in m/s)}$$

(b) The acceleration as a function of t is the derivative of the velocity function:

$$a(t) = \dot{v}(t) = \frac{d}{dt}(8t - 6) = 8 \text{ m/s}^2$$

Notice that the acceleration is constant (because it doesn't depend on t).

(c)   The object is at the origin when $x(t)$ is equal to 0; that is, when

$$4t^2 - 6t - 40 = 0$$

$$2(2t^2 - 3t - 20) = 0$$

$$2(2t + 5)(t - 4) = 0$$

$$t = -\frac{5}{2} \text{ or } 4$$

Disregarding the negative value for t, we can say that the object passes through the origin at $t = 4$ s. At this time, the object's velocity is

$$v(4) \equiv v(t)\big|_{t=4} = (8t - 6)\big|_{t=4} = 8 \cdot 4 - 6 = 26 \text{ m/s}$$

The object's acceleration is a constant 8 m/s^2 throughout its motion, so, in particular, at $t = 4$ s, the acceleration is 8 m/s^2.

Example 2.24 An object is moving along a straight axis with a constant acceleration of 3 m/s^2. If the object's initial velocity is 2 m/s and its initial position is $x = 3$ m, where will this object be at time $t = 4$ s?

Solution.

By integrating the acceleration with respect to time, we find the velocity function; then, integrating this with respect to time, we find the position function.

$$v(t) = \int a(t)\ dt = \int 3\ dt = 3t + c$$

To get a value for c, the arbitrary constant of integration, we use the fact that the object's initial velocity was 2 m/s:

$$v(0) = 2 \Rightarrow (3t + c)\big|_{t=0} = 2 \Rightarrow c = 2$$

(c is just v_0, the initial velocity.) So the velocity function is given by the equation $v(t) = 3t + 2$ (in m/s). Integrating again gives the position function:

$$x(t) = \int v(t)\ dt = \int (3t + 2)\ dt = \frac{3}{2}t^2 + 2t + c'$$

To evaluate c', the arbitrary constant in this integration, we use the fact that the object's initial position was $x = 3$ m:

$$x(0) = 3 \Rightarrow \left(\frac{3}{2}t^2 + 2t + 3\right)\bigg|_{t=0} = 3 \Rightarrow c' = 3$$

(Note that c' is just x_0, the initial position.) So the velocity function is given by the equation

$$x(t) = \frac{3}{2}t^2 + 2t + 3 \text{ (in m)}$$

and the object's position at time $t = 4$ s can be determined:

$$x(4) \equiv x(t)\big|_{t=4} = \left(\frac{3}{2}t^2 + 2t + 3\right)\bigg|_{t=4} = \frac{3}{2} \cdot 4^2 + 2 \cdot 4 + 3 = 35 \text{ m}$$

CHAPTER 2 REVIEW QUESTIONS

SECTION I: MULTIPLE CHOICE

1. An object that's moving with constant speed travels once around a circular path. Which of the following is/are true concerning this motion?

    I. The displacement is zero.
    II. The average speed is zero.
    III. The acceleration is zero.

    (A) I only
    (B) I and II only
    (C) I and III only
    (D) III only
    (E) II and III only

2. At time $t = t_1$, an object's velocity is given by the vector $\mathbf{v}_1$ shown below:

    A short time later, at $t = t_2$, the object's velocity is the vector $\mathbf{v}_2$:

    If $v_2 = v_1$, which one of the following vectors best illustrates the object's average acceleration between $t = t_1$ and $t = t_2$?

    (A)

    (B)

    (C)

    (D)

    (E)

3. Which of the following is/are true?

    I. If an object's acceleration is constant, then it must move in a straight line.
    II. If an object's acceleration is zero, then its speed must remain constant.
    III. If an object's speed remains constant, then its acceleration must be zero.

    (A) I and II only
    (B) I and III only
    (C) II only
    (D) III only
    (E) II and III only

4. A baseball is thrown straight upward. What is the ball's acceleration at its highest point?

    (A) 0
    (B) $\frac{1}{2}g$, downward
    (C) g, downward
    (D) $\frac{1}{2}g$, upward
    (E) g, upward

5. How long would it take a car, starting from rest and accelerating uniformly in a straight line at 5 m/s², to cover a distance of 200 m?

    (A) 9.0 s
    (B) 10.5 s
    (C) 12.0 s
    (D) 15.5 s
    (E) 20.0 s

6. A rock is dropped off a cliff and strikes the ground with an impact velocity of 30 m/s. How high was the cliff?

   (A) 15 m
   (B) 20 m
   (C) 30 m
   (D) 45 m
   (E) 60 m

7. A stone is thrown horizontally with an initial speed of 10 m/s from a bridge. If air resistance could be ignored, how long would it take the stone to strike the water 80 m below the bridge?

   (A) 1 s
   (B) 2 s
   (C) 4 s
   (D) 6 s
   (E) 8 s

8. A soccer ball, at rest on the ground, is kicked with an initial velocity of 10 m/s at a launch angle of 30°. Calculate its total flight time, assuming that air resistance is negligible.

   (A) 0.5 s
   (B) 1 s
   (C) 1.7 s
   (D) 2 s
   (E) 4 s

9. A stone is thrown horizontally with an initial speed of 30 m/s from a bridge. Find the stone's total speed when it enters the water 4 seconds later. (Ignore air resistance.)

   (A) 30 m/s
   (B) 40 m/s
   (C) 50 m/s
   (D) 60 m/s
   (E) 70 m/s

10. Which one of the following statements is true concerning the motion of an ideal projectile launched at an angle of 45° to the horizontal?

   (A) The acceleration vector points opposite to the velocity vector on the way up and in the same direction as the velocity vector on the way down.
   (B) The speed at the top of the trajectory is zero.
   (C) The object's total speed remains constant during the entire flight.
   (D) The horizontal speed decreases on the way up and increases on the way down.
   (E) The vertical speed decreases on the way up and increases on the way down.

SECTION II: FREE RESPONSE

1. This question concerns the motion of a car on a straight track; the car's velocity as a function of time is plotted below.

(a) Describe what happened to the car at time $t = 1$ s.

(b) How does the car's average velocity between time $t = 0$ and $t = 1$ s compare to its average velocity between times $t = 1$ s and $t = 5$ s?

(c) What is the displacement of the car from time $t = 0$ to time $t = 7$ s?

(d) Plot the car's acceleration during this interval as a function of time.

(e) Plot the object's position during this interval as a function of time. Assume that the car begins at $s = 0$.

2. Consider a projectile moving in a parabolic trajectory under constant gravitational acceleration. Its initial velocity has magnitude v_0, and its launch angle (with the horizontal) is θ_0.

(a) Calculate the maximum height, H, of the projectile.

(b) Calculate the (horizontal) range, R, of the projectile.

(c) For what value of θ_0 will the range be maximized?

(d) If $0 < h < H$, compute the time that elapses between passing through the horizontal line of height h in both directions (ascending and descending); that is, compute the time required for the projectile to pass through the two points shown in this figure:

3. A cannonball is shot with an initial speed of 50 m/s at a launch angle of 40° toward a castle wall 220 m away. The height of the wall is 30 m. Assume that effects due to the air are negligible.

    (a)   Show that the cannonball will strike the castle wall.

    (b)   How long will it take for the cannonball to strike the wall?

    (c)   At what height above the base of the wall will the cannonball strike?

    (d)   Assuming that neither the location of the cannon nor the launch speed of the cannonball can be varied—but the launch angle can—determine the launch angles that will allow the cannonball to just clear the top of the castle wall.

4. [C] A particle moves along a straight axis in such a way that its acceleration at time t is given by the equation $a(t) = 6t$ (m/s^2). If the particle's initial velocity is 2 m/s and its initial position is $x = 4$ m, determine

    (a)   the time at which the particle's velocity is 14 m/s, and

    (b)   the particle's position at time $t = 3$ s.

3

NEWTON'S LAWS

INTRODUCTION

In the previous chapter we studied the vocabulary and equations that describe motion. Now we will learn *why* things move the way they do; this is the subject of **dynamics**.

An interaction between two bodies, a push or a pull—is called a **force**. If you lift a book, you exert an upward force (created by your muscles) on it. If you pull on a rope that's attached to a crate, you create a *tension* in the rope that pulls the crate. When a skydiver is falling through the air, the earth is exerting a downward pull called *gravitational force*, and the air exerts an upward force called *air resistance*. When you stand on the floor, the floor provides an upward, supporting force called the *normal force*. If you slide a book across a table, the table exerts a *frictional force* against the book, so the book slows down and then stops. Static cling provides a directly observable example of the *electrostatic force*. Protons and neutrons are held together in the nuclei of atoms by the *strong nuclear force*, and radioactive nuclei decay through the action of the *weak nuclear force*.

The Englishman Sir Isaac Newton published a book in 1687 called *The Mathematical Principles of Natural Philosophy*—referred to nowadays as simply *The Principia*—which began the modern study of physics as a scientific discipline. Three of the laws that Newton stated in *The Principia* form the basis for dynamics and are known simply as *Newton's Laws of Motion*.

THE FIRST LAW

Newton's First Law says that *an object will continue in its state of motion unless compelled to change by a force impressed upon it*. That is, unless an unbalanced force acts on an object, the object's velocity will not change: If the object is at rest, then it will stay at rest; and if it is moving, then it will continue to move at a constant speed in a straight line.

Basically, no force means no change in velocity. This property of objects, their natural resistance to changes in their state of motion, is called **inertia**. In fact, the First Law is often referred to as the **Law of Inertia**.

THE SECOND LAW

Newton's Second Law predicts what will happen when a force *does* act on an object: The object's velocity will change; the object will accelerate. More precisely, it says that its acceleration, **a**, will be directly proportional to the strength of the total—or *net*—force ($\mathbf{F}_{net}$) and inversely proportional to the object's mass, *m*:

$$\mathbf{F}_{net} = m\mathbf{a}$$

This is the most important equation in mechanics!

The **mass** of an object is the quantitative measure of its inertia; intuitively, it measures how much matter is contained in an object. Two identical boxes, one empty and one full, have different masses. The box that's full has the greater mass, because it contains more stuff; more stuff, more mass. Mass is measured in *kilograms*, abbreviated kg. (Note: An object whose mass is 1 kg weighs about 2.2 pounds.) It takes twice as much force to produce the same change in velocity of a 2 kg object than of a 1 kg object. Mass is a measure of an object's inertia, its resistance to acceleration.

Forces are represented by vectors; they have magnitude and direction. If several different forces act on an object simultaneously, then the net force, $\mathbf{F}_{net}$, is the vector sum of all these forces. (The phrase *resultant force* is also used to mean *net force*.)

Since $\mathbf{F}_{net} = m\mathbf{a}$, and *m* is a *positive* scalar, the direction of **a** always matches the direction of $\mathbf{F}_{net}$. Finally, since $F = ma$, the units for F equal the units of m times the units of a:

$$[F] = [m][a]$$
$$= kg \cdot m/s^2$$

A force of $1 \ kg \cdot m/s^2$ is renamed 1 **newton** (abbreviated N). A medium-sized apple weighs about 1 N.

THE THIRD LAW

This is the law that's commonly remembered as, *to every action, there is an equal, but opposite, reaction*. More precisely, if Object 1 exerts a force on Object 2, then Object 2 exerts a force back on Object 1, equal in strength but opposite in direction. These two forces, $\mathbf{F}_{1\text{-on-}2}$ and $\mathbf{F}_{2\text{-on-}1}$, are called an **action/reaction pair**.

Example 3.1 What net force is required to maintain a 5000 kg object moving at a constant velocity of magnitude 7500 m/s?

Solution. The First Law says that any object will *continue* in its state of motion unless a force acts on it. Therefore, *no* net force is required to maintain a 5000 kg object moving at a constant velocity of magnitude 7500 m/s. Here's another way to look at it: Constant velocity means $\mathbf{a} = \mathbf{0}$, so the equation $\mathbf{F}_{net} = m\mathbf{a}$ immediately gives $\mathbf{F}_{net} = \mathbf{0}$.

Example 3.2 How much force is required to cause an object of mass 2 kg to have an acceleration of 4 m/s²?

Solution. According to the Second Law, $F_{net} = ma = (2 \text{ kg})(4 \text{ m/s}^2) = 8$ N.

Example 3.3 An object feels two forces; one of strength 8 N pulling to the left and one of strength 20 N pulling to the right. If the object's mass is 4 kg, what is its acceleration?

Solution. Forces are represented by vectors and can be added and subtracted. Therefore, an 8 N force to the left added to a 20 N force to the right yields a net force of 20 − 8 = 12 N to the right. Then Newton's Second Law gives $\mathbf{a} = \mathbf{F}_{net}/m = (12$ N to the right$)/(4$ kg$) = 3$ m/s² to the right.

WEIGHT

Mass and weight are not the same thing—there is a clear distinction between them in physics—but they are often used interchangeably in everyday life. The **weight** of an object is the gravitational force exerted on it by the earth (or by whatever planet it happens to be on). Mass, by contrast, is an intrinsic property of an object that measures its inertia. An object's mass does not change with location. Put a baseball in a rocket and send it to the Moon. The baseball's *weight* on the Moon is less than its weight here on Earth (because the Moon's gravitational pull is weaker than the earth's due to its much smaller mass), but the baseball's mass would be the same.

Since weight is a force, we can use $\mathbf{F} = m\mathbf{a}$ to compute it. What acceleration would the gravitational force impose on an object? The gravitational acceleration, of course! Therefore, setting $\mathbf{a} = \mathbf{g}$, the equation $\mathbf{F} = m\mathbf{a}$ becomes

$$\mathbf{F}_w = m\mathbf{g}$$

This is the equation for the weight of an object of mass m. (Weight is often symbolized merely by $\mathbf{w}$, rather than $\mathbf{F}_w$.) Notice that mass and weight are proportional but not identical. Furthermore, mass is measured in kilograms, while weight is measured in newtons.

Example 3.4 What is the mass of an object that weighs 500 N?

Solution. Since weight is m multiplied by g, mass is F_w (weight) divided by g. Therefore,

$$m = F_w/g = (500 \text{ N})/(9.8 \text{ m/s}^2) = 51 \text{ kg}$$

Example 3.5 A person weighs 150 pounds. Given that a pound is a unit of weight equal to 4.45 N, what is this person's mass?

Solution. This person's weight in newtons is (150 lb)(4.45 N/lb) = 667.5 N, so his mass is

$$m = F_w/g = (667.5 \text{ N})/(9.8 \text{ m/s}^2) = 68 \text{ kg}$$

Example 3.6 A book whose mass is 2 kg rests on a table. Find the magnitude of the force exerted by the table on the book.

Solution. The book experiences two forces: The downward pull of the earth's gravity and the upward, supporting force exerted by the table. Since the book is at rest on the table, its acceleration is zero, so the net force on the book must be zero. Therefore the magnitude of the support force must equal the magnitude of the book's weight, which is $F_w = mg = (2 \text{ kg})(9.8 \text{ m/s}^2) = 20 \text{ N}$.

Example 3.7 A can of paint with a mass of 6 kg hangs from a rope. If the can is to be pulled up to a rooftop with an acceleration of 1 m/s², what must the tension in the rope be?

Solution. First draw a picture. Represent the object of interest (the can of paint) as a heavy dot, and draw the forces that act on the object as arrows connected to the dot. This is called a **free-body** (or **force**) **diagram**.

We have the tension force in the rope, $\mathbf{F}_T$ (also symbolized merely by $\mathbf{T}$), which is upward, and the weight, $\mathbf{F}_w$, which is downward. Calling *up* the positive direction, the net force is $F_T - F_w$. The Second Law, $F_{net} = ma$, becomes $F_T - F_w = ma$, so

$$F_T = F_w + ma = mg + ma = m(g + a) = 6(9.8 + 1) = 65 \text{ N}$$

Example 3.8 A can of paint with a mass of 6 kg hangs from a rope. If the can is to be pulled up to a rooftop with a constant velocity of 1 m/s, what must the tension in the rope be?

Solution. The phrase "constant velocity" automatically means $a = 0$ and, therefore, $F_{net} = 0$. In the diagram above, $\mathbf{F}_T$ would need to have the *same* magnitude as $\mathbf{F}_w$ in order to keep the can moving at a constant velocity. Thus, in this case, $F_T = F_w = mg = (6)(9.8) = 59$ N.

> **Example 3.9** What force must be exerted to lift a 49 N object with an acceleration of 9.8 m/s²?

Solution. First draw a free-body diagram

"up" is the
positive direction

We have the tension force, $\mathbf{F}_T$, which is upward, and the weight, $\mathbf{F}_w$, which is downward. Calling *up* the positive direction, the net force is $F_T - F_w$. The Second Law, $F_{net} = ma$, becomes $F_T - F_w = ma$, so $F_T = F_w + ma$. Remembering that $m = F_w/g$, we find that

$$F_T = F_w + ma = F_w + \frac{F_w}{g}a = 49 \text{ N} + \frac{49 \text{ N}}{9.8 \text{ m}/\text{s}^2}\left(9.8 \text{ m}/\text{s}^2\right) = 98 \text{ N}$$

THE NORMAL FORCE

When an object is in contact with a surface, the surface exerts a contact force on the object. The component of the contact force that's *perpendicular* to the surface is called the **normal force** on the object. (In physics, the word *normal* means *perpendicular*.) The normal force is what prevents objects from falling through tabletops or you from falling through the floor. The normal force is denoted by $\mathbf{F}_N$, or simply by $\mathbf{N}$. (If you use the latter notation, be careful not to confuse it with N, the abbreviation for the newton.)

> **Example 3.10** A book whose mass is 2 kg rests on a table. Find the magnitude of the normal force exerted by the table on the book.

Solution. The book experiences two forces: The downward pull of Earth's gravity and the upward, supporting force exerted by the table. Since the book is at rest on the table, its acceleration is zero, so the net force on the book must be zero. Therefore, the magnitude of the support force must equal the magnitude of the book's weight, which is $F_w = mg = (2)(9.8) = 20$ N. This means the normal force must be 20 N as well: $F_N = 20$ N. (Notice that this is a repeat of Example 3.6, except now we have a name for the "upward, supporting force exerted by the table"; it's called the normal force.)

FRICTION

When an object is in contact with a surface, the surface exerts a contact force on the object. The component of the contact force that's *parallel* to the surface is called the **friction force** on the object. Friction, like the normal force, arises from electrical interactions between atoms that comprise the object and those that comprise the surface.

We'll look at two main categories of friction: (1) **static friction** and (2) **kinetic (sliding) friction**. If you attempt to push a heavy crate across a floor, at first you meet with resistance, but then you push hard enough to get the crate moving. The force that acted on the crate to cancel out your initial pushes was static friction, and the force that acts on the crate as it slides across the floor is kinetic friction. Static friction occurs when there is no relative motion between the object and the surface (no sliding); kinetic friction occurs when there *is* relative motion (when there's sliding).

The strength of the friction force depends, in general, on two things: The nature of the surfaces and the strength of the normal force. The nature of the surfaces is represented by the **coefficient of friction**, denoted by μ (*mu*). The greater this number is, the stronger the friction force will be. For example, the coefficient of friction between rubber-soled shoes and a wooden floor is 0.7, but between rubbed-soled shoes and ice, it's only 0.1. Also, since kinetic friction is generally weaker than static friction (it's easier to keep an object sliding once it's sliding than it is to start the object sliding in the first place), there are two coefficients of friction; one for static friction (μ_s) and one for kinetic friction (μ_k). For a given pair of surfaces, it's virtually always true that $\mu_k < \mu_s$. The strengths of these two types of friction forces are given by the following equations:

$$F_{\text{static friction, max}} = \mu_s F_N$$

$$F_{\text{kinetic friction}} = \mu_k F_N$$

Notice that the equation for the strength of the static friction force is for the *maximum* value only. This is because static friction can vary, precisely counteracting weaker forces that attempt to move an object. For example, suppose an object feels a normal force of $F_N = 100$ N and the coefficient of static friction between it and the surface it's on is 0.5. Then, the *maximum* force that static friction can exert is (0.5)(100 N) = 50 N. However, if you push on the object with a force of, say, 20 N, then the static friction force will be 20 N (in the opposite direction), *not* 50 N; the object won't move. The net force on a stationary object must be zero. Static friction can take on all values, up to a certain maximum, and you must overcome the maximum static friction force to get the object to slide. The direction of $F_{\text{kinetic friction}} = F_{f\ (\text{kinetic})}$ is opposite to that of motion (sliding), and the direction of $F_{\text{static friction}} = F_{f\ (\text{static})}$ is opposite to that of the intended motion.

Example 3.11 A crate of mass 20 kg is sliding across a wooden floor. The coefficient of kinetic friction between the crate and the floor is 0.3.

  (a) Determine the strength of the friction force acting on the crate.
  (b) If the crate is being pulled by a force of 90 N (parallel to the floor), find the acceleration of the crate.

Solution. First draw a free-body diagram:

(a) The normal force on the object balances the object's weight, so
$F_N = mg = (20\ \text{kg})(9.8\ \text{m/s}^2) = 196\ \text{N}$. Therefore, $F_{f\ (\text{kinetic})} = \mu_k F_N = (0.3)(196\ \text{N}) = 59$ N.

(b) The net horizontal force that acts on the crate is $F - F_f = 90\ \text{N} - 59\ \text{N} = 31\ \text{N}$, so the acceleration of the crate is $a = F_{\text{net}}/m = (31\ \text{N})/(20\ \text{kg}) = 1.6\ \text{m/s}^2$.

Example 3.12 A crate of mass 100 kg rests on the floor. The coefficient of static friction is 0.4. If a force of 250 N (parallel to the floor) is applied to the crate, what's the magnitude of the force of static friction on the crate?

Solution. The normal force on the object balances its weight, so $F_N = mg = (100\ \text{kg})(9.8\ \text{m/s}^2) = 980\ \text{N}$. Therefore, $F_{\text{static friction, max}} = F_{f\ (\text{static}),\ \text{max}} = \mu_s F_N = (0.4)(980\ \text{N}) = 390\ \text{N}$. This is the *maximum* force that static friction can exert, but in this case it's *not* the actual value of the static friction force. Since the applied force on the crate is only 250 N, which is less than the $F_{f\ (\text{static}),\ \text{max}}$, the force of static friction will be less also: $F_{f\ (\text{static})} = 250\ \text{N}$, and the crate will not slide.

PULLEYS

Pulleys are devices that change the direction of the tension force in the cords that slide over them. Here we'll consider each pulley to be frictionless and massless, which means that their masses are so much smaller than the objects of interest in the problem that they can be ignored.

Example 3.13 In the diagram above, assume that the tabletop is frictionless. Determine the acceleration of the blocks once they're released from rest.

Solution. There are two blocks, so we draw two free-body diagrams:

To get the acceleration of each one, we use Newton's Second Law, $\mathbf{F}_{net} = m\mathbf{a}$.

$$F_T = ma$$

$$Mg - F_T = Ma$$

Notice that there are two unknowns, F_T and a, but we can eliminate F_T by adding the two equations, and then we can solve for a.

$$F_T = ma$$
$$Mg - F_T = Ma$$

Add the equations to eliminate F_T.

$$Mg = ma + Ma$$
$$= a(m + M)$$

$$\frac{Mg}{m + M} = a$$

Example 3.14 Using the same diagram as in the previous example, assume that $m = 2$ kg, $M = 10$ kg, and the coefficient of kinetic friction between the small block and the tabletop is 0.5. Compute the acceleration of the blocks.

Solution. Once again, draw a free-body diagram for each object. Notice that the only difference between these diagrams and the ones in the previous example is the inclusion of the force of (kinetic) friction, $\mathbf{F}_f$, that acts on the block on the table.

$$F_T - F_f = ma$$
$$Mg - F_T = Ma$$

As before, we have two equations that contain two unknowns (a and F_T):

$$F_T - F_f = ma \quad (1)$$

$$Mg - F_T = Ma \quad (2)$$

Add the equations (thereby eliminating F_T) and solve for a. Notice that, by definition, $F_f = \mu F_N$, and from the free-body diagram for m, we see that $F_N = mg$, so $F_f = \mu mg$:

$$Mg - F_f = ma + Ma$$

$$Mg - \mu mg = a(m + M)$$

$$\frac{M - \mu m}{m + M} g = a$$

Substituting in the numerical values given for m, M, and μ, we find that $a = \frac{3}{4} g$ (or 7.4 m/s²).

> **Example 3.15** In the previous example, calculate the strength of the tension in the cord.

Solution. Since the value of a has been determined, we can use either of the two original equations to calculate F_T. Using Equation (2), $Mg - F_T = Ma$ (because it's simpler), we find

$$F_T = Mg - Ma = Mg - M \cdot \frac{3}{4} g = \frac{1}{4} Mg = \frac{1}{4}(10)(9.8) = 25 \text{ N}$$

As you can see, we would have found the same answer if Equation (1) had been used:

$$F_T - F_f = ma \Rightarrow F_T = F_f + ma = \mu mg + ma = \mu mg + m \cdot \frac{3}{4} g = mg\left(\mu + \frac{3}{4}\right)$$

$$= (2)(9.8)(0.5 + 0.75)$$

$$= 25 \text{ N}$$

INCLINED PLANES

An **inclined plane** is basically a ramp. If an object of mass m is on the ramp, then the force of gravity on the object, $\mathbf{F}_w = m\mathbf{g}$, has two components: One that's parallel to the ramp ($mg \sin \theta$) and one that's normal to the ramp ($mg \cos \theta$), where θ is the incline angle. The force driving the block down the inclined plane is the component of the block's weight that's parallel to the ramp: $mg \sin \theta$.

This angle is also θ.

Example 3.16 A block slides down a frictionless, inclined plane that makes a 30° angle with the horizontal. Find the acceleration of this block.

Solution. Let m denote the mass of the block, so the force that pulls the block down the incline is $mg \sin \theta$, and the block's acceleration down the plane is

$$a = \frac{F}{m} = \frac{mg \sin \theta}{m} = g \sin \theta = g \sin 30° = \frac{1}{2} g = 4.9 \text{ m/s}^2$$

Example 3.17 A block slides down an inclined plane that makes a 30° angle with the horizontal. If the coefficient of kinetic friction is 0.3, find the acceleration of the block.

Solution. First draw a free-body diagram. Notice that, in the diagram shown below, the weight of the block, $\mathbf{F_w} = m\mathbf{g}$, has been written in terms of its scalar components: $F_w \sin \theta$ parallel to the ramp and $F_w \cos \theta$ normal to the ramp:

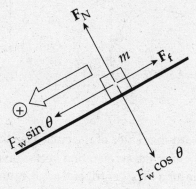

The force of friction, $\mathbf{F_f}$, that acts up the ramp (opposite to the direction in which the block slides) has magnitude $F_f = \mu F_N$. But the diagram shows that $F_N = F_w \cos \theta$, so $F_f = \mu (mg \cos \theta)$. Therefore the net force down the ramp is

$$F_w \sin \theta - F_f = mg \sin \theta - \mu mg \cos \theta = mg(\sin \theta - \mu \cos \theta)$$

Then, setting F_{net} equal to ma, we solve for a:

$$a = \frac{F_{net}}{m} = \frac{mg(\sin \theta - \mu \cos \theta)}{m}$$
$$= g(\sin \theta - \mu \cos \theta)$$
$$= (9.8 \text{ m/s}^2)(\sin 30° - 0.3 \cos 30°)$$
$$= 2.4 \text{ m/s}^2$$

UNIFORM CIRCULAR MOTION

In Chapter 2, we considered two types of motion; straight-line motion and parabolic motion. We will now look at motion that follows a circular path, such as a rock on the end of a string, a horse on a merry-go-round, and (to a good approximation) the Moon around Earth and Earth around the Sun.

Let's simplify matters and consider the object's speed around its path to be constant. This is called **uniform circular motion**. You should remember that although the speed may be constant, the velocity is not, because the direction of the velocity is always changing. Since the velocity is changing, there must be acceleration. This acceleration does not change the speed of the object; it only changes the direction of the velocity to keep the object on its circular path. Also, in order to produce an acceleration, there must be a force; otherwise, the object would move off in a straight line (Newton's First Law).

The figure on the left below shows an object moving along a circular trajectory, along with its velocity vectors at two nearby points. The vector $\mathbf{v}_1$ is the object's velocity at time $t = t_1$, and $\mathbf{v}_2$ is the object's velocity vector a short time later (at time $t = t_2$). The velocity vector is always tangential to the object's path (whatever the shape of the trajectory). Notice that since we are assuming constant speed, the lengths of $\mathbf{v}_1$ and $\mathbf{v}_2$ (their magnitudes) are the same.

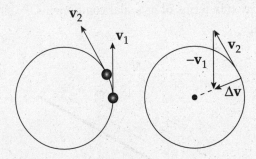

Since $\Delta \mathbf{v} = \mathbf{v}_2 - \mathbf{v}_1$ points toward the center of the circle (see the figure on the right), so does the acceleration, since $\mathbf{a} = \Delta \mathbf{v} / \Delta t$. Because the acceleration vector points toward the center of the circle, it's called **centripetal acceleration**, or $\mathbf{a}_c$. The centripetal acceleration is what turns the velocity vector to keep the object traveling in a circle. The magnitude of the centripetal acceleration depends on the object's speed, v, and the radius, r, of the circular path according to the equation

$$a_c = \frac{v^2}{r}$$

> **Example 3.18** An object of mass 5 kg moves at a constant speed of 6 m/s in a circular path of radius 2 m. Find the object's acceleration and the net force responsible for its motion.

Solution. By definition, an object moving at constant speed in a circular path is undergoing uniform circular motion. Therefore, it experiences a centripetal acceleration of magnitude v^2/r, always directed toward the center of the circle:

$$a_c = \frac{v^2}{r} = \frac{(6 \text{ m/s})^2}{2 \text{ m}} = 18 \text{ m/s}^2$$

The force that produces the centripetal acceleration is given by Newton's Second Law, coupled with the equation for centripetal acceleration:

$$F_c = ma_c = m\frac{v^2}{r}$$

This equation gives the magnitude of the force. As for the direction, recall that because $\mathbf{F} = m\mathbf{a}$, the directions of $\mathbf{F}$ and $\mathbf{a}$ are always the same. Since centripetal acceleration points toward the center of the circular path, so does the force that produces it. Therefore, it's called **centripetal force**. The centripetal force acting on this object has a magnitude of $F_c = ma_c = (5 \text{ kg})(18 \text{ m/s}^2) = 90 \text{ N}$.

Example 3.19 An 8.3 kg mass is attached to a string that has a breaking strength of 1500 N. If the mass is whirled in a horizontal circle of radius 80 cm, what maximum speed can it have?

Solution. The first thing to do in problems like this is to identify what force(s) provide the centripetal force. In this example, the tension in the string provides the centripetal force:

$$\mathbf{F}_T \text{ provides } \mathbf{F}_c \Rightarrow F_T = \frac{mv^2}{r} \Rightarrow v = \sqrt{\frac{rF_T}{m}} \Rightarrow v_{\text{max}} = \sqrt{\frac{rF_{T,\text{max}}}{m}}$$

$$= \sqrt{\frac{(0.80 \text{ m})(1500 \text{ N})}{8.3 \text{ kg}}}$$

$$= 12 \text{ m/s}$$

Example 3.20 An athlete who weighs 790 N is running around a curve at a speed of 6.0 m/s in an arc whose radius of curvature, r, is 4.9 m. Find the centripetal force acting on him. What provides the centripetal force? What could happen to him if r were smaller?

Solution. Using the equation for the strength of the centripetal force, we find that

$$F_c = m\frac{v^2}{r} = \frac{F_w}{g} \cdot \frac{v^2}{r} = \frac{790 \text{ N}}{9.8 \text{ N/kg}} \cdot \frac{(6.0 \text{ m/s})^2}{4.9 \text{ m}} = 590 \text{ N}$$

In this case, static friction provides the centripetal force. Since the coefficient of static friction between his shoes and the ground is most likely around 1, the maximum force that static friction can exert is $\mu_s F_N \approx F_N = F_w = 790 \text{ N}$. Fortunately, 790 N is greater than 590 N. But notice that if the radius of curvature of the arc were much smaller, then F_c would become greater than what static friction could handle, and he would slip.

Example 3.21 A roller-coaster car enters the circular-loop portion of the ride. At the very top of the circle (where the people in the car are upside down), the speed of the car is 25 m/s, and the acceleration points straight down. If the diameter of the loop is 50 m and the total mass of the car (plus passengers) is 1200 kg, find the magnitude of the normal force exerted by the track on the car at this point.

Solution. There are two forces acting on the car at its topmost point: The normal force exerted by the track and the gravitational force, both of which point downward.

The combination of these two forces, $\mathbf{F}_N + \mathbf{F}_w$, provides the centripetal force:

$$F_N + F_w = \frac{mv^2}{r} \Rightarrow F_N = \frac{mv^2}{r} - F_w$$

$$= \frac{mv^2}{r} - mg$$

$$= m\left(\frac{v^2}{r} - g\right)$$

$$= (1200 \text{ kg})\left[\frac{(25 \text{ m/s})^2}{\frac{1}{2}(50 \text{ m})} - 9.8 \text{ m/s}^2\right]$$

$$= 1.8 \times 10^4 \text{ N}$$

Example 3.22 In the previous example, if the net force on the car at its topmost point is straight down, why doesn't the car fall straight down?

Solution. Remember that force tells an object how to *accelerate*. If the car had zero velocity at this point, then it would certainly fall straight down, but the car has a nonzero velocity (to the left) at this point. The fact that the acceleration is downward means that, at the next moment **v** will point down to the left at a slight angle, ensuring that the car remains on a circular path, in contact with the track.

CHAPTER 3 REVIEW QUESTIONS

SECTION I: MULTIPLE CHOICE

1. A person standing on a horizontal floor feels two forces: the downward pull of gravity and the upward supporting force from the floor. These two forces

    (A) have equal magnitudes and form an action/reaction pair.
    (B) have equal magnitudes but do not form an action/reaction pair.
    (C) have unequal magnitudes and form an action/reaction pair.
    (D) have unequal magnitudes and do not form an action/reaction pair.
    (E) None of the above

2. A person who weighs 800 N steps onto a scale that is on the floor of an elevator car. If the elevator accelerates upward at a rate of 4.9 m/s², what will the scale read?

    (A) 400 N
    (B) 800 N
    (C) 1000 N
    (D) 1200 N
    (E) 1600 N

3. A frictionless inclined plane of length 20 m has a maximum vertical height of 5 m. If an object of mass 2 kg is placed on the plane, which of the following best approximates the net force it feels?

    (A) 5 N
    (B) 10 N
    (C) 15 N
    (D) 20 N
    (E) 30 N

4. A 20 N block is being pushed across a horizontal table by an 18 N force. If the coefficient of kinetic friction between the block and the table is 0.4, find the acceleration of the block.

    (A) 0.5 m/s²
    (B) 1 m/s²
    (C) 5 m/s²
    (D) 7.5 m/s²
    (E) 9 m/s²

5. The coefficient of static friction between a box and a ramp is 0.5. The ramp's incline angle is 30°. If the box is placed at rest on the ramp, the box will

    (A) accelerate down the ramp.
    (B) accelerate briefly down the ramp but then slow down and stop.
    (C) move with constant velocity down the ramp.
    (D) not move.
    (E) Cannot be determined from the information given

6.

Assuming a frictionless, massless pulley, determine the acceleration of the blocks once they are released from rest.

(A) $\dfrac{m}{M+m}g$

(B) $\dfrac{M}{M+m}g$

(C) $\dfrac{M}{m}g$

(D) $\dfrac{M+m}{M-m}g$

(E) $\dfrac{M-m}{M+m}g$

7. If all of the forces acting on an object balance so that the net force is zero, then

(A) the object must be at rest.
(B) the object's speed will decrease.
(C) the object will follow a parabolic trajectory.
(D) the object's direction of motion can change, but not its speed.
(E) None of the above

8. A block of mass m is at rest on a frictionless, horizontal table placed in a laboratory on the surface of the earth. An identical block is at rest on a frictionless, horizontal table placed on the surface of the Moon. Let $\mathbf{F}$ be the net force necessary to give the Earth-bound block an acceleration of $\mathbf{a}$ across the table. Given that g_{Moon} is one-sixth of g_{Earth}, the force necessary to give the Moon-bound block the same acceleration $\mathbf{a}$ across the table is

(A) $\mathbf{F}/12$
(B) $\mathbf{F}/6$
(C) $\mathbf{F}/3$
(D) $\mathbf{F}$
(E) $6\mathbf{F}$

9. A crate of mass 100 kg is at rest on a horizontal floor. The coefficient of static friction between the crate and the floor is 0.4, and the coefficient of kinetic friction is 0.3. A force $\mathbf{F}$ of magnitude 344 N is then applied to the crate, parallel to the floor. Which of the following is true?

(A) The crate will accelerate across the floor at 0.5 m/s^2.
(B) The static friction force, which is the reaction force to $\mathbf{F}$ as guaranteed by Newton's Third Law, will also have a magnitude of 344 N.
(C) The crate will slide across the floor at a constant speed of 0.5 m/s.
(D) The crate will not move.
(E) None of the above

10. Two crates are stacked on top of each other on a horizontal floor; Crate #1 is on the bottom, and Crate #2 is on the top. Both crates have the same mass. Compared to the strength of the force $\mathbf{F}_1$ necessary to push only Crate #1 at a constant speed across the floor, the strength of the force $\mathbf{F}_2$ necessary to push the stack at the same constant speed across the floor is greater than F_1 because

(A) the force of the floor on Crate #1 is greater.
(B) the coefficient of kinetic friction between Crate #1 and the floor is greater.
(C) the force of kinetic friction, but not the normal force, on Crate #1 is greater.
(D) the coefficient of static friction between Crate #1 and the floor is greater.
(E) the weight of Crate #1 is greater.

11. An object moves at constant speed in a circular path. Which of the following statements is/are true?

I. The velocity is constant.
II. The acceleration is constant.
III. The net force on the object is zero since its speed is constant.

(A) II only
(B) I and III only
(C) II and III only
(D) I and II only
(E) None of the above

A 60 cm rope is tied to the handle of a bucket which is then whirled in a vertical circle. The mass of the bucket is 3 kg.

12. At the lowest point in its path, the tension in the rope is 50 N. What is the speed of the bucket?

   (A) 1 m/s
   (B) 2 m/s
   (C) 3 m/s
   (D) 4 m/s
   (E) 5 m/s

13. What is the critical speed below which the rope would become slack when the bucket reaches the highest point in the circle?

   (A) 0.6 m/s
   (B) 1.8 m/s
   (C) 2.4 m/s
   (D) 3.2 m/s
   (E) 4.8 m/s

14. An object moves at a constant speed in a circular path of radius r at a rate of 1 revolution per second. What is its acceleration?

   (A) 0
   (B) $(2\pi^2\,s^{-2})r$
   (C) $(2\pi^2\,s^{-2})r^2$
   (D) $(4\pi^2\,s^{-2})r$
   (E) $(4\pi^2\,s^{-2})r^2$

SECTION II: FREE RESPONSE

1. This question concerns the motion of a crate being pulled across a horizontal floor by a rope. In the diagram below, the mass of the crate is m, the coefficient of kinetic friction between the crate and the floor is μ, and the tension in the rope is F_T.

   (a) Draw and label all of the forces acting on the crate.

   (b) Compute the normal force acting on the crate in terms of m, F_T, θ, and g.

   (c) Compute the acceleration of the crate in terms of m, F_T, θ, μ, and g.

   (d) [C] Assume that the magnitude of the tension in the rope is fixed but that the angle θ may be varied. For what value of θ would the resulting horizontal acceleration of the crate be maximized?

2. In the diagram below, a massless string connects two blocks—of masses m_1 and m_2, respectively—on a flat, frictionless tabletop. A force **F** pulls on Block #2, as shown:

   (a) Draw and label all of the forces acting on Block #1.

   (b) Draw and label all of the forces acting on Block #2.

   (c) What is the acceleration of Block #1?

   (d) What is the tension in the string connecting the two blocks?

   (e) If the string connecting the blocks were not massless, but instead had a mass of m, figure out

   (i) the acceleration of Block #1, and

   (ii) the difference between the strength of the force that the connecting string exerts on Block #2 and the strength of the force that the connecting string exerts on Block #1.

3. In the figure shown, assume that the pulley is frictionless and massless.

(a) If the surface of the inclined plane is frictionless, determine what value(s) of θ will cause the box of mass m_1 to

   (i) accelerate up the ramp;

   (ii) slide up the ramp at constant speed.

(b) If the coefficient of kinetic friction between the surface of the inclined plane and the box of mass m_1 is μ_k, derive (but do not solve) an equation satisfied by the value of θ which will cause the box of mass m_1 to slide up the ramp at constant speed.

4. A sky diver is falling with speed v_0 through the air. At that moment (time $t = 0$), she opens her parachute and experiences the force of air resistance whose strength is given by the equation $F = kv$, where k is a proportionality constant and v is her descent speed. The total mass of the sky diver and equipment is m. Assume that g is constant throughout her descent.

(a) Draw and label all the forces acting on the sky diver after her parachute opens.

(b) Determine the sky diver's acceleration in terms of m, v, k, and g.

(c) Determine the sky diver's terminal speed (that is, the eventual constant speed of descent).

(d) Sketch a graph of v as a function of time, being sure to label important values on the vertical axis.

(e) [C] Derive an expression for her descent speed, v, as a function of time t since opening her parachute in terms of m, k, and g.

5. An amusement park ride consists of a large cylinder that rotates around its central axis as the passengers stand against the inner wall of the cylinder. Once the passengers are moving at a certain speed v, the floor on which they were standing is lowered. Each passenger feels pinned against the wall of the cylinder as it rotates. Let r be the inner radius of the cylinder.

   (a) Draw and label all the forces acting on a passenger of mass m as the cylinder rotates with the floor lowered.

   (b) Describe what conditions must hold to keep the passengers from sliding down the wall of the cylinder.

   (c) Compare the conditions discussed in part (b) for an adult passenger of mass m and a child passenger of mass $m/2$.

6. A curved section of a highway has a radius of curvature of r. The coefficient of friction between standard automobile tires and the surface of the highway is μ_s.

   (a) Draw and label all the forces acting on a car of mass m traveling along this curved part of the highway.

   (b) Compute the maximum speed with which a car of mass m could make it around the turn without skidding in terms of μ_s, r, g, and m.

   City engineers are planning on banking this curved section of highway at an angle of θ to the horizontal.

   (c) Draw and label all of the forces acting on a car of mass m traveling along this banked turn. Do not include friction.

   (d) The engineers want to be sure that a car of mass m traveling at a constant speed v (the posted speed limit) could make it safely around the banked turn even if the road were covered with ice (that is, essentially frictionless). Compute this banking angle θ in terms of r, v, g, and m.

4

WORK, ENERGY, AND POWER

INTRODUCTION

It wasn't until over 100 years after Newton that the idea of energy became incorporated into physics, but today it permeates every branch of the subject.

It's difficult to give a precise definition of energy; there are different forms of energy because there are different kinds of forces. There's gravitational energy (a meteor crashing into the earth), elastic energy (a stretched rubber band), thermal energy (an oven), radiant energy (sunlight), electrical energy (a lamp plugged into a wall socket), nuclear energy (nuclear power plants), and mass energy (the heart of Einstein's equation $E = mc^2$). Energy can come into a system or leave it via various interactions that produce changes. One of the best definitions we know reads as follows: **Force** is the agent of change, **energy** is the measure of change, and **work** is the way of transferring energy from one system to another. And one of the most important laws in physics (the **Law of Conservation of**

Energy, also known as the **First Law of Thermodynamics**) says that if you account for all its various forms, the total amount of energy in a given process will stay constant; that is, it will be *conserved*. For example, electrical energy can be converted into light and heat (this is how a light bulb works), but the amount of electrical energy *coming in* to the light bulb equals the total amount of light and heat *given off*. Energy cannot be created or destroyed; it can only be transferred (from one system to another) or transformed (from one form to another).

WORK

When you lift a book from the floor, you exert a force on it, over a distance, and when you push a crate across a floor, you also exert a force on it, over a distance. The application of force over a distance, and the resulting change in energy of the system that the force acted on, give rise to the concept of **work**. When you hold a book in your hand, you exert a force on the book (normal force) but, since the book is at rest, the force does not act through a distance, so you do no work on the book. Although you did work on the book as you lifted it from the floor, once it's at rest in your hand, you are no longer doing work on it.

> *Definition.* If a force **F** acts over a distance *d*, and **F** is parallel to **d**, then the work done by **F** is the product of force and distance: $W = Fd$.

Notice that, although work depends on two vectors (**F** and **d**), work itself is *not* a vector. *Work is a scalar quantity.*

> **Example 4.1** You slowly lift a book of mass 2 kg at constant velocity a distance of 3 m. How much work did you do on the book?

Solution. In this case, the force you exert must balance the weight of the book (otherwise the velocity of the book wouldn't be constant), so $F = mg = (2 \text{ kg})(9.8 \text{ m/s}^2) = 20$ N. Since this force is straight upward and the displacement of the book is also straight upward, **F** and **d** are parallel, so the work done by your lifting force is $W = Fd = (20 \text{ N})(3 \text{ m}) = 60$ N·m. The unit for work, the newton-meter (N·m) is renamed a **joule**, and abbreviated J. So the work done here is 60 J.

The definition above takes care of cases in which **F** is parallel to the motion. If **F** is not parallel to the motion, then the definition needs to be generalized.

> *Definition.* If a force **F** acts over a distance *d*, and θ is the angle between **F** and **d**, then the work done by **F** is the product of the component of force in the direction of the motion and the distance: $W = (F \cos \theta)d$. [Notice that you can write this definition using the *dot product*: $W = \mathbf{F} \cdot \mathbf{d}$.]

> **Example 4.2** A 15 kg crate is moved along a horizontal floor by a warehouse worker who's pulling on it with a rope that makes a 30° angle with the horizontal. The tension in the rope is 200 N and the crate slides a distance of 10 m. How much work is done on the crate by the worker?

Solution. The figure below shows that $\mathbf{F}_T$ and $\mathbf{d}$ are not parallel. It's only the component of the force acting along the direction of motion, $F_T \cos \theta$, that does work.

Therefore,

$$W = (F_T \cos \theta)d = (200 \text{ N} \cdot \cos 30°)(10 \text{ m}) = 1730 \text{ J}$$

Example 4.3 In the previous example, assume that the coefficient of kinetic friction between the crate and the floor is 0.4.
 (a) How much work is done by the normal force?
 (b) How much work is done by the friction force?

Solution.

(a) Clearly, the normal force is not parallel to the motion, so we use the general definition of work. Since the angle between $\mathbf{F}_N$ and $\mathbf{d}$ is 90° (by definition of *normal*) and $\cos 90° = 0$, the normal force does zero work.

(b) The friction force, $\mathbf{F}_f$, is also not parallel to the motion; it's *antiparallel*. That is, the angle between $\mathbf{F}_f$ and $\mathbf{d}$ is 180°. Since $\cos 180° = -1$, and since the strength of the normal force is $F_N = F_w = mg = (15 \text{ kg})(9.8 \text{ m/s}^2) = 147 \text{ N}$, the work done by the friction force is:

$$W = -F_f d = -\mu_k F_N d = -(0.4)(147 \text{ N})(10 \text{ m}) = -590 \text{ J}$$

The two previous examples show that work, which is a scalar quantity, may be positive, negative, or zero. If the angle between $\mathbf{F}$ and $\mathbf{d}$ (θ) is less than 90°, then the work is positive (because $\cos \theta$ is positive in this case); if $\theta = 90°$, the work is zero (because $\cos 90° = 0$); and if $\theta > 90°$, then the work is negative (because $\cos \theta$ is negative). Intuitively, if a force helps the motion, the work done by the force is positive, but if the force opposes the motion, then the work done by the force is negative.

Example 4.4 A box slides down an inclined plane (incline angle = 40°). The mass of the block, m, is 35 kg, the coefficient of kinetic friction between the box and the ramp, μ_k, is 0.3, and the length of the ramp, d, is 8 m.

(a) How much work is done by gravity?
(b) How much work is done by the normal force?
(c) How much work is done by friction?
(d) What is the total work done?

Solution.

(a) Recall that the force that's directly responsible for pulling the box down the plane is the component of the gravitational force that's parallel to the ramp:

$F_w \sin \theta = mg \sin \theta$ (where θ is the incline angle). This component is parallel to the motion, so the work done by gravity is

$$W_{\text{by gravity}} = (mg \sin \theta)d = (35 \text{ kg})(9.8 \text{ N/kg})(\sin 40°)(8 \text{ m}) = 1760 \text{ J}$$

Notice that the work done by gravity is positive, as we would expect it to be, since gravity is helping the motion. Also, be careful with the angle θ. The general definition of work reads $W = (F \cos \theta)d$, where θ is the angle between $\mathbf{F}$ and $\mathbf{d}$. However, the angle between $\mathbf{F}_w$ and $\mathbf{d}$ is *not* 40° here, so the work done by gravity is not $(mg \cos 40°)d$. The angle θ used in the calculation above is the incline angle.

(b) Since the normal force is perpendicular to the motion, the work done by this force is zero.

(c) The strength of the normal force is $F_w \cos \theta$ (where θ is the incline angle), so the strength of the friction force is $F_f = \mu_k F_N = \mu_k F_w \cos \theta = \mu_k mg \cos \theta$. Since $\mathbf{F}_f$ is antiparallel to $\mathbf{d}$, the cosine of the angle between these vectors (180°) is –1, so the work done by friction is

$$W_{\text{by friction}} = -F_f d = -(\mu_k mg \cos \theta)(d) = -(0.3)(35 \text{ kg})(9.8 \text{ N/kg})(\cos 40°)(8 \text{ m}) = -630 \text{ J}$$

Notice that the work done by friction is negative, as we expect it to be, since friction is opposing the motion.

(d) The total work done is found simply by adding the values of the work done by each of the forces acting on the box:

$$W_{\text{total}} = \Sigma W = W_{\text{by gravity}} + W_{\text{by normal force}} + W_{\text{by friction}} = 1760 + 0 + (-630) = 1130 \text{ J}$$

WORK DONE BY A VARIABLE FORCE

If a force remains constant over the distance through which it acts, then the work done by the force is simply the product of force and distance. However, if the force does not remain constant, then the work done by the force is given by a definite integral. Focusing only on displacements that are along a straight line (call it the x axis), let $\mathbf{F}$ be a force whose component in the x direction varies with position according to the equation $F = F(x)$. Then the work done by this force as it acts from position $x = x_1$ to position $x = x_2$ is equal to

$$W = \int_{x_1}^{x_2} F(x)\, dx$$

If a graph of F *vs.* x is given, then the work done by $\mathbf{F}$ as it acts from $x = x_1$ to $x = x_2$ is equal to the area bounded by the graph of F, the x axis, and the vertical lines $x = x_1$ and $x = x_2$:

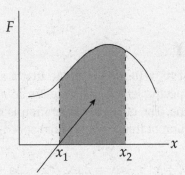

area = work done by $\mathbf{F}$

Example 4.5 The force exerted by a spring when it's displaced by x from its natural length is given by the equation $F(x) = -kx$, where k is a positive constant. What is the work done by a spring as it pushes out from $x = -x_2$ to $x = -x_1$ (where $x_2 > x_1$)?

Solution. Since the force is variable, we calculate the following definite integral:

$$W = \int_{-x_2}^{-x_1} F(x)\, dx = \int_{-x_2}^{-x_1} (-kx)\, dx = -\tfrac{1}{2}kx^2 \Big]_{-x_2}^{-x_1}$$

$$= \tfrac{1}{2}kx^2 \Big]_{-x_1}^{-x_2}$$

$$= \tfrac{1}{2}k\left(x_2^2 - x_1^2\right)$$

Another solution would involve sketching a graph of $F(x) = -kx$ and calculating the area under the graph from $x = -x_2$ to $x = -x_1$.

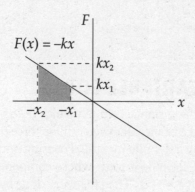

Here, the region is a trapezoid with area $A = \frac{1}{2}(\text{base}_1 + \text{base}_2) \times \text{height}$, so

$$W = A = \tfrac{1}{2}(kx_2 + kx_1)(x_2 - x_1)$$
$$= \tfrac{1}{2}k(x_2 + x_1)(x_2 - x_1)$$
$$= \tfrac{1}{2}k\left(x_2^2 - x_1^2\right)$$

KINETIC ENERGY

Consider an object at rest ($v_0 = 0$), and imagine that a steady force is exerted on it, causing it to accelerate. Let's be more specific; let the object's mass be m, and let $\mathbf{F}$ be the force acting on the object, pushing it in a straight line. The object's acceleration is $a = F/m$, so after the object has traveled a distance Δs under the action of this force, its final speed, v, is given by Big Five #5:

$$v^2 = v_0^2 + 2a\Delta s = 2a\Delta s = 2\frac{F}{m}\Delta s \quad \Rightarrow \quad F\Delta s = \tfrac{1}{2}mv^2$$

But the quantity $F\,\Delta s$ is the work done by the force, so $W = \frac{1}{2}mv^2$. The work done on the object has transferred energy to it, in the amount $\frac{1}{2}mv^2$. The energy an object possesses by virtue of its motion is therefore defined as $\frac{1}{2}mv^2$ and is called **kinetic energy**:

$$K = \tfrac{1}{2}mv^2$$

THE WORK–ENERGY THEOREM

Kinetic energy is expressed in joules just like work, since in the case we just looked at, $W = K$. In fact, the derivation above can be extended to an object with a nonzero initial speed, and the same analysis will show that the total work done on an object—or, equivalently, the work done by the net force—will equal its change in kinetic energy; this is known as the **work–energy theorem**:

$$W_{\text{total}} = \Delta K$$

Notice that kinetic energy, like work, is a scalar quantity.

Example 4.6 What is the kinetic energy of a baseball (mass = 0.15 kg) moving with a speed of 36 m/s?

Solution. From the definition,

$$K = \tfrac{1}{2}mv^2 = \tfrac{1}{2}(0.15 \text{ kg})(36 \text{ m/s})^2 = 97 \text{ J}$$

Example 4.7 A tennis ball (mass = 0.06 kg) is hit straight upward with an initial speed of 45 m/s. How high would it go if air resistance were negligible?

Solution. This could be done using the Big Five, but let's try to solve it using the concepts of work and energy. As the ball travels upward, gravity acts on it by doing negative work. [The work is negative because gravity is opposing the upward motion. $\mathbf{F}_w$ and $\mathbf{d}$ are in opposite directions, so $\theta = 180°$, which tells us that $W = (F_w \cos \theta)d = -F_w d$.] At the moment the ball reaches its highest point, its speed is 0, so its kinetic energy is also 0. The work–energy theorem then says

$$W = \Delta K \quad \Rightarrow \quad -F_w d = 0 - \tfrac{1}{2}mv_0^2 \quad \Rightarrow \quad d = \frac{\tfrac{1}{2}mv_0^2}{F_w} = \frac{\tfrac{1}{2}mv_0^2}{mg} = \frac{\tfrac{1}{2}v_0^2}{g} = \frac{\tfrac{1}{2}(45 \text{ m/s})^2}{9.8 \text{ m/s}^2} = 103 \text{ m}$$

Example 4.8 Consider the box sliding down the inclined plane in Example 4.4. If it starts from rest at the top of the ramp, with what speed does it reach the bottom?

Solution. It was calculated in Example 4.4 that $W_{total} = 1130$ J. According to the work–energy theorem,

$$W_{total} = \Delta K \quad \Rightarrow \quad W_{total} = K_f - K_i = K_f = \tfrac{1}{2}mv^2 \quad \Rightarrow \quad v = \sqrt{\frac{2W_{total}}{m}} = \sqrt{\frac{2(1130 \text{ J})}{35 \text{ kg}}} = 8 \text{ m/s}$$

Example 4.9 A pool cue striking a stationary billiard ball (mass = 0.25 kg) gives the ball a speed of 1.5 m/s. If the force of the cue on the ball was 20 N, over what distance did this force act?

Solution. The kinetic energy of the ball as it leaves the cue is

$$K = \tfrac{1}{2}mv^2 = \tfrac{1}{2}(0.25 \text{ kg})(1.5 \text{ m/s})^2 = 0.28 \text{ J}$$

The work W done by the cue gave the ball this kinetic energy, so

$$W = \Delta K \quad \Rightarrow \quad W = K_f \quad \Rightarrow \quad Fd = K \quad \Rightarrow \quad d = \frac{K}{F} = \frac{0.28 \text{ J}}{20 \text{ N}} = 0.014 \text{ m} = 1.4 \text{ cm}$$

POTENTIAL ENERGY

Kinetic energy is the energy an object has by virtue of its motion. Potential energy is independent of motion; it arises from the object's position (or the system's configuration). For example, a ball at the edge of a tabletop has energy, which could be transformed into kinetic energy if it falls off. An arrow in an archer's pulled back bow has energy that could be transformed into kinetic energy if the archer releases the arrow. Both of these examples illustrate the concept of **potential energy**, the energy an object or system has by virtue of its position or configuration. In each case, work was done on the object to put it in the given configuration (the ball was lifted to the tabletop, the bowstring was pulled back), and since work is the means of transferring energy, these things have *stored energy that can be retrieved*, as kinetic energy. This is **potential energy**, denoted by U.

Because there are different types of forces, there are different types of potential energy. The ball at the edge of the tabletop provides an example of **gravitational potential energy**, U_{grav}, which is the energy stored by virtue of an object's position in a gravitational field. This energy would be converted to kinetic energy as gravity pulled the ball down to the floor. For now, let's concentrate on gravitational potential energy.

Assume the ball has a mass m of 2 kg, and that the tabletop is $h = 1.5$ m above the floor. How much work did gravity do as the ball was lifted from the floor to the table? The strength of the gravitational force on the ball is $F_w = mg = (2\ \text{kg})(9.8\ \text{N/kg}) = 20$ N. The force $\mathbf{F}_w$ points downward, and the ball's motion was upward, so the work done by gravity during the ball's ascent was

$$W_{\text{by gravity}} = -F_w h = -mgh = -(20\ \text{N})(1.5\ \text{m}) = -30\ \text{J}$$

So someone performed +30 J of work to raise the ball from the floor to the tabletop. That energy is now stored and, if the ball was given a push to send it over the edge, by the time the ball reached the floor it would acquire a kinetic energy of 30 J. We therefore say that the change in the ball's gravitational potential energy in moving from the floor to the table was +30 J. That is,

$$\Delta U_{grav} = -W_{\text{by gravity}}$$

Notice that potential energy, like work (and kinetic energy), is expressed in joules.

In general, if an object of mass m is raised a height h (which is small enough that g stays essentially constant over this altitude change), then the increase in the object's gravitational potential energy is

$$\Delta U_{grav} = mgh$$

An important fact that makes the above equation possible is that the work done by gravity as the object is raised does not depend on the path taken by the object. The ball could be lifted straight upward, or in some curvy path; it would make no difference. Gravity is said to a **conservative** force because of this property.

If we decide on a reference level to call $h = 0$, then we can say that the gravitational potential energy of an object of mass m at a height h is $U_{grav} = mgh$. In order to use this last equation, it's essential that we choose a reference level for height. For example, consider a passenger in an airplane reading a book. If the book is 1 m above the floor of the plane then, to the passenger, the gravitational potential energy of the book is mgh, where $h = 1$ m. However, to someone on the ground looking up, the floor of the plane may be, say, 9000 m above the ground. So, to this person, the gravitational potential energy of the book is mgH, where $H = 9001$ m. What both would agree on, though, is that the difference in potential energy between the floor of the plane and the position of the book is $mg \times (1\ \text{m})$, since the airplane passenger would calculate the difference as $mg \times (1\ \text{m} - 0\ \text{m})$, while the person on the ground would calculate it as $mg \times (9001\ \text{m} - 9000\ \text{m})$. Differences, or changes, in potential energy are unambiguous, but values of potential energy are relative.

Example 4.10 A stuntwoman (mass = 60 kg) scales a 40-meter tall rock face. What is her gravitational potential energy (relative to the ground)?

Solution. Calling the ground $h = 0$, we find

$$U_{grav} = mgh = (60 \text{ kg})(9.8 \text{ N/kg})(40 \text{ m}) = 23{,}500 \text{ J}$$

Example 4.11 If the stuntwoman in the previous example were to jump off the cliff, what would be her final speed as she landed on a large, air-filled cushion lying on the ground?

Solution. The gravitational potential energy would be transformed into kinetic energy. So

$$U \to K \;\Rightarrow\; U \to \tfrac{1}{2}mv^2 \;\Rightarrow\; v = \sqrt{\frac{2 \cdot U}{m}} = \sqrt{\frac{2(23{,}500 \text{ J})}{60 \text{ kg}}} = 28 \text{ m/s}$$

CONSERVATION OF MECHANICAL ENERGY

We have seen energy in its two basic forms: Kinetic energy (K) and potential energy (U). The sum of an object's kinetic and potential energies is called its **mechanical energy**, E:

$$E = K + U$$

(Notice that because U is relative, so is E.) Assuming that no nonconservative forces (friction, for example) act on an object or system while it undergoes some change, then mechanical energy is conserved. That is, the initial mechanical energy, E_i, is equal to the final mechanical energy, E_f, or

$$K_i + U_i = K_f + U_f$$

This is the simplest form of the Law of Conservation of Total Energy, which we mentioned at the beginning of this section.

Example 4.12 A ball of mass 2 kg is gently pushed off the edge of a tabletop that is 1.5 m above the floor. Find the speed of the ball as it strikes the floor.

Solution. Ignoring the friction due to the air, we can apply Conservation of Mechanical Energy. Calling the floor our $h = 0$ reference level, we write

$$K_i + U_i = K_f + U_f$$
$$0 + mgh = \tfrac{1}{2}mv^2 + 0$$
$$v = \sqrt{2gh}$$
$$= \sqrt{2(9.8 \text{ m/s}^2)(1.5 \text{ m})}$$
$$= 5.4 \text{ m/s}$$

Notice that the ball's potential energy decreased, while its kinetic energy increased. This is the basic idea behind conservation of mechanical energy: One form of energy decreases while the other increases.

> **Example 4.13** A box is projected up a long ramp (incline angle with the horizontal = 20°) with an initial speed of 8 m/s. If the surface of the ramp is very smooth (essentially frictionless), how high up the ramp will the box go? What distance along the ramp will it slide?

Solution. Because friction is negligible, we can apply Conservation of Mechanical Energy. Calling the bottom of the ramp our $h = 0$ reference level, we write

$$K_i + U_i = K_f + U_f$$
$$\tfrac{1}{2}mv_0^2 + 0 = 0 + mgh$$
$$h = \frac{\tfrac{1}{2}v_0^2}{g}$$
$$= \frac{\tfrac{1}{2}(8 \text{ m/s})^2}{9.8 \text{ m/s}^2}$$
$$= 3.3 \text{ m}$$

Since the incline angle is $\theta = 20°$, the distance d it slides up the ramp is found in this way:

$$h = d \sin\theta$$
$$d = \frac{h}{\sin\theta} = \frac{3.3 \text{ m}}{\sin 20°} = 9.6 \text{ m}$$

> **Example 4.14** A skydiver jumps from a hovering helicopter that's 3000 m above the ground. If air resistance can be ignored, how fast will he be falling when his altitude is 2000 m?

Solution. Ignoring air resistance, we can apply Conservation of Mechanical Energy. Calling the ground our $h = 0$ reference level, we write

$$K_i + U_i = K_f + U_f$$
$$0 + mgH = \tfrac{1}{2}mv^2 + mgh$$
$$v = \sqrt{2g(H - h)}$$
$$= \sqrt{2(9.8 \text{ m/s}^2)(3000 \text{ m} - 2000 \text{ m})}$$
$$= 140 \text{ m/s}$$

(That's over 300 mph! This shows that air resistance *does* play a role, even before the parachute is opened.)

The equation $K_i + U_i = K_f + U_f$ holds if no nonconservative forces are doing work. However, if work is done by such forces during the process under investigation, then the equation needs to be modified to account for this work as follows:

$$K_i + U_i + W_{other} = K_f + U_f$$

Example 4.15 Wile E. Coyote (mass = 40 kg) falls off a 50-meter-high cliff. On the way down, the force of air resistance has an average strength of 100 N. Find the speed with which he crashes into the ground.

Solution. The force of air resistance opposes the downward motion, so it does negative work on the coyote as he falls: $W_r = -F_r h$. Calling the ground $h = 0$, we find that

$$K_i + U_i + W_r = K_f + U_f$$
$$0 + mgh + (-F_r h) = \tfrac{1}{2}mv^2 + 0$$
$$v = \sqrt{2h(g - F_r / m)} = \sqrt{2(50)(9.8 - 100 / 40)} = 27 \text{ m} / \text{s}$$

Example 4.16 A skier starts from rest at the top of a 20° incline and skis in a straight line to the bottom of the slope, a distance d (measured along the slope) of 400 m. If the coefficient of kinetic friction between the skis and the snow is 0.2, calculate the skier's speed at the bottom of the run.

Solution. The strength of the friction force on the skier is $F_f = \mu_k F_N = \mu_k(mg \cos \theta)$, so the work done by friction is $-F_f d = -\mu_k(mg \cos \theta) \cdot d$. The vertical height of the slope above the bottom of the run (which we designate the $h = 0$ level) is $h = d \sin \theta$. Therefore, Conservation of Mechanical Energy (including the negative work done by friction) gives

$$K_i + U_i + W_{friction} = K_f + U_f$$
$$0 + mgh + (-\mu_k mg \cos\theta \cdot d) = \tfrac{1}{2}mv^2 + 0$$
$$mg(d\sin\theta) + (-\mu_k mg \cos\theta \cdot d) = \tfrac{1}{2}mv^2$$
$$gd(\sin\theta - \mu_k \cos\theta) = \tfrac{1}{2}v^2$$
$$v = \sqrt{2gd(\sin\theta - \mu_k \cos\theta)}$$
$$= \sqrt{2(9.8)(400)[\sin 20° - (0.2)\cos 20°]}$$
$$= 35 \text{ m} / \text{s}$$

[C] POTENTIAL ENERGY CURVES

The behavior of a system can be analyzed if we are given a graph of its potential energy, $U(x)$ as a function of position and its mechanical energy, E. Since $K + U = E$, we have $\frac{1}{2}mv^2 + U(x) = E$ which can be solved for v, the velocity at position x:

$$v = \pm\sqrt{\frac{2}{m}[E - U(x)]}$$

For example, consider the following potential energy curve:

The graph shows how the potential energy, U, varies with position, x. A particular value of the total energy, $E = E_0$, is also shown. Motion of an object whose potential energy is given by $U(x)$ and which has a mechanical energy of E_0 is confined to the region $-x_0 \leq x \leq x_0$, because only in this range is $E_0 \geq U(x)$. At each position x in this range, the kinetic energy, $K = E_0 - U(x)$, is positive. However, if $x > x_0$ (or if $x < -x_0$), then $U(x) > E_0$, which is physically impossible because the difference $E_0 - U(x)$, which should give K, is negative.

This particular energy curve, with $U(x) = \frac{1}{2}kx^2$, describes one of the most important physical systems: a simple harmonic oscillator. The force felt by the oscillator can be recovered from the potential energy curve. Recall that, in the case of gravitational potential energy, we defined $\Delta U_{grav} = -W_{by\ grav}$. In general, $\Delta U = -W$. If we account for a variable force of the form $F = F(x)$, which does the work W, then over a small displacement Δx, we have $\Delta U(x) = -W = -F(x)\Delta x$, so $F(x) = -\Delta U(x)/\Delta x$. In the limit as $\Delta x \to 0$, this last equation becomes

$$F(x) = -\frac{dU}{dx}$$

Therefore, in this case, we find $F(x) = -(d/dx)(\frac{1}{2}kx^2) = -kx$, which specifies a linear restoring force, a prerequisite for simple harmonic motion. This equation, $F(x) = -kx$, is called Hooke's Law and is obeyed by ideal springs (see Example 4.5).

With this result, we can appreciate the oscillatory nature of the system whose energy curve is sketched above. If x is positive (and not greater than x_0), then $U(x)$ is increasing, so dU/dx is positive, which tells us that F is negative. So the oscillator feels a force—and an acceleration—in the negative direction, which pulls it back through the origin ($x = 0$). If x is negative (and not less than $-x_0$), then $U(x)$ is decreasing, so dU/dx is negative, which tells us that F is positive. So the oscillator feels a force—and an acceleration—in the positive direction, which pushes it back through the origin ($x = 0$).

Furthermore, the difference between E_0 and U, which is K, decreases as x approaches x_0 (or as x approaches $-x_0$), dropping to zero at these points. The fact that K decreases to zero at $\pm x_0$ tells us that the oscillator's speed decreases to zero as it approaches these endpoints, before changing direction and heading back toward the origin—where its kinetic energy and speed are maximized—for another oscillation. By looking at the energy curve with these observations in mind, you can almost see the oscillator moving back and forth between the barriers at $x = \pm x_0$.

The origin is a point at which $U(x)$ has a minimum, so the tangent line to the curve at this point is horizontal; the slope is zero. Since $F = -dU/dx$, the force F is 0 at this point [which we also know from the equation $F(x) = -kx$]; this means that this is a point of **equilibrium**. If the oscillator is pushed from this equilibrium point in either direction, the force $F(x)$ will attempt to restore it to $x = 0$, so this is a point of **stable** equilibrium. However, a point where the $U(x)$ curve has a maximum is also a point of equilibrium, but it's an **unstable** one, because if the system were moved from this point in either direction, the force would accelerate it *away* from the equilibrium position.

Consider the following potential energy curve:

Point C is a position of stable equilibrium and E is a point of unstable equilibrium. Since $U(x)$ is decreasing at Points A and F, $F(x)$ is positive, accelerating the system in the positive x direction. Points B and D mark the barriers of oscillation if the system has a mechanical energy E_0 of 0.

POWER

Simply put, **power** is the rate at which work gets done (or energy gets transferred, which is the same thing). Suppose you and I each do 1000 J of work, but I do the work in 2 minutes while you do it in 1 minute. We both did the same amount of work, but you did it more quickly; you were more powerful. Here's the definition of power:

$$\text{Power} = \frac{\text{Work}}{\text{time}} \quad \text{— in symbols} \rightarrow \quad P = \frac{W}{t}$$

The unit of power is the joule per second (J/s), which is renamed the **watt**, and symbolized W (not to be confused with the symbol for work, W). One watt is 1 joule per second: 1 W = 1 J/s. Here in the United States, which still uses older units like inches, feet, yards, miles, ounces, pounds, and so forth, you still hear of power ratings expressed in horsepower (particularly of engines). One horsepower is defined as, well, the power output of a large horse. Horses can pull a 150-pound weight at a speed of $2\frac{1}{2}$ mph for quite a while. Let's assume that **F** and **d** are parallel, so that $W = Fd$; then the definition $P = W/t$ becomes $P = Fd/t$, which is Fv. Therefore,

$$P = Fv \quad \Rightarrow \quad 1 \text{ horsepower (hp)} = (150 \text{ lb})(2\tfrac{1}{2} \text{ mph})$$

Now for some unit conversions:

$$150 \text{ lb} = 150 \text{ lb} \times \frac{4.45 \text{ N}}{\text{lb}} = 667.5 \text{ N}$$

$$2\tfrac{1}{2} \text{ mph} = \frac{2\tfrac{1}{2} \text{ mi}}{\text{hr}} \times \frac{1609 \text{ m}}{1 \text{ mi}} \times \frac{1 \text{ hr}}{3600 \text{ s}} = 1.117 \text{ m}/\text{s}$$

Therefore,

$$1 \text{ hp} = (667.5 \text{ N})(1.117 \text{ m}/\text{s}) = 746 \text{ W}$$

By contrast, a human in good physical condition can do work at a steady rate of about 75 W (about 1/10 that of a horse!) but can attain power levels as much as twice this much for short periods of time.

Example 4.17 A mover pushes a large crate (mass $m = 75$ kg) from the inside of the truck to the back end (a distance of 6 m), exerting a steady push of 300 N. If he moves the crate this distance in 20 s, what is his power output during this time?

Solution. The work done on the crate by the mover is $W = Fd = (300 \text{ N})(6 \text{ m}) = 1800$ J. If this much work is done in 20 s, then the power delivered is $P = W/t = (1800 \text{ J})/(20 \text{ s}) = 90$ W.

Example 4.18 What must be the power output of an elevator motor that can lift a total mass of 1000 kg and give the elevator a constant speed of 8.0 m/s?

Solution. The equation $P = Fv$, with $F = mg$, yields

$$P = mgv = (1000 \text{ kg})(9.8 \text{ N}/\text{kg})(8.0 \text{ m}/\text{s}) = 78,000 \text{ W} = 78 \text{ kW}$$

CHAPTER 4 REVIEW QUESTIONS

SECTION I: MULTIPLE CHOICE

1. A force **F** of strength 20 N acts on an object of mass 3 kg as it moves a distance of 4 m. If **F** is perpendicular to the 4 m displacement, the work it does is equal to

   (A) 0 J
   (B) 60 J
   (C) 80 J
   (D) 600 J
   (E) 2400 J

2. Under the influence of a force, an object of mass 4 kg accelerates from 3 m/s to 6 m/s in 8 s. How much work was done on the object during this time?

   (A) 27 J
   (B) 54 J
   (C) 72 J
   (D) 96 J
   (E) Cannot be determined from the information given

3. A box of mass m slides down a frictionless inclined plane of length L and vertical height h. What is the change in its gravitational potential energy?

   (A) $-mgL$
   (B) $-mgh$
   (C) $-mgL/h$
   (D) $-mgh/L$
   (E) $-mghL$

4. An object of mass m is traveling at constant speed v in a circular path of radius r. How much work is done by the centripetal force during one-half of a revolution?

   (A) πmv^2
   (B) $2\pi mv^2$
   (C) 0
   (D) $\pi mv^2 r$
   (E) $2\pi mv^2 r$

5. While a person lifts a book of mass 2 kg from the floor to a tabletop, 1.5 m above the floor, how much work does the gravitational force do on the book?

   (A) −30 J
   (B) −15 J
   (C) 0 J
   (D) 15 J
   (E) 30 J

6. A block of mass 3.5 kg slides down a frictionless inclined plane of length 6 m that makes an angle of 30° with the horizontal. If the block is released from rest at the top of the incline, what is its speed at the bottom?

   (A) 4.9 m/s
   (B) 5.2 m/s
   (C) 6.4 m/s
   (D) 7.7 m/s
   (E) 9.1 m/s

7. A block of mass 3.5 kg slides down an inclined plane of length 6 m that makes an angle of 60° with the horizontal. The coefficient of kinetic friction between the block and the incline is 0.3. If the block is released from rest at the top of the incline, what is its speed at the bottom?

   (A) 4.9 m/s
   (B) 5.2 m/s
   (C) 6.4 m/s
   (D) 7.7 m/s
   (E) 9.2 m/s

8. As a rock of mass 4 kg drops from the edge of a 40-meter-high cliff, it experiences air resistance, whose average strength during the descent is 20 N. At what speed will the rock hit the ground?

   (A) 8 m/s
   (B) 10 m/s
   (C) 12 m/s
   (D) 16 m/s
   (E) 20 m/s

9. An astronaut drops a rock from the top of a crater on the Moon. When the rock is halfway down to the bottom of the crater, its speed is what fraction of its final impact speed?

(A) $1/4\sqrt{2}$
(B) $1/4$
(C) $1/2\sqrt{2}$
(D) $1/2$
(E) $1/\sqrt{2}$

10. A force of 200 N is required to keep an object sliding at a constant speed of 2 m/s across a rough floor. How much power is being expended to maintain this motion?

(A) 50 W
(B) 100 W
(C) 200 W
(D) 400 W
(E) Cannot be determined from the information given

SECTION II: FREE RESPONSE

1. A box of mass m is released from rest at Point A, the top of a long, frictionless slide. Point A is at height H above the level of Points B and C. Although the slide is frictionless, the horizontal surface from Point B to C is not. The coefficient of kinetic friction between the box and this surface is μ_k, and the horizontal distance between Points B and C is x.

(a)   Find the speed of the box when its height above Point B is $\frac{1}{2}H$.

(b)   Find the speed of the box when it reaches Point B.

(c)   Determine the value of μ_k so that the box comes to rest at Point C.

(d)   Now assume that Points B and C were not on the same horizontal level. In particular, assume that the surface from B to C had a uniform upward slope so that Point C were still at a horizontal distance of x from B but now at a vertical height of y above B. Answer the question posed in part (c).

(e)   If the slide were not frictionless, determine the work done by friction as the box moved from Point A to Point B if the speed of the box as it reached Point B were half the speed calculated in part (b).

2. The diagram below shows a roller-coaster ride which contains a circular loop of radius r. A car (mass m) begins at rest from Point A and moves down the frictionless track from A to B where it then enters the vertical loop (also frictionless), traveling once around the circle from B to C to D to E and back to B, after which it travels along the flat portion of the track from B to F (which is not frictionless).

(a) Find the centripetal acceleration of the car when it is at Point C.

(b) Determine the speed of the car when its position relative to Point B is specified by the angle θ shown in the diagram.

(c) What is the minimum cut-off speed v_c that the car must have as it enters the loop at Point B to make it around the loop?

(d) What is the minimum height H necessary to ensure that the car makes it around the loop?

(e) If $H = 6r$ and the coefficient of friction between the car and the flat portion of the track from B to F is 0.5, how far along this flat portion of the track will the car travel before coming to rest at Point F?

3. [C] A particle of mass $m = 3$ kg has the potential energy function

$$U(x) = 3(x - 1) - (x - 3)^3$$

where x is measured in meters and U in joules. The following graph is a sketch of this potential energy function.

The energies indicated on the vertical axis are evenly spaced; that is, $E_3 - E_2 = E_2 - E_1$. The energy E_1 is equal to $U(x_1)$, and the energy E_3 is equal to $U(x_3)$.

(a) Determine the numerical values of x_1 and x_3.

(b) Describe the motion of the particle if its total energy is E_2.

(c) What is the particle's speed at $x = x_1$ if its total energy, E, equals 58 J?

(d) Sketch the graph of the particle's acceleration as a function of x. Be sure to indicate x_1 and x_3 on your graph.

(e) The particle is released from rest at $x = \frac{1}{2}x_1$. Find its speed as it passes through $x = x_1$.

5

LINEAR MOMENTUM

INTRODUCTION

When Newton first expressed his Second Law, he didn't write $\mathbf{F}_{net} = m\mathbf{a}$. Instead, he expressed the law in the words *The alteration of motion is . . . proportional to the . . . force impressed. . . .*   By "motion," he meant the product of mass and velocity, a vector quantity known as **linear momentum** and denoted by $\mathbf{p}$:

$$\mathbf{p} = m\mathbf{v}$$

So Newton's original formulation of the Second Law read $\Delta\mathbf{p} \propto \mathbf{F}$, or, equivalently, $\mathbf{F} \propto \Delta\mathbf{p}$. But a large force that acts for a short period of time can produce the same change in linear momentum as a small force acting for a greater period of time. Knowing this, we can turn the proportion above into an equation, if we take the average force that acts over the time interval Δt:

$$\overline{\mathbf{F}} = \frac{\Delta\mathbf{p}}{\Delta t}$$

This equation becomes $\mathbf{F} = m\mathbf{a}$, since $\Delta\mathbf{p}/\Delta t = \Delta(m\mathbf{v})/\Delta t = m(\Delta\mathbf{v}/\Delta t) = m\mathbf{a}$ (assuming that m remains constant). If we take the limit as $\Delta t \to 0$, then the equation above takes the form:

$$\mathbf{F} = \frac{d\mathbf{p}}{dt}$$

Example 5.1 A golfer strikes a golf ball of mass 0.05 kg, and the time of impact between the golf club and the ball is 1 ms. If the ball acquires a velocity of magnitude 70 m/s, calculate the average force exerted on the ball.

Solution. Using Newton's Second Law, we find

$$\bar{F} = \frac{\Delta p}{\Delta t} = \frac{\Delta(mv)}{\Delta t} = m\frac{v-0}{\Delta t} = (0.05 \text{ kg})\frac{70 \text{ m/s}}{10^{-3} \text{ s}} = 3500 \text{ N} \quad [\approx 790 \text{ lb (!)}]$$

IMPULSE

The product of force and the time during which it acts is known as **impulse**; it's a vector quantity that's denoted by **J**:

$$\mathbf{J} = \bar{\mathbf{F}}\Delta t$$

In terms of impulse, Newton's Second Law can be written in yet another form:

$$\mathbf{J} = \Delta\mathbf{p}$$

Sometimes this is referred to as the **impulse–momentum theorem**, but it's just another way of writing Newton's Second Law. If F varies with time over the interval during which it acts, then the impulse delivered by the force $\mathbf{F} = \mathbf{F}(t)$ from time $t = t_1$ to $t = t_2$ is given by the following definite integral:

$$\mathbf{J} = \int_{t_1}^{t_2} \mathbf{F}(t)\,dt$$

Example 5.2 A football team's kicker punts the ball (mass = 0.42 kg) and gives it a launch speed of 30 m/s. Find the impulse delivered to the football by the kicker's foot and the average force exerted by the kicker on the ball, given that the impact time is 8 ms.

Solution. Impulse is equal to change in linear momentum, so

$$J = \Delta p = p_f - p_i = p_f = mv = (0.42 \text{ kg})(30 \text{ m/s}) = 13 \text{ kg·m/s}$$

Using the equation $\bar{F} = J/\Delta t$, we find that the average force exerted by the kicker is

$$\bar{F} = J/\Delta t = (13 \text{ kg·m/s}) / (8\times10^{-3} \text{ s}) = 1600 \text{ N} \quad [\approx 370 \text{ lb}]$$

Example 5.3 An 80 kg stuntman jumps out of a window that's 50 m above the ground.

    (a) How fast is he falling when he reaches ground level?

    (b) He lands on a large, air-filled target, coming to rest in 1.5 sec. What average force does he feel while coming to rest?

    (c) What if he had instead landed on the ground (impact time = 10 ms)?

Solution.

(a) His gravitational potential energy turns into kinetic energy: $mgh = \frac{1}{2}mv^2$, so

$$v = \sqrt{2gh} = \sqrt{2(9.8)(50)} = 31 \text{ m/s} \quad [\approx 70 \text{ mph}]$$

(You could also have answered this question using Big Five #5.)

(b) Using $\overline{\mathbf{F}} = \Delta\mathbf{p}/\Delta t$, we find that

$$\overline{\mathbf{F}} = \frac{\Delta\mathbf{p}}{\Delta t} = \frac{\mathbf{p}_f - \mathbf{p}_i}{\Delta t} = \frac{0 - m\mathbf{v}_i}{\Delta t} = \frac{-(80 \text{ kg})(31 \text{ m/s})}{1.5 \text{ s}} = -1650 \text{ N} \quad \Rightarrow \quad \overline{F} = 1650 \text{ N}$$

(c) In this case,

$$\overline{\mathbf{F}} = \frac{\Delta\mathbf{p}}{\Delta t} = \frac{\mathbf{p}_f - \mathbf{p}_i}{\Delta t} = \frac{0 - m\mathbf{v}_i}{\Delta t} = \frac{-(80 \text{ kg})(31 \text{ m/s})}{10 \times 10^{-3} \text{ s}} = -248,000 \text{ N} \quad \Rightarrow \quad \overline{F} = 248,000 \text{ N}$$

This force is equivalent to about 28 tons(!), more than enough to break bones and cause fatal brain damage. Notice how crucial impact time is: Increasing the slowing-down time reduces the acceleration and the force, ideally enough to prevent injury. This is the purpose of air bags in cars, for instance.

Example 5.4 **[C]** A small block of mass $m = 0.07$ kg, initially at rest, is struck by an impulsive force **F** of duration 10 ms whose strength varies with time according to the following graph:

What is the resulting speed of the block?

Solution. The impulse delivered to the block is equal to

$$J = \int_0^{10} F(t)\,dt$$

which is the area under the curve. The region is a trapezoid, so its area, $\frac{1}{2}(\text{base}_1 + \text{base}_2) \times \text{height}$, can be calculated as follows:

$$J = \int_0^{10} F(t)\,dt = \tfrac{1}{2}[(10\text{ ms} - 0) + (6\text{ ms} - 2\text{ ms})] \times (20\text{ N}) = 0.14\text{ N}\cdot\text{s}$$

Now, by the impulse–momentum theorem,

$$J = \Delta p = p_f - p_i = p_f = mv_f \quad \Rightarrow \quad v_f = \frac{J}{m} = \frac{0.14\text{ N}\cdot\text{s}}{0.07\text{ kg}} = 2\text{ m/s}$$

CONSERVATION OF LINEAR MOMENTUM

Newton's Third Law says that when one object exerts a force on a second object, the second object exerts an equal but opposite force on the first. Since Newton's Second Law says that the impulse delivered to an object is equal to the resulting change in its linear momentum, $\mathbf{J} = \Delta\mathbf{p}$, the two interacting objects experience equal but opposite momentum changes (assuming that there are no external forces), which implies that the total linear momentum of the system remains constant. In fact, given any number of interacting objects, each pair that comes in contact will undergo equal but opposite momentum changes, so the result described for two interacting objects will actually hold for any number of objects, given that the only forces they feel are from each other. This means that, in an isolated system, *the total linear momentum will remain constant*. This is the **Law of Conservation of Linear Momentum**.

> **Example 5.5** An astronaut is floating in space near her shuttle when she realizes that the cord that's supposed to attach her to the ship has become disconnected. Her total mass (body + suit + equipment) is 90 kg. She reaches into her pocket, finds a 1 kg metal tool, and throws it out into space with a velocity of 6 m/s directly away from the ship. If the ship is 10 m away, how long will it take her to reach it?

Solution. Here, the astronaut + tool are the system. Because of Conservation of Linear Momentum,

$$m_{\text{astronaut}}\mathbf{v}_{\text{astronaut}} + m_{\text{tool}}\mathbf{v}_{\text{tool}} = 0$$

$$m_{\text{astronaut}}\mathbf{v}_{\text{astronaut}} = -m_{\text{tool}}\mathbf{v}_{\text{tool}}$$

$$\mathbf{v}_{\text{astronaut}} = -\frac{m_{\text{tool}}}{m_{\text{astronaut}}}\mathbf{v}_{\text{tool}}$$

$$= -\frac{1\text{ kg}}{90\text{ kg}}(-6\text{ m/s}) = +0.067\text{ m/s}$$

Using *distance = rate × time*, we find

$$t = \frac{d}{v} = \frac{10\text{ m}}{0.067\text{ m/s}} = 150\text{ s} = 2\tfrac{1}{2}\text{ min}$$

COLLISIONS

Conservation of Linear Momentum is routinely used to analyze **collisions**. The objects whose collision we will analyze form the *system*, and although the objects exert forces on each other during the impact, these forces are only *internal* (they occur within the system), and the system's total linear momentum is conserved.

Collisions are classified into two major categories: (1) **elastic** and (2) **inelastic**. A collision is said to be *elastic* if kinetic energy is conserved. Ordinary macroscopic collisions are never truly elastic, because there is always a change in energy due to energy transferred as heat, deformation of the objects, and the sound of the impact. However, if the objects do not deform very much (for example, two billiard balls or a hard glass marble bouncing off a steel plate), then the loss of initial kinetic energy is small enough to be ignored, and the collision can be treated as virtually elastic. *Inelastic* collisions, then, are ones in which the total kinetic energy is different after the collision. An extreme example of inelasticism is **completely** (or **perfectly** or **totally**) **inelastic**. In this case, the objects stick together after the collision and move as one afterwards. In all cases of isolated collisions (elastic or not), Conservation of Linear Momentum states that

$$\text{total } \mathbf{p}_{\text{before collision}} = \text{total } \mathbf{p}_{\text{after collision}}$$

> **Example 5.6** Two balls roll toward each other. The red ball has a mass of 0.5 kg and a speed of 4 m/s just before impact. The green ball has a mass of 0.3 kg and a speed of 2 m/s. After the head-on collision, the red ball continues forward with a speed of 2 m/s. Find the speed of the green ball after the collision. Was the collision elastic?

Solution. First remember that momentum is a vector quantity, so the direction of the velocity is crucial. Since the balls roll toward each other, one ball has a positive velocity while the other has a negative velocity. Let's call the red ball's velocity before the collision positive; then $\mathbf{v}_{\text{red}} = +4$ m/s, and $\mathbf{v}_{\text{green}} = -2$ m/s. Using a prime to denote *after the collision*, Conservation of Linear Momentum gives us the following:

$$\text{total } \mathbf{p}_{\text{before}} = \text{total } \mathbf{p}_{\text{after}}$$
$$m_{\text{red}}\mathbf{v}_{\text{red}} + m_{\text{green}}\mathbf{v}_{\text{green}} = m_{\text{red}}\mathbf{v}'_{\text{red}} + m_{\text{green}}\mathbf{v}'_{\text{green}}$$
$$(0.5)(+4) + (0.3)(-2) = (0.5)(+2) + (0.3)\mathbf{v}'_{\text{green}}$$
$$\mathbf{v}'_{\text{green}} = +1.3 \text{ m/s}$$

Notice that the green ball's velocity was reversed as a result of the collision; this typically happens when a lighter object collides with a heavier object. To see whether the collision was elastic, we need to compare the total kinetic energies before and after the collision. In this case, however, an explicit calculation is not needed since both objects experienced a decrease in speed as a result of the collision. Kinetic energy was lost (so the collision was inelastic); this is usually the case with macroscopic collisions. Most of the lost energy was transferred as heat; the two objects are both slightly warmer as a result of the collision.

Example 5.7 Two balls roll toward each other. The red ball has a mass of 0.5 kg and a speed of 4 m/s just before impact. The green ball has a mass of 0.3 kg and a speed of 2 m/s. If the collision is completely inelastic, determine the velocity of the composite object after the collision.

Solution. If the collision is completely inelastic, then, by definition, the masses stick together after impact, moving with a velocity, $\mathbf{v}'$. Applying Conservation of Linear Momentum, we find

$$\text{total } \mathbf{p}_{\text{before}} = \text{total } \mathbf{p}_{\text{after}}$$
$$m_{\text{red}}\mathbf{v}_{\text{red}} + m_{\text{green}}\mathbf{v}_{\text{green}} = (m_{\text{red}} + m_{\text{green}})\mathbf{v}'$$
$$(0.5)(+4) + (0.3)(-2) = (0.5 + 0.3)\mathbf{v}'$$
$$\mathbf{v}' = +1.8 \text{ m/s}$$

Example 5.8 An object of mass m_1 is moving with velocity v_1 toward a target object of mass m_2 which is stationary ($v_2 = 0$). The objects collide head-on, and the collision is elastic. Show that the relative velocity before the collision, $v_2 - v_1$, has the same magnitude as $v_2' - v_1'$, the relative velocity after the collision.

Solution. Since the collision is elastic, both total linear momentum and kinetic energy are conserved. Therefore,

$$m_1 v_1 = m_1 v_1' + m_2 v_2' \qquad (1)$$
$$\tfrac{1}{2} m_1 v_1^2 = \tfrac{1}{2} m_1 v_1'^2 + \tfrac{1}{2} m_2 v_2'^2 \qquad (2)$$

Now for some algebra. Cancel the $\tfrac{1}{2}$'s in the second equation and factor to get the following pair of equations:

$$m_1(v_1 - v_1') = m_2 v_2' \qquad (1')$$
$$m_1(v_1 - v_1')(v_1 + v_1') = m_2 v_2'^2 \qquad (2')$$

Next, dividing the second equation by the first gives $v_1 + v_1' = v_2'$, so we can write

$$v_1 - v_1' = (m_2/m_1)v_2' \qquad (1'')$$
$$v_1 + v_1' = v_2' \qquad (2'')$$

Adding Equations (1'') and (2'') gives

$$2v_1 = \left(\tfrac{m_2}{m_1} + 1\right)v_2' \quad \Rightarrow \quad v_2' = \frac{2v_1}{\tfrac{m_2}{m_1} + 1} = \frac{2m_1}{m_1 + m_2} v_1$$

Substituting this result into Equation (2″) gives

$$v_1 + v_1' = \frac{2m_1}{m_1 + m_2} v_1 \quad \Rightarrow \quad v_1' = \left(\frac{2m_1}{m_1 + m_2} - 1\right) v_1 = \frac{m_1 - m_2}{m_1 + m_2} v_1$$

Now we have calculated the final velocities, v_1' and v_2'. To verify the claim made in the statement of the question, we notice that

$$v_2' - v_1' = \frac{2m_1}{m_1 + m_2} v_1 - \frac{m_1 - m_2}{m_1 + m_2} v_1 = \frac{m_1 + m_2}{m_1 + m_2} v_1 = v_1 = v_1 - 0 = v_1 - v_2 = -(v_2 - v_1)$$

so the relative velocity after the collision, $v_2' - v_1'$, is equal (in magnitude) but opposite (in direction) to $v_2 - v_1$, the relative velocity before the collision. *This is a general property that characterizes elastic collisions.*

Example 5.9 An object of mass m moves with velocity **v** toward a stationary object of mass $2m$. After impact, the objects move off in the directions shown in the following diagram:

Before the collision

After the collision

(a) Determine the magnitudes of the velocities after the collision (in terms of v).

(b) Is the collision elastic? Explain your answer.

Solution.

(a) Conservation of Linear Momentum is a principle that establishes the equality of two vectors: $\mathbf{p}_{\text{total}}$ before the collision and $\mathbf{p}_{\text{total}}$ after the collision. Writing this single vector equation as two equations, one for the x component and one for the y, we have

$$x \text{ component: } \quad mv = mv_1' \cos 30° + 2mv_2' \cos 45° \quad (1)$$
$$y \text{ component: } \quad 0 = mv_1' \sin 30° - 2mv_2' \sin 45° \quad (2)$$

Adding these equations eliminates v_2',

$$mv = mv_1'(\cos 30° + \sin 30°)$$

and lets us determmie v_1':

$$v_1' = \frac{v}{\cos 30° + \sin 30°} = \frac{2v}{1+\sqrt{3}}$$

Substituting this result into Equation (2) gives us

$$0 = m\frac{2v}{1+\sqrt{3}}\sin 30° - 2mv_2'\sin 45°$$

$$2mv_2'\sin 45° = m\frac{2v}{1+\sqrt{3}}\sin 30°$$

$$v_2' = \frac{\dfrac{2v}{1+\sqrt{3}}\sin 30°}{2\sin 45°} = \frac{v}{\sqrt{2}(1+\sqrt{3})}$$

(b) The collision is elastic only if kinetic energy is conserved. The total kinetic energy after the collision, K', is calculated as follows:

$$K' = \frac{1}{2}\cdot mv_1'^2 + \frac{1}{2}\cdot 2mv_2'^2$$

$$= \frac{1}{2}m\left(\frac{v}{1+\sqrt{3}}\right)^2 + m\left(\frac{v}{\sqrt{2}(1+\sqrt{3})}\right)^2$$

$$= mv^2\left[\frac{1}{2(1+\sqrt{3})^2} + \frac{1}{2(1+\sqrt{3})^2}\right]$$

$$= \frac{mv^2}{(1+\sqrt{3})^2}$$

However, the kinetic energy before the collision is just $K = \frac{1}{2}mv^2$, so the fact that

$$\frac{1}{(1+\sqrt{3})^2} < \frac{1}{2}$$

tells us that K' is less than K, so some kinetic energy is lost; the collision is inelastic.

CENTER OF MASS

The center of mass is the point where all of the mass of an object can be considered to be concentrated; it's the dot that represents the object of interest in a free-body diagram.

For a homogeneous body (that is, one for which the density is uniform throughout), the center of mass is where you intuitively expect it to be: at the geometric center. Thus, the center of mass of a uniform sphere or cube or box is at its geometric center.

If we have a collection of discrete particles, the center of mass of the system can be determined mathematically as follows. First consider the case where the particles all lie on a straight line. Call this the x axis. Select some point to be the origin ($x = 0$) and determine the positions of each particle on the axis. Multiply each position value by the mass of the particle at that location, and get the sum for all the particles. Divide this sum by the total mass, and the resulting x value is the center of mass:

$$x_{cm} = \frac{m_1 x_1 + m_2 x_2 + \cdots + m_n x_n}{m_1 + m_2 + \cdots + m_n}$$

is equivalent to:

The system of particles behaves as if all its mass, $M = m_1 + m_2 + \ldots + m_n$, were concentrated at a single location, x_{cm}.

If the system consists of objects that are not confined to the same straight line, use the equation above to find the x coordinate of their center of mass, and the corresponding equation,

$$y_{cm} = \frac{m_1 y_1 + m_2 y_2 + \cdots + m_n y_n}{m_1 + m_2 + \cdots + m_n}$$

to find the y coordinate of their center of mass (and one more equation to calculate the z coordinate, if they are not confined to a single plane).

From the equation

$$x_{cm} = \frac{m_1 x_1 + m_2 x_2 + \cdots + m_n x_n}{M}$$

we can derive

$$M v_{cm} = m_1 v_1 + m_2 v_2 + \cdots + m_n v_n$$

So the total linear momentum of all the particles in the system $(m_1 v_1 + m_2 v_2 + \cdots + m_n v_n)$ is the same as $M v_{cm}$, the linear momentum of a single particle (whose mass is equal to the system's total mass) moving with the velocity of the center of mass.

We can also differentiate again and establish the following:

$$\mathbf{F}_{net} = M \mathbf{a}_{cm}$$

This says that the net (external) force acting on the system causes the center of mass to accelerate according to Newton's Second Law. In particular, *if the net external force on the system is zero, then the center of mass will not accelerate.*

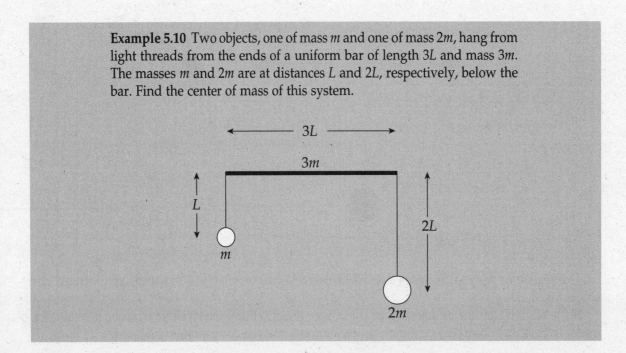

Example 5.10 Two objects, one of mass m and one of mass $2m$, hang from light threads from the ends of a uniform bar of length $3L$ and mass $3m$. The masses m and $2m$ are at distances L and $2L$, respectively, below the bar. Find the center of mass of this system.

Solution. The center of mass of the bar alone is at its midpoint (because it is uniform), so we may treat the total mass of the bar as being concentrated at its midpoint. Constructing a coordinate system with this point as the origin, we now have three objects: one of mass m at $(-3L/2, -L)$, one of mass $2m$ at $(3L/2, -2L)$, and one of mass $3m$ at $(0, 0)$:

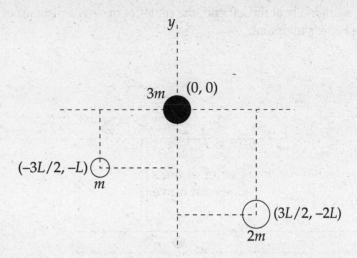

We figure out the x and y coordinates of the center of mass separately:

$$x_{cm} = \frac{m_1 x_1 + m_2 x_2 + m_3 x_3}{m_1 + m_2 + m_3} = \frac{(m)(-3L/2) + (2m)(3L/2) + (3m)(0)}{m + 2m + 3m} = \frac{3mL/2}{6m} = \frac{L}{4}$$

$$y_{cm} = \frac{m_1 y_1 + m_2 y_2 + m_3 y_3}{m_1 + m_2 + m_3} = \frac{(m)(-L) + (2m)(-2L) + (3m)(0)}{m + 2m + 3m} = \frac{-5mL}{6m} = -\frac{5L}{6}$$

Therefore, the center of mass is at

$$(x_{cm}, y_{cm}) = (L/4, -5L/6)$$

relative to the midpoint of the bar.

Example 5.11 A man of mass m is standing at one end of a stationary, floating barge of mass $3m$. He then walks to the other end of the barge, a distance of L meters. Ignore any frictional effects between the barge and the water.

(a) How far will the barge move?

(b) If the man walks at an average velocity of v, what is the average velocity of the barge?

Solution. (a) Since there are no external forces acting on the man + barge system, the center of mass of the system cannot accelerate. In particular, since the system is originally at rest, the center of mass cannot move. Letting $x = 0$ denote the midpoint of the barge (which is its own center of mass, assuming it is uniform), we figure out the center of mass of the man + barge system:

$$x_{cm} = \frac{m_1 x_1 + m_2 x_2}{m_1 + m_2} = \frac{(m)(-L/2) + (3m)(0)}{m + 3m} = -\frac{L}{8}$$

So the center of mass is a distance of $L/8$ from the midpoint of the barge, and since the mass is originally at the left end, the center of mass is a distance of $L/8$ to the left of the barge's midpoint.

When the man reaches the other end of the barge, the center of mass will, by symmetry, be $L/8$ to the *right* of the midpoint of the barge. But, since the position of the center of mass cannot move, this means the barge itself must have moved a distance of

$$L/8 + L/8 = 2L/8 = L/4$$

to the left.

(b) Let the time it takes the man to walk across the barge be denoted by t; then $t = L/v$. In this amount of time, the barge moves a distance of $L/4$ in the *opposite* direction, so the velocity of the barge is

$$v_{\text{barge}} = \frac{-L/4}{t} = \frac{-L/4}{L/v} = -\frac{v}{4}$$

CHAPTER 5 REVIEW QUESTIONS

SECTION I: MULTIPLE CHOICE

1. An object of mass 2 kg has a linear momentum of magnitude 6 kg·m/s. What is this object's kinetic energy?

    (A) 3 J
    (B) 6 J
    (C) 9 J
    (D) 12 J
    (E) 18 J

2. A ball of mass 0.5 kg, initially at rest, acquires a speed of 4 m/s immediately after being kicked by a force of strength 20 N. For how long did this force act on the ball?

    (A) 0.01 s
    (B) 0.02 s
    (C) 0.1 s
    (D) 0.2 s
    (E) 1 s

3. A box with a mass of 2 kg accelerates in a straight line from 4 m/s to 8 m/s due to the application of a force whose duration is 0.5 s. Find the average strength of this force.

    (A) 2 N
    (B) 4 N
    (C) 8 N
    (D) 12 N
    (E) 16 N

4. A ball of mass m traveling horizontally with velocity $\mathbf{v}$ strikes a massive vertical wall and rebounds back along its original direction with no change in speed. What is the magnitude of the impulse delivered by the wall to the ball?

    (A) 0
    (B) $\frac{1}{2}mv$
    (C) mv
    (D) $2mv$
    (E) $4mv$

5. Two objects, one of mass 3 kg and moving with a speed of 2 m/s and the other of mass 5 kg and speed 2 m/s, move toward each other and collide head-on. If the collision is perfectly inelastic, find the speed of the objects after the collision.

    (A) 0.25 m/s
    (B) 0.5 m/s
    (C) 0.75 m/s
    (D) 1 m/s
    (E) 2 m/s

6. Object #1 moves toward Object #2, whose mass is twice that of Object #1 and which is initially at rest. After their impact, the objects lock together and move with what fraction of Object #1's initial kinetic energy?

    (A) 1/18
    (B) 1/9
    (C) 1/6
    (D) 1/3
    (E) None of the above

7. Two objects move toward each other, collide, and separate. If there was no net external force acting on the objects, but some kinetic energy was lost, then

    (A) the collision was elastic and total linear momentum was conserved.
    (B) the collision was elastic and total linear momentum was not conserved.
    (C) the collision was not elastic and total linear momentum was conserved.
    (D) the collision was not elastic and total linear momentum was not conserved.
    (E) None of the above

8. Three thin, uniform rods each of length L are arranged in the shape of an inverted U:

The two rods on the arms of the U each have mass m; the third rod has mass $2m$. How far below the midpoint of the horizontal rod is the center of mass of this assembly?

(A) $L/8$
(B) $L/4$
(C) $3L/8$
(D) $L/2$
(E) $3L/4$

9. A wooden block of mass M is moving at speed V in a straight line.

How fast would the bullet of mass m need to travel to stop the block (assuming that the bullet became embedded inside)?

(A) $mV/(m + M)$
(B) $MV/(m + M)$
(C) mV/M
(D) MV/m
(E) $(m + M)V/m$

10. Which of the following best describes a perfectly inelastic collision free of external forces?

(A) Total linear momentum is never conserved.
(B) Total linear momentum is sometimes conserved.
(C) Kinetic energy is never conserved.
(D) Kinetic energy is sometimes conserved.
(E) Kinetic energy is always conserved.

SECTION II: FREE RESPONSE

1. A steel ball of mass m is fastened to a light cord of length L and released when the cord is horizontal. At the bottom of its path, the ball strikes a hard plastic block of mass $M = 4m$, initially at rest on a frictionless surface. The collision is elastic.

(a) Find the tension in the cord when the ball's height above its lowest position is $\frac{1}{2}L$. Write your answer in terms of m and g.

(b) Find the speed of the block immediately after the collision.

(c) To what height h will the ball rebound after the collision?

2. A *ballistic pendulum* is a device that may be used to measure the muzzle speed of a bullet. It is composed of a wooden block suspended from a horizontal support by cords attached at each end. A bullet is shot into the block, and as a result of the perfectly inelastic impact, the block swings upward. Consider a bullet (mass m) with velocity v as it enters the block (mass M). The length of the cords supporting the block each have length L. The maximum height to which the block swings upward after impact is denoted by y, and the maximum horizontal displacement is denoted by x.

(a) In terms of m, M, g, and y, determine the speed v of the bullet.

(b) What fraction of the bullet's original kinetic energy is lost as a result of the collision? What happens to the lost kinetic energy?

(c) If y is very small (so that y^2 can be neglected), determine the speed of the bullet in terms of m, M, g, x, and L.

(d) Once the block begins to swing, does the momentum of the block remain constant? Why or why not?

3. An object of mass m moves with velocity $\mathbf{v}$ toward a stationary object of the same mass. After their impact, the objects move off in the directions shown in the following diagram:

Before the collision

After the collision

Assume that the collision is elastic.

(a) If K_1 denotes the kinetic energy of Object 1 before the collision, what is the kinetic energy of this object after the collision? Write your answer in terms of K_1 and θ_1.

(b) What is the kinetic energy of Object 2 after the collision? Write your answer in terms of K_1 and θ_1.

(c) What is the relationship between θ_1 and θ_2?

6

ROTATIONAL MOTION

INTRODUCTION

So far we've studied only translational motion: objects sliding, falling, or rising, but in none of our examples have we considered spinning objects. We will now look at rotation, which will complete our study of motion. All motion is some combination of **translation** and **rotation**, which are illustrated in the figures below. Consider any two points in the object under study (on the left) and imagine connecting them by a straight line. If this line always remains parallel to itself while the object moves, then the object is translating only. However, if this line does not always remain parallel to itself while the object moves, then the object is rotating.

pure translation

pure rotation

translation and rotation

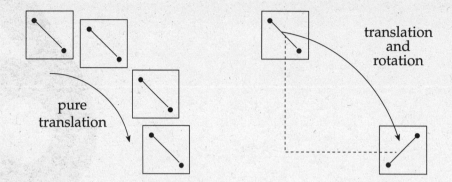

translation
and
rotation

pure
translation

[C] ROTATIONAL KINEMATICS

Mark several dots along a radius on a disk, and call this radius the *reference line*. If the disk rotates about its center, we can use the movement of these dots to talk about angular displacement, angular velocity, and angular acceleration.

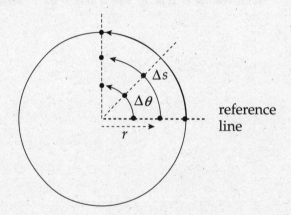

reference
line

If the disk rotates as a rigid body, then all three dots shown have the same **angular displacement**, $\Delta\theta$. In fact, this is the definition of a **rigid body**: All points along a radial line always have the same angular displacement.

Just as the time rate-]o-change of displacement gives velocity, the time rate-of-change of angular displacement gives angular velocity, denoted by ω (*omega*). The definition of the **average angular velocity** is:

$$\overline{\omega} = \frac{\Delta\theta}{\Delta t}$$

Notice that if we let the time interval Δt approach 0, then the equation above leads to the definition of the instantaneous angular velocity:

$$\omega = \frac{d\theta}{dt}$$

And, finally, just as the time rate-of-change of velocity gives acceleration, the time rate-of-change of angular velocity gives angular acceleration, or α (*alpha*). The definition of the **average angular acceleration** is:

$$\overline{\alpha} = \frac{\Delta\omega}{\Delta t}$$

If we let the time interval Δt approach 0, then the equation above leads to the definition of the instantaneous angular velocity:

$$\alpha = \frac{d\omega}{dt}$$

On the rotating disk illustrated above, we said that all points undergo the same angular displacement in any given time interval; this means that all points on the disk have the same angular velocity, ω, but not all points have the same linear velocity, v. This follows from the definition of **radian** measure. Expressed in radians, the angular displacement, $\Delta\theta$, is related to the arc length, Δs, by the equation

$$\Delta\theta = \frac{\Delta s}{r}$$

Rearranging this equation and dividing by Δt, we find that

$$\Delta s = r\Delta\theta \quad \Rightarrow \quad \frac{\Delta s}{\Delta t} = r\frac{\Delta\theta}{\Delta t} \quad \Rightarrow \quad \overline{v} = r\overline{\omega}$$

Or, using the equations $v = ds/dt$ and $\omega = d\theta/dt$;

$$v = r\omega$$

Therefore, the greater the value of r, the greater the value of v. Points on the rotating body farther from the rotation axis move more quickly than those closer to the rotation axis.

From the equation $v = r\omega$, we can derive the relationship that connects angular acceleration and linear acceleration. Differentiating both sides with respect to t (holding r constant), gives us

$$\frac{dv}{dt} = r\frac{d\omega}{dt} \quad \Rightarrow \quad a = r\alpha$$

(It's important to realize that the acceleration a in this equation is *not* centripetal acceleration, it's tangential acceleration, which arises from a change in speed caused by an angular acceleration. By contrast, centripetal acceleration does not produce a change in speed.) Often, tangential acceleration is written as a_t to distinguish it from centripetal acceleration (a_c).

Example 6.1 A rotating, rigid body makes one complete revolution in 2 s. What is its average angular velocity?

Solution. One complete revolution is equal to an angular displacement of 2π radians, so the body's average angular velocity is

$$\overline{\omega} = \frac{\Delta\theta}{\Delta t} = \frac{2\pi \text{ rad}}{2 \text{ s}} = \pi \text{ rad}/\text{s}$$

Example 6.2 The angular velocity of a rotating disk increases from 2 rad/s to 5 rad/s in 0.5 s. What's the disk's average angular acceleration?

Solution. By definition,

$$\bar{\alpha} = \frac{\Delta\omega}{\Delta t} = \frac{(5-2)\,\text{rad}/\text{s}}{0.5\,\text{s}} = 6\,\text{rad}/\text{s}^2$$

Example 6.3 A disk of radius 20 cm rotates at a constant angular velocity of 6 rad/s. How fast does a point on the rim of this disk travel (in m/s)?

Solution. The linear speed, v, is related to the angular speed, ω, by the equation $v = r\omega$. Therefore,

$$v = r\omega = (0.20\,\text{m})(6\,\text{rad}/\text{s}) = 1.2\,\text{m}/\text{s}$$

Notice that although we typically write the abbreviation *rad* when writing angular measurements, the radian is actually a dimensionless unit, since, by definition, $\theta = s/r$. So $\Delta\theta = 6$ means the same thing as $\Delta\theta = 6$ rad.

Example 6.4 The angular velocity of a rotating disk of radius 50 cm increases from 2 rad/s to 5 rad/s in 0.5 s. What is the linear acceleration of a point on the rim of the disk during this time interval?

Solution. The linear acceleration a is related to the angular acceleration α by the equation $a = r\alpha$. Since $\alpha = 6$ rad/s^2 (as calculated in Example 6.2), we find that

$$a = r\alpha = (0.50\,\text{m})(6\,\text{rad}/\text{s}^2) = 3\,\text{m}/\text{s}^2$$

Example 6.5 Derive an expression for centripetal acceleration in terms of angular speed.

Solution. For an object revolving with linear speed v at a distance r from the center of rotation, the centripetal acceleration is given by the equation $a_c = v^2/r$. Using the fundamental equation $v = r\omega$, we find that

$$a_c = \frac{v^2}{r} = \frac{(r\omega)^2}{r} = \omega^2 r$$

[C] THE BIG FIVE FOR ROTATIONAL MOTION

The simplest type of rotational motion to analyze is motion in which the angular acceleration is *constant* (possibly equal to zero). Another restriction that will make our analysis easier (and which, doesn't diminish the power and applicability of our results too much) is to consider rotational motion around a *fixed* axis of rotation. In this case, there are only two possible directions for motion. One direction, counterclockwise, is called *positive* (+), and the opposite direction, clockwise, is called *negative* (–).

Let's review the quantities we've seen so far. The fundamental quantities for rotational motion are angular displacement ($\Delta \theta$), angular velocity (ω), and angular acceleration (α). Because we're dealing with angular acceleration, we know about changes in angular velocity, from initial velocity (ω_i or ω_0) to final velocity (ω_f or simply ω—with no subscript). And, finally, the motion takes place during some elapsed time interval, Δt. Therefore, we have five kinematics quantities: $\Delta \theta$, ω_0, ω, α, and Δt.

These five quantities are interrelated by a group of five equations which we call *The Big Five*. They work in cases in which the angular acceleration is uniform. These equations are identical to The Big Five we studied in Chapter 2 but, in these cases, the translational variables (s, v, or a) are replaced by the corresponding rotational variables (θ, ω, or α, respectively).

		Variable that's missing
Big Five #1:	$\Delta\theta = \overline{\omega}\Delta t$	α
Big Five #2:	$\Delta\omega = \alpha\Delta t$	$\Delta\theta$
Big Five #3:	$\Delta\theta = \omega_0\Delta t + \frac{1}{2}\alpha(\Delta t)^2$	ω
Big Five #4:	$\Delta\theta = \omega\Delta t - \frac{1}{2}\alpha(\Delta t)^2$	ω_0
Big Five #5:	$\omega^2 = \omega_0^2 + 2\alpha\Delta\theta$	Δt

In Big Five #1, the average angular velocity is simply the average of the initial angular velocity and the final angular velocity: $\overline{\omega} = \frac{1}{2}(\omega_0 + \omega)$. (Because angular acceleration is constant.) Also, if we decide that $t_i = 0$, then $\Delta t = t_f - t_i = t - 0 = t$, so we can just write "$t$" instead of "$\Delta t$" in the first four equations. This simplification in notation makes the equations a little easier to memorize.

Each of the Big Five equations is missing exactly one of the five kinematics quantities and, like with the other Big Five you learned, the way you decide which equation to use is to determine which of the kinematics quantities is missing from the problem, and use the equation that's also missing that quantity. For example, if the problem never mentions the final angular velocity—ω is neither given nor asked for—then the equation that will work is the one that's missing ω; that's Big Five #3.

Notice that Big Five #1 and #2 are simply the definitions of $\overline{\omega}$ and $\overline{\alpha}$ written in forms that don't involve fractions.

> **Example 6.6** An object with an initial angular velocity of 1 rad/s rotates with constant angular acceleration. Three seconds later, its angular velocity is 5 rad/s. Calculate its angular displacement during this time interval.

Solution. We're given ω_0, t, and ω, and asked for $\Delta\theta$. So α is missing, and we use Big Five #1:

$$\Delta\theta = \overline{\omega}\Delta t = \tfrac{1}{2}(\omega_0 + \omega)\Delta t = \tfrac{1}{2}(1 \text{ rad}/\text{s} + 5 \text{ rad}/\text{s})(3 \text{ s}) = 9 \text{ rad}$$

Example 6.7 Starting with zero initial angular velocity, a sphere begins to spin with constant angular acceleration about an axis through its center, achieving an angular velocity of 10 rad/s when its angular displacement is 20 rad. What is the value of the sphere's angular acceleration?

Solution. We're given ω_0, $\Delta\theta$, and ω, and asked for α. Since t is missing, we use Big Five #5:

$$\omega^2 = \omega_0^2 + 2\alpha\Delta\theta \quad \Rightarrow \quad \omega^2 = 2\alpha\Delta\theta \text{ (since } \omega_0 = 0)$$

$$\alpha = \frac{\omega^2}{2\Delta\theta} = \frac{(10 \text{ rad}/\text{s})^2}{2(20 \text{ rad})} = 2.5 \text{ rad}/\text{s}^2$$

To summarize, here's a comparison of the fundamental quantities of translational and rotational motion and of the Big Five (assuming constant acceleration and a fixed axis of rotation):

	Translational	*Rotational*	*Connection*
displacement:	Δs	$\Delta\theta$	$\Delta s = r\Delta\theta$
velocity:	v	ω	$v = r\omega$
acceleration:	a	α	$a = r\alpha$
Big Five #1:	$\Delta s = \overline{v}\Delta t$	$\Delta\theta = \overline{\omega}\Delta t$	
Big Five #2:	$\Delta v = a\Delta t$	$\Delta\omega = \alpha\Delta t$	
Big Five #3:	$\Delta s = v_0\Delta t + \tfrac{1}{2}a(\Delta t)^2$	$\Delta\theta = \omega_0\Delta t + \tfrac{1}{2}\alpha(\Delta t)^2$	
Big Five #4:	$\Delta s = v\Delta t - \tfrac{1}{2}a(\Delta t)^2$	$\Delta\theta = \omega\Delta t - \tfrac{1}{2}\alpha(\Delta t)^2$	
Big Five #5:	$v^2 = v_0^2 + 2a\Delta s$	$\omega^2 = \omega_0^2 + 2\alpha\Delta\theta$	

ROTATIONAL DYNAMICS

The dynamics of translational motion involves describing the acceleration of an object in terms of its mass (inertia) and the forces that act on it; $F_{net} = ma$. By analogy, the dynamics of rotational motion involves describing the angular (rotational) acceleration of an object in terms of its **rotational inertia** and the **torques** that act on it.

TORQUE

Intuitively, torque describes the effectiveness of a force in producing rotational acceleration. Consider a uniform rod that pivots around one of its ends, which is fixed. For simplicity, let's assume that the rod is at rest. What effect, if any, would each of the four forces in the figure below have on the potential rotation of the rod?

Our intuition tells us that F_1, F_2, and F_3 would *not* cause the rod to rotate, but F_4 would. What's different about F_4? *It has torque.*

The torque of a force can be defined as follows. Let r be the distance from the pivot (axis of rotation) to the point of application of the force **F**, and let θ be the angle between vectors **r** and **F**.

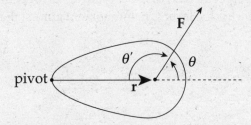

Then the torque of **F**, denoted by τ (*tau*), is defined as:

$$\tau = rF \sin \theta$$

In the figure above, the angle between the vectors **r** and **F** is θ. Imagine sliding **r** over so that its initial point is the same as that of **F**. *The angle between two vectors is the angle between them when they start at the same point.* However, the supplementary angle θ' can be used in place of θ in the definition of torque. This is because torque depends on $\sin \theta$, and the sine of an angle and the sine of its supplement are always equal. Therefore, when figuring out torque, use whichever of these angles is more convenient.

We will now see if this mathematical definition of torque supports our intuition about forces F_1, F_2, F_3, and F_4.

The angle between **r** and F_1 is 0, and $\theta = 0$ implies $\sin \theta = 0$, so by the definition of torque, $\tau = 0$ as well. The angle between **r** and F_2 is 180°, and $\theta = 180°$ gives us $\sin \theta = 0$, so $\tau = 0$. For F_3, $r = 0$ (because F_3 acts *at* the pivot, so the distance from the pivot to the point of application of F_3 is zero); since $r = 0$, the torque is 0 as well. However, for F_4, neither r nor $\sin \theta$ is zero, so F_4 has a nonzero torque. Of the four forces shown in that figure, only F_4 has torque and would produce rotational acceleration.

There's another way to determine the value of the torque. Of course, it gives the same result as the method given above, but this method is often easier to use. Look at the same object and force:

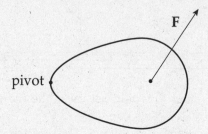

Instead of determining the distance from the pivot point to the point of application of the force, we will now determine the (perpendicular) distance from the pivot point to what's called the **line of action** of the force. This distance is the **lever arm** (or **moment arm**) of the force **F** relative to the pivot, and is denoted by l.

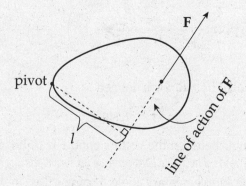

The torque of **F** is defined as the product

$$\tau = lF$$

(Just as the lever arm is often called the moment arm, the torque is called the **moment** of the force.) That these two definitions of torque, $\tau = rF \sin \theta$ and $\tau = lF$ are equivalent follows immediately from the fact that $l = r \sin \theta$:

Since l is the component of **r** that's perpendicular to **F**, it is also denoted by $r_\perp$ ("r perp"). So the definition of torque can be written as $\tau = r_\perp F$.

These two equivalent definitions of torque make it clear that only the component of **F** that's perpendicular to **r** produces torque. The component of **F** that's parallel to **r** does not produce torque. Notice that $\tau = rF \sin\theta = rF_\perp$, where $F_\perp$ ("F perp") is the component of **F** that's perpendicular to **r**:

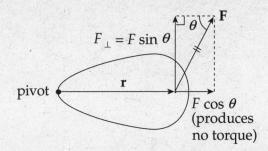

So the definition of torque can also be written as $\tau = rF_\perp$.

[C] **Remark.** Because only the component of **F** (perpendicular to **r**) produces torque, it is not surprising that the torque can be written as the cross product of **r** and **F**:

$$\tau = \mathbf{r} \times \mathbf{F}$$

Example 6.8 A student pulls down with a force of 40 N on a rope that winds around a pulley of radius 5 cm.

What's the torque of this force?

Solution. Since the tension force, F_T, is tangent to the pulley, it is perpendicular to the radius vector **r** at the point of contact:

Therefore, the torque produced by this tension force is simply

$$\tau = rF_T = (0.05 \text{ m})(40 \text{ N}) = 2 \text{ N·m}$$

Example 6.9 What is the net torque on the cylinder shown below?

Solution. Each of the two forces produces a torque, but these torques oppose each other. The torque of F_1 is counterclockwise, and the torque of F_2 is clockwise. This can be visualized either by imagining the effect of each force, assuming that the other was absent, or by using the vector definition of torque, $\tau = r \times F$. In the case of F_1, we have, by the right-hand rule,

$\tau_1 = r_1 \times F_1$ points out of the plane of the page: $\odot$, while

$\tau_2 = r_2 \times F_2$ points into the plane of the page: $\otimes$

If the torque vector points out of the plane of the page, this indicates a tendency to produce counterclockwise rotation and, if it points into the plane of the page, this indicates a tendency to produce clockwise rotation.

The **net torque** is the sum of the all the torques. Counting a counterclockwise torque as positive and a clockwise torque as negative, we have

$$\tau_1 = +r_1 F_1 = +(0.12 \text{ m})(100 \text{ N}) = +12 \text{ N·m}$$

and

$$\tau_2 = -r_2 F_2 = -(0.08 \text{ m})(80 \text{ N}) = -6.4 \text{ N·m}$$

so

$$\tau_{net} = \Sigma\, \tau = \tau_1 + \tau_2 = (+12 \text{ N·m}) + (-6.4 \text{ N·m}) = +5.6 \text{ N·m}$$

[C] ROTATIONAL INERTIA

Our goal is to develop a rotational analog of Newton's Second Law, $F_{net} = ma$. We're almost there; torque is the rotational analog of force and, therefore, τ_{net} is the rotational analog of F_{net}. The rotational analog of translational acceleration, a, is rotational (or angular) acceleration, α. We will now look at the rotational analog of inertial mass, m.

Consider a small point mass m at a distance r from the axis of rotation, being acted upon by a tangential force $\mathbf{F}$.

From Newton's Second Law, we have $F = ma$. Substituting $a = r\alpha$, this equation becomes $F = mr\alpha$. Now multiply both sides of this last equation by r to yield

$$rF = mr^2 \alpha$$

or, since $rF = \tau$,

$$\tau = mr^2 \alpha$$

In the equation $F = ma$, the quantity m is multiplied by the acceleration produced by the force F, while in the equation $\tau = mr^2\alpha$, the quantity mr^2 is multiplied by the rotational acceleration produced by the torque τ. So for a point mass at a distance r from the axis of rotation, its **rotational inertia** (also called **moment of inertia**) is defined as mr^2. If we now take into account all the point masses that comprise the object under study, we can get the total rotational inertia, I, of the body by adding them:

$$I = \sum m_i r_i^2$$

For a continuous solid body, this sum becomes the integral

$$I = \int r^2 \, dm$$

This formula can be used to calculate expressions for the rotational inertia of cylinders (disks), spheres, slender rods, and hoops. Notice that the rotational inertia depends not only on m, but also on r; both the mass *and how it's distributed about the axis of rotation* determine I. By summing over all point masses and all external torques, the equation $\tau = mr^2\alpha$ becomes

$$\sum \tau_i = \left(\sum m_i r_i^2\right)\alpha \quad \text{or} \quad \tau_{\text{net}} = I\alpha$$

We've reached our goal:

Translational motion	Rotational motion
force, F	torque, τ
acceleration, a	rotational acceleration, α
mass, m	rotational inertia, I
$F_{\text{net}} = ma$	$\tau_{\text{net}} = I\alpha$

Example 6.10 Three beads, each of mass m, are arranged along a rod of negligible mass and length L. Figure out the rotational inertia of the assembly when the axis of rotation is through the center bead and when the axis of rotation is through one of the beads on the ends.

Solution.

(a) In the first case, both the left bead and the right bead are at a distance of $L/2$ from the axis of rotation, while the center bead is at distance zero from the axis of rotation. Therefore,

$$I = \sum m_i r_i^2 = m\left(\tfrac{L}{2}\right)^2 + m(0)^2 + m\left(\tfrac{L}{2}\right)^2 = \tfrac{1}{2} mL^2$$

(b) In the second case, the left bead is at distance zero from the rotation axis, the center bead is at distance $L/2$, and the right bead is at distance L. Therefore,

$$I' = \sum m_i r_i^2 = m(0)^2 + m\left(\tfrac{L}{2}\right)^2 + m(L)^2 = \tfrac{5}{4} mL^2$$

Notice that, although both assemblies have the same mass (namely, $3m$), their rotational inertias are different, because of the different distribution of mass relative to the axis of rotation.

If the rotational inertia of a body is known relative to an axis that passes through the body's center of mass, then the rotational inertia, I', relative to any other rotation axis (parallel to the first one) can be calculated as follows. Let I_{cm} be the rotational inertia of a body relative to a rotation axis that passes through the body's center of mass, let the mass of the body be M, and let x be the distance from the axis through the center of mass to the rotation axis. Then

$$I' = I_{cm} + Mx^2$$

This is called the **parallel-axis theorem**. Let's use this result to calculate the rotational inertia of the three-bead assembly in part (b) from the value obtained in part (a), which is I_{cm}. Since $M = 3m$ and $x = L/2$, we have

$$I' = I_{cm} + Mx^2 = \tfrac{1}{2} mL^2 + (3m)\left(\tfrac{L}{2}\right)^2 = \tfrac{5}{4} mL^2$$

which agrees with the value calculated above.

Example 6.11 Show that the rotational inertia of a homogenous cylinder of radius R and mass M, rotating about its central axis, is given by the equation $I = \frac{1}{2}MR^2$.

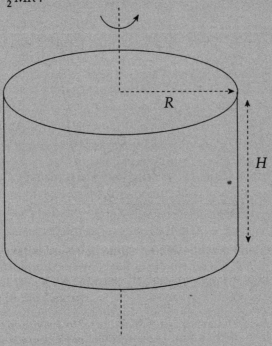

Solution. A solid is homogeneous if its density is constant throughout. Let ρ be the density of the cylinder. In order to compute I using the formula $I = \int r^2 \, dm$, we choose our mass element to be an infinitesimally thin cylindrical ring of radius r:

The mass of this ring is equal to its volume, $2\pi r\,dr \times H$, times the density; that is,

$$dm = \rho \times 2\pi rH\,dr,$$

Therefore,

$$I = \int r^2\,dm = \int_{r=0}^{r=R} r^2(\rho \cdot 2\pi rH\,dr)$$
$$= 2\pi\rho H\int_0^R r^3\,dr$$
$$= 2\pi\rho H\left[\tfrac{1}{4}r^4\right]_0^R$$
$$= \tfrac{1}{2}\pi\rho HR^4$$

To eliminate ρ, use the fact that the total mass of the cylinder is
$$M = \rho V = \rho \cdot \pi R^2 H$$

Putting this into the expression derived for I, we find that

$$I = \tfrac{1}{2}\pi\rho HR^4 = \tfrac{1}{2}(\rho \cdot \pi R^2 H)R^2 = \tfrac{1}{2}MR^2$$

The height of the cylinder (the dimension parallel to the axis of rotation) is irrelevant. Therefore, the formula $I = \tfrac{1}{2}MR^2$ gives the rotational inertia of any homogeneous solid cylinder revolving around its central axis. This includes a disk (which is just a really short cylinder).

Example 6.12 Again, consider the system of Example 6.9:

Assume that the mass of the cylinder is 50 kg. Given that the rotational inertia of a cylinder of radius R and mass M rotating about its central axis is given by the equation $I = \tfrac{1}{2}MR^2$, determine the rotational acceleration produced by the two forces shown.

Solution. In Example 6.9, we figured out that $\tau_{\text{net}} = +5.6$ N·m. The rotational inertia of the cylinder is

$$I = \tfrac{1}{2}MR^2 = \tfrac{1}{2}(50\text{ kg})(0.12\text{ m})^2 = 0.36\text{ kg·m}^2$$

Therefore, from the equation $\tau_{net} = I\alpha$, we find that

$$\alpha = \frac{\tau_{net}}{I} = \frac{5.6 \, \text{N} \cdot \text{m}}{0.36 \, \text{kg} \cdot \text{m}^2} = 16 \, \text{rad} / \text{s}^2$$

This angular acceleration will be counterclockwise, because τ_{net} is counterclockwise.

Example 6.13 A block of mass m is hung from a pulley of radius R and mass M and allowed to fall. What is the acceleration of the block?

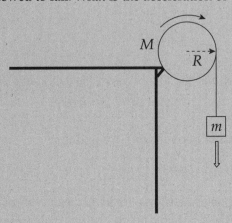

Solution. In Chapter 3, we treated pulleys as if they were massless, and no force was required to make them rotate. Now, however, we know how to take the mass of a pulley into account, by including its rotational inertia in our analysis. The pulley is a disk, so its rotational inertia is given by the formula $I = \frac{1}{2}MR^2$.

First we draw a free-body diagram for the falling block:

and apply Newton's Second Law:

$$mg - F_T = ma \quad (1)$$

Now the tension $\mathbf{F}_T$ in the cord produces a torque, $\tau = RF_T$, on the pulley:

Since this is the only torque on the pulley, the equation $\tau_{\text{net}} = I\alpha$ becomes $RF_{\text{T}} = I\alpha$. But $I = \frac{1}{2}MR^2$ and $\alpha = a/R$. (This last equation says that the cord doesn't slip as it slides over the pulley; the linear acceleration of a point on the rim, $a = R\alpha$, is equal to the acceleration of the connected block.) Therefore,

$$\tau = I\alpha \quad \Rightarrow \quad RF_{\text{T}} = \frac{1}{2}MR^2 \cdot \frac{a}{R} = \frac{1}{2}MRa$$

which tells us that

$$F_{\text{T}} = \frac{1}{2}Ma \quad (2)$$

Substituting Equation (2) into Equation (1), we find that

$$mg - \frac{1}{2}Ma = ma \quad \Rightarrow \quad \left(\frac{1}{2}M + m\right)a = mg \quad \Rightarrow \quad a = \frac{m}{\frac{1}{2}M + m}g$$

Example 6.14 A cylinder of mass M and radius R rolls (without slipping) down an inclined plane whose incline angle with the horizontal is θ. Determine the acceleration of the cylinder's center of mass.

Solution. First we draw a free-body diagram for the cylinder:

We know that the cylinder rolls without slipping, so the force of friction is not kinetic friction. Since the speed of the point on the cylinder in contact with the ramp is zero with respect to the ramp, *static* friction supplies the torque that allows the cylinder to roll smoothly.

The linear acceleration of the cylinder, a, is given by the equation $F_{net} = Ma$:

$$F_{net} = Ma \implies Mg\sin\theta - F_f = Ma$$

The rotational acceleration of the cylinder, α, is given by the equation $\tau_{net} = I\alpha$: Since $\tau = F_f R$, $I = \frac{1}{2}MR^2$, and $\alpha = a/R$, we have

$$\tau_{net} = I\alpha \implies F_f R = I\alpha \implies F_f R = \frac{1}{2}MR^2 \cdot \frac{a}{R} \implies F_f = \frac{1}{2}Ma$$

Substituting this result into the earlier equation gives

$$Mg\sin\theta - \frac{1}{2}Ma = Ma \implies \frac{3}{2}Ma = Mg\sin\theta \implies a = \frac{2}{3}g\sin\theta$$

[C] KINETIC ENERGY OF ROTATION

A rotating object has rotational kinetic energy, just as a translating object has translational kinetic energy. The formula for kinetic energy is, of course, $K = \frac{1}{2}mv^2$, but this can't be directly used to calculate the kinetic energy of rotation because each point mass that makes up the body can have a different v. For this reason, we need a definition of $K_{rotational}$ that involves ω instead of v.

$$K_{rotational} = \sum K_i = \sum \frac{1}{2}(m_i r_i^2)\omega^2 = \frac{1}{2}\left(\sum m_i r_i^2\right) \cdot \omega^2 = \frac{1}{2}I\omega^2$$

Notice that this expression for rotational kinetic energy follows the general pattern displayed by our previous results: I is the rotational analog of m and ω is the rotational analog of v. Therefore, the rotational analaog of $\frac{1}{2}mv^2$ should be $\frac{1}{2}I\omega^2$.

Example 6.15 A cylinder of mass M and radius R rolls (without slipping) down an inclined plane (of height h and length L) whose incline angle with the horizontal is θ. Determine the linear speed of the cylinder's center of mass when it reaches the bottom of the incline (assuming that it started from rest at the top).

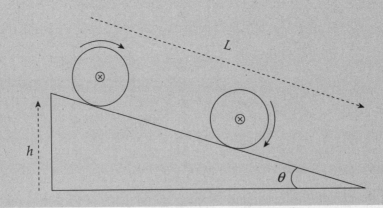

Solution. We will attack this problem using Conservation of Mechanical Energy. As the cylinder rolls down the ramp, its initial gravitational potential energy is converted into kinetic energy, which is a combination of translational kinetic energy (since the cylinder's center of mass is translating down the ramp) and rotational kinetic energy:

$$K_i + U_i = K_f + U_f$$
$$0 + Mgh = (\tfrac{1}{2}Mv_{cm}^2 + \tfrac{1}{2}I\omega^2) + 0$$

Since $I = \tfrac{1}{2}MR^2$ and $\omega = v_{cm}/R$, this equation becomes

$$Mgh = \tfrac{1}{2}Mv_{cm}^2 + \tfrac{1}{2}\left(\tfrac{1}{2}MR^2\right)\left(\frac{v_{cm}}{R}\right)^2 = \tfrac{1}{2}Mv_{cm}^2 + \tfrac{1}{4}Mv_{cm}^2 = \tfrac{3}{4}Mv_{cm}^2$$

Therefore,

$$v_{cm} = \sqrt{\tfrac{4}{3}gh}$$

We can verify this result using the result of the previous example. There we found that the acceleration of the cylinder's center of mass as it rolled down the ramp was $a = \tfrac{2}{3}g\sin\theta$. Applying Big Five #5 gives us:

$$v^2 = v_0^2 + 2a\Delta s = 2aL = 2a\frac{h}{\sin\theta} = 2\cdot\tfrac{2}{3}g\sin\theta\cdot\frac{h}{\sin\theta} = \tfrac{4}{3}gh \quad \Rightarrow \quad v = \sqrt{\tfrac{4}{3}gh}$$

[C] WORK AND POWER

Consider a small point mass m at distance r from the axis of rotation, acted upon by a tangential force **F**.

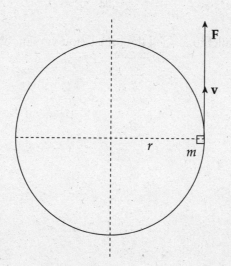

As it rotates through an angular displacement of $\Delta\theta$, the force does work on the point mass: $W = F\Delta s$, where $\Delta s = r\Delta\theta$. Therefore,

$$W = Fr\Delta\theta = \tau\Delta\theta$$

If the force is not purely tangential to the object's path, then only the tangential component of the force does work; the radial component does not (since it's perpendicular to the object's displacement). Therefore, for a general constant force F, the equation above would read $W = F_t r\Delta\theta = \tau\Delta\theta$, where F_t denotes the tangential component of F.

If we want to allow for a varying F—and a varying τ—then the work done is equal to the definite integral:

$$W = \int_{\theta_1}^{\theta_2} \tau\, d\theta$$

Again, notice the analogy between this equation and the one that defines work by F:

$$W = \int_{x_1}^{x_2} F\, dx$$

The work–energy theorem ($W = \Delta K$) also holds in the rotational case, where W is the work done by net torque and ΔK is the resulting change in the rotational kinetic energy.

The rate at which work is done, or the power (P) is defined by the equation

$$P = \frac{dW}{dt}$$

Over an infinitesimal angular displacement $d\theta$, the torque τ does an amount of work dW given by $dW = \tau\, d\theta$. This implies that

$$\frac{dW}{dt} = \tau\frac{d\theta}{dt} \quad\Rightarrow\quad P = \tau\omega$$

Once again, notice the parallel to $P = Fv$, the translation version of this equation.

Example 6.16 A block of mass $m = 5$ kg is hung from a pulley of radius $R = 15$ cm and mass $M = 8$ kg and then released from rest.

(a) What is the speed of the block as it strikes the floor, 2 m below its initial position?

(b) What is the rotational kinetic energy of the pulley just before the block strikes the floor?

(c) At what rate was work was done on the pulley?

Solution.

(a) Apply Conservation of Mechanical Energy. The initial gravitational potential energy of the block is transformed into the purely rotational kinetic energy of the pulley and translational kinetic energy of the falling block:

$$K_i + U_i = K_f + U_f$$
$$0 + mgh = (\tfrac{1}{2}mv^2 + \tfrac{1}{2}I\omega^2) + 0$$
$$= \tfrac{1}{2}mv^2 + \tfrac{1}{2}\cdot\tfrac{1}{2}MR^2 \cdot \left(\tfrac{v}{R}\right)^2$$
$$= \tfrac{1}{2}mv^2 + \tfrac{1}{4}Mv^2$$
$$= (\tfrac{1}{2}m + \tfrac{1}{4}M)v^2$$
$$v = \sqrt{\frac{mgh}{\tfrac{1}{2}m + \tfrac{1}{4}M}}$$

Substituting in the given numerical values, we get

$$v = \sqrt{\frac{(5)(9.8)(2)}{\tfrac{1}{2}(5) + \tfrac{1}{4}(8)}} = 4.7 \text{ m}/\text{s}$$

(b) The rotational kinetic energy of the pulley as the block strikes the floor is

$$K = \tfrac{1}{2} I \omega^2 = \tfrac{1}{2} \cdot \tfrac{1}{2} M R^2 \cdot \left(\tfrac{v}{R}\right)^2 = \tfrac{1}{4} M v^2 = \tfrac{1}{4}(8)(4.7)^2 = 44 \text{ J}$$

(c) The rate at which work is done on the pulley is the power produced by the torque. One way to compute this is to first use the work–energy theorem to determine the work done by the torque and then divide this by the time during which the block fell. So,

$$W = \Delta K = K_f - K_i = K_f = 44 \text{ J}$$

The time during which this work was done is the time required for the block to drop to the ground. Using Big Five #1 and the result of part (a), we find that

$$\Delta s = \bar{v} t \quad \Rightarrow \quad t = \frac{\Delta s}{\bar{v}} = \frac{h}{\tfrac{1}{2}(v_0 + v)} = \frac{h}{\tfrac{1}{2} v} = \frac{2 \text{ m}}{\tfrac{1}{2}(4.7 \text{ m}/\text{s})} = 0.85 \text{ s}$$

Therefore,

$$P = \frac{W}{t} = \frac{44 \text{ J}}{0.85 \text{ s}} = 52 \text{ W}$$

ANGULAR MOMENTUM

So far we've developed rotational analogs for displacement, velocity, acceleration, force, mass, and kinetic energy. We will finish by developing a rotational analog for linear momentum; it's called **angular momentum**.

Consider a small point mass m at distance r from the axis of rotation, moving with velocity **v** and acted upon by a tangential force **F**.

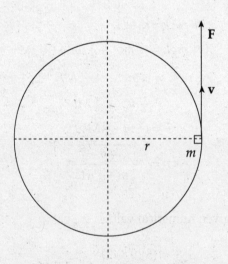

Then, by Newton's Second Law,

$$F = \frac{\Delta p}{\Delta t} = \frac{\Delta(mv)}{\Delta t}$$

If we multiply both sides of this equation by r and notice that $rF = \tau$, we get

$$\tau = \frac{\Delta(mvr)}{\Delta t}$$

Therefore, to form the analog of the law $F = \Delta p / \Delta t$ (force equals the rate-of-change of linear momentum), we say that torque equals the rate-of-change of angular momentum, and the angular momentum (denoted by L) of the point mass m is defined by the equation

$$L = rmv$$

If we now take into account all the point masses which comprise the object under study, we can get the angular momentum of the body by adding up all the individual contributions. This gives

$$L = I\omega$$

Notice that this expression for angular momentum follows the general pattern we saw previously: I is the rotational analog of m, and ω is the rotational analog of v. Therefore, the rotational analog of mv should be $I\omega$.

If the point mass m does not move in a circular path, we can still define its angular momentum relative to any reference point.

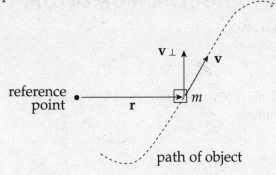

If $\mathbf{r}$ is the vector from the reference point to the mass, then the angular momentum is

$$L = rmv_\perp$$

where $v_\perp$ is the component of the velocity that's perpendicular to $\mathbf{r}$. The fact that it's the perpendicular component of $\mathbf{v}$ relative to $\mathbf{r}$ that's important for figuring out angular momentum motivates the general vector definition with the cross product. The equation $L = (r)(mv_\perp) = (r)(p_\perp)$ becomes

$$L = \mathbf{r} \times \mathbf{p}$$

Example 6.17 [C] A solid uniform sphere of mass $M = 8$ kg and radius $R = 50$ cm is revolving around an axis through its center at an angular speed of 10 rad/s. Given that the rotational inertia of the sphere is equal to $\frac{2}{5}MR^2$, what is the spinning sphere's angular momentum?

Solution. Apply the definition:

$$L = I\omega = \tfrac{2}{5}MR^2\omega = \tfrac{2}{5}(8 \text{ kg})(0.50 \text{ m})^2(10 \text{ rad} / \text{s}) = 8 \text{ kg} \cdot \text{m}^2 / \text{s}$$

If you want to specify the direction of the angular momentum vector, **L**, use the right-hand rule. Let the fingers of your right hand curl in the direction of rotation of the body. Your thumb gives the direction of **L**, pointing along the rotation axis:

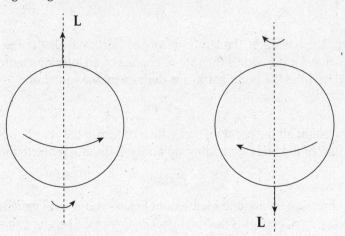

CONSERVATION OF ANGULAR MOMENTUM

Newton's Second Law says that

$$\mathbf{F}_{net} = \frac{d\mathbf{p}}{dt}$$

so if $F_{net} = 0$, then **p** is constant. This is Conservation of Linear Momentum.

The rotational analog of this is:

$$\tau_{net} = \frac{d\mathbf{L}}{dt}$$

so if $\tau_{net} = 0$, then **L** is constant. This is **Conservation of Angular Momentum**. Basically, this says that if the torques on a body balance so that the net torque is zero, then the body's angular momentum can't change.

An often cited example of this phenomenon is the spinning of a figure skater. As she pulls her arms inward, she moves more of her mass closer to the rotation axis and decreases her rotational inertia. Since the external torque on her is negligible, her angular momentum must be conserved. Since $L = I\omega$, a decrease in I causes an increase in ω, and she spins faster.

> **Example 6.18** **[C]** A child of mass $m = 30$ kg stands at the edge of small merry-go-round that's rotating at a rate of 1 rad/s. The merry-go-round is a disk of radius $R = 2.5$ m and mass $M = 100$ kg. If the child walks in, toward the center of the disk and stops 0.5 m from the center, what will happen to the angular velocity of the merry-go-round (if friction can be ignored)?

Solution. The child walking toward the center of the merry-go-round does not provide an external torque to the child + disk system, so angular momentum is conserved. Let's denote the child as a point mass, and consider the following two views of the merry-go-round (looking down from above):

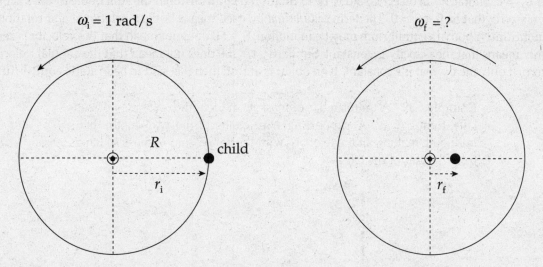

In the first picture, the total rotational inertia, I_i, is equal to the sum of the rotational inertia of the merry-go-round (MGR) and the child:

$$I_i = I_{\text{MGR}} + I_{\text{child}} = \tfrac{1}{2}MR^2 + mr_i^2 = \tfrac{1}{2}MR^2 + mR^2 = \left(\tfrac{1}{2}M + m\right)R^2$$

In the second picture, the total rotational inertia has decreased to

$$I_f = I_{\text{MGR}} + I'_{\text{child}} = \tfrac{1}{2}MR^2 + mr_f^2$$

So, by Conservation of Angular Momentum, we have

$$L_i = L_f$$
$$I_i\omega_i = I_f\omega_f$$
$$\left(\tfrac{1}{2}M + m\right)R^2\omega_i = \left(\tfrac{1}{2}MR^2 + mr_f^2\right)\omega_f$$
$$\omega_f = \frac{\left(\tfrac{1}{2}M + m\right)R^2}{\tfrac{1}{2}MR^2 + mr_f^2}\omega_i$$

and, substituting the given numerical values gives us

$$\omega_f = \frac{\left(\tfrac{1}{2}M + m\right)R^2}{\tfrac{1}{2}MR^2 + mr_f^2}\omega_i$$
$$= \frac{\left(\tfrac{1}{2}\cdot 100 + 30\right)(2.5)^2}{\tfrac{1}{2}\cdot 100 \cdot (2.5)^2 + 30 \cdot (0.5)^2}(1 \text{ rad}/\text{s})$$
$$= 1.6 \text{ rad}/\text{s}$$

Notice that ω increased as I decreased, just as Conservation of Angular Momentum predicts.

EQUILIBRIUM

An object is said to be in **translational equilibrium** if the sum of the forces acting on it is zero; that is, if $F_{net} = 0$. Similarly, an object is said to be in **rotational equilibrium** if the sum of the torques acting on it is zero; that is, if $\tau_{net} = 0$. The term *equilibrium* by itself means both translational and rotational equilibrium. A body in equilibrium may be in motion; $F_{net} = 0$ does not mean that the velocity is zero; it only means that the velocity is constant. Similarly, $\tau_{net} = 0$ does not mean that the angular velocity is zero; it only means that it's constant. If an object is at rest, then it is said to be in **static equilibrium**.

Example 6.19 A uniform bar of mass m and length L extends horizontally from a wall. A supporting wire connects the wall to the bar's midpoint, making an angle of 55° with the bar. A sign of mass M hangs from the end of the bar.

If the system is in static equilibrium, determine the tension in the wire and the strength of the force exerted on the bar by the wall if $m = 8$ kg and $M = 12$ kg.

Solution. Let $\mathbf{F}_C$ denote the (contact) force exerted by the wall on the bar. In order to simplify our work, we can write $\mathbf{F}_C$ in terms of its horizontal component, F_{Cx}, and its vertical component, F_{Cy}. Also, if $\mathbf{F}_T$ is the tension in the wire, then $F_{Tx} = F_T \cos 55°$ and $F_{Ty} = F_T \sin 55°$ are its components. This gives us the following force diagram:

The first condition for equilibrium requires that the sum of the horizontal forces is zero and the sum of the vertical forces is 0:

$$\sum F_x = 0: \qquad F_{Cx} - F_T \cos 55° = 0 \qquad (1)$$
$$\sum F_y = 0: \qquad F_{Cy} + F_T \sin 55° - mg - Mg = 0 \quad (2)$$

We notice immediately that we have more unknowns (F_{Cx}, F_{Cy}, F_T) than equations, so this system cannot be solved as is. The second condition for equilibrium requires that the sum of the torques about any point is equal to zero. Choosing the contact point between the bar and the wall as our pivot, only three of the forces in the diagram above produce torque: $\mathbf{F}_{Ty}$ produces a counterclockwise torque, and both mg and Mg produce clockwise torques, which must balance. From the definition $\tau = lF$, and taking counterclockwise torque as positive and clockwise torque as negative, we have

$$\sum \tau = 0: \qquad (L/2)F_{Ty} - (L/2)(mg) - LMg = 0 \quad (3)$$

This equation contains only one unknown and can be solved immediately:

$$\tfrac{L}{2} F_{Ty} = \tfrac{L}{2} mg + LMg$$
$$F_{Ty} = mg + 2Mg = (m + 2M)g$$

Since $F_{Ty} = F_T \sin 55°$, we can find that

$$F_T \sin 55° = (m + 2M)g \quad \Rightarrow \quad F_T = \frac{(m + 2M)g}{\sin 55°}$$

$$= \frac{(8 + 2 \cdot 12)(9.8)}{\sin 55°}$$

$$= 380 \text{ N}$$

Substituting this result into Equation (1) gives us F_{Cx}:

$$F_{Cx} = F_T \cos 55° = \frac{(m + 2M)g}{\sin 55°} \cos 55° = (8 + 2 \cdot 12)(9.8)\cot 55° = 220 \text{ N}$$

And finally, from Equation (2), we get

$$F_{Cy} = mg + Mg - F_T \sin 55°$$
$$= mg + Mg - \frac{(m + 2M)g}{\sin 55°} \sin 55°$$
$$= -Mg$$
$$= -(12)(9.8)$$
$$= -118 \text{ N}$$

The fact that F_{Cy} turned out to be negative simply means that in our original force diagram, the vector $\mathbf{F}_{Cy}$ points in the direction opposite to how we drew it. That is, $\mathbf{F}_{Cy}$ points downward. Therefore, the magnitude of the total force exerted by the wall on the bar is

$$F_C = \sqrt{(F_{Cx})^2 + (F_{Cy})^2} = \sqrt{220^2 + 118^2} = 250 \text{ N}$$

CHAPTER 6 REVIEW QUESTIONS

SECTION I: MULTIPLE CHOICE

1. [C] A compact disk has a radius of 6 cm. If the disk rotates about its central axis at an angular speed of 5 rev/s, what is the linear speed of a point on the rim of the disk?

   (A) 0.3 m/s
   (B) 1.9 m/s
   (C) 7.4 m/s
   (D) 52 m/s
   (E) 83 m/s

2. [C] A compact disk has a radius of 6 cm. If the disk rotates about its central axis at a constant angular speed of 5 rev/s, what is the total distance traveled by a point on the rim of disk in 40 min?

   (A) 180 m
   (B) 360 m
   (C) 540 m
   (D) 720 m
   (E) 4.5 km

3. [C] An object of mass 0.5 kg, moving in a circular path of radius 0.25 m, experiences a centripetal acceleration of constant magnitude 9 m/s². What is the object's angular speed?

   (A) 2.3 rad/s
   (B) 4.5 rad/s
   (C) 6 rad/s
   (D) 12 rad/s
   (E) Cannot be determined from the information given

4. [C] An object, originally at rest, begins spinning under uniform angular acceleration. In 10 s, it completes an angular displacement of 60 rad. What is the numerical value of the angular acceleration?

   (A) 0.3 rad/s²
   (B) 0.6 rad/s²
   (C) 1.2 rad/s²
   (D) 2.4 rad/s²
   (E) 3.6 rad/s²

5.

In an effort to tighten a bolt, a force **F** is applied as shown in the figure above. If the distance from the end of the wrench to the center of the bolt is 20 cm and $F = 20$ N, what is the magnitude of the torque produced by **F**?

   (A) 0 N·m
   (B) 1 N·m
   (C) 2 N·m
   (D) 4 N·m
   (E) 10 N·m

6.

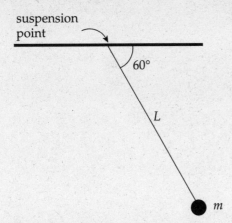

suspension point

60°

L

m

In the figure above, what is the torque about the pendulum's suspension point produced by the weight of the bob, given that the length of the pendulum, L, is 80 cm and $m = 0.50$ kg?

(A) 0.49 N·m
(B) 0.98 N·m
(C) 1.7 N·m
(D) 2.0 N·m
(E) 3.4 N·m

7.

m   M

A uniform meter stick of mass 1 kg is hanging from a thread attached at the stick's midpoint. One block of mass $m = 3$ kg hangs from the left end of the stick, and another block, of unknown mass M, hangs below the 80 cm mark on the meter stick. If the stick remains at rest in the horizontal position shown above, what is M?

(A) 4 kg
(B) 5 kg
(C) 6 kg
(D) 8 kg
(E) 9 kg

8. [C] What is the rotational inertia of the following body about the indicated rotation axis? (The masses of the connecting rods are negligible.)

rotation axis

m   m

$\frac{8}{3}L$

m   m

L   L

(A) $4mL^2$

(B) $\frac{32}{3}mL^2$

(C) $\frac{64}{9}mL^2$

(D) $\frac{128}{9}mL^2$

(E) $\frac{256}{9}mL^2$

9. [C] The moment of inertia of a solid uniform sphere of mass M and radius R is given by the equation $I = \frac{2}{5}MR^2$. Such a sphere is released from rest at the top of an inclined plane of height h, length L, and incline angle θ. If the sphere rolls without slipping, find its speed at the bottom of the incline.

(A) $\sqrt{\frac{10}{7}gh}$

(B) $\sqrt{\frac{5}{2}gh}$

(C) $\sqrt{\frac{7}{2}gh}$

(D) $\sqrt{\frac{2}{7}gL\sin\theta}$

(E) $\sqrt{\frac{7}{10}gL\sin\theta}$

10. [C] An object spins with angular velocity ω. If the object's moment of inertia increases by a factor of 2 without the application of an external torque, what will be the object's new angular velocity?

(A) $\omega/4$

(B) $\omega/2$

(C) $\omega/\sqrt{2}$

(D) $\sqrt{2}\,\omega$

(E) 2ω

SECTION II: FREE RESPONSE

1. [C] In the figure below, the pulley is a solid disk of mass M and radius R, with rotational inertia $MR^2/2$. Two blocks, one of mass m_1 and one of mass m_2, hang from either side of the pulley by a light cord. Initially the system is at rest, with Block 1 on the floor and Block 2 held at height h above the floor. Block 2 is then released and allowed to fall.

(a)   What is the speed of Block 2 just before it strikes the ground?

(b)   What is the angular speed of the pulley at this moment?

(c)   What's the angular displacement of the pulley?

(d)   How long does it take for Block 2 to fall to the floor?

2. **[C]** The diagram below shows a solid uniform cylinder of radius R and mass M rolling (without slipping) down an inclined plane of incline angle θ. A thread wraps around the cylinder as it rolls down the plane and pulls upward on a block of mass m. Ignore the rotational inertia of the pulley.

(a) Show that "rolling without slipping" means that the speed of the cylinder's center of mass, v_{cm}, is equal to $R\omega$, where ω is its angular speed.

(b) Show that, relative to P (the point of contact of the cylinder with the ramp), the speed of the top of the cylinder is $2v_{cm}$.

(c) What is the relationship between the magnitude of the acceleration of the block and the linear acceleration of the cylinder?

(d) What is the acceleration of the cylinder?

(e) What is the acceleration of the block?

3. **[C]** Two slender uniform bars, each of mass M and length $2L$, meet at right angles at their midpoints to form a rigid assembly that's able to rotate freely about an axis through the intersection point, perpendicular to the page. Attached to each end of each rod is a solid ball of clay of mass m. A bullet of mass m_b is shot with velocity $\mathbf{v}$ as shown in the figure (which is a view from above of the assembly) and becomes embedded in the targeted clay ball.

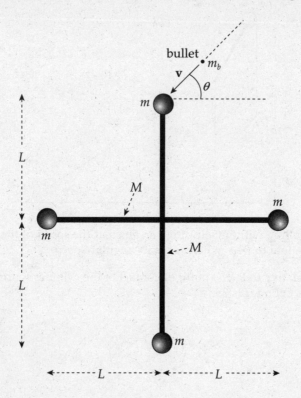

(a) Show that the moment of inertia of each slender rod about the given rotation axis is $ML^2/3$.

(b) Determine the angular velocity of the assembly after the bullet has become lodged in the targeted clay ball.

(c) What is the resulting linear speed of each clay ball?

(d) Determine the ratio of the final kinetic energy of the assembly to the kinetic energy of the bullet before impact.

7

NEWTON'S LAW OF GRAVITATION

KEPLER'S LAWS

Johannes Kepler spent years of exhaustive study distilling volumes of his mentor, Tycho Brahe's data into three simple laws that describe the motion of planets.

KEPLER'S FIRST LAW

Every planet moves in an elliptical orbit, with the Sun at one focus.

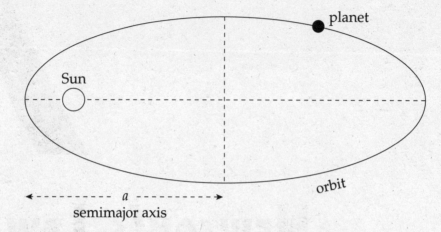

KEPLER'S SECOND LAW

As a planet moves in its orbit, a line drawn from the Sun to the planet sweeps out equal areas in equal time intervals.

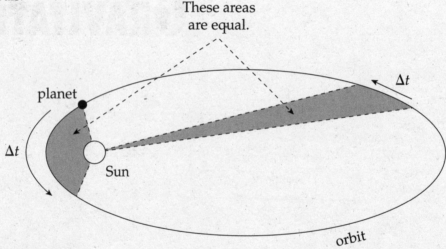

KEPLER'S THIRD LAW

If T is the period and a is the length of the semimajor axis of a planet's orbit, then the ratio T^2/a^3 is the same for all the planets.

NEWTON'S LAW OF GRAVITATION

Newton eventually proved that Kepler's first two laws imply a law of gravitation: Any two objects in the Universe exert an attractive force on each other—called the **gravitational force**—whose strength is proportional to the product of the objects' masses and inversely proportional to the square of the distance between them. If we let G be the **universal gravitational constant**, then the strength of the gravitational force is given by the equation:

$$F = G\frac{m_1 m_2}{r^2}$$

The forces $\mathbf{F}_{1\text{-on-}2}$ and $\mathbf{F}_{2\text{-on-}1}$ act along the line that joins the bodies and form an action/reaction pair.

The first reasonably accurate numerical value for G was determined by Cavendish more than one hundred years after Newton's Law was published. To three decimal places, the currently accepted value of G is

$$G = 6.67 \times 10^{-11} \ \mathrm{N \cdot m^2/kg^2}$$

Kepler's Third Law then follows from Newton's Law of Gravitation. We'll show how this works, for the case of a circular orbit of radius R (which can be considered an elliptical orbit with eccentricity zero). If the orbit is circular, then Kepler's Second Law says that the planet's orbit speed, v, must be constant. Therefore, the planet executes uniform circular motion, and centripetal force is provided by the gravitational attraction of the Sun. If we let M be the mass of the Sun and m the mass of the planet, then this last statement can be expressed mathematically as:

$$\frac{mv^2}{R} = G\frac{Mm}{R^2} \quad (1)$$

The period of a planet's orbit is the time it requires to make one revolution around the Sun, so dividing the distance covered, $2\pi R$, by the planet's orbit speed, v, we have

$$T = \frac{2\pi R}{v} \quad (2)$$

Equation (1) implies that $v^2 = GM/R$. Squaring both sides of Equation (2) and then substituting $v^2 = GM/R$, we find that

$$T^2 = \frac{4\pi^2 R^2}{v^2} = \frac{4\pi^2 R^2}{GM/R} = \frac{4\pi^2}{GM}R^3$$

Therefore,

$$\frac{T^2}{R^3} = \frac{4\pi^2}{GM}, \text{ a constant}$$

which is Kepler's Third Law for a circular orbit of radius R.

THE GRAVITATIONAL ATTRACTION DUE TO AN EXTENDED BODY

Newton's Law of Gravitation is really a statement about the force between two point particles; objects that are very small in comparison to the distance between them. Newton also proved that a uniform sphere attracts another body as if all of the sphere's mass were concentrated at its center.

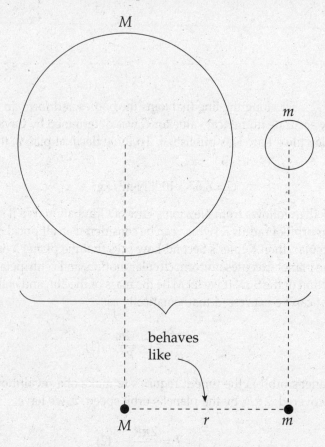

For this reason, we can apply Newton's Law of Gravitation to extended bodies, that is, to objects that are not small relative to the distance between them.

Additionally, a uniform shell of mass does not exert a gravitational force on a particle inside it. This means that if a spherical planet is uniform, then as we descend into it, only the mass of the sphere *underneath* us exerts a gravitational force; the shell *above* exerts no force because we're inside it.

> **Example 7.1** What is the gravitational force on a particle of mass m at a distance x from the center of a spherically-symmetric planet of uniform density ρ, total mass M, and radius R for
> (a) $x \geq R$
> (b) $x < R$

Solution. (a) If $x \geq R$, then the planet can be treated as a point particle with all its mass concentrated at its center, and

$$F = G\frac{Mm}{x^2} \quad (x \geq R)$$

(b) However, if $x < R$, then only the mass within the sphere of radius x exerts a gravitational force on the particle. Since the volume of such a sphere is $(4/3)\pi x^3$, its mass is $(4/3)\pi x^3 \rho$; we'll denote this by $M_{within\,x}$. Since the mass of the entire planet is $(4/3)\pi R^3 \rho$, we see that

$$\frac{M_{within\,x}}{M} = \frac{\frac{4}{3}\pi x^3 \rho}{\frac{4}{3}\pi R^3 \rho} = \frac{x^3}{R^3} \quad \Rightarrow \quad M_{within\,x} = \frac{x^3}{R^3}M$$

Therefore, the force that this much mass exerts on the particle of mass m is

$$F = G\frac{\dfrac{x^3}{R^3}M \cdot m}{x^2} = G\frac{Mm}{R^3}x \quad (x < R)$$

In summary then,

$$F_{grav} = \begin{cases} G\dfrac{Mm}{R^3}x & \text{for } x \leq R \\[2mm] G\dfrac{Mm}{x^2} & \text{for } x \geq R \end{cases}$$

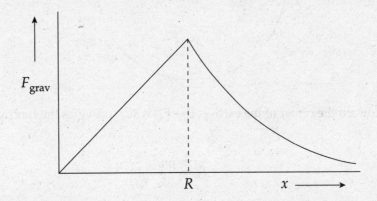

Example 7.2 Given that the radius of the earth is 6.37×10^6 m, determine the mass of the earth.

Solution. Consider a small object of mass m near the surface of the earth (mass M). Its weight is mg, but its weight is just the gravitational force it feels due to the earth, which is GMm/R^2. Therefore,

$$mg = G\frac{Mm}{R^2} \quad \Rightarrow \quad M = \frac{gR^2}{G}$$

Since we know that $g = 9.8$ m/s^2 and $G = 6.67 \times 10^{-11}$ N·m^2/kg^2, we can substitute to find

$$M = \frac{gR^2}{G} = \frac{(9.8 \text{ m/s}^2)(6.37 \times 10^6 \text{ m})^2}{6.67 \times 10^{-11} \text{ N·m}^2/\text{kg}^2} = 6.0 \times 10^{24} \text{ kg}$$

Example 7.3 We can derive the expression GM/R^2 by equating mg and GMm/R^2 (as we did in the previous example), and this gives the magnitude of the *absolute gravitational acceleration*, a quantity that's sometimes denoted g_0. The notation g is acceleration, but with the spinning of the earth taken into account. Show that if an object is at the equator, its *measured weight*, mg, is less than its *true weight*, mg_0, and compute the weight difference for a person of mass $m = 60$ kg.

Solution. Imagine looking down at the earth from above the North Pole.

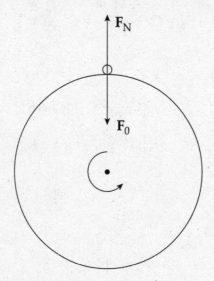

The net force toward the center of the earth is $\mathbf{F}_0 - \mathbf{F}_N$, which provides the centripetal force on the object. Therefore,

$$F_0 - F_N = \frac{mv^2}{R}$$

Since $v = 2\pi R/T$, where T is the earth's rotation period, we have

$$F_0 - F_N = \frac{m}{R}\left(\frac{2\pi R}{T}\right)^2 = \frac{4\pi^2 mR}{T^2}$$

or, since $F_0 = mg_0$ and $F_N = mg$,

$$mg_0 - mg = \frac{4\pi^2 mR}{T^2}$$

Since the quantity $4\pi^2 R/T^2$ is positive, mg must be less than mg_0. The difference between mg_0 and mg, for a person of mass $m = 60$ kg, is only:

$$\frac{4\pi^2 mR}{T^2} = \frac{4\pi^2(60\text{ kg})(6.37\times10^6\text{ m})}{\left(24\text{ hr}\times\frac{60\text{ min}}{\text{hr}}\times\frac{60\text{ s}}{\text{min}}\right)^2} = 2.0\text{ N}$$

and the difference between g_0 and g is

$$g_0 - g = \frac{mg_0 - mg}{m} = \frac{4\pi^2 R}{T^2} = \frac{4\pi^2(6.37\times10^6\text{ m})}{\left(24\text{ hr}\times\frac{60\text{ min}}{\text{hr}}\times\frac{60\text{ s}}{\text{min}}\right)^2} = 0.034\text{ m}/\text{s}^2$$

Example 7.4 Communications satellites are often parked in geosynchronous orbits above Earth's surface. Satellites have orbit periods that are equal to Earth's rotation period, so they remain above the same position on Earth's surface. Determine the altitude and the speed that a satellite must have to be in a geosynchronous orbit above a fixed point on Earth's equator. (The mass of the Earth is 5.98×10^{24} kg.)

Solution. Let m be the mass of the satellite, M the mass of Earth, and R the distance from the center of Earth to the position of the satellite. The gravitational pull of Earth provides the centripetal force on the satellite, so

$$G\frac{Mm}{R^2} = \frac{mv^2}{R} \quad \Rightarrow \quad G\frac{M}{R} = v^2$$

The orbit speed of the satellite is $2\pi R/T$, so

$$G\frac{M}{R} = \left(\frac{2\pi R}{T}\right)^2$$

which implies that

$$G\frac{M}{R} = \frac{4\pi^2 R^2}{T^2} \quad \Rightarrow \quad 4\pi^2 R^3 = GMT^2 \quad \Rightarrow \quad R = \sqrt[3]{\frac{GMT^2}{4\pi^2}}$$

Now the key feature of a geosynchronous orbit is that its period matches Earth's rotation period, $T = 24$ hr. Substituting the numerical values of G, M, and T into this expression, we find that

$$R = \sqrt[3]{\frac{GMT^2}{4\pi^2}} = \sqrt[3]{\frac{(6.67\times10^{-11})(5.98\times10^{24})(24\cdot60\cdot60)^2}{4\pi^2}}$$
$$= 4.23\times10^7\text{ m}$$

Therefore, if r_E is the radius of Earth, then the satellite's altitude above Earth's surface must be

$$h = R - r_E = (4.23\times10^7\text{ m}) - (6.37\times10^6\text{ m}) = 3.59\times10^7\text{ m}$$

which is equal to $5.6 r_E$. The speed of the satellite in this orbit is, from the first equation in our calculations,

$$v = \sqrt{G\frac{M}{R}} = \sqrt{(6.67\times10^{-11}\text{ N}\cdot\text{m}^2/\text{kg}^2)\frac{5.98\times10^{24}\text{ kg}}{4.23\times10^7\text{ m}}} = 3070\text{ m}/\text{s}$$

regardless of the mass of the satellite (well, as long as $m \ll M$).

Example 7.5 **[C]** A uniform, slender bar of mass M has length L. Determine the gravitational force it exerts on the point particle of mass m shown below:

Solution. Since the bar is an extended body (and not spherically symmetric), we must calculate F using an integral. Select an arbitrary segment of length dx and mass dM in the bar, at a distance x from its left-hand end.

Then, since the bar is uniform, $dM = (M/L)dx$, so the gravitational force between m and dM is

$$dF = G\frac{m \cdot dM}{(z+x)^2} = G\frac{m \cdot \dfrac{M}{L}dx}{(z+x)^2} = G\frac{mM}{L(z+x)^2}dx$$

Now, by adding (that is, by integrating) all of the contributions dF, we get the total gravitational force, F:

$$
\begin{aligned}
F &= \int dF \\
&= \int_{x=0}^{x=L} G\frac{mM}{L(z+x)^2}dx \\
&= G\frac{mM}{L}\int_{x=0}^{x=L}\frac{dx}{(z+x)^2} \\
&= G\frac{mM}{L}\left[\frac{-1}{z+x}\right]_{x=0}^{x=L} \\
&= G\frac{mM}{L}\left[\frac{-1}{z+L}+\frac{1}{z}\right] \\
&= G\frac{mM}{L}\frac{L}{z(z+L)} \\
&= G\frac{mM}{z(z+L)}
\end{aligned}
$$

GRAVITATIONAL POTENTIAL ENERGY

When we developed the equation $U = mgh$ for the gravitational potential energy of an object of mass m at height h above the surface of the earth, we took the surface of the earth to be our $U = 0$ reference level and assumed that the height, h, was small compared to the earth's radius. In that case, the variation in g was negligible, so g was treated as constant. The work done by gravity as an object was raised to height h was then simply $-F_{grav} \times \Delta s = -mgh$, so U_{grav}, which by definition equals $-W_{by\ grav}$, was mgh.

But now we'll take variations in g into account and develop a general equation for gravitational potential energy, one that isn't restricted to small altitude changes.

Consider an object of mass m at a distance r_1 from the center of the earth (or any spherical body) moving by some means to a position r_2:

How much work did the gravitational force perform during this displacement? The answer is given by the equation:

$$W_{by\ grav} = GMm\left(\frac{1}{r_2} - \frac{1}{r_1}\right) (*)$$

Therefore, since $\Delta U_{grav} = -W_{by\ grav}$, we get

$$U_2 - U_1 = -GMm\left(\frac{1}{r_2} - \frac{1}{r_1}\right)$$

Let's choose our $U = 0$ reference at infinity. That is, we decide to allow $U_2 \to 0$ as $r_2 \to \infty$. Then this equation becomes

$$U = -\frac{GMm}{r}$$

Notice that, according to this equation (and our choice of $U = 0$ when $r = \infty$), the gravitational potential energy is always negative. This just means that energy has to be added to bring an object (mass m) bound to the gravitational field of M to a point very far from M, at which $U = 0$.

[C] A PROOF OF EQUATION (*)

Because the gravitational force is not constant over the displacement, the work done by this force must be calculated using a definite integral:

$$dW = \mathbf{F} \cdot d\mathbf{r} \quad \Rightarrow \quad W = \int_{r=r_1}^{r=r_2} \mathbf{F} \cdot d\mathbf{r}$$

Displacement can be broken into a series of infinitesimal steps of two types: Those that are at a constant distance from the earth's center and those that are along a radial line going away from the earth's center. The result is that the displacement is equivalent to the sum of two curves, $C_1 + C_2$:

The gravitational force along C_1 does no work, because it's always perpendicular to the displacement. Along C_2, the inward gravitational force is in the opposite direction from the outward displacement, so along this ray,

$$\mathbf{F} \cdot d\mathbf{r} = F \cdot dr \cdot \cos 180°$$
$$= -F \, dr$$
$$= -\frac{GMm}{r^2} dr$$

Therefore,

$$W_{\text{by grav}} = \int_{r=r_1}^{r=r_2} \mathbf{F} \cdot d\mathbf{r}$$

$$= \int_{C_2} \mathbf{F} \cdot d\mathbf{r}$$

$$= \int_{r_1}^{r_2} -\frac{GMm}{r^2} dr$$

$$= GMm \int_{r=r_1}^{r=r_2} -\frac{1}{r^2} dr$$

$$= GMm \left[\frac{1}{r}\right]_{r_1}^{r_2}$$

$$= GMm \left(\frac{1}{r_2} - \frac{1}{r_1}\right)$$

Example 7.6 With what minimum speed must an object of mass m be launched in order to escape Earth's gravitational field? (This is called **escape speed**, v_{esc}.)

Solution. When launched, the object is at the surface of the earth ($r_i = r_E$) and has an upward, initial velocity of magnitude v_i. To get it far away from the earth, we want to bring its gravitational potential energy to zero, but to find the *minimum* launch speed, we want the object's final speed to be zero by the time it gets to this distant location. So, by Conservation of Energy,

$$K_i + U_i = K_f + U_f$$

$$\frac{1}{2}mv_i^2 + \frac{-GM_E m}{r_E} = 0 + 0$$

which gives

$$\frac{1}{2}mv_i^2 = \frac{GM_E m}{r_E} \quad \Rightarrow \quad v_i = \sqrt{\frac{2GM_E}{r_E}}$$

Substituting the known numerical values for G, M_E, and r_E gives us:

$$v_i = v_{\text{esc}} = \sqrt{\frac{2GM_E}{r_E}} = \sqrt{\frac{2(6.67 \times 10^{-11})(5.98 \times 10^{24})}{6.37 \times 10^6}}$$

$$= 1.12 \times 10^4 \text{ m/s}$$

(Note: This is the minimum speed needed to escape *Earth's* gravitational field but, in this situation, a projectile would also have to contend with the *Sun's* gravitational field, etc.)

> **Example 7.7** A satellite of mass m is in a circular orbit of radius R around the earth (radius r_E, mass M).
> (a) What is its total mechanical energy (where U_{grav} is considered zero as R approaches infinity)?
> (b) How much work would be required to move the satellite into a new orbit, with radius $2R$?

Solution.

(a) The mechanical energy, E, is the sum of the kinetic energy, K, and potential energy, U. You can calculate the kinetic energy since you know that the centripetal force on the satellite is provided by the gravitational attraction of the earth:

$$\frac{mv^2}{R} = \frac{GMm}{R^2} \quad \Rightarrow \quad mv^2 = \frac{GMm}{R} \quad \Rightarrow \quad K = \tfrac{1}{2}mv^2 = \frac{GMm}{2R}$$

Therefore,

$$E = K + U = \frac{GMm}{2R} + \frac{-GMm}{R} = -\frac{GMm}{2R}$$

(b) From the equation $K_i + U_i + W = K_f + U_f$, we see that

$$W = (K_f + U_f) - (K_i + U_i)$$
$$= E_f - E_i$$

Therefore, the amount of work necessary to effect the change in the satellite's orbit radius from R to $2R$, is

$$W = E_{at\,2R} - E_{at\,R}$$
$$= -\frac{GMm}{2(2R)} - \left(\frac{-GMm}{2R}\right)$$
$$= \frac{GMm}{4R}$$

[C] A NOTE ON ELLIPTICAL ORBITS

The expression for the total energy of a satellite in a circular orbit of radius R [derived in Example 7.7(a)] is:

$$E = -\frac{GMm}{2R} \quad \text{(circular orbit)}$$

and this also holds for a satellite traveling in an elliptical orbit, if the radius R is replaced by a, the length of the semimajor axis:

$$E = -\frac{GMm}{2a} \quad \text{(elliptical orbit)}$$

Example 7.8 An asteroid of mass m is in an elliptical orbit around the Sun (mass M). Assume that $m \ll M$.

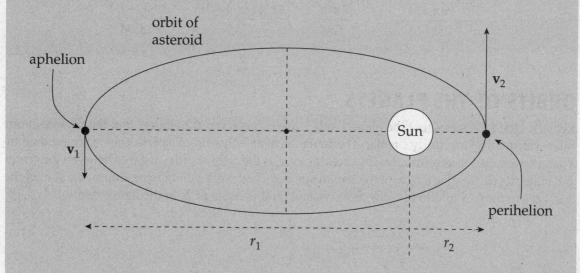

(a) What is the total energy of the asteroid?

(b) What is the ratio of v_1 (the asteroid's speed at aphelion) to v_2 (the asteroid's speed at perihelion)? Write your answer in terms of r_1 and r_2.

(c) What is the time necessary for the asteroid to make a complete orbit around the Sun?

Solution.

(a) The total energy of the asteroid is equal to $-GMm/2a$, where a is the semimajor axis. However, notice in the figure above that $2a = r_1 + r_2$. Therefore, the total energy of the asteroid is

$$E = -\frac{GMm}{r_1 + r_2}$$

(b) One way to answer this question is to invoke Conservation of Angular Momentum. When the asteroid is at aphelion, its angular momentum (with respect to the center of the Sun) is $L_1 = r_1 m v_1$. When the asteroid is at perihelion, its angular momentum is $L_2 = r_2 m v_2$. Therefore,

$$L_1 = L_2 \implies r_1 m v_1 = r_2 m v_2 \implies \frac{v_1}{v_2} = \frac{r_2}{r_1}$$

This tells us that the asteroid's speed at aphelion is less than its speed at perihelion (because $r_2/r_1 < 1$), as implied by Kepler's Second Law (a line drawn from the Sun to the asteroid must sweep out equal areas in equal time intervals). The closer the asteroid is to the Sun, the faster it has to travel to make this true.

(c) As you know, the time necessary for the asteroid to make a complete orbit around the Sun is the orbit period, T. Using Kepler's Third Law, with $a = \frac{1}{2}(r_1 + r_2)$, we find

$$\frac{T^2}{a^3} = \frac{4\pi^2}{GM} \;\Rightarrow\; T = \sqrt{\frac{4\pi^2 a^3}{GM}} = \sqrt{\frac{4\pi^2[\frac{1}{2}(r_1 + r_2)]^3}{GM}} = \sqrt{\frac{\pi^2(r_1 + r_2)^3}{2GM}}$$

ORBITS OF THE PLANETS

Kepler's First Law states that the planets' orbits are ellipses, but the ellipses that the planets in our solar system travel are nearly circular. The deviation of an ellipse from a perfect circle is measured by a parameter called its **eccentricity**. The eccentricity, e, is the ratio of c (the distance between the center and either focus, to a, the length of the semimajor axis). For every point on the ellipse, the sum of the distances to the foci (plural of focus) is a constant (and is equal to $2a$ in the figure below).

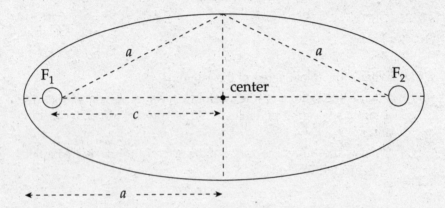

Kepler's First Law also states that one of the foci of a planet's elliptical orbit is located at the position of the Sun. Actually, one of the foci is at the center of mass of the Sun–planet system, because when one body orbits another, both bodies orbit around their center of mass, a point called the **barycenter**.

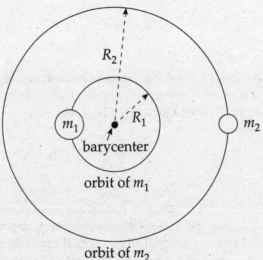

For most of the planets, which are much less massive than the Sun, this correction to Kepler's First Law has little significance, because the center of mass of the Sun and the planet system is close enough to the Sun's center. For example, let's figure out the center of mass of the Sun–Earth system. The mass of the Earth is $m = 5.98 \times 10^{24}$ kg, the mass of the Sun is $M = 1.99 \times 10^{30}$ kg, and the Sun–Earth distance averages $R = 1.496 \times 10^{11}$ m. Therefore, letting $x = 0$ be at the Sun's center, we have

$$x_{cm} = \frac{Mx_{Sun} + mx_{Earth}}{M + m} = \frac{M(0) + (5.98 \times 10^{24} \text{ kg})(1.496 \times 10^{11} \text{ m})}{(1.99 \times 10^{30} \text{ kg}) + (5.98 \times 10^{24} \text{ kg})} = 450 \text{ km}$$

So the center of mass of the Sun–Earth system is only 450 km from the center of the Sun, a distance of less than 0.1% of the Sun's radius!

Example 7.9 Derive a corrected version of Kepler's Third Law for the following orbiting system. Both bodies have orbit period T.

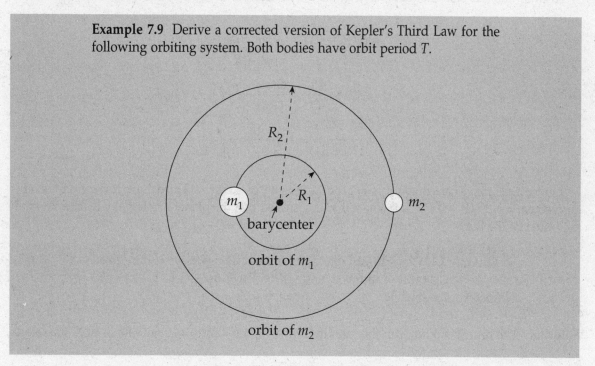

Solution. The centripetal force on each body is provided by the gravitational pull of the other body, so

$$\frac{m_1 v_1^2}{R_1} = G\frac{m_1 m_2}{(R_1 + R_2)^2} \qquad \text{and} \qquad \frac{m_2 v_2^2}{R_2} = G\frac{m_1 m_2}{(R_1 + R_2)^2}$$

which imply

$$\frac{v_1^2}{R_1} = G\frac{m_2}{(R_1 + R_2)^2} \qquad \text{and} \qquad \frac{v_2^2}{R_2} = G\frac{m_1}{(R_1 + R_2)^2}$$

But, since both bodies have the same orbit period, T, we have

$$v_1 = \frac{2\pi R_1}{T} \qquad \text{and} \qquad v_2 = \frac{2\pi R_2}{T}$$

Substituting these results into the preceding pair of equations gives us:

$$\frac{\left(2\pi R_1/T\right)^2}{R_1} = G\frac{m_2}{\left(R_1 + R_2\right)^2} \qquad \text{and} \qquad \frac{\left(2\pi R_2/T\right)^2}{R_2} = G\frac{m_1}{\left(R_1 + R_2\right)^2}$$

which simplify to

$$\frac{4\pi^2 R_1}{T^2} = G\frac{m_2}{\left(R_1 + R_2\right)^2} \qquad \text{and} \qquad \frac{4\pi^2 R_2}{T^2} = G\frac{m_1}{\left(R_1 + R_2\right)^2}$$

Adding this last pair of equations gives us the desired result:

$$\frac{4\pi^2 (R_1 + R_2)}{T^2} = G\frac{m_1 + m_2}{\left(R_1 + R_2\right)^2}$$

$$\frac{4\pi^2}{T^2} = \frac{G(m_1 + m_2)}{\left(R_1 + R_2\right)^3}$$

$$\frac{T^2}{\left(R_1 + R_2\right)^3} = \frac{4\pi^2}{G(m_1 + m_2)}$$

Notice that this final equation is a general version of Kepler's Third Law for a circular orbit derived earlier, $T^2/R^3 = 4\pi^2/GM$, where it was assumed that the planet orbited at a distance R from the center of the Sun.

Example 7.10 An artificial satellite of mass m travels at a constant speed in a circular orbit of radius R around the Earth (mass M). What is the speed of the satellite?

Solution. The centripetal force on the satellite is provided by Earth's gravitational pull. Therefore,

$$\frac{mv^2}{R} = G\frac{Mm}{R^2}$$

Solving this equation for v yields

$$v = \sqrt{G\frac{M}{R}}$$

Notice that the satellite's speed doesn't depend on its mass; even if it were a baseball, if its orbit radius were R, then its orbit speed would still be $\sqrt{GM/R}$.

CHAPTER 7 REVIEW QUESTIONS

SECTION I: MULTIPLE CHOICE

1. If the distance between two point particles is doubled, then the gravitational force between them

    (A) decreases by a factor of 4.
    (B) decreases by a factor of 2.
    (C) increases by a factor of 2.
    (D) increases by a factor of 4.
    (E) Cannot be determined without knowing the masses

2. At the surface of the earth, an object of mass m has weight w. If this object is transported to an altitude that's twice the radius of the earth, then, at the new location,

    (A) its mass is $m/2$ and its weight is $w/2$
    (B) its mass is m and its weight is $w/2$.
    (C) its mass is $m/2$ and its weight is $w/4$.
    (D) its mass is m and its weight is $w/4$.
    (E) its mass is m and its weight is $w/9$.

3. A moon of mass m orbits a planet of mass $100m$. Let the strength of the gravitational force exerted by the planet on the moon be denoted by F_1, and let the strength of the gravitational force exerted by the moon on the planet be F_2. Which of the following is true?

    (A) $F_1 = 100F_2$
    (B) $F_1 = 10F_2$
    (C) $F_1 = F_2$
    (D) $F_2 = 10F_1$
    (E) $F_2 = 100F_1$

4. The planet Pluto has 1/500 the mass and 1/15 the radius of Earth. What is the value of g on the surface of Pluto?

    (A) 0.3 m/s^2
    (B) 1.6 m/s^2
    (C) 2.4 m/s^2
    (D) 4.5 m/s^2
    (E) 7.1 m/s^2

5. A satellite is currently orbiting Earth in a circular orbit of radius R; its kinetic energy is K_1. If the satellite is moved and enters a new circular orbit of radius $2R$, what will be its kinetic energy?

    (A) $K_1/4$
    (B) $K_1/2$
    (C) K_1
    (D) $2K_1$
    (E) $4K_1$

6. A moon of Jupiter has a nearly circular orbit of radius R and an orbit period of T. Which of the following expressions gives the mass of Jupiter?

    (A) $2\pi R/T$
    (B) $4\pi^2R/T^2$
    (C) $2\pi R^3/(GT^2)$
    (D) $4\pi R^2/(GT^2)$
    (E) $4\pi R^3/(GT^2)$

7. Two large bodies, Body A of mass m and Body B, of mass $4m$, are separated by a distance R. At what distance from Body A, along the line joining the bodies, would the gravitational force on an object be equal to zero? (Ignore the presence of any other bodies.)

    (A) $R/16$
    (B) $R/8$
    (C) $R/5$
    (D) $R/4$
    (E) $R/3$

8. The mean distance from Saturn to the Sun is 9 times greater than the mean distance from Earth to the Sun. How long is a Saturn year?

    (A) 18 Earth years
    (B) 27 Earth years
    (C) 81 Earth years
    (D) 243 Earth years
    (E) 729 Earth years

9. The Moon has mass M and radius R. A small object is dropped from a distance of $3R$ from the Moon's center. The object's impact speed when it strikes the surface of the Moon is equal to

$$\sqrt{kGM/R} \text{ for } k =$$

(A) 1/3
(B) 2/3
(C) 3/4
(D) 4/3
(E) 3/2

10. [C] A planet orbits the Sun in an elliptical orbit of eccentricity e. What is the ratio of the planet's speed at perihelion to its speed at aphelion?

(A) $1/(1-e)$
(B) $e/(1-e)$
(C) $1/(1+e)$
(D) $e/(1+e)$
(E) $(1+e)/(1-e)$

SECTION II: FREE RESPONSE

1. Consider two uniform spherical bodies in deep space. Sphere 1 has mass m_1 and Sphere 2 has mass m_2. Starting from rest from a distance R apart, they are gravitationally attracted to each other.

   (a) Compute the acceleration of Sphere 1 when the spheres are a distance $R/2$ apart.

   (b) Compute the acceleration of Sphere 2 when the spheres are a distance $R/2$ apart.

   (c) Compute the speed of Sphere 1 when the spheres are a distance $R/2$ apart.

   (d) Compute the speed of Sphere 2 when the spheres are a distance $R/2$ apart.

   Now assume that these spheres orbit their center of mass with the same orbit period, T.

   (e) Determine the radii of their orbits. Write your answer in terms of m_1, m_2, T, and fundamental constants.

2. [C] A satellite of mass m is in the elliptical orbit shown below around Earth (radius r_E, mass M). Assume that $m \ll M$.

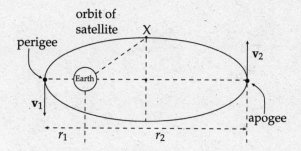

   (a) Determine v_1, the speed of the satellite at perigee (the point of the orbit closest to Earth). Write your answer in terms of r_1, r_2, M, and G.

   (b) Determine v_2, the speed of the satellite at apogee (the point of the orbit farthest from Earth). Write your answer in terms of r_1, r_2, M, and G.

   (c) Expres the ratio v_1/v_2 in simplest terms.

   (d) What is the satellite's angular momentum (with respect to Earth's center) when it's at apogee?

   (e) Determine the speed of the satellite when it's at the point marked X in the figure.

   (f) Determine the period of the satellite's orbit. Write your answer in terms of r_1, r_2, M, and fundamental constants.

   (g) What is the eccentricity of the satellite's orbit? Express your answer in terms of r_1 and r_2.

8

OSCILLATIONS

INTRODUCTION

In this chapter, we'll concentrate on a kind of periodic motion that's straightforward and that, fortunately, actually describes many real-life systems. This type of motion is called *simple harmonic motion*. The prototypical example of simple harmonic motion is a block that's oscillating on the end of a spring, and what we learn about this simple system, we can apply to many other oscillating systems.

SIMPLE HARMONIC MOTION (SHM): THE SPRING–BLOCK OSCILLATOR

When a spring is compressed or stretched from its natural length, a force is created. If the spring is displaced by **x** from its natural length, the force it exerts in response is given by the equation

$$\mathbf{F}_S = -k\mathbf{x}$$

This is known as **Hooke's Law**. The proportionality constant, k, is a positive number called the **spring (or force) constant** that indicates how stiff the spring is. The stiffer the spring, the greater the value of k. The minus sign in Hooke's Law tells us that $\mathbf{F}_s$ and $\mathbf{x}$ always point in opposite directions. For example, referring to the figure below, when the spring is stretched ($\mathbf{x}$ is to the right), the spring pulls back ($\mathbf{F}$ is to the left); when the spring is compressed ($\mathbf{x}$ is to the left), the spring pushes outward ($\mathbf{F}$ is to the right). In all cases, the spring wants to return to its original length. As a result, the spring tries to restore the attached block to the **equilibrium position**, which is the position at which the net force on the block is zero. For this reason, we say that the spring provides a **restoring force**.

Example 8.1 A 12 cm-long spring has a force constant (k) of 400 N/m. How much force is required to stretch the spring to a length of 14 cm?

Solution. The displacement of the spring has a magnitude of 14 − 12 = 2 cm = 0.02 m so, according to Hooke's Law, the spring exerts a force of magnitude $F = kx = (400 \text{ N/m})(0.02 \text{ m}) = 8$ N. Therefore, we'd have to exert this much force to keep the spring in this stretched state.

Springs that obey Hooke's Law (called **ideal** or **linear** springs) provide an ideal mechanism for defining the most important kind of vibrational motion: simple harmonic motion.

Consider a spring with force constant k, attached to a vertical wall, with a block of mass m on a frictionless table attached to the other end.

$x = 0$
equilibrium
position

Grab the block, pull it some distance from its original position, and release it. The spring will pull the block back toward equilibrium. Of course, because of its momentum, the block will pass through the equilibrium position and compress the spring. At some point, the block will stop, and the compressed spring will push the block back. In other words, the block will oscillate.

During the oscillation, the force on the block is zero when the block is at equilibrium (the point we designate as $x = 0$). This is because Hooke's Law says that the strength of the spring's restoring force is given by the equation $F_S = kx$, so $F_S = 0$ at equilibrium. The acceleration of the block is also equal to zero at $x = 0$, since $F_S = 0$ at $x = 0$ and $a = F_S/m$. At the endpoints of the oscillation region, where the block's displacement, x, has the greatest magnitude, the restoring force and the magnitude of the acceleration are both at their maximum.

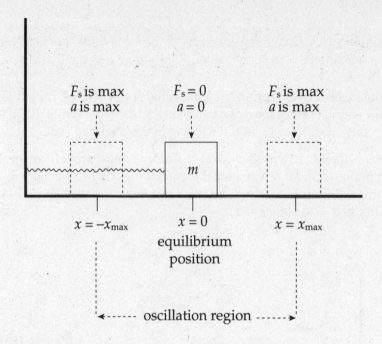

SHM IN TERMS OF ENERGY

Another way to describe the block's motion is in terms of energy transfers. A stretched or compressed spring stores **elastic potential energy**, which is transformed into kinetic energy (and back again); this shuttling of energy between potential and kinetic causes the oscillations. For a spring with spring constant k, the elastic potential energy it possesses—relative to its equilibrium position—is given by the equation

$$U_s = \tfrac{1}{2}kx^2$$

Notice that the farther you stretch or compress a spring, the more work you have to do, and, as a result, the more potential energy that's stored.

In terms of energy transfers, we can describe the block's oscillations as follows. When you initially pull the block out, you increase the elastic potential energy of the system. Upon releasing the block, this potential energy turns into kinetic energy, and the block moves. As it passes through equilibrium, $U_s = 0$, so all the potential energy is kinetic. Then, as the block continues through equilibrium, it compresses the spring and the kinetic energy is transformed back into elastic potential energy.

By Conservation of Mechanical Energy, the sum $K + U_s$ is a constant. Therefore, when the block reaches the endpoints of the oscillation region (that is, when $x = \pm x_{max}$), U_s is maximized, so K must be minimized; in fact, $K = 0$ at the endpoints. As the block is passing through equilibrium, $x = 0$, so $U_s = 0$ and K is maximized.

U_s is max
$K = 0$
$v = 0$

$U_s = 0$
K is max
v is max

U_s is max
$K = 0$
$v = 0$

m

$x = -x_{max}$ $x = 0$ $x = x_{max}$

equilibrium
position

The maximum displacement from equilibrium is called the **amplitude** of oscillation, and is denoted by A. So instead of writing $x = x_{max}$, we write $x = A$ (and $x = -x_{max}$ will be written as $x = -A$).

> **Example 8.2**   A block of mass $m = 1.5$ kg oscillates on a spring whose force constant k is 500 N/m. The amplitude of the oscillations is 4.0 cm. Calculate the maximum speed of the block.

Solution. First let's get an expression for the maximum elastic potential energy of the system:

$$U_S = \tfrac{1}{2}kx^2 \quad \Rightarrow \quad U_{S,\,max} = \tfrac{1}{2}kx_{max}^2 = \tfrac{1}{2}kA^2$$

When all this energy has been transformed into kinetic energy—which, as we discussed earlier, occurs just as the block is passing through equilibrium—the block will have maximum kinetic energy and maximum speed.

$$U_{S,\,max} \to K_{max} \quad \Rightarrow \quad \tfrac{1}{2}kA^2 = \tfrac{1}{2}mv_{max}^2$$

$$v_{max} = \sqrt{\frac{kA^2}{m}}$$

$$= \sqrt{\frac{(500 \text{ N}/\text{m})(0.04 \text{ m})^2}{1.5 \text{ kg}}}$$

$$= 0.73 \text{ m}/\text{s}$$

> **Example 8.3** **[C]** Show why $U_S = \tfrac{1}{2}kx^2$ if $\mathbf{F}_S = -k\mathbf{x}$.

Solution. By definition, $\Delta U_S = -W_S$, and, since **F** is not constant, the work done by **F** must be calculated using a definite integral. As the end of the spring moves from position $x = x_1$ to $x = x_2$, the work it does is equal to

$$W_S = \int_{x_1}^{x_2} \mathbf{F}(x) \cdot d\mathbf{x}$$

$$= \int_{x_1}^{x_2} -kx\, dx$$

$$= \left[-\tfrac{1}{2} kx^2 \right]_{x_1}^{x_2}$$

$$= -\left(\tfrac{1}{2} kx_2^2 - \tfrac{1}{2} kx_1^2 \right)$$

Therefore,

$$\Delta U_S = U_{S2} - U_{S1} = -W_S = \tfrac{1}{2} kx_2^2 - \tfrac{1}{2} kx_1^2$$

So if we designate $U_{S1} = 0$ at $x_1 = 0$, the equation above yields $U_S = \tfrac{1}{2} kx^2$, as desired. (Even if a spring does not obey Hooke's Law, this method can still be used to find the work done and the potential energy stored.)

> **Example 8.4** A block of mass $m = 2.0$ kg is attached to an ideal spring of force constant $k = 500\,\text{N/m}$. The amplitude of the resulting oscillations is 8.0 cm. Determine the total energy of the oscillator and the speed of the block when it's 4.0 cm from equilibrium.

Solution. The total energy of the oscillator is the sum of its kinetic and potential energies. By Conservation of Mechanical Energy, the sum $K + U_S$ is a constant, so if we can determine what this sum is at some point in the oscillation region, we'll know the sum at every point. When the block is at its amplitude position, $x = 8$ cm, its speed is zero; so at this position, E is easy to figure out:

$$E = K + U_S = 0 + \tfrac{1}{2} kA^2 = \tfrac{1}{2}(500\,\text{N/m})(0.08\,\text{m})^2 = 3.2\,\text{J}$$

This gives the total energy of the oscillator at *every* position. At any position x, we have

$$\tfrac{1}{2} mv^2 + \tfrac{1}{2} kx^2 = E$$

$$v = \sqrt{\frac{E - \tfrac{1}{2} kx^2}{\tfrac{1}{2} m}}$$

so when we substitute in the numbers, we get

$$v = \sqrt{\frac{E - \tfrac{1}{2} kx^2}{\tfrac{1}{2} m}} = \sqrt{\frac{(3.2\,\text{J}) - \tfrac{1}{2}(500\,\text{N/m})(0.04\,\text{m})^2}{\tfrac{1}{2}(2.0\,\text{kg})}}$$

$$= 1.7\,\text{m/s}$$

Example 8.5 A block of mass $m = 2.0$ kg is attached to an ideal spring of force constant $k = 500$ N/m. The block is at rest at its equilibrium position. An impulsive force acts on the block, giving it an initial speed of 2.0 m/s. Find the amplitude of the resulting oscillations.

Solution. The block will come to rest when all of its initial kinetic energy has been transformed into the spring's potential energy. At this point, the block is at its maximum displacement from equilibrium, that is, it's at one of its amplitude positions, and

$$K_i + U_i = K_f + U_f$$
$$\tfrac{1}{2}mv_i^2 + 0 = 0 + \tfrac{1}{2}kA^2$$
$$A = \sqrt{\frac{mv_i^2}{k}}$$
$$= \sqrt{\frac{(2.0 \text{ kg})(2.0 \text{ m}/\text{s})^2}{500 \text{ N}/\text{m}}}$$
$$= 0.13 \text{ m}$$

THE KINEMATICS OF SHM

Now that we've explored the dynamics of the block's oscillations in terms of force and energy, let's talk about motion—or kinematics. As you watch the block oscillate, you should notice that it repeats each **cycle** of oscillation in the same amount of time. A cycle is a *round-trip*: for example, from position $x = A$ over to $x = -A$ and back again to $x = A$. The amount of time it takes to complete a cycle is called the **period** of the oscillations, or T. If T is short, the block is oscillating rapidly, and if T is long, the block is oscillating slowly.

Another way of indicating the rapidity of the oscillations is to count the number of cycles that can be completed in a given time interval; the more completed cycles, the more rapid the oscillations. The number of cycles that can be completed per unit time is called the **frequency** of the oscillations, or f, and frequency is expressed in cycles per second. One cycle per second is one **hertz** (abbreviated **Hz**).

One of the most basic equations of oscillatory motion expresses the fact that the period and frequency are reciprocals of each other:

$$\text{period} = \frac{\text{\# seconds}}{\text{cycle}} \qquad \text{while} \qquad \text{frequency} = \frac{\text{\# cycles}}{\text{second}}$$

Therefore,

$$T = \frac{1}{f} \quad \text{and} \quad f = \frac{1}{T}$$

Example 8.6 A block oscillating on the end of a spring moves from its position of maximum spring stretch to maximum spring compression in 0.25 s. Determine the period and frequency of this motion.

Solution. The period is defined as the time required for one full cycle. Moving from one end of the oscillation region to the other is only half a cycle. Therefore, if the block moves from its position of maximum spring stretch to maximum spring compression in 0.25 s, the time required for a full cycle is twice as much; $T = 0.5$ s. Because frequency is the reciprocal of period, the frequency of the oscillations is $f = 1/T = 1/(0.5\ \text{s}) = 2$ Hz.

Example 8.7 A student observing an oscillating block counts 45.5 cycles of oscillation in one minute. Determine its frequency (in hertz) and period (in seconds).

Solution. The frequency of the oscillations, in hertz (which is the number of cycles per second), is

$$f = \frac{45.5\ \text{cycles}}{\text{min}} \times \frac{1\ \text{min}}{60\ \text{s}} = \frac{0.758\ \text{cycles}}{\text{s}} = 0.758\ \text{Hz}$$

Therefore,

$$T = \frac{1}{f} = \frac{1}{0.758\ \text{Hz}} = 1.32\ \text{s}$$

One of the defining properties of the spring–block oscillator is that the frequency and period can be determined from the mass of the block and the force constant of the spring. The equations are as follows:

$$f = \frac{1}{2\pi}\sqrt{\frac{k}{m}} \quad \text{and} \quad T = 2\pi\sqrt{\frac{m}{k}}$$

Let's analyze these equations. Suppose we had a small mass on a very stiff spring; then intuitively, we would expect that this strong spring would make the small mass oscillate rapidly, with high frequency and short period. Both of these predictions are substantiated by the equations above, because if m is small and k is large, then the ratio k/m is large (high frequency) and the ratio m/k is small (short period).

Example 8.8 A block of mass $m = 2.0$ kg is attached to a spring whose force constant, k, is 300 N/m. Calculate the frequency and period of the oscillations of this spring–block system.

Solution. According to the equations above,

$$f = \frac{1}{2\pi}\sqrt{\frac{k}{m}} = \frac{1}{2\pi}\sqrt{\frac{300 \text{ N}/\text{m}}{2.0 \text{ kg}}} = 1.9 \text{ Hz}$$

$$T = 2\pi\sqrt{\frac{m}{k}} = 2\pi\sqrt{\frac{2.0 \text{ kg}}{300 \text{ N}/\text{m}}} = 0.51 \text{ s}$$

Notice that $f \approx 2$ Hz and $T \approx 0.5$ s, and that these values satisfy the basic equation $T = 1/f$.

Example 8.9 A block is attached to a spring and set into oscillatory motion, and its frequency is measured. If this block were removed and replaced by a second block with 1/4 the mass of the first block, how would the frequency of the oscillations compare to that of the first block?

Solution. Since the same spring is used, k remains the same. According to the equation given above, f is inversely proportional to the square root of the mass of the block: $f \propto 1/\sqrt{m}$. Therefore, if m decreases by a factor of 4, then f increases by a factor of $\sqrt{4} = 2$.

The equations we saw above for the frequency and period of the spring–block oscillator do not contain A, the amplitude of the motion. In simple harmonic motion, *both the frequency and the period are independent of the amplitude.* The reason that the frequency and period of the spring–block oscillator are independent of amplitude is that F, the strength of the restoring force, is proportional to x, the displacement from equilibrium, as given by Hooke's Law: $F_S = kx$.

Example 8.10 A student performs an experiment with a spring–block simple harmonic oscillator. In the first trial, the amplitude of the oscillations is 3.0 cm, while in the second trial (using the same spring and block), the amplitude of the oscillations is 6.0 cm. Compare the values of the period, frequency, and maximum speed of the block between these two trials.

Solution. If the system exhibits simple harmonic motion, then the period and frequency are independent of amplitude. This is because the same spring and block were used in the two trials, so the period and frequency will have the same values in the second trial as they had in the first. But the maximum speed of the block will be greater in the second trial than in the first. Since the amplitude is greater in the second trial, the system possess more total energy ($E = \frac{1}{2}kA^2$). So when the block is passing through equilibrium (its position of greatest speed), the second system has more energy to convert to kinetic, meaning that the block will have a greater speed. In fact, from Example 8.2, we know that $v_{max} = A\sqrt{k/m}$ so, since A is twice as great in the second trial than in the first, v_{max} will be twice as great in the second trial than in the first.

Example 8.11 For each of the following arrangements of two springs, determine the **effective spring constant**, k_{eff}. This is the force constant of a single spring that would produce the same force on the block as the pair of springs shown in each case.

(a)

(b)

(c)

(d) Determine k_{eff} in each of these cases if $k_1 = k_2 = k$.

Solution.

(a) Imagine that the block was displaced a distance x to the right of its equilibrium position. Then the force exerted by the first spring would be $F_1 = -k_1x$ and the force exerted by the second spring would be $F_2 = -k_2x$. The net force exerted by the springs would be

$$F_1 + F_2 = -k_1x + -k_2x = -(k_1 + k_2)x$$

Since $F_{eff} = -(k_1 + k_2)x$, we see that $k_{eff} = k_1 + k_2$.

(b) Imagine that the block was displaced a distance x to the right of its equilibrium position. Then the force exerted by the first spring would be $F_1 = -k_1x$ and the force exerted by the second spring would be $F_2 = -k_2x$. The net force exerted by the springs would be

$$F_1 + F_2 = -k_1x + -k_2x = -(k_1 + k_2)x$$

As in part (a), we see that, since $F_{eff} = -(k_1 + k_2)x$, we get $k_{eff} = k_1 + k_2$.

(c) Imagine that the block was displaced a distance x to the right of its equilibrium position. Let x_1 be the distance that the first spring is stretched, and let x_2 be the distance that the second spring is stretched. Then $x = x_1 + x_2$. But $x_1 = -F/k_1$ and $x_2 = -F/k_2$, so

$$\frac{-F}{k_1} + \frac{-F}{k_2} = x$$

$$-F\left(\frac{1}{k_1} + \frac{1}{k_2}\right) = x$$

$$F = -\left(\frac{1}{\frac{1}{k_1} + \frac{1}{k_2}}\right)x$$

$$F = -\frac{k_1 k_2}{k_1 + k_2} x$$

Therefore,

$$k_{\text{eff}} = \frac{k_1 k_2}{k_1 + k_2}$$

(d) If the two springs have the same force constant, that is, if $k_1 = k_2 = k$, then in the first two cases, the pairs of springs are equivalent to one spring that has twice their force constant: $k_{\text{eff}} = k_1 + k_2 = k + k = 2k$. In (c), the pair of springs is equivalent to a single spring with half their force constant:

$$k_{\text{eff}} = \frac{k_1 k_2}{k_1 + k_2} = \frac{kk}{k + k} = \frac{k^2}{2k} = \frac{k}{2}$$

THE SPRING–BLOCK OSCILLATOR: VERTICAL MOTION

So far we've looked at a block sliding back and forth on a horizontal table, but the block could also oscillate vertically. The only difference would be that gravity would cause the block to move downward, to an equilibrium position at which, in contrast with the horizontal SHM we've examined, the spring would *not* be at its natural length.

Consider a spring of negligible mass hanging from a stationary support. A block of mass m is attached to its end and allowed to come to rest, stretching the spring a distance d. At this point, the block is in equilibrium; the upward force of the spring is balanced by the downward force of gravity. Therefore,

$$kd = mg \quad \Rightarrow \quad d = \frac{mg}{k}$$

equilibrium position - - - - - - | m | - - - - - - $y = 0$ - - - -

Next, imagine that the block is pulled down a distance A and released. The spring force increases (because the spring was stretched farther); it's stronger than the block's weight, and, as a result, the block accelerates upward. As the block's momentum carries it up, through the equilibrium position, the spring becomes less stretched than it was at equilibrium, so F_s is less than the block's weight. As a result, the block decelerates, stops, and accelerates downward again, and the up-and-down motion repeats.

When the block is at a distance y below its equilibrium position, the spring is stretched a total distance of $d + y$, so the upward spring force is equal to $k(d + y)$, while the downward force stays the same, mg. The net force on the block is

$$F = k(d + y) - mg$$

but this equation becomes $F = ky$, because $kd = mg$ (as we saw above). Since the resulting force on the block, $F = ky$, has the form of Hooke's Law, we know that the vertical simple harmonic oscillations of the block have the same characteristics as do horizontal oscillations, with the equilibrium position, $y = 0$, not at the spring's natural length, but at the point where the hanging block is in equilibrium.

> **Example 8.12** A block of mass $m = 1.5$ kg is attached to the end of a vertical spring of force constant $k = 300$ N/m. After the block comes to rest, it is pulled down a distance of 3.0 cm and released.
>
> (a) What is the frequency of the resulting oscillations?
> (b) What are the minimum and maximum amounts of stretch of the spring during the oscillations of the block?

Solution.

(a) The frequency is given by

$$f = \frac{1}{2\pi}\sqrt{\frac{k}{m}} = \frac{1}{2\pi}\sqrt{\frac{300 \text{ N}/\text{m}}{1.5 \text{ kg}}} = 2.3 \text{ Hz}$$

(b) Before the block is pulled down, to begin the oscillations, it stretches the spring by a distance

$$d = \frac{mg}{k} = \frac{(1.5 \text{ kg})(9.8 \text{ N}/\text{kg})}{300 \text{ N}/\text{m}} = 0.049 \text{ m} = 4.9 \text{ cm}$$

Since the amplitude of the motion is 2.0 cm, the spring is stretched a maximum of 4.9 cm + 2.0 cm = 6.9 cm when the block is at the lowest position in its cycle, and a minimum of 4.9 cm − 2.0 cm = 2.9 cm when the block is at its highest position.

THE SINUSOIDAL DESCRIPTION OF SHM

The position of the block during its oscillation can be written as a function of time. Take a look at the experimental set-up below.

constant speed

block undergoes
simple harmonic
oscillations

A small pen is attached to the oscillating block, and it makes a mark on the paper as the paper is pulled along by the roller on the right. Clearly, the simple harmonic motion of the block is sinusoidal.

The basic mathematical equation for describing simple harmonic motion is:

$$y = A \sin (\omega t)$$

where y is the position of the oscillator, A is the amplitude, ω is the **angular frequency** (defined as $2\pi f$, where f is the frequency of the oscillations), and t is time. Since $\sin(\omega t)$ oscillates between -1 and $+1$, the quantity $A \sin(\omega t)$ oscillates between $-A$ and $+A$; this describes the oscillation region.

If $t = 0$, then the quantity $A \sin (\omega t)$ is also equal to zero. This means that $y = 0$ at time $t = 0$. However, what if $y \neq 0$ at time $t = 0$? For example, if the oscillator is pulled to one of its amplitude positions, say $y = A$, and released at time $t = 0$, then $y = A$ at $t = 0$. To account for the fact that the oscillator can begin anywhere in the oscillation region, the basic equation for the position of the oscillator given above is generalized as follows:

$$y = A \sin (\omega t + \phi_0)$$

where ϕ_0 is called the **initial phase**. The argument of the sine function, $\omega t + \phi_0$, is called the **phase** (or **phase angle**). By carefully choosing ϕ_0, we can be sure that the equation correctly specifies the oscillator's position no matter where it may have been at time $t = 0$. The value of ϕ_0 can be calculated from the equation

$$\phi_0 = \sin^{-1}\left(\frac{y_{\text{at } t=0}}{A}\right)$$

Example 8.13 A simple harmonic oscillator has an amplitude of 3.0 cm and a frequency of 4.0 Hz. At time $t = 0$, its position is $y = 3.0$ cm. Where is it at time $t = 0.3$ s?

Solution. First, $A = 3$ cm and $\omega = 2\pi f = 2\pi(4.0 \text{ s}^{-1}) = 8\pi \text{ s}^{-1}$. The value of the initial phase is

$$\phi_0 = \sin^{-1}\left(\frac{y_{\text{at } t=0}}{A}\right) = \sin^{-1}\frac{3 \text{ cm}}{3 \text{ cm}} = \sin^{-1}1 = \tfrac{1}{2}\pi$$

Therefore, the position of the oscillator at any time t is given by the equation

$$y = (3 \text{ cm}) \cdot \sin[(8\pi \text{ s}^{-1})t + \tfrac{1}{2}\pi]$$

So, at time $t = 0.3$ s, we find that $y = (3 \text{ cm}) \cdot \sin[(8\pi \text{ s}^{-1})(0.3 \text{ s}) + \tfrac{1}{2}\pi] = 0.93$ cm. (Make sure your calculator is in *radian mode* when you evaluate this expression!)

Example 8.14 The position of a simple harmonic oscillator is given by the equation

$$y = (4 \text{ cm}) \cdot \sin[(6\pi \text{ s}^{-1})t - \tfrac{1}{2}\pi]$$

(a) Where is the oscillator at time $t = 0$?
(b) What is the amplitude of the motion?
(c) What is the frequency?
(d) What is the period?

Solution.

(a) To determine y at time $t = 0$, we simply substitute $t = 0$ into the given equation and evaluate:

$$y_{\text{at } t=0} = (4 \text{ cm}) \cdot \sin(-\tfrac{1}{2}\pi) = -4 \text{ cm}$$

(b) The amplitude of the motion, A, is the coefficient in front of the $\sin(\omega t + \phi_0)$ expression. In this case, we read directly from the given equation that $A = 4$ cm.

(c) The coefficient of t is the angular frequency, ω. In this case, we see that $\omega = 6\pi \text{ s}^{-1}$. Since $\omega = 2\pi f$ by definition, we have $f = \omega/(2\pi) = 3$ Hz.

(d) Since $T = 1/f$, we calculate that $T = 1/f = 1/(3 \text{ Hz}) = 0.33$ s.

[C] INSTANTANEOUS VELOCITY AND ACCELERATION

If the position of a simple harmonic oscillator is given by the equation $y = A\sin(\omega t + \phi_0)$, its velocity and acceleration can be found by differentiation:

$$v(t) = \dot{y}(t) = \frac{d}{dt}[A\sin(\omega t + \phi_0)] = A\omega\cos(\omega t + \phi_0)$$

and

$$a(t) = \dot{v}(t) = \frac{d}{dt}[A\omega\cos(\omega t + \phi_0)] = -A\omega^2\sin(\omega t + \phi_0)$$

Notice that both the velocity and acceleration vary with time.

Example 8.15 [C] The position of a simple harmonic oscillator is given by the equation

$$y = 4\sin(6\pi t - \tfrac{1}{2}\pi)$$

where y is in cm and t is in seconds. What are the maximum speed and maximum acceleration of the oscillator?

Solution. Since the maximum value of $\cos(\omega t + \phi_0)$ is 1, the maximum value of v is $v_{max} = A\omega$; similarly, since the minimum value of $\sin(\omega t + \phi_0)$ is –1, the maximum value of a is $a_{max} = A\omega^2$. From the equation for y, we see that $A = 4$ cm $= 0.04$ m and $\omega = 6\pi$ s^{-1}. Therefore, $v_{max} = A\omega = (0.04$ m$)$ $(6\pi$ s$^{-1}) = 0.75$ m/s and $a_{max} = A\omega^2 = (0.04$ m$)(6\pi$ s$^{-1})^2 = 14$ m/s^2.

PENDULUMS

A **simple pendulum** consists of a weight of mass m attached to a massless rod that swings, without friction, about the vertical equilibrium position. The restoring force is provided by gravity and, as the figure below shows, the magnitude of the restoring force when the bob is at an angle θ to the vertical is given by the equation:

$$F_{restoring} = mg\sin\theta$$

θ $L = $ length of pendulum

$F_{restoring} = mg\sin\theta$

θ

mg

equilibrium
position

Although the displacement of the pendulum is measured by the angle that it makes with the vertical, rather than by its linear distance from the equilibrium position (as was the case for the spring–block oscillator), the simple pendulum shares many of the important features of the spring–block oscillator. For example,

- displacement is zero at the equilibrium position;

- at the endpoints of the oscillation region (where $\theta = \pm \theta_{max}$), the restoring force and the tangential acceleration (a_t) have their greatest magnitudes, the speed of the pendulum is zero, and the potential energy is maximized;

- as the pendulum passes through the equilibrium position, its kinetic energy and speed are maximized.

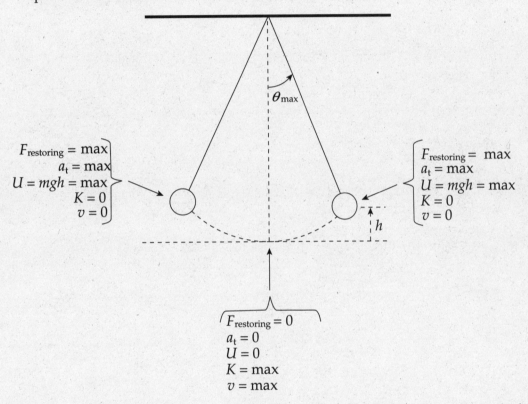

Despite these similarities, there is one important difference. Simple harmonic motion results from a restoring force that has a strength that's proportional to the displacement. The magnitude of the restoring force on a pendulum is $mg \sin \theta$, which is *not* proportional to the displacement θ. Strictly speaking, then, the motion of a simple pendulum is not really simple harmonic. However, if θ is small, then $\sin \theta \approx \theta$ (measured in radians) so, in this case, the magnitude of the restoring force is approximately $mg\theta$, which *is* proportional to θ. So if θ_{max} is small, the motion can be treated as simple harmonic.

If the restoring force is given by $mg\theta$, rather than $mg \sin \theta$, then the frequency and period of the oscillations depend only on the length of the pendulum and the value of the gravitational acceleration, according to the following equations:

$$f = \frac{1}{2\pi}\sqrt{\frac{g}{L}} \qquad \text{and} \qquad T = 2\pi\sqrt{\frac{L}{g}}$$

Notice that neither frequency nor period depends on the amplitude (the maximum angular displacement, θ_{max}); this is a characteristic feature of simple harmonic motion. Also notice that neither depends on the mass of the weight.

Example 8.16 A simple pendulum has a period of 1 s on Earth. What would its period be on the Moon (where g is one-sixth of its value here)?

Solution. The equation $T = 2\pi\sqrt{L/g}$ shows that T is inversely proportional to $\sqrt{g}$, so if g decreases by a factor of 6, then T increases by a factor of $\sqrt{6}$. That is,

$$T_{\text{on Moon}} = \sqrt{6} \times T_{\text{on Earth}} = \sqrt{6}(1 \text{ s}) = 2.4 \text{ s}$$

CHAPTER 8 REVIEW QUESTIONS

SECTION I: MULTIPLE CHOICE

1. Which of the following is/are characteristics of simple harmonic motion?

   I. The acceleration is constant.
   II. The restoring force is proportional to the displacement.
   III. The frequency is independent of the amplitude.

   (A) II only
   (B) I and II only
   (C) I and III only
   (D) II and III only
   (E) I, II, and III

2. A block attached to an ideal spring undergoes simple harmonic motion. The acceleration of the block has its maximum magnitude at the point where

   (A) the speed is the maximum.
   (B) the potential energy is the minimum.
   (C) the speed is the minimum.
   D) the restoring force is the minimum.
   (E) the kinetic energy is the maximum.

3. A block attached to an ideal spring undergoes simple harmonic motion about its equilibrium position ($x = 0$) with amplitude A. What fraction of the total energy is in the form of kinetic energy when the block is at position $x = \frac{1}{2}A$?

   (A) 1/3
   (B) 3/8
   (C) 1/2
   (D) 2/3
   (E) 3/4

4. A student measures the maximum speed of a block undergoing simple harmonic oscillations of amplitude A on the end of an ideal spring. If the block is replaced by one with twice the mass but the amplitude of its oscillations remains the same, then the maximum speed of the block will

   (A) decrease by a factor of 4.
   (B) decrease by a factor of 2.
   (C) decrease by a factor of $\sqrt{2}$.
   (D) remain the same.
   (E) increase by a factor of 2.

5. A spring–block simple harmonic oscillator is set up so that the oscillations are vertical. The period of the motion is T. If the spring and block are taken to the surface of the Moon, where the gravitational acceleration is 1/6 of its value here, then the vertical oscillations will have a period of

   (A) $T/6$
   (B) $T/3$
   (C) $T/\sqrt{6}$
   (D) T
   (E) $T\sqrt{6}$

6. A linear spring of force constant k is used in a physics lab experiment. A block of mass m is attached to the spring and the resulting frequency, f, of the simple harmonic oscillations is measured. Blocks of various masses are used in different trials, and in each case, the corresponding frequency is measured and recorded. If f^2 is plotted versus $1/m$, the graph will be a straight line with slope

   (A) $4\pi^2/k^2$
   (B) $4\pi^2/k$
   (C) $4\pi^2 k$
   (D) $k/(4\pi^2)$
   (E) $k^2/(4\pi^2)$

7. A block of mass $m = 4$ kg on a frictionless, horizontal table is attached to one end of a spring of force constant $k = 400$ N/m and undergoes simple harmonic oscillations about its equilibrium position ($x = 0$) with amplitude $A = 6$ cm. If the block is at $x = 6$ cm at time $t = 0$, then which of the following equations (with x in centimeters and t in seconds) gives the block's position as a function of time?

(A) $x = 6 \sin(10t + \frac{1}{2}\pi)$

(B) $x = 6 \sin(10\pi t + \frac{1}{2}\pi)$

(C) $x = 6 \sin(10\pi t - \frac{1}{2}\pi)$

(D) $x = 6 \sin(10t)$

(E) $x = 6 \sin(10t - \frac{1}{2}\pi)$

8. [C] A block attached to an ideal spring undergoes simple harmonic motion about its equilibrium position with amplitude A and angular frequency ω. What is the maximum magnitude of the block's acceleration?

(A) $A\omega$
(B) $A^2\omega$
(C) $A\omega^2$
(D) A/ω
(E) A/ω^2

9. A simple pendulum swings about the vertical equilibrium position with a maximum angular displacement of 5° and period T. If the same pendulum is given a maximum angular displacement of 10°, then which of the following best gives the period of the oscillations?

(A) $T/2$
(B) $T/\sqrt{2}$
(C) T
(D) $T\sqrt{2}$
(E) $2T$

10. A simple pendulum of length L and mass m swings about the vertical equilibrium position ($\theta = 0$) with a maximum angular displacement of θ_{max}. What is the tension in the connecting rod when the pendulum's angular displacement is $\theta = \theta_{max}$?

(A) $mg \sin \theta_{max}$
(B) $mg \cos \theta_{max}$
(C) $mgL \sin \theta_{max}$
(D) $mgL \cos \theta_{max}$
(E) $mgL(1 - \cos \theta_{max})$

SECTION II: FREE RESPONSE

1. The figure below shows a block of mass m (Block 1) that's attached to one end of an ideal spring of force constant k and natural length L. The block is pushed so that it compresses the spring to 3/4 of its natural length and then released from rest. Just as the spring has extended to its natural length L, the attached block collides with another block (also of mass m) at rest on the edge of the frictionless table. When Block 1 collides with Block 2, half of its kinetic energy is lost to heat; the other half of Block 1's kinetic energy at impact is divided between Block 1 and Block 2. The collision sends Block 2 over the edge of the table, where it falls a vertical distance H, landing at a horizontal distance R from the edge.

(a) What is the acceleration of Block 1 at the moment it's released from rest from its initial position? Write your answer in terms of k, L, and m.

(b) If v_1 is the velocity of Block 1 just before impact, show that the velocity of Block 1 just after impact is $\frac{1}{2}v_1$.

(c) Determine the amplitude of the oscillations of Block 1 after Block 2 has left the table. Write your answer in terms of L only.

(d) Determine the period of the oscillations of Block 1 after the collision, writing your answer in terms of T_0, the period of the oscillations that Block 1 would have had if it did not collide with Block 2.

(e) Find an expression for R in terms of H, k, L, m, and g.

2. A bullet of mass m is fired horizontally with speed v into a block of mass M initially at rest, at the end of an ideal spring on a frictionless table. At the moment the bullet hits, the spring is at its natural length, L. The bullet becomes embedded in the block, and simple harmonic oscillations result.

(a) Determine the speed of the block immediately after the impact by the bullet.

(b) Determine the amplitude of the resulting oscillations of the block.

(c) Compute the frequency of the resulting oscillations.

(d) Derive an equation which gives the position of the block as a function of time (relative to $x = 0$ at time $t = 0$).

3. A block of mass M oscillates with amplitude A on a frictionless horizontal table, connected to an ideal spring of force constant k. The period of its oscillations is T. At the moment when the block is at position $x = \frac{1}{2}A$ and moving to the right, a ball of clay of mass m dropped from above lands on the block.

(a) What is the velocity of the block just before the clay hits?

(b) What is the velocity of the block just after the clay hits?

(c) What is the new period of the oscillations of the block?

(d) What is the new amplitude of the oscillations? Write your answer in terms of A, k, M, and m.

(e) Would the answer to part (c) be different if the clay had landed on the block when it was at a different position? Support your answer briefly.

(f) Would the answer to part (d) be different if the clay had landed on the block when it was at a different position? Support your answer briefly.

4. [C] An object of total mass M is allowed to swing around a fixed suspension point P. The object's moment of inertia with respect to the rotation axis perpendicular to the page through P is denoted by I. The distance between P and the object's center of mass, C, is d.

(a) Compute the torque τ produced by the weight of the object when the line PC makes an angle θ with the vertical. (Take the counterclockwise direction as positive for both θ and τ.)

(b) If θ is small, so that $\sin \theta$ may be replaced by θ, write the restoring torque τ computed in part (a) in the form $\tau = -k\theta$.

A simple harmonic oscillator whose displacement from equilibrium, z, satisfies an equation of the form

$$\frac{d^2z}{dt^2} = -bz \quad (*)$$

has a period of oscillation given by the formula $T = 2\pi / \sqrt{b}$.

(c) Taking z equal to θ in Equation (*), use the result of part (b) to derive an expression for the period of small oscillations of the object shown above.

(d) Answer the question posed in part (c) if the object were a uniform bar of mass M and length L (whose moment of inertia about one of its ends is given by the equation $I = \frac{1}{3}ML^2$.)

9

THERMAL PHYSICS [B]

INTRODUCTION

This chapter looks at heat and temperature, concepts that seem familiar from our everyday experience. Technically, **heat** is defined as thermal energy that's transmitted from one body to another. While an object can contain **thermal energy** (due to the random motion of its molecules), an object doesn't *contain* heat; heat is energy that's *in transit*. **Temperature**, on the other hand, is a measure of the concentration of an object's internal thermal energy, and is one of the basic SI units.

TEMPERATURE SCALES

In the United States, temperatures are still often expressed in **degrees Fahrenheit** (°F). On this scale, water freezes at 32°F and boils at 212°F. In other countries, temperature is expressed in **degrees Celsius** (°C); water freezes at 0°C and boils at 100°C. The size of a Fahrenheit degree is smaller than a Celsius degree, and the conversion between these two scales is given by the formula

$$T \ (°F) = \tfrac{9}{5} T \ (°C) + 32$$

The Celsius scale is sometimes used in scientific work, but it's giving way to the **absolute temperature scale**, in which temperatures are expressed in **kelvins** (K). On the kelvin scale, water freezes at 273.15 K and boils at 373.15 K. Notice that the degree sign is *not* used for absolute temperature. The kelvin scale assigns a value of 0 K to the lowest theoretically-possible temperature and a value of 273.16 K to the **triple point of water** (the temperature at which the three phases of water—liquid water, ice, and vapor—coexist). A kelvin is equal in size to a Celsius degree, and the conversion between kelvins and degrees Celsius is

$$T\ (\text{K}) = T\ (^\circ\text{C}) + 273.15$$

For most purposes, you can ignore the .15 and use the simpler conversion equation $T = T_{^\circ\text{C}} + 273$.

Example 9.1 Room temperature is 68°F. What's this temperature in kelvins?

Solution. Let's convert this to Celsius. Since $T_{^\circ\text{F}} = \frac{9}{5}T_{^\circ\text{C}} + 32$, it's also true that $T_{^\circ\text{C}} = \frac{5}{9}(T_{^\circ\text{F}} - 32)$, so 68°F is equal to $\frac{5}{9}(68 - 32) = 20°\text{C}$. Converting this to kelvins, we add 273; room temperature is 293 K.

PHYSICAL CHANGES DUE TO HEAT TRANSFER

When a substance absorbs or gives off heat, one of two things can happen:

    (1)   the temperature of the substance can change
            or
    (2)   the substance can undergoes a phase change.

There are three phases of matter: **solid**, **liquid**, and **vapor** (or **gas**). When a solid **melts** (or **liquefies**), it becomes a liquid; the reverse process occurs when a liquid **freezes** (or **solidifies**) to become a solid. A liquid can **evaporate** (to become vapor), and vapor can **condense** to become liquid. These are the most common phase changes, but others exist: A solid can **sublimate**, going directly to vapor form, and vapor can experience **deposition**, going directly to solid.

Since either change (1) or change (2)—but *not both*—takes place upon heat transfer, let's study these changes separately.

CALORIMETRY I: HEAT TRANSFER AND TEMPERATURE CHANGE

The change in temperature that a substance experiences upon a transfer of heat depends upon two things: the identity and the amount of the substance present. For example, we could transfer 200 J of heat to a gold nugget and a piece of wood of equal mass and, even though they were infused with the same amount of thermal energy, the temperature of the gold would rise much more than the temperature of the wood. Also, if this heat were transferred to two nuggets of gold of unequal mass, the temperature of the smaller nugget would rise more than that of the bigger one. The equation that connects the amount of heat, Q, and the resulting temperature change, ΔT, is

$$Q = mc\,\Delta T$$

where m is the mass of the sample and c is an intrinsic property of the substance called its **specific heat**. Notice that positive Q is interpreted as heat coming *in* (ΔT is positive, so T increases), while negative Q corresponds to heat going *out* (ΔT is negative, so T decreases).

Example 9.2 Gold has a specific heat of 130 J/kg·°C, and wood has a specific heat of 1800 J/kg·°C. If a piece of gold and a piece of wood, each of mass 0.05 kg, both absorb 200 J of heat, by how much will their temperatures rise?

Solution. We're given c, m, and Q, and we know that $\Delta T = Q/(mc)$.

$$\Delta T_{gold} = \frac{Q}{mc_{gold}} = \frac{200 \text{ J}}{(0.05 \text{ kg})(130 \text{ J} / \text{kg} \cdot °\text{C})} = 31°\text{C}$$

$$\Delta T_{wood} = \frac{Q}{mc_{wood}} = \frac{200 \text{ J}}{(0.05 \text{ kg})(1800 \text{ J} / \text{kg} \cdot °\text{C})} = 2.2°\text{C}$$

Notice that the temperature of gold increased by 31°C, but the temperature of the wood increased by only 2.2°C.

Example 9.3 A nugget of gold of mass 0.05 kg at a temperature of 600°C is placed in a beaker of water at room temperature (20°C). After a while, the gold and water reach **thermal equilibrium** (they're at the same temperature). If the beaker contains 500 g of water (specific heat = 4186 J/kg·°C), what's the common final temperature of the gold and the water?

Solution. Heat always flows naturally from hot to cold. Therefore, when the hot nugget of gold is placed in the cool water, the gold loses heat and the water absorbs it. If we let T_f be the final temperature of both the gold and the water, then

$$Q_{\text{lost by gold}} = m_{gold}c_{gold}(T_f - 600°\text{C})$$

and

$$Q_{\text{gained by water}} = m_{water}c_{water}(T_f - 20°\text{C})$$

By conservation of energy (ignoring the heat transfer to the air or the beaker), the heat lost by the gold is equal to the heat absorbed by the water. Since $Q_{\text{lost by gold}}$ is heat going *out*, it's negative, and since $Q_{\text{gained by water}}$ is heat coming *in*, it's positive. To account for the signs, we have to write

$$Q_{\text{lost by gold}} = -Q_{\text{gained by water}}$$

and

$$m_{gold}c_{gold}(T_f - 600°\text{C}) = -m_{water}c_{water}(T_f - 20°\text{C})$$

$$T_f - 600°\text{C} = \frac{-m_{water}c_{water}}{m_{gold}c_{gold}}(T_f - 20°\text{C})$$

$$= -\frac{(0.5 \text{ kg})(4186 \text{ J} / \text{kg} \cdot °\text{C})}{(0.05 \text{ kg})(130 \text{ J} / \text{kg} \cdot °\text{C})} \cdot (T_f - 20°\text{C})$$

$$T_f - 600°\text{C} = -322(T_f - 20°\text{C})$$

$$323T_f = 7040°\text{C}$$

$$T_f = 21.8°\text{C}$$

Notice how little the temperature of the water changed! Water has a very high specific heat and can absorb large amounts of thermal energy without undergoing much of a temperature change. This experiment could also have been used to determine the specific heat of gold. Drop a known mass of gold at a given temperature into the water and then measure the temperature of the water once thermal equilibrium is reached. Knowing this final temperature, we could solve for c_{gold}.

CALORIMETRY II: HEAT TRANSFER AND PHASE CHANGES

Consider an ice cube. Since water freezes at 0°C, the temperature of the ice cube is 0°C. If we add heat to the ice, its temperature does not rise. Instead, the thermal energy absorbed by the ice goes into loosening the intermolecular bonds of the solid, thereby transforming it into liquid. The temperature remains at 0°C throughout this melting process. Once the ice cube is completely melted, additional heat will increase the temperature of the liquid, until it reaches its boiling point temperature (100°C). At this point, additional heat does not increase the temperature; it breaks the intermolecular bonds, transforming it into steam. In each of the phase changes (solid to liquid, liquid to vapor), absorbed heat causes no temperature change, so $Q = mc \, \Delta T$ does not apply at these transitions. The equation that *does* apply is

$$Q = mL$$

where L is the **latent heat of transformation**. This equation tells us how much heat must be transferred in order to cause a sample of mass m to completely undergo a phase change. In the case of a solid to liquid (or vice versa) phase change, L is called the latent **heat of fusion**. For a phase change between liquid and vapor, L is called the latent **heat of vaporization**.

> **Example 9.4** The heat of fusion for water is 334 kJ/kg. How much thermal energy is required to completely melt a 100-gram ice cube?

Solution. The change in phase from solid to liquid requires the input of heat; in this case, $Q = mL = (0.1 \text{ kg})(334 \text{ kJ/kg}) = 33.4 \text{ kJ}$.

> **Example 9.5** A beaker contains 100 g of water, initially at room temperature (20°C). If the heat of vaporization of water is 2260 kJ/kg, how much thermal energy would the water need to absorb in order to turn completely to steam?

Solution. First we need to heat the water to 100°C, and second, we need to continue to add heat until all the liquid is vaporized. The amount of thermal energy required for the first step is

$$\begin{aligned} Q_1 &= m_{water} c_{water} (100°C - 20°C) \\ &= (0.1 \text{ kg})(4186 \text{ J/kg} \cdot °C)(80°C) \\ &= 33 \text{ kJ} \end{aligned}$$

and the amount of energy required for the second step is

$$Q_2 = m_{water} L_{vap} = (0.1 \text{ kg})(2260 \text{ kJ/kg}) = 226 \text{ kJ}$$

Therefore, the total amount of thermal energy required is

$$Q_{total} = Q_1 + Q_2 = 33 \text{ kJ} + 226 \text{ kJ} = 259 \text{ kJ}$$

HEAT TRANSFER AND THERMAL EXPANSION

When a substance undergoes a temperature change, it changes in size. Steel beams that form railroad tracks or bridges expand when they get warmer; a balloon filled with air shrinks when it's placed in a freezer. The change in size of a substance due to a temperature change depends on the amount of the temperature change and the identity of the substance.

Let's first consider changes in length (of the steel beam, for example). When its temperature is T_i, its length is L_i. Then, if its temperature changes to T_f, the length changes to L_f, such that

$$L_f - L_i = \alpha L_i (T_f - T_i)$$

where α is the **coefficient of linear expansion** of the material. This equation is usually used in the simpler form

$$\Delta L = \alpha L_i \Delta T$$

Nearly all substances have a positive value of α, which means they expand upon heating.

> **Example 9.6** A steel beam used in the construction of a bridge has a length of 30.0 m when the temperature is 15°C. On a very hot day, when the temperature is 36°C, how long will the beam be? (The coefficient of linear expansion for structural steel is +1.2 × 10⁻⁵/°C.)

Solution. The change in length of the beam is

$$\Delta L = \alpha L_i \Delta T = \frac{1.2 \times 10^{-5}}{°C}(30.0 \text{ m})(36°C - 15°C) = 7.6 \times 10^{-3} \text{ m} = 7.6 \text{ mm}$$

As we've mentioned, substances also undergo volume changes when heat is lost or absorbed. The change in volume, ΔV, corresponding to a temperature change ΔT is given by the equation

$$\Delta V = \beta V_i \Delta T$$

where V_i is the sample's initial volume and β is the **coefficient of volume expansion** of the substance. Since we're now looking at the change in a 3-dimensional quantity (volume) rather than a 1-dimensional quantity (length), for most solids, $\beta \approx 3\alpha$. Nearly all substances have a positive value of β, which means that they expand upon heating. An extremely important example of a substance with a *negative* value of β is liquid water between 0°C and 4°C. Unlike the vast majority of substances, liquid water *expands* as it nears its freezing point and solidifies (which is why ice has a lower density and floats in water).

Example 9.7 The mercury in a household glass-tube thermometer has a volume of 50 mm³ (= 5.0×10^{-8} m³) at $T = 15°C$. The hollow column within which the mercury can rise or fall has a cross-sectional area of 1.0 mm² (= 1.0×10^{-6} m²). Ignoring the volume expansion of the glass, how much will the mercury rise in the thermometer when its temperature is 39°C? (The coefficient of volume expansion of mercury is $1.8 \times 10^{-4}/°C$.)

Solution. First let's figure out how much the volume of the mercury increases:

$$\Delta V = \beta V_i \Delta T = \frac{1.82 \times 10^{-4}}{°C}(5.0 \times 10^{-8} \text{ m}^3)(39°C - 15°C) = 2.2 \times 10^{-10} \text{ m}^3$$

Now, since *volume = cross-sectional area × height*, the change in height of the mercury column will be

$$\Delta h = \frac{\Delta V}{A} = \frac{2.2 \times 10^{-10} \text{ m}^3}{1.0 \times 10^{-8} \text{ m}^2} = 2.2 \times 10^{-2} \text{ m} = 2.2 \text{ cm}$$

THE KINETIC THEORY OF GASES

Unlike the condensed phases of matter—solid and liquid—the atoms or molecules that make up a gas do not move around relatively fixed positions. Rather, the molecules of a gas move freely and rapidly, in a chaotic swarm.

A confined gas exerts a force on the walls of its container, because the molecules are zipping around inside the container, striking the walls and rebounding. The magnitude of the force per unit area is called **pressure**, and is denoted by P:

$$P = \frac{F}{A}$$

The SI unit for pressure is the N/m², the **pascal** (abbreviated Pa). As we'll see, the faster the gas molecules are moving, the more pressure they exert.

We also need a way to talk about the typically vast numbers of molecules in a given sample of gas. One **mole** of atoms or molecules contains

$$N_A = 6.022 \times 10^{23}$$

of these elementary quantities. The number N_A is known as **Avogadro's constant**, and one mole of any substance has a mass in grams that defines its atomic or molecular mass (these values are given in the Periodic Table of Elements). For example, the mass of a carbon-12 atom (the most abundant isotope of carbon) has a mass of exactly 12 atomic mass units, and a mole of these atoms has a mass of 12 grams. Oxygen has an atomic mass of 16 g, so a mole of carbon dioxide (CO_2), each molecule of which is composed of one carbon atom and two oxygen atoms, has a mass of 12 g + 2(16 g) = 44 g.

THE IDEAL GAS LAW

Three physical properties—pressure (P), volume (V), and temperature (T)—describe a gas. At low densities, all gases approach *ideal* behavior; this means that these three variables are related by the equation

$$PV = nRT$$

where n is the number of moles of gas and R is a constant (8.31 J/mol·K) called the **universal gas constant**. This equation is known as the **Ideal Gas Law**.

An important consequence of this equation is that, for a fixed volume of gas, an increase in P gives a proportional increase in T. The pressure increases when the gas molecules strike the walls of their container with more force, which occurs if they move more rapidly. Using Newton's Second Law (*rate of change of momentum = force*) to find the average force—and, consequently, the pressure—the product of the pressure exerted by N molecules of gas in a container of volume V is related to the average kinetic energy of the molecules by the equation $PV = \frac{2}{3}NK_{avg}$. Comparing this to the Ideal Gas Law, we see that $\frac{2}{3}NK_{avg} = nRT$. We can rewrite this equation in the form $\frac{2}{3}N_A K_{avg} = RT$, since, by definition, $N = nN_A$. The ratio R/N_A is a fundamental constant of nature called **Boltzmann's constant** ($k_B = 1.38 \times 10^{-23}$ J/K), so our equation becomes

$$K_{avg} = \tfrac{3}{2}k_B T$$

This tells us that the average translational kinetic energy of the gas molecules is a direct indication of the temperature of the sample.

Since the average kinetic energy of the gas molecules is $K_{avg} = \frac{1}{2}m(v^2)_{avg}$, where m is the mass of each molecule, the equation above becomes $\frac{1}{2}m(v^2)_{avg} = \frac{3}{2}k_B T$, so

$$\sqrt{(v^2)_{avg}} = \sqrt{\frac{3k_B T}{m}}$$

The quantity on the left-hand side of this equation, the square root of the average of the square of v, is called the **root-mean-square speed**, v_{rms}, so

$$v_{rms} = \sqrt{\frac{3k_B T}{m}}$$

Because $k_B = R/N_A$ and $mN_A = M$ (the mass of one mole of the molecules—the **molar mass**), the equation for v_{rms} is also commonly written in the form

$$v_{rms} = \sqrt{\frac{3RT}{M}}$$

Notice that these last two equations can only determine v_{rms}. It's important to realize that the molecules in the container have a wide range of speeds; some are much slower and others are much faster than v_{rms}. The root-mean-square speed is important because it gives us a type of average speed that's easy to calculate from the temperature of the gas.

Example 9.8 Given that O_2 has a molecular mass of 32 g/mol, how fast do oxygen molecules travel at room temperature (20°C)?

Solution. Always use absolute temperatures (that is, temperatures expressed in kelvins) when dealing with the equations in this section. The conversion between kelvins and degrees Celsius is $T = T_{°C} + 273$, so a temperature of 20°C is 293 K. Therefore, the root-mean-square speed of oxygen molecules at room temperature is

$$v_{rms} = \sqrt{\frac{3RT}{M}} = \sqrt{\frac{3(8.31 \text{ J} / \text{mol} \cdot \text{K})(273 \text{ K})}{32 \times 10^{-3} \text{ kg} / \text{mol}}} = 460 \text{ m} / \text{s}$$

That's over 1000 miles per hour!

> **Example 9.9** Standard atmospheric pressure is 1.013×10^5 Pa (this is one **atmosphere**). At 0°C = 273.15 K, one mole of any ideal gas occupies the same volume. What is this volume?

Solution. Use the Ideal Gas Law:

$$V = \frac{nRT}{P} = \frac{(1.00 \text{ mol})(8.31 \text{ J} / \text{mol} \cdot \text{K})(273.15 \text{ K})}{1.013 \times 10^5 \text{ Pa}} = 22.4 \times 10^{-3} \text{ m}^3$$

The quantity 10^{-3} m³ is the definition of a **liter** (L), so the volume occupied by any gas at **STP** (standard **t**emperature and **p**ressure, 0°C and 1 atm) is 22.4 L.

> **Example 9.10** A 0.1-mole sample of gas is confined to a jar whose volume is 4.0 L. To what temperature must the gas be raised to cause the pressure of the gas to increase to 2 atm?

Solution. Use the Ideal Gas Law:

$$T = \frac{PV}{nR} = \frac{[2(1.013 \times 10^5 \text{ Pa})](4.0 \times 10^{-3} \text{ m}^3)}{(0.10 \text{ mol})(8.31 \text{ J} / \text{mol} \cdot \text{K})} = 975 \text{ K} = 702°C$$

> **Example 9.11** A cylindrical container of radius 15 cm and height 30 cm contains 0.6 mole of gas at 433 K. How much force does the confined gas exert on the lid of the container?

Solution. The volume of the cylinder is $\pi r^2 h$, where r is the radius and h is the height. Since we know V and T, we can the Ideal Gas Law to find P. Because pressure is force per unit area, we can find the force on the lid by multiplying the gas pressure times the area of the lid.

$$P = \frac{nRT}{V} = \frac{(0.6 \text{ mol})(8.31 \text{ J} / \text{mol} \cdot \text{K})(433 \text{ K})}{\pi(0.15 \text{ m})^2(0.30 \text{ m})} = 1.018 \times 10^5 \text{ Pa}$$

So, since the area of the lid is πr^2, the force exerted by the confined gas on the lid is:

$$F = PA = (1.018 \times 10^5 \text{ Pa}) \cdot \pi(0.15 \text{ m})^2 = 7200 \text{ N}$$

This is about 1600 pounds of force, which seems like a lot. Why doesn't this pressure pop the lid off? Because, while the bottom of the lid is feeling a pressure (due to the confined gas) of 1.018×10^5 Pa that exerts a force upward, the top of the lid feels a pressure of 1.013×10^5 Pa (due to the atmosphere) that exerts a force downward. The net force on the lid is

$$F_{\text{net}} = (\Delta P)A = (0.005 \times 10^5 \text{ Pa}) \cdot \pi(0.15 \text{ m})^2 = 35 \text{ N}$$

which is only about 8 pounds.

THE LAWS OF THERMODYNAMICS

We've learned about two ways in which energy may be transferred between a system and its environment. One is work, which takes place when a force acts over a distance. The other is heat, which takes place when energy is transferred due to a difference in temperature. The study of the energy transfers involving work and heat, and the resulting changes in internal energy, temperature, volume, and pressure is called **thermodynamics**.

THE ZEROTH LAW OF THERMODYNAMICS

When two objects are brought into contact, heat will flow from the warmer object to the cooler one until they reach thermal equilibrium. This property of temperature is expressed by the Zeroth Law of Thermodynamics: *If Objects 1 and 2 are each in thermal equilibrium with Object 3, then Objects 1 and 2 are in thermal equilibrium with each other.*

THE FIRST LAW OF THERMODYNAMICS

Simply put, the First Law of Thermodynamics is a statement of the Conservation of Energy that includes heat. Consider the following example, which is the prototype that's studied extensively in thermodynamics.

An insulated container filled with an ideal gas rests on a heat reservoir (that is, something that can can act as a heat source or a heat sink). The container is fitted with a snug, but frictionless, weighted piston that can be raised or lowered. The confined gas is the *system*, and the piston and heat reservoir are the *surroundings*.

weight

piston

insulated walls

gas

heat reservoir

heat exchange can occur here

temperature control knob

The **state** of the gas is given once its pressure, volume, and temperature are known, and the equation that connects these state variables is the Ideal Gas Law, $PV = nRT$. We'll imagine performing different experiments with the gas, such as heating it or allowing it to cool, increasing or decreasing the weight on the piston, etc., and study the energy transfers (work and heat) and the changes in the state variables. If each process is carried out such that, at each moment, the system and its surroundings are in thermal equilibrium, we can plot the pressure (P) vs. the volume (V) on a diagram. By following the path of this **P-V diagram**, we can study how the system is affected as it moves from one state to another.

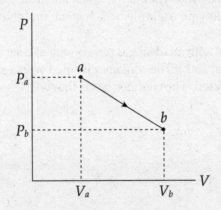

Work is done on or by the system when the piston is moved and the volume of the gas changes. For example, imagine that the gas pushes the piston upward, causing an increase in volume. The work done by the gas during its expansion is $W = F \Delta s$, but since $F = PA$, we have $W = PA \Delta s$, and because $A \Delta s = \Delta V$, we have

$$W = P \Delta V$$

This equation is also true if the piston is pushed down and the volume of the gas decreases. In this case, ΔV is negative, so W is negative. In general, then, W is positive when the system does work against its surroundings, and W is negative when the surroundings do work on the system.

The equation $W = P\Delta V$ assumes that the pressure P does not change during the process. If P *does* change, then the work is equal to the integral of $P\, dV$ from $V = V_i$ to $V = V_f$. This integral can be evaluated simply by finding the area under the curve in the P–V diagram; moving left to right gives a positive area (and positive work), while moving right to left gives a negative area (and negative work).

Example 9.12 What's the value of W for the process ab following path 1 and for the same process following path 2, shown in the P–V diagram below?

Solution.

Path 1. Since, in path 1, P remains constant, the work done is just $P\Delta V$:

$$W = P\Delta V = (1.5 \times 10^5 \text{ Pa})[(30 \times 10^{-3} \text{ m}^3) - (10 \times 10^{-3} \text{ m}^3)] = 3000 \text{ J}$$

Path 2. If the gas is brought from state a to state b, along path 2, then work is done only along the part from a to d. From d to b, the volume of the gas does not change, so no work can be performed. The area under the graph from a to d is

$$W = \tfrac{1}{2}h(b_1 + b_2) = \tfrac{1}{2}(\Delta V)(P_a + P_d)$$
$$= \tfrac{1}{2}(20 \times 10^{-3}\ \text{m}^3)[(1.5 \times 10^5\ \text{Pa}) + (0.7 \times 10^5\ \text{Pa})]$$
$$= 2200\ \text{J}$$

As this example shows, the value of W depends not only on the initial and final states of the system, but also on the path between the two. In general, different paths give different values for W.

CALORIMETRY III: HEAT TRANSFER AND TEMPERATURE CHANGE FOR GASES

The value of the heat transfer in a system, Q, is also path-dependent. When we studied the temperature change of a solid or liquid corresponding to a transfer of heat, the equation we used was $Q = mc\Delta T$. For gases, however, the situation is a little more complicated, because the value of the proportionality constant between Q and ΔT depends on whether the pressure or the volume is kept constant. If the volume remains constant during the heat transfer, then

$$Q = nC_V\Delta T$$

where n is the number of moles of gas and C_V is the **molar heat capacity at constant volume**, which varies, depending on whether the gas is monatomic, diatomic, or polyatomic.

If the *pressure* remains constant during the heat transfer, then

$$Q = nC_P\Delta T$$

where C_P is the **molar heat capacity at constant pressure**. The value of C_P is different from the value of C_V even for the same gas; in fact $C_P = C_V + R$ (where R is the universal gas constant), so C_P is always greater than C_V.

> **Example 9.13** For a diatomic gas (like oxygen), the value of C_V is 20.8 J/mol·K. What's the change in temperature of a 0.5 mol sample of oxygen if it absorbs 1000 J of heat at constant volume?

Solution. Using the equation $Q = nC_V\Delta T$, we find that

$$\Delta T = \frac{Q}{nC_V} = \frac{1000\ \text{J}}{(0.5\ \text{mol})(20.8\ \text{J}/\text{mol}\cdot\text{K})} = 96\ \text{K}$$

> **Example 9.14** What's the change in temperature of a 0.5 mol sample of oxygen if it absorbs 1000 J of heat at constant pressure? (Remember that $C_P = C_V + R$.)

Solution. Using the equation $Q = nC_P\Delta T$, we find that

$$\Delta T = \frac{Q}{nC_P} = \frac{Q}{n(C_V + R)} = \frac{1000\ \text{J}}{(0.5\ \text{mol})(20.8\ \text{J}/\text{mol}\cdot\text{K} + 8.31\ \text{J}/\text{mol}\cdot\text{K})} = 69\ \text{K}$$

These examples show that, like W, the value of Q is also path dependent. But experiments have shown that the value of $Q - W$ is *not* path dependent; it depends only on the initial and the final state of the system, so it describes a change in a fundamental property. This property is called the system's **internal energy**, denoted U, and the change in the system's internal energy, ΔU, is equal to $Q - W$. This is true regardless of the process that brought the system from its initial to final state. This statement is known as

The First Law of Thermodynamics

$$\Delta U = Q - W$$

Example 9.15 A 0.5 mol sample of an ideal gas (C_V = 12.5 J/mol·K, C_p = 20.8 J/mol·K) is brought from state a to state b along the path shown in the following $P-V$ diagram:

What are the values of each of the following?

(a) the temperature at a

(b) the temperature at b

(c) the work done by the gas during process ab

(d) the heat added to the gas during process ab

(e) the change in the internal energy of the gas

Solution.

(a, b) Both of these questions can be answered using the Ideal Gas Law, $T = PV/(nR)$:

$$T_a = \frac{P_a V_a}{nR} = \frac{(1.5 \times 10^5 \text{ Pa})(10 \times 10^{-3} \text{ m}^3)}{(0.5 \text{ mol})(8.31 \text{ J / mol} \cdot \text{K})} = 360 \text{ K}$$

$$T_b = \frac{P_b V_b}{nR} = \frac{(1.5 \times 10^5 \text{ Pa})(30 \times 10^{-3} \text{ m}^3)}{(0.5 \text{ mol})(8.31 \text{ J / mol} \cdot \text{K})} = 1080 \text{ K}$$

(c) Since the pressure remains constant during the process, we can use the equation $W = P\Delta V$. Because $\Delta V = (30 - 10) \times 10^{-3}\,\text{m}^3 = 20 \times 10^{-3}\,\text{m}^3$, we find that

$$W = P\Delta V = (1.5 \times 10^5\,\text{Pa})(20 \times 10^{-3}\,\text{m}^3) = 3000\,\text{J}$$

The expanding gas did positive work against its surroundings, pushing the piston upward. [Important note: If the pressure remains constant (which is designated by a horizontal line in the P–V diagram), the process is called **isobaric**.]

(d) Because the pressure of the gas remains constant,

$$Q = nC_P\Delta T = (0.5\,\text{mol})(20.8\,\text{J}/\text{mol}\cdot\text{K})(1080\,\text{K} - 360\,\text{K}) = 7500\,\text{J}$$

(e) By the First Law of Thermodynamics

$$\Delta U = Q - W = 7500\,\text{J} - 3000\,\text{J} = 4500\,\text{J}$$

Example 9.16 A 0.5 mol sample of an ideal monatomic gas ($C_V = 12.5\,\text{J}/\text{mol}\cdot\text{K}$, $C_p = 20.8\,\text{J}/\text{mol}\cdot\text{K}$) is brought from state a to state b along the path shown in the following P–V diagram:

What are the values of each of the following?
  (a) the work done by the gas during process ab
  (b) the change in the internal energy of the gas
  (c) the heat added to the gas during process ab

Solution. Notice that the initial and final states of the gas are the same as in the preceding example, but the path is different.

(a) Let's break the path into 3 pieces:

Over paths 1 and 3, the volume does not change, so no work is done. Work is done only over path 2:

$$W = P\,\Delta V = (0.5 \times 10^5 \text{ Pa})(20 \times 10^{-3} \text{ m}^3) = 1000 \text{ J}$$

Once again, the expanding gas does positive work against its surroundings, pushing the piston upward.

(b) Because the initial and final states of the gas are the same here as they were in the preceding example, the change in internal energy, ΔU, *must* be the same. Therefore, $\Delta U = 4500$ J.

(c) By the First Law of Thermodynamics, $\Delta U = Q - W$, so

$$Q = \Delta U + W = 4500 \text{ J} + 1000 \text{ J} = 5500 \text{ J}$$

An alternative solution for part (c) is to determine Q for paths 1, 2, and 3, and then figure out the total. The temperatures at points c and d are

$$T_c = \frac{P_c V_c}{nR} = \frac{(0.5 \times 10^5 \text{ Pa})(10 \times 10^{-3} \text{ m}^3)}{(0.5 \text{ mol})(8.31 \text{ J} / \text{mol} \cdot \text{K})} = 120 \text{ K}$$

$$T_d = \frac{P_d V_d}{nR} = \frac{(0.5 \times 10^5 \text{ Pa})(30 \times 10^{-3} \text{ m}^3)}{(0.5 \text{ mol})(8.31 \text{ J} / \text{mol} \cdot \text{K})} = 360 \text{ K}$$

Since $T_a = 360$ K and $T_b = 1080$ K, we have

$$Q_{ac} = nC_V \Delta T_{ac} = (0.5 \text{ mol})(12.5 \text{ J} / \text{mol} \cdot \text{K})(120 \text{ K} - 360 \text{ K}) = -1500 \text{ J}$$
$$Q_{cd} = nC_P \Delta T_{cd} = (0.5 \text{ mol})(20.8 \text{ J} / \text{mol} \cdot \text{K})(360 \text{ K} - 120 \text{ K}) = +2500 \text{ J}$$
$$Q_{db} = nC_V \Delta T_{db} = (0.5 \text{ mol})(12.5 \text{ J} / \text{mol} \cdot \text{K})(1080 \text{ K} - 360 \text{ K}) = +4500 \text{ J}$$

so the total heat involved in the process ab is

$$Q_{ab} = Q_{ac} + Q_{cd} + Q_{db} = 5500 \text{ J}$$

in agreement with the value figured out using the First Law of Thermodynamics.

Example 9.17 As isochoric process is one that takes place with no change in volume. What can you say about the change in the internal energy of a gas if it undergoes an isochoric change of state?

Solution. An isochoric process is illustrated by a vertical line in a P–V diagram and, since no change in volume occurs, $W = 0$. By the First Law of Thermodynamics, $\Delta U = Q - W = Q$. Therefore, the change in internal energy is entirely due to (and equal to) the heat transferred. If heat is transferred into the system (positive Q), then ΔU is positive; if heat is transferred out of the system (negative Q), then ΔU is negative.

Example 9.18 A 0.5 mol sample of an ideal gas (C_V = 12.5 J/mol·K, C_p = 20.8 J/mol·K) is brought from state a back to state a along the path shown in the following P–V diagram:

What are the values of each of the following?
  (a) the change in the internal energy of the gas
  (b) the work done on the gas during the process
  (c) the heat added to the gas during the process

Solution. A process such as this, which begins and ends at the same state, is said to be **cyclical**.

(a) Because the final state is the same as the initial state, the internal energy of the system cannot have changed, so $\Delta U = 0$.

(b) The total work involved in the process is equal to the work done from c to d plus the work done from b to a, because only along these paths does the volume change. Along these portions, we find that

$$W_{cd} = P \Delta V_{cd} = (0.5 \times 10^5 \text{ Pa})(+20 \times 10^{-3} \text{ m}^3) = +1000 \text{ J}$$

$$W_{ba} = P \Delta V_{ba} = (1.5 \times 10^5 \text{ Pa})(-20 \times 10^{-3} \text{ m}^3) = -3000 \text{ J}$$

so the total work done is $W = -2000$ J. The fact that W is negative means that, overall, work was done *on* the gas by the surroundings. Notice that for a cyclical process, the total work done is equal to the area enclosed by the loop, with clockwise travel taken as positive and counterclockwise travel taken as negative.

(c) The First Law of Thermodynamics states that $\Delta U = Q - W$. Since $\Delta U = 0$, it must be true that $Q = W$ (which will always be the case for a cyclical process), so $Q = -2000$ J.

Example 9.19 A 0.5 mol sample of an ideal gas ($C_V = 12.5$ J/mol·K, $C_P = 20.8$ J/mol·K) is brought from state a to state d along an **isotherm**, then isobarically to state c and isochorically back to state a, as shown in the following P–V diagram:

A process that takes place with no variation in temperature is said to be **isothermal**. Given that the work done during the isothermal part of the cycle is 1650 J, how much heat is transferred during the isothermal process, from a to d?

Solution. Be careful that you don't confuse *isothermal* with *adiabatic*. A process is isothermal if the *temperature* remains constant; a process is **adiabatic** if $Q = 0$. You might ask, *How could a process be isothermal without also being adiabatic at the same time?* Remember that the temperature is determined by the internal energy of the gas, which is affected by changes in Q , W, or both. Therefore, it's possible for U to remain unchanged even if Q is not 0 (because there can be an equal W to cancel it out). In fact, this is the key to this problem. Since T doesn't change from a to d, neither can the internal energy, which depends entirely on T. Because $\Delta U_{ad} = 0$, it must be true that $Q_{ad} = W_{ad}$. Since W_{ad} equals 1650 J, so must Q_{ad}. The gas absorbs heat from the reservoir and uses all this energy to do positive work as it expands, pushing the piston upward.

THE SECOND LAW OF THERMODYNAMICS

The form of the Second Law of Thermodynamics that we'll study for the AP Physics test deals with heat engines.

Converting work to heat is easy—rubbing your hands together shows that work can be completely converted to heat. What we'll look at it is the reverse process: How efficiently can heat be converted into work? A device that uses heat to produce useful work is called a **heat engine**. The internal-combustion engine in a car is an example. In particular, we're only interested in engines that take their working substance (a mixture of air and fuel in this case) through a cyclic process, so that the cycle can be repeated. The basic components of any cyclic heat engine are simple: Energy in the form of heat comes into the engine from a high-temperature source, some of this energy is converted into useful work, the remainder is ejected as exhaust heat into a low-temperature sink, and the system returns to its original state to run through the cycle again.

Since we're looking at cyclic engines only, the system returns to its original state at the end of each cycle, so ΔU must be 0. Therefore, by the First Law of Thermodynamics, $Q_{net} = W$. That is, the net heat absorbed by the system is equal to the work performed by the system. The heat that's absorbed from the high-temperature source is denoted Q_H (H for *hot*), and the heat that is discharged into the low-temperature reservoir is denoted Q_C (C for *cold*). Because heat coming *in* is positive and heat going *out* is negative, Q_H is positive and Q_C is negative, and the net heat absorbed is $Q_H + Q_C$. Instead of writing Q_{net} in this way, it's customary to write it as $Q_H - |Q_C|$, to show explicitly that Q_{net} is less than Q_H. The **thermal efficiency**, e, of the heat engine is equal to the ratio of what we get out, to what we have to put in; that is, $e = W/Q_H$. Since $W = Q_{net} = Q_H - |Q_C|$, we have

$$e = \frac{Q_H - |Q_C|}{Q_H} = 1 - \frac{|Q_C|}{Q_H}$$

Notice that unless $Q_C = 0$, the engine's efficiency is *always* less than 1. This is one of the forms of

The Second Law of Thermodynamics

For any cyclic heat engine, some exhaust heat is always produced. Because $Q_C \neq 0$, no cyclic heat engine can operate at 100% efficiency; it's impossible to completely convert heat into useful work.

Example 9.20 A heat engine draws 800 J of heat from its high-temperature source and discards 450 J of exhaust heat into its cold-temperature reservoir during each cycle. How much work does this engine perform per cycle, and what is its thermal efficiency?

Solution. The work output per cycle is equal to the difference between the heat energy drawn in and the heat energy discarded:

$$W = Q_H - |Q_C| = 800 \text{ J} - 450 \text{ J} = 350 \text{ J}$$

The efficiency of this engine is

$$e = \frac{W}{Q_H} = \frac{350 \text{ J}}{800 \text{ J}} = 0.44 \doteq 44\%$$

THE CARNOT CYCLE

The Second Law of Thermodynamics tells us that there are no perfect heat engines. But how can we construct, in principle, the best possible heat engine, meaning one with the maximum possible efficiency (that doesn't violate the Second Law)? Such an engine is called a **Carnot engine**, and the cycle through which its working substance (gas) is carried is called the **Carnot cycle**. It can be shown that a heat engine utilizing the Carnot cycle has the highest possible efficiency consistent with the Second Law of Thermodynamics.

The cycle has four steps.

Step 1: Isothermal expansion

The system absorbs heat from the high-temperature source and expands isothermally. Because the temperature doesn't increase, all the heat drawn from the source goes into work performed by the expansion of the gas.

Step 2: Adiabatic expansion

The system is allowed to expand without exchanging heat with its surroundings. Because the system expands (that is, does positive work), its internal energy and temperature decrease because it receives no influx of heat from the surroundings.

Step 3: Isothermal compression

Work is done on the gas by the environment and, rather than increasing its internal energy, the system discards heat to the low-temperature reservoir.

Step 4: Adiabatic compression

The system is compressed to its initial state without exchanging heat with its surroundings. Because the system is compressed, its internal energy and temperature increase, because no heat is discarded.

These four steps can be illustrated on a *P–V* diagram as follows:

Carnot cycle

What is the efficiency of a Carnot engine? The answer is given by the equation

$$e_C = \frac{T_H - T_C}{T_H} = 1 - \frac{T_C}{T_H}$$

Notice that the **Carnot efficiency** depends only on the absolute temperatures of the heat source and heat sink. The expression $1 - (T_C/T_H)$ gives the maximum theoretical efficiency of any cyclic heat engine. This cannot equal 1 unless $T_C = 0$, that is, unless the temperature of the cold reservoir is **absolute zero**. But the Third Law of Thermodynamics says, in part, that absolute zero can never be reached.

> **Example 9.21** An inventor proposes a design for a heat engine that operates between a heat source at 500°C and a cold reservoir at 25°C with an efficiency of 2/3. What's your reaction to the inventor's claim?

Solution. The highest possible efficiency for any heat engine is the Carnot efficiency, and a Carnot engine operating between the temperatures $T_H = 500°C = 773$ K and $T_C = 25°C = 298$ K has an efficiency of

$$e_C = 1 - \frac{T_C}{T_H} = 1 - \frac{298 \text{ K}}{773 \text{ K}} = 0.61 = 61\%$$

The inventor's claim is that his engine has a efficiency of 2/3 = 67%, which is higher than e_C. Your reaction should therefore be one of extreme skepticism!

CHAPTER 9 REVIEW QUESTIONS

SECTION I: MULTIPLE CHOICE

1. How much heat is required to raise the temperature of a 0.04 kg stainless steel spoon from 20°C to 50°C if the specific heat of stainless steel is 0.50 kJ/kg·°C?

   (A) 200 J
   (B) 400 J
   (C) 600 J
   (D) 800 J
   (E) 1000 J

2. The melting point of copper is 1080°C and its heat of fusion is 200 kJ/kg. If a copper coin at this temperature is completely melted by the absorption of 2000 J of heat, what is the mass of the coin?

   (A) 1/1080 kg
   (B) 1/540 kg
   (C) 1/108 kg
   (D) 1/100 kg
   (E) 1/50 kg

3. Water has the specific heat 4.186 kJ/kg·°C, a boiling point of 100°C, and a heat of vaporization of 2260 kJ/kg. A sealed beaker contains 100 g of water that's initially at 20°C. If the water absorbs 100 kJ of heat, what will its final temperature be?

   (A) 100°C
   (B) 119°C
   (C) 143°C
   (D) 183°C
   (E) 239°C

4. On a cold winter day (5°C), the foundation block for a statue is filled with 2.0 m^3 of concrete. By how much will the concrete's volume increase on a very warm summer day (35°C) if its coefficient of volume expansion is 4.0×10^{-5}/°C?

   (A) 160 cm^3
   (B) 1200 cm^3
   (C) 1600 cm^3
   (D) 2400 cm^3
   (E) 3200 cm^3

5. An ideal gas is confined to a container whose volume is fixed. If the container holds n moles of gas, by what factor will the pressure increase if the absolute temperature is increased by a factor of 2?

   (A) $2/(nR)$
   (B) 2
   (C) $2nR$
   (D) $2/n$
   (E) $2/R$

6. Two large glass containers of equal volume each hold 1 mole of gas. Container 1 is filled with hydrogen gas (2 g/mol), and Container 2 holds helium (4 g/mol). If the pressure of the gas in Container 1 equals the pressure of the gas in Container 2, which of the following is true?

   (A) The temperature of the gas in Container 1 is lower than the temperature of the gas in Container 2.
   (B) The temperature of the gas in Container 1 is greater than the temperature of the gas in Container 2.
   (C) The value of R for the gas in Container 1 is $\frac{1}{2}$ the value of R for the gas in Container 2.
   (D) The rms speed of the gas molecules in Container 1 is lower than the rms speed of the gas molecules in Container 2.
   (E) The rms speed of the gas molecules in Container 1 is greater than the rms speed of the gas molecules in Container 2.

7. Through a series of thermodynamic processes, the internal energy of a sample of confined gas is increased by 560 J. If the net amount of work done on the sample by its surroundings is 320 J, how much heat was transferred between the gas and its environment?

(A) 240 J absorbed
(B) 240 J dissipated
(C) 880 J absorbed
(D) 880 J dissipated
(E) None of the above

8. What's the total work performed on the gas as it's transformed from state *a* to state *c*, along the path indicated?

(A) 1500 J
(B) 3000 J
(C) 4500 J
(D) 5000 J
(E) 9500 J

9. In one of the steps of the Carnot cycle, the gas undergoes an isothermal expansion. Which of the following statements is true concerning this step?

(A) No heat is exchanged between the gas and its surroundings, because the process is isothermal.
(B) The temperature decreases because the gas expands.
(C) This step violates the Second Law of Thermodynamics because all the heat absorbed is transformed into work.
(D) The internal energy of the gas remains constant.
(E) The internal energy of the gas decreases due to the expansion.

10. What's the maximum possible efficiency for a heat engine operating between heat reservoirs whose temperatures are 800°C and 200°C?

(A) 25%
(B) 33%
(C) 50%
(D) 56%
(E) 75%

SECTION II: FREE RESPONSE

1. A student is performing a physics lab exercise to measure the specific heat of silver. The student knows that silver has a density of 10.5×10^3 kg/m^3 and that it melts at 962°C. The lab equipment includes a cube of silver 2.0 cm on each side, and a 75-gram beaker made of glass (specific heat = 0.84 kJ/kg·°C) filled with 100 g of water (specific heat = 4.186 kJ/kg·°C). Both the beaker and the water are at 20°C.

    (a) What is the mass of the silver cube?

    The silver cube is heated in an oven to a temperature of 500°C. The cube is quickly lifted out of the oven and placed into the water. A thermometer is placed in the water. The student then records the maximum temperature reading on the thermometer, 41°C.

    (b) (i) Write down equations for the heat gained by the water, the heat gained by the glass, and the heat lost by the silver cube.

    (ii) How are these related? (Assume that heat losses to the air and thermometer are negligible.)

    (c) Determine the specific heat of silver.

    (d) If the silver cube was at 20°C just before it was placed in the oven, and it reached its final temperature of 500°C in 5 minutes, find the rate (in watts) at which thermal energy was absorbed by the cube during heating.

2. A 0.4 mol sample of an ideal diatomic gas undergoes slow changes from state a to state b to state c and back to a along the cycle shown in the P–V diagram below:

Path ab is an isotherm, and it can be shown that the work done by the gas as it changes isothermally from state a to state b is given by the equation

$$W_{ab} = nRT \cdot \ln \frac{V_b}{V_a}$$

The molar heat capacities for the gas are $C_V = 20.8$ J/mol·K and $C_P = 29.1$ J/mol·K.

(a) What's the temperature of

   (i) state a?

   (ii) state b?

   (iii) state c?

(b) Determine the change in the internal energy of the gas for

   (i) step ab

   (ii) step bc

   (iii) step ca

(c) How much work, W_{ab}, is done by the gas during step ab?

(d) What is the total work done over cycle $abca$?

(e) (i) Is heat absorbed or discarded during step ab?

   (ii) If so, how much?

(f) What is the maximum possible efficiency (without violating the Second Law of Thermodynamics) for a cyclical heat engine that operates between the temperatures of states a and c?

10
ELECTRIC FORCES
AND FIELDS

ELECTRIC CHARGE

The basic components of atoms are protons, neutrons, and electrons. Protons and neutrons form the nucleus (and are referred to collectively as *nucleons*), while the electrons keep their distance, swarming around the nucleus. Most of an atom consists of empty space. In fact, if a nucleus were the size of the period at the end of this sentence, then the electrons would be 5 meters away. So what holds such an apparently tenuous structure together? One of the most powerful forces in nature: the *electromagnetic force*. Protons and electrons have a quality called **electric charge** that gives them an attractive force. Electric charge comes in two varieties; postitive and negative. A positive particle always attracts a negative particle, and particles of the same charge always repel each other. Protons are positively charged and electrons are negatively charged.

Protons and electrons are intrinsically charged, but bulk matter is not. This is because the amount of charge on a proton exactly balances the charge on an electron, which is quite remarkable in light of the fact that protons and electrons are very different particles. Since most atoms contain an equal number of protons and electrons, their overall electric charge is 0, because the negative charges cancel out the positive charges. Therefore, in order for matter to be **charged**, an imbalance between the numbers of protons and electrons must exist. This can be accomplished by either the removal or addition of electrons (that is, by the **ionization of** some of the object's atoms). If you remove electrons, then the object becomes positively-charged, while if you add electrons, then it becomes negatively-charged. Furthermore, charge is **conserved**. For example, if you rub a glass rod with a piece of silk, then the silk will acquire a negative charge and the glass will be left with an *equal* positive charge. *Net charge cannot be created or destroyed.* (*Charge* can be created or destroyed—it happens all the time—but *net* charge cannot.)

The magnitude of charge on an electron (and therefore on a proton) is denoted e. This stands for **elementary charge**, because it's the basic unit of electric charge. The charge of an ionized atom must be a whole number times e, because charge can be added or subtracted only in lumps of size e. For this reason we say that charge is **quantized**. To remind us of the quantized nature of electric charge, the charge of a particle (or object) is denoted by the letter q. In the SI system of units, charge is expressed in **coulombs** (abbreviated **C**). One coulomb is a tremendous amount of charge; the value of e is about 1.6×10^{-19} C.

COULOMB'S LAW

The electric force between two charged particles obeys the same mathematical law as the gravitational force between two masses, that is, it's an inverse-square law. The **electric force** between two particles with charges of q_1 and q_2, separated by a distance r, is given by the equation

$$F_E = k \frac{q_1 q_2}{r^2}$$

This is **Coulomb's Law**. We interpret a negative F_E as an attraction between the charges and a positive F_E as a repulsion. The value of the proportionality constant, k, depends on the material between the charged particles. In empty space (vacuum)—or air, for all practical purposes—it is called **Coulomb's constant** and has the approximate value $k_0 = 9 \times 10^9$ N $\cdot$ m^2/C^2. For reasons that will become clear later in this chapter, k_0 is usually written in terms of a fundamental constant known as the **permittivity of free space**, denoted ε_0, whose numerical value is approximately 8.85×10^{-12} C^2/N$\cdot$m^2. The equation that gives k_0 in terms of ε_0 is:

$$k_0 = \frac{1}{4\pi\varepsilon_0}$$

Coulomb's Law for the force between two point charges is then written as

$$F_E = \frac{1}{4\pi\varepsilon_0} \frac{q_1 q_2}{r^2}$$

Recall that the value of the universal gravitational constant, G, is 6.7×10^{-11} N $\cdot$ m^2/kg^2. The relative sizes of these fundamental constants show the relative strengths of the electric and gravitational forces. The value of k_0 is twenty orders of magnitude larger than G!

Example 10.1 Consider two small spheres, one carrying a charge of +1.5 nC and the other a charge of –2.0 nC, separated by a distance of 2 cm. Find the electric force between them. ("n" is the abbreviation for "nano," which means 10^{-9}.)

Solution. The electric force between the spheres is given by Coulomb's Law:

$$F_E = \frac{1}{4\pi\varepsilon_0}\frac{q_1 q_2}{r^2} = (9\times 10^9 \text{ N}\cdot\text{m}^2/\text{C}^2)\frac{(1.5\times 10^{-9}\text{ C})(-2.0\times 10^{-9}\text{ C})}{(2.0\times 10^{-2}\text{ m})^2} = -6.8\times 10^{-5}\text{ N}$$

The fact that F_E is negative means that the force is one of *attraction*, which we naturally expect, since one charge is positive and the other is negative. The force between the spheres is along the line that joins the charges, as we've illustrated below. The two forces shown form an action/reaction pair.

$$q_1 \oplus \xrightarrow{\ \mathbf{F}_E\ } \qquad \xleftarrow{\ \mathbf{F}_E\ } \ominus q_2$$

SUPERPOSITION

Consider three point charges: q_1, q_2, and q_3. The total electric force acting on, say, q_2 is simply the sum of $\mathbf{F}_{1\text{-on-2}}$, the electric force on q_2 due to q_1, and $\mathbf{F}_{3\text{-on-2}}$, the electric force on q_2 due to q_3:

$$\mathbf{F}_{\text{on 2}} = \mathbf{F}_{1\text{-on-2}} + \mathbf{F}_{3\text{-on-2}}$$

The fact that electric forces can be added in this way is known as **superposition**.

$$q_1 \oplus \qquad \begin{array}{c} \mathbf{F}_{\text{on 2}} \\ \mathbf{F}_{3\text{-on-2}} \\ \mathbf{F}_{1\text{-on-2}} \ominus \\ q_2 \end{array}$$

$$q_3 \ominus$$

Example 10.2 Consider four equal, positive point charges that are situated at the vertices of a square. Find the net electric force on a negative point charge placed at the square's center.

Solution. Refer to the diagram below. The attractive forces due to the two charges on each diagonal cancel out: $\mathbf{F}_1 + \mathbf{F}_3 = 0$, and $\mathbf{F}_2 + \mathbf{F}_4 = 0$, because the distances between the negative charge and the positive charges are all the same and the positive charges are all equivalent. Therefore, by symmetry, the net force on the center charge is zero. (See diagram next page.)

Solution. If we break $\mathbf{F}_1$ and $\mathbf{F}_2$ down into horizontal and vertical components, then by symmetry the two horizontal components will cancel each other out, and the two vertical components will add:

It is clear from the diagram on the left that $F_{1y} = F_1 \sin 45°$ and $F_{2y} = F_2 \sin 45°$. Also, the magnitude of $\mathbf{F}_1$ equals that of $\mathbf{F}_2$. So the net electric force on the negative charge is $F_{1y} + F_{2y} = 2F \sin 45°$, where F is the strength of the force between the negative charge and each of the positive charges. If s is the length of each side of the square, then the distance r between each positive charge and the negative charge is $r = \frac{1}{2}s\sqrt{2}$, and

$$F_E = 2F \sin 45° = 2 \frac{1}{4\pi\varepsilon_0} \frac{qQ}{r^2} \sin 45°$$

$$= 2(9 \times 10^9 \text{ N} \cdot \text{m}^2 / \text{C}^2) \frac{(1.5 \times 10^{-6} \text{ C})(6.2 \times 10^{-9} \text{ C})}{(\frac{1}{2} \cdot 4.0 \times 10^{-2} \cdot \sqrt{2} \text{ m})^2} \sin 45°$$

$$= 0.15 \text{ N}$$

The direction of the net force is straight upward, toward the center of the line that joins the two positive charges.

Example 10.4 Two pith balls of mass m are each given a charge of $+q$. They are hung side-by-side from two threads each of length L, and move apart as a result of their electrical repulsion. Find the equilibrium separation distance x in terms of m, q, and L. (Use the fact that if θ is small, then $\tan \theta \approx \sin \theta$.)

Solution. Three forces act on each ball: weight, tension, and electrical repulsion:

When the balls are in equilibrium, the net force each feels is zero. Therefore, the vertical component of $\mathbf{F}_T$ must cancel out $\mathbf{F}_w$ and the horizontal component of $\mathbf{F}_T$ must cancel out $\mathbf{F}_E$:

$$F_T \cos \theta = F_w \qquad \text{and} \qquad F_T \sin \theta = F_E$$

Dividing the second equation by the first, we get $\tan \theta = F_E / F_w$. Therefore,

$$\tan \theta = \frac{k \dfrac{q^2}{x^2}}{mg} = \frac{kq^2}{mgx^2}$$

Now, to approximate: If θ is small, then $\tan \theta \approx \sin \theta$ and, from the diagram, $\sin \theta = \frac{1}{2} x / L$. Therefore, the equation above becomes

$$\frac{\frac{1}{2}x}{L} = \frac{kq^2}{mgx^2} \quad \Rightarrow \quad \tfrac{1}{2}mgx^3 = kq^2 L \quad \Rightarrow \quad x = \sqrt[3]{\frac{2kq^2 L}{mg}}$$

THE ELECTRIC FIELD

The presence of a massive body such as the earth causes objects to experience a gravitational force directed toward the earth's center. For objects located outside the earth, this force varies inversely with the square of the distance and directly with the mass of the gravitational source. A vector diagram of the gravitational field surrounding the earth looks like this:

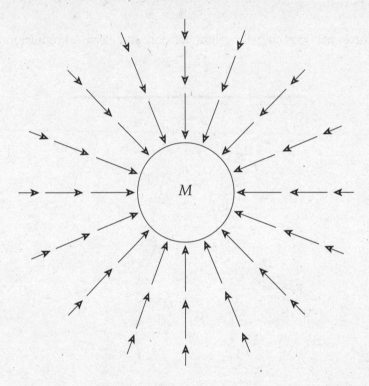

We can think of the space surrounding the earth as permeated by a **gravitational field** that's created by the earth. Any mass that's placed in this field then experiences a gravitational force due to this field.

The same process is used to describe the electric force. Rather than having two charges reach out across empty space to each other to produce a force, we can instead interpret the interaction in the following way: The presence of a charge creates an **electric field** in the space that surrounds it. Another charge placed in the field created by the first will experience a force due to the field.

Consider a point charge Q in a fixed position and assume that it's positive. Now imagine moving a tiny positive test charge q around to various locations near Q. At each location, measure the force that the test charge experiences, and call it $\mathbf{F}_{on\,q}$. Divide this force by the test charge q; the resulting vector is the **electric field vector**, $\mathbf{E}$, at that location:

$$\mathbf{E} = \frac{\mathbf{F}_{on\,q}}{q}$$

The reason for dividing by the test charge is simple. If we were to use a different test charge with, say, twice the charge of the first one, then each of the forces $\mathbf{F}$ we'd measure would be twice as much as before. But when we divided this new, stronger force by the new, greater test charge, the factors of 2 would cancel, leaving the same ratio as before. So this ratio tells us the intrinsic strength of the field due to the source charge, independent of whatever test charge we may use to measure it.

What would the electric field of a positive charge Q look like? Since the test charge used to measure the field is positive, every electric field vector would point radially away from the source charge. *If the source charge is positive, the electric field vectors point away from it; if the source charge is negative, then the field vectors point toward it.* And, since the force decreases as we get further away from the charge (as $1/r^2$), so does the electric field. This is why the electric field vectors farther from the source charge are shorter than those that are closer.

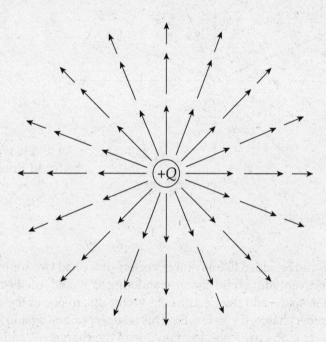

Since the force on the test charge q has a strength of $qQ/4\pi\varepsilon_0 r^2$, when we divide this by q, we get the expression for the strength of the electric field created by a point-charge source of magnitude Q:

$$E = \frac{1}{4\pi\varepsilon_0}\frac{Q}{r^2}$$

To make it easier to sketch an electric field, lines are drawn through the vectors such that the electric field vector is tangent to the line everywhere it's drawn.

Now, your first thought might be that obliterating the individual field vectors deprives us of information, since the length of the field vectors told us how strong the field was. Well, although the individual field vectors are gone, the strength of the field can be figured out by looking at the density of the field lines. Where the field lines are denser, the field is stronger.

Field is strong here
(field lines are dense).

+Q

Field is weak here
(field lines are sparse).

Electric field vectors can be added like any other vectors. If we had two source charges, their fields would overlap and effectively add; a third charge wandering by would feel the effect of the combined field. At each position in space, add the electric field vector due to one of the charges to the electric field vector due to the other charge: $E_{total} = E_1 + E_2$. (This is superposition again.) In the diagram below, E_1 is the electric field vector at a particular location due to the charge $+Q$, and E_2 is the electric field vector at that same location due to the other charge, $-Q$. Adding these vectors gives the overall field vector E_{total} at that location.

E_1

E_{total}

E_2

+Q

−Q

------source charges------

If this is done at enough locations, the electric field lines can be sketched.

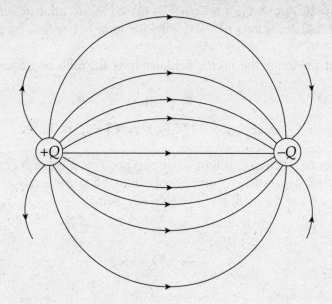

Notice that, like electric field vectors, electric field lines always point away from positive source charges and toward negative ones. Two equal but opposite charges, like the ones shown in the diagram above, form a pair called an **electric dipole**.

If a positive charge +q were placed in the electric field above, it would experience a force that is tangent to, and in the same direction as, the field line passing through +q's location. After all, electric fields are sketched from the point of view of what a positive test charge would do. On the other hand, if a negative charge −q were placed in the electric field, it would experience a force that is tangent to, but in the direction opposite from, the field line passing through −q's location.

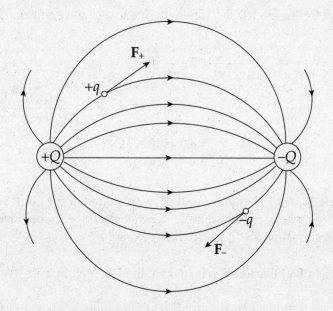

Finally, notice that electric field lines never cross.

Example 10.5 A charge $q = +3.0$ nC is placed at a location at which the electric field strength is 400 N/C. Find the force felt by the charge q.

Solution. From the definition of the electric field, we have the following equation:

$$\mathbf{F}_{\text{on } q} = q\mathbf{E}$$

Therefore, in this case, $F_{\text{on } q} = qE = (3 \times 10^{-9} \text{ C})(400 \text{ N/C}) = 1.2 \times 10^{-6} \text{ N}$.

Example 10.6 A dipole is formed by two point charges, each of magnitude 4.0 nC, separated by a distance of 6.0 cm. What is the strength of the electric field at the point midway between them?

Solution. Let the two source charges be denoted $+Q$ and $-Q$. At Point P, the electric field vector due to $+Q$ would point directly away from $+Q$, and the electric field vector due to $-Q$ would point directly toward $-Q$. Therefore, these two vectors point in the same direction (from $+Q$ to $-Q$), so their magnitudes would add.

Using the equation for the electric field strength due to a single point charge, we find that

$$E_{\text{total}} = \frac{1}{4\pi\varepsilon_0}\frac{Q}{r^2} + \frac{1}{4\pi\varepsilon_0}\frac{Q}{r^2} = 2\frac{1}{4\pi\varepsilon_0}\frac{Q}{r^2}$$

$$= 2(9 \times 10^9 \text{ N} \cdot \text{m}^2/\text{C}^2)\frac{4.0 \times 10^{-9} \text{ C}}{[\frac{1}{2}(6.0 \times 10^{-2} \text{ m})]^2}$$

$$= 8.0 \times 10^4 \text{ N/C}$$

Example 10.7 If a charge $q = -5.0$ pC were placed at the midway point described in the previous example, describe the force it would feel. ("p" is the abbreviation for "pico-," which means 10^{-12}.)

Solution. Since the field **E** at this location is known, the force felt by q is easy to calculate:

$$\mathbf{F}_{\text{on } q} = q\mathbf{E} = (-5.0 \times 10^{-12} \text{ C})(8.0 \times 10^4 \text{ N/C to the right}) = 4.0 \times 10^{-7} \text{ N to the } \textit{left}$$

Example 10.8 What can you say about the electric force that a charge would feel if it were placed at a location at which the electric field was zero?

Solution. Remember that $\mathbf{F}_{on\,q} = q\mathbf{E}$. So if $\mathbf{E} = 0$, then $\mathbf{F}_{on\,q} = 0$. (Zero field means zero force.)

Example 10.9 Positive charge is distributed uniformly over a large, horizontal plate, which then acts as the source of a vertical electric field. An object of mass 5 g is placed at a distance of 2 cm above the plate. If the strength of the electric field at this location is 10^6 N/C, how much charge would the object need to have in order for the electrical repulsion to balance the gravitational pull?

Solution. Clearly, since the plate is positively charged, the object would also have to carry a positive charge so that the electric force would be repulsive.

Let q be the charge on the object. Then, in order for F_E to balance mg, we must have

$$qE = mg \implies q = \frac{mg}{E} = \frac{(5\times10^{-3}\text{ kg})(9.8\text{ N}/\text{kg})}{10^6\text{ N}/\text{C}} = 5\times10^{-8}\text{ C} = 50\text{ nC}$$

Example 10.10 [C] A thin, nonconducting rod that carries a uniform linear charge density λ is bent into a semicircle of radius R. Find the electric field at the center of curvature of the semicircle.

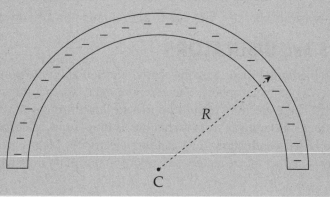

Solution. Refer to the figure below. Consider a small section of the rod subtended by an angle $d\theta$. The length of this section is (by the definition of radian measure) $R\,d\theta$, so the charge it carries is equal to $\lambda\,R\,d\theta$. The field it creates at C is $(1/4\pi\varepsilon_0)(\lambda\,R\,d\theta/R^2)$, pointing directly toward this section.

However, another section of the rod creates a field of the same strength and, as the figure shows, cancels out the horizontal component of the field created by the first section. Only the two vertical components, $dE\sin\theta$, remain, giving a net field due to these two symmetrically-located sections of the rod of $2\,dE\sin\theta$, where $dE = (1/4\pi\varepsilon_0)(\lambda\,R\,d\theta/R^2)$, pointing upward. The total electric field at C, due to all sections of the rod, is found by adding up the individual contributions:

$$
\begin{aligned}
E &= \int 2\,dE\sin\theta \\
&= \int_{\theta=0}^{\theta=\pi/2} 2\left(\frac{1}{4\pi\varepsilon_0}\cdot\frac{\lambda R d\theta}{R^2}\right)\sin\theta \\
&= \frac{\lambda}{2\pi\varepsilon_0 R}\int_0^{\pi/2}\sin\theta\,d\theta \\
&= \frac{\lambda}{2\pi\varepsilon_0 R}\left[-\cos\theta\right]_0^{\pi/2} \\
&= \frac{\lambda}{2\pi\varepsilon_0 R}
\end{aligned}
$$

Since the rod is negatively charged, the field **E**, at C, points upward, toward the rod.

CONDUCTORS AND INSULATORS

Materials can be classified into broad categories based on their ability to permit the flow of charge. If electrons were placed on a metal sphere, they would quickly spread out and cover the outside of the sphere uniformly. These electrons would be free to flow through the metal and redistribute themselves, moving to get as far away from each other as they could. Materials that permit the flow of excess charge are called **conductors**; they conduct electricity. Metals are the best examples of conductors, but others conductors are aqueous solutions that contain dissolved electrolytes (such as salt water). Metals conduct electricity because the structure of a typical metal consists of a lattice of nuclei and inner-shell electrons, with about one electron per atom not bound to its nucleus. Electrons are free to move about the lattice, creating a sort of sea of mobile (or conduction) electrons. This freedom allows excess charge to flow freely.

Insulators, on the other hand, closely guard their electrons—and even extra ones that might be added. Electrons are not free to roam throughout the atomic lattice. Examples of insulators are glass, wood, rubber, and plastic. If excess charge is placed on an insulator, it stays put.

Midway between conductors and insulators is a class of materials known as **semiconductors**. As the name indicates, they're kinda conductors. That is, they are less conducting than most metals, but more conducting than most insulators. Examples of semiconducting materials are silicon and germanium.

An extreme example of a conductor is the **superconductor**. This is a material that offers absolutely no resistance to the flow of charge; they are *perfect* conductors of electric charge. Many metals and ceramics become superconducting when they are brought to extremely low temperatures.

> **Example 10.11** A solid sphere of copper is given a negative charge. Discuss the electric field inside and outside the sphere.

Solution. The excess electrons that are deposited on the sphere move quickly to the outer surface (copper is a great conductor). *Any excess charge on a conductor resides entirely on the outer surface.*

excess charge
moves to outer
surface of conductor

Electric field
inside = 0

Once these excess electrons establish a uniform distribution on the outer surface of the sphere, there will be no net electric field within the sphere. Why not? Since there is no additional excess charge inside the conductor, there are no excess charges to serve as a source or sink of an electric field line cutting down into the sphere, because field lines begin or end on excess charges.

> *There can be no electrostatic field within the body of a conductor.*

In fact, you can shield yourself from electric fields simply by surrounding yourself with metal. Charges may move around on the outer surface of your cage, but within the cage, the electric field will be zero. For points outside the sphere, it can be shown that the sphere behaves as if all its excess charge were concentrated at its center. (Remember that this is just like the gravitational field due to a uniform spherical mass.) Also, *the electric field is always perpendicular to the surface, no matter what shape the surface may be.* See the diagram on the next page.

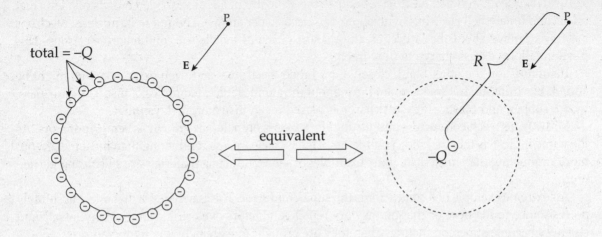

total = $-Q$

equivalent

R

$-Q$

[C] GAUSS'S LAW

For individual point charges, we can compute the electric field they produce by using the equation $E = Q/4\pi\varepsilon_0 r^2$ for each source charge, Q, then add up the resulting electric field vectors to obtain the net field. However, if the source charge is spread over a wire or a plate or throughout a cylinder or a sphere, then we need another method for determining the resulting electric field.

First, let's discuss the concept of **flux**. Consider the flow of a fluid through a pipe and imagine a small rectangular surface perpendicular to the flow. Multiplying the area of this rectangle (A) by the speed of the flow (v) gives the volume of fluid flowing through the surface per unit time. This is called the **fluid-volume flux**, symbolized Φ (the uppercase Greek letter *phi*):

area = A

$\mathbf{v}$

$\Phi = Av$

In general, the fluid-volume flux through the surface is given by the equation $\Phi = Av\cos\theta$, where θ is the angle between the velocity $\mathbf{v}$ of the flow and the normal to the surface. If this rectangular surface were tilted at an angle θ to the flow, then less fluid would flow through it per unit time. In fact, if θ were 90°, then no fluid would flow through the surface. (You might also recognize this as the dot product, $\Phi = \mathbf{A} \cdot \mathbf{v}$, where $\mathbf{A}$ is the vector whose magnitude is A and whose direction is normal to the surface.)

All the fluid that used to cross the surface down here (below the dotted line) now no longer passes through the tilted surface.
So, the flux through the surface has been decreased. It's now the same as the flux through the rectangular portion perpendicular to **v** that lies above the dotted line. This area is $A \cos \theta$.

$$\Phi = \mathbf{A} \cdot \mathbf{v}$$
$$= Av \cos \theta$$

Let's now apply this same idea to an electric field. Consider a source charge $+Q$ and imagine a tiny patch (area = A) of a spherical surface of radius r. The diagram below shows a cross-section of the situation.

Then we can think of the electric field vectors flowing through the area A and, since **E** is everywhere perpendicular to this patch area A, the **electric flux** (Φ_E) would simply be the product: $\Phi_E = EA$. Although the electric field isn't really flowing like the fluid in the previous discussion, we can still use the same terminology. It might be more appropriate to think of the electric flux as a measure of the amount of electric field passing through the surface.

In general, the electric flux through a patch of area dA is given by the equation

$$d\Phi_E = \mathbf{E} \cdot d\mathbf{A}$$

The total electric flux is then found by adding (that is, integrating) all of the contributions:

$$\Phi_E = \int d\Phi_E = \int \mathbf{E} \cdot d\mathbf{A}$$

Let's now imagine a *closed* surface—a sphere, for simplicity—surrounding the charge $+Q$. Place this closed spherical surface at a distance r from $+Q$.

imaginary spherical surface
surrounding the charge $+Q$

E

r

$+Q \oplus$

The total flux outward through this closed surface is

$$\Phi_E = EA = E(4\pi r^2)$$

We know what the electric field is at the position of this imaginary sphere; it's $E = Q/4\pi\varepsilon_0 r^2$. Therefore, the previous equation becomes

$$\Phi_E = \frac{1}{4\pi\varepsilon_0}\frac{Q}{r^2} \cdot 4\pi r^2 = \frac{Q}{\varepsilon_0}$$

(Now you can finally see why we write Coulomb's constant, k_0, as $1/4\pi\varepsilon_0$. It makes the 4π's cancel out in this equation.) It can be shown that the previous equation holds true for *any closed surface*; the total electric flux through the surface is equal to $1/\varepsilon_0$ times the charge enclosed:

$$\Phi_E = \frac{Q_{enclosed}}{\varepsilon_0}$$

This is **Gauss's Law**. The quantity $Q_{enclosed}$ is the algebraic sum of the charges inside. For example, if the imaginary closed surface we construct encloses, say, charges of $+Q$ and $-3Q$, then the total charge enclosed is $-2Q$, the algebraic sum, so this is $Q_{enclosed}$ in this case. In fact, many people place a Σ in front of $Q_{enclosed}$ to remind them that they need to take the *sum* of the charges enclosed when using Gauss's Law. The power of Gauss's Law to determine electric fields is evident if we can write Φ_E in terms of E—and this requires symmetry—because then the equation can be solved for E. The imaginary closed surface that we will construct when using Gauss's Law to determine an electric field is known as a **Gaussian surface**.

Example 10.12 Consider a long, straight wire carrying a total charge of $+Q$, distributed uniformly along its entire length, L. Use Gauss's Law to find an expression for the electric field created by the wire.

Solution. By symmetry, the electric field must point radially away from the wire. To take advantage of this symmetry, we will construct a cylindrical Gaussian surface—of length x and radius r—around the wire:

The electric field is always perpendicular to the lateral surface area, A, of the cylinder. Therefore, the electric flux through the cylinder is equal to $EA = E(2\pi rx)$. The flux through each of the two lids of the cylinder is zero, because there **E** is parallel to the end surfaces (so $\mathbf{E} \cdot d\mathbf{A} = E\, dA \cos 90° = 0$). So the total electric flux through the Gaussian surface is $\Phi_E = 0 + E(2\pi rx) + 0 = E(2\pi rx)$. Next we need to know the charge enclosed by the Gaussian surface. Since a total charge of Q is distributed uniformly along the entire length L of the wire, the amount of charge on a section of length x is $(x/L)Q$. Therefore, Gauss's Law becomes

$$\Phi_E = \frac{Q_{\text{enclosed}}}{\varepsilon_0}$$

$$E \cdot 2\pi rx = \frac{(x/L)Q}{\varepsilon_0}$$

$$E = \frac{Q/L}{2\pi\varepsilon_0 r}$$

The ratio Q/L (charge per unit length) is called the *linear charge density*, and is denoted by λ; using this notation, the electric field at a distance r from the wire is given by the equation $E = \lambda/(2\pi\varepsilon_0 r)$. (If the charge on the wire were $-Q$, then the field would point radially inward.)

> **Example 10.13** A very large rectangular plate has a surface charge density of $+\sigma$ (this is the charge per unit area). Use Gauss's Law to determine an expression for the electric field it creates.

Solution. By symmetry, the electric field lines must be perpendicular to the plate. We will construct a cylindrical Gaussian surface, with cross-sectional area A and total length $2r$, perpendicular to the plate:

The electric flux through the lateral surface area is now zero, since **E** is parallel to the cylindrical surface here. However, there is flux through the end caps: $EA + EA = 2EA$. (Flux outward from the closed surface is counted as positive; flux inward is counted as negative.) Therefore,

$$\Phi_E = \frac{Q_{enclosed}}{\varepsilon_0}$$

$$2EA = \frac{\sigma A}{\varepsilon_0}$$

$$E = \frac{\sigma}{2\varepsilon_0}$$

The electric field does not depend on the distance r from the plate. This would only be true if the plate had infinite area. In practical terms, this result means that if we are close to a very large plate (and away from its edges), then the plate looks infinite, and moving a small amount toward or away from the plate won't make much difference; the electric field will remain essentially constant.

> **Example 10.14** A nonconducting sphere of radius a has excess charge distributed throughout its volume so that the volume charge density ρ as a function of r (the distance from the sphere's center) is given by the equation $\rho(r) = \rho_0(r/a)^2$, where ρ_0 is a constant. Determine the electric field at points inside and outside the sphere.

Solution. In order to apply Gauss's Law, we need to find the total charge enclosed by a Gaussian surface of radius r. Since the charge density depends on r only, consider a thin spherical shell of radius R and thickness dR.

Gaussian surface

The shell's volume is $dV = 4\pi R^2\, dR$, so the charge contained in the shell is

$$dQ = \rho\ dV = \rho_0 (R/a)^2 \cdot 4\pi R^2\, dR$$

The total charge enclosed within a sphere of radius r is found by adding up all the charges on these shells, from $R = 0$ to $R = r$:

$$Q(\text{within } r) = \int dQ = \int_{R=0}^{R=r} \rho_0 (R/a)^2 \cdot 4\pi R^2\, dR \qquad (*)$$

$$= (4\pi\rho_0 / a^2)\int_{R=0}^{R=r} R^4\, dR$$

$$= \frac{4\pi\rho_0}{5a^2} r^5$$

The electric flux through the spherical Gaussian surface of radius r is

$$\Phi_E = EA = E(4\pi r^2)$$

so, by Gauss's Law,

$$\Phi_E = \frac{Q_{\text{encl}}}{\varepsilon_0}$$

$$E(4\pi r^2) = \frac{1}{\varepsilon_0} \frac{4\pi\rho_0}{5a^2} r^5$$

$$E = \frac{\rho_0}{5\varepsilon_0 a^2} r^3$$

This gives the electric field at all points within the given sphere. For points outside, we first figure out the charge on the entire sphere, which from the integral (*) above, with $r = a$ is

$$Q(\text{within } a) = \int dQ = \int_{R=0}^{R=a} \rho_0 (R/a)^2 \cdot 4\pi R^2 \, dR$$

$$= (4\pi\rho_0 / a^2) \int_{R=0}^{R=a} R^4 \, dR$$

$$= \frac{4\pi\rho_0 a^3}{5}$$

Then, applying Gauss's Law again on a spherical Gaussian surface of radius $r > a$, we get

$$\Phi_E = \frac{Q_{\text{encl}}}{\varepsilon_0}$$

$$E(4\pi r^2) = \frac{1}{\varepsilon_0} \frac{4\pi\rho_0 a^3}{5}$$

$$E = \frac{\rho_0 a^3}{5\varepsilon_0 r^2}$$

To summarize then, we have found

$$E(r) = \begin{cases} \dfrac{\rho_0}{5\varepsilon_0 a^2} r^3 & \text{for } r \le a \\[3mm] \dfrac{\rho_0 a^3}{5\varepsilon_0 r^2} & \text{for } r \ge a \end{cases}$$

Example 10.15 Use Gauss's Law to show that the electric field inside a charged hollow metal sphere is zero.

Solution. Recall that for a conductor, any excess charge resides on its surface. Therefore, if a Gaussian surface is constructed anywhere *within* the metal, it contains no net charge, so **E = 0** everywhere inside the sphere.

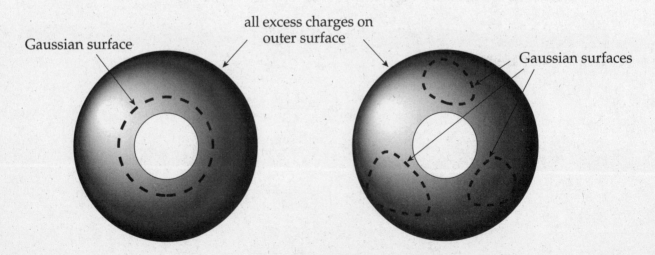

Gaussian surface

all excess charges on outer surface

Gaussian surfaces

Example 10.16 Consider a neutral, hollow metal sphere. Imagine that a charge of $+q$ could be introduced into the cavity, insulated from the inner wall. What will happen?

Solution. *A static electric field cannot be sustained within the body of a conductor.* Therefore, enough electrons will migrate to the inner wall of the cavity to form a *shield* of charge $-q$ around the inside charge $+q$.

Gaussian surface

E = 0 inside

+q

A charge of $-q$ forms on the inner surface to "guard" the interior of the conductor. . .

. . . leaving a charge of $+q$ on the exterior of the sphere.

To see why this must be so, if any Gaussian surface surrounding the cavity is drawn within the conductor then, because E *must* be 0 inside, the electric flux must be 0, so $Q_{enclosed}$ must be 0. The only way to ensure that $Q_{enclosed} = 0$ is to have a charge of $-q$ on the inner wall of the cavity. Since the sphere was originally neutral, an excess charge of $+q$ will then appear on the outer surface.

Example 10.17 A solid metal sphere of radius a, carrying a charge of $+q$, is placed inside and concentric with a neutral hollow metal sphere of inner radius b and outer radius c. Determine the electric field for $r < a$, $a < r < b$, and $r < b < c$. Also, describe the charge distributions.

Solution. For $r < a$, the electric field is 0, since there can be no electric field within the body of a conductor. For r between a and b, the inner sphere acts like a point charge of $+q$ at its center, so $E = q/(4\pi\varepsilon_0 r^2)$. For r between b and c, the electric field is again zero, since there can be no electric field within the body of a conductor. For $r > c$, the ensemble behaves as if all its charge were concentrated at its center, so once again, $E = q/(4\pi\varepsilon_0 r^2)$.

The charge on the sphere of radius a will be at its surface. To protect the interior of the outer spherical shell from an electric field, a charge of $-q$ will reside on the surface of radius b (shielding the charge of $+q$ that's introduced into the cavity), leaving $+q$ to appear on the outer surface (radius c).

CHAPTER 10 REVIEW QUESTIONS

SECTION I: MULTIPLE CHOICE

1. If the distance between two positive point charges is tripled, then the strength of the electrostatic repulsion between them will decrease by a factor of

    (A) 3
    (B) 6
    (C) 8
    (D) 9
    (E) 12

2. Two 1 kg spheres each carry a charge of magnitude 1 C. How does F_E, the strength of the electric force between the spheres, compare to F_G, the strength of their gravitational attraction?

    (A) $F_E < F_G$
    (B) $F_E = F_G$
    (C) $F_E > F_G$
    (D) If the charges on the spheres are of the same sign, then $F_E > F_G$; but if the charges on the spheres are of opposite sign, then $F_E < F_G$.
    (E) Cannot be determined without knowing the distance between the spheres

3. The figure above shows three point charges, all positive. If the net electric force on the center charge is zero, what is the value of y/x?

    (A) 4/9
    (B) $\sqrt{2/3}$
    (C) $\sqrt{3/2}$
    (D) 3/2
    (E) 9/4

4.

    The figure above shows two point charges, $+Q$ and $-Q$. If the negative charge were absent, the electric field at Point P due to $+Q$ would have strength E. With $-Q$ in place, what is the strength of the total electric field at P, which lies at the midpoint of the line segment joining the charges?

    (A) 0
    (B) $E/4$
    (C) $E/2$
    (D) E
    (E) $2E$

5. A sphere of charge $+Q$ is fixed in position. A smaller sphere of charge $+q$ is placed near the larger sphere and released from rest. The small sphere will move away from the large sphere with

    (A) decreasing velocity and decreasing acceleration.
    (B) decreasing velocity and increasing acceleration.
    (C) decreasing velocity and constant acceleration.
    (D) increasing velocity and decreasing acceleration.
    (E) increasing velocity and increasing acceleration.

6. An object of charge $+q$ feels an electric force $\mathbf{F}_E$ when placed at a particular location in an electric field, $\mathbf{E}$. Therefore, if an object of charge $-2q$ were placed at the same location where the first charge was, it would feel an electric force of

    (A) $-\mathbf{F}_E/2$
    (B) $-2\mathbf{F}_E$
    (C) $-2q\mathbf{F}_E$
    (D) $-2\mathbf{F}_E/q$
    (E) $-\mathbf{F}_E/(2q)$

7. A charge of $-3Q$ is transferred to a solid metal sphere of radius r. Where will this excess charge reside?

(A) $-Q$ at the center, and $-2Q$ on the outer surface

(B) $-2Q$ at the center, and $-Q$ on the outer surface

(C) $-3Q$ at the center

(D) $-3Q$ on the outer surface

(E) $-Q$ at the center, $-Q$ in a ring of radius $\frac{1}{2}r$, and $-Q$ on the outer surface

8. [C] The figure below shows four point charges and the cross section of a Gaussian surface:

Which of the following statements is true concerning the situation depicted?

(A) The net electric flux through the Gaussian surface depends on all four charges shown, but the electric field at point P depends only on charges Q_2 and Q_3.

(B) The net electric flux through the Gaussian surface depends only on charges Q_2 and Q_3, but the electric field at point P depends on all four charges.

(C) The net electric flux through the Gaussian surface depends only on charges Q_2 and Q_3, and the electric field at point P depends only on charges Q_2, Q_3, and Q_4.

(D) The net electric flux through the Gaussian surface depends only on charges Q_1 and Q_4, and the electric field at point P depends only on charges Q_2 and Q_3.

(E) Both the net electric flux through the Gaussian surface and the electric field at point P depend on all four charges.

9. [C] A nonconducting sphere of radius R contains a total charge of $-Q$ distributed uniformly throughout its volume (that is, the volume charge density, ρ, is constant).

The magnitude of the electric field at point P, at a distance $r < R$ from the sphere's center, is equal to

(A) $\dfrac{1}{4\pi\varepsilon_0}\dfrac{Q}{R^3}r$

(B) $\dfrac{1}{4\pi\varepsilon_0}\dfrac{Q}{R^2}r^2$

(C) $\dfrac{1}{4\pi\varepsilon_0}\dfrac{Q}{R^3}r^3$

(D) $\dfrac{1}{4\pi\varepsilon_0}\dfrac{Q}{R^3r^2}$

(E) $\dfrac{1}{4\pi\varepsilon_0}\dfrac{Q}{r^2}$

10. [C] Calculate the electric flux through a Gaussian surface of area A enclosing an electric dipole where each charge has magnitude q.

(A) 0
(B) $Aq/(4\pi\varepsilon_0)$
(C) $Aq^2/(4\pi\varepsilon_0)$
(D) $Aq/(4\pi\varepsilon_0 r)$
(E) $Aq/(4\pi\varepsilon_0 r^2)$

SECTION II: FREE RESPONSE

1. In the figure shown, all four charges ($+Q$, $+Q$, $-q$, and $-q$) are situated at the corners of a square. The net electric force on each charge $+Q$ is zero.

   (a) Express the magnitude of q in terms of Q.

   (b) Is the net electric force on each charge $-q$ also equal to zero? Justify your answer.

   (c) Determine the electric field at the center of the square.

2. Two charges, $+Q$ and $+2Q$, are fixed in place along the y axis of an x-y coordinate system as shown in the figure below. Charge 1 is at the point $(0, a)$, and Charge 2 is at the point $(0 -2a)$.

   (a) Find the electric force (magnitude and direction) felt by Charge 1 due to Charge 2.

   (b) Find the electric field (magnitude and direction) at the origin created by both Charges 1 and 2.

   (c) Is there a point on the x axis where the total electric field is zero? If so, where? If not, explain briefly.

   (d) Is there a point on the y axis where the total electric field is zero? If so, where? If not, explain briefly.

   (e) If a small negative charge, $-q$, of mass m were placed at the origin, determine its initial acceleration (magnitude and direction).

3. A conducting spherical shell of inner radius a and outer radius b is inside (and concentric with) a larger conducting spherical shell of inner radius c and outer radius d. The inner shell carries a net charge of $+2q$, and the outer shell has a net charge of $+3q$.

(a)   Determine the electric field for

   (i) $r < a$

   (ii) $a < r < b$

   (iii) $b < r < c$

   (iv) $c < r < d$

   (v) $r > d$

(b)   Show in the figure the charges that reside on or inside each of the two shells.

4.[C] A positively-charged, thin nonconducting rod of length ℓ lies along the y axis with its midpoint at the origin. The linear charge density within the rod is uniform and denoted by λ. Points P_1 and P_2 lie on the positive x axis, at distances x_1 and x_2, respectively, from the rod.

(a) Use Gauss's Law to approximate the electric field at Point P_1, given that x_1 is very small compared to ℓ. Write your answer in terms of λ, x_1, and fundamental constants.

(b) What is the total charge Q on the rod?

(c) Compute the electric field at Point P_2, given that x_2 is not small compared to ℓ. For $x_2 = \ell$, write your answer in terms of Q, ℓ, and fundamental constants. You may use the fact that

$$\int (x^2 + y^2)^{-3/2}\,dy = \frac{y}{x^2\sqrt{x^2+y^2}} + c$$

5. [C] A solid glass sphere of radius a contains excess charge distributed throughout its volume such that the volume charge density depends on the distance r from the sphere's center according to the equation

$$\rho(r) = \rho_s(r/a)$$

where ρ_s is a constant.

(a) What are the units of ρ_s?

(b) Compute the total charge Q on the sphere.

(c) Determine the magnitude of the electric field for

(i) $r < a$

(ii) $r \geq a$

Write your answers to both (i) and (ii) in terms of Q, a, r, and fundamental constants.

(d) Sketch the electric field magnitude E as a function of r on the graph below. Be sure to indicate on the vertical axis the value of E at $r = a$.

11

ELECTRIC POTENTIAL AND CAPACITANCE

INTRODUCTION

When an object moves in a gravitational field, it usually experiences a change in kinetic energy and in gravitational potential energy due to the work done on the object by gravity. Similarly, when a charge move in an electric field, it generally experiences a change in kinetic energy and in electrical potential energy due to the work done on it by the electric field. By exploring the idea of electric potential, we can simplify our calculations of work and energy changes within electric fields.

ELECTRICAL POTENTIAL ENERGY

When a charge moves in an electric field, then unless its displacement is always perpendicular to the field, the electric force does work on the charge. If W_E is the work done by the electric force, then the change in the charge's **electrical potential energy** is defined by

$$\Delta U_E = -W_E$$

Notice that this is the same equation that defined the change in the gravitational potential energy of an object of mass m undergoing a displacement in a gravitational field ($\Delta U_G = -W_G$).

Example 11.1 A positive charge $+q$ moves from position A to position B in a uniform electric field **E**:

What is its change in electrical potential energy?

Solution. Since the field is uniform, the electric force that the charge feels, $F_E = qE$, is constant. Since q is positive, F_E points in the same direction as **E**, and, as the figure shows, they point in the same direction as the displacement, **r**. This makes the work done by the electric field equal to $W_E = F_E r = qEr$, so the change in the electrical potential energy is

$$\Delta U_E = -qEr$$

Notice that the change in potential energy is negative, which means that potential energy has decreased; this always happens when the field does positive work. It's just like when you drop a rock to the ground: Gravity does positive work, and the rock loses gravitational potential energy.

Example 11.2 Do the previous problem, but consider the case of a negative charge, $-q$.

Solution. In this case, an outside agent must be pushing the charge to make it move, because the electric force *naturally* pushes negative charges against field lines. Therefore, we expect that the work done by the electric field is negative. The electric force, $F_E = (-q)E$, points in the direction opposite to the displacement, so the work it does is $W_E = -F_E r = -qEr = -qEr$, so the change in electrical potential energy is positive: $\Delta U_E = -W_E = -(-qEr) = qEr$. Since the change in potential energy is positive, the potential energy increased; this always happens when the field does negative work. It's like when you lift a rock off the ground: Gravity does negative work, and the rock gains gravitational potential energy.

Example 11.3 A positive charge $+q$ moves from position A to position B in a uniform electric field **E**:

What is its change in electrical potential energy?

Solution. The electric force felt by the charge q is $\mathbf{F}_E = q\mathbf{E}$ and this force is parallel to **E**, because q is positive. In this case, because $\mathbf{F}_E$ is not parallel to **r** (as it was in Example 11.1), we will use the more general definition of work:

$$W_E = \mathbf{F}_E \cdot \mathbf{r} = F_E\, r \cos\theta = qEr \cos\theta$$

But $r \cos\theta = d$, so

$$W_E = qEd$$

and

$$\Delta U_E = -W_E = -qEd$$

Because the electric force is a conservative force, which means that the work done does not depend on the path that connects the positions A and B, the work calculated above could have been figured out by considering the path from A to B composed of the segments $\mathbf{r}_1$ and $\mathbf{r}_2$:

Along $\mathbf{r}_1$, the electric force does no work since this displacement is perpendicular to the force. Thus, the work done by the electric field as q moves from A to B is simply equal to the work it does along $\mathbf{r}_2$. And since the length of $\mathbf{r}_2$ is $d = r \cos\theta$, we have $W_E = F_E d = qEd$, just as before.

Example 11.4 A positive charge $+q$ moves from position A to B in the electric field, **E**, created by the source charge $+Q$ (only a portion of the electric field is drawn):

What is its change in electrical potential energy?

Solution. As you know, movement that's perpendicular to the field lines causes the electric field to do no work. So replace the path pictured by another path, composed of $\mathbf{r}_1$ and $\mathbf{r}_2$:

At every point along the arc $\mathbf{r}_1$, the electric force is radial and thus perpendicular to the displacement, so $\mathbf{F}_E$ does no work on the charge as it moves along $\mathbf{r}_1$. But along radial line $\mathbf{r}_2$, the electric force is parallel to the displacement. The work done by the electric force is

$$W_E = \int_{\mathbf{r}_2} \mathbf{F}_E \cdot d\mathbf{r} = \int_{r=r_A}^{r=r_B} \frac{1}{4\pi\varepsilon_0} \frac{Qq}{r^2} dr$$

$$= \frac{Qq}{4\pi\varepsilon_0} \int_{r=r_A}^{r=r_B} \frac{1}{r^2} dr$$

$$= \frac{Qq}{4\pi\varepsilon_0} \left[-\frac{1}{r} \right]_{r_A}^{r_B}$$

$$= \frac{Qq}{4\pi\varepsilon_0} \left(\frac{1}{r_A} - \frac{1}{r_B} \right)$$

and the change in electrical potential energy is

$$\Delta U_E = -W_E = \frac{Qq}{4\pi\varepsilon_0} \left(\frac{1}{r_B} - \frac{1}{r_A} \right)$$

This equation holds true regardless of the signs of Q and q. Our illustration had both Q and q positive, but this procedure can be used with any combination of signs and the result will be the same. Since the equation can be written in the form

$$U_B - U_A = \frac{1}{4\pi\varepsilon_0} \frac{Qq}{r_B} - \frac{1}{4\pi\varepsilon_0} \frac{Qq}{r_A}$$

we can define the potential energy of two charges (let's just call them q_1 and q_2), separated by a distance r to be

$$U = \frac{1}{4\pi\varepsilon_0} \frac{q_1 q_2}{r}$$

This definition says that when the charges are infinitely far apart, their potential energy is zero.

> **Example 11.5** A positive charge $q_1 = +2 \times 10^{-6}$ C is held stationary, while a negative charge, $q_2 = -1 \times 10^{-8}$ C, is released from rest at a distance of 10 cm from q_1. Find the kinetic energy of charge q_2 when it's 1 cm from q_1.

Solution. The gain in kinetic energy is equal to the loss in potential energy; you know this from Conservation of Energy. The change in electrical potential energy is

$$\Delta U = \frac{q_1 q_2}{4\pi\varepsilon_0} \left(\frac{1}{r_B} - \frac{1}{r_A} \right)$$

$$= (9 \times 10^9 \text{ N} \cdot \text{m}^2 / \text{C}^2)(+2 \times 10^{-6} \text{ C})(-1 \times 10^{-8} \text{ C}) \left(\frac{1}{0.01 \text{ m}} - \frac{1}{0.10 \text{ m}} \right)$$

$$= -0.016 \text{ J}$$

So the gain in kinetic energy is +0.016 J. Since q_2 started from rest (with no kinetic energy), this is the kinetic energy of q_2 when it's 1 cm from q_1.

Example 11.6 Two positive charges, q_1 and q_2, are held in the positions shown below. How much work would be required to bring (from infinity) a third positive charge, q_3, and place it so that the three charges form the corners of an equilateral triangle of side length s?

Solution. An external agent would need to do positive work, equal in magnitude to the negative work done by the electric force on q_3 as it is brought into place, so let's first compute this quantity. Let's first compute the work done *by the electric force* as q_3 is brought in. Since q_3 is fighting against both q_1's and q_2's electric field, the total work done on q_3 by the electric force, W_E, is equal to the work done on q_3 by q_1 ($W_{1\text{-}3}$) plus the work done on q_3 by q_2 ($W_{2\text{-}3}$). Using the equation $W_E = -\Delta U_E$ and the one we derived above for ΔU_E, we have

$$W_{1\text{-}3} + W_{2\text{-}3} = -\Delta U_{1\text{-}3} + -\Delta U_{2\text{-}3}$$

$$= -\frac{q_1 q_3}{4\pi\varepsilon_0}\left(\frac{1}{s}-0\right) + -\frac{q_2 q_3}{4\pi\varepsilon_0}\left(\frac{1}{s}-0\right)$$

$$= -\left(\frac{1}{4\pi\varepsilon_0}\frac{q_1 q_3}{s} + \frac{1}{4\pi\varepsilon_0}\frac{q_2 q_3}{s}\right)$$

Therefore, the work that an external agent must do to bring q_3 into position is

$$-W_E = \frac{1}{4\pi\varepsilon_0}\frac{q_1 q_3}{s} + \frac{1}{4\pi\varepsilon_0}\frac{q_2 q_3}{s}$$

In general, the work required by an external agent to assemble a collection of point charges $q_1, q_2, \ldots, q_n$ (bringing each one from infinity), such that the final fixed distance between q_i and q_j is r_{ij}, is equal to the total electrical potential of the arrangement:

$$W_{\text{by external agent}} = U_{\text{total}} = \frac{1}{4\pi\varepsilon_0}\sum_{i<j}\frac{q_i q_j}{r_{ij}}$$

ELECTRIC POTENTIAL

Let W_E be the work done by the electric field on a charge q as it undergoes a displacement. If another charge, say $2q$, were to undergo the same displacement, the electric force would be twice as great on this second charge, and the work done by the electric field would be twice as much, $2W_E$. Since the work would be twice as much in the second case, the change in electrical potential energy would be twice as great as well, but the ratio of the change in potential energy to the charge would be the same: $\Delta U_E/q = 2\Delta U_E/2q$. This ratio says something about the *field* and the *displacement*, but not the charge that made the move. The change in **electric potential**, ΔV, is defined as this ratio:

$$\Delta V = \frac{\Delta U_E}{q}$$

Electric potential is electrical potential energy *per unit charge*; the units of electric potential are joules per coulomb. One joule per coulomb is called one **volt** (abbreviated V); so $1\ \text{J/C} = 1\ \text{V}$.

Consider the electric field that's created by a point source charge Q. If a charge q moves from a distance r_A to a distance r_B from Q, then the change in the potential energy is

$$U_B - U_A = \frac{Qq}{4\pi\varepsilon_0}\left(\frac{1}{r_B} - \frac{1}{r_A}\right)$$

The difference in electric potential between positions A and B in the field created by Q is

$$V_B - V_A = \frac{U_B - U_A}{q} = \frac{Q}{4\pi\varepsilon_0}\left(\frac{1}{r_B} - \frac{1}{r_A}\right)$$

If we designate $V_A \to 0$ as $r_A \to \infty$ (an assumption that's stated on the AP exam), then the electric potential at a distance r from Q is

$$V = \frac{1}{4\pi\varepsilon_0}\frac{Q}{r}$$

Notice that the potential depends on the source charge making the field and the distance from it.

> **Example 11.7** Let $Q = 2 \times 10^{-9}$ C. What is the potential at a point P that is 2 cm from Q?

Solution. Relative to $V = 0$ at infinity, we have

$$V = \frac{1}{4\pi\varepsilon_0}\frac{Q}{r} = \left(9\times10^9\ \text{N}\cdot\text{m}^2/\text{C}^2\right)\frac{2\times10^{-9}\ \text{C}}{0.02\ \text{m}} = 900\ \text{V}$$

This means that the work done by the electric field on a charge of q coulombs brought to a point 2 cm from Q would be $-900q$ joules.

Notice that, like potential energy, potential is a *scalar*. In the preceding example, we didn't have to specify the direction of the vector from the position of Q to the point P, because it didn't matter. At *any* point on a sphere that's 2 cm from Q, the potential will be 900 V. These spheres around Q are called **equipotential surfaces**, and they're surfaces of constant potential. Their cross sections in any plane are circles and are (therefore) perpendicular to the electric field lines. The equipotentials are always perpendicular to the electric field lines.

Example 11.8 How much work is done by the electric field as a charge moves along an equipotential surface?

Solution. If the charge always remains on a single equipotential, then, by definition, the potential, V, never changes. Therefore, $\Delta V = 0$, so $\Delta U_E = 0$. Since $W_E = -\Delta U_E$, the work done by the electric field is zero.

Example 11.9 If charges $q_1 = 4 \times 10^{-9}$ C and $q_2 = -6 \times 10^{-9}$ C are stationary, calculate the potential at point P in the figure below:

Solution. Potentials add like ordinary numbers. Therefore, the potential at A is just the sum of the potentials at A due to q_1 and q_2. Note that the distance from q_1 to A is 5 cm.

$$V = \frac{1}{4\pi\varepsilon_0}\frac{q_1}{r_{1A}} + \frac{1}{4\pi\varepsilon_0}\frac{q_2}{r_{2A}}$$

$$= \frac{1}{4\pi\varepsilon_0}\left(\frac{q_1}{r_{1A}} + \frac{q_2}{r_{2A}}\right)$$

$$= (9\times10^9 \text{ N}\cdot\text{m}^2/\text{C}^2)\left(\frac{4\times10^{-9} \text{ C}}{0.05 \text{ m}} + \frac{-6\times10^{-9} \text{ C}}{0.03 \text{ m}}\right)$$

$$= -1080 \text{ V}$$

Example 11.10 How much work would it take to move a charge $q = +1 \times 10^{-2}$ C from Point A to Point B (the point midway between q_1 and q_2)?

Solution. $\Delta U_E = q\Delta V$, so if we calculate the potential difference between Points A and B and multiply by q, we will have found the change in the electrical potential energy: $\Delta U_{A \to B} = q\Delta V_{A \to B}$. Then, since the work by the electric field is $-\Delta U$, the work required by an external agent is ΔU. In this case, the potential at point B is

$$V_B = \frac{1}{4\pi\varepsilon_0}\left(\frac{q_1}{r_{1B}} + \frac{q_2}{r_{2B}}\right)$$

$$= (9 \times 10^9 \text{ N} \cdot \text{m}^2 / \text{C}^2)\left(\frac{4 \times 10^{-9} \text{ C}}{0.02 \text{ m}} + \frac{-6 \times 10^{-9} \text{ C}}{0.02 \text{ m}}\right)$$

$$= -900 \text{ V}$$

In the preceding example, we calculated the potential at Point A: $V_A = -1080$ V, so $\Delta V_{A \to B} = V_B - V_A = (-900 \text{ V}) - (-1080 \text{ V}) = +180$ V. This means that the change in electrical potential energy as q moves from A to B is

$$\Delta U_{A \to B} = qV_{A \to B} = (+1 \times 10^{-2} \text{ C})(+180 \text{ V}) = 1.8 \text{ J}$$

This is the work required by an external agent to move q from A to B.

THE POTENTIAL IN A UNIFORM FIELD

Example 11.11 Consider a very large, flat plate that contains a uniform surface charge density σ. At points that are not too far from the plate, the electric field is uniform and given by the equation

$$E = \frac{\sigma}{2\varepsilon_0}$$

What is the potential at a point which is a distance d from the sheet, relative to the potential of the sheet itself?

Solution. Let A be a point on the plate and let B be a point a distance d from the sheet. Then

$$V_B - V_A = \frac{-W_{E,\,A\to B} \text{ on } q}{q}$$

Since the field is constant, the force that a charge q would feel is also constant, and is equal to

$$F_E = qE = q\frac{\sigma}{2\varepsilon_0}$$

Therefore,

$$W_{E,\,A\to B} = \int_A^B \mathbf{F}_E \cdot d\mathbf{r}$$

$$= \int_{r=0}^{r=d} q \cdot \frac{\sigma}{2\varepsilon_0} dr$$

$$= \frac{q\sigma}{2\varepsilon_0}[r]_0^d$$

$$= \frac{q\sigma}{2\varepsilon_0}d$$

so applying the definition gives us

$$V_B - V_A = \frac{-W_{E,\,A\to B}}{q} = -\frac{\sigma}{2\varepsilon_0}d$$

This says that the potential decreases linearly as we move away from the plate.

Example 11.12 Two large flat plates—one carrying a charge of $+Q$, the other $-Q$—are separated by a distance d. The electric field between the plates, **E**, is uniform. Determine the potential difference between the plates.

Solution. Imagine a positive charge q moving from the positive plate to the negative plate:

Since the work done by the electric field is

$$W_{E, + \to -} = F_E d = qEd$$

the potential difference between the plates is

$$V_- - V_+ = \frac{-W_{E, + \to -}}{q} = \frac{-qEd}{q} = -Ed$$

This tells us that the potential of the positive plate is greater than the potential of the negative plate, by the amount Ed. This equation can also be written as

$$E = -\frac{V_- - V_+}{d}$$

Therefore, if the potential difference and the distance between the plates are known, then the magnitude of the electric field can be determined quickly.

[C] THE POTENTIAL OF A SPHERE

Think about a conducting spherical shell of radius R. If the shell carries an excess charge Q, we know that this excess charge will be found on the outer surface and that the electric field inside the sphere will be zero. What is the potential due to the shell? At points outside the shell, the field exists as if all of the charge of the sphere were concentrated at the center. That is, for points outside the shell, the potential is the same as it would be due to a single point charge Q:

$$V = \frac{1}{4\pi\varepsilon_0} \frac{Q}{r} \quad \text{for } r > R$$

What about at points inside the shell? Since $\mathbf{E} = \mathbf{0}$ everywhere inside, there would be no electric force and no work done on a charge moving inside the shell. *The potential is constant within the sphere.* So if we moved a charge q from the surface of the spherical shell to its inside, the potential wouldn't change. The potential everywhere inside the shell is equal to the potential on the surface, which is $(1/4\pi\varepsilon_0)(Q/R)$. Therefore,

$$V = \begin{cases} \dfrac{1}{4\pi\varepsilon_0} \dfrac{Q}{R} & \text{for } r \leq R \\[2ex] \dfrac{1}{4\pi\varepsilon_0} \dfrac{Q}{r} & \text{for } r > R \end{cases}$$

The same is also true for a solid conducting sphere.

Example 11.13 The figure below shows two concentric, conducting, thin spherical shells. The inner shell has a radius of a and carries a charge of q. The outer shell has a radius of b and carries a charge of Q. The inner shell is supported on an insulating stand.

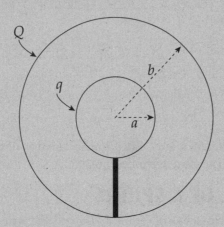

(a) What would the potential of the inner shell be if the outer shell were absent?

(b) What is the potential of the inner shell with the outer shell present?

(c) Show that the potential difference between the inner shell and the outer shell, $V_a - V_b$, does not depend on the charge on the outer shell.

Solution.

(a) The potential on (and within) a sphere of radius a containing a charge q is given by the equation $V_a = (1/4\pi\varepsilon_0)(q/a)$.

(b) The potential inside the outer sphere (if the inner sphere were absent) is equal to $(1/4\pi\varepsilon_0)(Q/b)$. The potential of the inner sphere if the outer sphere were absent is $(1/4\pi\varepsilon_0)(q/a)$. So the potential of the inner sphere with the outer sphere present is the sum: $(1/4\pi\varepsilon_0)(Q/b) + (1/4\pi\varepsilon_0)(q/a)$.

Here's another way to arrive at this result. Outside (and on) the outer sphere, the potential is the same as if the total charge were concentrated at the center, $(1/4\pi\varepsilon_0)(q + Q)/r$. So at a point *on* the outer sphere, the potential is found by substituting b for r in this expression; this gives $V_b = (1/4\pi\varepsilon_0)(q + Q)/b$. Now, the electric field between the spheres is, by Gauss's Law, simply equal to $(1/4\pi\varepsilon_0)(q/r^2)$. Therefore, the work required *by an external agent* to move a charge (let's call it q_0) from infinity to the inner sphere is equal to

$$W_{\text{from } \infty \text{ to } a} = W_{\text{from } \infty \text{ to } b} + W_{\text{from } b \text{ to } a}$$

$$= q_0 V_b + - \int_{r=b}^{r=a} q_0 E \, dr$$

$$= q_0 V_b - q_0 \int_{r=b}^{r=a} \frac{1}{4\pi\varepsilon_0} \frac{q}{r^2} \, dr$$

$$= q_0 V_b - q_0 \frac{q}{4\pi\varepsilon_0} \left[-\frac{1}{r} \right]_b^a$$

$$= q_0 V_b - q_0 \frac{q}{4\pi\varepsilon_0} \left(\frac{1}{b} - \frac{1}{a} \right)$$

Therefore,

$$V_a = \frac{W_{\text{from } \infty \text{ to } a}}{q_0}$$

$$= V_b - \frac{q}{4\pi\varepsilon_0} \left(\frac{1}{b} - \frac{1}{a} \right)$$

$$= \left[\frac{1}{4\pi\varepsilon_0} \frac{q+Q}{b} \right] - \frac{q}{4\pi\varepsilon_0} \left(\frac{1}{b} - \frac{1}{a} \right)$$

$$= \frac{1}{4\pi\varepsilon_0} \left(\frac{Q}{b} + \frac{q}{a} \right)$$

(c) At points outside the outer sphere, the two spheres behave as if all their charge was concentrated at the center. So at points outside the sphere ($r > b$) the potential is equal to $(1/4\pi\varepsilon_0)(q + Q)/r$. This must also give the potential at the surface of the outer sphere when $r = b$. Therefore, the potential difference between the inner sphere and the outer sphere is

$$V_a - V_b = \left[\frac{1}{4\pi\varepsilon_0} \frac{q}{a} - \frac{1}{4\pi\varepsilon_0} \frac{Q}{b} \right] - \frac{1}{4\pi\varepsilon_0} \frac{q+Q}{b}$$

$$= \frac{1}{4\pi\varepsilon_0} \frac{q}{a} - \frac{1}{4\pi\varepsilon_0} \frac{q}{b}$$

$$= \frac{q}{4\pi\varepsilon_0} \left(\frac{1}{a} - \frac{1}{b} \right)$$

This expression does not depend on Q, which is what we were asked to show.

Example 11.14 A *nonconducting* sphere of radius R has an excess charge of Q distributed uniformly throughout its volume (that is, the volume charge density, ρ, is a constant). The electric field at a distance $r < R$ from the center is given by the equation

$$E = \frac{1}{4\pi\varepsilon_0}\frac{Q}{R^3}r$$

What is the potential inside the sphere? That is, what is the potential at a distance r from the sphere's center?

Solution. The potential at some distance, let's call it r_0, from the center is equal to the negative of the work done by the electric field as a charge q is brought to r_0 from infinity, divided by q. (By definition, $V = U_E/q = -W_E/q$, where we take $V = 0$ at infinity.) So our first step (the big one) is to figure out the work done by the electric field in bringing a charge q in, from infinity. At points outside the sphere, the electric field is simply $(1/4\pi\varepsilon_0)(Q/r^2)$, since the sphere behaves as if all of its charge were concentrated at its center. Once we get inside, however, the electric field is given by the formula in the question. Therefore,

$$W_E = W_{E,\,\infty\,\text{to}\,R} + W_{E,\,R\,\text{to}\,r_0}$$

$$= \int_\infty^R q \cdot \frac{1}{4\pi\varepsilon_0}\frac{Q}{r^2}\,dr + \int_R^{r_0} q \cdot \frac{1}{4\pi\varepsilon_0}\frac{Q}{R^3}r\,dr$$

$$= \frac{qQ}{4\pi\varepsilon_0}\int_\infty^R \frac{1}{r^2}\,dr + \frac{qQ}{4\pi\varepsilon_0 R^3}\int_R^{r_0} r\,dr$$

$$= \frac{qQ}{4\pi\varepsilon_0}\left[-\frac{1}{r}\right]_\infty^R + \frac{qQ}{4\pi\varepsilon_0 R^3}\left[\frac{r^2}{2}\right]_R^{r_0}$$

$$= -\frac{qQ}{4\pi\varepsilon_0}\frac{1}{R} + \frac{qQ}{8\pi\varepsilon_0 R^3}(r_0^2 - R^2)$$

$$= \frac{qQ}{4\pi\varepsilon_0}\left(\frac{r_0^2 - 3R^2}{2R^3}\right)$$

Taking the negative of this result, dividing by q, and replacing r_0 by r gives us our answer:

$$V = \frac{-W_E}{q} = \frac{Q}{4\pi\varepsilon_0}\left(\frac{3R^2 - r^2}{2R^3}\right)$$

Notice how this result differs from the potential of a *conducting* sphere. In that case, the potential was constant throughout the interior of the sphere (and was equal to the value of the potential on the surface). In this case the potential is not constant; it depends on r.

[C] THE POTENTIAL OF A CYLINDER

Example 11.15 Consider a very long conducting cylinder of radius R, which carries a uniform linear charge density λ. The electric field at a distance r from the center of the cylinder is given by the equation

$$E = \frac{\lambda}{2\pi\varepsilon_0 r}$$

Determine a formula for the potential at a point outside the cylinder, relative to the potential on the cylinder.

Solution. Let A be a point on the cylinder (at $r = R$) and let B be a point outside the cylinder (at $r = r_0 > R$). Then, by definition,

$$V_B - V_A = \frac{-W_{E,\,A\to B}\text{ on }q}{q}$$

So we figure out the work done by the electric field as a charge q moves from A to B:

$$
\begin{aligned}
W_{E,\,A\to B}\text{ on }q &= \int_A^B \mathbf{F}_E \cdot d\mathbf{r} \\
&= \int_{r=R}^{r=r_0} q \cdot \frac{\lambda}{2\pi\varepsilon_0 r}\, dr \\
&= \frac{q\lambda}{2\pi\varepsilon_0} \int_{r=R}^{r=r_0} \frac{dr}{r} \\
&= \frac{q\lambda}{2\pi\varepsilon_0} \left[\ln r\right]_R^{r_0} \\
&= \frac{q\lambda}{2\pi\varepsilon_0} (\ln r_0 - \ln R) \\
&= \frac{q\lambda}{2\pi\varepsilon_0} \ln\frac{r_0}{R}
\end{aligned}
$$

Replacing r_0 with r, we get

$$
\begin{aligned}
V_B - V_A &= \frac{-W_{E,\,A\to B}\text{ on }q}{q} \\
&= -\frac{\lambda}{2\pi\varepsilon_0} \ln\frac{r}{R} \\
&= \frac{\lambda}{2\pi\varepsilon_0} \ln\frac{R}{r}
\end{aligned}
$$

[C] DERIVING THE FIELD FROM THE POTENTIAL

From the definition of potential,

$$V_B - V_A = \frac{-W_{E, A \to B} \text{ on } q}{q}$$

$$= -\frac{1}{q} \int_A^B F_E \, dr$$

$$= -\frac{1}{q} \int_A^B qE \, dr$$

$$= \int_A^B (-E) \, dr$$

If A and B are separated by an infinitesimal distance dr, then

$$V_B - V_A = \int_A^B dV$$

and this gives us

$$\int_A^B (-E) \, dr = \int_A^B dV$$

from which we can conclude that

$$(-E) \, dr = dV$$

$$E = -\frac{dV}{dr}$$

So, if we know how the potential varies as a function of r, we can determine the electric field variation with r.

> **Example 11.16** If the potential at a distance r from a source point charge Q is given by the equation $V(r) = (1/4\pi\varepsilon_0)(Q/r)$, determine a formula for the electric field.

Solution. Using the relationship derived above,

$$E = -\frac{dV}{dr} = -\frac{d}{dr}\left(\frac{1}{4\pi\varepsilon_0}\frac{Q}{r}\right) = -\frac{Q}{4\pi\varepsilon_0}\frac{d}{dr}\left(\frac{1}{r}\right) = -\frac{Q}{4\pi\varepsilon_0}\left(-\frac{1}{r^2}\right) = \frac{1}{4\pi\varepsilon_0}\frac{Q}{r^2}$$

a result we know well!

CAPACITANCE

Consider two conductors, separated by some distance, that carry equal but opposite charges, $+Q$ and $-Q$. Such a pair of conductors comprise a system called a **capacitor**. Work must be done to create this separation of charge, and, as a result, potential energy is stored. Capacitors are basically storage devices for electrical potential energy.

The conductors may have any shape, but the most common conductors are parallel metal plates or sheets. These types of capacitors are called **parallel-plate capacitors**. We'll assume that the distance d between the plates is small compared to the dimensions of the plates since, in this case, the electric field between the plates is uniform. The electric field due to *one* such plate, if its surface charge density is $\sigma = Q/A$, is given by the equation $E = \sigma/(2\varepsilon_0)$, with **E** pointing away from the sheet if σ is positive and toward the plate if σ is negative.

Therefore, with two plates, one with surface charge density $+\sigma$ and the other, $-\sigma$, the electric fields combine to give a field that's zero outside the plates and that has the magnitude

$$E_{\text{total}} = \frac{\sigma}{2\varepsilon_0} + \frac{\sigma}{2\varepsilon_0} = \frac{\sigma}{\varepsilon_0}$$

in-between. In Example 11.12, we learned that the magnitude of the potential difference, ΔV, between the plates satisfies the relationship $\Delta V = Ed$, so combining this with the previous equation, we get

$$E = \frac{\sigma}{\varepsilon_0} \quad \Rightarrow \quad \frac{\Delta V}{d} = \frac{\sigma}{\varepsilon_0} \quad \Rightarrow \quad \frac{\Delta V}{d} = \frac{Q/A}{\varepsilon_0} \quad \Rightarrow \quad \frac{Q}{\Delta V} = \frac{\varepsilon_0 A}{d}$$

The ratio of Q to ΔV, for *any* capacitor, is called its **capacitance** (C),

$$C = Q/\Delta V$$

so for a parallel-plate capacitor, we get

$$C = \frac{\varepsilon_0 A}{d}$$

The capacitance measures the capacity for holding charge. The greater the capacitance, the more charge can be stored on the plates at a given potential difference. The capacitance of any capacitor depends only on the size, shape, and separation of the conductors. From the definition, $C = Q/\Delta V$, the units of C are joules per volt. One joule per volt is renamed one **farad** (abbreviated F): 1 J/V = 1 F.

Example 11.17 A 10-nanofarad parallel-plate capacitor holds a charge of magnitude 50 μC on each plate.
(a) What is the potential difference between the plates?
(b) If the plates are separated by a distance of 0.2 mm, what is the area of each plate?

Solution.

(a) From the definition, $C = Q / \Delta V$, we find that

$$\Delta V = \frac{Q}{C} = \frac{50 \times 10^{-6} \ \text{C}}{10 \times 10^{-9} \ \text{F}} = 5000 \ \text{V}$$

(b) From the equation $C = \varepsilon_0 A / d$, we can calculate the area, A, of each plate:

$$A = \frac{Cd}{\varepsilon_0} = \frac{(10 \times 10^{-9} \ \text{F})(0.2 \times 10^{-3} \ \text{m})}{8.85 \times 10^{-12} \ \text{C}^2 / \text{N} \cdot \text{m}^2} = 0.23 \ \text{m}^2$$

[C] CAPACITORS OF OTHER GEOMETRIES

Example 11.18 A long cable consists of a solid conducting cylinder of radius a, which carries a linear charge density of $+ \lambda$, concentric with an outer cylindrical shell of radius b, which carries a linear charge density of $- \lambda$. This is a **coaxial** cable. Determine the capacitance of the cable.

Solution. We first apply the definition, $C = Q / \Delta V$. In Example 10.12, we zthat the electric field outside of a conducting cylinder is given by the equation

$$E = \frac{\lambda}{2\pi\varepsilon_0 r}$$

Therefore, we can get the potential difference between the inner cylinder and the outer cylindrical shell by integrating the electric field. Since

$$V_{\text{B}} - V_{\text{A}} = \Delta V_{\text{A} \rightarrow \text{B}} = \frac{-W_{\text{E, A} \rightarrow \text{B}} \ \text{on} \ q}{q} = -\frac{1}{q} \int_{\text{A}}^{\text{B}} q\mathbf{E} \cdot d\mathbf{r} = \int_{\text{B}}^{\text{A}} \mathbf{E} \cdot d\mathbf{r}$$

we have

$$V_{\text{inner}} - V_{\text{outer}} = \int_{r=a}^{r=b} \frac{\lambda}{2\pi\varepsilon_0 r} \, dr = \frac{\lambda}{2\pi\varepsilon_0} [\ln r]_a^b = \frac{\lambda}{2\pi\varepsilon_0} \ln \frac{b}{a}$$

Therefore, over a length ℓ of cable, the magnitude of the charge Q on each cylinder is $\lambda \ell$, so by the definition of capacitance, we get

$$C = \frac{Q}{\Delta V} = \frac{\lambda \ell}{\frac{\lambda}{2\pi \varepsilon_0} \ln \frac{b}{a}} = \frac{2\pi \varepsilon_0 \ell}{\ln \frac{b}{a}}$$

Example 11.19 A spherical conducting shell of radius a, which carries a charge of $+Q$, is concentric with an outer spherical shell of radius b, which carries a charge of $-Q$. What is the capacitance of this spherical capacitor?

Solution. We first apply the definition, $C = Q / \Delta V$. We know that, in the region between the shells, the field is due to the inner shell alone:

$$E = \frac{1}{4\pi \varepsilon_0} \frac{Q}{r^2}$$

Therefore, the potential difference between the inner sphere and the outer sphere shell is obtained by integrating the electric field as follows. Since

$$V_B - V_A = \Delta V_{A \to B} = \frac{-W_{E, A \to B} \text{ on } q}{q} = -\frac{1}{q} \int_A^B q\mathbf{E} \cdot d\mathbf{r} = \int_B^A \mathbf{E} \cdot d\mathbf{r}$$

we have

$$V_{inner} - V_{outer} = \int_{r=a}^{r=b} \frac{1}{4\pi \varepsilon_0} \frac{Q}{r^2} \, dr = \frac{Q}{4\pi \varepsilon_0} \int_{r=a}^{r=b} \frac{1}{r^2} \, dr = \frac{Q}{4\pi \varepsilon_0} \left[-\frac{1}{r} \right]_a^b = \frac{Q}{4\pi \varepsilon_0} \left(\frac{1}{a} - \frac{1}{b} \right)$$

So, by definition of capacitance, we get

$$C = \frac{Q}{\Delta V} = \frac{Q}{\frac{Q}{4\pi \varepsilon_0} \left(\frac{1}{a} - \frac{1}{b} \right)} = \frac{4\pi \varepsilon_0}{\frac{1}{a} - \frac{1}{b}} = 4\pi \varepsilon_0 \frac{ab}{b-a}$$

The capacitance of a single, isolated conductor can also be defined; we can just think of the other conductor as being infinitely far away. In this case, if a conductor holds a charge Q at a potential of V, then its capacitance is defined as $C = Q/V$. For a single sphere of radius a, we determined earlier in this chapter that the potential at its surface is $V = (1/4\pi \varepsilon_0)Q/a$, so its capacitance is

$$C = \frac{Q}{V} = \frac{Q}{\frac{1}{4\pi \varepsilon_0} \frac{Q}{a}} = 4\pi \varepsilon_0 a$$

which says that C is proportional to the radius of the sphere. This makes sense; a larger sphere would have the capacity to hold more charge and should therefore have a greater capacitance. This same result for the capacitance of a single sphere can be obtained from the equation we derived above for the spherical shell capacitor simply by letting the radius b of the outer sphere go to infinity:

$$\lim_{b \to \infty} \frac{4\pi \varepsilon_0}{\frac{1}{a} - \frac{1}{b}} = \frac{4\pi \varepsilon_0}{\frac{1}{a} - 0} = 4\pi \varepsilon_0 a$$

COMBINATIONS OF CAPACITORS

Capacitors are often arranged in combination in electric circuits. Here we'll look at two types of arrangements, the parallel combination and the series combination.

A collection of capacitors are said to be in **parallel** if they all share the same potential difference. The following diagram shows two capacitors wired in parallel:

The top plates are connected by a wire and form a single equipotential; the same is true for the bottom plates. Therefore, the potential difference across one capacitor is the same as the potential difference across the other capacitor.

We want to find the capacitance of a *single* capacitor that would perform the same function as this combination. If the capacitances are C_1 and C_2, then the charge on the first capacitor is $Q_1 = C_1 \Delta V$ and the charge on the second capacitor is $Q_2 = C_2 \Delta V$. The total charge on the combination is $Q_1 + Q_2$, so the equivalent capacitance, C_p, must be

$$C_P = \frac{Q}{\Delta V} = \frac{Q_1 + Q_2}{\Delta V} = \frac{Q_1}{\Delta V} + \frac{Q_2}{\Delta V} = C_1 + C_2$$

So the **equivalent** capacitance of a collection of capacitors in parallel is found by adding the individual capacitances.

A collection of capacitors are said to be in **series** if they all share the same charge magnitude. The following diagram shows two capacitors wired in series:

When a potential difference is applied, as shown, negative charge will be deposited on the bottom plate of the bottom capacitor; this will push a equal amount of negative charge away from the top plate of the bottom capacitor toward the bottom plate of the top capacitor. When the system has reached equilibrium, the charges on all the plates will have the same magnitude:

If the top and bottom capacitors have capacitances of C_1 and C_2, respectively, then the potential difference across the top capacitor is $\Delta V_1 = Q/C_1$, and the potential difference across the bottom capacitor is $\Delta V_2 = Q/C_2$. The total potential difference across the combination is $\Delta V_1 + \Delta V_2$, which must equal ΔV. Therefore, the equivalent capacitance, C_S, must be

$$C_S = \frac{Q}{\Delta V} = \frac{Q}{\Delta V_1 + \Delta V_2} = \frac{Q}{\frac{Q}{C_1} + \frac{Q}{C_2}} = \frac{1}{\frac{1}{C_1} + \frac{1}{C_2}}$$

We can write this in another form:

$$\frac{1}{C_S} = \frac{1}{C_1} + \frac{1}{C_2}$$

In words, the *reciprocal* of the capacitance of a collection of capacitors in series is found by adding the reciprocals of the individual capacitances.

Example 11.20 Given that $C_1 = 2\ \mu F$, $C_2 = 4\ \mu F$, and $C_3 = 6\ \mu F$, calculate the equivalent capacitance for the following combination:

Solution. Notice that C_2 and C_3 are in series, and they are in parallel with C_1. That is, the capacitor equivalent to the series combination of C_2 and C_3 (which we'll call $C_{2\text{-}3}$) is in parallel with C_1. We can represent this as follows:

So the first step is to find $C_{2\text{-}3}$:

$$\frac{1}{C_{2\text{-}3}} = \frac{1}{C_2} + \frac{1}{C_3} \quad \Rightarrow \quad C_{2\text{-}3} = \frac{C_2 C_3}{C_2 + C_3}$$

Now this is in parallel with C_1, so the overall equivalent capacitance ($C_{1\text{-}2\text{-}3}$) is

$$C_{1\text{-}2\text{-}3} = C_1 + C_{2\text{-}3} = C_1 + \frac{C_2 C_3}{C_2 + C_3}$$

Substituting in the given numerical values, we get

$$C_{1\text{-}2\text{-}3} = (2\ \mu\text{F}) + \frac{(4\ \mu\text{F})(6\ \mu\text{F})}{(4\ \mu\text{F}) + (6\ \mu\text{F})} = 4.4\ \mu\text{F}$$

THE ENERGY STORED IN A CAPACITOR

To figure out the electrical potential energy stored in a capacitor, imagine taking a small amount of negative charge off the positive plate and transferring it to the negative plate. This requires that positive work is done by an external agent, and this is the reason that the capacitor stores energy. Imagine that the plates currently hold a charge of magnitude q (so one plate holds $+q$ and the other holds $-q$). Then the potential difference is $\Delta V = q/C$. The work required by an external agent to transfer a small amount of additional charge, dq, is $dW = \Delta V dq$. Therefore, the total work required to bring the capacitor from $q = 0$ to its final value, $q = Q$, is

$$W = \int dW = \int_{q=0}^{q=Q} \frac{q}{C}\,dq = \frac{1}{C}\left[\frac{q^2}{2}\right]_0^Q = \frac{Q^2}{2C}$$

This is the electrical potential energy stored in a capacitor. Because of the definition $C = Q/\Delta V$, the equation for the stored potential energy can be written in two other forms:

$$U_E = \frac{(C\Delta V)^2}{2C} = \tfrac{1}{2}C(\Delta V)^2 \quad \text{or} \quad U_E = \frac{Q^2}{2(Q/\Delta V)} = \tfrac{1}{2}Q\Delta V$$

[C] DIELECTRICS

One method of keeping the plates of a capacitor apart, which is necessary to maintain charge separation and store potential energy, is to insert an insulator (called a **dielectric**) between the plates.

A dielectric always increases the capacitance of a capacitor. Let's see why this happens. Imagine charging a capacitor to a potential difference of ΔV with charge $+Q$ on one plate and $-Q$ on the other. Now disconnect the capacitor from the charging source and insert a dielectric. What happens? Although the dielectric is not a conductor, the electric field that existed between the plates causes the molecules within the dielectric material to polarize; there is more electron density on the side of the molecule near the positive plate.

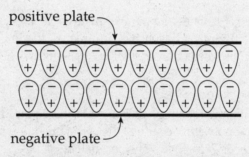

The effect of this is to form a layer of negative charge along the top surface of the dielectric and a layer of positive charge along the bottom surface; this separation of charge induces its own electric field ($\mathbf{E_i}$), within the dielectric, that opposes the original electric field, $\mathbf{E}$, within the capacitor:

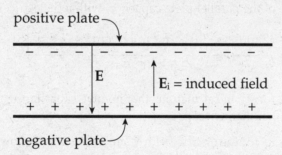

So the overall electric field has been reduced from its previous value: $\mathbf{E}_{total} = \mathbf{E} + \mathbf{E}_i$, and $E_{total} = E - E_i$. Let's say that the electric field has been reduced by a factor of κ (the Greek letter *kappa*) from its original value:

$$E_{\text{with dielectric}} = E_{\text{without dielectric}} - E_i = \frac{E}{\kappa}$$

Since $\Delta V = Ed$ for a parallel-plate capacitor, we see that ΔV must have decreased by a factor of κ. But $C = Q/\Delta V$, so if ΔV decreases by a factor of κ, then C increases by a factor of κ:

$$C_{\text{with dielectric}} = \kappa C_{\text{without dielectric}}$$

The value of κ, called the **dielectric constant**, varies from material to material, but it's always greater than 1.

Although the description for why the capacitance increases with the insertion of a dielectric assumed that the source which charged the capacitor was disconnected (so that Q remains constant), the same result holds if the source of potential remains connected to the capacitor. The capacitance still increases, but because ΔV must now remain constant, the equation $Q = C \Delta V$ tells us that more charge will appear on the plates (because C increases).

The presence of a dielectric also limits the potential difference that can be applied across the plates. If ΔV gets too high, then $E = \Delta V / d$ gets so strong that electrons in the dielectric material can be ripped right out of their atoms and propelled toward the positive plate. This discharges the capacitor (and typically burns a hole through the dielectric). This event is called **dielectric breakdown**.

The capacitance formulas derived in this chapter have assumed that no dielectric was present; the permittivity constant that appears in the formulas is ε_0, the permittivity of *free space* (vacuum). If a dielectric is present, then the permittivity increases to $\varepsilon = \kappa \varepsilon_0$, so the occurrence of ε_0 in each formula is simply replaced by $\varepsilon = \kappa \varepsilon_0$.

> **Example 11.21** The plates of a parallel-plate capacitor are separated by a distance of 2.0 mm and each has an area of 10 cm². If a layer of polystyrene (whose dielectric constant is 2.6) is sandwiched between the plates, figure out
>
> (a) the capacitance,
>
> (b) the maximum amount of charge that can be placed on the plates, given that polystyrene suffers dielectric breakdown if the electric field exceeds 20 million volts per meter.

Solution.

(a) The capacitance of the parallel-plate capacitor, with a dielectric, is

$$C = \frac{\kappa \varepsilon_0 A}{d} = \frac{(2.6)(8.85 \times 10^{-12} \text{ F/m})\left[10 \text{ cm}^2 \cdot \left(\frac{1 \text{ m}}{100 \text{ cm}}\right)^2\right]}{2.0 \times 10^{-3} \text{ m}} = 1.2 \times 10^{-11} \text{ F}$$

Notice the units for ε_0; in calculations that involve capacitance, it is usually easier to write F/m rather than C²/N·m².

(b) First note the units for the electric field: V/m. These units follow from the equation $\Delta V = Ed$. In the past, we've written the units of E as N/C. These two units are actually equivalent: 1 V/m = 1 N/C. We were asked to determine Q_{max} if E_{max} is 20×10^6 V/m and, from the equations $\Delta V = Ed$ and $Q = C \Delta V$, we get

$$
\begin{aligned}
Q_{max} = C \Delta V_{max} &= C E_{max} d \\
&= (1.2 \times 10^{-11} \text{ F})(20 \times 10^6 \text{ V/m})(2 \times 10^{-3} \text{ m}) \\
&= 4.8 \times 10^{-7} \text{ C}
\end{aligned}
$$

CHAPTER 11 REVIEW QUESTIONS

SECTION I: MULTIPLE CHOICE

1. Which of the following statements is/are true?

   I. If the electric field at a certain point is zero, then the electric potential at the same point is also zero.
   II. If the electric potential at a certain point is zero, then the electric field at the same point is also zero.
   III. The electric potential is inversely proportional to the strength of the electric field.

   (A) I only
   (B) II only
   (C) I and II only
   (D) I and III only
   (E) None are true

2. If the electric field does negative work on a negative charge as the charge undergoes a displacement from Position A to Position B within an electric field, then the electrical potential energy

   (A) is negative.
   (B) is positive.
   (C) increases.
   (D) decreases.
   (E) Cannot be determined from the information given

3.

The work required to assemble the system shown above, bringing each charge in from an infinite distance, is equal to

   (A) $\dfrac{1}{4\pi\varepsilon_0}\dfrac{4q^2}{s}$

   (B) $\dfrac{1}{4\pi\varepsilon_0}\dfrac{(4+\sqrt{2})q^2}{s}$

   (C) $\dfrac{1}{4\pi\varepsilon_0}\dfrac{6q^2}{s}$

   (D) $\dfrac{1}{4\pi\varepsilon_0}\dfrac{(4+2\sqrt{2})q^2}{s}$

   (E) $\dfrac{1}{4\pi\varepsilon_0}\dfrac{(8+2\sqrt{2})q^2}{s}$

4. Negative charges are accelerated by electric fields toward points

   (A) at lower electric potential.
   (B) at higher electric potential.
   (C) where the electric field is zero.
   (D) where the electric field is weaker.
   (E) where the electric field is stronger.

5. A charge q experiences a displacement within an electric field from Position A to Position B. The change in the electrical potential energy is ΔU_E, and the work done by the electric field during this displacement is W_E. Then

(A) $V_B - V_A = W_E/q$
(B) $V_A - V_B = qW_E$
(C) $V_B - V_A = qW_E$
(D) $V_A - V_B = \Delta U_E/q$
(E) $V_B - V_A = \Delta U_E/q$

6.

Which points in this uniform electric field (between the plates of the capacitor) shown above lie on the same equipotential?

(A) 1 and 2 only
(B) 1 and 3 only
(C) 2 and 4 only
(D) 3 and 4 only
(E) 1, 2, 3 and 4 all lie on the same equipotential since the electric field is uniform.

7. [C] Two isolated and widely separated conducting spheres each carry a charge of $-Q$. Sphere #1 has a radius of a and Sphere #2 has a radius of $4a$. If the spheres are now connected by a conducting wire, what will be the final charge on each sphere?

	Sphere 1	Sphere 2
(A)	$-Q$	$-Q$
(B)	$-2Q/3$	$-4Q/3$
(C)	$-4Q/3$	$-2Q/3$
(D)	$-2Q/5$	$-8Q/5$
(E)	$-8Q/5$	$-2Q/5$

8. [C] A parallel-plate capacitor is charged to a potential difference of ΔV; this results in a charge of $+Q$ on one plate and a charge of $-Q$ on the other. The capacitor is disconnected from the charging source, and a dielectric is then inserted. What happens to the potential difference and the stored electrical potential energy?

(A) The potential difference decreases, and the stored electrical potential energy decreases.
(B) The potential difference decreases, and the stored electrical potential energy increases.
(C) The potential difference increases, and the stored electrical potential energy decreases.
(D) The potential difference increases, and the stored electrical potential energy increases.
(E) The potential difference decreases, and the stored electrical potential energy remains unchanged.

9.

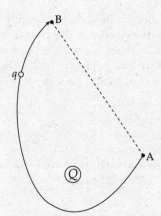

How much work would the electric field (created by the stationary charge Q) perform as a charge q is moved from Point A to B along the curved path shown? $V_A = 200$ V, $V_B = 100$ V, $q = -0.05$ C, length of line segment AB = 10 cm, length of curved path = 20 cm.

(A) -10 J
(B) -5 J
(C) $+5$ J
(D) $+10$ J
(E) $+20$ J

10.

If each of the capacitors in the array
shown above is C, what is the capacitance
of the entire combination?

(A) C/2
(B) 2C/3
(C) 5C/6
(D) 2C
(E) 5C/3

SECTION II: FREE RESPONSE

1. In the figure shown, all four charges are situated at the corners of a square with sides s.

(a) What is the total electrical potential energy of this array of fixed charges?

(b) What is the electric field at the center of the square?

(c) What is the electric potential at the center of the square?

(d) Sketch (on the diagram) the portion of the equipotential surface that lies in the plane of the figure and passes through the center of the square.

(e) How much work would the electric field perform on a charge q as it moved from the midpoint of the right side of the square to the midpoint of the top of the square?

2. The figure below shows a parallel-plate capacitor. Each rectangular plate has length L and width w, and the plates are separated by a distance d.

(a) Determine the capacitance.

An electron (mass m, charge $-e$) is shot horizontally into the empty space between the plates, midway between them, with an initial velocity of magnitude v_0. The electron just barely misses hitting the end of the top plate as it exits. (Ignore gravity.)

(b) In the diagram, sketch the electric field vector at the position of the electron when it has traveled a horizontal distance of $L/2$.

(c) In the diagram, sketch the electric force vector on the electron at the same position as in part (b).

(d) Determine the strength of the electric field between the plates. Write your answer in terms of L, d, m, e, and v_0.

(e) Determine the charge on the top plate.

(f) How much potential energy is stored in the capacitor?

3. A solid conducting sphere of radius a carries an excess charge of Q.

(a) Determine the electric field magnitude, $E(r)$, as a function of r, the distance from the sphere's center.

(b) Determine the potential, $V(r)$, as a function of r. Take the zero of potential at $r = \infty$.

(c) On the diagrams below, sketch $E(r)$ and $V(r)$. (Cover at least the range $0 < r < 2a$.)

4. [C] A solid, nonconducting sphere of radius a has a volume charge density given by the equation $\rho(r) = \rho_0(r/a)^3$, where r is the distance from the sphere's center.

(a) Determine the electric field magnitude, $E(r)$, as a function of r.

(b) Determine the potential, $V(r)$, as a function of r. Take the zero of potential at $r = \infty$.

(c) On the diagrams below, sketch $E(r)$ and $V(r)$. Be sure to indicate on the vertical axis in each plot the value at $r = a$.

12

DIRECT CURRENT CIRCUITS

INTRODUCTION

In the previous chapter, when we studied electrostatic fields, we learned that, within a conductor, an electrostatic field cannot be sustained; the source charges move to the surface and the conductor forms a single equipotential. We will now look at conductors within which an electric field can be sustained because a power source maintains a potential difference across the conductor, allowing charges to continually move through it. This ordered motion of charge through a conductor is called electric current.

ELECTRIC CURRENT

Picture a piece of metal wire. Within the metal, electrons are zooming around at speeds of about a million m/s in random directions, colliding with other electrons and positive ions in the lattice. This constitutes charge in motion, but it doesn't constitute *net* movement of charge, because the electrons move randomly. If there's no net motion of charge, there's no current. However, if we were to create a potential difference between the ends of the wire, meaning if we set up an electric field,

the electrons would experience an electric force, and they would start to drift through the wire. This is current. Although the electric field would travel through the wire at nearly the speed of light, the electrons themselves would still have to make their way through a crowd of atoms and other free electrons, so their **drift speed**, v_d, would be relatively slow: on the order of a millimeter per second.

To measure the current, we have to measure how much charge crosses a plane per unit time. If an amount of charge of magnitude ΔQ crosses an imaginary plane in a time interval Δt, then the **current** is

$$I = \frac{\Delta Q}{\Delta t}$$

If the amount of current is changing during the time interval Δt, then the equation above gives the average current. We can define the instantaneous current as

$$I = \frac{dQ}{dt}$$

Because current is charge per unit time, it's expressed in coulombs per second. One coulomb per second is an **ampere** (abbreviated **A**), or amp. So 1 C/s = 1 A.

Although the charge carriers that constitute the current within a metal are electrons, the direction of the current is taken to be the direction that *positive* charge carriers would move. (This is explicitly stated on the AP exam.) So, if the conduction electrons drift to the right, we'd say the current points toward the left.

RESISTANCE

Let's say we had a copper wire and a glass fiber that had the same length and cross-sectional area, and that we hooked up the ends of the metal wire to a source of potential difference and measured the resulting current. If we were to do the same thing with the glass fiber, the current would probably be too small to measure, but why? Well, the glass provided more resistance to the flow of charge. If the potential difference is ΔV and the current is I, then the **resistance** is

$$R = \frac{\Delta V}{I}$$

Notice that if the current is large, the resistance is low, and if the current is small, then resistance is high. The Δ in the equation above is often omitted, but you should always assume that, in this context, $V = \Delta V$ = potential difference, also called voltage.

Because resistance is voltage divided by current, it is expressed in volts per amp. One volt per amp is one **ohm** (Ω, *omega*). So, 1 V/A = 1 Ω.

RESISTIVITY

The resistance of an object depends on two things: the material it's made of and its shape. For example, again think of the copper wire and glass fiber of the same length and area. They have the same shape, but their resistances are different because they're made of different materials. Glass has a much greater intrinsic resistance than copper does; it has a greater **resistivity**. Each material has its own characteristic resistivity, and resistance depends on how the material is shaped. For a wire of length L and cross-sectional area A made of a material with resistivity ρ, resistance is given by:

$$R = \frac{\rho L}{A}$$

The resistivity of copper is around 10^{-8} $\Omega \cdot$m, while the resistivity of glass is much greater, around 10^{12} $\Omega \cdot$m.

> **Example 12.1** A wire of radius 1 mm and length 2 m is made of platinum (resistivity = 1×10^{-7} $\Omega \cdot$m). If a voltage of 9 V is applied between the ends of the wire, what will be the resulting current?

Solution. First, the resistance of the wire is given by the equation

$$R = \frac{\rho L}{A} = \frac{\rho L}{\pi r^2} = \frac{(1 \times 10^{-7}\ \Omega \cdot \text{m})(2\ \text{m})}{\pi (0.001\ \text{m})^2} = 0.064\ \Omega$$

Then, from $I = V/R$, we get

$$I = \frac{V}{R} = \frac{9\ \text{V}}{0.064\ \Omega} = 140\ \text{A}$$

ELECTRIC CIRCUITS

An electric current is maintained when the terminals of a voltage source (a battery, for example) are connected by a conducting pathway, in what's called a **circuit**. If the current always travels in the same direction through the pathway, it's called a **direct current**.

The job of the voltage source is to provide a potential difference called an **emf**, or **electromotive force**, which drives the flow of charge. The emf isn't really a force, it's the work done per unit charge, and it's measured in volts.

To try to imagine what's happening in a circuit in which a steady-state current is maintained, let's follow one of the charge carriers that's drifting through the pathway. (Remember we're pretending that the charge carriers are positive.) The charge is introduced by the positive terminal of the battery and enters the wire, where it's pushed by the electric field. It encounters resistance, bumping into the relatively stationary atoms that make up the metal's lattice and setting them into greater motion. So the electrical potential energy that the charge had when it left the battery is turning into heat. By the time the charge reaches the negative terminal, all of its original electrical potential energy is lost. In order to keep the current going, the voltage source must do positive work on the charge, forcing it to move from the negative terminal toward the positive terminal. The charge is now ready to make another journey around the circuit.

ENERGY AND POWER

When a carrier of positive charge q drops by an amount V in potential, it loses potential energy in the amount qV. If this happens in time t, then the rate at which this energy is transformed is equal to $(qV)/t = (q/t)V$. But q/t is equal to the current, I, so the rate at which electrical energy is transferred is given by the equation

$$P = IV$$

This equation works for the power delivered by a battery to the circuit as well as for resistors. The power dissipated in a resistor, as electrical potential energy is turned into heat, is given by $P = IV$, but, because of the relationship $V = IR$, we can express this in two other ways:

$$P = IV = I(IR) = I^2R$$

or

$$P = IV = \frac{V}{R} \cdot V = \frac{V^2}{R}$$

Resistors become hot when current passes through them; the thermal energy generated is called **joule heat**.

CIRCUIT ANALYSIS

We will now develop a way of specifying the current, voltage, and power associated which each element in a circuit. Our circuits will contain three basic elements: batteries, resistors, and connecting wires. As we've seen, the resistence of an ordinary metal wire is negligible; resistance is provided by devices that control the current; **resistors**. All the resistance of the system is concentrated in the resistors, which are symbolized in a circuit diagram by this symbol:

Batteries are denoted by the symbol:

where the longer line represents the **positive** (higher potential) terminal, and the shorter line is the **negative** (lower potential) terminal. Sometimes a battery is denoted by more than one pair of such lines:

Here's a simple circuit diagram:

The emf ($\mathcal{E}$) of the battery is indicated, as is the resistance (R) of the resistor. Determining the current in this case is straightforward, because there's only one resistor. The equation $V = IR$, with V given by $\mathcal{E}$, gives us

$$I = \frac{\mathcal{E}}{R}$$

COMBINATIONS OF RESISTORS

Two common ways of combining resistors within a circuit is to place them either in **series** (one after the other), or in **parallel** (that is, side-by-side):

In order to simplify the circuit, our goal is to find the equivalent resistance of combinations. Resistors are said to be in series if they all share the same current and if the total voltage drop across them is equal to the sum of the individual voltage drops.

In this case, then, if V denotes the voltage drop across the combination, we have

$$R_{\text{equiv}} = \frac{V}{I} = \frac{V_1 + V_2}{I} = \frac{V_1}{I} + \frac{V_2}{I} = R_1 + R_2$$

This idea can be applied to any number of resistors in series (not just two):

$$R_S = \sum_i R_i$$

Resistors are said to be in parallel if they all share the same voltage drop, and the total current entering the combination is split among the resistors. Imagine that a current I enters the combination. It splits; some of the current, I_1, would go through R_1, and the remainder, I_2, would go through R_2.

So if V is the voltage drop across the combination, we have

$$I = I_1 + I_2 \quad \Rightarrow \quad \frac{V}{R_{\text{equiv}}} = \frac{V}{R_1} + \frac{V}{R_2} \quad \Rightarrow \quad \frac{1}{R_{\text{equiv}}} = \frac{1}{R_1} + \frac{1}{R_2}$$

This idea can be applied to any number of resistors in parallel (not just two): The reciprocal of the equivalent resistance for resistors in parallel is equal to the sum of the reciprocals of the individual resistances:

$$\frac{1}{R_P} = \sum_i \frac{1}{R_i}$$

Example 12.2 Calculate the equivalent resistance for the following circuit:

Solution. First find the equivalent resistance of the two parallel resistors:

$$\frac{1}{R_P} = \frac{1}{3\ \Omega} + \frac{1}{6\ \Omega} \quad \Rightarrow \quad \frac{1}{R_P} = \frac{1}{2\ \Omega} \quad \Rightarrow \quad R_P = 2\ \Omega$$

This resistance is in series with the 4 Ω resistor, so the overall equivalent resistance in the circuit is $R = 4\ \Omega + 2\ \Omega = 6\ \Omega$.

Example 12.3 Determine the current through each resistor, the voltage drop across each resistor, and the power given off (dissipated) as heat in each resistor of this circuit:

Solution. You might want to redraw the circuit each time we replace a combination of resistors by its equivalent resistance. From our work in the preceding example, we have

From diagram ③, which has just one resistor, we can figure out the current:

$$I = \frac{\varepsilon}{R} = \frac{12 \text{ V}}{6\,\Omega} = 2 \text{ A}$$

Now we can work our way back to the original circuit (diagram ①). In going from ③ to ②, we are going back to a series combination, and what do resistors in series share? That's right, the same current. So we take the current, $I = 2$ A, back to diagram ②. The current through each resistor in diagram ② is 2 A.

Since we know the current through each resistor, we can figure out the voltage drop across each resistor using the equation $V = IR$. The voltage drop across the 4 Ω resistor is (2 A)(4 Ω) = 8 V, and the voltage drop across the 2 Ω resistor is (2 A)(2 Ω) = 4 V. Notice that the total voltage drop across the two resistors is 8 V + 4 V = 12 V, which matches the emf of the battery, which is to be expected.

Now for the last step; going from diagram ② back to diagram ①. Nothing needs to be done with the 4 Ω resistor; nothing about it changes in going from diagram ② to ①, but the 2 Ω resistor in diagram ② goes back to the parallel combination. And what do resistors in parallel share? The same voltage drop. So we take the voltage drop, $V = 4$ V, back to diagram ①. The voltage drop across each of the two parallel resistors in diagram ① is 4 V.

Since we know the voltage drop across each resistor, we can figure out the current through each resistor by using the equation $I = V/R$. The current through the 3 Ω resistor is (4 V)/(3 Ω) = $\frac{4}{3}$ A, and the current through the 6 Ω resistor is (4 V)/(6 Ω) = $\frac{2}{3}$ A. Note that the current entering the parallel combination (2 A) equals the total current passing through the individual resistors ($\frac{4}{3}$ A + $\frac{2}{3}$ A). Again this was expected.

Finally, we will calculate the power dissipated as heat by each resistor. We can use any of the equivalent formulas: $P = IV$, $P = I^2R$, or $P = V^2/R$.

For the 4 Ω resistor: $P = IV = $ (2 A)(8 V) = 16 W

For the 3 Ω resistor: $P = IV = (\frac{4}{3}$ A)(4 V) = $\frac{16}{3}$ W

For the 6 Ω resistor: $P = IV = (\frac{2}{3}$ A)(4 V) = $\frac{8}{3}$ W

So the resistors are dissipating a total of

$$16 \text{ W} + \tfrac{16}{3} \text{ W} + \tfrac{8}{3} \text{ W} = 24 \text{ W}$$

If the resistors are dissipating a total of 24 J every second, then they must be provided with that much power. This is easy to check: $P = IV = (2 \text{ A})(12 \text{ V}) = 24 \text{ W}$.

Example 12.4 For the following circuit,
(a) In which direction will current flow and why?
(b) What's the overall emf?
(c) What's the current in the circuit?
(d) At what rate is energy consumed by, and provided to, this circuit?

Solution. (a) The battery whose emf is $\mathcal{E}_1$ wants to send current clockwise, while the battery whose emf is $\mathcal{E}_2$ wants to send current counterclockwise. Since $\mathcal{E}_2 > \mathcal{E}_1$, the battery whose emf is $\mathcal{E}_2$ is the more powerful battery, so the current will flow counterclockwise.

(b) Charges forced through $\mathcal{E}_1$ will lose, rather than gain, 4 V of potential, so the overall emf of this circuit is $\mathcal{E}_2 - \mathcal{E}_1 = 8$ V.

(c) Since the total resistance is 3 Ω + 1 Ω = 4 Ω, the current will be $I = (8 \text{ V})/(4 \text{ Ω}) = 2$ A. $\mathcal{E}_2$ will provide energy at a rate of $P_2 = IV_2 = (2 \text{ A})(12 \text{ V}) = 24$ W, while $\mathcal{E}_1$ will absorb at a rate of $P_1 = IV_1 = (2 \text{ A})(4 \text{ V}) = 8$ W.

(d) Finally, energy will be dissipated in these resistors at a rate of $I^2R_1 + I^2R_2 = (2 \text{ A})^2(3 \text{ Ω}) + (2 \text{ A})^2(1 \text{ Ω}) = 16$ W. Once again, energy is conserved; the power delivered (24 W) equals the power taken (8 W + 16 W = 24 W).

Example 12.5 All real batteries contain **internal resistance**, r. Determine the current in the following circuit when the switch S is closed:

Solution. Before the switch is closed, there is no complete conducting pathway from the positive terminal of the battery to the negative terminal, so no current flows through the resistors. However, once the switch is closed, the resistance of the circuit is 2 Ω + 3 Ω + 5 Ω = 10 Ω, so the current in the circuit is $I = (20 \text{ V})/(10 \text{ Ω}) = 2$ A. Often the battery and its internal resistance are enclosed in a dotted line:

In this case, a distinction can be made between the emf of the battery and the actual voltage it provides once the current has begun. Since $I = 2$ A, the voltage drop across the internal resistance is $Ir = (2 \text{ A})(2 \text{ Ω}) = 4$ V, so the effective voltage provided by the battery to the rest of the circuit—called the **terminal voltage**—is lower than the ideal emf. It is $V = \mathcal{E} - Ir = 20 \text{ V} - 4 \text{ V} = 16$ V.

> **Example 12.6** A student has three 30 Ω resistors and an ideal 90 V battery. (A battery is *ideal* if it has a negligible internal resistance.) Compare the current drawn from—and the power supplied by—the battery when the resistors are arranged in parallel versus in series.

Solution. Resistors in series always provide an equivalent resistance that's greater than any of the individual resistances, and resistors in parallel always provide an equivalent resistance that's smaller than their individual resistances. So, hooking up the resistors in parallel will create the smallest resistance and draw the greatest total current:

In this case, the equivalent resistance is

$$\frac{1}{R_P} = \frac{1}{30\ \Omega} + \frac{1}{30\ \Omega} + \frac{1}{30\ \Omega} \quad \Rightarrow \quad \frac{1}{R_P} = \frac{1}{10\ \Omega} \quad \Rightarrow \quad R_P = 10\ \Omega$$

and the total current is $I = \mathcal{E}/R_P = (90\text{ V})/(10\ \Omega) = 9$ A. (You could verify that 3 A of current would flow in each of the three branches of the combination.) The power supplied by the battery will be $P = IV = (9\text{ A})(90\text{ V}) = 810$ W.

If the resistors are in series, the equivalent resistance is $R_S = 30\ \Omega + 30\ \Omega + 30\ \Omega = 90\ \Omega$, and the current drawn is only $I = \mathcal{E}/R_S = (90\text{ V})/(90\ \Omega) = 1$ A. The power supplied by the battery in this case is just $P = IV = (1\text{ A})(90\text{ V}) = 90$ W.

Example 12.7 A **voltmeter** is a device that's used to measure the voltage between two points in a circuit. An **ammeter** is used to measure current. Determine the readings on the voltmeter (denoted —Ⓥ—) and the ammeter (denoted —Ⓐ—) in the circuit below.

Solution. We consider the ammeter to be ideal; this means it has negligible resistance, so it doesn't alter the current that it's trying to measure. Similarly, we consider the voltmeter to have an extremely high resistance, so it draws negligible current away from the circuit.

Our first goal is to find the equivalent resistance in the circuit. The 600 Ω and 300 Ω resistors are in parallel; they're equivalent to a single 200 Ω resistor. This is in series with the battery's internal resistance, r, and R_3. The overall equivalent resistance is therefore $R = 50\ \Omega + 200\ \Omega + 150\ \Omega = 400\ \Omega$, so the current supplied by the battery is $I = \mathcal{E}/R = (2400\text{ V})/(400\ \Omega) = 6$ A. At the junction marked J, this current splits. Since R_1 is twice R_2, half as much current will flow through R_1 as through R_2; the current through R_1 is $I_1 = 2$ A, and the current through R_2 is $I_2 = 4$ A. The voltage drop across each of these resistors is $I_1R_1 = I_2R_2 = 1200$ V (matching voltages verify the values of currents I_1 and I_2). Since the ammeter is in the branch that contains R_2, it will read $I_2 = 4$ A.

The voltmeter will read the voltage drop across R_3, which is $V_3 = IR_3 = (6\text{ A})(150\ \Omega) = 900$ V. So the potential at point b is 900 V lower than at point a.

Example 12.8 The diagram below shows a point a at potential $V = 20$ V connected by a combination of resistors to a point (denoted G) that is **grounded**. *The ground is considered to be at potential zero.* If the potential at point a is maintained at 20 V, what is the current through R_3?

Solution. R_1 and R_2 are in parallel; their equivalent resistance is R_p, where

$$\frac{1}{R_p} = \frac{1}{4\ \Omega} + \frac{1}{6\ \Omega} \quad \Rightarrow \quad R_p = \frac{24}{10}\ \Omega = 2.4\ \Omega$$

R_p is in series with R_3, so the equivalent resistance is:

$$R = R_p + R_3 = (2.4\ \Omega) + (8\ \Omega) = 10.4\ \Omega$$

and the current that flows through R_3 is

$$I_3 = \frac{V}{R} = \frac{20\ \text{V}}{10.4\ \Omega} = 1.9\ \text{A}$$

KIRCHHOFF'S RULES

When the resistors in a circuit cannot be classified as either in series or in parallel, we need another method for analyzing the circuit. The rules of Gustav Kirchhoff (pronounced "Keer koff") can be applied to any circuit:

The Loop Rule. The sum of the potential differences (positive and negative) that traverse any closed loop in a circuit must be zero.

The Junction Rule. The total current that enters a junction must equal the total current that leaves the junction. (This is also known as the **Node Rule**.)

The Loop Rule just says that, starting at any point, by the time we get back to that same point by following any closed loop, we have to be back to the same potential. Therefore, the total drop in potential must equal the total rise in potential. Put another way, the Loop Rule says that all the decreases in electrical potential energy (for example, caused by resistors in the direction of the current) must be balanced by all the increases in electrical potential energy (for example, caused by a source of emf from the negative to positive terminal). So the Loop Rule is bascially a statement of the Law of Conservation of Energy.

Similarly, the Junction Rule simply says that the charge (per unit time) that goes into a junction must equal the charge (per unit time) that comes out. This is basically a statement of the Law of Conservation of Charge.

In practice, the Junction Rule is straightforward to apply. The most important things to remember about the Loop Rule can be summarized as follows:

♦ When going across a resistor in the *same* direction as the current, the potential *drops* by *IR*.

♦ When going across a resistor in the *opposite* direction from the current, the potential *increases* by *IR*.

♦ When going from the negative to the positive terminal of a source of emf, the potential *increases* by $\mathcal{E}$.

♦ When going from the positive to the negative terminal of a source of emf, the potential *decreases* by $\mathcal{E}$.

Example 12.9 Use Kirchhoff's Rules to determine the current through R_2 in the following circuit:

Solution. First let's label some points in the circuit.

$$\mathcal{E}_1 = 20 \text{ V} \qquad \mathcal{E}_2 = 10 \text{ V}$$

$R_2 = 20 \ \Omega$

$R_1 = 10 \ \Omega \qquad R_3 = 30 \ \Omega$

The points c and f are junctions (nodes). We have 2 nodes and 3 branches: one branch is *fabc*, another branch is *cdef*, and the third branch is *cf*. Each branch has one current throughout. If we label the current in *fabc* I_1 and the current in branch *cdef* I_2 (with the directions as shown in the diagram below), then the current in branch *cf* must be $I_1 - I_2$, by the Junction Rule: I_1 comes into c, and a total of $I_2 + (I_1 - I_2) = I_1$ comes out.

Now pick a loop; say, *abcfa*. Starting at a, we go to b, then across R_1 in the direction of the current, so the potential drops by $I_1 R_1$. Then we move to c, then up through R_2 in the direction of the current, so the potential drops by $(I_1 - I_2)R_2$. Then we reach f, turn left and travel through $\mathcal{E}_1$ from the negative to the positive terminal, so the potential increases by $\mathcal{E}_1$. We now find ourselves back at a. By the Loop Rule, the total change in potential around this closed loop must be zero, and

$$-I_1 R_1 - (I_1 - I_2)R_2 + \mathcal{E}_1 = 0 \quad (1)$$

Since we have two unknowns (I_1 and I_2), we need two equations, so now pick another loop; let's choose *cdefc*. From c to d, we travel across the resistor in the direction of the current, so the potential drops by $I_2 R_3$. From e to f, we travel through $\mathcal{E}_2$ from the positive to the negative terminal, so the potential *drops* by $\mathcal{E}_2$. Heading down from f to c, we travel across R_2 but in the direction opposite to the current, so the potential *increases* by $(I_1 - I_2)R_2$. At c, our loop is completed, so

$$-I_2 R_3 - \mathcal{E}_2 + (I_1 - I_2)R_2 = 0 \quad (2)$$

Substituting in the given numerical values for R_1, R_2, R_3, $\mathcal{E}_1$, and $\mathcal{E}_2$, and simplifying, these two equations become

$$3I_1 - 2I_2 = 2 \quad (1')$$

$$2I_1 - 5I_2 = 1 \quad (2')$$

Solving this pair of simultaneous equations, we get

$$I_1 = \tfrac{8}{11} \text{ A} = 0.73 \text{ A} \quad \text{and} \quad I_2 = \tfrac{1}{11} \text{ A} = 0.09 \text{ A}$$

So the current through R_2 is $I_1 - I_2 = \tfrac{7}{11}$ A = 0.64 A.

The choice of directions of the currents at the beginning of the solution was arbitrary. Don't worry about trying to guess the actual direction of the current in a particular branch. Just pick a direction, stick with it, and obey the Junction Rule. At the end, when you solve for the values of the branch current, a negative value will alert you that the direction of the current is actually opposite to the direction you originally chose for it in your diagram.

Example 12.10 In the circuit diagram below, Resistors ① and ③ have fixed resistances (R_1 and R_3, respectively), which are known. Resistor ② is a **variable** (or **adjustable**) resistor, and the resistance of Resistor ④ is unknown.

Show that if Resistor ② is adjusted until the ammeter shown registers no current through its branch, then

$$R_1 R_4 = R_2 R_3$$

(This circuit arrangement is known as a **Wheatstone bridge**.)

Solution. If no current flows through the ammeter, then Resistors ① and ③ are in series, and so are Resistors ② and ④. Therefore, the current flowing through ① and ③ is equal to $I_{1-3} = \mathcal{E}/(R_1 + R_3)$. Similarly, the current flowing through ② and ④ is $I_{2-4} = \mathcal{E}/(R_2 + R_4)$. Now consider the three points marked a, b, and c below:

Since no current flows between Points a and b, there must be no potential difference between a and b; they're at the same potential. So the voltage drop from a to c must equal the voltage drop from b to c. The voltage drop from a to c is

$$V_{ac} = I_{2\text{-}4}R_4 = \frac{\varepsilon}{R_2 + R_4}R_4$$

and the voltage drop from b to c is

$$V_{bc} = I_{1\text{-}3}R_3 = \frac{\varepsilon}{R_1 + R_3}R_3$$

Setting these equal to each other, we get

$$\frac{\varepsilon}{R_2 + R_4}R_4 = \frac{\varepsilon}{R_1 + R_3}R_3$$

$$\frac{R_4}{R_2 + R_4} = \frac{R_3}{R_1 + R_3}$$

$$R_4(R_1 + R_3) = R_3(R_2 + R_4)$$

$$R_1R_4 + R_3R_4 = R_2R_3 + R_3R_4$$

$$R_1R_4 = R_2R_3$$

By knowing R_1, R_2, and R_3, we can solve for the unknown resistance: $R_4 = R_2R_3/R_1$.

RESISTANCE–CAPACITANCE (RC) CIRCUITS

Capacitors are typically charged by batteries. Once the switch in the diagram on the left is closed, electrons are attracted to the positive terminal of the battery and leave the top plate of the capacitor. Electrons also accumulate on the bottom plate of the capacitor, and this continues until the voltage across the capacitor plates matches the emf of the battery. When this condition is reached, the current stops and the capacitor is fully charged.

Example 12.11 Find the charge stored and the voltage across each capacitor in the following circuit, given that $\mathcal{E} = 180$ V, $C_1 = 30\,\mu F$, $C_2 = 60\,\mu F$, and $C_3 = 90\,\mu F$.

Solution. Once the charging currents stop, the voltage across C_3 is equal to the voltage across the battery, so $V_3 = 180$ V. This gives us $Q_3 = C_3 V_3 = (90\,\mu F)(180$ V$) = 16.2$ mC. Since C_1 and C_2 are in series, they must store identical amounts of charge, and, from the diagram, the sum of their voltages must equal the voltage of the battery. So if we let Q be the charge on each of these two capacitors, then $Q = C_1 V_1 = C_2 V_2$, and $V_1 + V_2 = 180$ V. The equation $C_1 V_1 = C_2 V_2$ becomes $(30\,\mu F)V_1 = (60\,\mu F)V_2$, so $V_1 = 2V_2$. Substituting this into $V_1 + V_2 = 180$ V gives us $V_1 = 120$ V and $V_2 = 60$ V. The charge stored on each of these capacitors is

$$(30\,\mu F)(120\text{ V}) = C_1 V_1 = C_2 V_2 = (60\,\mu F)(60\text{ V}) = 3.6\text{ mC}$$

Example 12.12 In the diagram below, $C_1 = 2$ mF and $C_2 = 4$ mF. When Switch S is open, a battery (which is not shown) is connected between points a and b and charges capacitor C_1 so that $V_{ab} = 12$ V. The battery is then disconnected.

After the switch is closed, what will be the common voltage across each of the parallel capacitors (once electrostatic conditions are reestablished)?

Solution. When C_1 is fully charged, the charge on (each of the plates of) C_1 has the magnitude $Q = C_1 V = (2$ mF$)(12$ V$) = 24$ mC. After the switch is closed, this charge will be redistributed in such a way that the resulting voltages across the two capacitors, V', are equal. This happens because the capacitors are in parallel. So if Q_1' is the new charge magnitude on C_1 and Q_2' is the new charge magnitude on C_2, we have $Q_1' + Q_2' = Q$, so $C_1 V' + C_2 V' = Q$, which gives us:

$$V' = \frac{Q}{C_1 + C_2} = \frac{24\text{ mC}}{2\text{ mF} + 4\text{ mF}} = 4\text{ V}$$

[C] CHARGING OR DISCHARGING A CAPACITOR IN AN RC CIRCUIT

When a battery is hooked up to an uncharged capacitor and current begins to flow, the current is not constant. So far, we have assumed that the currents in our circuits have been constant, but RC circuits are different.

CHARGING A CAPACITOR

Consider the RC circuit shown below, where the charge on the capacitor is zero:

When the switch is closed (time $t = 0$), there is no charge on the capacitor, which means that there's no voltage across the capacitor, so Kirchhoff's Loop Rule gives us $\mathcal{E} - IR = 0$, and the initial current in the circuit is $I = \mathcal{E}/R$. But, as time passes, charge begins to accumulate on the capacitor, and a voltage is created that opposes the emf of the battery. At any time t after the switch is closed, Kirchhoff's Loop Rule gives us:

$$\mathcal{E} - I(t)R - V(t) = 0$$

where $I(t)$ is the current at time t and $V(t)$ is the voltage across the capacitor at time t. Since $V(t) = Q(t)/C$ and $I(t) = dQ(t)/dt$, the equation above becomes

$$\mathcal{E} - R\frac{dQ}{dt} - \frac{Q}{C} = 0 \quad \Rightarrow \quad \frac{dQ}{dt} = \frac{C\mathcal{E} - Q}{RC}$$

Solving this equation for $Q(t)$ gives us:

$$Q(t) = C\mathcal{E}(1 - e^{-t/RC})$$

The product $C\mathcal{E}$ is equal to the final charge on the capacitor (remember that $Q = CV$). The quantity RC that appears in the exponent is called the **time constant** for the circuit and is represented by τ:

$$\tau = RC$$

Therefore, letting Q_f replace the quantity $C\mathcal{E}$, the equation above becomes

$$Q(t) = Q_f(1 - e^{-t/\tau}) \qquad (*)$$

What does the time constant, τ, say about the circuit? It says that, after a time interval of τ has elapsed, the charge on the capacitor is

$$Q(\tau) = Q_f(1 - e^{-\tau/\tau}) = Q_f(1 - e^{-1}) \approx 0.63 Q_f$$

Therefore, the greater the value of τ, the more slowly the capacitor charges. By differentiating (*) with respect to t,

$$\frac{dQ}{dt} = \frac{Q_f}{\tau}e^{-t/\tau} = \frac{Q_f}{RC}e^{-t/\tau} = \frac{\mathcal{E}}{R}e^{-t/\tau}$$

we can get the current in the circuit as a function of time:

$$I(t) = \frac{\mathcal{E}}{R}e^{-t/\tau}$$

Therefore, the charge builds up gradually on the capacitor,

as the current in the circuit drops gradually to zero:

DISCHARGING A CAPACITOR

Consider the RC circuit shown below, where the charge on the capacitor is Q_0:

When the switch is closed (time $t = 0$), the voltage across the capacitor is $V_0 = Q_0/C$, so $V_0 - IR = 0$, and the initial current in the circuit is $I_0 = V_0/R$. But as time passes, charge leaks off the capacitor and its voltage decreases, which causes the current to decrease.

The equation for $Q(t)$ is

$$Q(t) = Q_0 e^{-t/RC} = Q_0 e^{-t/\tau}$$

The voltage across the plates as a function of time is

$$V(t) = \frac{Q(t)}{C} = \frac{Q_0}{C} e^{-t/\tau}$$

and, by using the equation $I(t) = -dQ/dt$, the current in the circuit is

$$I(t) = \frac{Q_0}{\tau} e^{-t/\tau} = \frac{Q_0}{RC} e^{-t/\tau} = \frac{V_0}{R} e^{-t/\tau}$$

Example 12.13 In the circuit below, $\mathcal{E} = 20\ \text{V}$, $R = 1000\ \Omega$, and $C = 2\ \text{mF}$. If the capacitor is initially uncharged, how long will it take (after the switch S is closed) for the capacitor to be 99% charged?

Solution. The equation $Q(t) = Q_f(1 - e^{-t/\tau})$, where $\tau = RC$, gives the charge on the capacitor as a function of time. If we want $Q(t)$ to equal $0.99Q_f$, then we have to wait until time t, when $e^{-t/\tau} = 0.01$. Solving this equation for t, we get

$$e^{-t/\tau} = 0.01$$

$$-\frac{t}{\tau} = \ln(0.01)$$

$$t = -\ln(0.01)\tau$$

$$= (4.6)\tau$$

Since the time constant is

$$\tau = RC = (1000\ \Omega)(2\ \text{mF}) = 2\ \text{s}$$

the time required is $(4.6)\tau = (4.6)(2\ \text{s}) = 9.2\ \text{s}$.

CHAPTER 12 REVIEW QUESTIONS

SECTION I: MULTIPLE CHOICE

1. A wire made of brass and a wire made of silver have the same length, but the diameter of the brass wire is 4 times the diameter of the silver wire. The resistivity of brass is 5 times greater than the resistivity of silver. If R_B denotes the resistance of the brass wire and R_S denotes the resistance of the silver wire, which of the following is true?

   (A) $R_B = \frac{5}{16}R_S$
   (B) $R_B = \frac{4}{5}R_S$
   (C) $R_B = \frac{5}{4}R_S$
   (D) $R_B = \frac{5}{2}R_S$
   (E) $R_B = \frac{16}{5}R_S$

2. For an ohmic conductor, doubling the voltage without changing the resistance will cause the current to

   (A) decrease by a factor of 4.
   (B) decrease by a factor of 2.
   (C) remain unchanged.
   (D) increase by a factor of 2.
   (E) increase by a factor of 4.

3. If a 60-watt light bulb operates at a voltage of 120 V, what is the resistance of the bulb?

   (A) 2 Ω
   (B) 30 Ω
   (C) 240 Ω
   (D) 720 Ω
   (E) 7200 Ω

4. A battery whose emf is 40 V has an internal resistance of 5 Ω. If this battery is connected to a 15 Ω resistor R, what will the voltage drop across R be?

   (A) 10 V
   (B) 30 V
   (C) 40 V
   (D) 50 V
   (E) 70 V

5.

Determine the equivalent resistance between points a and b.

   (A) 0.167 Ω
   (B) 0.25 Ω
   (C) 0.333 Ω
   (D) 1.5 Ω
   (E) 2 Ω

6.

Three identical light bulbs are connected to a source of emf, as shown in the diagram above. What will happen if the middle bulb burns out?

   (A) All the bulbs will go out.
   (B) The light intensity of the other two bulbs will decrease (but they won't go out).
   (C) The light intensity of the other two bulbs will increase.
   (D) The light intensity of the other two bulbs will remain the same.
   (E) More current will be drawn from the source of emf.

7.

What is the voltage drop across the 12-ohm resistor in the portion of the circuit shown above?

(A) 24 V
(B) 36 V
(C) 48 V
(D) 72 V
(E) 144 V

8.

What is the current through the 8-ohm resistor in the circuit shown above?

(A) 0.5 A
(B) 1.0 A
(C) 1.25 A
(D) 1.5 A
(E) 3.0 A

9. How much energy is dissipated as heat in 20 s by a 100 Ω resistor that carries a current of 0.5 A?

(A) 50 J
(B) 100 J
(C) 250 J
(D) 500 J
(E) 1000 J

10.

What is the time constant for the circuit above?

(A) 0.01 s
(B) 0.025 s
(C) 0.04 s
(D) 0.05 s
(E) 0.1 s

SECTION II: FREE RESPONSE

1. Consider the following circuit:

(a) At what rate does the battery deliver energy to the circuit?

(b) Find the current through the 20 Ω resistor.

(c) (i) Determine the potential difference between points a and b.

(ii) At which of these two points is the potential higher?

(d) Find the energy dissipated by the 100 Ω resistor in 10 s.

(e) Given that the 100 Ω resistor is a solid cylinder that's 4 cm long, composed of a material whose resistivity is 0.45 Ω · m, determine its radius.

2. [C] The diagram below shows an uncharged capacitor, two resistors, and a battery whose emf is $\mathcal{E}$.

The switch S is turned to point a at time $t = 0$.

(Express all answers in terms of C, r, R, $\mathcal{E}$, and fundamental constants.)

(a) Determine the current through r at time $t = 0$.

(b) Compute the time required for the charge on the capacitor to reach one-half its final value.

(c) When the capacitor is fully charged, which plate is positively charged?

(d) Determine the electrical potential energy stored in the capacitor when the current through r is zero.

When the current through r is zero, the switch S is then moved to point b; for the following parts, consider this event time $t = 0$.

(e) Determine the current through R as a function of time.

(f) Find the power dissipated in R as a function of time.

(g) Determine the total amount of energy dissipated as heat by R.

13

MAGNETIC FORCES AND FIELDS

INTRODUCTION

In chapter 10, we learned that electric charges are the source of electric fields and that other charges experience an electric force in those fields. The charges generating the field were assumed to be at rest, because if they weren't, then another force field would have been generated in addition to the electric field. Electric charges *that move* are the source of **magnetic fields**, and other charges that move experience a magnetic force in these fields.

THE MAGNETIC FORCE ON A MOVING CHARGE

If a particle with charge q moves with velocity **v** through a magnetic field **B**, it will experience a magnetic force, $\mathbf{F}_B$, with magnitude:

$$F_B = |q|vB\sin\theta \quad (1)$$

where θ is the angle between **v** and **B**. From this equation, we can see that if the charge is at rest, then $v = 0$ immediately gives us $F_B = 0$. This tells us that magnetic forces only act on moving charges. Also, if **v** is parallel (or antiparallel) to **B**, then $F_B = 0$ since, in either of these cases, $\sin\theta = 0$. So only charges that cut across the magnetic field lines will experience a magnetic force. Furthermore, the magnetic force is maximized when **v** is perpendicular to **B**, since if $\theta = 90°$, then $\sin\theta$ is equal to 1; its maximum value.

The direction of $\mathbf{F}_B$ is always perpendicular to both **v** and **B** and depends on the sign of the charge q and the direction of $\mathbf{v} \times \mathbf{B}$ (which is given by the right-hand rule).

$$\text{direction of } \mathbf{F}_B = \begin{cases} \text{same as the direction of } \mathbf{v} \times \mathbf{B} \text{ if } q \text{ is positive} \\ \text{opposite to the direction of } \mathbf{v} \times \mathbf{B} \text{ if } q \text{ is negative} \end{cases} \quad (2)$$

Equations (1) and (2) can be summarized by a single equation:

$$\mathbf{F}_B = q(\mathbf{v} \times \mathbf{B})$$

Notice that there are fundamental differences between the electric force and magnetic force on a charge. First, a magnetic force acts on a charge only if the charge is moving; the electric force acts on a charge whether it moves or not. Second, the direction of the magnetic force is always perpendicular to the magnetic field, while the electric force is always parallel (or antiparallel) to the electric field.

The SI unit for the magnetic field is the **tesla** (abbreviated **T**) which is one newton per ampere-meter. Another common unit for magnetic field strength is the **gauss** (abbreviated **G**); $1\text{ G} = 10^{-4}\text{ T}$.

Example 13.1 A charge $+q = +6 \times 10^{-6}$ C moves with speed $v = 4 \times 10^5$ m/s through a magnetic field of strength $B = 0.4$ T, as shown in the figure below. What is the magnetic force experienced by q?

Solution. The magnitude of $\mathbf{F}_B$ is

$$F_B = qvB \sin\theta = (6 \times 10^{-6}\text{ C})(4 \times 10^5\text{ m/s})(0.4\text{ T}) \sin 30° = 0.48\text{ N}$$

By the right-hand rule, the direction of $\mathbf{v} \times \mathbf{B}$ is into the plane of the page, which is symbolized by $\otimes$. Because q is a positive charge, the direction of $\mathbf{F}_B$ on q is also into the plane of the page.

Example 13.2 A particle of mass m and charge $+q$ is projected with velocity $\mathbf{v}$ (in the plane of the page) into a uniform magnetic field $\mathbf{B}$ that points into the page. How will the particle move?

Solution. Since $\mathbf{v}$ is perpendicular to $\mathbf{B}$, the particle will feel a magnetic force of strength qvB, which will be directed perpendicular to $\mathbf{v}$ (and to $\mathbf{B}$) as shown:

Since $\mathbf{F}_B$ is always perpendicular to $\mathbf{v}$, the particle will undergo uniform circular motion; $\mathbf{F}_B$ will provide the centripetal force. Notice that, because $\mathbf{F}_B$ is always perpendicular to $\mathbf{v}$, the magnitude of $\mathbf{v}$ will not change, just its direction. *Magnetic forces alone cannot change the speed of a charged particle, they can only change its direction of motion.* The radius of the particle's circular path is found from the equation $F_B = F_C$:

$$ qvB = \frac{mv^2}{r} \quad \Rightarrow \quad r = \frac{mv}{qB} $$

Example 13.3 A particle of charge $-q$ is shot into a region that contains an electric field, $\mathbf{E}$, crossed with a perpendicular magnetic field, $\mathbf{B}$. If $E = 2 \times 10^4\ \mathrm{N/C}$ and $B = 0.5\ \mathrm{T}$, what must be the speed of the particle if it is to cross this region without being deflected?

Solution. If the particle is to pass through undeflected, the electric force it feels has to be canceled by the magnetic force. In the diagram above, the electric force on the particle is directed upward (since the charge is negative and **E** is downward), and the magnetic force is directed downward (since the charge is negative and **v** × **B** is upward). So $\mathbf{F}_E$ and $\mathbf{F}_B$ point in opposite directions, and in order for their magnitudes to balance, qE must equal qvB, so v must equal E/B, which in this case gives

$$v = \frac{E}{B} = \frac{2 \times 10^4 \text{ N/C}}{0.5 \text{ T}} = 4 \times 10^4 \text{ m/s}$$

Example 13.4 A particle with charge $+q$, traveling with velocity **v**, enters a uniform magnetic field **B**, as shown below. Describe the particle's subsequent motion.

Solution. If the particle's velocity were parallel to **B**, then it would be unaffected by **B**. If **v** were perpendicular to **B**, then it would undergo uniform circular motion (as we saw in Example 13.2). In this case, **v** is neither purely parallel nor perpendicular to **B**. It has a component ($\mathbf{v}_1$) that's parallel to **B** and a component ($\mathbf{v}_2$) that's perpendicular to **B**.

Component $\mathbf{v}_1$ will not be changed by **B**, so the particle will continue upward in the direction of **B**. However, the presence of $\mathbf{v}_2$ will create circular motion. The superposition of these two types of motion will cause the particle's trajectory to be a *helix*; it will spin in circular motion while traveling upward with the speed $v_1 = v \sin \phi$:

THE MAGNETIC FORCE ON A CURRENT-CARRYING WIRE

Since magnetic fields affect moving charges, they should also affect current-carrying wires. After all, a wire that contains a current contains charges that move.

Let a wire of length ℓ be immersed in magnetic field **B**. If the wire carries a current I, then the magnitude of the magnetic force it feels is

$$F_B = I\ell B \sin \theta$$

where θ is the angle between ℓ and **B**. Here, the direction of ℓ is the direction of the current, I. The direction of $\mathbf{F}_B$ is the same as the direction of $\ell \times \mathbf{B}$, and these properties can be summarized into a single equation:

$$\mathbf{F}_B = I(\ell \times \mathbf{B})$$

Example 13.5 A U-shaped wire of mass m is lowered into a magnetic field **B** that points out of the plane of the page. How much current I must pass through the wire in order to cause the net force on the wire to be zero?

Solution. The total magnetic force on the wire is equal to the sum of the magnetic forces on each of the three sections of wire. The force on the first section (the right, vertical one), $\mathbf{F}_{B1}$, is directed to the left (applying the right-hand rule to $\ell_1 \times \mathbf{B}$; ℓ_1 points downward), and the force on the third piece (the left, vertical one), $\mathbf{F}_{B3}$, is directed to the right. Since these pieces are the same length, these two oppositely-directed forces have the same magnitude, $I\ell_1 B = I\ell_3 B$, and they cancel. So the net magnetic force on the wire is the magnetic force on the middle piece. Since ℓ_2 points to the left and **B** is out of the page, $\ell_2 \times \mathbf{B}$ [and, therefore, $\mathbf{F}_{B2} = I(\ell_2 \times \mathbf{B})$] is directed upward.

Since the magnetic force on the wire is $I\ell_2 B$, directed upward, the amount of current must create an upward magnetic force that exactly balances the downward gravitational force on the wire. Because the total mass of the wire is m, the resultant force (magnetic + gravitational) will be zero if

$$I\ell_2 B = mg \quad \Rightarrow \quad I = \frac{mg}{\ell_2 B}$$

Example 13.6 A rectangular loop of wire that carries a current I is placed in a uniform magnetic field, **B**, as shown in the diagram below. What torque does it experience?

Solution. Ignoring the tiny gap in the vertical left-hand wire, we have two wires of length ℓ_1 and two of length ℓ_2. There is no magnetic force on either of the sides of the loop of length ℓ_2, because the current in the top side is parallel to **B** and the current in the bottom side is antiparallel to **B**. The magnetic force on the right-hand side points out of the plane of the page, while the magnetic force on the left-hand side points into the plane of the page.

If the loop is free to rotate, then each of these two forces exerts a torque that tends to turn the loop in such a way that the right-hand side rises out of the plane of the page and the left-hand side rotates into the page. Relative to the axis shown above (which cuts the loop in half), the torque of F_{B1} is

$$\tau_1 = rF_{B1} \sin \theta = (\tfrac{1}{2} \ell_2)(I \ell_1 B) \sin 90° = \tfrac{1}{2} I \ell_1 \ell_2 B$$

and the torque of F_{B2} is

$$\tau_2 = rF_{B2} \sin \theta = (\tfrac{1}{2} \ell_2)(I \ell_1 B) \sin 90° = \tfrac{1}{2} I \ell_1 \ell_2 B$$

Since both these torques rotate the loop in the same direction, the net torque on the loop is

$$\tau_1 + \tau_2 = I \ell_1 \ell_2 B$$

Example 13.7 [C] The middle portion of the wire shown below is bent into the shape of a semicircle of radius r. The wire carries a current I. What's the total magnetic force that acts on the wire in the field, B?

Solution. Let's first find the magnetic force that acts on the two straight sections. The magnitude of the magnetic force on each section is $I \ell B = IrB$, and since ℓ points to the right in both sections, the magnetic force on each of them points upward.

On the semicircle, the direction of ℓ is not constant, so we have to split this section into small pieces with lengths $d\ell = r\, d\theta$ and then use the equation $d\mathbf{F} = I(d\boldsymbol{\ell} \times \mathbf{B})$. In the diagram on the next page, the direction of $d\mathbf{F}$ is radially away from the center of the semicircle.

The total horizontal force on the semicircle, F_{Bx}, can be found by integrating $dF_{Bx} = dF \cos \theta$ from $\theta = 0$ to $\theta = \pi$:

$$F_{Bx} = \int dF_{Bx} = \int dF \cos\theta = \int I(r\,d\theta)B\cos\theta$$

$$= IrB \int_0^\pi \cos\theta\,d\theta$$

$$= IrB[\sin\theta]_0^\pi$$

$$= 0$$

The total vertical force on the semicircle, F_{By}, can be found by integrating $dF_{By} = dF \sin \theta$ from $\theta = 0$ to $\theta = \pi$:

$$F_{By} = \int dF_{By} = \int dF \sin\theta = \int I(r\,d\theta)B\sin\theta$$

$$= IrB \int_0^\pi \sin\theta\,d\theta$$

$$= IrB[-\cos\theta]_0^\pi$$

$$= 2IrB$$

So the total magnetic force on the wire is (IrB, upward) + ($2IrB$, upward) + (IrB, upward) = $4IrB$, upward.

MAGNETIC FIELDS CREATED BY CURRENT–CARRYING WIRES

As we said at the beginning of this chapter, the source of magnetic fields are electric charges that move; they may spin, circulate, move through space, or flow down a wire. For example, consider a long straight wire that carries a current I. The current generates a magnetic field in the surrounding space, of magnitude:

$$B = \frac{\mu_0}{2\pi} \frac{I}{r}$$

where r is the distance from the wire. The symbol μ_0 denotes a fundamental constant called the permeability of free space. Its value is:

$$\mu_0 = 4\pi \times 10^{-7}\,\mathrm{N}/\mathrm{A}^2 = 4\pi \times 10^{-7}\,\mathrm{T}\cdot\mathrm{m}/\mathrm{A}$$

The magnetic field lines are actually circles whose centers are on the wire. The direction of these circles is determined by a variation of the right-hand rule. Imagine grabbing the wire in your right hand with your thumb pointing in the direction of the current. Then the direction in which your fingers curl around the wire gives the direction of the magnetic field lines.

wire (perpendicular to page, with current directed outward)

wire (perpendicular to page, with current directed inward)

Example 13.8 The diagram below shows a proton moving with a speed of 2×10^5 m/s, initially parallel to, and 4 cm from, a long straight wire. If the current in the wire is 20 A, what's the magnetic force on the proton?

proton

$+e$ $\mathbf{v}_0$

I

Solution. Above the wire (where the proton is), the magnetic field lines generated by the current-carrying wire point out of the plane of the page, so $\mathbf{v}_0 \times \mathbf{B}$ points downward. Since the proton's charge is positive, the magnetic force $\mathbf{F}_B = q(\mathbf{v}_0 \times \mathbf{B})$ is also directed down, toward the wire.

The strength of the magnetic force on the proton is

$$F_B = qv_0B = ev_0\frac{\mu_0}{2\pi}\frac{I}{r} = (1.6\times10^{-19}\ \text{C})(2\times10^5\ \text{m/s})\frac{4\pi\times10^{-7}\ \text{N/A}^2}{2\pi}\frac{20\ \text{A}}{0.04\ \text{m}}$$

$$= 3.2\times10^{-18}\ \text{N}$$

Example 13.9 The diagram below shows a pair of long, straight, parallel wires, separated by a small distance, r. If currents I_1 and I_2 are established in the wires, what is the magnetic force per unit length they exert on each other?

Solution. To find the force on Wire 2, consider the current in Wire 1 as the source of the magnetic field. Below Wire 1, the magnetic field lines generated by Wire 1 point into the plane of the page. Therefore, the force on Wire 2, as given by the equation $\mathbf{F}_{B2} = I_2(\boldsymbol{\ell}_2 \times \mathbf{B}_1)$, points upward.

The magnitude of the magnetic force per unit length felt by Wire 2, due to the magnetic field generated by Wire 1, is found this way:

$$F_{B2} = I_2\ell_2B_1 = I_2\ell_2\frac{\mu_0}{2\pi}\frac{I_1}{r} \quad\Rightarrow\quad \frac{F_{B2}}{\ell_2} = \frac{\mu_0}{2\pi}\frac{I_1I_2}{r}$$

By Newton's Third Law, this is the same force that Wire 1 feels due to the magnetic field generated by Wire 2. The force is attractive because the currents point in the same direction; if one of the currents were reversed, then the force between the wires would be repulsive.

[C] THE MAGNETIC FIELD OF A SOLENOID

Imagine taking a long piece of wire and winding it in a helix around the length of a hollow tube; this is a **solenoid**. Let N be the total number of turns and L the length of the solenoid; then the number of turns per unit length is N/L, which we'll call n. If a current I is established in the wire, then a magnetic field is generated in the space that surrounds the solenoid. If the solenoid is much longer than it is wide, then the magnetic field inside will be parallel to the central axis and nearly uniform. The strength of the field inside is given by the equation

$$B = \mu_0 nI$$

So the magnetic field inside a solenoid can be increased either by winding the wire more tightly (to increase n) or by increasing the current.

> **Example 13.10** A tightly-wound solenoid has a length of 30 cm, a diameter of 2 cm, and contains a total of 10,000 turns. If it carries a current of 5 A, what's the magnitude of the magnetic field inside the solenoid?

Solution. Since the solenoid is so much longer than it is wide, the equation $B = \mu_0 nI$ can be used to calculate the field inside:

$$B = \mu_0 nI = \mu_0 \frac{N}{L} I = (4\pi \times 10^{-7} \text{ T} \cdot \text{m} / \text{A}) \frac{10,000}{0.30 \text{ m}} (5 \text{ A}) = 0.2 \text{ T}$$

[C] THE BIOT–SAVART LAW

In this section, you'll learn one way to determine the magnetic field created by an electric current. Let's say we want to determine the magnitude and direction of the magnetic field, at point P, created by the current I in the diagram below.

Consider a small section of the current, an infinitesimal section of length $d\ell$, and assign it the direction of the current so we obtain a **current element**, $d\boldsymbol{\ell}$. Let $\mathbf{r}$ be the position vector from the current element to the point P, and form the unit vector $\hat{\mathbf{r}} = \mathbf{r}/r$. Then the magnitude and direction of the magnetic field at P, due to the current element is

$$d\mathbf{B} = \frac{\mu_0}{4\pi} \frac{I(d\boldsymbol{\ell} \times \hat{\mathbf{r}})}{r^2}$$

This is called the **Biot–Savart Law**. By adding all the contributions to the magnetic field, we can get the total magnetic field due to the entire current.

Example 13.11 Use the Biot–Savart Law to show that the magnetic field due to an infinitely-long straight wire carrying a current I is given by the equation $B = (\mu_0/2\pi)I/R$, where R is the distance from the wire. You should use the integration formula

$$\int_{-\infty}^{\infty} \frac{dx}{(x^2 + a^2)^{3/2}} = \frac{2}{a^2}$$

Solution. Refer to the diagram below:

The direction of $d\boldsymbol{\ell} \times \hat{\mathbf{r}}$ is out of the plane of the page (because P is above the wire). The contribution from the current element to the total magnetic field at P is given by the Biot–Savart Law:

$$dB = \frac{\mu_0}{4\pi} \frac{I|d\boldsymbol{\ell} \times \hat{\mathbf{r}}|}{r^2} = \frac{\mu_0}{4\pi} \frac{I \, d\ell \sin\theta}{r^2}$$

From the diagram, we see that $\sin\theta = R/r = R/\sqrt{\ell^2 + R^2}$, so

$$dB = \frac{\mu_0 IR}{4\pi} \frac{d\ell}{(\ell^2 + R^2)^{3/2}}$$

and, integrating along the entire wire, we get:

$$B = \int dB = \int_{-\infty}^{\infty} \frac{\mu_0 IR}{4\pi} \frac{d\ell}{(\ell^2 + R^2)^{3/2}} = \frac{\mu_0 IR}{4\pi} \int_{-\infty}^{\infty} \frac{d\ell}{(\ell^2 + R^2)^{3/2}} = \frac{\mu_0 IR}{4\pi} \left[\frac{2}{R^2} \right] = \frac{\mu_0}{2\pi} \frac{I}{R}$$

Example 13.12 A circular loop of wire has radius R. If the loop carries a current I, what's the magnetic field created at the center of the loop?

Solution.

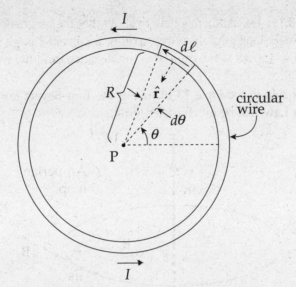

Every current element $d\ell$ is perpendicular to $\hat{\mathbf{r}}$, and $r = R$, so the Biot–Savart Law gives us:

$$dB = \frac{\mu_0}{4\pi}\frac{I\,d\ell\sin\theta}{r^2} = \frac{\mu_0}{4\pi}\frac{I\,d\ell\sin 90°}{R^2} = \frac{\mu_0 I}{4\pi R^2}\,d\ell$$

Writing $d\ell = R\,d\theta$, we integrate around the circle to get

$$B = \int dB = \int_0^{2\pi} \frac{\mu_0 I}{4\pi R^2}R\,d\theta = \frac{\mu_0 I}{4\pi R}\int_0^{2\pi} d\theta = \frac{\mu_0 I}{2R}$$

If the current is counterclockwise (as shown above), then $d\ell \times \hat{\mathbf{r}}$, and the magnetic field points out of the plane of the page, but if the current is clockwise, the magnetic field at the center points into the page.

[C] AMPERE'S LAW

In chapter 10, we learned about Gauss's Law, which can be used to calculate the electric field due to a configuration of electric charges. Gauss's law says that the electric flux through a closed Gaussian surface (which is actually the integral of $\mathbf{E} \cdot d\mathbf{A}$ over the area of the surface) is equal to a constant $(1/\varepsilon_0)$ times the total electric charge enclosed by the surface.

There's an analogous law for calculating the magnetic field due to a configuration of electric currents. This law says that the integral of $\mathbf{B} \cdot d\mathbf{s}$ around a closed loop (called an **Amperian loop**) is equal to a constant (μ_0) times the total current that passes through the loop:

$$\oint_{\text{loop}} \mathbf{B} \cdot d\mathbf{s} = \mu_0 I_{\text{through loop}}$$

This is **Ampere's Law** and we'll use it to find the magnetic field at points on an Amperian loop surrounding the source current. (The circle on the integral sign in Ampere's Law emphasizes that the integral must always be taken around a *closed* path.)

Example 13.13 Use Ampere's Law to show that the magnetic field due to an infinitely-long straight wire carrying a current I is given by the equation $B = (\mu_0/2\pi)I/R$, where R is the distance from the wire.

Solution. When we did this in Example 13.10 (using the Biot–Savart law), we ran into a messy integral. Using Ampere's Law will be much easier. First,

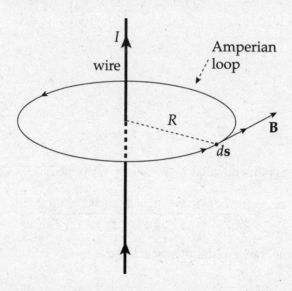

The magnetic field must have the same magnitude at every point on the Amperian circle, and the direction of the field must always be perpendicular to the circle (which means it points radially away from or toward the wire) or always tangent to the circle. We can rule out the first case in two ways: (1) Magnetic field lines *always* form closed curves that encircle the current that generates them; (2) If **B** were perpendicular to the Amperian circle, then **B** · d**s** would be zero everywhere along the circle, so Ampere's Law would give $0 = \mu_0 I$, a contradiction. So **B** must be tangent to the Amperian circle.

Since **B** has constant magnitude on the circle and is always parallel to d**s** (which is a small section of the Amperian loop),

$$\mathbf{B} \cdot d\mathbf{s} = B \, ds \cos \theta = B \, ds$$

The current that passes through the loop is I, so Ampere's Law gives us

$$\oint_{\text{loop}} B \, ds = \mu_0 I$$

$$B \oint_{\text{loop}} ds = \mu_0 I$$

$$B(2\pi R) = \mu_0 I$$

$$B = \frac{\mu_0 I}{2\pi R}$$

Example 13.14 The figure below is a cut-away view of a long coaxial cable that's composed of a solid cylindrical conductor (of radius R_1) surrounded by a thin conducting cylindrical shell (of radius R_2).

The inner cylinder carries a current of I_1 and the outer cylindrical shell carries a smaller current of I_2 in the opposite direction. Use Ampere's Law to find the magnitude of the magnetic field (a) in the space between the inner cylinder and the shell, and (b) outside the outer shell.

Solution.

(a) Construct an Amperian loop of radius r in the space between the solid cylinder and the outer shell. The magnetic field must be of constant magnitude along (and tangent to) this loop.

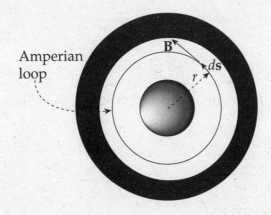

The only current that passes through the loop is I_1 (the current I_2 in the outer shell does not pierce the interior of the Amperian loop), so Ampere's Law gives us:

$$\oint_{loop} B\,ds = \mu_0 I_1$$
$$B(2\pi r) = \mu_0 I_1$$
$$B = \frac{\mu_0}{2\pi}\frac{I_1}{r} \quad (R_1 < r < R_2)$$

(b)   Now construct an Amperian loop that encircles the entire cable.

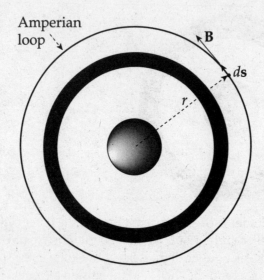

Unlike in the loop constructed in part (a), *both* currents pass through this loop. If they had the same direction, we'd add them to get the total current, but since the currents here have *opposite* directions, the net current through the loop is $I_1 - I_2$. Ampere's Law then gives us:

$$\oint_{loop} B\,ds = \mu_0(I_1 - I_2)$$
$$B(2\pi r) = \mu_0(I_1 - I_2)$$
$$B = \frac{\mu_0}{2\pi}\frac{I_1 - I_2}{r} \quad (r > R_2)$$

Notice that if $I_1 = I_2$, then the magnetic field outside the cable is zero.

Example 13.15 The figure below is a cross section of a *toroidal solenoid* (a solenoid bent into a donut shape) of inner radius R_1 and outer radius R_2. It consists of N windings, and the wire carries a current I. What's the magnetic field in each of the following regions?

(a) $r < R_1$

(b) $R_1 < r < R_2$

(c) $r > R_2$

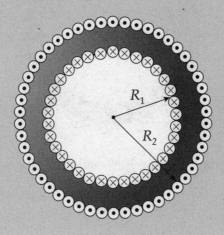

Solution.

(a) If we construct a circular Amperian loop of radius $r < R_1$, then no current will pass through it.

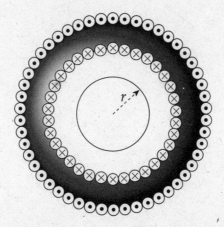

Since $\oint_{\text{loop}} \mathbf{B} \cdot d\mathbf{s} = \oint_{\text{loop}} B \, ds = B(2\pi r)$ and $I_{\text{through loop}} = 0$, Ampere's law immediately tells us that $B = 0$ in this region (the hole of the donut).

(b) Construct a circular Amperian loop of radius r such that $R_1 < r < R_2$. Each of the N windings that brings current into the plane of the page passes through the loop, but the N windings that bring current out of the plane of the page do not pass through the loop.

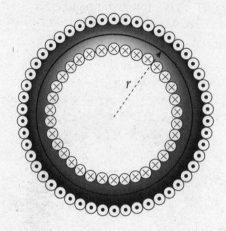

So the net current through the loop is NI, and Ampere's law gives us:

$$\oint_{\text{loop}} B\,ds = \mu_0 NI$$

$$B(2\pi r) = \mu_0 NI$$

$$B = \frac{\mu_0}{2\pi}\frac{NI}{r} \quad (R_1 < r < R_2)$$

(c) Construct a circular Amperian loop of radius $r > R_2$.

For every current contribution of I punching upward through the loop, there is an equal current punching downward through the loop, so the net current through the loop is zero, and $B = 0$ in this region.

Notice that the results of this example show that for an ideal toroidal solenoid, the magnetic field is contained within the space enclosed by the windings.

CHAPTER 13 REVIEW QUESTIONS

SECTION I: MULTIPLE CHOICE

1. Which of the following is/are true concerning magnetic forces and fields?

   I. The magnetic field lines due to a current-carrying wire radiate away from the wire.
   II. The kinetic energy of a charged particle can be increased by a magnetic force.
   III. A charged particle can move through a magnetic field without feeling a magnetic force.

   (A) I only
   (B) II and III only
   (C) I and II only
   (D) III only
   (E) I and III only

2. The velocity of a particle of charge $+4.0 \times 10^{-9}$ C and mass 2×10^{-4} kg is perpendicular to a 0.1-tesla magnetic field. If the particle's speed is 3×10^4 m/s, what is the acceleration of this particle due to the magnetic force?

   (A) 0.0006 m/s^2
   (B) 0.006 m/s^2
   (C) 0.06 m/s^2
   (D) 0.6 m/s^2
   (E) None of the above

3. In the figure below, what is the direction of the magnetic force $\mathbf{F}_B$?

   (A) To the right
   (B) Downward, in the plane of the page
   (C) Upward, in the plane of the page
   (D) Out of the plane of the page
   (E) Into the plane of the page

4. In the figure below, what must be the direction of the particle's velocity, $\mathbf{v}$?

   (A) To the right
   (B) Downward, in the plane of the page
   (C) Upward, in the plane of the page
   (D) Out of the plane of the page
   (E) Into the plane of the page

5. Due to the magnetic force, a positively-charged particle executes uniform circular motion within a uniform magnetic field, $\mathbf{B}$. If the charge is q and the radius of its path is r, which of the following expressions gives the magnitude of the particle's linear momentum?

   (A) qBr
   (B) qB/r
   (C) $q/(Br)$
   (D) $B/(qr)$
   (E) $r/(qB)$

6. A straight wire of length 2 m carries a 10-amp current. How strong is the magnetic field at a distance of 2 cm from the wire?

   (A) 1×10^{-6} T
   (B) 1×10^{-5} T
   (C) 2×10^{-5} T
   (D) 1×10^{-4} T
   (E) 2×10^{-4} T

7. Two long, straight wires are hanging parallel to each other and are 1 cm apart. The current in Wire #1 is 5 A, and the current in Wire #2 is 10 A, in the opposite direction. Which of the following best describes the magnetic force per unit length felt by the wires?

(A) The force per unit length on Wire #1 is twice the force per unit length on Wire #2.
(B) The force per unit length on Wire #2 is twice the force per unit length on Wire #1.
(C) The force per unit length on Wire #1 is 0.0003 N/m, away from Wire #2.
(D) The force per unit length on Wire #1 is 0.001 N/m, toward Wire #2.
(E) The force per unit length on Wire #1 is 0.001 N/m, away from Wire #2.

8. In the figure below, what is the magnetic field at the point P, which is midway between the two wires?

(A) $2\mu_0 I/(\pi d)$, out of the plane of the page
(B) $2\mu_0 I/(\pi d)$, into the plane of the page
(C) $\mu_0 I/(2\pi d)$, out of the plane of the page
(D) $\mu_0 I/(2\pi d)$, into the plane of the page
(E) Zero

9. [C] How many windings must a solenoid of length 80 cm have in order to establish a magnetic field of strength 0.2 T inside the solenoid, if it carries a current of 20 amps?

(A) 1000
(B) 6400
(C) 10,000
(D) 32,000
(E) 64,000

10. [C] The value of $\oint \mathbf{B} \cdot d\mathbf{s}$ along a closed path in a magnetic field **B** is 6.28×10^{-6} T · m. What is the total current that passes through this closed path?

(A) 0.1 A
(B) 0.5 A
(C) 1 A
(D) 4 A
(E) 5 A

SECTION II: FREE RESPONSE

1. The diagram below shows a simple mass spectrograph. It consists of a source of ions (charged atoms) that are accelerated (essentially from rest) by the voltage V and enter a region containing a uniform magnetic field, **B**. The polarity of V may be reversed so that both positively-charged ions (cations) and negatively-charged ions (anions) can be accelerated. Once the ions enter the magnetic field, they follow a semicircular path and strike the front wall of the spectrograph, on which photographic plates are constructed to record the impact.

(a) What is the acceleration of an ion of charge q just before it enters the magnetic field?

(b) Find the speed with which an ion of charge q enters the magnetic field.

(c) (i) Which semicircular path, 1 or 2, would a cation follow?

(ii) Which semicircular path, 1 or 2, would an anion follow?

(d) Determine the mass of a cation entering the apparatus in terms of y, q, B, and V.

(e) Once a cation of charge q enters the magnetic field, how long does it take to strike the photographic plate?

(f) What is the work done by the magnetic force in the spectrograph on a cation of charge q?

2. A wire of diameter d and resistivity ρ is bent into a rectangular loop (of side lengths a and b) and fitted with a small battery that provides a voltage V. The loop is placed at a distance c from a very long straight wire that carries a current I in the direction indicated in the diagram.

(Express all answers in terms of a, b, c, d, ρ, V, I, and fundamental constants.)

(a) When the switch S is closed, find the current in the rectangular loop.

(b) What is the magnetic force (magnitude and direction) exerted on the loop by the long straight wire?

(c) The wire of the rectangular loop is then reshaped into a circle. What will be the radius of the circular loop?

(d) If the loop constructed in part (c) were then threaded around the long straight wire (so that the straight wire passed through the center of the circular loop), what would be the magnetic force on the loop now?

(e) In the following diagram, two fixed L-shaped wires, separated by a distance x, are connected by a wire that's free to slide vertically.

The mass of the sliding wire, S, is m. If the sliding wire S crosses a region that contains a uniform magnetic field $\mathbf{B}$, how much current must be carried by the wire to keep S from sliding down (due to its weight)?

3. [C] The figure below shows two long straight wires connected by a circular arc of radius x that subtends a central angle ϕ. The current in the wire is I.

(a) Find the magnetic field (magnitude and direction) created at point C. Write your answer in terms of x, ϕ, I, and fundamental constants.

(b) A particle of charge $+q$ is placed at point C and released. Find the magnetic force on the particle.

(c) A second, long straight wire is set up perpendicular to the plane of the page through C, carrying the same current, I (directed out of the page), as the wire pictured in the diagram. Determine the magnetic force per unit length between the wires.

4. [C] For a conducting rod that carries a current I, the **current density** is defined as the current per unit area: $J = I/A$.

Part 1. A nonhomogenous cylindrical rod of radius R carries a current whose current density, J, is uniform (constant); that is, J does not vary with the radial distance, r, from the center of the rod.

(a) Determine the current, I, in the rod.

(b) Calculate the magnitude of the magnetic field for

    (i) $r < R$

    (ii) $r > R$, writing your answers in terms of r, R, and I.

Part 2. A nonhomogenous cylindrical rod of radius R carries a current whose current density, J, varies with the radial distance, r, from the center of the rod according to the equation $J = \sigma r$, where σ is a constant.

(c) What are the units of σ?

(d) Determine the current, I, in the rod.

(e) Calculate the magnitude of the magnetic field for

    (i) $r < R$

    (ii) $r > R$, writing your answers in terms of r, R, and I.

14

ELECTROMAGNETIC INDUCTION

INTRODUCTION

In Chapter 13, we learned that electric currents generate magnetic fields, and we will now see how magnetism can generate electric currents.

MOTIONAL EMF

The figure below shows a conducting wire of length ℓ, moving with constant velocity **v** in the plane of the page through a uniform magnetic field **B** that's perpendicular to the page. The magnetic field exerts a force on the moving conduction electrons in the wire. With **B** pointing into the page, the direction of $\mathbf{v} \times \mathbf{B}$ is upward, so the magnetic force, $\mathbf{F_B}$, on these electrons (which are negatively-charged) is downward.

As a result, electrons will be pushed to the lower end of the wire, which will leave an excess of positive charge at its upper end. This separation of charge creates a uniform electric field, **E**, within the wire (pointing downward).

A charge q in the wire feels two forces: an electric force, $\mathbf{F_E} = q\mathbf{E}$, and a magnetic force,

$$\mathbf{F_B} = q(\mathbf{v} \times \mathbf{B})$$

If q is negative, $\mathbf{F_E}$ is upward and $\mathbf{F_B}$ is downward; if q is positive, $\mathbf{F_E}$ is downward and $\mathbf{F_B}$ is upward. So, in both cases, the forces act in opposite directions. Once the magnitude of $\mathbf{F_E}$ equals the magnitude of $\mathbf{F_B}$, the charges in the wire are in electromagnetic equilibrium. This occurs when $qE = qvB$; that is, when $E = vB$.

The presence of the electric field creates a potential difference between the ends of the rod. Since negative charge accumulates at the lower end (which we'll call point a) and positive charge accumulates at the upper end (point b), point b is at a higher electric potential.

The potential difference V_{ba} is equal to $E\ell$ and, since $E = vB$, the potential difference can be written as $vB\ell$.

Now imagine that the rod is sliding along a pair of conducting rails connected at the left by a stationary bar. The sliding rod now completes a rectangular circuit, and the potential difference V_{ba} causes current to flow.

The motion of the sliding rod through the magnetic field creates an electromotive force, called **motional emf**:

$$\mathcal{E} = vB\ell$$

The existence of a current in the sliding rod causes the magnetic field to exert a force on it. Using the formula $\mathbf{F}_B = I(\ell \times \mathbf{B})$, the fact that ℓ points upward (in the direction of the current) and $\mathbf{B}$ is into the page, tells us that the direction of $\mathbf{F}_B$ on the rod is to the left. An external agent must provide this same amount of force to the right to maintain the rod's constant velocity and keep the current flowing. The power that the external agent must supply is $P = Fv = I\ell Bv$, and the electrical power delivered to the circuit is $P = IV_{ba} = I\mathcal{E} = IvB\ell$. Notice that these two expressions are identical. The energy provided by the external agent is transformed first into electrical energy and then thermal energy as the conductors making up the circuit dissipate heat.

FARADAY'S LAW OF ELECTROMAGNETIC INDUCTION

Electromotive force can be created by the motion of a conductor through a magnetic field, but there's another way to create an emf from a magnetic field.

MAGNETIC FLUX

Think back to Chapter 10 and electric flux. The electric flux through a surface of area A is equal to the product of A and the electric field that's perpendicular to it. That is, $\Phi_E = E_\perp A = \mathbf{E} \cdot \mathbf{A} = EA \cos \theta$. If $\mathbf{E}$ varies over the area A, then we write $\Phi_E = \int \mathbf{E} \cdot d\mathbf{A}$.

The idea of magnetic flux is exactly the same. The **magnetic flux**, Φ_B, through an area A is equal to the product of A and the magnetic field perpendicular to it: $\Phi_B = B_\perp A = \mathbf{B} \cdot \mathbf{A} = BA \cos \theta$. Again, if $\mathbf{B}$ varies over the area, then we must write $\Phi_B = \int \mathbf{B} \cdot d\mathbf{A}$.

Example 14.1 The figure below shows two views of a circular loop of radius 3 cm placed within a uniform magnetic field, **B** (magnitude 0.2 T).

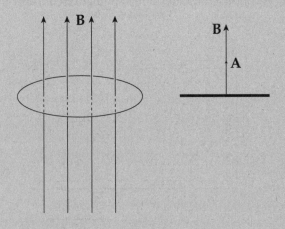

(a) What's the magnetic flux through the loop?

(b) What would be the magnetic flux through the loop if the loop were rotated 45°?

(c) What would be the magnetic flux through the loop if the loop were rotated 90°?

Solution.

(a) Since **B** is parallel to **A**, the magnetic flux is equal to BA:

$$\Phi_B = BA = B \cdot \pi r^2 = (0.2 \text{ T}) \cdot \pi (0.03 \text{ m})^2 = 5.7 \times 10^{-4} \text{ T·m}^2$$

The SI unit for magnetic flux, the tesla·meter², is called a **weber** (abbreviated **Wb**). So $\Phi_B = 5.7 \times 10^{-4}$ Wb.

(b) Since the angle between **B** and **A** is 45°, the magnetic flux through the loop is

$$\Phi_B = BA \cos 45° = B \cdot \pi r^2 \cos 45° = (0.2 \text{ T}) \cdot \pi (0.03 \text{ m})^2 \cos 45° = 4.0 \times 10^{-4} \text{ Wb}$$

(c) If the angle between **B** and **A** is 90°, the magnetic flux through the loop is zero, since cos 90° = 0.

The concept of magnetic flux is crucial, because changes in magnetic flux induce emf. According to **Faraday's Law of Electromagnetic Induction**, the magnitude of the emf induced in a circuit is equal to the rate of change of the magnetic flux through the circuit. This can be written mathematically in the form

$$\left| \mathcal{E}_{avg} \right| = \frac{\Delta \Phi_B}{\Delta t}$$

or, if we let $\Delta t \to 0$, we get

$$\left| \mathcal{E} \right| = \frac{d \Phi_B}{dt}$$

This induced emf can produce a current, which will then create its own magnetic field. The direction of the induced current is determined by the polarity of the induced emf and is given by **Lenz's Law**: The induced current will always flow in the direction that opposes the change in magnetic flux that produced it. If this were not so, then the magnetic flux created by the induced current would magnify the change that produced it, and energy would not be conserved. Lenz's Law can be integrated mathematically with Faraday's Law by the introduction of a minus sign; this leads to a single equation that expresses both results:

$$\mathcal{E}_{avg} = -\frac{\Delta \Phi_B}{\Delta t} \quad \text{or} \quad \mathcal{E} = -\frac{d \Phi_B}{dt}$$

Example 14.2 The circular loop of Example 14.1 rotates at a constant angular speed through 45° in 0.5 s.

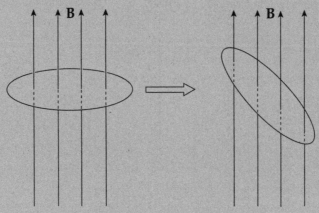

(a) What's the induced emf in the loop?

(b) In which direction will current be induced to flow?

Solution.

(a) As we found in Example 14.1, the magnetic flux through the loop changes when the loop rotates. Using the values we determined earlier, Faraday's Law gives

$$\mathcal{E}_{avg} = -\frac{\Delta \Phi_B}{\Delta t} = -\frac{(4.0 \times 10^{-4} \text{ Wb}) - (5.7 \times 10^{-4} \text{ Wb})}{0.5 \text{ s}} = 3.4 \times 10^{-4} \text{ V}$$

(b) The original magnetic flux was 5.7×10^{-4} Wb upward, and was decreased to 4.0×10^{-4} Wb. So the change in magnetic flux is -1.7×10^{-4} Wb upward, or, equivalently, $\Delta \Phi_B = 1.7 \times 10^{-4}$ Wb, downward. To oppose this change we would need to create some magnetic flux upward. The current would be induced in the counterclockwise direction (looking down on the loop), because the right-hand rule tells us that then the current would produce a magnetic field that would point up.

Current will flow only while the loop rotates, because emf is induced only when magnetic flux is changing. If the loop rotates 45° and then stops, the current will disappear.

Example 14.3 Again consider the conducting rod that's moving with constant velocity **v** along a pair of parallel conducting rails (separated by a distance ℓ), within a uniform magnetic field, **B**:

Find the induced emf and the direction of the induced current in the rectangular circuit.

Solution. The area of the rectangular loop is ℓx, where x is the distance from the left-hand bar to the moving rod:

Because the area is changing, the magnetic flux through the loop is changing, which means that an emf will be induced in the loop. To calculate the induced emf, we first write $\Phi_B = BA = B\ell x$, then since $\Delta x / \Delta t = v$, we get

$$\mathcal{E}_{avg} = -\frac{\Delta\Phi_B}{\Delta t} = -\frac{\Delta(B\ell x)}{\Delta t} = -B\ell\frac{\Delta x}{\Delta t} = -B\ell v$$

We can figure out the direction of the induced current from Lenz's Law. As the rod slides to the right, the magnetic flux into the page increases. How do we oppose an increasing into-the-page flux? By producing out-of-the-page flux. In order for the induced current to generate a magnetic field that points out of the plane of the page, the current must be directed counterclockwise (according to the right-hand rule).

Notice that the magnitude of the induced emf and the direction of the current agree with the results we derived earlier, in the section on motional emf.

This example also shows how a violation of Lenz's law would lead directly to a violation of the law of conservation of energy. The current in the sliding rod is directed upward, as given by Lenz's law, so the conduction electrons are drifting downward. The force on these drifting electrons—and thus the rod itself—is directed to the left, opposing the force that's pulling the rod to the right. If the current were directed downward, in violation of Lenz's law, then the magnetic force on the rod would be to the right, causing the rod to accelerate to the right with ever-increasing speed and kinetic energy, without the input of an equal amount of energy from an external agent.

Example 14.4 A permanent magnet creates a magnetic field in the surrounding space. The end of the magnet at which the field lines emerge is designated the **north pole** (N), and the other end is the **south pole** (S):

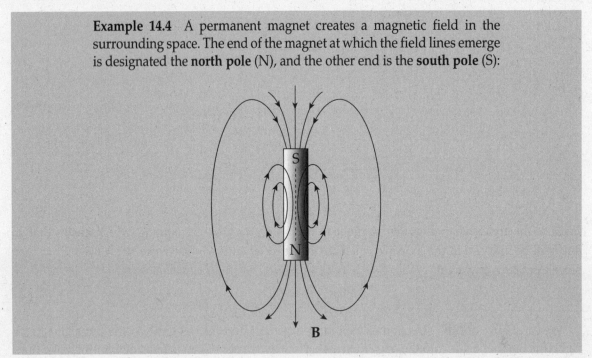

(a) The figure below shows a bar magnet moving down, through a circular loop of wire. What will be the direction of the induced current in the wire?

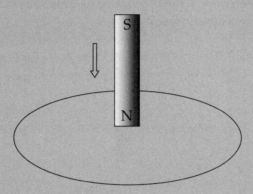

(b) What will be the direction of the induced current in the wire if the magnet is moved as shown in the following diagram?

Solution.

(a) The magnetic flux down, through the loop, increases as the magnet is moved. By Lenz's Law, the induced emf will generate a current that opposes this change. How do we oppose a change of *more flux downward*? By creating flux upward. So, according to the right-hand rule, the induced current must flow counterclockwise (because this current will generate an upward-pointing magnetic field):

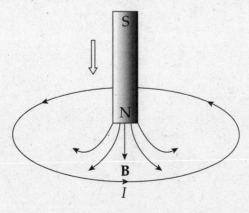

(b) In this case, the magnetic flux through the loop is upward and, as the south pole moves closer to the loop, the magnetic field strength increases so the magnetic flux through the loop increases upward. How do we oppose a change of *more flux upward*? By creating flux downward. Therefore, in accordance with the right-hand rule, the induced current will flow clockwise (because this current will generate a downward-pointing magnetic field):

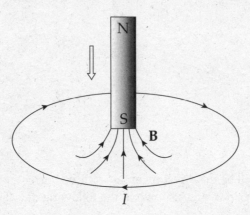

Example 14.5 A square loop of wire 2 cm on each side contains 5 tight turns and has a total resistance of 0.0002 Ω. It is placed 20 cm from a long, straight, current-carrying wire. If the current in the straight wire is increased at a steady rate from 20 A to 50 A in 2 s, determine the direction of the current induced in the square loop. (Because the square loop is at such a great distance from the straight wire, assume that the magnetic field through the loop is uniform and equal to the magnetic field at its center.)

Solution. At the position of the square loop, the magnetic field due to the straight wire is directed out of the plane of the page and its strength is given by the equation $B = (\mu_0 / 2\pi)(I/r)$. As the current in the straight wire increases, the magnetic flux through the turns of the square loop change, inducing an emf and current. There are $N = 5$ turns; Faraday's Law becomes $\mathcal{E}_{avg} = -N(\Delta \Phi_B / \Delta t)$, and

$$\mathcal{E}_{avg} = -N\frac{\Delta\Phi_B}{\Delta t} = -N\frac{\Delta(BA)}{\Delta t} = -NA\frac{\Delta B}{\Delta t} = -NA\frac{\mu_0}{2\pi r}\frac{\Delta I}{\Delta t}$$

Substituting the given numerical values, we get

$$\mathcal{E}_{avg} = -NA\frac{\mu_0}{2\pi r}\frac{\Delta I}{\Delta t}$$

$$= -(5)(0.02 \text{ m})^2 \frac{4\pi \times 10^{-7} \text{ T} \cdot \text{m}/\text{A}}{2\pi(0.20 \text{ m})} \frac{(50 \text{ A} - 20 \text{ A})}{2 \text{ s}}$$

$$= -6 \times 10^{-9} \text{ V}$$

The magnetic flux through the loop is out of the page and increases as the current in the straight wire increases. To oppose an increasing out-of-the-page flux, the direction of the induced current should be clockwise, thereby generating an into-the-page magnetic field (and flux).

The value of the current in the loop will be

$$I = \frac{\mathcal{E}}{R} = \frac{6 \times 10^{-9} \text{ V}}{0.0002 \ \Omega} = 3 \times 10^{-5} \text{ A}$$

Example 14.6 [C] A rectangular loop of wire 10 cm by 4 cm has a total resistance of 0.005 Ω. It is placed 2 cm from a long, straight, current-carrying wire. If the current in the straight wire is increased at a steady rate from 20 A to 50 A in 2 s, determine the direction of the current induced in the rectangular loop.

Solution. Unlike in the previous example, in this case the magnetic field varies greatly over the interior of the rectangular loop, so we have to use integration to calculate the magnetic flux. Take a narrow strip of width dx and height y, whose area is $dA = y \, dx$:

The magnetic field strength everywhere in this strip is $B = (\mu_0/2\pi)(I/x)$, so the magnetic flux through the strip is

$$d\Phi_B = B \cdot dA = B \cdot (y\,dx) = \frac{\mu_0}{2\pi}\frac{I}{x} \cdot y\,dx$$

Integrating from $x = r$ to $x = r + \ell$ gives the total magnetic flux through the loop:

$$\Phi_B = \int d\Phi_B = \int_{x=r}^{x=r+\ell} \frac{\mu_0}{2\pi}\frac{I}{x} \cdot y\,dx = \frac{\mu_0 Iy}{2\pi}\int_r^{r+\ell}\frac{dx}{x} = \frac{\mu_0 Iy}{2\pi}\left[\ln x\right]_r^{r+\ell} = \frac{\mu_0 Iy}{2\pi}\ln\frac{r+\ell}{r}$$

Faraday's Law then gives us:

$$\varepsilon = -\frac{d\Phi_B}{dt} = -\frac{d}{dt}\left(\frac{\mu_0 Iy}{2\pi}\ln\frac{r+\ell}{r}\right) = -\left(\frac{\mu_0 y}{2\pi}\ln\frac{r+\ell}{r}\right)\frac{dI}{dt}$$

Ignoring the minus sign (which only reminds us that Lenz's law has to be obeyed), the value of the current induced in the loop is

$$I = \frac{\varepsilon}{R} = \left(\frac{\mu_0 y}{2\pi R}\ln\frac{r+\ell}{r}\right)\frac{dI}{dt}$$

$$= \frac{(4\pi\times10^{-7}\ \text{T}\cdot\text{m}\,/\,\text{A})(0.04\ \text{m})}{2\pi(0.005\ \Omega)} \cdot \ln\frac{2\ \text{cm}+10\ \text{cm}}{2\ \text{cm}} \cdot \frac{50\ \text{A} - 20\ \text{A}}{2\ \text{s}}$$

$$= 4.3\times10^{-5}\ \text{A}$$

At the position of the rectangular loop, the magnetic field due to the straight wire is directed into the plane of the page. So the magnetic flux through the loop is into the page and increases as the current in the straight wire increases. To oppose an increasing into-the-page flux, the direction of the induced current will be counterclockwise, generating an out-of-the-page magnetic field (and flux).

[C] INDUCED ELECTRIC FIELDS

In examples 14.4, 14.5, and 14.6, electric current was induced in a stationary conducting loop by a changing magnetic flux through the loop, but what was the source of the force that pushed these charges around the loop? It was not the magnetic force, because the loop was stationary. It must therefore have been an electric force that was produced by an electric field. The changing magnetic field produced the electric field, which acted on the free charges in the conducting loop and caused the current.

Let's look at a specific situation. The figure below is a view down the central axis of an ideal solenoid (*ideal* means that the magnetic field is uniform and parallel to the axis and that no magnetic field exists outside). Surrounding the solenoid is a loop of wire.

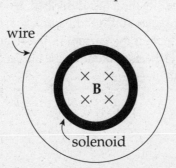

Now suppose that the current in the solenoid is increased, which increases the strength of its magnetic field. This changes the magnetic flux through the wire, and induces a current (which is directed counterclockwise). The force that pushes the charges around this wire is $\mathbf{F}_E = q\mathbf{E}$; $\mathbf{E}$ is the induced electric field.

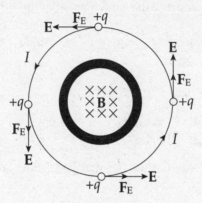

The work done on a charge q as it makes one revolution is F_E times the distance around the wire, $F_E \cdot 2\pi r = qE \cdot (2\pi r)$. So the work per unit charge, which is the definition of emf, is equal to $E(2\pi r)$. But Faraday's Law says that the emf is equal to $-d\Phi_B/dt$:

$$E(2\pi r) = -d\Phi_B/dt$$

This equation can be generalized by saying that the work done per unit charge by the induced electric field around a closed path is equal to $\oint \mathbf{E} \cdot d\boldsymbol{\ell}$. Therefore,

$$\oint \mathbf{E} \cdot d\boldsymbol{\ell} = -\frac{d\Phi_B}{dt}$$

This is a restatement of Faraday's Law that includes the electric field, $\mathbf{E}$, induced by the changing magnetic flux. Notice that this electric field is different from the ones we studied in the previous chapters. Electric fields created by stationary source charges, called electrostatic fields, are conservative, meaning that the work done by them on charges moved along closed paths is always zero. However, as we've just seen in the example of the solenoid above, the electric field induced by a *changing magnetic flux* does not share this property. The work done by $\mathbf{E}_{induced}$ on a charge as it moves around a closed path is equal to $\oint \mathbf{E} \cdot d\boldsymbol{\ell}$, which is not zero because $d\Phi_B/dt$ is not zero. Because of this, the electric field induced by a changing magnetic flux is nonconservative.

Example 14.7 For the situation just described, assume that the solenoid has 15,000 turns per meter and a radius of $r = 2$ cm. The radius of the circular loop is $R = 4$ cm. If the current in the solenoid is increased at a rate of 10 A/s, what is the magnitude of the induced electric field at each position along the circular wire?

Solution. From Faraday's Law, we have

$$\oint \mathbf{E} \cdot d\boldsymbol{\ell} = -\frac{d\Phi_B}{dt}$$

$$E(2\pi R) = -\frac{d\Phi_B}{dt}$$

$$|E| = \frac{1}{2\pi R}\left|\frac{d\Phi_B}{dt}\right|$$

Assuming that the magnetic field exists only inside the solenoid, the magnetic flux through the circular wire is $BA = B(\pi r^2)$, where $B = \mu_0 nI$:

$$\Phi_B = (\mu_0 nI) \cdot (\pi r^2)$$

Therefore,

$$\begin{aligned}
|E| &= \frac{1}{2\pi R}\left|\frac{d\Phi_B}{dt}\right| \\
&= \frac{1}{2\pi R} \cdot \frac{d}{dt}(\mu_0 nI \cdot \pi r^2) \\
&= \frac{\mu_0 n r^2}{2R}\frac{dI}{dt} \\
&= \frac{(4\pi \times 10^{-7} \text{ T} \cdot \text{m} / \text{A})(15{,}000)(0.02 \text{ m})^2}{2(0.04 \text{ m})}(10 \text{ A} / \text{s}) \\
&= 9.4 \times 10^{-4} \text{ V} / \text{m}
\end{aligned}$$

[C] INDUCTANCE

Placing a capacitor in series with a resistor and battery in an electric circuit causes the current to drop exponentially from $\mathcal{E}/R$ (when the switch is closed) to zero, as charge builds up on the capacitor and causes the voltage across the capacitor to oppose the emf of the battery. The same thing happens when an inductor is placed in series with a resistor and a seat of emf in an electric circuit.

An **inductor** is a circuit element that opposes changes in current. The prototypical inductor is a coil (a solenoid) that looks like this in diagrams:

How does this coil oppose changes in current in a circuit? Well, when current exists in the coil, a magnetic field is created, and magnetic flux passes through the loops. If the current changes, then the magnetic field changes proportionately, as does the magnetic flux through the loops. But, according to Faraday's Law of Induction, a changing magnetic flux induces an emf that opposes the change that produced it. In other words, the changing magnetic flux through the coil, due to the current in the coil itself, produces a **self-induced emf**. Since this self-induced emf opposes the change in the current that produced it, it's also called **back emf**.

Assume that the inductor contains N turns and that Φ_B is the magnetic flux through each turn. Then the total magnetic flux through the entire coil is $N\Phi_B$; this is proportional to the current, so

$N\Phi_B = LI$ for some constant, L. The proportionality constant L is called the **inductance** (or **self-inductance**) of the coil:

$$L = \frac{N\Phi_B}{I}$$

The SI unit for inductance is the weber per ampere, which is renamed a **henry** (**H**).

> **Example 14.8** An ideal solenoid of cross sectional area A and length ℓ contains n turns per unit length. What is its self-inductance?

Solution. The magnetic field inside an ideal solenoid is parallel to its central axis and has strength $B = \mu_0 nI$. Since the solenoid's length is ℓ, the total number of turns, N, is $n\ell$. Therefore,

$$L = \frac{N\Phi_B}{I} = \frac{N \cdot BA}{I} = \frac{n\ell \cdot BA}{I} = \frac{n\ell \cdot (\mu_0 nI)A}{I} = \mu_0 n^2 A\ell$$

Or, in terms of the total number of turns in the solenoid, $L = \mu_0 N^2 A / \ell$.

The self-induced emf in an inductor now follows directly from the definition of L and Faraday's Law. Since $N\Phi_B = LI$, we have $N(d\Phi_B/dt) = L(dI/dt)$. But by Faraday's Law, $\mathcal{E} = -N(d\Phi_B/dt)$. So,

$$\mathcal{E} = -L\frac{dI}{dt}$$

The self-induced emf is proportional to the rate of change of the current. The faster the current tries to change, the greater is the self-induced (back) emf. But if the current is steady, then $\mathcal{E} = 0$.

RL CIRCUITS

Consider the following circuit, which contains a battery, an inductor, and a resistor:

Move the switch S to point a. If the inductor were absent, the current would rise quickly to $\mathcal{E}/R$, but the inductor opposes this rapid increase in current by producing a back emf. The result is a current that increases gradually in time, according to the equation

$$I(t)=\frac{\mathcal{E}}{R}\left(1-e^{-t/\frac{L}{R}}\right)$$

The ratio of L to R (in the exponent) is called the **inductive time constant**: $\tau_L = L/R$, and the equation for the rising current in the **RL circuit** (a circuit that contains a resistor and an inductor) can be written as:

$$I(t)=\frac{\mathcal{E}}{R}\left(1-e^{-t/\frac{L}{R}}\right)$$

which is similar to the equation for the gradually rising charge on the plates of a capacitor in an RC circuit.

As current builds in the circuit, the source of emf provides electrical energy. Some of this energy is dissipated as heat by the resistor, and the remainder is stored in the magnetic field of the inductor. The amount of stored energy is

$$U_B = \frac{1}{2}LI^2$$

where L is the inductance of the inductor carrying a current I.

> **Example 14.9** In a particular circuit, assume that $\mathcal{E} = 12$ V, $R = 40\ \Omega$, and $L = 5$ mH. How much energy is stored in the inductor's magnetic field when the current reaches its maximum steady-state value?

Solution. When the current in the circuit reaches its maximum steady-state value, $I = \mathcal{E}/R$. At this point, the energy stored in the magnetic field of the **inductor is**

$$U_B=\frac{1}{2}LI^2=\frac{1}{2}L\cdot\left(\frac{\mathcal{E}}{R}\right)^2=\frac{L\mathcal{E}^2}{2R^2}=\frac{(5\times10^{-3}\ \text{H})(12\ \text{V})^2}{2(40\ \Omega)^2}=2.3\times10^{-4}\text{J}$$

Once the current has reached its steady-state value of $\mathcal{E}/R$, imagine that you move the switch to point b. Without the inductor, the current would drop abruptly to zero (because the source of emf has been taken out of the circuit). But the inductor would oppose this abrupt decrease in the current by producing a self-induced emf. The presence of this emf would cause the current to die out gradually, according to the equation

$$I(t)=\frac{\mathcal{E}}{R}e^{-t/\tau_L}$$

LC CIRCUITS

The RC circuit we looked at in Chapter 12 and the RL circuit above are similar in that they both experience an exponential increase or decrease of current. However, an LC circuit, which is a circuit that contains both an inductor and a capacitor, behaves quite differently.

The following figure shows a capacitor and an inductor in a simple series circuit.

Let's assume that initially there is no current and that the capacitor is charged; at time $t = 0$, the switch S is closed and the circuit is complete. The presence of the inductor prevents the capacitor from discharging abruptly, so the current rises gradually and the energy in the electric field of the capacitor is transferred to energy in the magnetic field of the inductor. Once the capacitor has discharged, all the energy is in the inductor's magnetic field. The current in the inductor (now at its maximum), delivers charge to the capacitor, but in the opposite direction from its original charge configuration. The current gradually returns to zero as the magnetic-field energy in the inductor is transformed back to electric-field energy in the capacitor.

The capacitor starts to discharge again, but this time it sends current in the opposite direction. The current rises gradually, reaching a maximum value as the charge on the capacitor reaches zero. The inductor continues to deliver charge to the capacitor as the current gradually returns to zero, and it finds itself right back where it started. The circuit oscillates, and this defines one cycle of oscillation.

Frequency of oscillation is related to inductance and capacitance by the equation

$$f = \frac{1}{2\pi\sqrt{LC}}$$

The charge on the capacitor, as a function of time (assuming that it possessed its maximum charge, Q_{max}, at time $t = 0$) is

$$Q(t) = Q_{max} \cos(\omega t)$$

where $\omega = 2\pi f$.

Example 14.10 Find an equation for the current in the LC circuit as a function of time. How long does it take for the circuit to complete a full oscillation?

Solution. By definition, the current is the time derivative of the charge. So,

$$I(t) = \frac{dQ}{dt} = \frac{d}{dt}\left[Q_{max} \cos(\omega t)\right] = -\omega Q_{max} \sin(\omega t)$$

The time required to complete a cycle (the period) would be the reciprocal of the frequency:

$$T = \frac{1}{f} = 2\pi\sqrt{LC}$$

[C] MAXWELL'S EQUATIONS

We'll finish up this chapter with a set of four equations that embody the subject of electromagnetism.

1. GAUSS'S LAW

This law, first studied in Chapter 10, gives us a method for calculating electric fields and is particularly useful when the system we're working with possesses symmetry.

$$\int_{\substack{\text{closed} \\ \text{surface}}} \mathbf{E} \cdot d\mathbf{A} = \frac{Q_{\text{enclosed}}}{\varepsilon_0}$$

2. GAUSS'S LAW FOR MAGNETIC FIELDS

We mentioned (Chapter 13) that magnetic fields lines always form closed loops that encircle the current that generates them. (Remember: This property is not shared by electrostatic fields, which radiate away from positive source charges and toward negative ones.) The fact that magnetic field lines always close upon themselves tells us that the magnetic flux through any closed surface must be zero; as much magnetic flux will enter the closed surface as will exit it. Mathematically, this says:

$$\int_{\substack{\text{closed} \\ \text{surface}}} \mathbf{B} \cdot d\mathbf{A} = 0$$

Another statement of this law is that there are no magnetic monopoles. If there were, a single isolated magnetic north pole would generate a magnetic field that radiates away, and an isolated magnetic south pole would generate a magnetic field that radiates inward, toward the pole. A closed surface surrounding such a magnetic charge (if one existed) would have a nonzero flux through it. No magnetic monopoles like this have ever been observed.

3. FARADAY'S LAW

As we discussed in this chapter, a changing magnetic flux induces an emf; this also means that a changing magnetic field produces an electric field. The equation is

$$\oint E \cdot d\ell = -\frac{d\Phi_B}{dt}$$

4. THE AMPERE–MAXWELL LAW

The final equation in this set begins with Ampere's Law, which provides us with a method for calculating magnetic fields and is particularly useful when systems are symmetrical. It reads

$$\oint \mathbf{B} \cdot d\mathbf{s} = \mu_0 I_{\text{enclosed}}$$

You may notice that the first two equations listed in this section possess a sort of symmetry; there's a Gauss's Law for E-fields and one for B-fields. The third equation says that a changing B-field produces an E-field. One question we haven't asked yet, which is of interest here is *Does a changing E-field produce a B-field?* The answer is *yes*, and the equation can be amended in the following way [Maxwell added the missing piece, which is proportional to the rate of change of the electric flux, $\mu_0 \varepsilon_0 (d\Phi_E/dt)$]:

$$\oint \mathbf{B} \cdot d\mathbf{s} = \mu_0 I + \mu_0 \varepsilon_0 \frac{d\Phi_E}{dt}$$

This shows that a changing electric field, which appears on the right-hand side of the equation [in the term $\mu_0 \varepsilon_0 (d\Phi_E / dt)$], will produce a magnetic field, which appears on the left-hand side of the equation.

The quantity $\varepsilon_0 (d\Phi_E / dt)$ has units of current and is called displacement current, I_D. It differs from the current I, which is conduction current (I_C), because while I_C is composed of moving electric charge, I_D is not. The Ampere–Maxwell equation can be written in terms of conduction current and displacement current as follows:

$$\oint \mathbf{B} \cdot d\mathbf{s} = \mu_0 (I_C + I_D)$$

CHAPTER 14 REVIEW QUESTIONS

SECTION I: MULTIPLE CHOICE

1. A metal rod of length L is pulled upward with constant velocity **v** through a uniform magnetic field **B** which points out of the plane of the page.

   What is the potential difference between points a and b?

   (A) 0

   (B) $\frac{1}{2}vBL$, with point a at the higher potential

   (C) $\frac{1}{2}vBL$, with point b at the higher potential

   (D) vBL, with point a at the higher potential

   (E) vBL, with point b at the higher potential

2. [C] A circular disk of radius a is rotating at a constant angular speed ω in a uniform magnetic field, **B**, which is directed out of the plane of the page.

   Determine the induced emf between the center of the disk and the rim.

   (A) $\frac{1}{2}\omega Ba$

   (B) $\frac{1}{2}Ba$

   (C) $\frac{1}{2}\omega Ba^2$

   (D) ωBa^2

   (E) $2\pi\omega Ba^2$

3. The figure below shows a small circular loop of wire (radius r) in the plane of a long, straight wire that carries a current I. The resistance of the loop is R. If the loop is moved from x_2 to x_1 in t seconds, what will be the induced current in the loop?

   (A) $\dfrac{\mu_0 Ir^2(x_2 - x_1)}{2\pi x_1 x_2 tR}$, clockwise

   (B) $\dfrac{\mu_0 Ir^2(x_2 - x_1)}{2\pi x_1 x_2 tR}$, counterclockwise

   (C) $\dfrac{\mu_0 Ir^2(x_2 - x_1)}{2x_1 x_2 tR}$, clockwise

   (D) $\dfrac{\mu_0 Ir^2(x_2 - x_1)}{2x_1 x_2 tR}$, counterclockwise

   (E) $\dfrac{\mu_0 Ir(x_2 - x_1)}{2x_1 x_2 t}$, clockwise

4. In the figure below, a small circular loop of wire (radius r) is placed on an insulating stand inside a hollow solenoid of radius R. The solenoid has n turns per unit length and carries a current I. If the current in the solenoid is decreased at a steady rate of a amps/s, determine the induced emf, $\mathcal{E}$, and the direction of the induced current in the loop.

solenoid
(radius = R)

wire loop
(radius = r)

(A) $\mathcal{E} = \mu_0 \pi n r^2 a$; induced current is clockwise

(B) $\mathcal{E} = \mu_0 \pi n r^2 a$; induced current is counterclockwise

(C) $\mathcal{E} = \mu_0 \pi n R^2 a$; induced current is clockwise

(D) $\mathcal{E} = \mu_0 \pi n R^2 a$; induced current is counterclockwise

(E) $\mathcal{E} = \mu_0 \pi I n R^2 a$; induced current is counterclockwise

5. In the figure below, a permanent bar magnet is pulled upward with a constant velocity through a loop of wire.

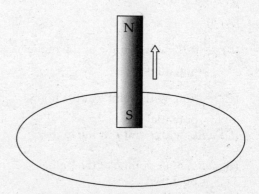

Which of the following best describes the direction(s) of the current induced in the loop (looking down on the loop from above)?

(A) Always clockwise
(B) Always counterclockwise
(C) First clockwise, then counterclockwise
(D) First counterclockwise, then clockwise
(E) No current will be induced in the loop.

6. A square loop of wire (side length = s) surrounds a long straight wire such that the wire passes through the center of the square.

If the current in the wire is I, determine the current induced in the square loop.

(A) $\dfrac{2\mu_0 Is}{\pi\left(1+\sqrt{2}\right)}$

(B) $\dfrac{\mu_0 Is}{\pi\sqrt{2}}$

(C) $\dfrac{\mu_0 Is}{\pi}$

(D) $\dfrac{\mu_0 Is\sqrt{2}}{\pi}$

(E) 0

[C] Questions 7–9
A circuit contains a solenoid of inductance L in series with a resistor of resistance R and a battery with terminal voltage $\mathcal{E}$. At time $t = 0$, a switch is closed and the circuit is completed.

7. How long does it take for the current to reach 3/4 of its maximum (steady-state) value?

(A) $(\ln 4)(L/R)$

(B) $(\ln \frac{3}{4})(L/R)$

(C) $(\ln \frac{4}{3})(L/R)$

(D) $(\ln \frac{4}{3})(R/L)$

(E) $(\ln 4)(R/L)$

8. When the current reaches its maximum value, how much energy is stored in the magnetic field of the solenoid?

(A) $L^2\mathcal{E}^2/(4R^2)$
(B) $L^2\mathcal{E}^2/(2R^2)$
(C) $L\mathcal{E}^2/(4R^2)$
(D) $L\mathcal{E}^2/(2R^2)$
(E) 0

9. When the current reaches its maximum value, what is the total magnetic flux through the solenoid?

(A) $L\mathcal{E}$
(B) $L\mathcal{E}/R$
(C) $\mathcal{E}/(RL)$
(D) $RL/\mathcal{E}$
(E) 0

10. [C] Which one of Maxwell's equations states that a changing electric field produces a magnetic field?

(A) Gauss's Law
(B) Gauss's Law for Magnetism
(C) Biot–Savart Law
(D) Ampere–Maxwell Law
(E) Faraday's Law

SECTION II: FREE RESPONSE

1. [C] The diagram below shows two views of a metal rod of length ℓ rotating with constant angular speed ω about an axis that is in the plane of the page. The rotation takes place in a uniform magnetic field **B** whose direction is parallel to the angular velocity ω.

view from
above

(a) What is the emf induced between the ends of the rod?

(b) What is the polarity (+ or –) of the rotating end?

In the following diagram, a metal rod of length ℓ moves with constant velocity **v** parallel to a long, straight wire carrying a steady current I. The lower end of the rod maintains a distance of a from the straight wire.

(c) What is the emf induced between the ends of the rod?

(d) What is the polarity (+ or –) of the end that is farther from the straight wire?

2. **[C]** A rectangular loop of wire (side lengths a and b) rotates with constant angular speed ω in a uniform magnetic field **B**. At time $t = 0$, the plane of the loop is perpendicular to **B**, as shown in the figure on the left. The magnetic field **B** is directed to the right (in the $+x$ direction), and the rotation axis is the y axis (with ω in the $+y$ direction), and the four corners of the loop are labeled 1, 2, 3 and 4. (Express answers in terms of a, b, ω, B, and fundamental constants.)

side view
at time $t = 0$

(a) Find a formula that gives the magnetic flux through the loop as a function of time, t.

(b) Find a formula that gives the emf induced in the loop as a function of time, t.

(c) If the total resistance of the loop is R, what is the current induced in the loop?

(d) When $\omega t = \pi/2$, is the induced current in the loop directed from Point 1 to Point 2 ($-y$ direction) or from Point 2 to Point 1 ($+y$ direction)?

(e) Find the rate at which energy is dissipated (as joule heat) in the wires that comprise the loop), and the amount of energy dissipated per revolution.

(f) Find the external torque required to keep the loop rotating at the constant angular speed ω.

3. [C] The figure below shows a toroidal solenoid of mean radius R and N total windings. The cross-sections of the toroid are circles of radius a (which is much smaller than R, so variations in the magnetic field strength within the space enclosed by the windings may be neglected).

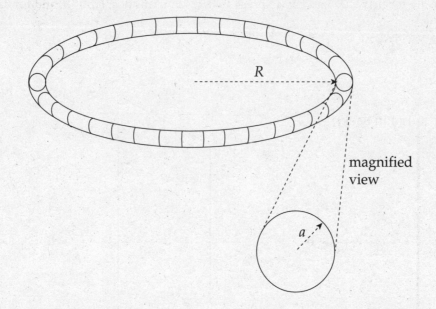

(a)   Use Ampere's Law to find the magnetic field strength within the toroid. Write your answer in terms of N, I, R, and fundamental constants.

A circular loop of wire of radius $2a$ is placed around the toroid as shown:

Assume that the current in the toroid is varied sinusoidally according to the equation $I(t) = I_0 \sin \omega t$, where I_0 and ω are fixed constants.

(b)   Determine the emf induced in the circular wire loop.

(c)   Determine the electric field induced at the position of the circular wire loop.

(d)   What is the self-inductance of the toroidal solenoid?

15

WAVES [B]

INTRODUCTION

Imagine holding the end of a long rope in your hand, with the other end attached to a wall. Move your hand up and down, and you'll create a wave that travels along the rope, from your hand to the wall. This simple example displays the basic idea of a **mechanical wave**: a disturbance transmitted by a medium from one point to another, without the medium itself being transported. In the case of water waves, wind or an earthquake can cause a disturbance in the ocean, and the resulting waves can travel thousands of miles. Now, of course, no water actually makes that journey; the water is only the medium that conducts the disturbance.

TRANSVERSE TRAVELING WAVES

Let's return to our long rope. Someone standing near the system would see peaks and valleys actually moving along the rope, in what's called a **traveling wave**.

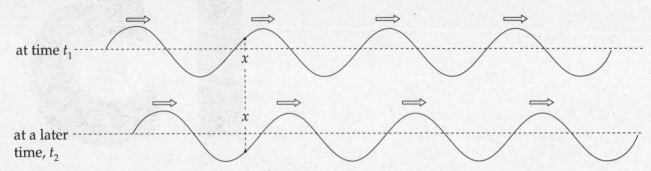

At any point (x) along the rope, the rope has a certain, and varying, vertical displacement. It's this variation in the vertical displacement that defines the shape of the wave. In the figure above, one particular location along the rope—marked x—is shown. Notice that, at time t_1, the vertical position y of the rope at x is slightly positive (that is, it's above the horizontal). But at a later time, t_2, the vertical position of the rope at this same x is slightly negative (that is, it's below the horizontal). It's clear that for a traveling wave, the displacement y of each point depends not only on x but also on t. An equation that gives y must therefore be a function of both position (x) and time (t). Because y depends on *two* independent variables, wave analysis can be difficult. But there's a way of looking at waves that simplifies things.

Instead of looking at a wave in which both variables (x and t) are changing, we'll look at a wave and allow *only one* of the variables to change. We'll use two points of view:

> *Point of View #1:* x varies, t does not
>
> *Point of View #2:* t varies, x does not

POINT OF VIEW #1: x VARIES, t DOES NOT

In order to keep t from varying, we must freeze time. How do we do this? By imagining a photograph of the wave. In fact, the figure above shows two snapshots; one taken at time t_1 and the second taken at a slightly later time, t_2. All the x's along the rope are visible (that is, x varies), but t does not. What features of the wave can we see in this point of view? Well, we can see the points at which the rope has its maximum vertical displacement above the horizontal; these points are called **crests**. The points at which the rope has its maximum vertical displacement below the horizontal are called **troughs**. These crests and troughs repeat themselves at regular intervals along the rope, and the distance between two adjacent crests (or two adjacent troughs) is the length of one wave, and is called the **wavelength** (λ, *lambda*). Also, the maximum displacement from the horizontal equilibrium position of the rope is also measurable; this is known as the **amplitude** (A) of the wave.

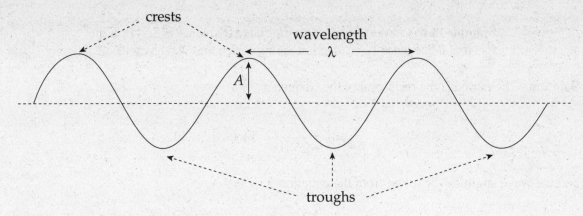

POINT OF VIEW #2: *t* VARIES, *x* DOES NOT

Now we will designate one position *x* along the rope to watch as time varies. One way to do this is to visualize two screens in front of the rope, with only a narrow gap between them. We can then observe how a single point on the rope varies as a wave travels behind the screen (the wave is traveling because we're not freezing time here). This point on the rope moves up and down. Since the direction in which the rope oscillates (vertically) is perpendicular to the direction in which the wave **propagates** (or travels, horizontally), this wave is **transverse**. The time it takes for one complete vertical oscillation of a point on the rope is called the **period**, *T*, of the wave, and the number of cycles it completes in one second is called its **frequency**, *f*. The period and frequency are established by the source of the wave and, of course, $T = 1/f$.

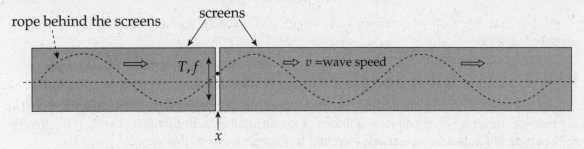

Four of the most important characteristics of any wave are its wavelength, amplitude, period, and frequency. The first two of these were identified in Point of View #1, and the second two were identified in Point of View #2.

A fifth important characteristic of a traveling wave is its speed, *v*. Look at the figure above and imagine the visible point on the rope moving from its crest position, down to its trough position, and then back up to the crest position. How long did this take? The period, *T*. Behind the screen, the wave moved a distance of one wavelength. *T* is the time required for one wave to travel by a point, and λ is the distance traveled by one wave. Therefore, the equation *distance = rate × time* becomes

$$\lambda = vT$$
$$\lambda \cdot \frac{1}{T} = v$$
$$\lambda f = v$$

The simple equation $v = \lambda f$ shows how the wave speed, wavelength, and frequency are interconnected. *It's the most basic equation in wave theory.*

Solution. The period is the reciprocal of the frequency:

$$T = \frac{1}{f} = \frac{1}{2.5 \text{ Hz}} = 0.4 \text{ s}$$

and the wavelength can be found from the equation $\lambda f = v$:

$$\lambda = \frac{v}{f} = \frac{1.5 \text{ m/s}}{2.5 \text{ Hz}} = 0.6 \text{ m}$$

Solution. The frequency is the reciprocal of the period: $f = 1/T = 1/(0.5 \text{ s}) = 2$ Hz. The wave speed can be found from the equation $v = \lambda f$:

$$v = \lambda f = (0.4 \text{ m})(2 \text{ Hz}) = 0.8 \text{ m/s}$$

(Notice that the frequency, period, wavelength, and wave speed have nothing to do with the amplitude.)

WAVE SPEED ON A STRETCHED STRING

We can also derive an equation for the speed of a transverse wave on a stretched string or rope. Let the mass of the string be m and its length be L; then its *linear mass density* (μ) is m/L. If the tension in the string is F_T, then the speed of a traveling transverse wave on this string is given by

$$v = \sqrt{\frac{F_T}{\mu}}$$

Notice that v depends only on the physical characteristics of the string—its tension and linear density. So, because $v = \lambda f$ for a given stretched string, varying f will create different waves that have different wavelengths, but v will not vary.

Solution.

(a) Wave speed is established by the physical characteristics of the rope:

$$v = \sqrt{\frac{F_T}{\mu}} = \sqrt{\frac{60\text{ N}}{0.5\text{ kg}/\text{m}}} = 11\text{ m}/\text{s}$$

With v, we can find the wavelength: $\lambda = v/f = (11\text{ m}/\text{s})/(4\text{ Hz}) = 2.8\text{ m}$.

(b) If f were increased to 5 Hz, then v would not change, but λ would; the new wavelength would be

$$\lambda' = v/f' = (11\text{ m}/\text{s})/(5\text{ Hz}) = 2.2\text{ m}$$

Example 15.4 Two ropes of unequal linear densities are connected, and a wave is created in the rope on the left, which propagates to the right, toward the interface with the heavier rope.

When a wave strikes the boundary to a new medium (in this case, the heavier rope), some of the wave's energy is reflected and some is transmitted. The frequency of the transmitted wave is the same, but the speed and wavelength are not. How do the speed and wavelength of the incident wave compare to the speed and wavelength of the wave as it travels through Rope #2?

Solution. Since the wave enters a new medium, it will have a new wave speed. Because Rope #2 has a greater linear mass density than Rope #1, and because v is inversely proportional to the square root of the linear mass density, the speed of the wave in Rope #2 will be less than the speed of the wave in Rope #1. Since $v = \lambda f$ must always be satisfied and f does not change, the fact that v changes means that λ must change, too. In particular, since v decreases upon entering Rope #2, so will λ.

THE MATHEMATICAL DESCRIPTION OF A TRAVELING WAVE

Remember that the location of a point in a medium that conducts a wave depends on two variables, position and time (x and t). It has the basic form

$$y = A\sin(\omega t \pm \kappa x)$$

To show that y depends on both x and t, the dependent variable, y, is often written as $y(x, t)$, and read "y of x and t." If the minus sign is used in the equation above, the wave travels in the $+x$ direction; if the plus sign is used, the wave travels in the $-x$ direction.

What do the coefficients A, ω, and κ stand for? Well, A is the amplitude, ω (*omega*) is the **angular frequency** and is defined as 2π times the frequency: $\omega = 2\pi f$. The coefficient κ (*kappa*) is called the **angular wave number**; it's equal to 2π times the **wave number** (or **propagation constant**), k, which is the number of wavelengths per unit distance. By definition, then, $k = 1/\lambda$, and $\kappa = 2\pi k$. So, the equation given above for y contains quantities that characterize all of the important features of a wave: the amplitude, the frequency f (through ω), the period T (which is $1/f = 2\pi/\omega$), the wavelength ($\lambda = 2\pi/\kappa$), and the wave speed v (which is $\lambda f = \omega/k$). Since, at this point, it's easier to relate to f and λ than to ω and κ, it's helpful to rewrite the equation above in the following equivalent forms:

$$y = A\sin 2\pi(ft \pm \frac{1}{\lambda}x) \quad \text{or} \quad y = A\sin \frac{2\pi}{\lambda}(vt \pm x)$$

which now include the quantities f and λ (or, in the second form, v and λ).

Example 15.5 Write the equation for a transverse wave traveling in the $+x$ direction with a frequency of 6 Hz, wavelength 0.2 m, and amplitude 8 cm, given that the left-end of the rope (the point $x = 0$) has zero displacement at time $t = 0$.

Solution. According to the description above, the equation of this wave is

$$y = 0.08\sin\left[2\pi(6t - 5x)\right]$$

where x and y are expressed in meters and t in seconds. Notice that, at $(x, t) = (0, 0)$, the value of y is zero, as it should be. [If y were *not* 0 at $(x, t) = (0, 0)$, then we would have to include an initial phase in the equation.]

Example 15.6 The vertical position y of any point on a rope that supports a transverse wave traveling horizontally is given by the equation

$$y = 0.1\sin(6\pi t + 8\pi x)$$

with x and y in meters and t in seconds. Find the amplitude, frequency, angular frequency, period, wavelength, wave speed, wave number, and angular wave number. Does this wave travel in the $+x$ or the $-x$ direction?

Solution. The coefficient of the sine term is the amplitude, so

amplitude: $A = 0.1$ m

Next, we recognize that the coefficient of t is the angular frequency (ω) and that the coefficient of x is the angular wave number (κ). Therefore,

angular frequency: $\omega = 6\pi$ s^{-1}
frequency: $f = \omega/(2\pi) = (6\pi\text{ s}^{-1})/(2\pi) = 3$ Hz
angular wave number: $\kappa = 8\pi$ m^{-1}
wave number: $k = \kappa/(2\pi) = (8\pi\text{ m}^{-1})/(2\pi) = 4$ m^{-1}
wavelength: $\lambda = 1/k = 1/(4\text{ m}^{-1}) = 0.25$ m
period: $T = 1/f = 1/(3\text{ Hz}) = 0.33$ s
wave speed: $v = \lambda f = (0.25\text{ m})(3\text{ Hz}) = 0.75$ m/s

Since the plus sign is used in the argument of the sine function, this wave is going in the $-x$ direction.

SUPERPOSITION OF WAVES

When two or more waves meet, the displacement at any point of the medium is equal to the algebraic sum of the displacements due to the individual waves. This is **superposition**. The figure below shows two wave pulses traveling toward each other along a stretched string. Notice that when they meet and overlap (**interfere**), the displacement of the string is equal to the sum of the individual displacements, but after they pass, the wave pulses continue, unchanged by their meeting.

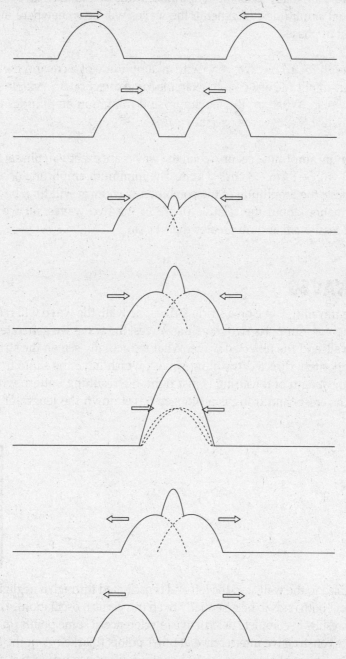

If the two waves have displacements of the same sign when they overlap, the combined wave will have a displacement of greater magnitude than either individual wave; this is called **constructive interference**. Similarly, if the waves have opposite displacements when they meet, the combined waveform will have a displacement of smaller magnitude than either individual wave; this is called **destructive interference**. If the waves travel in the same direction, the amplitude of the combined wave depends on the relative phase of the two waves. If the waves are exactly **in phase**—that is, if crest meets crest and trough meets trough—then the waves will constructively interfere completely, and the amplitude of the combined wave will be the sum of the individual amplitudes. However, if the waves are exactly **out of phase**—that is, if crest meets trough and trough meets crest—then they will destructively interfere completely, and the amplitude of the combined wave will be the difference between the individual amplitudes. In general, the waves will be somewhere in-between exactly in phase and exactly out of phase.

> **Example 15.7** Two waves, one with an amplitude of 8 cm and the other with an amplitude of 3 cm, travel in the same direction on a single string and overlap. What are the maximum and minimum amplitudes of the string while these waves overlap?

Solution. The maximum amplitude occurs when the waves are exactly in phase; the amplitude of the combined waveform will be 8 cm + 3 cm = 11 cm. The minimum amplitude occurs when the waves are exactly out of phase; the amplitude of the combined waveform will then be 8 cm – 3 cm = 5 cm. Without more information about the relative phase of the two waves, all we can say is that the amplitude will be at least 5 cm and no greater than 11 cm.

STANDING WAVES

When our prototype traveling wave on a string strikes the wall, the wave will reflect and travel back toward us. The string now supports two traveling waves; the wave we generated at our end, which travels toward the wall, and the reflected wave. What we actually see on the string is the superposition of these two oppositely-directed traveling waves, which have the same frequency, amplitude, and wavelength. If the length of the string is just right, the resulting pattern will oscillate vertically and remain fixed. The crests and troughs no longer travel down the length of the string. This is a **standing wave**.

The right end is fixed to the wall, and the left end is oscillated through a negligibly small amplitude so that we can consider both ends to be essentially fixed (no vertical oscillation). The interference of the two traveling waves results in complete destructive interference at some points (marked N in the figure below), and complete constructive interference at other points (marked A in the figure). Other points have amplitudes between these extremes. Notice another difference between a traveling wave and a standing wave: While every point on the string had the same amplitude as the traveling wave went by, each point on a string supporting a standing wave has an individual amplitude. The points marked N are called **nodes**, and those marked A are called **antinodes**.

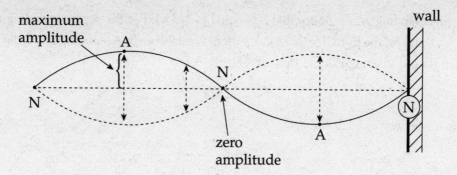

Nodes and antinodes always alternate, they're equally spaced, and the distance between two successive nodes (or antinodes) is equal to $\frac{1}{2}\lambda$. This information can be used to determine how standing waves can be generated. The following figures show the three simplest standing waves that our string can support. The first standing wave has one antinode, the second has two, and the third has three. The length of the string in all three diagrams is L.

For the first standing wave, notice that L is equal to $1(\frac{1}{2}\lambda)$. For the second standing wave, L is equal to $2(\frac{1}{2}\lambda)$, and for the third, $L = 3(\frac{1}{2}\lambda)$. A pattern is established: A standing wave can only form when the length of the string is a multiple of $\frac{1}{2}\lambda$:

$$L = n(\tfrac{1}{2}\lambda)$$

Solving this for the wavelength, we get

$$\lambda_n = \frac{2L}{n}$$

These are called the **harmonic** (or **resonant**) **wavelengths**, and the integer n is known as the **harmonic number**.

Since we typically have control over the frequency of the waves we create, it's more helpful to figure out the *frequencies* that generate a standing wave. Because $\lambda f = v$, and because v is fixed by the physical characteristics of the string, the special λ's found above correspond to equally special frequencies. From $f_n = v / \lambda_n$, we get

$$f_n = \frac{nv}{2L}$$

These are the **harmonic** (or **resonant**) **frequencies**. A standing wave will form on a string if we create a traveling wave whose frequency is the same as a resonant frequency. The first standing wave, the one for which the harmonic number, n, is 1, is called the **fundamental** standing wave. From the equation for the harmonic frequencies, we see that the nth harmonic frequency is simply n times the fundamental frequency:

$$f_n = nf_1$$

Similarly, the nth harmonic wavelength is equal to λ_1 divided by n. Therefore, by knowing the fundamental frequency (or wavelength), all the other resonant frequencies and wavelengths can be determined.

Example 15.8 A string of length 12 m that's fixed at both ends supports a standing wave with a total of 5 nodes. What are the harmonic number and wavelength of this standing wave?

Solution. First, draw a picture.

This shows that the length of the string is equal to $4(\frac{1}{2}\lambda)$, so

$$L = 4(\tfrac{1}{2}\lambda) \quad \Rightarrow \quad \lambda = \frac{2L}{4}$$

This is the fourth-harmonic standing wave, with wavelength λ_4 (because the expression above matches $\lambda_n = 2L/n$ for $n = 4$). Since $L = 12$ m, the wavelength is

$$\lambda_4 = \frac{2(12 \text{ m})}{4} = 6 \text{ m}$$

Example 15.9 A string of length 10 m and mass 300 g is fixed at both ends, and the tension in the string is 40 N. What is the frequency of the standing wave for which the distance between a node and the closest antinode is 1 m?

Solution. Because the distance between two successive nodes (or successive antinodes) is equal to $\frac{1}{2}\lambda$, the distance between a node and the closest antinode is half this, or $\frac{1}{4}\lambda$. Therefore, $\frac{1}{4}\lambda = 1$ m, so $\lambda = 4$ m. Since the harmonic wavelengths are given by the equation $\lambda_n = 2L/n$, we can find that

$$4 \text{ m} = \frac{2(10 \text{ m})}{n} \quad \Rightarrow \quad n = 5$$

The frequency of the fifth harmonic is

$$f_5 = \frac{5v}{2L} = \frac{5}{2L}\sqrt{\frac{F_T}{\mu}} = \frac{5}{2L}\sqrt{\frac{F_T}{m/L}} = \frac{5}{2(10 \text{ m})}\sqrt{\frac{40 \text{ N}}{0.3 \text{ kg}/10 \text{ m}}} = 9.1 \text{ Hz}$$

SOUND WAVES

Sound waves are produced by the vibration of an object, such as your vocal cords, a plucked string, or a jackhammer. The vibrations cause pressure variations in the conducting medium (which can be gas, liquid, or solid), and if the frequency is between 20 Hz and 20,000 Hz, the vibrations may be detected by human ears and perceived as sound. The variations in the conducting medium can be positions at which the molecules of the medium are bunched together (where the pressure is above normal), which are called **compressions**, and positions where the pressure is below normal, called **rarefactions**. In the figure below, a vibrating diaphragm sets up a sound wave in an air-filled tube. Each dot represents many, many air molecules:

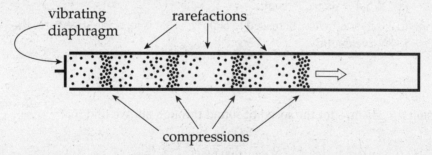

An important difference between sound waves and the waves we've been studying on stretched strings is that the molecules of the medium transmitting a sound wave move *parallel* to the direction of wave propagation, rather than perpendicular to it. For this reason, sound waves are said to be **longitudinal**. Despite this difference, all of the basic characteristics of a wave—amplitude, wavelength, period, frequency—apply to sound waves as they did for waves on a string. Furthermore, the all-important equation $\lambda f = v$ also holds true. However, because it's very difficult to draw a picture of a longitudinal wave, an alternate method is used: We can graph the pressure as a function of position:

The speed of a sound wave depends on the medium through which it travels. In particular, it depends on the density (ρ) and on the **bulk modulus** (B); a measure of the medium's response to compression. A medium that is easily compressible, like a gas, has a low bulk modulus; liquids and solids, which are much less easily compressed, have significantly greater bulk modulus values. For this reason, sound generally travels faster through solids than through liquids and faster through liquids than through gases. The equation that gives a sound wave's speed in terms of ρ and B is

$$v = \sqrt{\frac{B}{\rho}}$$

The speed of sound through air can also be written in terms of air's mean pressure, which depends on its temperature. At room temperature (approximately 20°C) and normal atmospheric pressure, sound travels at 343 m/s. This value increases as air warms or pressure increases.

Example 15.10 A sound wave with a frequency of 300 Hz travels through the air.
  (a) What is its wavelength?
  (b) If its frequency increased to 600 Hz, what is its wave speed and the wavelength?

Solution.

(a) Using $v = 343$ m/s for the speed of sound through air, we find that

$$\lambda = \frac{v}{f} = \frac{343 \text{ m/s}}{300 \text{ Hz}} = 1.14 \text{ m}$$

(b) Unless the ambient pressure or the temperature of the air changed, the speed of sound would not change. Wave speed depends on the characteristics of the medium, not on the frequency, so, v would still be 343 m/s. However, a change in frequency would cause a change in wavelength. Since f increased by a factor of 2, λ would decrease by a factor of 2, to $\frac{1}{2}(1.14 \text{ m}) = 0.57 \text{ m}$.

> **Example 15.11** A sound wave traveling through water has a frequency of 500 Hz and a wavelength of 3 m. How fast does sound travel through water?

Solution. $v = \lambda f = (3\text{ m})(500\text{ Hz}) = 1500\text{ m/s}$.

SOUND LEVEL

Sound waves transmit energy; the rate at which they transmit energy, per unit area, is called the **intensity**. It is denoted by I and has the unit W/m^2. Intensity depends on the wave's amplitude: The greater the amplitude (A), the greater the intensity (and, therefore, the louder the sound); in fact, I is proportional to A^2. Also, since sound waves spread out to form a spherical wavefront whose area is proportional to r^2, the intensity is proportional to $1/r^2$, where r is the distance from the source. The loudness of a sound is usually expressed not in terms of W/m^2 but in **decibels** (abbreviated **dB**). The **loudness level** of an acoustic wave whose intensity is I is defined as:

$$\beta = 10\log\frac{I}{I_0}$$

where $I_0 = 1 \times 10^{-12}\text{ W/m}^2$, a value known as the *threshold of hearing*. A sound wave at the threshold of hearing has $I = I_0$, so its sound level is $\beta = 0$ dB (because $\log 1 = 0$). Since the decibel scale is logarithmic, when intensity increases by a factor of 10, the decibel level increases by *the addition of* 10. Similarly, if the intensity decreases by a factor of 10, the decibel level decreases by *the subtraction of* 10.

> **Example 15.12** The loudness level in a library is 30 dB. If the loudness level of normal conversation is 60 dB, how many times more intense are the sound waves produced by normal conversation than those that exist in a library?

Solution. The difference between the decibel levels is $60 - 30 = 30$ dB. Each change by 10 in the decibel level corresponds to a factor of 10 in intensity. Since 30 dB represents 3 changes of 10, the intensity of normal conversation must be 3 *factors* of 10, or $10^3 = 1000$ times, greater than that in the library.

BEATS

If two sound waves whose frequencies are close but not identical interfere, the resulting sound modulates in amplitude, becoming loud, then soft, then loud, then soft. This is due to the fact that as the individual waves travel, they are in phase, then out of phase, then in phase again, and so on. Therefore, by superposition, the waves interfere constructively, then destructively, then constructively, etc. When the waves interfere constructively, the amplitude increases, and the sound is loud; when the waves interfere destructively, the amplitude decreases, and the sound is soft. Each time the waves interfere constructively, producing an increase in sound level, we say that a **beat** has occurred. The number of beats per second, known as the **beat frequency**, is equal to the difference between the frequencies of the two combining sound waves:

$$f_{\text{beat}} = |f_1 - f_2|$$

If frequencies f_1 and f_2 match, then the combined waveform doesn't waver in amplitude, and no beats are heard.

Example 15.13 A piano tuner uses a tuning fork to adjust the key that plays the A note above middle C (whose frequency should be 440 Hz). The tuning fork emits a perfect 440 Hz tone. When the tuning fork and the piano key are struck, beats of frequency 3 Hz are heard.

(a) What is the frequency of the piano key?

(b) If it's known that the piano key's frequency is too high, should the piano tuner tighten or loosen the wire inside the piano in order to tune it?

Solution.

(a) Since f_{beat} = 3 Hz, the tuning fork and the piano string are off by 3 Hz. Since the fork emits a tone of 440 Hz, the piano string must emit a tone of either 437 Hz or 443 Hz. Without more information, we can't decide which.

(b) If we know that the frequency of the tone emitted by the out-of-tune string is too high (that is, it's 443 Hz), we need to find a way to lower the frequency. Remember that the resonant frequencies for a stretched string fixed at both ends are given by the equation $f_n = nv/2L$, and that $v = \sqrt{F_T / \mu}$. Since f is too high, v must be too high. To lower v, we must reduce F_T. The piano tuner should loosen the string and listen for beats again, adjusting the string until the beats disappear.

RESONANCE FOR SOUND WAVES

Just as standing waves can be set up on a vibrating string, standing *sound* waves can be established within an enclosure. In the figure below, a vibrating source at one end of an air-filled tube produces sound waves that travel the length of the tube.

These waves reflect off the far end, and the superposition of the forward and reflected waves can produce a standing wave pattern if the length of the tube and the frequency of the waves are related in a certain way.

Notice that air molecules at the far end of the tube can't oscillate horizontally because they're up against a wall. So the far end of the tube is a displacement node. But the other end of the tube (where the vibrating source is located) is a displacement antinode. A standing wave with one antinode (A) and one node position (N) can be depicted as follows:

Although sound waves in air are longitudinal, here we'll show the wave as transverse so that it's easier to determine the wavelength. Since the distance between an antinode and an adjacent node is always $\frac{1}{4}$ of the wavelength, the length of the tube, L, in the figure above is $\frac{1}{4}$ the wavelength. This is the longest standing wavelength that can fit in the tube, so it corresponds to the lowest standing wave frequency, the fundamental.

$$L = \frac{\lambda_1}{4} \quad \Rightarrow \quad \lambda_1 = 4L \quad \Rightarrow \quad f_1 = \frac{v}{\lambda_1} = \frac{v}{4L}$$

The next higher frequency standing wave that can be supported in this tube must have two antinodes and two nodes:

In this case, the length of the tube is equal to $3(\frac{1}{4}\lambda')$, so

$$L = \frac{3\lambda'}{4} \quad \Rightarrow \quad \lambda' = \frac{4L}{3} \quad \Rightarrow \quad f' = \frac{v}{\lambda'} = \frac{3v}{4L}$$

Here's the pattern: Standing sound waves can be established in a tube that's closed at one end if the tube's length is equal to an *odd* multiple of $\frac{1}{4}\lambda$. The resonant wavelengths and frequencies are given by the equations

$$\left.\begin{array}{l} \lambda_n = \dfrac{4L}{n} \\[2mm] f_n = n\dfrac{v}{4L} \end{array}\right\} \text{ for any } \textit{odd} \text{ integer } n$$

If the far end of the tube is not sealed, standing waves can still be established in the tube, because sound waves can be reflected from the open air. A closed end is a displacement node, but an open end is a displacement antinode. In this case, then, the standing waves will have two displacement antinodes (at the ends of the tube), and the resonant wavelengths and frequencies will be given by

$$\left.\begin{array}{l} \lambda_n = \dfrac{2L}{n} \\[2mm] f_n = n\dfrac{v}{2L} \end{array}\right\} \text{ for any integer } n$$

Notice that, while an open-ended tube can support any harmonic, a closed-end tube can only support *odd* harmonics.

Example 15.14 A closed-end tube resonates at a fundamental frequency of 440.0 Hz. The air in the tube is at a temperature of 20°C, and it conducts sound at a speed of 343 m/s.

(a) What is the length of the tube?

(b) What is the next higher harmonic frequency?

(c) Answer the questions posed in (a) and (b) assuming that the tube were open at its far end.

Solution.

(a) For a closed-end tube, the harmonic frequencies obey the equation $f_n = nv/(4L)$. The fundamental corresponds to $n = 1$, so

$$f_1 = \frac{v}{4L} \quad \Rightarrow \quad L = \frac{v}{4f_1} = \frac{343 \text{ m/s}}{4(440.0 \text{ Hz})} = 0.195 \text{ m} = 19.5 \text{ cm}$$

(b) Since a closed-end tube can support only *odd* harmonics, the next higher harmonic frequency (the first **overtone**) is the *third* harmonic, f_3, which is $3f_1 = 3(440.0 \text{ Hz}) = 1320 \text{ Hz}$.

(c) For an opened-end tube, the harmonic frequencies obey the equation $f_n = nv/(2L)$. The fundamental corresponds to $n = 1$, so

$$f_1 = \frac{v}{2L'} \quad \Rightarrow \quad L' = \frac{v}{2f_1} = \frac{343 \text{ m/s}}{2(440.0 \text{ Hz})} = 0.390 \text{ m} = 39.0 \text{ cm}$$

And, since an opened-end tube can support any harmonic, the first overtone would be the second harmonic, $f_2 = 2f_1 = 2(440.0 \text{ Hz}) = 880.0 \text{ Hz}$.

THE DOPPLER EFFECT

When a source of sound waves and a detector are not in relative motion, the frequency that the source emits matches the frequency that the detector receives.

However, if there *is* relative motion between the source and the detector, then the waves that the detector receives are different in frequency (and wavelength). For example, if the detector moves toward the source, then the detector intercepts the waves at a rate higher than the one at which they were emitted; the detector hears a higher frequency than the source emitted. In the same way, if the source moves toward the detector, the wavefronts pile up, and this results in the detector receiving waves with shorter wavelengths and higher frequencies:

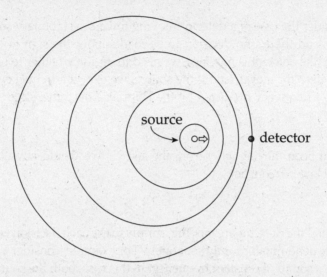

Conversely, if the detector is moving away from the source or if the source is moving away from the detector,

then the detected waves have a longer wavelength and a lower frequency than they had when they were emitted by the source. The shift in frequency and wavelength that occurs when the source and detector are in relative motion is known as the **Doppler Effect**. In general, relative motion *toward* each other results in a frequency shift upward, and relative motion *away* from each other results in a frequency shift downward.

Let f_S be the frequency of waves that the source emits and f_D the frequency that the detector hears. To determine f_D from f_S, use the following equation:

$$f_D = \frac{v \pm v_D}{v \pm v_S} \cdot f_S$$

where v is the speed of sound, v_D is the speed of the detector, and v_S is the speed of the source. The signs in the numerator and denominator depend on the directions in which the source and detector are moving.

For example, consider the case of a detector moving toward a stationary source. Since the source doesn't move, $v_S = 0$, and there's no decision to be made about the sign in the denominator. But, because v_D is not zero (the detector is moving), we need to decide whether to use the + or the − in the numerator. Since the detector moves *toward* the source, we expect a frequency shift upward. Therefore, to give the higher frequency predicted by the Doppler Effect, the + sign must be used:

$$f_D = \frac{v + v_D}{v} \cdot f_S$$

If the detector had been moving *away* from the source, we would have used the − sign in the numerator, to get the lower frequency

$$f_D = \frac{v - v_D}{v} \cdot f_S$$

If both the source and the detector are moving, simply make each decision (+ or − in the numerator for v_D and + or − in the denominator for v_S) separately. For example, consider a car following a police car whose siren emits a sound of constant frequency. In this case, both the source (the police car) and the detector (the driver of the pursuing car) are moving. Because the detector is moving toward the source, we should use the + sign on v_D in the numerator for an upward contribution to f_D. Since the source is moving away from the detector, we should use the + sign on v_S in the denominator for a downward contribution to f_D. Therefore, we get

$$f_D = \frac{v + v_D}{v + v_S} \cdot f_S$$

We can learn something else from this. What if the car were moving at the same speed as the police car? Then, although both are moving relative to the road, *they are not moving relative to each other*. If there is no relative motion between the source and the detector, then there should be no Doppler shift. This conclusion is supported by the equation above, since $v_D = v_S$ implies that $f_D = f_S$.

Example 15.15 A source of 4 kHz sound waves travels at $\frac{1}{9}$ the speed of sound toward a detector that's moving at $\frac{1}{9}$ the speed of sound, toward the source.
  (a) What is the frequency of the waves as they're received by the detector?
  (b) How does the wavelength of the detected waves compare to the wavelength of the emitted waves?

Solution.

(a) Because the detector moves toward the source, we use the + sign in the numerator of the Doppler Effect formula, and since the source moves toward the detector, we use the − sign in the denominator. This gives us:

$$f_D = \frac{v + v_D}{v - v_S} \cdot f_S = \frac{v + \frac{1}{9}v}{v - \frac{1}{9}v} \cdot f_S = \frac{5}{4} f_S = \frac{5}{4}(4 \text{ kHz}) = 5 \text{ kHz}$$

(b) Since the frequency shifted up by a factor of $\frac{5}{4}$, the wavelength will shift down by the same factor. That is,

$$\lambda_D = \frac{\lambda_S}{\frac{5}{4}} = \frac{4}{5}\lambda_S$$

Example 15.16 A person yells, emitting a constant frequency of 200 Hz, as he runs at 5 m/s toward a stationary brick wall. When the reflected waves reach the person, how many beats per second will he hear? (Use 343 m/s for the speed of sound.)

Solution. We need to determine what the frequency of the reflected waves will be when they reach the runner. First, the person is the source of the sound, and the wall is the detector. So:

$$f_{\text{wall}} = \frac{v}{v - v_{\text{runner}}} f$$

Then, as the sound waves reflect off the wall (with no change in frequency upon reflection), the wall acts as the source and the runner acts as the detector:

$$f' = \frac{v + v_{\text{runner}}}{v} f_{\text{wall}}$$

Combining these two equations gives

$$f' = \frac{v + v_{\text{runner}}}{v - v_{\text{runner}}} f$$

With $v = 343$ m/s and $v_{\text{runner}} = 5$ m/s, we get

$$f' = \frac{(343 + 5) \text{ m/s}}{(343 - 5) \text{ m/s}}(200 \text{ Hz}) = 206 \text{ Hz}$$

Therefore, the beat frequency is

$$f_{\text{beat}} = f' - f = 206 \text{ Hz} - 200 \text{ Hz} = 6 \text{ Hz}$$

THE DOPPLER EFFECT FOR LIGHT

Light, or electromagnetic waves, also experience the Doppler Effect. The detected wavelength, λ_D, is related to the emitted wavelength, λ_s, by the equation $\lambda_D = (1 \pm u/c)\lambda_s$, where u is the relative speed of the source and detector, and $c = 3.00 \times 10^8$ m/s, the speed of light. This formula assumes that u is much less than c. Again, the choice of + and – depends on whether the source and detector are moving away from or toward each other. As with sound, motion *toward* corresponds to a frequency shift upward (and a wavelength shift downward), and motion *away* corresponds to a frequency shift downward (and to a wavelength shift upward).

> **Example 15.17** Light from a distant galaxy is received on Earth with a wavelength of 679 nm. It's known that the wavelength of this light upon emission was 657 nm. Is the galaxy moving toward or away from us? At what speed?

Solution. The fact that the light has a longer wavelength upon detection than it had at emission tells us that the source is receding. Its speed is determined as follows:

$$\lambda_D = \left(1 + \frac{u}{c}\right)\lambda_S \quad \Rightarrow \quad u = c\left(\frac{\lambda_D}{\lambda_S} - 1\right) = (3.00 \times 10^8 \text{ m/s})\left(\frac{679 \text{ nm}}{657 \text{ nm}} - 1\right) = 1.00 \times 10^7 \text{ m/s}$$

Astronomers would say that the light has been **red-shifted**; that is, the wavelength was shifted upward, toward the red end of the visible spectrum.

CHAPTER 15 REVIEW QUESTIONS

SECTION I: MULTIPLE CHOICE

1. What is the wavelength of a 5 Hz wave that travels with a speed of 10 m/s?

    (A) 0.25 m
    (B) 0.5 m
    (C) 1 m
    (D) 2 m
    (E) 50 m

2. A rope of length 5 m is stretched to a tension of 80 N. If its mass is 1 kg, at what speed would a 10 Hz transverse wave travel down the string?

    (A) 2 m/s
    (B) 5 m/s
    (C) 20 m/s
    (D) 50 m/s
    (E) 200 m/s

3. A transverse wave on a long horizontal rope has a wavelength of 8 m travels at 2 m/s. At $t = 0$, a particular point on the rope has a vertical displacement of $+A$, where A is the amplitude of the wave. At what time will the vertical displacement of this same point on the rope be $-A$?

    (A) $t = \frac{1}{8}$ s
    (B) $t = \frac{1}{4}$ s
    (C) $t = \frac{1}{2}$ s
    (D) $t = 2$ s
    (E) $t = 4$ s

4. The vertical displacement, y, of a transverse traveling wave is given by the equation $y = 6 \sin (10 \pi t - \frac{1}{2} \pi x)$, with x and y in centimeters and t in seconds. What is the wavelength?

    (A) 0.25 cm
    (B) 0.5 cm
    (C) 2 cm
    (D) 4 cm
    (E) 8 cm

5. A string, fixed at both ends, supports a standing wave with a total of 4 nodes. If the length of the string is 6 m, what is the wavelength of the wave?

    (A) 0.67 m
    (B) 1.2 m
    (C) 1.5 m
    (D) 3 m
    (E) 4 m

6. A string, fixed at both ends, has a length of 6 m and supports a standing wave with a total of 4 nodes. If a transverse wave can travel at 40 m/s down the rope, what is the frequency of this standing wave?

    (A) 6.7 Hz
    (B) 10 Hz
    (C) 13.3 Hz
    (D) 20 Hz
    (E) 26.7 Hz

7. A sound wave travels through a metal rod with wavelength λ and frequency f. Which of the following best describes the wave when it passes into the surrounding air?

	Wavelength	Frequency
(A)	Less than λ	Equal to f
(B)	Less than λ	Less than f
(C)	Greater than λ	Equal to f
(D)	Greater than λ	Less than f
(E)	Greater than λ	Greater than f

8. In the figure below, two speakers, S_1 and S_2, emit sound waves of wavelength 2 m, in phase with each other.

Let A_P be the amplitude of the resulting wave at point P, and A_Q the amplitude of the resultant wave at point Q. How does A_P compare to A_Q?

(A) $A_P < A_Q$
(B) $A_P = A_Q$
(C) $A_P > A_Q$
(D) $A_P < 0, A_Q > 0$
(E) A_P and A_Q vary with time, so no comparison can be made.

9. An observer is 2 m from a source of sound waves. By how much will the sound level decrease if the observer moves to a distance of 20 m?

(A) 1 dB
(B) 2 dB
(C) 10 dB
(D) 18 dB
(E) 20 dB

10. An organ pipe that's closed at one end has a length of 17 cm. If the speed of sound through the air inside is 340 m/s, what is the pipe's fundamental frequency?

(A) 250 Hz
(B) 500 Hz
(C) 1000 Hz
(D) 1500 Hz
(E) 2000 Hz

11. A bat emits a 40 kHz "chirp" with a wavelength of 8.75 mm toward a tree and receives an echo 0.4 s later. How far is the bat from the tree?

(A) 35 m
(B) 70 m
(C) 105 m
(D) 140 m
(E) 175 m

12. A car is traveling at 20 m/s away from a stationary observer. If the car's horn emits a frequency of 600 Hz, what frequency will the observer hear? (Use $v = 340$ m/s for the speed of sound.)

(A) (34/36)(600 Hz)
(B) (34/32)(600 Hz)
(C) (36/34)(600 Hz)
(D) (32/34)(600 Hz)
(E) (32/36)(600 Hz)

SECTION II: FREE RESPONSE

1. A rope is stretched between two vertical supports. The points where it's attached (P and Q) are fixed. The linear density of the rope, μ, is 0.4 kg/m, and the speed of transverse waves on the rope is 12 m/s.

(a) What's the tension in the rope?

(b) With what frequency must the rope vibrate to create a traveling wave with a wavelength of 2 m?

The rope can support standing waves of lengths 4 m and 3.2 m, whose harmonic numbers are consecutive integers.

(c) Find

    (i) the length of the rope;

    (ii) the mass of the rope.

(d) What is the harmonic number of the 4 m standing wave?

(e) On the diagram above, draw a sketch of the 4 m standing wave, labeling the nodes and antinodes.

2. For a physics lab experiment on the Doppler Effect, students are brought to a racetrack. A car is fitted with a horn that emits a tone with a constant frequency of 500 Hz, and the goal of the experiment is for the students to observe the pitch (frequency) of the car's horn.

(a) If the car drives at 50 m/s directly away from the students (who remain at rest), what frequency will they hear? (Note: speed of sound = 345 m/s)

(b) Would it make a difference if the car remained stationary and the students were driven in a separate vehicle at 50 m/s away from the car?

The following diagram shows a long straight track along which the car is driven. The students stand 40 m from the track.

As the car drives by, the frequency which the students hear, f', is related to the car horn's frequency, f', by the equation

$$f' = \frac{v}{v - v_C \cos\theta} \cdot f$$

where v is the speed of sound, v_C is the speed of the car (50 m/s), and θ is the angle shown in the diagram.

(c) Find f' when $\theta = 60°$.

(d) Find f' when $\theta = 120°$.

(e) On the axes below, sketch the graph of f' as a function of x, the horizontal position of the car relative to the students' location.

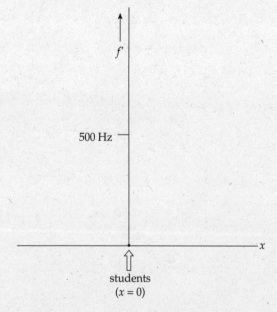

16

OPTICS [B]

INTRODUCTION

Light (or visible light) makes up only a small part of the entire spectrum of electromagnetic waves, which ranges from radio waves to gamma rays. The waves we studied in the preceding chapter required a material medium for their transmission, but electromagnetic waves can propagate through empty space. Electromagnetic waves consist of time-varying electric and magnetic fields that oscillate perpendicular to each other and to the direction of propagation of the wave. Through vacuum, all electromagnetic waves travel at a fixed speed:

$$c = 3.00 \times 10^8 \, \text{m/s}$$

regardless of their frequency.

THE ELECTROMAGNETIC SPECTRUM

Electromagnetic waves can be categorized by their frequency (or wavelength); the full range of waves is called the **electromagnetic** (or **EM**) **spectrum**. Types of waves include **radiowaves**, **microwaves**, **infrared**, **visible light**, **ultraviolet**, **X-rays**, and **γ-rays** (**gamma rays**) and, although they've been delineated in the spectrum below, there's no universal agreement on all the boundaries, so many of these bands overlap. You should be familiar with the names of the major categories, and, in particular, memorize the order of the colors within the visible spectrum (which, as you can see, accounts for only a tiny sliver of the full EM spectrum). In order of increasing wave frequency, the colors are red, orange, yellow, green, blue, and violet, which is commonly remembered as ROYGBV ("roy-gee-biv"). The wavelengths of the colors in the visible spectrum are usually expressed in nanometers. For example, electromagnetic waves whose wavelengths are between 577 nm and 597 nm are seen as yellow light.

ELECTROMAGNETIC SPECTRUM

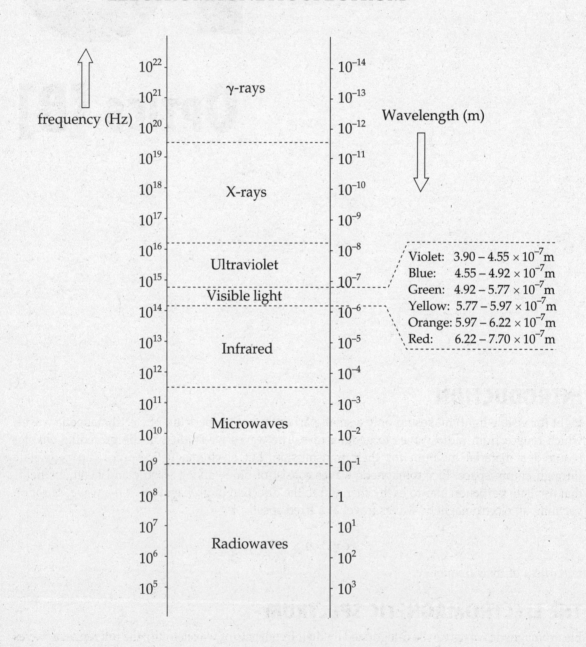

Example 16.1 What's the frequency range for green light?

Solution. According to the spectrum, light is green if its wavelength is between 4.92×10^{-7} m and 5.77×10^{-7} m. Using the equation $\lambda f = c$, we find that the upper end of this wavelength range corresponds to a frequency of

$$f_1 = \frac{c}{\lambda_1} = \frac{3.00 \times 10^8 \text{ m/s}}{5.77 \times 10^{-7} \text{ m}} = 5.20 \times 10^{14} \text{ Hz}$$

while the lower end corresponds to

$$f_2 = \frac{c}{\lambda_2} = \frac{3.00 \times 10^8 \text{ m/s}}{4.92 \times 10^{-7} \text{ m}} = 6.10 \times 10^{14} \text{ Hz}$$

So the frequency range for green light is

$$5.20 \times 10^{14} \text{ Hz} \leq f_{\text{green}} \leq 6.10 \times 10^{14} \text{ Hz}$$

Solution. According to the electromagnetic spectrum presented above, electromagnetic waves with $\lambda = 10^{-2}$ m are microwaves.

INTERFERENCE AND DIFFRACTION

As we learned in the preceding chapter, waves experience interference when they meet, and whether they interfere constructively or destructively depends on their relative phase. If they meet *in phase* (crest meets crest), they combine constructively, but if they meet *out of phase* (crest meets trough), they combine destructively. The key to the interference patterns we'll study in the next section rests on this observation. In particular, if waves that have the same wavelength meet, then the difference in the distances they've traveled determine whether the waves are in phase. Assuming that the waves are **coherent** (which means that their phase difference remains constant over time and does not vary), if the difference in their path lengths, $\Delta \ell$, is a whole number of wavelengths—0, $\pm\lambda$, $\pm 2\lambda$, etc.— they'll arrive in phase at the meeting point. On the other hand, if this difference is a whole number plus one-half a wavelength—$\pm\frac{1}{2}\lambda$, $\pm(1 + \frac{1}{2})\lambda$, $\pm(2 + \frac{1}{2})\lambda$, etc.—then they'll arrive out exactly of phase. That is,

$$\left. \begin{array}{ll} \text{constructive interference:} & \Delta\ell = m\lambda \\ \text{destructive interference:} & \Delta\ell = (m + \frac{1}{2})\lambda \end{array} \right\} \text{where } m \text{ is an integer}$$

YOUNG'S DOUBLE-SLIT INTERFERENCE EXPERIMENT

The following figure shows light incident on a barrier that contains two narrow slits (perpendicular to the plane of the page), separated by a distance d. On the right is a screen whose distance from the barrier, L, is much greater than d. The question is, What will we see on the screen? You might expect that we'll just see two bright narrow strips of light, directly opposite the slits in the barrier. As reasonable as this may sound, it doesn't take into account the wave nature of light.

When a wave encounters an aperture whose width is comparable to its wavelength, the wave will fan out after it passes through. The alteration in the straight-line propagation of a wave when it encounters a barrier is called **diffraction**. In the set-up above, the waves will diffract through the slits, and spread out and interfere as they travel toward the screen.

The screen will show the results of this interference: There will be bright bands (bright **fringes**) centered at those points at which the waves interfere constructively, alternating with dark fringes, where the waves interfere destructively. Let's determine the locations of these fringes.

In the figure below, we've labeled the slits S_1 and S_2. A point P on the screen is selected, the path lengths from S_1 and S_2 to P are called ℓ_1 and ℓ_2, respectively, and the angle that the line from the midpoint of the slits to P makes with the horizontal is θ. Segment S_1Q is perpendicular to line S_2P. Because L is so much larger than d, the angle that line S_2P makes with the horizontal is also approximately θ, which tells us that $\angle S_2S_1Q$ is approximately θ and that the path difference, $\Delta \ell = \ell_2 - \ell_1$, is nearly equal to S_2Q.

Because $S_2Q = d \sin \theta$, we get $\Delta \ell = d \sin \theta$. Now, using what we learned earlier about how constructive or destructive interference depends on $\Delta \ell$, we can write:

constructive interference
(intensity maximum —
bright fringe — on screen): $d \sin \theta = m\lambda$

destructive interference
(intensity minimum —
dark fringe — on screen): $d \sin \theta = (m + \frac{1}{2})\lambda$

} where m is an integer

To locate the positions of, say, the bright fringes on the screen, we use the fact that $y = L \tan \theta$. If θ is small, then $\tan \theta \approx \sin \theta$, so we can write $y = L \sin \theta$ (we can tell this from the figure). Since $\sin \theta = m\lambda/d$ for bright fringes, we get

$$y_m = \frac{m\lambda L}{d}$$

Also, the intensity of the bright fringes decreases as m increases in magnitude. The bright fringe directly opposite the midpoint of the slits—the **central maximum**—will have the greatest intensity, the bright fringes with $m = \pm 1$ will have a lower intensity, those with $m = \pm 2$ will be fainter still, and so on. If more than two slits are cut in the barrier, the interference pattern becomes sharper, and the distinction between dark and bright fringes becomes more pronounced. Barriers containing thousands of tiny slits per centimeter—called **diffraction gratings**—are used precisely for this purpose.

Example 16.3 For the experimental set-up we've been studying, assume that $d = 1.5$ mm, $L = 6.0$ m, and that the light used has a wavelength of 589 nm.

(a) How far above the center of the screen will the first intensity maximum appear?

(b) What's the width of this bright fringe?

(c) How far below the center of the screen is the third dark fringe?

(d) What would happen to the interference pattern if the slits were moved closer together?

Solution.

(a) The central maximum corresponds to $m = 0$ ($y_0 = 0$). The first maximum above the central one is labeled y_1 (since $m = 1$), and the first maximum below the central one is labeled y_{-1} (that is, $m = -1$). The other bright fringes on the screen are labeled accordingly.

The value of y_1 is

$$y_1 = \frac{1 \cdot \lambda L}{d} = \frac{(589 \times 10^{-9} \text{ m})(6.0 \text{ m})}{1.5 \times 10^{-3} \text{ m}} = 2.4 \times 10^{-3} \text{ m} = 2.4 \text{ mm}$$

(b) The distance between the centers of adjacent bright fringes is

$$\Delta y = y_{m+1} - y_m = \frac{(m+1)\lambda L}{d} - \frac{m\lambda L}{d} = \frac{\lambda L}{d} = 2.4 \text{ mm}$$

So, as the figure above shows, the width of each fringe is half this, or 1.2 mm.

(c) The third dark fringe occurs just before the third bright fringe, so

$$y_{\substack{\text{3rd minimum} \\ \text{below central max}}} = \frac{(-3+\frac{1}{2})\lambda L}{d} = \frac{(-3+\frac{1}{2})(589 \times 10^{-9} \text{ m})(6.0 \text{ m})}{1.5 \times 10^{-3} \text{ m}} = -5.9 \times 10^{-3} \text{ m} = -5.9 \text{ mm}$$

(d) Since $y_m = m\lambda L/d$, a decrease in d would cause an increase in y_m. That is, the fringes would become larger; the interference pattern would be more spread out.

SINGLE-APERTURE DIFFRACTION

A diffraction pattern will also form on the screen if the barrier contains only one slit. The central maximum will be very pronounced, but lower-intensity maxima will also be seen because of interference from waves arriving from different locations within the slit itself. The width of the central maximum will become wider as the width of the slit is decreased.

For a circular pinhole aperture, the diffraction pattern will consist of a central, bright circular disk surrounded by rings of decreasing intensity.

REFLECTION AND REFRACTION

Imagine a beam of light directed toward a smooth transparent surface. When it hits this surface, some of its energy will be reflected off the surface and some will be transmitted into the new medium. We can figure out the directions of the reflected and transmitted beams by calculating the angles that the beams make with the normal to the interface. In the following figure, an incident beam strikes the boundary of another medium; it could be a beam of light in air striking a piece of glass.

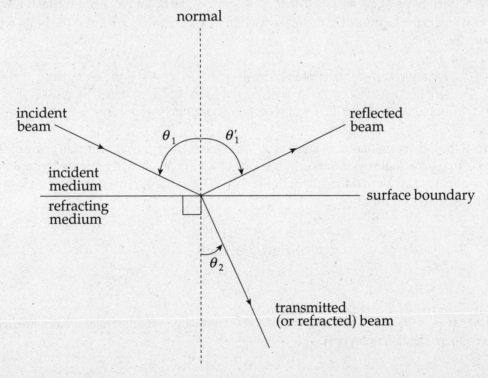

The angle that the **incident beam** makes with the normal is called the **angle of incidence**, or θ_1. The angle that the **reflected beam** makes with the normal is called the **angle of reflection**, θ_1', and the angle that the **transmitted beam** makes with the normal is called the **angle of refraction**, θ_2. The incident, reflected, and transmitted beams of light all lie in the same plane.

The relationship between θ_1 and θ_1' is pretty easy; it is called the **Law of Reflection**:

$$\theta_1 = \theta_1'$$

In order to describe how θ_1 and θ_2 are related, we first need to talk about a medium's index of refraction.

When light travels through empty space (vacuum), its speed is $c = 3.00 \times 10^8$ m/s; this is one of the fundamental constants of nature. But when light travels through a material medium (such as water or glass), it's constantly being absorbed and re-emitted by the atoms that compose the material and, as a result, its apparent speed, v, is some fraction of c. This fraction,

$$n = \frac{c}{v}$$

is called the medium's **index of refraction**. For example, since the speed of light in water is $v = 2.25 \times 10^8$ m/s, the index of refraction of water is

$$n = \frac{3.00 \times 10^8 \text{ m/s}}{2.25 \times 10^8 \text{ m/s}} = 1.33$$

Notice that n has no units; it's also never less than 1.

The equation that relates θ_1 and θ_2 involves the index of refraction of the incident medium (n_1) and the index of refraction of the refracting medium (n_2); it's called **Snell's Law**:

$$n_1 \sin \theta_1 = n_2 \sin \theta_2$$

If $n_2 > n_1$, then Snell's Law tells us that $\theta_2 < \theta_1$; that is, the beam will bend (**refract**) toward the normal as it enters the medium. On the other hand, if $n_2 < n_1$, then $\theta_2 > \theta_1$, and the beam will bend away from the normal.

Example 16.4 A beam of light in air is incident upon a piece of glass, striking the surface at an angle of 30°. If the index of refraction of the glass is 1.5, what are the angles of reflection and refraction?

Solution. If the light beam makes an angle of 30° with the surface, then it makes an angle of 60° with the normal; this is the angle of incidence. By the Law of Reflection, then, the angle of reflection is also 60°. We use Snell's Law to find the angle of refraction. The index of refraction of air is close to to 1, so we can say that $n = 1$ for air.

$$n_1 \sin \theta_1 = n_2 \sin \theta_2$$
$$1 \cdot \sin 60° = 1.5 \sin \theta_2$$
$$\sin \theta_2 = 0.5774$$
$$\theta_2 = 35°$$

Notice that $\theta_2 < \theta_1$, as we would expect since the refracting medium (glass) has a greater index than does the incident medium (air).

Example 16.5 A fisherman drops a flashlight into a lake that's 10 m deep. The flashlight sinks to the bottom where its emerging light beam is directed almost vertically upward toward the surface of the lake, making a small angle (θ_1) with the normal. How deep will the flashlight appear to be to the fisherman? (Use the fact that tan θ is almost equal to sin θ if θ is small.)

Solution. Take a look at the figure below.

Since the refracting medium (air) has a lower index than the incident medium (water), the beam of light will bend away from the normal as it emerges from the water. As a result, the fisherman will think that the flashlight is at a depth of only y_1, rather than its actual depth of $y_2 = 10$ m. By simple trigonometry, we know that

$$\tan\theta_1 = \frac{x}{y_2} \quad \text{and} \quad \tan\theta_2 = \frac{x}{y_1}$$

So,

$$\frac{y_1}{y_2} = \frac{\tan\theta_1}{\tan\theta_2}$$

Snell's Law tells us that $n_1 \sin\theta_1 = \sin\theta_2$ (since $n_2 = n_{air} = 1$), so

$$\frac{\sin\theta_1}{\sin\theta_2} = \frac{1}{n_1}$$

Using the approximations sin $\theta_1 \approx$ tan θ_1 and sin $\theta_2 \approx$ tan θ_2, we can write

$$\frac{\tan\theta_1}{\tan\theta_2} \approx \frac{\sin\theta_1}{\sin\theta_2}$$

which means

$$\frac{y_1}{y_2} = \frac{1}{n_1}$$

Because $y_2 = 10$ m and $n_1 = n_{water} = 1.33$,

$$y_1 = \frac{y_2}{n_1} = \frac{10 \text{ m}}{1.33} = 7.5 \text{ m}$$

DISPERSION OF LIGHT

One thing we learned when we studied waves is that wave speed is independent of frequency. For a given medium, different frequencies give rise to different wavelengths, because the equation $\lambda f = v$ must always be satisfied and v doesn't vary. But when light travels through a material medium, it displays **dispersion**, which is a variation in wave speed with frequency (or wavelength). So, the definition of the index of refraction, $n = c/v$, should be accompanied by a statement of the frequency of the light used to measure v, since different frequencies have different speeds and different indices. A piece of glass may have the following indices for visible light:

	red	orange	yellow	green	blue	violet
$n =$	1.502	1.506	1.511	1.517	1.523	1.530

Notice that as the wavelength decreases, refractive index increases. In general, higher frequency waves have higher indices of refraction. Most lists of refractive index values are tabulated using yellow light of wavelength 589 nm (frequency 5.1×10^{14} Hz).

Although the variation in the values of the refractive index across the visible spectrum is pretty small, when white light (which is a combination of all the colors of the visible spectrum) hits a glass prism, the beam is split into its component colors.

Why? Because each color has its own index, Snell's Law tells us that each color will have its own angle of refraction. Therefore, each color emerges from the prism at a slightly different angle, so the light disperses into its component colors.

Example 16.6 In the figure above, assume that the incident beam strikes the prism with an angle of incidence of 60.00°. If the top angle of the prism has a measure of 60.00°, what are the angles of refraction of red light and violet light when the beam emerges from the other side? (Use $n = 1.502$ for red light and 1.530 for violet light.)

Solution. The beam refracts twice, once when it enters the prism and again when it exits.

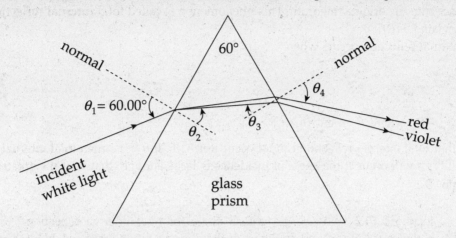

Snell's Law tells us that

$$1 \cdot \sin 60.00° = n \sin \theta_2 \quad \text{and} \quad n \sin \theta_3 = 1 \cdot \sin \theta_4$$

where n is the index of the glass. We'll ignore the minuscule variation in n for light in air, and just use $n = 1$ for all colors. The relationship between θ_2 and θ_3 follows from the fact that the sum of the measures of the angles in any triangle is 180°, so

$$(90° - \theta_2) + 60° + (90° - \theta_3) = 180°$$

which implies that $\theta_3 = 60° - \theta_2$. We can now make the following table of values:

color	n	θ_2	θ_3	θ_4
red	1.502	35.210°	24.790°	39.03°
violet	1.530	34.474°	25.526°	41.25°

TOTAL INTERNAL REFLECTION

When a beam of light strikes the boundary to a medium that has a lower index of refraction, the beam bends away from the normal. As the angle of incidence increases, the angle of refraction becomes larger. At some point, when the angle of incidence reaches a **critical angle,** θ_c, the angle of refraction becomes 90°, which means the refracted beam is directed along the surface.

For angles of incidence that are greater than θ_c, there is *no* angle of refraction; the entire beam is reflected back into the original medium. This phenomenon is called **total internal reflection** (sometimes abbreviated **TIR**).

Total internal reflection occurs when:

1) $n_1 > n_2$

and

2) $\theta_1 > \theta_c$, where $\theta_c = \sin^{-1}(n_2/n_1)$

Notice that total internal reflection cannot occur if $n_1 < n_2$. If $n_1 > n_2$, then total internal reflection is a possibility; it will occur if the angle of incidence is large enough, that is, if it's greater than the critical angle, θ_c.

> **Example 16.7** What is the critical angle for total internal reflection between air and water? In which of these media must light be incident for total internal reflection to occur?

Solution. First, total internal reflection can only occur when the light is incident in the medium that has the greater refractive index and strikes the boundary to a medium that has a lower index. So, in this case, total internal reflection can occur only when the light source is in the water and the light is incident upon the water/air surface. The critical angle is found as follows:

$$\sin\theta_c = \frac{n_2}{n_1} \implies \sin\theta_c = \frac{n_{air}}{n_{water}} = \frac{1}{1.33} \implies \sin\theta_c = 0.75 \implies \theta_c = 49°$$

Total internal reflection will occur if the light from the water strikes the water/air boundary at an angle of incidence greater than 49°.

> **Example 16.8** How close must the fisherman be to the flashlight in Example 16.5 in order to see the light it emits?

Solution. In order for the fisherman to see the light, the light must be transmitted into the air from the water; that is, it cannot undergo total internal reflection. The figure below shows that, within a circle of radius x, light from the flashlight will emerge from the water. Outside this circle, the angle of incidence is greater than the critical angle, and the light would be reflected back into the water, rendering it undetectable by the fisherman above.

Because the critical angle for total internal reflection at a water/air interface is 49° (as we found in the preceding example), we can solve for x:

$$\tan 49° = \frac{x}{y} \quad \Rightarrow \quad x = y\tan 49° = (10\text{ m})\tan 49° = 11.5\text{ m}$$

Example 16.9 The refractive index for the glass prism shown below is 1.55. In order for a beam of light to experience total internal reflection at the right-hand face of the prism, the angle θ_1 must be smaller than what value?

Solution. Total internal reflection will occur at the glass/air boundary if θ_3 is greater than the critical angle, θ_c, which we can calculate this way:

$$\sin\theta_c = \frac{n_{air}}{n_{glass}} = \frac{1}{1.55} \quad \Rightarrow \quad \theta_c = 40°$$

Because $\theta_3 = 60° - \theta_2$, total internal reflection will take place if θ_2 is smaller than 20°. Now, by Snell's Law, $\theta_2 = 20°$ if

$$n_{air}\sin\theta_1 = n_{glass}\sin\theta_2$$
$$\sin\theta_1 = 1.55\sin 20°$$
$$\theta_1 = 32°$$

Therefore, total internal reflection will occur at the right-hand face of the prism if θ_1 is smaller than 32°.

MIRRORS

A **mirror** is an optical device that forms an image by reflecting light. We've all looked into a mirror and seen images of nearby objects, and the purpose of this section is to analyze these images mathematically. We begin with a plane mirror, which is flat, and is the simplest type of mirror. Then we'll examine curved mirrors; we'll have to use geometrical methods or algebraic equations to analyze the patterns of reflection from these.

PLANE MIRRORS

The figure below shows an object (denoted by the bold arrow) in front of a flat mirror. Light that's reflected off of the object strikes the mirror and is reflected back to our eyes. The directions of the rays reflected off the mirror determines where we perceive the image to be.

There are four questions we'll answer about the image formed by a mirror:

(1) Where is the image?

(2) Is the image real or is it virtual?

(3) Is the image upright or is it inverted?

(4) What is the height of the image (compared to that of the object)?

When we look at ourselves in a mirror, it seems like our image is *behind* the mirror, and, if we take a step back, our image also takes a step back. The Law of Reflection can be used to show that the image seems as far behind the mirror as the object is in front of the mirror. This answers question (1).

An image is said to be **real** if light rays actually focus at the image. A real image can be projected onto a screen. For a flat mirror, light rays bounce off the front of the mirror; so, of course, no light focuses behind it. Therefore, the images produced by a flat mirror are not real; they are **virtual**. This answers question (2).

When we look into a flat mirror, our image isn't upside down; flat mirrors produce upright images, and question (3) is answered.

Finally, the image formed by a flat mirror is neither magnified nor diminished (minified) relative to the size of the object. This answers question (4).

SPHERICAL MIRRORS

A **spherical mirror** is a mirror that's curved in such a way that its surface forms part of a sphere.

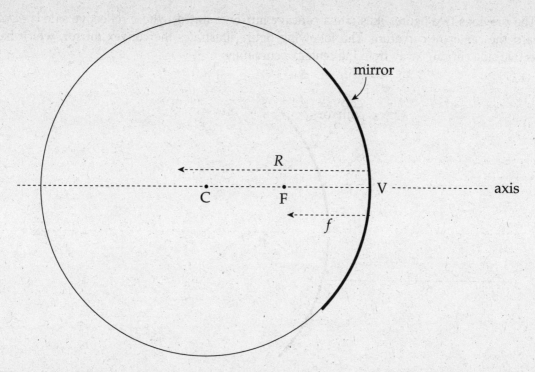

The center of this imaginary sphere is the mirror's **center of curvature**, and the radius of the sphere is called the mirror's **radius of curvature**, R. Halfway between the mirror and the center of curvature, C, is the **focus** (or **focal point**), F. The intersection of the mirror's optic **axis** (its axis of symmetry) with the mirror itself is called the **vertex**, V, and the distance from V to F is called the **focal length**, f, equal to one-half of the radius of curvature:

$$f = \frac{R}{2}$$

If the mirror had a parabolic cross-section, then any ray parallel to the axis would be reflected by the mirror through the focal point. Spherical mirrors do this for incident light rays near the axis (**paraxial rays**) because, in the region of the mirror that's close to the axis, the shapes of a parabolic mirror and a spherical mirror are nearly identical.

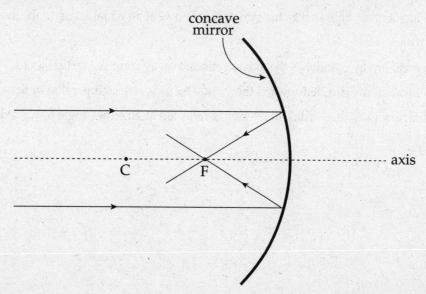

The previous two figures illustrate a **concave mirror**, a mirror whose reflective side is *caved in* toward the center of curvature. The following figure illustrates the **convex mirror**, which has a reflective side curving away from the center of curvature.

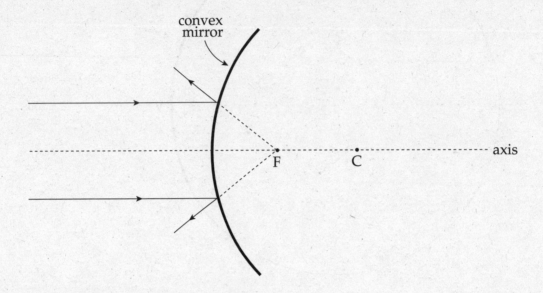

RAY TRACING FOR MIRRORS

One method of answering the four questions listed above concerning the image formed by a mirror involves a geometric approach called **ray tracing**. Representative rays of light are sketched in a diagram that depicts the object and the mirror; the point at which the reflected rays intersect (or appear to intersect) is the location of the image. Some rules governing rays are:

Concave mirrors:

- An incident ray parallel to the axis is reflected through the focus.
- An incident ray that passes through the focus is reflected parallel to the axis.
- An incident ray that strikes the vertex is reflected at an equal angle to the axis.

Convex mirrors:

- An incident ray parallel to the axis is reflected away from the virtual focus.
- An incident ray directed toward the virtual focus is reflected parallel to the axis.
- An incident ray that strikes the vertex is reflected at an equal angle to the axis.

Example 16.10 The figure below shows a concave mirror and an object (the bold arrow). Use a ray diagram to locate the image of the object

Solution. It only takes two distinct rays to locate the image:

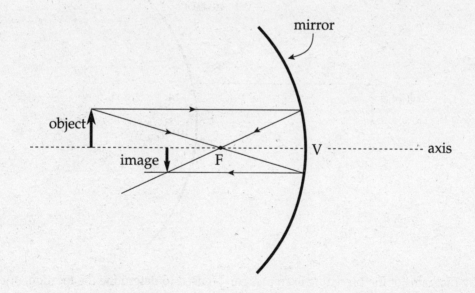

Example 16.11 The figure below shows a convex mirror and an object (the arrow). Use a ray diagram to locate the image of the object.

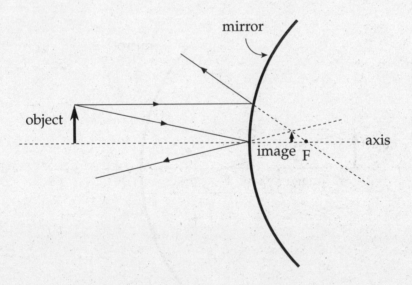

Solution.

The ray diagrams of the preceding examples can be used to determine the location, orientation, and size of the image. The nature of the image—that is, whether it's real or virtual—can be determined by seeing on which side of the mirror the image is formed. If the image if formed on the same side of the mirror as the object, then the image is real, but if the image is formed on the opposite side of the mirror, it's virtual. Therefore, the image in Example 16.10 is real, and the image in Example 16.11 is virtual.

USING EQUATIONS TO ANSWER QUESTIONS ABOUT THE IMAGE

The fastest and easiest way to get information about an image is to use two equations and some simple conventions. The first equation, called the **mirror equation**, is

$$\frac{1}{s_o} + \frac{1}{s_i} = \frac{1}{f}$$

where s_o is the object's distance from the mirror, s_i is the image's distance from the mirror, and f is the focal length of the mirror. The value of s_o is *always* positive for a real object, but s_i can be positive or negative. The sign of s_i tells us whether the image is real or virtual: If s_i is positive, the image is real; and if s_i is negative, the image is virtual.

The second equation is called the **magnification equation**:

$$m = -\frac{s_i}{s_o}$$

This gives the magnification; the height of the image, h_i, is $|m|$ times the height of the object, h_o. If m is positive, then the image is upright relative to the object; if m is negative, it's inverted. Because s_o is always positive, we can come to two important conclusions. If s_i is positive, then m is negative, so real images are always inverted, and, if s_i is negative, then m is positive, so virtual images are always upright.

Finally, to distinguish *mathematically* between concave and convex mirrors, we always write the focal length f as a positive value for concave mirrors and a negative value for convex mirrors. With these two equations and their accompanying conventions, all four questions about an image can be answered. The mirror equation answers questions (1) and (2), and the magnification equation answers (3) and (4).

MIRRORS

concave $\Leftrightarrow$ f positive

convex $\Leftrightarrow$ f negative

$$\frac{1}{s_o} + \frac{1}{s_i} = \frac{1}{f} \begin{cases} s_o \text{ always positive (real object)} \\ s_i \text{ positive} \implies \text{image is real} \\ s_i \text{ negative} \implies \text{image is virtual} \end{cases}$$

$$m = -\frac{s_i}{s_o} \begin{cases} |m| \times h_o = h_i \\ m \text{ positive} \implies \text{image is upright} \\ m \text{ negative} \implies \text{image is inverted} \end{cases}$$

Example 16.12 A object of height 4 cm is placed 30 cm in front of a concave mirror whose focal length is 10 cm.

(a) Where's the image?

(b) Is it real or virtual?

(c) Is it upright or inverted?

(d) What's the height of the image?

Solution.

(a) With $s_o = 30$ cm and $f = 10$ cm, the mirror equation gives

$$\frac{1}{s_o} + \frac{1}{s_i} = \frac{1}{f} \quad \Rightarrow \quad \frac{1}{30 \text{ cm}} + \frac{1}{s_i} = \frac{1}{10 \text{ cm}} \quad \Rightarrow \quad \frac{1}{s_i} = \frac{1}{15 \text{ cm}} \quad \Rightarrow \quad s_i = 15 \text{ cm}$$

The image is located 15 cm in front of the mirror.

(b) Because s_i is positive, the image is real.

(c) Real images are inverted.

(d) The magnification is

$$m = -\frac{s_i}{s_o} = -\frac{15 \text{ cm}}{10 \text{ cm}} = -\frac{3}{2}$$

[The fact that the magnification is negative confirms that the image is inverted, as we said in part (c).] The height of the image is

$$h_i = |m| \cdot h_o = \tfrac{3}{2}(4 \text{ cm}) = 6 \text{ cm}$$

Example 16.13 A object of height 4 cm is placed 20 cm in front of a convex mirror whose focal length is –30 cm.

(a) Where's the image?

(b) Is it real or virtual?

(c) Is it upright or inverted?

(d) What's the height of the image?

Solution.

(a) With $s_o = 20$ cm and $f = -30$ cm, the mirror equation gives us:

$$\frac{1}{s_o} + \frac{1}{s_i} = \frac{1}{f} \quad \Rightarrow \quad \frac{1}{20 \text{ cm}} + \frac{1}{s_i} = \frac{1}{-30 \text{ cm}} \quad \Rightarrow \quad \frac{1}{s_i} = -\frac{1}{12 \text{ cm}} \quad \Rightarrow \quad s_i = -12 \text{ cm}$$

So, the image is located 12 cm behind the mirror.

(b) Because s_i is negative, the image is virtual.

(c) Virtual images are upright.

(d) The magnification is

$$m = -\frac{s_i}{s_o} = -\frac{-12 \text{ cm}}{20 \text{ cm}} = \frac{3}{5}$$

[The fact that the magnification is positive tells us that the image is upright, as we said in part (c).] The height of the image is

$$h_i = |m| \cdot h_o = \tfrac{3}{5}(4 \text{ cm}) = 2.4 \text{ cm}$$

Example 16.14 Show how the statements made earlier about plane mirrors can be derived from the mirror and magnification equations.

Solution. A plane mirror can be considered a spherical mirror with an infinite radius of curvature (and an infinite focal length). If $f = \infty$, then $1/f = 0$, so the mirror equation becomes

$$\frac{1}{s_o} + \frac{1}{s_i} = 0 \quad \Rightarrow \quad s_i = -s_o$$

So, the image is as far behind the mirror as the object is in front. Also, since s_o is always positive, s_i is negative, so the image is virtual. The magnification is

$$m = -\frac{s_i}{s_o} = -\frac{-s_o}{s_o} = 1$$

and the image is upright and has the same height as the object. The mirror and magnification equations confirm our description of images formed by plane mirrors.

Example 16.15 Show why convex mirrors can only form virtual images.

Solution. Because f is negative and s_o is positive, the mirror equation

$$\frac{1}{s_o} + \frac{1}{s_i} = \frac{1}{f}$$

immediately tells us that s_i cannot be positive (if it were, the left-hand side would be the sum of two positive numbers, while the right-hand side would be negative). Since s_i must be negative, the image must be virtual.

Example 16.16 An object placed 60 cm in front of a spherical mirror forms a real image at a distance of 30 cm from the mirror.
(a) Is the mirror concave or convex?
(b) What's the mirror's focal length?
(c) Is the image taller or shorter than the object?

Solution.

(a) The fact that the image is real tells us that the mirror cannot be convex, since convex mirrors form only virtual images. The mirror is concave.

(b) With $s_o = 60$ cm and $s_i = 30$ cm (s_i is positive since the image is real), the mirror equation tells us that

$$\frac{1}{s_o} + \frac{1}{s_i} = \frac{1}{f} \implies \frac{1}{60 \text{ cm}} + \frac{1}{30 \text{ cm}} = \frac{1}{f} \implies \frac{1}{f} = \frac{1}{20 \text{ cm}} \implies f = 20 \text{ cm}$$

Notice that f is positive; it must be, since the mirror is concave.

(c) The magnification is

$$m = -\frac{s_i}{s_o} = -\frac{30 \text{ cm}}{60 \text{ cm}} = -\frac{1}{2}$$

Since the absolute value of m is less than 1, the mirror makes the object look smaller (minifies the height of the object). The image is only half as tall as the object (and is upside down, because m is negative).

> **Example 16.17** A concave mirror with a focal length of 25 cm is used to create a real image that has twice the height of the object. How far is the image from the mirror?

Solution. Since h_i (the height of the image) is twice h_o (the height of the object) the value of the magnification is either +2 or –2. To figure out which, we just notice that the image is real; real images are inverted, so the magnification, m, must be negative. Therefore, $m = -2$, so

$$-\frac{s_i}{s_o} = -2 \implies s_o = \tfrac{1}{2} s_i$$

Substituting this into the mirror equation gives us:

$$\frac{1}{s_o} + \frac{1}{s_i} = \frac{1}{f} \implies \frac{1}{\frac{1}{2}s_i} + \frac{1}{s_i} = \frac{1}{f} \implies \frac{3}{s_i} = \frac{1}{f} \implies s_i = 3f = 3(25 \text{ cm}) = 75 \text{ cm}$$

THIN LENSES

A lens is an optical device that forms an image by *refracting* light. We'll now talk about the equations and conventions that are used to analyze images formed by the two major categories of lenses: converging and diverging.

A **converging lens**—like the bi-convex one shown below—converges parallel paraxial rays of light to a focal point on the far side. (This lens is *bi-convex*; both of its faces are convex. Converging lens all have at least one convex face.) Because light rays actually focus at F, this point is called a **real focus**. Its distance from the lens is the focal length, f.

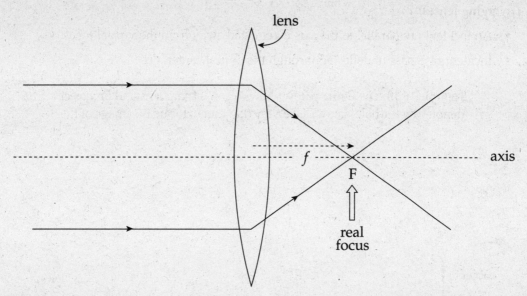

A **diverging lens**—like the *bi-concave* one shown below—causes parallel paraxial rays of light to diverge away from a **virtual focus**, F, on the same side as the incident rays. (Diverging lens all have at least one concave face.)

RAY TRACING FOR LENSES

Just as is the case with mirrors, representative rays of light can be sketched in a diagram along with the object and the lens; the point at which the reflected rays intersect (or appear to intersect) is the location of the image. The rules that govern these rays are as follows:

Converging lenses:

- An incident ray parallel to the axis is refracted through the real focus.

- Incident rays pass undeflected through the **optical center**, O (the central point within the lens where the axis intersects the lens).

Diverging lenses:

- An incident ray parallel to the axis is refracted away from the virtual focus.

- Incident rays pass undeflected through the optical center, O.

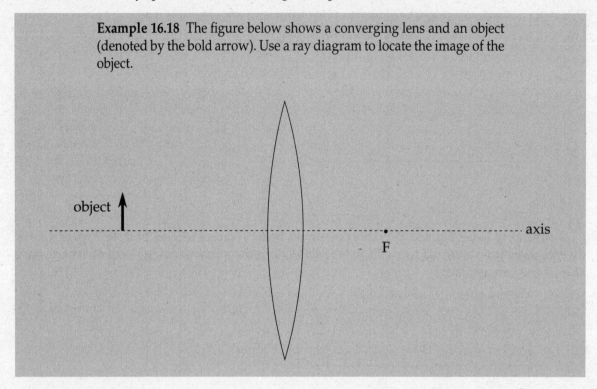

Example 16.18 The figure below shows a converging lens and an object (denoted by the bold arrow). Use a ray diagram to locate the image of the object.

Solution.

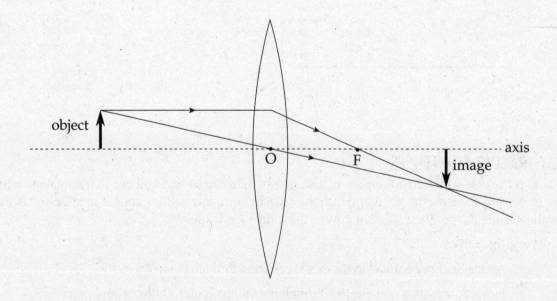

Example 16.19 The figure below shows a diverging lens and an object. Use a ray diagram to locate the image of the object.

Solution.

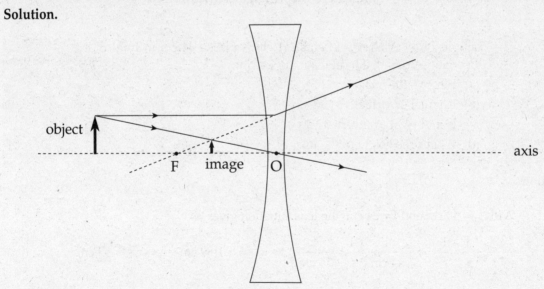

The nature of the image—that is, whether it's real or virtual—is determined by the side of the lens upon which the image is formed. If the image is formed on the side of the lens that's opposite the object, then the image is real, and if the image is formed on the same side of the lens as the object, then it's virtual. Therefore, the image in Example 16.18 is real, while the image in Example 16.19 is virtual.

USING EQUATIONS TO ANSWER QUESTIONS ABOUT THE IMAGE

Using the notation we used for mirrors, we can summarize the equations and conventions for analyzing the images formed by lenses. Except for the reversal of the physical locations of real vs. virtual images, everything else is the same!

LENSES

$$\text{converging} \Leftrightarrow f \text{ positive}$$
$$\text{diverging} \Leftrightarrow f \text{ negative}$$

$$\frac{1}{s_o} + \frac{1}{s_i} = \frac{1}{f} \begin{cases} s_o \text{ always positive (real object)} \\ s_i \text{ positive} \Rightarrow \text{ image is real} \\ s_i \text{ negative} \Rightarrow \text{ image is virtual} \end{cases}$$

$$m = -\frac{s_i}{s_o} \begin{cases} |m| \times h_o = h_i \\ m \text{ positive} \Rightarrow \text{ image is upright} \\ m \text{ negative} \Rightarrow \text{ image is inverted} \end{cases}$$

> **Example 16.20** A object of height 11 cm is placed 44 cm in front of a converging lens with a focal length of 24 cm.
> (a) Where's the image?
> (b) Is it real or virtual?
> (c) Is it upright or inverted?
> (d) What's the height of the image?

Solution.

(a) With $s_o = 44$ cm and $f = 24$ cm, the lens equation gives us:

$$\frac{1}{s_o} + \frac{1}{s_i} = \frac{1}{f} \Rightarrow \frac{1}{44 \text{ cm}} + \frac{1}{s_i} = \frac{1}{24 \text{ cm}} \Rightarrow \frac{1}{s_i} = 0.0189 \text{ cm}^{-1} \Rightarrow s_i = 53 \text{ cm}$$

So the image is located 53 cm from the lens, on the opposite side from the object.

(b) Because s_i is positive, the image is real.

(c) Real images are inverted.

(d) The magnification is

$$m = -\frac{s_i}{s_o} = -\frac{53 \text{ cm}}{44 \text{ cm}} = -1.2$$

(The fact that the magnification is negative confirms that the image is inverted.) The height of the image is

$$h_i = |m| \cdot h_o = 1.2(11 \text{ cm}) = 13 \text{ cm}$$

These results are illustrated in Example 16.18.

Example 16.21 A object of height 11 cm is placed 48 cm in front of a diverging lens with a focal length of –24.5 cm.
    (a) Where's the image?
    (b) Is it real or virtual?
    (c) Is it upright or inverted?
    (d) What's the height of the image?

Solution.

(a) With s_o = 48 cm and f = –24.5 cm, the lens equation gives us:

$$\frac{1}{s_o} + \frac{1}{s_i} = \frac{1}{f} \implies \frac{1}{48 \text{ cm}} + \frac{1}{s_i} = \frac{1}{-24.5 \text{ cm}} \implies \frac{1}{s_i} = -0.0616 \text{ cm}^{-1} \implies s_i = -16 \text{ cm}$$

The image is 16 cm from the lens, on the same side as the object.

(b) Because s_i is negative, the image is virtual.

(c) Virtual images are upright.

(d) The magnification is

$$m = -\frac{s_i}{s_o} = -\frac{-16 \text{ cm}}{48 \text{ cm}} = \frac{1}{3}$$

(The fact that the magnification is positive confirms that the image is upright.) The height of the image is

$$h_i = |m| \cdot h_o = \tfrac{1}{3}(11 \text{ cm}) = 3.7 \text{ cm}$$

These results are illustrated in Example 16.19.

Example 16.22 The **power** of a lens, P, is defined as $1/f$, where f is the lens's focal length (in meters). Lens power is expressed in **diopters** (abbreviated D), where 1 D = 1 m^{-1}. When an object is placed 10 cm from a converging lens, the real image formed is twice the height of the object. What's the power of this lens?

Solution. Since h_i, the height of the image, is twice h_o, the height of the object, the value of the magnification is either +2 or –2. To decide, we simply notice that the image is real; real images are inverted, so the magnification, m, must be negative. Since $m = -2$, we find that

$$-\frac{s_i}{s_o} = -2 \quad \Rightarrow \quad s_o = \tfrac{1}{2}s_i$$

Because $s_o = 10$ cm, it must be true that $s_i = 20$ cm, so the lens equation gives us:

$$\frac{1}{s_o} + \frac{1}{s_i} = \frac{1}{f} \quad \Rightarrow \quad \frac{1}{10 \text{ cm}} + \frac{1}{20 \text{ cm}} = \frac{1}{f} \quad \Rightarrow \quad f = \frac{20}{3} \text{ cm}$$

Expressing the focal length in meters and then taking the reciprocal gives the lens power in diopters:

$$f = \frac{20}{3} \text{ cm} \times \frac{1 \text{ m}}{100 \text{ cm}} = \frac{1}{15} \text{ m} \quad \Rightarrow \quad P = \frac{1}{f} = \frac{1}{\frac{1}{15} \text{ m}} = 15 \text{ D}$$

CHAPTER 16 REVIEW QUESTIONS

SECTION I: MULTIPLE CHOICE

1. What is the wavelength of an X-ray whose frequency is 1.0×10^{18} Hz?

   (A) 3.3×10^{-11} m
   (B) 3.0×10^{-10} m
   (C) 3.3×10^{-9} m
   (D) 3.0×10^{-8} m
   (E) 3.0×10^{26} m

2. In Young's double-slit interference experiment, what is the difference in path length of the light waves from the two slits at the center of the first bright fringe above the central maximum?

   (A) 0
   (B) $\frac{1}{4}\lambda$
   (C) $\frac{1}{2}\lambda$
   (D) λ
   (E) $\frac{3}{2}\lambda$

3. A beam of light in air is incident upon the smooth surface of a piece of flint glass, as shown:

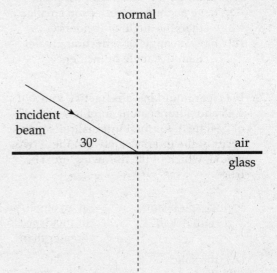

   If the reflected beam and refracted beam are perpendicular to each other, what is the index of refraction of the glass?

   (A) $\frac{1}{2}$
   (B) $\frac{1}{2}\sqrt{3}$
   (C) $\sqrt{3}$
   (D) 2
   (E) $2\sqrt{3}$

4. When green light (wavelength = 500 nm in air) travels through diamond (refractive index = 2.4), what is its wavelength?

   (A) 208 nm
   (B) 357 nm
   (C) 500 nm
   (D) 700 nm
   (E) 1200 nm

5. A beam of light traveling in Medium 1 strikes the interface to another transparent medium, Medium 2. If the speed of light is less in Medium 2 than in Medium 1, the beam will

(A) refract toward the normal.
(B) refract away from the normal.
(C) undergo total internal reflection.
(D) have an angle of reflection smaller than the angle of incidence.
(E) have an angle of reflection greater than the angle of incidence.

6. If a clear liquid has a refractive index of 1.45 and a transparent solid has an index of 2.90 then, for total internal reflection to occur at the interface between these two media, which of the following must be true?

incident beam originates in	at an angle of incidence greater than
(A) the solid	30°
(B) the liquid	30°
(C) the solid	60°
(D) the liquid	60°
(E) Total internal reflection cannot occur.	

7. An object is placed 60 cm in front of a concave spherical mirror whose focal length 40 cm. Which of the following best describes the image?

Nature of image	Distance from mirror
(A) Virtual	24 cm
(B) Real	24 cm
(C) Virtual	120 cm
(D) Real	120 cm
(E) Real	240 cm

8. An object is placed 60 cm from a spherical convex mirror. If the mirror forms a virtual image 20 cm from the mirror, what's the magnitude of the mirror's radius of curvature?

(A) 7.5 cm
(B) 15 cm
(C) 30 cm
(D) 60 cm
(E) 120 cm

9. The image created by a converging lens is projected onto a screen that's 60 cm from the lens. If the height of the image is 1/4 the height of the object, what's the focal length of the lens?

(A) 36 cm
(B) 45 cm
(C) 48 cm
(D) 72 cm
(E) 80 cm

10. Which of the following is true concerning a bi-concave lens?

(A) Its focal length is positive.
(B) It cannot form real images.
(C) It cannot form virtual images.
(D) It can magnify objects.
(E) None of the above

SECTION II: FREE RESPONSE

1. Two trials of a double-slit interference experiment are set up as follows. The slit separation is $d = 0.50$ mm, and the distance to the screen, L, is 4.0 m.

(a) What is the purpose of the first (single-slit) barrier? Why not use two light sources, one at each slit at the second barrier? Explain briefly.

In the first trial, white light is used.

(b) What is the vertical separation on the screen (in mm) between the first-order maxima for red light ($\lambda = 750$ nm) and violet light ($\lambda = 400$ nm)?

(c) Locate the nearest point to the central maximum where an intensity maximum for violet light ($\lambda = 400$ nm) coincides with an intensity maximum for orange-yellow light ($\lambda = 600$ nm).

In the second trial, the entire region between the double-slit barrier and the screen is filled with a large slab of glass of refractive index $n = 1.5$, and monochromatic green light ($\lambda = 500$ nm in air) is used.

(d) What is the separation between adjacent bright fringes on the screen?

2. In order to determine the criteria for constructive and destructive interference, the following rules are used:

   1) When light strikes the boundary to a medium with a higher refractive index than the incident medium, it undergoes a 180° phase change upon reflection (this is equivalent to a shift by one-half wavelength).

   2) When light strikes the boundary to a medium with a lower refractive index than the incident medium, it undergoes no phase change.

   These rules can be applied to the two situations described below.

   A thin soap film of thickness T, consisting of a mixture of water and soap (refractive index = 1.38), has air on both sides. Incident sunlight is reflected off the front face and the back face, causing interference.

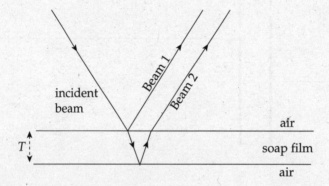

   (a) Which beam, 1 or 2, suffers a 180° phase change upon reflection?

   (b) Since the beams are out of phase, destructive interference will occur if the difference in their path lengths, $\Delta \ell \approx 2T$ for near-normal incidence, is equal to a whole number of wavelengths (wavelength as measured in the soap film). What is the criterion of *constructive* interference? Write your answer as an algebraic equation.

(c) If $T = 462$ nm, what wavelength of visible light is most strongly reflected by this film? What color does the soap film appear to be? You may use the following table:

Wavelengths	in air
violet:	390–455 nm
blue:	455–492 nm
green:	492–577 nm
yellow:	577–597 nm
orange:	597–622 nm
red:	622–770 nm

(d) A thin coating is to be placed on the glass lens of a camera:

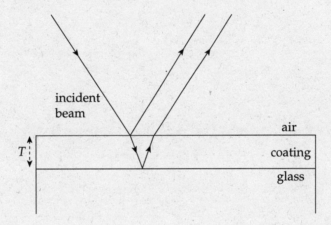

If the refractive indices of the coating and the glass are 1.42 and 1.58, respectively, what is the minimum coating thickness necessary to suppress reflection of yellow-green light of wavelength 570 nm?

3. An object of height 5 cm is placed 40 cm in front of a spherical concave mirror. An image is formed 72 cm behind the mirror.

   (a)   Is the image real or virtual?

   (b)   Is the image upright or inverted?

   (c)   What's the height of the image?

   (d)   What is the mirror's radius of curvature?

   (e)   In the figure below, sketch the mirror, labeling its vertex and focal point, and then construct a ray diagram (with a minimum of two rays) showing the formation of the image.

17

ATOMIC AND
NUCLEAR PHYSICS [B]

INTRODUCTION

The subject matter of the previous chapters was developed in the seventeenth, eighteenth, and nineteenth centuries, but as we delve into the physics of the very small, we enter the twentieth century. Let's first look at the structure of the atom, then travel into the nucleus itself.

THE RUTHERFORD MODEL OF THE ATOM

Around 1900, the atom was just considered a small conglomerate of positively-charged "stuff" embedded with negatively-charged electrons. This theoretical structure was known as the *raisin pudding model*; the pudding was the positively-charged part of the atom, and the raisins were the electrons. However, laboratory experiments in 1909–1911 led Ernest Rutherford to propose an radical revision of this model.

Rutherford fired **alpha particles** (α), which were known to be relatively massive and carry an electric charge of $+2e$, at an extremely thin sheet of gold foil. An alpha particle is actually a composite body; it consists of two protons and two neutrons, tightly bound together. If the atom is really just a glob of positive charge dotted with tiny negative electrons, then the heavy alpha particles should sail right through the target atoms, with little deviation.

For the most part, this is what the experiments revealed. However, a small percentage of the alpha particles exhibited behavior that was completely unexpected: Some were deflected through very large angles (90° to 180°). This was explained by postulating that the positive charge of the atom was not spread throughout its volume, but was concentrated in a very tiny volume, at the atom's center. Alpha particles that came close to this concentration of positive charge experienced a strong Coulombic repulsive force and were deflected through large angles.

The tiny volume in which the positive charge is concentrated in an atom is known as the **nucleus**, and the nucleus is surrounded by a swarm of negatively-charged electrons. This model is known as the **Rutherford nuclear model**.

We can use this model to estimate the size of the nucleus. If an alpha particle's trajectory is directed right at the nucleus, then the electric repulsion will cause the alpha to slow down, stop, and then be pushed away. At the moment it stops, the kinetic energy of the alpha particle is transformed into electric potential energy. Since the alpha particle has a charge of $+2e$ and the atom's nucleus has a charge of $+Ze$ (where Z is the number of protons), their electrical potential energy at the point at which they're closest (separation distance r) is

$$U_E = \frac{1}{4\pi\varepsilon_0}\frac{(+2e)(+Ze)}{r}$$

Therefore, the equation $K = U_E$ becomes

$$\tfrac{1}{2}m_\alpha v_\alpha^2 = \frac{1}{4\pi\varepsilon_0}\frac{(+2e)(+Ze)}{r}$$

$$r = \frac{1}{4\pi\varepsilon_0}\frac{(+2e)(+Ze)}{\tfrac{1}{2}m_\alpha v_\alpha^2}$$

The mass of an alpha particle is about 6.6×10^{-27} kg, and the speed with which the particles were shot at the gold foil was about 1.5×10^7 m/s. Since ε_0 and e are known constants and $Z = 79$ for gold, we get

$$r = \frac{1}{4\pi(8.85\times10^{-12}\ \text{C}^2/\text{N}\cdot\text{m}^2)}\frac{[+2(1.6\times10^{-19}\ \text{C})][(+79(1.6\times10^{-19}\ \text{C})]}{\tfrac{1}{2}(6.6\times10^{-27}\ \text{kg})(1.5\times10^7\ \text{m}/\text{s})^2}$$

$$\approx 5\times10^{-14}\ \text{m}$$

The radius of the nucleus can be no larger than this value. Since the radius of a typical atom is about 10^{-10} m, the nuclear radius is roughly one ten-thousandth the radius of the atom; the positive charge within the atom is certainly concentrated in a tiny volume! In fact, if the nucleus were the size of a golf ball, the atom would be more than a quarter of a mile in diameter. Over 99% of an atom's volume is empty space.

PHOTONS AND THE PHOTOELECTRIC EFFECT

The particle-like nature of light was revealed and studied through the work of Max Panck in 1900, and later Albert Einstein (who won the Nobel prize for work in this area in 1921.) Electromagnetic radiation is emitted and absorbed by matter as though it existed in individual bundles called **quanta**. A quantum of electromagnetic energy is known as a **photon**. Light behaves like a stream of photons, and this is illustrated by the **photoelectric effect**.

When a piece of metal is illuminated by electromagnetic radiation (either visible light, ultraviolet light, or X-rays), the energy absorbed by electrons near the surface of the metal can liberate them from their bound state, and these electrons can fly off. The released electrons are known as **photoelectrons**. In this case, the classical, wave-only theory of light would predict three results:

(1) There would be a significant time delay between the moment of illumination and the ejection of photoelectrons, as the electrons absorbed incident energy until their kinetic energy was sufficient to release them from the atoms' grip.

(2) Increasing the intensity of the light would cause the electrons to leave the metal surface with greater kinetic energy.

(3) Photoelectrons would be emitted regardless of the frequency of the incident energy, as long as the intensity was high enough.

Surprisingly, none of these predictions was observed. Photoelectrons were ejected within just a few billionths of a second of illumination, disproving prediction (1). Secondly, increasing the intensity of the light did not cause photoelectrons to leave the metal surface with greater kinetic energy. Although more electrons were ejected as the intensity was increased, there was a maximum photoelectron kinetic energy; prediction (2) was false. And, for each metal, there was certain **threshold**

frequency, f_0: If light of frequency lower than f_0 were used to illuminate the metal surface, *no* photoelectrons were ejected, regardless of how intense the incident radiation was; prediction (3) was also false. Clearly, something was wrong with the wave-only theory of light.

Einstein explained these observations by postulating that the energy of the incident electromagnetic wave was absorbed in individual bundles (photons). The energy of a photon is proportional to the frequency of the wave,

$$E = hf$$

where h is **Planck's constant** (about 6.63×10^{-34} J·s). A certain amount of energy had to be imparted to an electron on the metal surface in order to liberate it; this was known as the metal's **work function**, or ϕ. If an electron absorbed a photon whose energy E was greater than ϕ, it would leave the metal with a maximum kinetic energy equal to $E - \phi$. This process could occur *very* quickly, which accounts for the rapidity with which photoelectrons are seen after illumination.

Increasing the intensity of the incident energy means bombardment with more photons and results in the ejection of more photoelectrons—but since the energy of each incident photon is fixed by the equation $E = hf$, the value of K_{max} will still be $E - \phi$. This accounts for the observation that disproved prediction (2).

Finally, if the incident energy had a frequency that was less than ϕ / h, the incident photons would each have an energy that was less than ϕ; this would not be enough energy to liberate electrons. Blasting the metal surface with more photons (that is, increasing the intensity of the incident beam) would also do nothing; none of the photons would have enough energy to eject electrons, so whether there were one or one million of them wouldn't make any difference. This accounts for the observation of a threshold frequency, which we now know is ϕ / h.

Before we get to some examples, it's worthwhile to introduce a new unit for energy. The SI unit for energy is the joule, but it's too large to be convenient in the domains we're studying now. We'll use a much smaller unit, the **electronvolt** (abbreviated **eV**). The eV is equal to the energy gained (or lost) by an electron accelerated through a potential difference of one volt. Using the equation $\Delta U_E = q \Delta V$, we find that

$$1 \text{ eV} = (1 \text{ e})(1 \text{ V}) = (1.6 \times 10^{-19} \text{ C})(1 \text{ V}) = 1.6 \times 10^{-19} \text{ J}$$

In terms of electronvolts, the value of Planck's constant is 4.14×10^{-15} eV·s.

Example 17.1 The work function for aluminum is 4.08 eV.

(a) What is the threshold frequency required to produce photoelectrons from aluminum?

(b) Classify the electromagnetic radiation that can produce photoelectrons.

(c) If light of frequency $f = 4.00 \times 10^{15}$ Hz is used to illuminate a piece of aluminum,

    (i) what is K_{max}, the maximum kinetic energy of ejected photoelectrons?

    (ii) what's the maximum speed of the photoelectrons? (Electron mass = 9.11×10^{-31} kg.)

(d) If the light described in part (b) were increased by a factor of 2 in intensity, what would happen to the value of K_{max}?

Solution.

(a) We know from the statement of the question that, in order for a photon to be successful in liberating an electron from the surface of the aluminum, its energy cannot be less than 4.08 eV. Therefore, the minimum frequency of the incident light—the threshold frequency—must be

$$f_0 = \frac{\phi}{h} = \frac{4.08 \text{ eV}}{4.14 \times 10^{-15} \text{ eV} \cdot \text{s}} = 9.86 \times 10^{14} \text{ Hz}$$

(b) The illuminating energy cannot be visible light, as the following calculation will show. Of all the colors, violet has the shortest wavelength and the highest frequency. The maximum frequency of violet light is

$$f_{\text{violet, max}} = \frac{c}{\lambda_{\text{violet, min}}} = \frac{3.00 \times 10^8 \text{ m/s}}{380 \times 10^{-9} \text{ m}} = 7.89 \times 10^{14} \text{ Hz}$$

Since the threshold frequency, f_0, is greater than this, the electromagnetic radiation used to produce photoelectrons from aluminum must be at least in the ultraviolet region of the EM spectrum.

(c) (i) The maximum kinetic energy of photoelectrons is found from the equation

$$K_{\text{max}} = hf - \phi$$
$$= (4.14 \times 10^{-15} \text{ eV} \cdot \text{s})(4.00 \times 10^{15} \text{ Hz}) - (4.08 \text{ eV})$$
$$= 12.5 \text{ eV}$$

(ii) Using the above result, we can find v_{max}:

$$v_{\text{max}} = \sqrt{\frac{2}{m_e} K_{\text{max}}}$$

$$= \sqrt{\frac{2}{9.11 \times 10^{-31} \text{ kg}} \left(12.5 \text{ eV} \cdot \frac{1.6 \times 10^{-19} \text{ J}}{1 \text{ eV}} \right)}$$

$$= 2.1 \times 10^6 \text{ m/s}$$

(d) Nothing will happen. Increasing the intensity of the illuminating radiation will cause more photons to impinge on the metal surface, thereby ejecting more photoelectrons, but their maximum kinetic energy will remain the same. The only way to increase K_{max} would be to increase the frequency of the incident energy.

THE BOHR MODEL OF THE ATOM

In the years immediately following Rutherford's announcement of his nuclear model of the atom, a young physicist, Niels Bohr, added an important piece to the atomic puzzle.

For fifty years it had been known that atoms in a gas discharge tube emitted and absorbed light only at specific wavelengths. The light from a glowing gas, passed through a prism to disperse the beam into its component wavelengths, produced patterns of sharp lines called **atomic spectra**. The visible wavelengths that appeared in the emission spectrum of hydrogen had been summarized by the *Balmer formula*

$$\frac{1}{\lambda_n} = R\left(\frac{1}{2^2} - \frac{1}{n^2}\right)$$

where R is the *Rydberg constant* (about 1.1×10^7 m^{-1}). But *why* do atoms emit (or absorb) radiation only at certain discrete wavelengths?

Bohr's model of the atom explains the spectroscopists' observations. Using the simplest atom, hydrogen (which has one electron), Bohr postulated that the electron orbits the nucleus at certain discrete radii. When the electron is in one of these special orbits, it does not lose energy (as the classical theory would predict). However, if the electron absorbs a certain amount of energy, it is **excited** to a higher orbit, one with a greater radius. After spending a short time in this excited state, it returns to a lower orbit, emitting a photon in the process. Since each allowed orbit—or **energy level**—has a specific radius (and corresponding energy), the photons emitted in each jump also have specific wavelengths.

The basis for his model is that the electron's angular momentum, $L = m_e v_n r_n$, must be a whole number times $h/2\pi$, where h is Planck's constant. [The quantity $h/2\pi$ turns up so often in atomic physics that a special symbol, $\hbar$ ("h-bar") was invented for it.] If an electron is in a circular orbit of radius r_n, then the electrical attraction by the nucleus (charge $= Ze$, where Z is the number of protons) provides the centripetal force:

$$\frac{1}{4\pi\varepsilon_0}\frac{(e)(Ze)}{r_n^2} = \frac{m_e v_n^2}{r_n}$$

Now, assuming the Bohr hypothesis, $m_e v_n r_n = n\hbar$,

$$\frac{1}{4\pi\varepsilon_0}\frac{(e)(Ze)}{r_n^2} = \frac{m_e(n\hbar/m_e r_n)^2}{r_n} \quad\Rightarrow\quad r_n = n^2\frac{4\pi\varepsilon_0\hbar^2}{Ze^2 m_e} = n^2 r_1$$

The quantity r_1 is the smallest possible radius of an orbit. An electron is normally in this **ground-state** energy level, and can reach the higher orbits (**excited states**), whose radii are

$$r_n = n^2 r_1 \ (n = 2, 3, \ldots)$$

by absorbing quantified energy. For hydrogen ($Z = 1$), the value of the **Bohr radius** (the ground-state energy level), r_1, is

$$r_1 = \frac{4\pi\varepsilon_0\hbar^2}{e^2 m_e} = \frac{4\pi(8.85\times10^{-12}\ \mathrm{C^2/N\cdot m^2})}{(1.6\times10^{-19}\ \mathrm{C})^2(9.11\times10^{-31}\ \mathrm{kg})}\left(\frac{6.63\times10^{-34}\ \mathrm{J\cdot s}}{2\pi}\right)^2 = 5.3\times10^{-11}\ \mathrm{m}$$

The energy of an orbiting electron is equal to its kinetic energy plus its electrical potential energy (due to the attraction of the nucleus):

$$E_n = K_n + U_n = \tfrac{1}{2}m_e v_n^2 + \frac{1}{4\pi\varepsilon_0}\frac{(-e)(Ze)}{r_n}$$

Because of the Bohr hypothesis, which tells us that the electron's orbit radii and speeds are **quantized** (that is, they can only assume specific values), electron *energies* are also quantized;

$$E_n = \frac{Z^2}{n^2}\left[-\frac{e^4 m_e}{32\pi^2 \hbar^2 \varepsilon_0^2}\right] = \frac{Z^2}{n^2} E_1$$

Notice that E_1 (and, therefore, all of the E_n) are negative. This corresponds with the fact that the electron is bound "within" the atom. Energy must be supplied to cause it to leave; that is, to bring its energy to zero. For hydrogen ($Z = 1$), the value of the **ground-state energy**, E_1, is –13.6 eV. This is also known as the **ionization energy** of hydrogen, the minimum amount of energy that must be supplied to release its electron. The energy levels within the hydrogen atom are given by the formula

$$E_n = \frac{1}{n^2}(-13.6 \text{ eV})$$

and for other one-electron atoms—ionized helium ($Z = 2$), doubly-ionized lithium ($Z = 3$), etc.—the energy levels are

$$E_n = \frac{Z^2}{n^2}(-13.6 \text{ eV})$$

where Z is the number of protons in the atom's nucleus.

When an excited electron drops from energy level $n = j$ to a lower one, $n = i$, the transition causes a photon of energy to be emitted, and the energy of photon is the difference between the two energy levels:

$$E_{\text{emitted photon}} = \Delta E = E_j - E_i$$

The wavelength of this photon is

$$\lambda = \frac{c}{f} = \frac{c}{E_{\text{photon}}/h} = \frac{hc}{E_j - E_i}$$

Returning to the hydrogen atom, assume that an excited electron drops to the $n = 2$ energy level from some higher level, n. The wavelength of the photon emitted in the transition is

$$\lambda_n = \frac{hc}{E_n - E_2}$$

Therefore,

$$\frac{1}{\lambda_n} = \frac{1}{hc}(E_n - E_2) = \frac{1}{hc}\left[\left(\frac{1}{n^2}E_1\right) - \left(\frac{1}{2^2}E_1\right)\right] = \frac{E_1}{hc}\left(\frac{1}{n^2} - \frac{1}{2^2}\right)$$

Since the value of $E_1/(hc)$ is

$$\frac{E_1}{hc} = \frac{-13.6 \text{ eV}}{(4.14\times10^{-15} \text{ eV}\cdot\text{s})(3\times10^8 \text{ m}/\text{s})} = -1.1\times10^7 \text{ m}^{-1}$$

we can find that

$$\frac{1}{\lambda_n} = (1.1\times10^7 \text{ m}^{-1})\left(\frac{1}{2^2} - \frac{1}{n^2}\right)$$

But this is the Balmer formula, from the beginning of this section! Bohr's hypothesis that the electron's angular momentum is quantized leads to the fact that the electron's orbit radii and energy levels must be quantized as must hydrogen's spectrum.

Example 17.2

(a) How much energy must a ground-state electron in a hydrogen atom absorb to be excited to the $n = 4$ energy level?

(b) When the electron in the $n = 4$ level, what wavelengths are possible for the photon emitted when the electron drops to a lower energy level? In what regions of the EM spectrum do these photons lie?

Solution.

(a) The ground-state energy level ($n = 1$) for hydrogen is -13.6 eV, and using the equation $E_n = (1/n^2)E_1$, the $n = 4$ energy level (the third excited state) is

$$E_4 = \frac{1}{4^2}(-13.6 \text{ eV}) = -0.85 \text{ eV}$$

Therefore, in order for an electron to make the transition from E_1 to E_4, it must absorb energy in the amount $E_4 - E_1 = (-0.85 \text{ eV}) - (-13.6 \text{ eV}) = 12.8 \text{ eV}$.

(b) An electron in the $n = 4$ energy level can make several different transitions: It can drop to $n = 3$, $n = 2$, or all the way down to the ground state, $n = 1$. The energies of the $n = 2$ and $n = 3$ levels are

$$E_2 = \frac{1}{2^2}(-13.6 \text{ eV}) = -3.4 \text{ eV} \qquad \text{and} \qquad E_3 = \frac{1}{3^2}(-13.6 \text{ eV}) = -1.5 \text{ eV}$$

The following diagram shows the electron dropping from $n = 4$ to $n = 3$:

There are three possible values for the energy of the emitted photon, $E_{4\to3}$, $E_{4\to2}$, or $E_{4\to1}$:

$$E_{4\to3} = E_4 - E_3 = (-0.85 \text{ eV}) - (-1.5 \text{ eV}) = 0.65 \text{ eV}$$
$$E_{4\to2} = E_4 - E_2 = (-0.85 \text{ eV}) - (-3.4 \text{ eV}) = 2.55 \text{ eV}$$
$$E_{4\to1} = E_4 - E_1 = (-0.85 \text{ eV}) - (-13.6 \text{ eV}) = 12.8 \text{ eV}$$

From the equation $E = hf = hc/\lambda$, we get $\lambda = hc/E$, so

$$\lambda_{4\to3} = \frac{hc}{E_{4\to3}} = \frac{(4.14\times10^{-15} \text{ eV}\cdot\text{s})(3.00\times10^8 \text{ m/s})}{0.65 \text{ eV}} = 1910 \text{ nm}$$

$$\lambda_{4\to2} = \frac{hc}{E_{4\to2}} = \frac{(4.14\times10^{-15} \text{ eV}\cdot\text{s})(3.00\times10^8 \text{ m/s})}{2.55 \text{ eV}} = 487 \text{ nm}$$

$$\lambda_{4\to1} = \frac{hc}{E_{4\to1}} = \frac{(4.14\times10^{-15} \text{ eV}\cdot\text{s})(3.00\times10^8 \text{ m/s})}{12.8 \text{ eV}} = 97 \text{ nm}$$

Notice that $\lambda_{4\to2}$ is in the visible spectrum; this wavelength corresponds to the color blue-green; $\lambda_{4\to1}$ is an ultraviolet wavelength, and $\lambda_{4\to3}$ is infrared.

WAVE–PARTICLE DUALITY

Light and other electromagnetic waves exhibit wave-like characteristics through interference and diffraction. However, as we saw in the photoelectric effect, light also behaves as if its energy were granular, composed of particles. This is **wave–particle duality**: Electromagnetic radiation propagates like a wave but exchanges energy like a particle.

Since an electromagnetic wave can behave like a particle, can a particle of matter behave like a wave? In 1923, the French physicist Louis de Broglie proposed that the answer is *yes*. His conjecture, which has since been supported by experiment, is that a particle of mass m and speed v—and thus with linear momentum $p = mv$—has an associated wavelength, which is called its **de Broglie wavelength**:

$$\lambda = \frac{h}{p}$$

Particles in motion can display wave characteristics, and behave as if they had a wavelength $\lambda = h/p$.

Since the value of h is so small, ordinary macroscopic objects do not display wave-like behavior. For example, a baseball (mass = 0.15 kg) thrown at a speed of 40 m/s has a de Broglie wavelength of

$$\lambda = \frac{h}{p} = \frac{h}{mv} = \frac{6.63\times10^{-34} \text{ J}\cdot\text{s}}{(0.15 \text{ kg})(40 \text{ m/s})} = 1.1\times10^{-34} \text{ m}$$

This is much too small to measure. However, with subatomic particles, the wave nature is clearly evident. The 1937 Noble prize was awarded for experiments that reveal that a stream of electrons exhibited diffraction patterns when scattered by crystals; a behavior that's characteristic of waves.

There's an interesting connection between the de Broglie wavelength for electrons and Bohr's model of quantized orbital radii (once tested on the AP exam!). Remember that Bohr postulated that the electron's orbital angular momentum, $m_e v_n r_n$, had to be an integral multiple of $\hbar = h/2\pi$. The equation

$$m_e v_n r_n = n\frac{h}{2\pi}$$

can be rewritten as follows:

$$2\pi r_n = n\frac{h}{m_e v_n} \quad \Rightarrow \quad 2\pi r_n = n\frac{h}{p_e} \quad \Rightarrow \quad 2\pi r_n = n\lambda_e$$

In this last form, the equation says that the circumference of the electron's orbit must be equal to a whole number of wavelengths in order for it to be stable, a restriction that should remind you of sustained standing waves.

Example 17.3 Electrons in a diffraction experiment are accelerated through a potential difference of 200 V. What is the de Broglie wavelength of these electrons?

Solution. By definition, the kinetic energy of these electrons is 200 eV. Since the relationship between linear momentum and kinetic energy is $p = \sqrt{2mK}$,

$$\lambda = \frac{h}{p} = \frac{h}{\sqrt{2mK}} = \frac{6.63 \times 10^{-34} \text{ J} \cdot \text{s}}{\sqrt{2(9.11 \times 10^{-31} \text{ kg})\left[200 \text{ eV} \cdot \dfrac{1.6 \times 10^{-19} \text{ J}}{1 \text{ eV}}\right]}} = 8.7 \times 10^{-11} \text{ m} = 0.087 \text{ nm}$$

This wavelength is characteristic of X-rays.

NUCLEAR PHYSICS

The nucleus of the atom is composed of particles called **protons** and **neutrons**, which are collectively called **nucleons**. The number of protons in a given nucleus is called the atom's **atomic number**, and is denoted Z, and the number of neutrons (the **neutron number**) is denoted N. The total number of nucleons, $Z + N$, is called the **mass number** (or **nucleon number**), and is denoted A. The number of protons in the nucleus of an atom defines the element. For example, the element chlorine (abbreviated Cl) is characterized by the fact that the nucleus of every chlorine atom contains 17 protons, so the atomic number of chlorine is 17; but, different chlorine atoms may contain different numbers of neutrons. In fact, about three-fourths of all naturally-occurring chlorine atoms have 18 neutrons in their nuclei (mass number = 35), and most of the remaining one-fourth contain 20 neutrons (mass number = 37). Nuclei that contain the same numbers of protons but different numbers of neutrons are called **isotopes**. The notation for a **nuclide**—the term for a nucleus with specific numbers of protons and neutrons—is to write Z and A before the chemical symbol of the element:

$$^A_Z X$$

The isotopes of chlorine mentioned above would be written as follows:

$$^{35}_{17}\text{Cl} \quad \text{and} \quad ^{37}_{17}\text{Cl}$$

Example 17.4 How many protons and neutrons are contained in the nuclide $^{63}_{29}\text{Cu}$?

Solution. The subscript (the atomic number, Z) gives the number of protons, which is 29. The superscript (the mass number, A) gives the total number of nucleons. Since $A = 63 = Z + N$, we find that $N = 63 - 29 = 34$.

Example 17.5 The element neon (abbreviated Ne, atomic number 10) has several isotopes. The most abundant isotope contains 10 neutrons, and two others contain 11 and 12. Write symbols for these three nuclides.

Solution. The mass numbers of these isotopes are $10 + 10 = 20$, $10 + 11 = 21$, and $10 + 12 = 22$. So, we'd write them as follows:

$$^{20}_{10}\text{Ne}, \quad ^{21}_{10}\text{Ne}, \quad \text{and} \quad ^{22}_{10}\text{Ne}$$

Another common notation—which we also use—is to write the mass number after the name of the element. These three isotopes of neon would be written as neon-20, neon-21, and neon-22.

THE NUCLEAR FORCE

Why wouldn't any nucleus that has more than one proton be unstable? After all, protons are positively-charged and would therefore experience a repulsive Coulomb force from each other. Why don't these nuclei explode? And what holds neutrons—which have no electric charge—in the nucleus? These issues are resolved by the presence of another fundamental force, the **nuclear force**, which binds neutrons and protons together to form nuclei. Although the strength of the Coulomb force can be expressed by a simple mathematical formula (it's inversely proportional to the square of their separation), the nuclear force is much more complicated; no simple formula can be written for the strength of the nuclear force.

BINDING ENERGY

The masses of the proton and neutron are listed below.

$$\text{proton: } m_p = 1.6726 \times 10^{-27} \text{ kg}$$

$$\text{neutron: } m_n = 1.6749 \times 10^{-27} \text{ kg}$$

Because these masses are so tiny, a much smaller mass unit is used. With the most abundant isotope of carbon (carbon-12) as a reference, the **atomic mass unit** (abbreviated **amu** or simply **u**) is defined as 1/12 the mass of a ^{12}C atom. The conversion between kg and u is $1 \text{ u} = 1.6605 \times 10^{-27}$ kg. In terms of atomic mass units,

$$m_p = 1.00728 \text{ u}$$

$$m_n = 1.00867 \text{ u}$$

Now consider the **deuteron**, the nucleus of **deuterium**, an isotope of hydrogen that contains 1 proton and 1 neutron. The mass of a deuteron is 2.01356 u, which is a little *less* than the sum of the individual masses of the proton and neutron. The difference between the mass of any bound nucleus and the sum of the masses of its constituent nucleons is called the **mass defect**, Δm. In the case of the deuteron (symbolized **d**), the mass defect is

$$\Delta m = (m_p + m_n) - m_d$$
$$= (1.00728 \text{ u} + 1.00867 \text{ u}) - (2.01356 \text{ u})$$
$$= 0.00239 \text{ u}$$

What happened to this missing mass? It was converted to energy when the deuteron was formed. It also represents the amount of energy needed to break the deuteron into a separate proton and neutron. Since this tells us how strongly the nucleus is bound, it is called the **binding energy** of the nucleus. The conversion between mass and energy is given by Einstein's **mass–energy equivalence** equation, $E = mc^2$ (where c is the speed of light); the binding energy, E_B, is equal to the mass defect, Δm:

$$E_B = (\Delta m)c^2$$

Using $E = mc^2$, the energy equivalent of 1 atomic mass unit is

$$E = (1.6605 \times 10^{-27} \text{ kg})(2.9979 \times 10^8 \text{ m/s})^2$$
$$= 1.4924 \times 10^{-10} \text{ J}$$
$$= 1.4924 \times 10^{-10} \text{ J} \cdot \frac{1 \text{ eV}}{1.6022 \times 10^{-19} \text{ J}}$$
$$= 9.31 \times 10^8 \text{ eV}$$
$$= 931 \text{ MeV}$$

In terms of electronvolts, then, the binding energy of the deuteron is

$$E_B \text{ (deuteron)} = 0.00239 \text{ u} \times \frac{931 \text{ MeV}}{1 \text{ u}} = 2.23 \text{ MeV}$$

Since the deuteron contains 2 nucleons, the **binding energy per nucleon** is

$$\frac{2.23 \text{ MeV}}{2 \text{ nucleons}} = 1.12 \text{ MeV/nucleon}$$

This is lowest value of all nuclides. The highest, 8.8 MeV/nucleon, is for an isotope of nickel, ^{62}Ni. Typically, when nuclei smaller than nickel are fused to form a single nucleus, the binding energy per nucleon increases, which tells us that energy is released in the process. On the other hand, when nuclei *larger* than nickel are *split*, binding energy per nucleon again increases, releasing energy.

Example 17.6 What is the maximum wavelength of EM radiation that could be used to photodisintegrate a deuteron?

Solution. The binding energy of the deuteron is 2.23 MeV, so a photon would need to have at least this much energy to break the deuteron into a proton and neutron. Since $E = hf$ and $f = c/\lambda$,

$$E = \frac{hc}{\lambda} \implies \lambda_{max} = \frac{hc}{E_{min}} = \frac{(4.14 \times 10^{-15} \text{ eV} \cdot \text{s})(3.00 \times 10^8 \text{ m/s})}{2.23 \times 10^6 \text{ eV}} = 5.57 \times 10^{-13} \text{ m}$$

Example 17.7 The atomic mass of $^{27}_{13}\text{Al}$ is 26.9815 u. What is its nuclear binding energy per nucleon? (Mass of electron = 0.0005486 u.)

Solution. The nuclear mass of $^{27}_{13}\text{Al}$ is equal to its atomic mass minus the mass of its electrons. Since an aluminum atom has 13 protons, it must also have 13 electrons. So,

$$\text{nuclear mass of } ^{27}_{13}\text{Al} = (\text{atomic mass of } ^{27}_{13}\text{Al}) - 13m_e$$
$$= 26.9815 \text{ u} - 13(0.0005486 \text{ u})$$
$$= 26.9744 \text{ u}$$

Now, the nucleus contains 13 protons and $27 - 13 = 14$ neutrons, so the total mass of the individual nucleons is

$$M = 13m_p + 14m_n$$
$$= 13(1.00728 \text{ u}) + 14(1.00867 \text{ u})$$
$$= 27.2160 \text{ u}$$

and, the mass defect of the aluminum nucleus is

$$\Delta m = M - m = 27.2160 \text{ u} - 26.9744 \text{ u} = 0.2416 \text{ u}$$

Converting this mass to energy, we can see that

$$E_B = 0.2416 \text{ u} \times \frac{931 \text{ MeV}}{1 \text{ u}} = 225 \text{ MeV}$$

so the binding energy per nucleon is

$$\frac{225 \text{ MeV}}{27} = 8.3 \text{ MeV / nucleon}$$

RADIOACTIVITY

The stability of a nucleus depends on the ability of the nuclear force to balance the repulsive Coulomb forces between the protons. As a result, many nuclides are ultimately unstable and will undergo spontaneous restructuring to become more stable. An unstable nucleus that will spontaneously change into a lower-energy configuration is said to be **radioactive**. Nuclei that are too large (A is too great) or ones in which the neutron-to-proton ratio is unfavorable are radioactive, and there are several different modes of radioactive decay. We'll look at the most important ones: **alpha** decay, **beta** decay (three forms), and **gamma** decay.

ALPHA DECAY

When a nucleus undergoes alpha decay, it emits an alpha particle, which consists of two protons and two neutrons and is the same as the nucleus of a helium-4 atom. An alpha particle can be represented as:

$$\alpha, \ ^4_2\alpha, \text{ or } ^4_2\text{He}$$

Very large nuclei can shed nucleons quickly by emitting one or more alpha particles, for example, radon-222 ($^{222}_{86}$Rn) is radioactive and undergoes alpha decay:

$$^{222}_{86}\text{Rn} \rightarrow {}^{218}_{84}\text{Po} + {}^4_2\alpha$$

This reaction illustrates two important features of any nuclear reaction:

(1)   Mass number is conserved (in this case, 222 = 218 + 4)

(2)   Charge is conserved (in this case, 86 = 84 + 2)

The decaying nuclide is known as the **parent**, and the resulting nuclide is known as the **daughter**. (Here, radon-222 is the parent nuclide and polonium-218 is the daughter.) Alpha decay decreases the mass by 4 and the atomic number by 2. Therefore, alpha decay always has the form

$$^A_Z\text{X} \rightarrow {}^{A-4}_{Z-2}\text{X}' + {}^4_2\alpha$$

BETA DECAY

There are three subcategories of **beta** (β) decay, called β^-, β^+, and **electron capture** (EC).

β^- DECAY

When the neutron-to-proton ratio is too large, the nucleus undergoes β^- decay, which is the most common form of beta decay. β^- decay occurs when a neutron transforms into a proton and an electron, and the electron is ejected from the nucleus. The expelled electron is called a **beta particle**. The transformation of a neutron into a proton and an electron (and another particle, the **electron-antineutrino**, $\bar{\nu}_e$) is caused by the action of the **weak nuclear force**, another of nature's fundamental forces. A common example of a nuclide that undergoes β^- decay is carbon-14, which is used to date archaeological artifacts:

$$^{14}_6\text{C} \rightarrow {}^{14}_7\text{N} + {}^0_{-1}\text{e} + \bar{\nu}_e$$

Notice how the ejected electron is written: The superscript is its nucleon number (which is zero), and the subscript is its charge. The reaction is balanced, since 14 = 14 + 0 and 6 = 7 + (–1).

β^+ DECAY

When the neutron-to-proton ratio is too small, the nucleus will undergo β^+ decay. In this form of beta decay, a proton is transformed into a neutron and a **positron**, $^0_{+1}\text{e}$ (the electron's **antiparticle**), plus another particle, the **electron-neutrino**, ν_e, which are then both ejected from the nucleus. An example of a positron emitter is fluorine-17:

$$^{17}_9\text{F} \rightarrow {}^{17}_8\text{O} + {}^0_{+1}\text{e} + \nu_e$$

ELECTRON CAPTURE

Another way in which a nucleus can increase its neutron-to-proton ratio is to capture an orbiting electron and then cause the transformation of a proton into a neutron. Beryllium-7 undergoes this process:

$$^7_4\text{Be} + {}^0_{-1}\text{e} \rightarrow {}^7_3\text{Li} + \nu_e$$

GAMMA DECAY

In each of the decay processes defined above, the daughter was a different element from the parent. Radon becomes polonium as a result of α decay, carbon becomes nitrogen as a result of β^- decay, fluorine becomes oxygen from β^+ decay, and beryllium becomes lithium from electron capture. By contrast, gamma decay does not alter the identity of the nucleus; it just allows the nucleus to relax and shed energy. Imagine that potassium-42 undergoes β^- decay to form calcium-42:

$$^{42}_{19}\text{K} \rightarrow {}^{42}_{20}\text{Ca}^* + {}^{0}_{-1}\text{e} + \bar{\nu}_e$$

The asterisk indicates that the daughter calcium nucleus is left in a high-energy, excited state. In order for this excited nucleus to drop to its ground state, it must emit a photon of energy, a **gamma ray**, symbolized by γ:

$$^{42}_{20}\text{Ca}^* \rightarrow {}^{42}_{20}\text{Ca} + \gamma$$

Example 17.8 What's the daughter nucleus in each of the following radioactive decays?

(a) Strontium-90 ($^{90}_{38}\text{Sr}$); β^- decay

(b) Argon-37 ($^{37}_{18}\text{Ar}$); electron capture

(c) Plutonium-239 ($^{239}_{94}\text{Pu}$); alpha decay

(d) Cobalt-58 ($^{58}_{27}\text{Co}$); β^+ decay

Solution.

(a) $^{90}_{38}\text{Sr} \rightarrow {}^{90}_{39}\text{Y} + {}^{0}_{-1}\text{e} + \bar{\nu}_e \Rightarrow$ daughter = yttrium-90

(b) $^{37}_{18}\text{Ar} + {}^{0}_{-1}\text{e} \rightarrow {}^{37}_{17}\text{Cl} + \nu_e \Rightarrow$ daughter = chlorine-37

(c) $^{239}_{94}\text{Pu} \rightarrow {}^{235}_{92}\text{U} + {}^{4}_{2}\alpha \Rightarrow$ daughter = uranium-235

(d) $^{58}_{27}\text{Co} \rightarrow {}^{58}_{26}\text{Fe} + {}^{0}_{+1}\text{e}^+ + \nu_e \Rightarrow$ daughter = iron-58

RADIOACTIVE DECAY RATES

Although it's impossible to say precisely when a particular radioactive nuclide will decay, it *is* possible to predict the decay rates of a radioactive sample that contains large numbers of identical radioactive nuclei. As a radioactive sample disintegrates, the number of decays per second decreases, but the *fraction* of nuclei that decay per second—the **decay constant**—does not change. The decay constant is uniquely determined by the identity of the radioisotope. Boron-9 has a decay constant of 7.5×10^{17} s^{-1} (rapid), while uranium-238 has a decay constant of about 5×10^{-18} s^{-1} (slow).

The **activity** (A) of a radioactive sample is the number of disintegrations it undergoes per second; it decreases with time according to the equation

$$A = A_0 e^{-\lambda t}$$

where A_0 is the activity at time $t = 0$ and λ is the decay constant (not to be confused with wavelength). Activity is expressed in disintegrations per second: 1 disintegration per second is one **becquerel (Bq)**.

The greater the value of λ, the faster the sample decays. This equation also describes the number (N) of radioactive nuclei in a given sample, $N = N_0 e^{-\lambda t}$, or the mass (m) of the sample, $m = m_0 e^{-\lambda t}$.

The most common way to indicate the rapidity with which radioactive samples decay is to give their **half-life**. Just as the name suggests, the half-life is the time required for half of a given sample to decay. Half-life, $T_{1/2}$, is inversely proportional to the decay constant, λ:

$$T_{1/2} = \frac{\ln 2}{\lambda} \approx \frac{0.693}{\lambda}$$

In terms of the half-life, the exponential decay of a sample's mass (or activity) can be written in the form

$$m = m_0 \left(\tfrac{1}{2}\right)^{t/T_{1/2}}$$

A sample's activity or mass can be graphed as a function of time; the result is the **exponential decay curve**, which you should study carefully:

Example 17.9 The half-life of iodine-131 (a β^- emitter) is 8 days.

(a) If a sample of ^{131}I has a mass of 1 gram, what will the mass be 40 days later?

(b) What is the decay constant (in s^{-1})?

Solution.

(a) Every 8 days, the sample's mass decreases by a factor of 2. We can illustrate the decay in the following diagram:

This agrees with the result we'd get by using the formula:

$$m = m_0\left(\tfrac{1}{2}\right)^{t/T_{1/2}} = (1 \text{ g})\left(\tfrac{1}{2}\right)^{40 \text{ d}/8 \text{ d}} = (1 \text{ g})\left(\tfrac{1}{2}\right)^5 = \tfrac{1}{32} \text{ g}$$

(b) The decay constant is

$$\lambda = \frac{0.693}{T_{1/2}} = \frac{0.693}{8 \text{ d} \times \dfrac{24 \text{ h}}{1 \text{ d}} \times \dfrac{60 \text{ min}}{1 \text{ h}} \times \dfrac{60 \text{ s}}{1 \text{ min}}} = 1 \times 10^{-6} \text{ s}^{-1}$$

Example 17.10 Home smoke detectors contain a small radioactive sample of americium-241 ($^{241}_{95}\text{Am}$), an alpha-particle emitter that has a half-life of 430 years.
  (a) What is the daughter nucleus of the decay?
  (b) If a homeowner keeps a smoke detector for 25 years, how much of the original americium sample is left?

Solution.

(a) $^{241}_{95}\text{Am} \rightarrow {}^{237}_{93}\text{Np} + {}^4_2\alpha \Rightarrow$ daughter = neptunium-237

(b) Using the equation $m = m_0\left(\tfrac{1}{2}\right)^{t/T_{1/2}}$, we find that

$$m = m_0\left(\tfrac{1}{2}\right)^{25 \text{ y}/430 \text{ y}} = m_0\left(\tfrac{1}{2}\right)^{0.058} = m_0(0.96)$$

Therefore, 96% of the original sample remains after 25 years.

NUCLEAR REACTIONS

Natural radioactive decay provides one example of a nuclear reaction. Other examples of nuclear reactions include the bombardment of target nuclei with subatomic particles to artificially induce radioactivity (this is **nuclear fission**), and the **nuclear fusion** of small nuclei at extremely high temperatures. In all cases of nuclear reactions that we'll study, nucleon number and charge must be conserved. In order to balance nuclear reactions, we write ^1_1p or ^1_1H for a proton and ^1_0n for a neutron. Gamma-ray photons can also be produced in nuclear reactions; they have no charge or nucleon number, and are represented as $^0_0\gamma$.

Example 17.11 A mercury-198 nucleus is bombarded by a neutron, which causes a nuclear reaction:

$$^1_0\text{n} + {}^{198}_{80}\text{Hg} \rightarrow {}^{197}_{79}\text{Au} + {}^?_?\text{X}$$

What's the unknown product particle, X?

Solution. In order to balance the superscripts, we must have $1 + 198 = 197 + A$, so $A = 2$, and the subscripts are balanced if $0 + 80 = 79 + Z$, so $Z = 1$:

$$\,^1_0 n + \,^{198}_{80} Hg \rightarrow \,^{197}_{79} Au + \,^2_1 X$$

Therefore, X must be a deuteron, $\,^2_1 H$ (or just d).

DISINTEGRATION ENERGY

Nuclear reactions not only produce new nuclei and other subatomic product particles, they also involve the absorption or emission of energy. Nuclear reactions must conserve total energy, so changes in mass are accompanied by changes in energy according to Einstein's equation $\Delta E = (\Delta m)c^2$. A general nuclear reaction is written

$$A + B \rightarrow C + D + Q$$

where Q denotes the **disintegration energy**. If Q is positive, the reaction is **exothermic** (or **exoergic**) and the reaction can occur spontaneously; if Q is negative, the reaction is **endothermic** (or **endoergic**) and the reaction cannot occur spontaneously. The energy Q is calculated as follows:

$$Q = [(m_A + m_B) - (m_C + m_D)]c^2 = (\Delta m)c^2$$

For spontaneous reactions—ones that liberate energy—most of the energy is revealed as kinetic energy of the least massive product nuclei.

> **Example 17.12** The process that powers the Sun—and upon which all life on Earth is dependent—is the fusion reaction:
>
> $$4\,^1_1 H \rightarrow \,^4_2 \alpha + 2\,^0_{+1} e + 2\nu_e + \gamma$$
>
> (a) Show that this reaction releases energy.
> (b) How much energy is released per proton?
>
> Use the fact that $m_\alpha = 4.0015$ u and ignore the mass of the electron-neutrino, ν_e.

Solution.

(a) We need to find the mass difference between the reactants and products:

$$\begin{aligned}
\Delta m &= 4m_p - (m_\alpha + 2m_e) \\
&= 4(1.00728 \text{ u}) - [4.0015 \text{ u} + 2(0.0005486 \text{ u})] \\
&= 0.02652 \text{ u}
\end{aligned}$$

Since Δm is positive, the reaction is exothermic: Energy is released.

(b) Converting the mass difference to energy gives

$$Q = 0.02652 \text{ u} \times \frac{931 \text{ MeV}}{1 \text{ u}} = 24.7 \text{ MeV}$$

Since four protons went into the reaction, the energy liberated per proton is

$$\frac{24.7 \text{ MeV}}{4 \text{ p}} = 6.2 \text{ MeV} / \text{proton}$$

Example 17.13 Can the following nuclear reaction occur spontaneously?

$$\begin{smallmatrix}4\\2\end{smallmatrix}\alpha + \begin{smallmatrix}14\\7\end{smallmatrix}\text{N} \rightarrow \begin{smallmatrix}17\\8\end{smallmatrix}\text{O} + \begin{smallmatrix}1\\1\end{smallmatrix}\text{H}$$

(The mass of the nitrogen nucleus is 13.9992 u, and the mass of the oxygen nucleus is 16.9947 u.)

Solution. We first figure out the mass equivalent of the disintegration energy:

$$\begin{aligned}
\Delta m &= (m_\alpha + m_N) - (m_O + m_p) \\
&= (4.0015 \text{ u} + 13.9992 \text{ u}) - (16.9947 \text{ u} + 1.00728 \text{ u}) \\
&= -0.00128 \text{ u}
\end{aligned}$$

Since Δm is negative, this reaction is nonspontaneous; energy must be *supplied* in order for this reaction to proceed. But how much?

$$|Q| = 0.00128 \text{ u} \times \frac{931 \text{ MeV}}{1 \text{ u}} = 1.19 \text{ MeV}$$

CHAPTER 17 REVIEW QUESTIONS

SECTION I: MULTIPLE CHOICE

1. What's the energy of a photon whose wavelength is 2.07 nm?

   (A) 60 eV
   (B) 600 eV
   (C) 960 eV
   (D) 6000 eV
   (E) 9600 eV

2. A metal whose work function is 6.0 eV is struck with light of frequency 7.2×10^{15} Hz. What is the maximum kinetic energy of photoelectrons ejected from the metal's surface?

   (A) 7 eV
   (B) 13 eV
   (C) 19 eV
   (D) 24 eV
   (E) No photoelectrons will be produced.

3. An atom with one electron has an ionization energy of 25 eV. How much energy will be released when the electron makes the transition from an excited energy level, where $E = -16$ eV, to the ground state?

   (A) 9 eV
   (B) 11 eV
   (C) 16 eV
   (D) 25 eV
   (E) 41 eV

4. The single electron in an atom has an energy of –40 eV when it's in the ground state, and the first excited state for the electron is at –10 eV. What will happen to this electron if the atom is struck by a stream of photons, each of energy 15 eV?

   (A) The electron will absorb the energy of one photon and become excited halfway to the first excited state, then quickly return to the ground state, without emitting a photon.
   (B) The electron will absorb the energy of one photon and become excited halfway to the first excited state, then quickly return to the ground state, emitting a 15 eV photon in the process.
   (C) The electron will absorb the energy of one photon and become excited halfway to the first excited state, then quickly absorb the energy of another photon to reach the first excited state.
   (D) The electron will absorb two photons and be excited to the first excited state.
   (E) Nothing will happen.

5. What is the de Broglie wavelength of a proton whose linear momentum has a magnitude of 3.3×10^{-23} kg·m/s?

   (A) 0.0002 nm
   (B) 0.002 nm
   (C) 0.02 nm
   (D) 0.2 nm
   (E) 2 nm

6. The difference between the mass of an intact phosphorus-31 nucleus and the sum of the masses of its individual protons and neutrons is 0.2825 u. What is the nuclear binding energy per nucleon?

(A) 4.6 MeV/nucleon
(B) 6.3 MeV/nucleon
(C) 8.5 MeV/nucleon
(D) 12.1 MeV/nucleon
(E) 17.4 MeV/nucleon

7. Compared to the parent nucleus, the daughter of a β^- decay has

(A) the same mass number but a greater atomic number.
(B) the same mass number but a smaller atomic number.
(C) a smaller mass number but the same atomic number.
(D) a greater mass number but the same atomic number.
(E) None of the above

8. The reaction $^{218}_{85}\text{At} \rightarrow {}^{214}_{83}\text{Bi}$ is an example of what type of radioactive decay?

(A) alpha
(B) β^-
(C) β^+
(D) electron capture
(E) gamma

9. Tungsten-176 has a half-life of 2.5 hours. After how many hours will the disintegration rate of a tungsten-176 sample drop to 1/10 its initial value?

(A) 5
(B) 8.3
(C) 10
(D) 12.5
(E) 25

10. What's the missing particle in the following nuclear reaction?

$$^{2}_{1}\text{H} + {}^{63}_{29}\text{Cu} \rightarrow {}^{64}_{30}\text{Zn} + (?)$$

(A) proton
(B) neutron
(C) electron
(D) positron
(E) deuteron

11. What's the missing particle in the following nuclear reaction?

$$^{196}_{78}\text{Pt} + {}^{1}_{0}\text{n} \rightarrow {}^{197}_{78}\text{Pt} + (?)$$

(A) proton
(B) neutron
(C) electron
(D) positron
(E) gamma

SECTION II: FREE RESPONSE

1. The Bohr model of electron energy levels can be applied to any one-electron atom, such as doubly-ionized lithium (Li^{2+}). The energy levels for the electron are given by the equation

$$E_n = \frac{Z^2}{n^2}(-13.6 \text{ eV})$$

where Z is the atomic number. The emission spectrum for Li^{2+} contains four spectral lines corresponding to the following wavelengths:

$$11.4 \text{ nm}, \quad 13.5 \text{ nm}, \quad 54.0 \text{ nm}, \quad 72.9 \text{ nm}$$

(a) What's the value of Z for Li^{2+}?

(b) Identify which energy-level transitions give rise to the four wavelengths cited.

(c) Can the emission spectrum for Li^{2+} contain a line corresponding to a wavelength between 54.0 nm and 72.9 nm? If so, calculate its wavelength. If not, briefly explain.

(c) What is the next shortest wavelength in the emission spectrum (closest to, but shorter than, 11.4 nm)?

2. Thorium-229 (^{229}Th, mass = 229.03 u) is naturally radioactive. It has a half-life of 7340 years and decays by emitting an alpha particle (mass of alpha: m_α = 4.0015 u, where 1 u = 1.66×10^{-27} kg). The atomic numbers, names, and symbols of some elements are given below:

Atomic number	Name of element	Chemical Symbol
85	astatine	At
86	radon	Rn
87	francium	Fr
88	radium	Ra
89	actinium	Ac
90	thorium	Th
91	protactinium	Pa
92	uranium	U
93	neptunium	Np
94	plutonium	Pu
95	americium	Am

(a)   How many protons and neutrons does a thorium-229 nucleus have?

(b)   What is the daughter nucleus of the decay of ^{229}Th? Be sure to specify the mass number and atomic number of the daughter.

(c)   If the mass of the daughter is M = 225.02 u, what is the distintegration energy, Q, associated with the decay of ^{229}Th?

(d)   If the daughter nucleus undergoes β^- decay with a half-life of 15 days, what is *its* daughter (^{229}Th's granddaughter)?

Assume that a ^{229}Th nucleus is at rest when it spontaneously decays.

(e)   If v is the speed of the ejected alpha particle and V the recoil speed of the daughter nucleus, use conservation of linear momentum to find a relationship between v and V.

(f)   If the total kinetic energy of the alpha particle and the daughter is equal to the disintegration energy computed in part (c), find the speeds v and V.

(g)   What percentage of the initial mass of a sample of thorium-229's daughter will remain after

(i)   30 days?

(ii)   40 days?

18

SOLUTIONS TO THE CHAPTER REVIEW QUESTIONS

CHAPTER 2 REVIEW QUESTIONS

SECTION I: MULTIPLE CHOICE

1. **(A)** Traveling once around a circular path means that the final position coincides with the initial position. Therefore, the displacement is zero. The average speed, which is *total* distance traveled divided by elapsed time, cannot be zero. And since the velocity changed (because its direction changed), there was a nonzero acceleration. Therefore, only Statement I is true.

2. **(C)** By definition, $\bar{\mathbf{a}} = \Delta \mathbf{v} / \Delta t$. We determine $\Delta \mathbf{v} = \mathbf{v}_2 - \mathbf{v}_1 = \mathbf{v}_2 + (-\mathbf{v}_1)$ geometrically as follows:

   Since Δt is a positive scalar, the direction of $\bar{\mathbf{a}}$ is the same as the direction of $\Delta \mathbf{v}$, which is displayed above; choice (C) is best.

3. **(C)** Statement I is false since a projectile experiencing only the constant acceleration due to gravity can travel in a parabolic trajectory. Statement II is true: Zero acceleration means no change in speed (or direction). Statement III is false: An object whose speed remains constant but whose velocity vector is changing direction is accelerating.

4. **(C)** The baseball is still under the influence of Earth's gravity. Its acceleration throughout the *entire* flight is constant, equal to g downward.

5. **(A)** Use Big Five #3 with $v_0 = 0$:

   $$\Delta s = v_0 t + \tfrac{1}{2} a t^2 = \tfrac{1}{2} a t^2 \quad \Rightarrow \quad t = \sqrt{\frac{2\Delta s}{a}} = \sqrt{\frac{2(200 \text{ m})}{5 \text{ m}/\text{s}^2}} = 9 \text{ s}$$

6. **(D)** Use Big Five #5 with $v_0 = 0$ (calling *down* the positive direction):

   $$v^2 = v_0^2 + 2a\Delta s = 2a\Delta s \quad \Rightarrow \quad \Delta s = \frac{v^2}{2a} = \frac{v^2}{2g} = \frac{(30 \text{ m}/\text{s})^2}{2(9.8 \text{ m}/\text{s}^2)} \approx 45 \text{ m}$$

7. **(C)** Apply Big Five #3 to the vertical motion, calling *down* the positive direction:

   $$\Delta y = v_{0y} t + \tfrac{1}{2} a_y t^2 = \tfrac{1}{2} a_y t^2 = \tfrac{1}{2} g t^2 \quad \Rightarrow \quad t = \sqrt{\frac{2\Delta y}{g}} = \sqrt{\frac{2(80 \text{ m})}{9.8 \text{ m}/\text{s}^2}} = 4 \text{ s}$$

   Notice that the stone's initial horizontal speed ($v_{0x} = 10 \text{ m}/\text{s}$) is irrelevant.

8. **(B)** First we determine the time required for the ball to reach the top of its parabolic trajectory (which is the time required for the vertical velocity to drop to zero).

   $$v_y \overset{\text{set}}{=} 0 \quad \Rightarrow \quad v_{0y} - gt = 0 \quad \Rightarrow \quad t = \frac{v_{0y}}{g}$$

The total flight time is equal to twice this value:

$$T = 2t = 2\frac{v_{0y}}{g} = 2\frac{v_0 \sin\theta_0}{g} = \frac{2(10 \text{ m/s})\sin 30°}{9.8 \text{ m/s}^2} = 1 \text{ s}$$

9. **(C)** After 4 seconds, the stone's vertical speed has changed by $\Delta v_y = a_y t = (10 \text{ m/s}^2)(4 \text{ s}) = 40 \text{ m/s}$. Since $v_{0y} = 0$, the value of v_y at $t = 4$ is 40 m/s. The horizontal speed does not change. Therefore, when the rock hits the water, its velocity has a horizontal component of 30 m/s and a vertical component of 40 m/s.

By the Pythagorean theorem, the magnitude of the total velocity, v, is 50 m/s.

10. **(E)** Since the acceleration of the projectile is always downward (because it's gravitational acceleration), the vertical speed decreases as the projectile rises and increases as the projectile falls. Statements A, B, C, and D are all false.

SECTION II: FREE RESPONSE

1. (a) At time $t = 1$ s, the car's velocity starts to decrease as the acceleration (which is the slope of the given v vs. t graph) changes from positive to negative.

(b) The average velocity between $t = 0$ and $t = 1$ s is $\frac{1}{2}(v_{t=0} + v_{t=1}) = \frac{1}{2}(0 + 20 \text{ m/s}) = 10 \text{ m/s}$, and the average velocity between $t = 1$ and $t = 5$ is $\frac{1}{2}(v_{t=1} + v_{t=5}) = \frac{1}{2}(20 \text{ m/s} + 0) = 10 \text{ m/s}$. The two average velocities are the same.

(c) The displacement is equal to the area bounded by the graph and the t axis, taking areas above the t axis as positive and those below as negative. In this case, the displacement from $t = 0$ to $t = 5$ s is equal to the area of the triangular region whose base is the segment along the t axis from $t = 0$ to $t = 5$ s:

$$\Delta s \,(t = 0 \text{ to } t = 5 \text{ s}) = \tfrac{1}{2} \times \text{base} \times \text{height} = \tfrac{1}{2}(5 \text{ s})(20 \text{ m/s}) = 50 \text{ m}$$

The displacement from $t = 5$ s to $t = 7$ s is equal to the negative of the area of the triangular region whose base is the segment along the t axis from $t = 0$ to $t = 5$ s:

$$\Delta s \,(t = 5 \text{ s to } t = 7 \text{ s}) = -\tfrac{1}{2} \times \text{base} \times \text{height} = -\tfrac{1}{2}(2 \text{ s})(10 \text{ m/s}) = -10 \text{ m}$$

Therefore, the displacement from $t = 0$ to $t = 7$ s is

$$\Delta s\ (t = 0 \text{ to } t = 5 \text{ s}) + \Delta s\ (t = 5 \text{ s to } t = 7 \text{ s}) = 50 \text{ m} + (-10 \text{ m}) = 40 \text{ m}$$

(d)   The acceleration is the slope of the v vs. t graph.   The segment of the graph from $t = 0$ to $t = 1$ s has a slope of $a = \Delta v / \Delta t = (20 \text{ m/s} - 0)/(1 \text{ s} - 0) = 20 \text{ m/s}^2$, and the segment of the graph from $t = 1$ s to $t = 7$ s has a slope of $a = \Delta v / \Delta t = (-10 \text{ m/s} - 20 \text{ s})/(7 \text{ s} - 1 \text{ s}) = -5 \text{ m/s}^2$.   Therefore, the graph of a vs. t is

(e) One way to determine the displacement is to determine equations for $v(t)$ and integrate to get $s(t)$. The segment from $t = 0$ to $t = 1$ s connects the points $(0, 0)$ and $(1, 20)$; the slope is 20, and we get $v = 20t$. The segment from $t = 1$ to $t = 7$ connects the points $(1, 20)$ and $(7, -10)$; the slope is -5, and we get $v = -5t + 25$. In summary,

$$v(t) = \begin{cases} 20t & 0 \le t \le 1 \\ -5t + 25 & 1 \le t \le 7 \end{cases}$$

Therefore, since $s(t) = \displaystyle\int v(t)\,dt$, we find that

$$s(t) = \begin{cases} 10t^2 & 0 \le t \le 1 \\ -\frac{5}{2}t^2 + 25t - \frac{25}{2} & 1 \le t \le 7 \end{cases}$$

2. (a) The maximum height of the projectile occurs at the time at which its vertical velocity drops to zero:

$$v_y \overset{\text{set}}{=} 0 \;\Rightarrow\; v_{0y} - gt = 0 \;\Rightarrow\; t = \frac{v_{0y}}{g}$$

The vertical displacement of the projectile at this time is computed as follows:

$$\Delta y = v_{0y}t - \tfrac{1}{2}gt^2 \;\Rightarrow\; H = v_{0y}\frac{v_{0y}}{g} - \tfrac{1}{2}g\left(\frac{v_{0y}}{g}\right)^2 = \frac{v_{0y}^2}{2g} = \frac{v_0^2 \sin^2\theta_0}{2g}$$

(b) The total flight time is equal to twice the time computed in part (a):

$$T = 2t = 2\frac{v_{0y}}{g}$$

The horizontal displacement at this time gives the projectile's range:

$$\Delta x = v_{0x}t \;\Rightarrow\; R = v_{0x}T = \frac{v_{0x}\cdot 2v_{0y}}{g} = \frac{2v_0^2 \sin\theta_0 \cos\theta_0}{g} \;\text{ or }\; \frac{v_0^2 \sin 2\theta_0}{g}$$

(c) For any given value of v_0, the range,

$$\Delta x = v_{0x}t \quad \Rightarrow \quad R = v_{0x}T = \frac{v_{0x} \cdot 2v_{0y}}{g} = \frac{2v_0^2 \sin\theta_0 \cos\theta_0}{g} \quad \text{or} \quad \frac{v_0^2 \sin 2\theta_0}{g},$$

will be maximized when $\sin 2\theta_0$ is maximized. This occurs when $2\theta_0 = 90°$, that is, when $\theta_0 = 45°$.

(d) Set the general expression for the projectile's vertical displacement equal to h and solve for the two value of t:

$$v_{0y}t - \tfrac{1}{2}gt^2 \overset{\text{set}}{=} h \quad \Rightarrow \quad \tfrac{1}{2}gt^2 - v_{0y}t + h = 0$$

Applying the quadratic formula, we find that

$$t = \frac{v_{0y} \pm \sqrt{(-v_{0y})^2 - 4(\tfrac{1}{2}g)(h)}}{2(\tfrac{1}{2}g)} = \frac{v_{0y} \pm \sqrt{v_{0y}^2 - 2gh}}{g}$$

Therefore, the two times at which the projectile crosses the horizontal line at height h are

$$t_1 = \frac{v_{0y} - \sqrt{v_{0y}^2 - 2gh}}{g} \quad \text{and} \quad t_2 = \frac{v_{0y} + \sqrt{v_{0y}^2 - 2gh}}{g}$$

so the amount of time that elapses between these events is

$$\Delta t = t_2 - t_1 = \frac{2\sqrt{v_{0y}^2 - 2gh}}{g}$$

3. (a) The cannonball will certainly reach the wall (which is only 220 m away) since the ball's range is

$$R = \frac{v_0^2 \sin 2\theta_0}{g} = \frac{(50 \text{ m}/\text{s})^2 \sin 2(40°)}{9.8 \text{ m}/\text{s}^2} = 251 \text{ m}$$

We simply need to make sure that the cannonball's height is less than 30 m at the point where its horizontal displacement is 220 m (so that the ball actually hits the wall rather than flying over it). To do this, we find the time at which $x = 220$ m by first writing

$$x = v_{0x}t \quad \Rightarrow \quad t = \frac{x}{v_{0x}} = \frac{x}{v_0 \cos\theta_0} \qquad (1)$$

Thus, the cannonball's vertical position can be written in terms of its horizontal position as follows:

$$y = v_{0y}t - \tfrac{1}{2}gt^2 = v_0 \sin\theta_0 \frac{x}{v_0 \cos\theta_0} - \tfrac{1}{2}g\left(\frac{x}{v_0 \cos\theta_0}\right)^2$$

$$= x \tan\theta_0 - \frac{gx^2}{2v_0^2 \cos^2\theta_0} \qquad (2)$$

Substituting the known values for x, θ_0, g, and v_0, we get

$$y(\text{at } x = 220\text{ m}) = (220\text{ m})\tan 40° - \frac{(9.8\text{ m}/\text{s}^2)(220\text{ m})^2}{2(50\text{ m}/\text{s})^2 \cos^2 40°}$$

$$= 23\text{ m}$$

This is indeed less than 30 m, as desired.

(b) From Equation (1) derived in part (a),

$$t = \frac{x}{v_0 \cos\theta_0} = \frac{220\text{ m}}{(50\text{ m}/\text{s})\cos 40°} = 5.7\text{ s}$$

(c) The height at which the cannonball strikes the wall was determined in part (a) to be 23 m.

(d) We use Equation (2) from part (a):

$$y = x\tan\theta_0 - \frac{gx^2}{2v_0^2 \cos^2\theta_0}$$

Using the identities $1/\cos^2\theta_0 = \sec^2\theta_0$ and $\sec^2\theta_0 = 1 + \tan^2\theta_0$, this equation can be written in the form

$$y = x\tan\theta_0 - \frac{gx^2}{2v_0^2}(1 + \tan^2\theta_0)$$

or

$$\frac{gx^2}{2v_0^2}(\tan\theta_0)^2 - x\tan\theta_0 + \left(y + \frac{gx^2}{2v_0^2}\right) = 0$$

Substituting $x = 220$ m and $y = 30$ m (which is the top of the castle wall), this equation becomes

$$(94.864)(\tan\theta_0)^2 - 220\tan\theta_0 + 124.864 = 0$$

The quadratic formula then gives

$$\tan\theta_0 = \frac{220 \pm \sqrt{220^2 - 4(94.864)(124.864)}}{2(94.864)}$$

$$= 0.9913,\ 1.328$$

$$\theta_0 = 44.7°,\ 53.0°$$

4. (a) Integrating $a(t)$ with respect to time gives the velocity, $v(t)$:

$$v(t) = \int a(t)\,dt = \int 6t\,dt = 3t^2 + v_0 \quad \Rightarrow \quad v(t) = 3t^2 + 2$$

Setting this equal to 14, we solve for t:

$$v(t) = 14 \quad \Rightarrow \quad 3t^2 + 2 = 14 \quad \Rightarrow \quad t = 2\ \text{s}$$

(Notice that we discarded the solution $t = -2$.)

(b) Integrating $v(t)$ with respect to time gives the position, $x(t)$:

$$x(t) = \int v(t)\,dt = \int (3t^2 + 2)\,dt = t^3 + 2t + x_0 \quad \Rightarrow \quad x(t) = t^3 + 2t + 4$$

Therefore, the particle's position at $t = 3$ s is

$$x(3) = \left[t^3 + 2t + 4\right]_{t=3} = 37\ \text{m}$$

CHAPTER 3 REVIEW QUESTIONS
SECTION I: MULTIPLE CHOICE

1. **(B)** Because the person is not accelerating, the net force he feels must be zero. Therefore, the magnitude of the upward normal force from the floor must balance that of the downward gravitational force. Although these two forces have equal magnitudes, they do not form an action/reaction pair because they both act on the same object (namely, the person). The forces in an action/reaction pair always act on different objects.

2. **(D)** First draw a free-body diagram:

The person exerts a downward force on the scale, and the scale pushes up on the person with an equal (but opposite) force, F_N. Thus, the scale reading is F_N, the magnitude of the normal force. Since $F_N - F_w = ma$, we have $F_N = F_w + ma = (800 \text{ N}) + [800 \text{ N}/(9.8 \text{ m/s}^2)](4.9 \text{ m/s}^2) = 1200 \text{ N}$.

3. **(A)** The net force that the object feels on the inclined plane is $mg \sin \theta$, the component of the gravitational force that is parallel to the ramp. Since $\sin \theta = (5 \text{ m})/(20 \text{ m}) = 1/4$, we have $F_{net} = (2 \text{ kg})(9.8 \text{ N/kg})(1/4) = 5 \text{ N}$.

4. **(C)** The net force on the block is $F - F_f = F - \mu_k F_N = F - \mu_k F_w = (18 \text{ N}) - (0.4)(20 \text{ N}) = 10 \text{ N}$. Since $F_{net} = ma = (F_w/g)a$, we find that $10 \text{ N} = [(20 \text{ N})/(9.8 \text{ m/s}^2)]a$, which gives $a = 5 \text{ m/s}^2$.

5. **(A)** The force pulling the block down the ramp is $mg \sin \theta$, and the maximum force of static friction is $\mu_s F_N = \mu_s mg \cos \theta$. If $mg \sin \theta$ is greater than $\mu_s mg \cos \theta$, then there is a net force down the ramp, and the block will accelerate down. So, the question becomes, "Is $\sin \theta$ greater than $\mu_s \cos \theta$?" Since $\theta = 30°$ and $\mu_s = 0.5$, the answer is *yes*.

6. **(E)** One way to attack this question is to notice that if the two masses happen to be equal, that is, if $M = m$, then the blocks won't accelerate (because their weights balance). The only expression given that becomes zero when $M = m$ is the one given in choice (E). If we draw a free-body diagram,

Newton's Second Law gives us the following two equations:

$$F_T - mg = ma \qquad (1)$$

$$Mg - F_T = Ma \qquad (2)$$

Adding these equations yields $Mg - mg = ma + Ma = (M + m)a$, so

$$a = \frac{Mg - mg}{M + m} = \frac{M - m}{M + m}g.$$

7. **(E)** If $\mathbf{F}_{net} = 0$, then $\mathbf{a} = 0$. No acceleration means constant speed (possibly, but not necessarily, zero) with no change in direction. Therefore, statements B, C, and D are false, and statement A is not necessarily true.

8. **(D)** The horizontal motion across the frictionless tables is unaffected by (vertical) gravitational acceleration. It would take as much force to accelerate the block across the table on Earth as it would on the Moon. (If friction *were* taken into account, then the smaller weight of the block on the Moon would imply a smaller normal force by the table and hence a smaller frictional force. Less force would be needed on the Moon in this case.)

9. **(D)** The maximum force which static friction can exert on the crate is $\mu_s F_N = \mu_s F_w = \mu_s mg = (0.4)(100 \text{ kg})(9.8 \text{ N/kg}) = 392 \text{ N}$. Since the force applied to the crate is only 344 N, static friction is able to apply that same magnitude of force on the crate, keeping it stationary. [Choice (B) is incorrect because the static friction force is *not* the reaction force to **F**; both **F** and $\mathbf{F}_{f(static)}$ act on the same object (the crate) and therefore cannot form an action/reaction pair.]

10. **(A)** With Crate #2 on top of Crate #1, the force pushing downward on the floor is greater, so the normal force exerted by the floor on Crate #1 is greater, which increases the friction force. Statements B, C, D, and E are all false.

11. **(E)** Neither the velocity nor the acceleration is constant because the direction of each of these vectors is always changing as the object moves along its circular path. And the net force on the object is not zero, because a centripetal force must be acting to provide the necessary centripetal acceleration to maintain the object's circular motion.

12. **(B)** When the bucket is at the lowest point in its vertical circle, it feels a tension force $\mathbf{F}_T$ upward and the gravitational force $\mathbf{F}_w$ downward. The net force toward the center of the circle, which is the centripetal force, is $F_T - F_w$. Thus,

$$F_T - F_w = m\frac{v^2}{r} \implies v = \sqrt{\frac{r(F_T - mg)}{m}} = \sqrt{\frac{(0.60 \text{ m})[50 \text{ N} - (3 \text{ kg})(9.8 \text{ N/kg})]}{3 \text{ kg}}} = 2 \text{ m/s}$$

13. **(C)** When the bucket reaches the topmost point in its vertical circle, the forces acting on the bucket are its weight, $\mathbf{F}_w$, and the downward tension force, $\mathbf{F}_T$. The net force, $\mathbf{F}_w + \mathbf{F}_T$, provides the centripetal force. In order for the rope to avoid becoming slack, $\mathbf{F}_T$ must not vanish. Therefore, the cut-off speed for ensuring that the bucket makes it around the circle is the speed

at which $\mathbf{F}_T$ just becomes zero; any greater speed would imply that the bucket would make it around. Thus,

$$F_w + F_T = m\frac{v^2}{r} \implies F_w + 0 = m\frac{v^2_{\text{cut-off}}}{r} \implies v_{\text{cut-off}} = \sqrt{\frac{rF_w}{m}} = \sqrt{gr}$$

$$= \sqrt{(9.8 \text{ m/s}^2)(0.60 \text{ m})}$$

$$= 2.4 \text{ m/s}$$

14. **(D)** Centripetal acceleration is given by the equation $a_c = v^2/r$. Since the object covers a distance of $2\pi r$ in 1 revolution, its speed is $2\pi r$ s^{-1}. Therefore,

$$a_c = \frac{v^2}{r} = \frac{(2\pi r \text{ s}^{-1})^2}{r} = 4\pi^2 r \text{ s}^{-2}$$

SECTION II: FREE RESPONSE

1. (a) The forces acting on the crate are $\mathbf{F}_T$ (the tension in the rope), $\mathbf{F}_w$ (the weight of the block), $\mathbf{F}_N$ (the normal force exerted by the floor), and $\mathbf{F}_f$ (the force of kinetic friction):

(b) First break $\mathbf{F}_T$ into its horizontal and vertical components:

Since the net vertical force on the crate is zero, we have $F_N + F_T \sin \theta = F_w$, so $F_N = F_w - F_T \sin \theta = mg - F_T \sin \theta$.

(c) From part (b), we see that the net horizontal force acting on the crate is

$$F_T \cos\theta - F_f = F_T \cos\theta - \mu F_N = F_T \cos\theta - \mu(mg - F_T \sin\theta)$$

so the crate's horizontal acceleration across the floor is

$$a = \frac{F_{net}}{m} = \frac{F_T \cos\theta - \mu(mg - F_T \sin\theta)}{m}$$

(d) In order to maximize the crate's acceleration, we want to maximize the net horizontal force, $F_T \cos\theta - \mu(mg - F_T \sin\theta) = F_T(\cos\theta + \mu\sin\theta) - \mu mg$. Since F_T, μ, m and g are all fixed, maximizing the net horizontal force depends on maximizing the expression

$$\cos\theta + \mu\sin\theta$$

Call this $f(\theta)$. To determine the value of θ at which $f(\theta) = \cos\theta + \mu\sin\theta$ attains an extreme value, we take the derivative of f and set it equal to zero:

$$f'(\theta) = -\sin\theta + \mu\cos\theta \overset{set}{=} 0$$
$$\mu\cos\theta = \sin\theta$$
$$\mu = \tan\theta$$
$$\theta = \tan^{-1}\mu$$

[That this value of θ does indeed maximize f can be verified by noticing that for θ in the interval $0 \le \theta \le \frac{1}{2}\pi$, $f''(\theta) = -\cos\theta - \mu\sin\theta$ is always negative, and

$$f(\tan^{-1}\mu) = \cos(\tan^{-1}\mu) + \mu\sin(\tan^{-1}\mu)$$
$$= \frac{1}{\sqrt{1+\mu^2}} + \mu\frac{\mu}{\sqrt{1+\mu^2}}$$
$$= \sqrt{1+\mu^2}$$

is greater than $f(0) = 1$ or $f(\frac{1}{2}\pi) = \mu$, the values of f at the endpoints of the interval.]

2. (a) The forces acting on Block #1 are F_T (the tension in the string connecting it to Block #2), F_{w1} (the weight of the block), and F_{N1} (the normal force exerted by the tabletop):

(b) The forces acting on Block #2 are **F** (the pulling force), F_T (the tension in the string connecting it to Block #1), F_{w2} (the weight of the block), and F_{N2} (the normal force exerted by the tabletop):

(c) Newton's Second Law applied to Block #2 yields $F - F_T = m_2 a$, and applied to Block #1 yields $F_T = m_1 a$. Adding these equations, we find that $F = (m_1 + m_2)a$, so

$$a = \frac{F}{m_1 + m_2}$$

(d) Substituting the result of part (c) into the equation $F_T = m_1 a$, we get

$$F_T = m_1 a = \frac{m_1}{m_1 + m_2} F$$

(e) (i) Since the force **F** must accelerate all three masses—m_1, m, and m_2—the common acceleration of all parts of the system is

$$a = \frac{F}{m_1 + m + m_2} \, \mu$$

(e) (ii) Let $\mathbf{F}_{T1}$ denote the tension force in the connecting string acting on Block #1, and let $\mathbf{F}_{T2}$ denote the tension force in the connecting string acting on Block #2. Then, Newton's Second Law applied to Block #1 yields $F_{T1} = m_1 a$ and applied to Block #2 yields $F - F_{T2} = m_2 a$. Therefore, using the value for a computed above, we get

$$\begin{aligned}
F_{T2} - F_{T1} &= (F - m_2 a) - m_1 a \\
&= F - (m_1 + m_2)a \\
&= F - (m_1 + m_2)\frac{F}{m_1 + m + m_2} \\
&= F\left(1 - \frac{m_1 + m_2}{m_1 + m + m_2}\right) \\
&= F\frac{m}{m_1 + m + m_2}
\end{aligned}$$

3. (a) First draw free-body diagrams for the two boxes:

Applying Newton's Second Law to the boxes yields the following two equations:

$$F_T - m_1 g \sin\theta = m_1 a \qquad (1)$$

$$m_2 g - F_T = m_2 a \qquad (2)$$

Adding the equations allows us to solve for a:

$$m_2 g - m_1 g \sin\theta = (m_1 + m_2)a$$

$$a = \frac{m_2 - m_1 \sin\theta}{m_1 + m_2} g$$

(i) For a to be positive, we must have $m_2 - m_1 \sin\theta > 0$, which implies that $\sin\theta < m_2/m_1$, or, equivalently, $\theta < \sin^{-1}(m_2/m_1)$.

(ii) For a to be zero, we must have $m_2 - m_1 \sin\theta = 0$, which implies that $\sin\theta = m_2/m_1$, or, equivalently, $\theta = \sin^{-1}(m_2/m_1)$.

(b) Including the force of kinetic friction, the force diagram for m_1 is

Since $F_f = \mu_k F_N = \mu_k m_1 g \cos\theta$, applying Newton's Second Law to the boxes yields these two equations:

$$F_T - m_1 g \sin\theta - \mu_k mg \cos\theta = m_1 a \qquad (1)$$

$$m_2 g - F_T = m_2 a \qquad (2)$$

Adding the equations allows us to solve for a:

$$m_2 g - m_1 g \sin\theta - \mu_k m_1 g \cos\theta = (m_1 + m_2)a$$

$$a = \frac{m_2 - m_1(\sin\theta + \mu_k \cos\theta)}{m_1 + m_2} g$$

If we want a to be equal to zero (so that the box of mass m_1 slides up the ramp with constant velocity), then

$$m_2 - m_1(\sin\theta + \mu_k \cos\theta) = 0$$

$$\sin\theta + \mu_k \cos\theta = \frac{m_2}{m_1}$$

4. (a) The forces acting on the sky diver are $\mathbf{F}_r$, the force of air resistance (upward), and $\mathbf{F}_w$, the weight of the sky diver (downward):

(b) Since $F_{net} = F_w - F_r = mg - kv$, the sky diver's acceleration is

$$a = \frac{F_{net}}{m} = \frac{mg - kv}{m}$$

(c) Terminal speed occurs when the sky diver's acceleration becomes zero, since then the decent velocity becomes constant. Setting the expression derived in part (b) equal to 0, we find the speed $v = v_t$ at which this occurs:

$$v = v_t \text{ when } a = 0 \quad \Rightarrow \quad \frac{mg - kv_t}{m} = 0 \quad \Rightarrow \quad v_t = \frac{mg}{k}$$

(d) The sky diver's descent speed is initially v_0 and the acceleration is (close to) g. However, once the parachute opens, the force of air resistance provides a large (speed-dependent) upward acceleration, causing her descent velocity to decrease. The slope of the v vs. t graph (the acceleration) is not constant but instead decreases to zero as her descent speed decreases from v_0 to v_t. Therefore, the graph is not linear.

(e) Since $a = dv/dt$ and, from part (b), $a = (mg - kv)/m$, we have

$$\frac{dv}{dt} = \frac{mg - kv}{m} \quad \Rightarrow \quad \frac{dv}{mg - kv} = \frac{dt}{m}$$

Integrating both sides of this equation gives

$$-\tfrac{1}{k}\ln|mg - kv| = \tfrac{1}{m}t + c$$

where c is a constant of integration. This equation can be rewritten in the form

$$mg - kv = Ce^{(-k/m)t}$$
$$kv = mg - Ce^{(-k/m)t}$$

Since $v = v_0$ at $t = 0$, we can determine the constant C:

$$kv_0 = mg - C \quad \Rightarrow \quad C = mg - kv_0$$

Therefore, the equation for the sky diver's descent speed as a function of time is

$$v(t) = \tfrac{1}{k}\left[mg - (mg - kv_0)e^{(-k/m)t}\right]$$

5. (a) The forces acting on a person standing against the cylinder wall are gravity ($\mathbf{F}_w$, downward), the normal force from the wall ($\mathbf{F}_N$, directed toward the center of the cylinder), and the force of static friction ($\mathbf{F}_f$, directed upward):

(b) In order to keep the passenger from sliding down the wall, the maximum force of static friction must be at least as great as the passenger's weight: $F_{f(\text{max})} \geq mg$. Since $F_{f(\text{max})} = \mu_s F_N$, this condition becomes

$$\mu_s F_N \geq mg$$

Now, consider the circular motion of the passenger. Neither $\mathbf{F}_f$ nor $\mathbf{F}_w$ has a component toward the center of the path, so the centripetal force is provided entirely by the normal force:

$$F_N = \frac{mv^2}{r}$$

Substituting this expression for F_N into the previous equation, we get

$$\mu_s \frac{mv^2}{r} \geq mg$$

$$\mu_s \geq \frac{gr}{v^2}$$

Therefore, the coefficient of static friction between the passenger and the wall of the cylinder must satisfy this condition in order to keep the passenger from sliding down.

(c) Since the mass m canceled out in deriving the expression for μ_s, the conditions are independent of mass. Thus, the inequality $\mu_s \geq gr/v^2$ holds for both the adult passenger of mass m and the child of mass $m/2$.

6. (a) The forces acting on the car are gravity ($\mathbf{F}_w$, downward), the normal force from the road ($\mathbf{F}_N$, upward), and the force of static friction ($\mathbf{F}_f$, directed toward the center of curvature of the road):

(b) The force of static friction [we assume static friction because we *don't* want the car to slide (that is, skid)] provides the necessary centripetal force:

$$F_f = \frac{mv^2}{r}$$

Therefore, to find the maximum speed at which static friction can continue to provide the necessary force, we write

$$F_{f\,(max)} = \frac{mv_{max}^2}{r}$$

$$\mu_s F_N = \frac{mv_{max}^2}{r}$$

$$\mu_s mg = \frac{mv_{max}^2}{r}$$

$$v_{max} = \sqrt{\mu_s g r}$$

(c) Ignoring friction, the forces acting on the car are gravity ($\mathbf{F}_w$, downward) and the normal force from the road ($\mathbf{F}_N$, which is now tilted toward the center of curvature of the road):

(d) Because of the banking of the turn, the normal force is tilted toward the center of curvature of the road. The component of $\mathbf{F}_N$ toward the center can provide the centripetal force, making reliance on friction unnecessary.

There's no vertical acceleration, so $F_N \cos \theta = F_w = mg$, so $F_N = mg/\cos \theta$. The component of F_N toward the center of curvature of the turn, $F_N \sin \theta$, provides the centripetal force:

$$F_N \sin \theta = \frac{mv^2}{r}$$

$$\frac{mg}{\cos \theta} \sin \theta = \frac{mv^2}{r}$$

$$g \tan \theta = \frac{v^2}{r}$$

$$\theta = \tan^{-1} \frac{v^2}{gr}$$

CHAPTER 4 REVIEW QUESTIONS

SECTION I: MULTIPLE CHOICE

1. **(A)** Since the force **F** is perpendicular to the displacement, the work it does is zero.

2. **(B)** By the work–energy theorem,

$$W = \Delta K = \tfrac{1}{2}m(v^2 - v_0^2) = \tfrac{1}{2}(4 \text{ kg})[(6 \text{ m}/\text{s})^2 - (3 \text{ m}/\text{s})^2] = 54 \text{ J}$$

3. **(B)** Since the box (mass m) falls through a vertical distance of h, its gravitational potential energy decreases by mgh. The length of the ramp is irrelevant here.

4. **(C)** Since the centripetal force always points along a radius toward the center of the circle, and the velocity of the object is always tangent to the circle (and thus perpendicular to the radius), the work done by the centripetal force is zero. Alternatively, since the object's speed remains constant, the work–energy theorem tells us that no work is being performed.

5. **(A)** The gravitational force points downward while the book's displacement is upward. Therefore, the work done by gravity is $-mgh = -(2 \text{ kg})(9.8 \text{ N/kg})(1.5 \text{ m}) = -30 \text{ J}$.

6. **(D)** The work done by gravity as the block slides down the inclined plane is

$$W = (mg \sin \theta)(L) = [(3.5 \text{ kg})(9.8 \text{ N/kg}) \sin 30°](6 \text{ m}) = 103 \text{ J}$$

Now, applying the work–energy theorem, we find that

$$W = \Delta K = \tfrac{1}{2}m(v^2 - v_0^2) = \tfrac{1}{2}mv^2 \implies v = \sqrt{\frac{2W}{m}} = \sqrt{\frac{2(103 \text{ J})}{3.5 \text{ kg}}} = 7.7 \text{ m}/\text{s}$$

7. **(E)** Apply Conservation of Mechanical Energy (including the negative work done by $\mathbf{F}_f$, the force of sliding friction):

$$K_i + U_i + W_f = K_f + U_f$$
$$0 + mgh - F_f L = \tfrac{1}{2}mv^2 + 0$$
$$mg(L\sin\theta) - (\mu mg\cos\theta)L = \tfrac{1}{2}mv^2$$
$$v = \sqrt{2gL(\sin\theta - \mu\cos\theta)}$$
$$= \sqrt{2(9.8\ \text{m}/\text{s}^2)(6\ \text{m})[\sin 60° - (0.3)\cos 60°]}$$
$$= 9.2\ \text{m}/\text{s}$$

8. **(E)** Apply Conservation of Mechanical Energy (including the negative work done by $\mathbf{F}_r$, the force of air resistance):

$$K_i + U_i + W_r = K_f + U_f$$
$$0 + mgh - F_r h = \tfrac{1}{2}mv^2 + 0$$
$$v = \sqrt{\frac{2h(mg - F_r)}{m}}$$
$$= \sqrt{\frac{2(40\ \text{m})[(4\ \text{kg})(9.8\ \text{N}/\text{kg}) - 20\ \text{N}]}{4\ \text{kg}}}$$
$$= 20\ \text{m}/\text{s}$$

9. **(E)** Because the rock has lost half of its gravitational potential energy, its kinetic energy at the halfway point is half of its kinetic energy at impact. Since K is proportional to v^2, if $K_{\text{at halfway point}}$ is equal to $\tfrac{1}{2}K_{\text{at impact}}$, then the rock's speed at the halfway point is $\sqrt{1/2} = 1/\sqrt{2}$ its speed at impact.

10. **(D)** Using the equation $P = Fv$, we find that $P = (200\ \text{N})(2\ \text{m}/\text{s}) = 400\ \text{W}$.

SECTION II: FREE RESPONSE

1. (a) Applying Conservation of Energy,

$$K_A + U_A = K_{\text{at }H/2} + U_{\text{at }H/2}$$
$$0 + mgH = \tfrac{1}{2}mv^2 + mg(\tfrac{1}{2}H)$$
$$\tfrac{1}{2}mgH = \tfrac{1}{2}mv^2$$
$$v = \sqrt{gH}$$

(b) Applying Conservation of Energy again,

$$K_A + U_A = K_B + U_B$$
$$0 + mgH = \tfrac{1}{2}mv_B^2 + 0$$
$$v_B = \sqrt{2gH}$$

(c) By the work–energy theorem, we want the work done by friction to be equal (but opposite) to the kinetic energy of the box at Point B:

$$W = \Delta K = \tfrac{1}{2}m(v_C^2 - v_B^2) = -\tfrac{1}{2}mv_B^2 = -\tfrac{1}{2}m(\sqrt{2gH})^2 = -mgH$$

Therefore,

$$W = -mgH \quad \Rightarrow \quad -F_f x = -mgH \quad \Rightarrow \quad -\mu_k mg x = -mgH \quad \Rightarrow \quad \mu_k = H/x$$

(d) Apply Conservation of Energy (including the negative work done by friction as the box slides up the ramp from B to C):

$$K_B + U_B + W_f = K_C + U_C$$
$$\tfrac{1}{2}m(\sqrt{2gH})^2 + 0 - F_f L = 0 + mgy$$
$$mgH + 0 - F_f L = 0 + mgy$$
$$mg(H - y) - (\mu_k mg \cos\theta)(L) = 0$$
$$\mu_k = \frac{H - y}{L\cos\theta} = \frac{H - y}{x}$$

(e) The result of part (b) reads $v_B = \sqrt{2gH}$. Therefore, by Conservation of Mechanical Energy (with the work done by the frictional force on the slide included), we get

$$K_A + U_A + W_f = K_B' + U_B$$
$$0 + mgH + W_f = \tfrac{1}{2}m\left(\tfrac{1}{2}v_B\right)^2 + 0$$
$$mgH + W_f = \tfrac{1}{2}m\left(\tfrac{1}{2}\sqrt{2gH}\right)^2$$
$$mgH + W_f = \tfrac{1}{4}mgH$$
$$W_f = -\tfrac{3}{4}mgH$$

2. (a) The centripetal acceleration of the car at Point C is given by the equation $a = v_C^2/r$, where v_C is the speed of the car at C. To find v_C^2, we apply Conservation of Energy:

$$K_A + U_A = K_C + U_C$$
$$0 + mgH = \tfrac{1}{2}mv_C^2 + mgr$$
$$mg(H - r) = \tfrac{1}{2}mv_C^2$$
$$v_C^2 = 2g(H - r)$$

Therefore,

$$a_c = \frac{v_C^2}{r} = \frac{2g(H - r)}{r}$$

(b) In terms of θ, the car's height above the bottom of the track (Point B) is given by the equation $h = r + (-r \cos \theta)$,

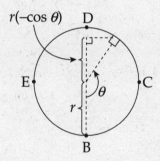

so we get

$$K_A + U_A = K + U$$
$$0 + mgH = \tfrac{1}{2}mv^2 + mg(r - r\cos\theta)$$
$$mg[H - r(1 - \cos\theta)] = \tfrac{1}{2}mv^2$$
$$v = \sqrt{2g[H - r(1 - \cos\theta)]}$$

(c) When the car reaches Point D, the forces acting on the car are its weight, $\mathbf{F}_w$, and the downward normal force, $\mathbf{F}_N$, from the track. Thus, the net force, $\mathbf{F}_w + \mathbf{F}_N$, provides the centripetal force. In order for the car to maintain contact with the track, $\mathbf{F}_N$ must not vanish. Therefore, the cut-off speed for ensuring that the car makes it safely around the track is the speed at which $\mathbf{F}_N$ just becomes zero; any greater speed would imply that the car would make it around. Thus,

$$F_w + F_N = m\frac{v^2}{r} \implies F_w + 0 = m\frac{v_{\text{cut-off}}^2}{r} \implies v_{\text{cut-off}} = \sqrt{\frac{rF_w}{m}} = \sqrt{gr}$$

(d) Using the cut-off speed calculated in part (c), we now apply Conservation of Mechanical Energy:

$$K_A + U_A = K_D + U_D$$

$$0 + mgH = \tfrac{1}{2}mv_{\text{cut-off}}^2 + mg(2r)$$

$$mgH = \tfrac{1}{2}m(gr) + mg(2r)$$

$$= \tfrac{5}{2}mgr$$

$$H = \tfrac{5}{2}r$$

(e) First, we calculate the car's kinetic energy at Point B; then, we determine the distance x the car must travel from B to F for the work done by friction to eliminate this kinetic energy. So, applying Conservation of Mechanical Energy, we find

$$K_A + U_A = K_B + U_B$$

$$0 + mg(6r) = \tfrac{1}{2}mv_B^2 + 0$$

$$6mgr = \tfrac{1}{2}mv_B^2$$

Now, by the work–energy theorem,

$$W = \Delta K = \tfrac{1}{2}mv_F^2 - \tfrac{1}{2}mv_B^2 = -\tfrac{1}{2}mv_B^2 \quad \Rightarrow \quad -F_f x = -\tfrac{1}{2}mv_B^2$$

$$-\mu mgx = -6mgr$$

$$x = \frac{6r}{\mu} = \frac{6r}{0.5} = 12r$$

3. (a) The point where $x = x_1$ is a local minimum of the function $U(x)$, and the point where $x = x_3$ is a local maximum. Therefore, at each of these locations, the derivative of $U(x)$ must be equal to 0.

$$\frac{dU}{dx} = 0 \quad \Rightarrow \quad 3 - 3(x-3)^2 = 0 \quad \Rightarrow \quad (x-3)^2 = 1 \quad \Rightarrow \quad x = 2 \text{ or } 4$$

Therefore, $x_1 = 2$ m and $x_3 = 4$ m.

(b) If the particle's total energy is $E_2 = \tfrac{1}{2}(E_1 + E_3) = \tfrac{1}{2}[U(\tfrac{1}{2}x_1) + U(x_1)] = \tfrac{1}{2}[U(2) + U(4)] = \tfrac{1}{2}(4\text{ J} + 8\text{ J}) = 6$ J, then the particle can oscillate between the points marked a and b in the figure below.

At points a and b, the object has no kinetic energy (since $U = E$ at these points), so these are the turning points at which the object momentarily comes to rest before being accelerated back toward $x = x_1$ (where the potential energy is minimized). The particle cannot be found at $x <$ a or within the interval $b < x < c$, since $U > E_2$ in these intervals (and this would imply a negative K, which is impossible). If $x > c$, then since U decreases, K increases: the particle would move off with increasing speed.

(c) Since $K + U = E$, we have $K = E - U$. Therefore,

$$
\begin{aligned}
K(x_1) &= E - U(x_1) \\
&= E - \left[3(x-1) - (x-3)^3 \right]_{x=2} \\
&= 58 \text{ J} - [(3-(-1)] \text{ J} \\
&= 54 \text{ J}
\end{aligned}
$$

Therefore,

$$
K = \tfrac{1}{2} m v_1^2 \quad \Rightarrow \quad v_1 = \sqrt{\frac{2K}{m}} = \sqrt{\frac{2(54 \text{ J})}{3 \text{ kg}}} = 6 \text{ m/s}
$$

(d) Since $F(x) = -dU/dx = -[3 - 3(x - 3)^2] = 3(x - 3)^2 - 3$, dividing by m gives a:

$$
a(x) = \frac{F(x)}{m} = \frac{[3(x-3)^2 - 3] \text{ J}}{3 \text{ kg}} = (x-3)^2 - 1 \ \ (\text{in m/s}^2)
$$

(e) At $x = \frac{1}{2}x_1$, the particle's energy is $E_3 = U(\frac{1}{2}x_1) = U(1) = \left[3(x-1)-(x-3)^3\right]_{x=1} = 8$ J.

This is the particle's total energy because it has no initial kinetic energy (it is released from rest). As the particle passes through $x = x_1$, its potential energy decreases to

$$U(x_1) = U(2) = \left[3(x-1)-(x-3)^3\right]_{x=2} = 4 \text{ J}$$

Therefore, since its total energy is 8 J, the particle's kinetic energy at $x = x_1$ must be $K = E - U = 8$ J $- 4$ J $= 4$ J. This implies that its speed is

$$K = \frac{1}{2}mv^2 \quad \Rightarrow \quad v = \sqrt{\frac{2K}{m}} = \sqrt{\frac{2(4 \text{ J})}{3 \text{ kg}}} = 1.6 \text{ m/s}$$

CHAPTER 5 REVIEW QUESTIONS

SECTION I: MULTIPLE CHOICE

1. **(C)** The magnitude of the object's linear momentum is $p = mv$. Since $p = 6$ kg $\cdot$ m/s and $m = 2$ kg, then $v = 3$ m/s. Therefore, the object's kinetic energy is $K = \frac{1}{2}mv^2 = \frac{1}{2}(2 \text{ kg})(3 \text{ m/s})^2 = 9$ J.

2. **(C)** The impulse delivered to the ball, $J = F\,\Delta t$, equals its change in momentum. Since the ball started from rest, we have

$$F\Delta t = mv \quad \Rightarrow \quad \Delta t = \frac{mv}{F} = \frac{(0.5 \text{ kg})(4 \text{ m/s})}{20 \text{ N}} = 0.1 \text{ s}$$

3. **(E)** The impulse delivered to the ball, $J = \bar{F}\Delta t$, equals its change in momentum. Thus,

$$\bar{F}\Delta t = \Delta p = p_f - p_i = m(v_f - v_i) \quad \Rightarrow \quad \bar{F} = \frac{m(v_f - v_i)}{\Delta t} = \frac{(2 \text{ kg})(8 \text{ m/s} - 4 \text{ m/s})}{0.5 \text{ s}} = 16 \text{ N}$$

4. **(D)** The impulse delivered to the ball is equal to its change in momentum. The momentum of the ball was $m\mathbf{v}$ before hitting the wall and $m(-\mathbf{v})$ after. Therefore, the change in momentum is $m(-\mathbf{v}) - m\mathbf{v} = -2m\mathbf{v}$, so the magnitude of the momentum change (and the impulse) is $2mv$.

5. **(B)** By definition of *perfectly inelastic*, the objects move off together with one common velocity, $\mathbf{v}'$, after the collision. By Conservation of Linear Momentum,

$$m_1\mathbf{v}_1 + m_2\mathbf{v}_2 = (m_1 + m_2)\mathbf{v}'$$
$$\mathbf{v}' = \frac{m_1 v_1 + m_2 v_2}{m_1 + m_2}$$
$$= \frac{(3 \text{ kg})(2 \text{ m/s}) + (5 \text{ kg})(-2 \text{ m/s})}{3 \text{ kg} + 5 \text{ kg}}$$
$$= -0.5 \text{ m/s}$$

6. **(D)** First, apply Conservation of Linear Momentum to calculate the speed of the combined object after the (perfectly inelastic) collision:

$$m_1 v_1 + m_2 v_2 = (m_1 + m_2)v'$$
$$v' = \frac{m_1 v_1 + m_2 v_2}{m_1 + m_2}$$
$$= \frac{m_1 v_1 + (2m_1)(0)}{m_1 + 2m_1}$$
$$= \frac{1}{3}v_1$$

Therefore, the ratio of the kinetic energy after the collision to the kinetic energy before the collision is

$$\frac{K'}{K} = \frac{\frac{1}{2}m'v'^2}{\frac{1}{2}m_1v_1^2} = \frac{\frac{1}{2}(m_1 + 2m_1)(\frac{1}{3}v_1)^2}{\frac{1}{2}m_1v_1^2} = \frac{1}{3}$$

7. **(C)** Total linear momentum is conserved in a collision during which the net external force is zero. If kinetic energy is lost, then by definition, the collision is not elastic.

8. **(B)** First replace each rod by concentrating its mass at its center of mass position:

The center of mass of the two m's is at their midpoint, at a distance of $\frac{1}{2}L$ below the center of mass of the rod of mass $2m$:

Now, applying the equation for locating the center of mass (letting $y = 0$ denote the position of the center of mass of the top horizontal rod), we find

$$y_{cm} = \frac{(2m)(0) + (2m)(\frac{1}{2}L)}{2m + 2m} = \frac{1}{4}L$$

9. **(D)** The linear momentum of the bullet must have the same magnitude as the linear momentum of the block in order for their combined momentum after impact to be zero. The block has momentum MV to the left, so the bullet must have momentum MV to the right. Since the bullet's mass is m, its speed must be $v = MV/m$.

10. **(C)** In a perfectly inelastic collision, kinetic energy is never conserved; some of the initial kinetic energy is always lost to heat and some is converted to potential energy in the deformed shapes of the objects as they lock together.

SECTION II: FREE RESPONSE

1. (a) First draw a free-body diagram:

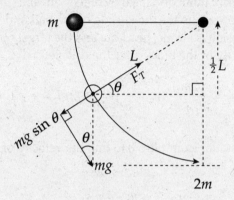

The net force toward the center of the steel ball's circular path provides the centripetal force. From the geometry of the diagram, we have

$$F_T - mg\sin\theta = \frac{mv^2}{L} \qquad (*)$$

In order to determine the value of mv^2, we use Conservation of Mechanical Energy:

$$K_i + U_i = K_f + U_f$$
$$0 + mgL = \tfrac{1}{2}mv^2 + mg(\tfrac{1}{2}L)$$
$$\tfrac{1}{2}mgL = \tfrac{1}{2}mv^2$$
$$mgL = mv^2$$

Substituting this result into Equation (*), we get

$$F_T - mg\sin\theta = \frac{mgL}{L}$$
$$F_T = mg(1+\sin\theta)$$

Now, from the free-body diagram we see that $\sin\theta = \tfrac{1}{2}L/L = \tfrac{1}{2}$, so

$$F_T = mg(1+\tfrac{1}{2}) = \tfrac{3}{2}mg$$

(b) Applying Conservation of Energy, we find the speed of the ball just before impact:

$$K_i + U_i = K_f + U_f$$
$$0 + mgL = \tfrac{1}{2}mv^2 + 0$$
$$v = \sqrt{2gL}$$

We can now use Conservation of Linear Momentum and the fact that kinetic energy is conserved to derive expressions for the speeds of the ball and block immediately after their collision. Since the collision is elastic, head-on, and the target object is at rest, this was done in Example 5.8. The velocity of the block after the collision is

$$v_2' = \frac{2m_1}{m_1 + m_2}v_1 = \frac{2m}{m + 4m}\sqrt{2gL} = \tfrac{2}{5}\sqrt{2gL}$$

(c) We can quote the result of Example 5.8 to find the velocity of the ball immediately after the collision:

$$v_1' = \frac{m_1 - m_2}{m_1 + m_2}v_1 = \frac{m - 4m}{m + 4m}\sqrt{2gL} = -\tfrac{3}{5}\sqrt{2gL}$$

Now, applying Conservation of Mechanical Energy, we find

$$K_i + U_i = K_f + U_f$$
$$\tfrac{1}{2}mv_1'^2 + 0 = 0 + mgh$$

$$h = \frac{v_1'^2}{2g} = \frac{\left(\tfrac{3}{5}\sqrt{2gL}\right)^2}{2g} = \tfrac{9}{25}L$$

2. (a) By Conservation of Linear Momentum, $mv = (m + M)$, v' so $v' = \dfrac{mv}{m + M}$.

Now, by Conservation of Mechanical Energy,

$$K_i + U_i = K_f + U_f$$
$$\tfrac{1}{2}(m + M)v'^2 + 0 = 0 + (m + M)gy$$
$$\tfrac{1}{2}v'^2 = gy$$
$$\tfrac{1}{2}\left(\frac{mv}{m + M}\right)^2 = gy$$
$$v = \frac{m + M}{m}\sqrt{2gy}$$

(b) Use the result derived in part (a) to compute the kinetic energy of the block and bullet immediately after the collision:

$$K' = \tfrac{1}{2}(m+M)v'^2 = \tfrac{1}{2}(m+M)\left(\frac{mv}{m+M}\right)^2 = \tfrac{1}{2}\frac{m^2v^2}{m+M}$$

Since $K = \tfrac{1}{2}mv^2$, the difference is

$$\Delta K = K' - K = \tfrac{1}{2}\frac{m^2v^2}{m+M} - \tfrac{1}{2}mv^2$$

$$= \tfrac{1}{2}mv^2\left(\frac{m}{m+M} - 1\right)$$

$$= K\left(\frac{-M}{m+M}\right)$$

Therefore, the fraction of the bullet's original kinetic energy that was lost is $M/(m+M)$. This energy is manifested as heat (the bullet and block are warmer after the collision than before), and some was used to break the intermolecular bonds within the wooden block to allow the bullet to penetrate.

(c) From the geometry of the diagram,

the Pythagorean theorem implies that $(L-y)^2 + x^2 = L^2$. Therefore,

$$L^2 - 2Ly + y^2 + x^2 = L^2 \quad \Rightarrow \quad y = \frac{x^2}{2L}$$

(where we have used the fact that y^2 is small enough to be neglected). Substituting this into the result of part (a), we derive the following equation for the speed of the bullet in terms of x and L instead of y:

$$v = \frac{m+M}{m}\sqrt{2gy} = \frac{m+M}{m}\sqrt{2g\frac{x^2}{2L}} = \frac{m+M}{m}x\sqrt{\frac{g}{L}}$$

(d) No; momentum is conserved only when the net external force on the system is zero (or at least negligible). In this case, the block and bullet feel a net nonzero force that causes it to slow down as it swings upward. Since its speed is decreasing as it swings upward, its linear momentum cannot remain constant.

3. (a) To apply Conservation of Linear Momentum to the collision, we recognize that momentum is a vector quantity and, therefore, linear momentum must be conserved separately in the horizontal (x) and vertical (y) directions. Before the collision, the linear momentum was horizontal only. Therefore, in the x direction:

$$mv = mv_1'\cos\theta_1 + mv_2'\cos\theta_2 \quad \Rightarrow \quad v = v_1'\cos\theta_1 + v_2'\cos\theta_2 \qquad (1)$$

in the y direction:

$$0 = mv_1'\sin\theta_1 - mv_2'\sin\theta_2 \quad \Rightarrow \quad 0 = v_1'\sin\theta_1 - v_2'\sin\theta_2 \qquad (2)$$

Since the collision is elastic, kinetic energy is also conserved; thus,

$$K = K_1' + K_2'$$
$$\tfrac{1}{2}mv^2 = \tfrac{1}{2}mv_1'^2 + \tfrac{1}{2}mv_2'^2$$
$$v^2 = v_1'^2 + v_2'^2 \qquad (3)$$

In order to find $K_1' = \tfrac{1}{2}mv_1'^2$ in terms of K_1 and θ_1 only, we need to manipulate the equations to eliminate v_2' and θ_2. The following approach will do this. Rewrite Equations (1) and (2) in the following forms:

$$v_2'\cos\theta_2 = v - v_1'\cos\theta_1 \quad (1')$$
$$v_2'\sin\theta_2 = v_1'\sin\theta_1 \qquad (2')$$

Square both equations and add, exploiting the trig identity $\cos^2\theta + \sin^2\theta = 1$:

$$v_2'^2\cos^2\theta_2 = v^2 - 2vv_1'\cos\theta_1 + v_1'^2\cos^2\theta_1$$
$$v_2'^2\sin^2\theta_2 = v_1'^2\sin^2\theta_1$$
$$v_2'^2 = v^2 - 2vv_1'\cos\theta_1 + v_1'^2 \quad (4)$$

This eliminates θ_2. Now, to eliminate v_2', substitute the value of $v_2'^2$ from Equation (3) into Equation (4):

$$v^2 - v_1'^2 = v^2 - 2vv_1'\cos\theta_1 + v_1'^2$$
$$-2v_1'^2 = -2vv_1'\cos\theta_1$$
$$v_1' = v\cos\theta_1$$

Therefore, we can write

$$K_1' = \tfrac{1}{2}mv_1'^2 = \tfrac{1}{2}m(v\cos\theta_1)^2 = (\cos^2\theta_1)\cdot\tfrac{1}{2}mv^2 = (\cos^2\theta_1)K_1$$

(b) Since, by Equation (3), $v_2'^2 = v^2 - v_1'^2$, the result of part (a) gives

$$K_2' = \tfrac{1}{2}mv_2'^2 = \tfrac{1}{2}m(v^2 - v_1'^2) = \tfrac{1}{2}mv^2 - \tfrac{1}{2}mv_1'^2$$
$$= K_1 - K_1'$$
$$= K_1 - (\cos^2\theta_1)K_1$$
$$= (1 - \cos^2\theta_1)K_1$$
$$= (\sin^2\theta_1)K_1$$

(c) Square Equation (1) and Equation (2) from part (a) and add:

$$v^2 = v_1'^2\cos^2\theta_1 + 2v_1'v_2'\cos\theta_1\cos\theta_2 + v_2'^2\cos^2\theta_2$$
$$0 = v_1'^2\sin^2\theta_1 - 2v_1'v_2'\sin\theta_1\sin\theta_2 + v_2'^2\sin^2\theta_2$$

Adding gives:

$$v^2 = v_1'^2 + 2v_1'v_2'(\cos\theta_1\cos\theta_2 - \sin\theta_1\sin\theta_2) + v_2'^2$$
$$v^2 = v_1'^2 + 2v_1'v_2'\cos(\theta_1 + \theta_2) + v_2'^2 \qquad (5)$$

Now, since by Equation (3), $v^2 = v_1'^2 + v_2'^2$, combining this with equation (5) gives

$$2v_1'v_2'\cos(\theta_1 + \theta_2) = 0$$
$$\cos(\theta_1 + \theta_2) = 0$$
$$\theta_1 + \theta_2 = 90°$$

Thus, the objects' post-collision velocity vectors are perpendicular to each other.

CHAPTER 6 REVIEW QUESTIONS

Section I: Multiple Choice

1. **(B)** We use the equation $v = r\omega$:

$$v = r\omega = 0.06 \text{ m} \times \left(\frac{5 \text{ rev}}{\text{s}} \times \frac{2\pi \text{ rad}}{\text{rev}} \right) = (0.6)\pi \text{ m/s} = 1.9 \text{ m/s}$$

2. **(E)** Use the equation *distance* = *rate* × *time* with $v = r\omega$:

$$s = vt = r\omega t = 0.06 \text{ m} \times \left(\frac{5 \text{ rev}}{\text{s}} \times \frac{2\pi \text{ rad}}{\text{rev}} \right) \times \left(40 \text{ min} \times \frac{60 \text{ s}}{\text{min}} \right) = 4500 \text{ m}$$

3. **(C)** By combining the equation for centripetal acceleration, $a_c = v^2/r$, with $v = r\omega$, we find

$$a_c = \frac{v^2}{r} = \frac{(r\omega)^2}{r} = \omega^2 r \quad \Rightarrow \quad \omega = \sqrt{\frac{a_c}{r}} = \sqrt{\frac{9 \text{ m/s}^2}{0.25 \text{ m}}} = 6 \text{ s}^{-1}$$

4. **(C)** Use Big Five #3 for rotational motion:

$$\Delta\theta = \omega_0 t + \tfrac{1}{2}\alpha t^2 = \tfrac{1}{2}\alpha t^2 \quad \Rightarrow \quad \alpha = \frac{2\Delta\theta}{t^2} = \frac{2(60 \text{ rad})}{(10 \text{ s})^2} = 1.2 \text{ rad/s}^2$$

5. **(D)** The torque is $\tau = rF = (0.20 \text{ m})(20 \text{ N}) = 4 \text{ N} \cdot \text{m}$.

6. **(D)** From the diagram,

we calculate that

$$\tau = rF \sin\theta = Lmg \sin\theta$$

$$= (0.80 \text{ m})(0.50 \text{ kg})(9.8 \text{ N/kg})(\sin 30^\circ)$$

$$= 2.0 \text{ N} \cdot \text{m}$$

7. **(B)** The stick will remain at rest in the horizontal position if the torques about the suspension point are balanced:

$$\tau_{CCW} = \tau_{CW}$$
$$r_1 F_1 = r_2 F_2$$
$$r_1 m_1 g = r_2 m_2 g$$
$$m_2 = \frac{r_1 m_1}{r_2} = \frac{(50 \text{ cm})(3 \text{ kg})}{30 \text{ cm}} = 5 \text{ kg}$$

8. **(E)** Each of the four masses is at distance L from the rotation axis, so

$$I = \sum m_i r_i^2 = mL^2 + mL^2 + mL^2 + mL^2 = 4mL^2$$

Notice that the length of the rectangular frame, $\frac{8}{3}L$, is irrelevant here.

9. **(A)** By Conservation of Mechanical Energy,

$$K_i + U_i = K_f + U_f$$
$$0 + Mgh = (\tfrac{1}{2}I\omega^2 + \tfrac{1}{2}Mv_{cm}^2) + 0$$
$$= \tfrac{1}{2}(\tfrac{2}{5}MR^2)\left(\frac{v_{cm}}{R}\right)^2 + \tfrac{1}{2}Mv_{cm}^2$$
$$= \tfrac{7}{10}Mv_{cm}^2$$
$$v_{cm} = \sqrt{\tfrac{10}{7}gh}$$

10. **(B)** By Conservation of Angular Momentum,

$$L_i = L_f \quad \Rightarrow \quad I_i \omega_i = I_f \omega_f \quad \Rightarrow \quad \omega_f = \frac{I_i \omega_i}{I_f} = \frac{I_i \omega}{2I_i} = \frac{\omega}{2}$$

SECTION II: FREE RESPONSE

1. (a) Apply conservation of mechanical energy, remembering to take into account the translational kinetic energy of the falling block (m_2), the rising block (m_1), and the rotating pulley:

$$K_i + U_i = K_f + U_f$$

$$0 + m_2 gh = \left(\tfrac{1}{2} m_1 v^2 + \tfrac{1}{2} m_2 v^2 + \tfrac{1}{2} I \omega^2 \right) + m_1 gh$$

$$= \left[\tfrac{1}{2} m_1 v^2 + \tfrac{1}{2} m_2 v^2 + \tfrac{1}{2} \left(\tfrac{1}{2} MR^2 \right) \left(\frac{v}{R} \right)^2 \right] + m_1 gh$$

$$(m_2 - m_1) gh = \tfrac{1}{2} v^2 \left(m_1 + m_2 + \tfrac{1}{2} M \right)$$

$$v = \sqrt{ \frac{2(m_2 - m_1) gh}{m_1 + m_2 + \tfrac{1}{2} M} }$$

(b) Using the equation $v = R\omega$, we find

$$\omega = \frac{v}{R} = \frac{1}{R} \sqrt{ \frac{2(m_2 - m_1) gh}{m_1 + m_2 + \tfrac{1}{2} M} }$$

(c) Since Block 2 (and Block 1) moved a distance h during the motion, a point on the rim of the pulley must also move through a distance h. Therefore, $\Delta \theta = h/R$.

(d) Use Big Five #1 (for translational motion):

$$\Delta t = \frac{\Delta s}{\overline{v}} = \frac{\Delta s}{\tfrac{1}{2} v} = \frac{2\Delta s}{v} = \frac{2h}{v} = 2h \sqrt{ \frac{m_1 + m_2 + \tfrac{1}{2} M}{2(m_2 - m_1) gh} } = h \sqrt{ \frac{2m_1 + 2m_2 + M}{(m_2 - m_1) gh} }$$

2. (a) Consider the following diagram of the disk rolling down the ramp:

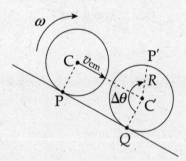

In a time interval Δt, the center of mass moves from C to C′, a distance equal to $v_{cm} \Delta t$. While this is occurring, the point P on the rim moves to the new position P′. In order for there to be no slipping, the arc length P′Q, which is $R \Delta \theta$, must equal the straight line distance PQ. But PQ = CC′, so we have

$$v_{cm} \Delta t = R\Delta \theta \quad \Rightarrow \quad v_{cm} \Delta t = R\omega \Delta t \quad \Rightarrow \quad v_{cm} = R\omega$$

(b) One way to derive the desired result is to notice that the velocity of T relative to P is equal to the velocity of T relative to C plus the velocity of C relative to P ($\mathbf{v}_{TP} = \mathbf{v}_{TC} + \mathbf{v}_{CP}$).

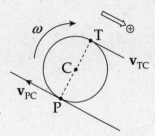

Since the velocity of C relative to P is the opposite of the velocity of P relative to C ($\mathbf{v}_{CP} = -\mathbf{v}_{PC}$), we have $\mathbf{v}_{TP} = \mathbf{v}_{TC} - \mathbf{v}_{PC}$. Relative to C, point T is moving forward with speed $R\omega$ and point P is moving backward with speed $R\omega$. Therefore, $\mathbf{v}_{TP} = (+R\omega) - (-R\omega) = +2R\omega = 2\mathbf{v}_{cm}$.

Another method is to think of the disk as executing pure rotation instantaneously about the contact Point P. From this point of view (with P as pivot), the distance to C is R, and the distance to T is $2R$. Therefore, the linear speed of C is $R\omega$ and that of T is $2R\omega$, which implies that the linear speed of point T is twice that of point C, as desired.

(c) The speed with which the block rises, v_b, is equal to the speed at which the thread wraps around the cylinder, which is $2v_{cm}$, as shown in part (b). Therefore, differentiating the equation $v_b = 2v_{cm}$ with respect to time, we get $a_b = 2a_{cm}$. That is, the acceleration of the block is equal to twice that of the (center of mass of the) cylinder.

(d) First draw free-body diagrams for the block and the cylinder:

Newton's Second Law applied to the block yields $F_T - mg = ma_b$. Since $a_b = 2a_{cm}$, we write

$$F_T - mg = 2ma_{cm} \quad (1)$$

Newton's Second Law applied to the forces on the cylinder gives us

$$Mg \sin\theta - F_f - F_T = Ma_{cm} \quad (2)$$

The tension force and friction force each exert a torque about the center of mass of the cylinder. The torque of the friction force is counterclockwise (positive), and the torque of the tension force is negative. Therefore, $\tau_{net} = I\alpha$ becomes

$$RF_f - RF_T = \tfrac{1}{2}MR^2 \cdot \frac{a_{cm}}{R}$$

$$F_f - F_T = \tfrac{1}{2}Ma_{cm} \qquad (3)$$

Now for the algebra. Adding Equations (2) and (3) gives $Mg\sin\theta - 2F_T = \tfrac{3}{2}Ma_{cm}$. Multiplying both sides of the equation by 1 gives $2F_T - 2mg = 4ma_{cm}$. Adding these last two equations allows us to find a_{cm}, the linear acceleration of the cylinder:

$$Mg\sin\theta - 2mg = \left(\tfrac{3}{2}M + 4m\right)a_{cm} \quad \Rightarrow \quad a_{cm} = \frac{M\sin\theta - 2m}{\tfrac{3}{2}M + 4m}g$$

(d) Since $a_b = 2a_{cm}$, the acceleration of the block is

$$a_b = \frac{2(M\sin\theta - 2m)}{\dfrac{3}{2}M + 4m}g$$

3. (a) Consider a rod of length $2L$ with the pivot at its center. Since the rod is uniform, its linear mass density is $M/(2L)$, so the mass of a segment of length dx is $M\,dx/(2L)$.

Applying the definition of I, we find

$$I = \int r^2\,dm = \int_{-L}^{L} x^2 \cdot \tfrac{m}{2L}\,dx = \tfrac{m}{2L}\left[\tfrac{1}{3}x^3\right]_{-L}^{L} = \tfrac{m}{2L}\left[\tfrac{2}{3}L^3\right] = \tfrac{1}{3}ML^2$$

(b) We apply conservation of angular momentum to the collision of the bullet and assembly. Since the rods were at rest prior to the bullet's impact, only the bullet had angular momentum. With respect to the pivot point, its angular momentum was $Lm_b v_\perp$, where $v_\perp$ is the component of $\mathbf{v}$ that is perpendicular to the radius vector. From the definition of θ in the figure given with the question, $v_\perp = v\cos\theta$. After the collision, the angular momentum is equal to the angular velocity of the assembly times the rotational inertia of the four clay balls, the two rods, and the embedded bullet. We get:

$$Lm_b v\cos\theta = \left[4mL^2 + 2\left(\tfrac{1}{3}ML^2\right) + m_b L^2\right]\omega_f$$

$$\omega_f = \frac{m_b v\cos\theta}{L\left(4m + \tfrac{2}{3}M + m_b\right)}$$

(c) Using the equation $v = R\omega$, we find that

$$v_f = L\omega_f = \frac{m_b v \cos\theta}{4m + \frac{2}{3}M + m_b}$$

(d) After the collision, the assembly has rotational kinetic energy. The ratio of this energy to the (translational) kinetic energy of the bullet before impact is

$$\frac{K'}{K} = \frac{\frac{1}{2}I\omega_f^2}{\frac{1}{2}m_b v^2} = \frac{\left(4mL^2 + \frac{2}{3}ML^2 + m_b L^2\right)\left[\dfrac{m_b v \cos\theta}{L\left(4m + \frac{2}{3}M + m_b\right)}\right]^2}{m_b v^2}$$

$$= \frac{m_b \cos^2\theta}{4m + \frac{2}{3}M + m_b}$$

CHAPTER 7 REVIEW QUESTIONS

SECTION I: MULTIPLE CHOICE

1. **(A)** Gravitational force obeys an inverse-square law: $F_{grav} \propto 1/r^2$. Therefore, if r increases by a factor of 2, then F_{grav} decreases by a factor of $2^2 = 4$.

2. **(E)** Mass is an intrinsic property of an object and does not change with location. This eliminates choices A and C. If an object's height above the surface of the earth is equal to $2R_E$, then its distance from the center of the earth is $3R_E$. Thus, the object's distance from the earth's center increases by a factor of 3, so its weight decreases by a factor of $3^2 = 9$.

3. **(C)** The gravitational force that the moon exerts on the planet is equal in magnitude to the gravitational force that the planet exerts on the moon (Newton's Third Law).

4. **(D)** The gravitational acceleration at the surface of a planet of mass M and radius R is given by the equation $g = GM/R^2$. Therefore,

$$g_{Pluto} = G\frac{M_{Pluto}}{R_{Pluto}^2} = G\frac{\frac{1}{500}M_{Earth}}{\left(\frac{1}{15}R_{Earth}\right)^2} = \frac{15^2}{500} \cdot G\frac{M_{Earth}}{R_{Earth}^2} = \frac{225}{500}(9.8 \text{ m}/\text{s}^2) = 4.4 \text{ m}/\text{s}^2$$

5. **(B)** The gravitational pull by the earth provides the centripetal force on the satellite, so $GMm/R^2 = mv^2/R$. This gives $\frac{1}{2}mv^2 = GMm/2R$, so the kinetic energy K of the satellite is inversely proportional to R. Therefore if R increases by a factor of 2, then K decreases by a factor of 2.

6. **(E)** The gravitational pull by Jupiter provides the centripetal force on its moon:

$$G\frac{Mm}{R^2} = \frac{mv^2}{R}$$

$$G\frac{M}{R} = v^2$$

$$= \left(\frac{2\pi R}{T}\right)^2$$

$$= \frac{4\pi^2 R^2}{T^2}$$

$$M = \frac{4\pi^2 R^3}{GT^2}$$

7. **(E)** Let the object's distance from Body A be x; then its distance from Body B is $R - x$. In order for the object to feel no net gravitational force, the gravitational pull by A must balance the gravitational pull by B. Therefore, if we let M denote the mass of the object, then

$$G\frac{m_A M}{x^2} = G\frac{m_B M}{(R-x)^2}$$

$$\frac{m}{x^2} = \frac{4m}{(R-x)^2}$$

$$\frac{(R-x)^2}{x^2} = \frac{4m}{m}$$

$$\left(\frac{R-x}{x}\right)^2 = 4$$

$$\left(\frac{R}{x} - 1\right)^2 = 4$$

$$\frac{R}{x} - 1 = 2$$

$$x = R/3$$

8. **(B)** Kepler's Third Law says that $T^2 \propto R^3$ for a planet with a circular orbit of radius R. Since $T \propto R^{3/2}$, if R increases by a factor of 9, then T increases by a factor of $9^{3/2} = (3^2)^{3/2} = 3^3 = 27$.

9. **(D)** Apply conservation of mechanical energy:

$$K_i + U_i = K_f + U_f$$

$$0 - G\frac{Mm}{3R} = \tfrac{1}{2}mv_f^2 - G\frac{Mm}{R}$$

$$\tfrac{1}{2}mv_f^2 = G\frac{2Mm}{3R}$$

$$v_f = \sqrt{\frac{\tfrac{4}{3}GM}{R}}$$

10. **(E)** Recall Example 7.8, where we used conservation of angular momentum to find that the ratio of a satellite's speed at aphelion to its speed at perihelion is given by the expression r_2/r_1, where r_2 is the satellite's perihelion distance and r_1 is its aphelion distance from the Sun.

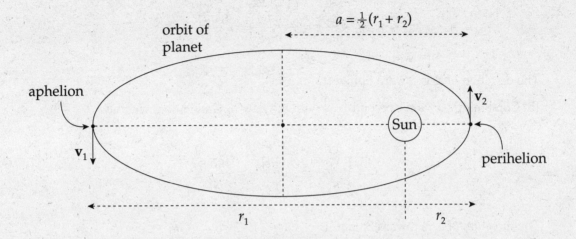

The ratio asked for in the present question is therefore r_1/r_2, which we must write in terms of the eccentricity, e, of the planet's orbit. The semimajor axis is $a = \frac{1}{2}(r_1 + r_2)$, so the distance from the center of the ellipse to the Sun is $c = a - r_2 = \frac{1}{2}(r_1 + r_2) - r_2 = \frac{1}{2}(r_1 - r_2)$. Since, by definition, $e = c/a$, we have

$$e = \frac{\frac{1}{2}(r_1 - r_2)}{\frac{1}{2}(r_1 + r_2)} = \frac{r_1 - r_2}{r_1 + r_2} = \frac{\frac{r_1}{r_2} - \frac{r_2}{r_2}}{\frac{r_1}{r_2} + \frac{r_2}{r_2}} = \frac{\frac{r_1}{r_2} - 1}{\frac{r_1}{r_2} + 1} = \frac{b - 1}{b + 1}$$

where $b = r_1/r_2$. Solving this equation for b in terms of e, we get

$$e = \frac{b-1}{b+1} \quad \Rightarrow \quad be + e = b - 1 \quad \Rightarrow \quad b - be = 1 + e \quad \Rightarrow \quad b = \frac{1+e}{1-e}$$

Therefore,

$$\frac{v_{\text{at perihelion}}}{v_{\text{at aphelion}}} = \frac{v_2}{v_1} = \frac{r_1}{r_2} = \frac{1+e}{1-e}$$

SECTION II: FREE RESPONSE

1. (a) Combining Newton's Second Law with the Law of Gravitation, we find

$$a_1 = \frac{F_{2\text{-on-}1}}{m_1} = \frac{G\frac{m_1 m_2}{(\frac{1}{2}R)^2}}{m_1} = \frac{4Gm_2}{R^2}$$

The direction of $\mathbf{a}_1$ is toward Sphere 2.

(b) Combining Newton's Second Law with the Law of Gravitation, we find

$$a_2 = \frac{F_{1\text{-on-}2}}{m_2} = \frac{G\frac{m_1 m_2}{(\frac{1}{2}R)^2}}{m_2} = \frac{4Gm_1}{R^2}$$

The direction of $\mathbf{a}_2$ is toward Sphere 1.

(c) Since the two spheres start from rest, the total linear momentum of the system is clearly zero. Since no external forces act (we're in "deep space"), the total momentum must remain zero during their motion toward each other. Therefore, the magnitude of Sphere 1's linear momentum, $m_1 v_1$, must always equal the magnitude of Sphere 2's linear momentum, $m_2 v_2$. Thus, $v_2 = (m_1/m_2)v_1$. With this result, we can apply conservation of mechanical energy:

$$K_i + U_i = K_f + U_f$$

$$0 - \frac{Gm_1 m_2}{R} = \tfrac{1}{2}m_1 v_1^2 + \tfrac{1}{2}m_2 v_2^2 - \frac{Gm_1 m_2}{R/2}$$

$$\frac{Gm_1 m_2}{R} = \tfrac{1}{2}m_1 v_1^2 + \tfrac{1}{2}m_2 \left(\tfrac{m_1}{m_2}v_1\right)^2$$

$$\frac{Gm_2}{R} = \tfrac{1}{2}v_1^2 \left(1 + \tfrac{m_1}{m_2}\right)$$

$$v_1 = \sqrt{\frac{2Gm_2}{R\left(1 + \tfrac{m_1}{m_2}\right)}}$$

$$= m_2\sqrt{\frac{2G}{R(m_1 + m_2)}}$$

(d) Using the result of part (c) and the relationship $v_2 = (m_1/m_2)v_1$, we get

$$v_2 = \tfrac{m_1}{m_2}v_1 = \tfrac{m_1}{m_2} \cdot m_2\sqrt{\frac{2G}{R(m_1 + m_2)}} = m_1\sqrt{\frac{2G}{R(m_1 + m_2)}}$$

(e) The centripetal force on each sphere is provided by the gravitational pull by the other sphere.

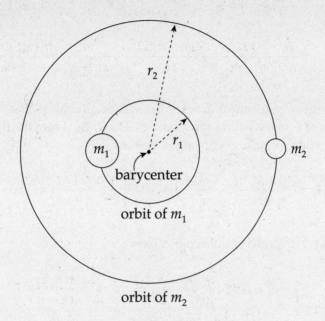

barycenter

orbit of m_1

orbit of m_2

Therefore,

$$\frac{m_1 v_1^2}{r_1} = \frac{G m_1 m_2}{(r_1 + r_2)^2} = \frac{m_2 v_2^2}{r_2}$$

Since both spheres have the same orbit period, T, we get

$$\frac{m_1 v_1^2}{r_1} = \frac{m_2 v_2^2}{r_2} \quad \Rightarrow \quad \frac{m_1}{r_1}\left(\frac{2\pi r_1}{T}\right)^2 = \frac{m_2}{r_2}\left(\frac{2\pi r_2}{T}\right)^2 \quad \Rightarrow \quad m_1 r_1 = m_2 r_2 \qquad (1)$$

We can also derive (as we did in Example 7.9), that

$$\frac{T^2}{(r_1 + r_2)^3} = \frac{4\pi^2}{G(m_1 + m_2)} \quad \Rightarrow \quad r_1 + r_2 = \sqrt[3]{\frac{G(m_1 + m_2)T^2}{4\pi^2}} \qquad (2)$$

Substituting the result of Equation (1), $r_2 = (m_1/m_2)r_1$, into Equation (2), we can solve for r_1:

$$r_1 + r_2 = \sqrt[3]{\frac{G(m_1 + m_2)T^2}{4\pi^2}}$$

$$r_1 + \tfrac{m_1}{m_2} r_1 =$$

$$r_1\left(1 + \tfrac{m_1}{m_2}\right) =$$

$$r_1 = \frac{m_2}{m_1 + m_2} \sqrt[3]{\frac{G(m_1 + m_2)T^2}{4\pi^2}}$$

and then for r_2:

$$r_2 = \frac{m_1}{m_2} r_1 = \frac{m_1}{m_2} \cdot \frac{m_2}{m_1 + m_2} \sqrt[3]{\frac{G(m_1 + m_2)T^2}{4\pi^2}} = \frac{m_1}{m_1 + m_2} \sqrt[3]{\frac{G(m_1 + m_2)T^2}{4\pi^2}}$$

2. (a) The total energy of a satellite of mass m in an elliptical orbit with semimajor axis a around a planet of mass M is given by the equation $E = -GmM/2a$. From the figure, we see that $2a = r_1 + r_2$, so the satellite's kinetic energy at perigee is

$$K_1 = E - U_1 = -\frac{GmM}{r_1 + r_2} - \left(-\frac{GmM}{r_1}\right) = GmM\left(\frac{1}{r_1} - \frac{1}{r_1 + r_2}\right) = GmM\frac{r_2}{r_1(r_1 + r_2)}$$

Its speed at this point is then calculated as follows:

$$\tfrac{1}{2}mv_1^2 = GmM\frac{r_2}{r_1(r_1 + r_2)} \quad \Rightarrow \quad v_1 = \sqrt{\frac{2GMr_2}{r_1(r_1 + r_2)}}$$

(b) Employing the same method as used in part (a), we find

$$K_2 = E - U_2 = -\frac{GmM}{r_1 + r_2} - \left(-\frac{GmM}{r_2}\right) = GmM\left(\frac{1}{r_2} - \frac{1}{r_1 + r_2}\right) = GmM\frac{r_1}{r_2(r_1 + r_2)}$$

so

$$\tfrac{1}{2}mv_2^2 = GmM\frac{r_1}{r_2(r_1 + r_2)} \quad \Rightarrow \quad v_2 = \sqrt{\frac{2GMr_1}{r_2(r_1 + r_2)}}$$

(c) The ratio of v_1 to v_2 is

$$\frac{v_1}{v_2} = \frac{\sqrt{\dfrac{2GMr_2}{r_1(r_1 + r_2)}}}{\sqrt{\dfrac{2GMr_1}{r_2(r_1 + r_2)}}} = \frac{\sqrt{\dfrac{r_2}{r_1}}}{\sqrt{\dfrac{r_1}{r_2}}} = \sqrt{\frac{r_2}{r_1}} \cdot \sqrt{\frac{r_2}{r_1}} = \frac{r_2}{r_1}$$

(d) Since $\mathbf{v}_2$ is perpendicular to $\mathbf{r}_2$, the satellite's angular momentum is

$$L_2 = r_2 m v_2 = r_2 m \sqrt{\frac{2GMr_1}{r_2(r_1 + r_2)}} = m\sqrt{\frac{2GMr_1 r_2}{r_1 + r_2}}$$

(e) The distance from X to the center of the earth is equal to the semimajor axis, $a = \frac{1}{2}(r_1 + r_2)$. (This is because the sum of the distances from *any* point on the ellipse to the two foci must equal $2a = r_1 + r_2$, and X is equidistant from the two foci, one of which is at the center of the earth.) Therefore, the kinetic energy of the satellite when it's at X is

$$K_X = E - U_X = -\frac{GmM}{r_1 + r_2} - \left[-\frac{GmM}{\frac{1}{2}(r_1 + r_2)} \right] = \frac{GmM}{r_1 + r_2}$$

so its speed at this point is can be determined:

$$\frac{1}{2}mv_X^2 = \frac{GmM}{r_1 + r_2} \quad \Rightarrow \quad v_X = \sqrt{\frac{2GM}{r_1 + r_2}}$$

(f) [See Example 7.8(c)] Use Kepler's Third Law for elliptical orbits:

$$\frac{T^2}{a^3} = \frac{4\pi^2}{GM} \quad \Rightarrow \quad T = \sqrt{\frac{4\pi^2 a^3}{GM}} = \sqrt{\frac{4\pi^2 [\frac{1}{2}(r_1 + r_2)]^3}{GM}} = \sqrt{\frac{\pi^2 (r_1 + r_2)^3}{2GM}}$$

(g) By definition, $e = c/a$, where c is the distance from the center of the ellipse to either focus and a is the length of the semimajor axis. From the figure given with the question, we have

$$e = \frac{c}{a} = \frac{a - r_1}{a} = \frac{\frac{1}{2}(r_1 + r_2) - r_1}{\frac{1}{2}(r_1 + r_2)} = \frac{\frac{1}{2}(r_2 - r_1)}{\frac{1}{2}(r_2 + r_1)} = \frac{r_2 - r_1}{r_2 + r_1},$$

CHAPTER 8 REVIEW QUESTIONS

SECTION I: MULTIPLE CHOICE

1. **(D)** The acceleration of a simple harmonic oscillator is not constant, since the restoring force—and, consequently, the acceleration—depends on position. Therefore Statement I is false. However, both Statements II and III are fundamental, defining characteristics of simple harmonic motion.

2. **(C)** The acceleration of the block has its maximum magnitude at the points where its displacement from equilibrium has the maximum magnitude (since $a = F/m = kx/m$). At the endpoints of the oscillation region, the potential energy is maximized and the kinetic energy (and hence the speed) is zero.

3. **(E)** By conservation of mechanical energy, $K + U_s$ is a constant for the motion of the block. At the endpoints of the oscillation region, the block's displacement, x, is equal to $\pm A$. Since $K = 0$ here, all the energy is in the form of potential energy of the spring, $\frac{1}{2}kA^2$. Because $\frac{1}{2}kA^2$ gives the total energy at these positions, it also gives the total energy at any other position. Using the equation $U_s(x) = \frac{1}{2}kx^2$, we find that, at $x = \frac{1}{2}A$,

$$K + U_S = \tfrac{1}{2}kA^2$$
$$K + \tfrac{1}{2}k(\tfrac{1}{2}A)^2 = \tfrac{1}{2}kA^2$$
$$K = \tfrac{3}{8}kA^2$$

Therefore,

$$K/E = \tfrac{3}{8}kA^2 \big/ \tfrac{1}{2}kA^2 = \tfrac{3}{4}.$$

4. **(C)** As we derived in Example 8.2, the maximum speed of the block is given by the equation $v_{max} = A\sqrt{k/m}$. Therefore, v_{max} is inversely proportional to $\sqrt{m}$. If m is increased by a factor of 2, then v_{max} will decrease by a factor of $\sqrt{2}$.

5. **(D)** The period of a spring–block simple harmonic oscillator is independent of the value of g. (Recall that $T = 2\pi\sqrt{m/k}$.) Therefore, the period will remain the same.

6. **(D)** The frequency of a spring–block simple harmonic oscillator is given by the equation $f = (1/2\pi)\sqrt{k/m}$. Squaring both sides of this equation, we get $f^2 = (k/4\pi^2)(1/m)$. Therefore, if f^2 is plotted vs. $(1/m)$, then the graph will be a straight line with slope $k/4\pi^2$. (Note: The slope of the line whose equation is $y = ax$ is a.)

7. **(A)** First we find the angular frequency:

$$\omega = 2\pi f = \sqrt{\frac{k}{m}} = \sqrt{\frac{400 \text{ N}/\text{m}}{4 \text{ kg}}} = 10 \text{ s}^{-1}$$

Therefore, the equation that gives the block's position, $x = A \sin(\omega t + \phi_0)$, becomes $x = 6 \sin(10t + \phi_0)$. Because the block is at $x = 6$ cm at time $t = 0$, the initial phase angle ϕ_0 must be $\tfrac{1}{2}\pi$.

8. **(A)** Starting with the equation $x = A\sin(\omega t + \phi_0)$, we differentiate with respect to t to find the velocity function: $v = \dot{x} = A\omega\cos(\omega t + \phi_0)$. Since the maximum value of $\cos(\omega t + \phi_0)$ is 1, the maximum value of v is $v_{max} = A\omega$.

9. **(C)** For small angular displacements, the period of a simple pendulum is essentially independent of amplitude.

10. **(B)** First draw a free-body diagram:

The net force toward the center of the bob's circular path is $F_T - mg \cos \theta_{max}$. This must provide the centripetal force, mv^2/L. But since the speed of the bob at this moment is zero ($v = 0$), we get $F_T = mg \cos \theta_{max}$. [The acceleration is purely tangential here, equal to $(mg \sin \theta_{max})/m = g \sin \theta_{max}$.]

SECTION II: FREE RESPONSE

1. (a) Since the spring is compressed to $\frac{3}{4}$ its natural length, the block's position relative to equilibrium is $x = -\frac{1}{4}L$. Therefore, from $F_S = -kx$, we find

$$a = \frac{F_S}{m} = \frac{-k(-\frac{1}{4}L)}{m} = \frac{kL}{4m}$$

(b) Let v_1 denote the velocity of Block 1 just before impact, and let v_1' and v_2' denote, respectively, the velocities of Block 1 and Block 2 immediately after impact. By conservation of linear momentum, we write $mv_1 = mv_1' + mv_2'$, or

$$v_1 = v_1' + v_2' \qquad (1)$$

The initial kinetic energy of Block 1 is $\frac{1}{2}mv_1^2$. If half is lost to heat, then $\frac{1}{4}mv_1^2$ is left to be shared by Block 1 and Block 2 after impact: $\frac{1}{4}mv_1^2 = \frac{1}{2}mv_1'^2 + \frac{1}{2}mv_2'^2$, or

$$v_1^2 = 2v_1'^2 + 2v_2'^2 \qquad (2)$$

Square Equation (1) and multiply by 2 to give

$$2v_1^2 = 2v_1'^2 + 4v_1'v_2' + 2v_2'^2 \qquad (1')$$

then subtract Equation (2) from Equation (1′):

$$v_1^2 = 4v_1'v_2' \qquad (3)$$

Square Equation (1) again,

$$v_1^2 = v_1'^2 + 2v_1'v_2' + v_2'^2$$

and substitute into this the result of Equation (3):

$$4v_1'v_2' = v_1'^2 + 2v_1'v_2' + v_2'^2$$
$$0 = v_1'^2 - 2v_1'v_2' + v_2'^2$$
$$0 = (v_1' - v_2')^2$$
$$v_1' = v_2' \qquad (4)$$

Thus, combining Equations (1) and (4), we find that

$$v_1' = v_2' = \tfrac{1}{2}v_1$$

(c) When Block 1 reaches its new amplitude position, A', all of its kinetic energy is converted to elastic potential energy of the spring. That is,

$$K_1' \to U_S' \quad \Rightarrow \quad \tfrac{1}{2}mv_1'^2 = \tfrac{1}{2}kA'^2$$
$$A'^2 = \frac{m}{k}v_1'^2$$
$$A'^2 = \frac{m}{k}(\tfrac{1}{2}v_1)^2$$
$$A'^2 = \frac{mv_1^2}{4k} \qquad (1)$$

But the original potential energy of the spring, $U_S = \tfrac{1}{2}k(-\tfrac{1}{4}L)^2$, gave K_1:

$$U_S \to K_1 \quad \Rightarrow \quad \tfrac{1}{2}k(-\tfrac{1}{4}L)^2 = \tfrac{1}{2}mv_1^2 \quad \Rightarrow \quad mv_1^2 = \tfrac{1}{16}kL^2 \qquad (2)$$

Substituting this result into Equation (1) gives

$$A'^2 = \frac{\tfrac{1}{16}kL^2}{4k} = \frac{L^2}{64} \quad \Rightarrow \quad A' = \tfrac{1}{8}L$$

(d) The period of a spring–block simple harmonic oscillator depends only on the spring constant k and the mass of the block. Since neither of these changes, the period will remain the same; that is, $T' = T_0$.

(e) As we showed in part (a), Block 2's velocity as it slides off the table is $\frac{1}{2}v_1$ (horizontally). The time required to drop the vertical distance H is found as follows (calling *down* the positive direction):

$$\Delta y = v_{0y} + \tfrac{1}{2}gt^2 \quad \Rightarrow \quad H = \tfrac{1}{2}gt^2 \quad \Rightarrow \quad t = \sqrt{\frac{2H}{g}}$$

Therefore,

$$R = (\tfrac{1}{2}v_1)t = \tfrac{1}{2}v_1\sqrt{\frac{2H}{g}}$$

Now, from Equation (2) of part (c), $v_1 = \sqrt{kL^2/16m}$, so

$$R = \tfrac{1}{2}\sqrt{\frac{kL^2}{16m}}\sqrt{\frac{2H}{g}} = \frac{L}{8}\sqrt{\frac{2kH}{mg}}$$

2. (a) By conservation of linear momentum,

$$mv = (m+M)v' \quad \Rightarrow \quad v' = \frac{mv}{m+M}$$

(b) When the block is at its amplitude position (maximum compression of spring), the kinetic energy it (and the embedded bullet) had just after impact will become potential energy of the spring:

$$K' \to U_S$$

$$\tfrac{1}{2}(m+M)\left(\frac{mv}{m+M}\right)^2 = \tfrac{1}{2}kA^2$$

$$A = \frac{mv}{\sqrt{k(m+M)}}$$

(c) Since the mass on the spring is $m + M$, $f = \dfrac{1}{2\pi}\sqrt{\dfrac{k}{m+M}}$.

(d) The position of the block is given by the equation $x = A\sin(\omega t + \phi_0)$, where $\omega = 2\pi f$ and A is the amplitude. Since $x = 0$ at time $t = 0$, the initial phase, ϕ_0, is 0. From the results of parts (b) and (c), we have

$$x = A\sin(2\pi ft) = \frac{mv}{\sqrt{k(m+M)}}\sin\left(t\sqrt{\frac{k}{m+M}}\right)$$

3. (a) By conservation of mechanical energy, $K + U = E$, so

$$\tfrac{1}{2}Mv^2 + \tfrac{1}{2}k(\tfrac{1}{2}A)^2 = \tfrac{1}{2}kA^2$$

$$\tfrac{1}{2}Mv^2 = \tfrac{3}{8}kA^2$$

$$v = A\sqrt{\frac{3k}{4M}}$$

(b) Since the clay ball delivers no horizontal linear momentum to the block, horizontal linear momentum is conserved. Thus,

$$Mv = (M+m)v'$$

$$v' = \frac{Mv}{M+m} = \frac{MA}{M+m}\sqrt{\frac{3k}{4M}} = \frac{A}{M+m}\sqrt{\frac{3kM}{4}}$$

(c) Applying the general equation for the period of spring–block simple harmonic oscillator,

$$T = 2\pi\sqrt{\frac{M+m}{k}}$$

(d) The total energy of the oscillator after the clay hits is $\tfrac{1}{2}kA'^2$, where A' is the new amplitude. Just after the clay hits the block, the total energy is

$$K' + U_S = \tfrac{1}{2}(M+m)v'^2 + \tfrac{1}{2}k(\tfrac{1}{2}A)^2$$

Substitute for v' from part (b), set the resulting sum equal to $\tfrac{1}{2}kA'^2$, and solve for A':

$$\tfrac{1}{2}(M+m)\left(\frac{A}{M+m}\sqrt{\frac{3kM}{4}}\right)^2 + \tfrac{1}{2}k(\tfrac{1}{2}A)^2 = \tfrac{1}{2}kA'^2$$

$$\frac{A^2 \cdot 3kM}{8(M+m)} + \tfrac{1}{8}kA^2 = \tfrac{1}{2}kA'^2$$

$$A^2\left(\frac{3M}{M+m}+1\right) = 4A'^2$$

$$A' = \tfrac{1}{2}A\sqrt{\frac{3M}{M+m}+1}$$

(e) No, since the period depends only on the mass and the spring constant k.

(f) Yes. For example, if the clay had landed when the block was at $x = A$, the speed of the block would have been zero immediately before the collision and immediately after. No change in the block's speed would have meant no change in K, so no change in E, so no change in $A = \sqrt{2E/k}$.

4. (a) Since the weight provides a clockwise torque (which is negative), we have $\tau = -dMg \sin \theta$.

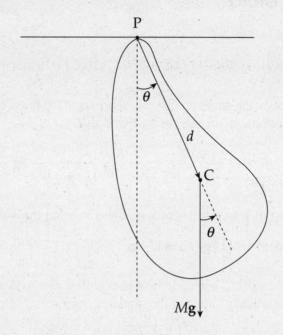

(b) If $\sin\theta \approx \theta$, then the equation in part (a) becomes

$$\tau = -dMg\,\theta \qquad (1)$$

(c) Since $\tau = I\alpha$, Equation (1) implies $I\alpha = -dMg\theta$. But by definition, $\alpha = d^2\theta/dt^2$, so we get

$$\frac{d^2\theta}{dt^2} = -\frac{dMg}{I}\theta \qquad (2)$$

Equation (3) is identical to Equation (*) given in the statement of the question with $z = \theta$ and $b = dMg/I$. Therefore,

$$T = \frac{2\pi}{\sqrt{b}} = \frac{2\pi}{\sqrt{dMg/I}} = 2\pi\sqrt{\frac{I}{dMg}}$$

(d) Using the result of part (c) with $I = \frac{1}{3}ML^2$ and $d = \frac{1}{2}L$, we get

$$T = 2\pi\sqrt{\frac{\frac{1}{3}ML^2}{\frac{1}{2}L \cdot Mg}} = 2\pi\sqrt{\frac{2L}{3g}}$$

CHAPTER 9 REVIEW QUESTIONS

SECTION I: MULTIPLE CHOICE

1. **(C)** Use the equation $Q = mc\,\Delta T$:

$$Q = (0.04 \text{ kg})(0.50 \text{ kJ}/\text{kg}\cdot{}^\circ\text{C})(50{}^\circ\text{C}-20{}^\circ\text{C}) = 0.6 \text{ kJ} = 600 \text{ J}$$

2. **(D)** Phase changes obey the equation $Q = mL$, where m is the mass of the sample and L is the latent heat of transformation. In this case, we find that

$$m = \frac{Q}{L} = \frac{2000 \text{ J}}{200 \text{ kJ}/\text{kg}} = \frac{2000 \text{ J}}{200\times10^3 \text{ J}/\text{kg}} = \frac{1}{100} \text{ kg}$$

3. **(A)** First, let's figure out how much heat is required to bring the water to its boiling point:

$$Q = mc\Delta T = (0.1 \text{ kg})(4.186 \text{ kJ}/\text{kg}\cdot{}^\circ\text{C})(100{}^\circ\text{C}-20{}^\circ\text{C}) = 33 \text{ kJ}$$

Once the water reaches 100°C, any additional heat will be absorbed and begin the transformation to steam. To completely vaporize the sample requires

$$Q = mL = (0.1 \text{ kg})(2260 \text{ kJ}/\text{kg}) = 226 \text{ kJ}$$

Since the 20°C water absorbed only 100 kJ of heat, enough heat was provided to bring the water to boiling, but not enough to completely vaporize it (at which point, the absorption of more heat would begin to increase the temperature of the steam). Thus, the water will reach and remain at 100°C.

4. **(D)** The equation for volume expansion is $\Delta V = \beta V_i \Delta T$, so

$$\Delta V = \beta V_i \Delta T = \frac{4.0\times10^{-5}}{{}^\circ\text{C}}(2.0 \text{ m}^3)(35{}^\circ\text{C}-5{}^\circ\text{C}) = 0.0024 \text{ m}^3 \times \left(\tfrac{10^2 \text{ cm}}{1\text{ m}}\right)^3 = 2400 \text{ cm}^3$$

5. **(B)** Because the gas is confined, n remains constant, and because we're told the volume is fixed, V remains constant as well. Since R is a universal constant, the Ideal Gas Law, $PV = nRT$, tells us that P and T are proportional. Therefore, if T increases by a factor of 2, then so does P.

6. **(E)** Neither choice A nor B can be correct. Using $PV = nRT$, both containers have the same V, n is the same, P is the same, and R is a universal constant. Therefore, T must be the same for both samples. Choice C is also wrong, since R is a universal constant. The kinetic theory of gases predicts that the rms speed of the gas molecules in a sample of molar mass M and temperature T is

$$v_{\text{rms}} = \sqrt{\frac{3RT}{M}}$$

Hydrogen has a smaller molar mass than does helium, so v_{rms} for hydrogen must be greater than v_{rms} for helium (because both samples are at the same T).

7. **(A)** By convention, work done *on* the gas sample is designated as negative, so in the First Law of Thermodynamics, $\Delta U = Q - W$, we must write $W = -320$ J. Therefore, $Q = \Delta U + W = 560$ J $+ (-320$ J$) = +240$ J. Positive Q denotes heat *in*.

8. **(C)** No work is done during the step from state b to state c because the volume doesn't change. Therefore, the work done from a to c is equal to the work done from a to b. Since the pressure remains constant (this step is isobaric), we find that $W = P\Delta V = (3.0 \times 10^5$ Pa$)[(25 - 10) \times 10^{-3}$ m$^3] = 4500$ J.

9. **(D)** Statement A is wrong because "no heat exchanged between the gas and its surroundings" is the definition of *adiabatic*, not *isothermal*. Statement B cannot be correct since the step described in the question is isothermal; by definition, the temperature does not change. This also eliminates statement E and supports statement D. Statement C is false, because although the heat absorbed is converted completely to work ($\Delta U = 0$ since $\Delta T = 0$, so, by the First Law of Thermodynamics, $W = Q_H$), the Second Law of Thermodynamics is not violated. If the sample could be brought back to its initial state and have a 100% conversion of heat to work, *that* would violate the Second Law. The Second law states that heat cannot be completely converted to work with no other change taking place. In this case, there are changes taking place: The pressure decreases and the volume increases.

10. **(D)** Be careful! Make sure that you always use absolute temperatures (in kelvins) when computing the Carnot efficiency, *not* temperatures in degrees Celsius. Since $T_H = 800°C = 1073$ K and $T_C = 200°C = 473$ K, the Carnot efficiency is

$$e_C = \frac{T_H - T_C}{T_H} = \frac{1073 - 473}{1073} = \frac{600}{1073} \lessapprox 60\%$$

SECTION II: FREE RESPONSE

1. (a) By definition, mass is equal to density times volume:

$$m = \rho V = \rho \ell^3 = (10.5 \times 10^3 \text{ kg}/\text{m}^3)(0.02 \text{ m})^3 = 0.084 \text{ kg}$$

(b) (i) We use the fundamental equation $Q = mc\,\Delta T$ to obtain

$$Q_{silver} = m_{silver}c_{silver}\Delta T_{silver} = m_S c_S \Delta T_S$$

$$Q_{water} = m_{water}c_{water}\Delta T_{water} = m_W c_W \Delta T_W$$

$$Q_{glass} = m_{glass}c_{glass}\Delta T_{glass} = m_G c_G \Delta T_G$$

(ii) Clearly, the hot silver cube loses heat, and the cooler water and glass absorb it. Since heat *out* is negative, and heat *in* is positive, the equation that relates these quantities is $Q_{silver} = -(Q_{water} + Q_{glass})$, or

$$m_S c_S \Delta T_S = -(m_W c_W \Delta T_W + m_G c_G \Delta T_G)$$

(c) Solving for c_S, we find that

$$c_S = \frac{-(m_W c_W \Delta T_W + m_G c_G \Delta T_G)}{m_S \Delta T_S}$$

$$= \frac{-[(0.1 \text{ kg})(4.186 \text{ kJ}/\text{kg}\cdot{}^\circ\text{C})(41{}^\circ\text{C}-20{}^\circ\text{C})+(0.075 \text{ kg})(0.84 \text{ kJ}/\text{kg}\cdot{}^\circ\text{C})(41{}^\circ\text{C}-20{}^\circ\text{C})]}{(0.084 \text{ kg})(41{}^\circ\text{C}-500{}^\circ\text{C})}$$

$$= 0.26 \text{ kJ}/\text{kg}\cdot{}^\circ\text{C}$$

(d) Using the value for c_S computed in part (c), we can figure out the amount of heat the silver cube had to absorb in order for its temperature to increase from 20°C to 500°C:

$$Q_{\text{silver}} = m_{\text{silver}} c_{\text{silver}} \Delta T_{\text{silver}}$$

$$= (0.084 \text{ kg})(0.26 \text{ kJ}/\text{kg}\cdot{}^\circ\text{C})(500{}^\circ\text{C}-20{}^\circ\text{C})$$

$$= 10.5 \text{ kJ}$$

Since 5 min = 300 s, the rate (in watts) at which thermal energy was absorbed by the cube was

$$\text{power} = \frac{\text{energy}}{\text{time}} = \frac{10.5 \text{ kJ}}{300 \text{ s}} = 0.035 \text{ kW} = 35 \text{ W}$$

2. (a) (i) Use the Ideal Gas Law:

$$T_a = \frac{P_a V_a}{nR} = \frac{(2.4\times10^5 \text{ Pa})(12\times10^{-3} \text{ m}^3)}{(0.4 \text{ mol})(8.31 \text{ J}/\text{mol}\cdot\text{K})} = 870 \text{ K}$$

(ii) Since state b is on the isotherm with state a, the temperature of state b must also be 870 K.

(iii) Use the Ideal Gas Law:

$$T_c = \frac{P_c V_c}{nR} = \frac{(0.6\times10^5 \text{ Pa})(12\times10^{-3} \text{ m}^3)}{(0.4 \text{ mol})(8.31 \text{ J}/\text{mol}\cdot\text{K})} = 220 \text{ K}$$

(b) (i) Since step ab takes place along an isotherm, the temperature of the gas does not change, so neither does the internal energy; $\Delta U_{ab} = 0$.

(ii) By the First Law of Thermodynamics, $\Delta U_{bc} = Q_{bc} - W_{bc}$. Since step bc is isobaric (constant pressure), we have

$$Q_{bc} = nC_P \Delta T_{bc} = (0.4 \text{ mol})(29.1 \text{ J}/\text{mol}\cdot\text{K})(220 \text{ K}-870 \text{ K}) = -7600 \text{ J}$$

Next,

$$W_{bc} = P\Delta V_{bc} = (0.6\times10^5 \text{ Pa})[(12-48)\times10^{-3} \text{ m}^3] = -2200 \text{ J}$$

Therefore,

$$\Delta U_{bc} = Q_{bc} - W_{bc} = (-7600 \text{ J}) - (-2200 \text{ J}) = -5400 \text{ J}$$

(iii) By the First Law of Thermodynamics, $\Delta U_{ca} = Q_{ca} - W_{ca}$. Since step ca is isochoric (constant volume), we have

$$Q_{ca} = nC_V \Delta T_{ca} = (0.4 \text{ mol})(20.8 \text{ J}/\text{mol} \cdot \text{K})(870 \text{ K} - 220 \text{ K}) = 5400 \text{ J}$$

and $W_{ca} = 0$. Therefore, $\Delta U_{ca} = Q_{ca} - W_{ca} = (5400 \text{ J}) - 0 = 5400 \text{ J}$.

Notice that part (iii) could have been answered as follows:

$$\begin{aligned} \Delta U_{aa} &= \Delta U_{ab} + \Delta U_{bc} + \Delta U_{ca} \\ 0 &= 0 + \Delta U_{bc} + \Delta U_{ca} \\ \Delta U_{ca} &= -\Delta U_{bc} \\ &= -(-5400 \text{ J}) \\ &= 5400 \text{ J} \end{aligned}$$

(c) Using the equation given, we find that

$$\begin{aligned} W_{ab} &= nRT \cdot \ln \frac{V_b}{V_a} = (0.4 \text{ mol})(8.31 \text{ J}/\text{mol} \cdot \text{K})(870 \text{ K}) \cdot \ln \frac{48 \times 10^{-3} \text{ m}^3}{12 \times 10^{-3} \text{ m}^3} \\ &= 4000 \text{ J} \end{aligned}$$

(d) The total work done over the cycle is equal to the sum of the values of the work done over each step:

$$\begin{aligned} W_{cycle} &= W_{ab} + W_{bc} + W_{ca} \\ &= W_{ab} + P_{bc} \Delta V_{bc} + 0 \\ &= (4000 \text{ J}) + (0.6 \times 10^5 \text{ Pa})[(12 - 48) \times 10^{-3} \text{ m}^3] \\ &= (4000 \text{ J}) + (-2200 \text{ J}) \\ &= 1800 \text{ J} \end{aligned}$$

(e) (i) and (ii) By the First Law of Thermodynamics,

$$\begin{aligned} \Delta U_{ab} &= Q_{ab} - W_{ab} \\ 0 &= Q_{ab} - W_{ab} \\ Q_{ab} &= W_{ab} \\ &= 4000 \text{ J} \quad \text{[from part (c)]} \end{aligned}$$

Since Q is positive, this represents heat *absorbed* by the gas.

(f) The maximum possible efficiency is the efficiency of a Carnot engine:

$$e_C = 1 - \frac{T_C}{T_H} = 1 - \frac{220\text{ K}}{870\text{ K}} = 75\%$$

CHAPTER 10 REVIEW QUESTIONS
SECTION I: MULTIPLE CHOICE

1. **(D)** Electrostatic force obeys an inverse-square law: $F_E \propto 1/r^2$. Therefore, if r increases by a factor of 3, then F_E decreases by a factor of $3^2 = 9$.

2. **(C)** The strength of the electric force is given by kq^2/r^2, and the strength of the gravitational force is Gm^2/r^2. Since both of these quantities have r^2 in the denominator, we simply need to compare the numerical values of kq^2 and Gm^2. There's no contest: Since

$$kq^2 = (9 \times 10^9 \text{ N·m}^2/\text{C}^2)(1\text{ C})^2 = 9 \times 10^9 \text{ N·m}^2$$

and

$$Gm^2 = (6.7 \times 10^{-11} \text{ N·m}^2/\text{kg}^2)(1\text{ kg})^2 = 6.7 \times 10^{-11} \text{ N·m}^2$$

we see that $kq^2 \gg Gm^2$, so F_E is much stronger than F_G.

3. **(C)** If the net electric force on the center charge is zero, the electrical repulsion by the $+2q$ charge must balance the electrical repulsion by the $+3q$ charge:

$$\frac{1}{4\pi\varepsilon_0}\frac{(2q)(q)}{x^2} = \frac{1}{4\pi\varepsilon_0}\frac{(3q)(q)}{y^2} \implies \frac{2}{x^2} = \frac{3}{y^2} \implies \frac{y^2}{x^2} = \frac{3}{2} \implies \frac{y}{x} = \sqrt{\frac{3}{2}}$$

4. **(E)** Since P is equidistant from the two charges, and the magnitudes of the charges are identical, the strength of the electric field at P due to $+Q$ is the same as the strength of the electric field at P due to $-Q$. The electric field vector at P due to $+Q$ points away from $+Q$, and the electric field vector at P due to $-Q$ points toward $-Q$. Since these vectors point in the same direction, the net electric field at P is (E to the right) + (E to the right) = ($2E$ to the right).

5. **(D)** The acceleration of the small sphere is

$$a = \frac{F_E}{m} = \frac{1}{4\pi\varepsilon_0}\frac{Qq}{mr^2}$$

As r increases (that is, as the small sphere is pushed away), a decreases. However, since a is always positive, the small sphere's speed, v, is always increasing.

6. **(B)** Since $\mathbf{F}_E$ (on q) = $q\mathbf{E}$, it must be true that $\mathbf{F}_E$ (on $-2q$) = $-2q\mathbf{E} = -2\mathbf{F}_E$.

7. **(D)** All excess electric charge on a conductor resides on the outer surface.

8. **(B)** The net electric flux through the Gaussian surface, Φ_E, is equal to $(1/\varepsilon_0)$ times the net charge *enclosed by the surface*, $Q_2 + Q_3$. However, the net electric field vector at P is equal to the sum of the electric field vectors due to each of the four charges individually.

9. **(A)** Since the charge is distributed uniformly throughout the sphere, the magnitude of its volume charge density is $\rho = Q/(\frac{4}{3}\pi R^3)$. Therefore, if we construct a spherical Gaussian surface of radius $r < R$, Gauss's Law gives

$$\Phi_E = \frac{Q_{enclosed}}{\varepsilon_0} \quad \Rightarrow \quad E(4\pi r^2) = \frac{\rho \cdot \frac{4}{3}\pi r^3}{\varepsilon_0} \quad \Rightarrow \quad E = \rho \frac{r}{3\varepsilon_0}$$

$$E = \frac{Q}{\frac{4}{3}\pi R^3}\frac{r}{3\varepsilon_0}$$

$$E = \frac{1}{4\pi\varepsilon_0}\frac{Q}{R^3}r$$

(Since the charge on the sphere is negative, the direction of **E** at any point is directed radially inward.)

10. **(A)** By definition, an electric dipole consists of two equal but opposite charges. Therefore a Gaussian surface enclosing both charges would enclose zero net charge. By Gauss's Law, the electric flux is zero as well (since $\Phi_E = Q_{enclosed}/\varepsilon_0$).

SECTION II: FREE RESPONSE

1. (a) From the figure below, we have $F_{1\text{-}2} = F_1/\cos 45°$.

Since the net force on $+Q$ is zero, we want $F_{1\text{-}2} = F_3$. If s is the length of each side of the square, then

$$F_{1-2} = F_3 \implies \frac{F_1}{\cos 45°} = F_3 \implies \frac{1}{\cos 45°} \frac{1}{4\pi\varepsilon_0} \frac{Qq}{s^2} = \frac{1}{4\pi\varepsilon_0} \frac{Q^2}{(s\sqrt{2})^2}$$

$$\sqrt{2} \cdot q = \frac{Q}{2}$$

$$q = \frac{Q}{2\sqrt{2}}$$

(b) No. If $q = Q/2\sqrt{2}$, as found in part (a), then the net force on $-q$ is not zero. **F**$_1$

This is because $F_{1-2} \neq F_4$, as the following calculations show:

$$F_{1-2} = \frac{F_1}{\cos 45°} = \sqrt{2} \frac{1}{4\pi\varepsilon_0} \frac{Qq}{s^2} = \sqrt{2} \frac{1}{4\pi\varepsilon_0} \frac{Q\frac{Q}{2\sqrt{2}}}{s^2} = \frac{1}{8\pi\varepsilon_0} \frac{Q^2}{s^2}$$

but

$$F_4 = \frac{1}{4\pi\varepsilon_0} \frac{q^2}{(s\sqrt{2})^2} = \frac{1}{4\pi\varepsilon_0} \frac{\left(\frac{Q}{2\sqrt{2}}\right)^2}{(s\sqrt{2})^2} = \frac{1}{64\pi\varepsilon_0} \frac{Q^2}{s^2}$$

(c) By symmetry, $E_1 = E_2$ and $E_3 = E_4$, so the net electric field at the center of the square is zero:

2. (a) The magnitude of the electric force on Charge 1 is

$$F_1 = \frac{1}{4\pi\varepsilon_0} \frac{(Q)(2Q)}{(a+2a)^2} = \frac{1}{18\pi\varepsilon_0} \frac{Q^2}{a^2}$$

The direction of $\mathbf{F}_1$ is directly away from Charge 2; that is, in the $+y$ direction, so

$$\mathbf{F}_1 = \frac{1}{18\pi\varepsilon_0} \frac{Q^2}{a^2} \hat{\mathbf{j}}$$

(b) The electric field vectors at the origin due to Charge 1 and due to Charge 2 are

$$\mathbf{E}_1 = \frac{1}{4\pi\varepsilon_0} \frac{Q}{a^2}(-\hat{\mathbf{j}}) \quad \text{and} \quad \mathbf{E}_2 = \frac{1}{4\pi\varepsilon_0} \frac{2Q}{(2a)^2}(+\hat{\mathbf{j}}) = \frac{1}{8\pi\varepsilon_0} \frac{Q}{a^2}(+\hat{\mathbf{j}})$$

Therefore, the net electric field at the origin is

$$\mathbf{E} = \mathbf{E}_1 + \mathbf{E}_2 = \frac{1}{4\pi\varepsilon_0} \frac{Q}{a^2}(-\hat{\mathbf{j}}) + \frac{1}{8\pi\varepsilon_0} \frac{Q}{a^2}(+\hat{\mathbf{j}}) = \frac{1}{8\pi\varepsilon_0} \frac{Q}{a^2}(-\hat{\mathbf{j}})$$

(c) No. At no point on the x axis will the individual electric field vectors due to each of the two charges point in exactly opposite directions.

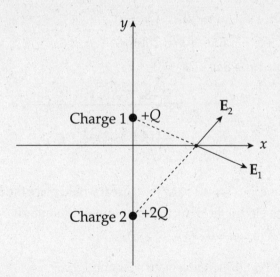

Therefore, at no point on the x axis could the total electric field be zero.

(d) Yes. There will be a point P on the y axis between the two charges, where the electric fields due to the individual charges will cancel each other out.

$$E_1 = E_2$$

$$\frac{1}{4\pi\varepsilon_0}\frac{Q}{(a+y)^2} = \frac{1}{4\pi\varepsilon_0}\frac{2Q}{(2a-y)^2}$$

$$\frac{1}{(a+y)^2} = \frac{2}{(2a-y)^2}$$

$$(2a-y)^2 = 2(a+y)^2$$

$$y^2 + 8ay - 2a^2 = 0$$

$$y = \frac{-8a \pm \sqrt{(8a)^2 - 4(-2a^2)}}{2}$$

$$= (-4 \pm 3\sqrt{2})a$$

Disregarding the value $y = (-4 - 3\sqrt{2})a$ (because it would place the point P below Charge 2 on the y axis, where the electric field vectors do not point in opposite directions), we have that $\mathbf{E} = 0$ at the point P = $(0, -y) = (0, (4 - 3\sqrt{2})a)$.

(e) Use the result of part (b) with Newton's Second Law:

$$\mathbf{a} = \frac{\mathbf{F}}{m} = \frac{-q\mathbf{E}}{m} = \frac{-q}{m}\left[\frac{1}{8\pi\varepsilon_0}\frac{Q}{a^2}(-\hat{\mathbf{j}})\right] = \frac{1}{8\pi\varepsilon_0}\frac{qQ}{ma^2}(+\hat{\mathbf{j}})$$

3. (a) The charges on the surfaces of the shells will be distributed on as follows:

Therefore, by Gauss's Law, the electric field in the various regions are as follows:

(i) $r < a$ $E = 0$ (no charge inside)

(ii) $a < r < b$ $E = 0$ (within metallic shell)

(iii) $b < r < c$ $E = (1 / 4\pi\varepsilon_0)(2q / r^2)$

(iv) $c < r < d$ $E = 0$ (within metallic shell)

(v) $r > d$ $E = (1 / 4\pi\varepsilon_0)(3q / r^2)$

(b) Within each metallic shell, there is no excess charge. The inner surface of the inner shell also has no excess charge. See the figure above for part (a) for the charges residing on the other surfaces of the shells.

4. (a) Very close to the rod, the rod behaves as if it were "infinitely long." Construct a cylindrical Gaussian surface of radius x_1 and length L centered on the rod. By symmetry the electric field at P_1 must point radially away from the rod, so the field at P_1 must point in the positive x direction.

There is no electric flux through the ends of the cylinder (since **E** is parallel to the lids of the cylinder); the electric flux is perpendicular to the lateral surface area of the cylinder, so $\Phi_E = 0 + EA + 0 = E(2\pi x_1 \ell)$. Since the charge enclosed by the surface is λL, Gauss's Law gives

$$E(2\pi x_1 \ell) = \frac{\lambda \ell}{\varepsilon_0} \quad \Rightarrow \quad E = \frac{\lambda}{2\pi \varepsilon_0 x_1}$$

(b) The total charge on the rod is equal to its linear charge density times its total length: $Q = \lambda \ell$.

(c) If x_2 is not small compared to ℓ, then we must calculate the electric field at P_2 by integration. Consider two symmetrically-located line elements along the rod, each of length dy, at a distance y above and below the origin.

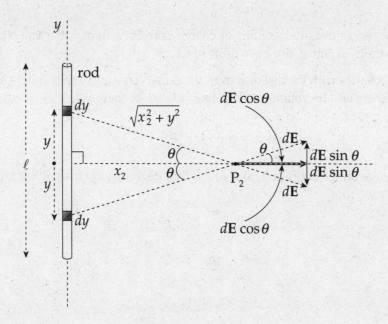

The vertical components of the electric fields at P_2 will cancel (by symmetry), leaving the net electric field at P_2 due to this pair of line elements equal to the sum of the horizontal components. Therefore,

$$dE_{total} = 2dE \cos\theta$$

$$E_{total} = \int_{y=0}^{y=\ell/2} 2\left[\frac{1}{4\pi\varepsilon_0}\frac{\lambda\,dy}{x_2^2+y^2}\right]\frac{x_2}{\sqrt{x_2^2+y^2}}$$

$$= \frac{\lambda x_2}{2\pi\varepsilon_0}\int_{y=0}^{y=\ell/2}\frac{dy}{(x_2^2+y^2)^{3/2}}$$

$$= \frac{\lambda x_2}{2\pi\varepsilon_0}\left[\frac{y}{x_2^2\sqrt{x_2^2+y^2}}\right]_{y=0}^{y=\ell/2}$$

$$= \frac{\lambda}{2\pi\varepsilon_0 x_2}\left[\frac{\ell/2}{\sqrt{x_2^2+(\ell/2)^2}}\right]$$

If $x_2 = \ell$, then

$$E_{\text{total}} = \frac{\lambda}{2\pi\varepsilon_0\ell}\left[\frac{\ell/2}{\sqrt{\ell^2 + (\ell/2)^2}}\right] = \frac{\lambda}{4\pi\varepsilon_0}\frac{1}{\sqrt{5\ell^2/4}} = \frac{\lambda}{2\pi\varepsilon_0\ell\sqrt{5}} = \frac{Q/\ell}{2\pi\varepsilon_0\ell\sqrt{5}} = \frac{Q}{2\pi\varepsilon_0\ell^2\sqrt{5}}$$

5. (a) Volume charge density has units of charge per unit volume, that is, $[\rho] = \text{C/m}^3$. Since r/a has no units, ρ_s must also have units of C/m^3.

(b) Since ρ varies with the distance from the center, consider a thin spherical shell of radius R and thickness dR. Its volume is $dV = 4\pi R^2\, dR$, so its charge is

$$dQ = \rho\, dV = \rho_s\frac{R}{a}\cdot 4\pi R^2\, dR = \frac{4\pi\rho_s}{a}R^3\, dR$$

The charge on the entire sphere is found by integrating dQ from $R = 0$ to $R = a$:

$$Q = \int dQ = \int_{R=0}^{R=a}\frac{4\pi\rho_s}{a}R^3\, dR \qquad (1)$$
$$= \frac{4\pi\rho_s}{a}\frac{a^4}{4}$$
$$= \pi\rho_s a^3$$

(c) (i) Replace "$R = a$" with "$R = r$" in Equation (1) above to find the charged enclosed by a spherical Gaussian surface of radius $r < a$:

$$Q_{\text{within }r} = \int_{R=0}^{R=r}\frac{4\pi\rho_s}{a}R^3\, dR = \frac{4\pi\rho_s}{a}\frac{r^4}{4}$$

Using the result of part (b), we can write this expression for $Q_{\text{within }r}$ in terms of Q, the total charge on the full sphere:

$$Q_{\text{within }r} = \frac{4\pi\rho_s}{a}\frac{r^4}{4} = \frac{4\dfrac{Q}{a^3}}{a}\frac{r^4}{4} = \frac{Q}{a^4}r^4$$

So, by Gauss's Law,

$$\Phi_E = \frac{1}{\varepsilon_0}\cdot Q_{\text{enclosed}}$$
$$E(4\pi r^2) = \frac{1}{\varepsilon_0}\cdot\frac{Q}{a^4}r^4$$
$$E = \frac{1}{4\pi\varepsilon_0}\frac{Q}{a^4}r^2 \quad (r < a)$$

(ii) Outside the sphere, $Q_{enclosed} = Q$, so

$$E = \frac{1}{4\pi\varepsilon_0}\frac{Q}{r^2} \quad (r \geq a)$$

(d)

CHAPTER 11 REVIEW QUESTIONS
SECTION I: MULTIPLE CHOICE

1. **(E)** A counterexample for Statement I is provided by two equal positive charges; at the point midway between the charges, the electric field is zero, but the potential is not. A counterexample for Statement II is provided by an electric dipole (a pair of equal but opposite charges); at the point midway between the charges, the electric potential is zero, but the electric field is not. As for Statement III, consider a single positive point charge $+Q$. Then at a distance r from this source charge, the electric field strength is $E = kQ/r^2$ and the potential is $V = kQ/r$. Thus, $V = rE$, so V is not inversely proportional to E.

2. **(C)** By definition, $\Delta U_E = -W_E$, so if W_E is negative, then ΔU_E is positive. This implies that the potential energy, U_E, increases.

3. **(B)** The work required to assemble the configuration is equal to the potential energy of the system:

$$W = U_E = \frac{1}{4\pi\varepsilon_0}\sum_{i<j}\frac{q_i q_j}{r_{ij}}$$

$$= \frac{1}{4\pi\varepsilon_0}\left(\frac{q_1 q_2}{r_{12}} + \frac{q_1 q_3}{r_{13}} + \frac{q_1 q_4}{r_{14}} + \frac{q_2 q_3}{r_{23}} + \frac{q_2 q_4}{r_{24}} + \frac{q_3 q_4}{r_{34}}\right)$$

$$= \frac{1}{4\pi\varepsilon_0}\left(\frac{q^2}{s} + \frac{q^2}{s\sqrt{2}} + \frac{q^2}{s} + \frac{q^2}{s} + \frac{q^2}{s\sqrt{2}} + \frac{q^2}{s}\right)$$

$$= \frac{1}{4\pi\varepsilon_0}\frac{q^2}{s}(4 + \sqrt{2})$$

4. **(B)** Use the definition $\Delta V = -W_E/q$. If an electric field accelerates a negative charge doing positive work on it, then $W_E > 0$. If $q < 0$, then $-W_E/q$ is positive. Therefore, ΔV is positive, which implies that V increases.

5. **(E)** By definition,

$$V_{A \to B} = \Delta U_E/q, \text{ so } V_B - V_A = \Delta U_E/q$$

6. **(C)** Because **E** is uniform, the potential varies linearly with distance from either plate ($\Delta V = Ed$). Since Points 2 and 4 are at the same distance from the plates, they lie on the same equipotential. (The equipotentials in this case are planes parallel to the capacitor plates.)

7. **(D)** Once the spheres are connected by a conducting wire, they quickly form a single equipotential surface. Since the potential on a sphere of radius r carrying charge q is given by the equation $(1/4\pi\varepsilon_0)(q/r)$, we have

$$V_{\text{Sphere \#1}} = V_{\text{Sphere \#2}} \quad \Rightarrow \quad \frac{1}{4\pi\varepsilon_0}\frac{q_1}{a} = \frac{1}{4\pi\varepsilon_0}\frac{q_2}{4a} \quad \Rightarrow \quad q_1 = \frac{q_2}{4}$$

Now, since $q_1 + q_2 = -Q + -Q = -2Q$, the fact that q_1 must equal $q_2/4$ means that $(q_2/4) + q_2 = -2Q$, which gives $q_2 = (-8/5)Q$ and $q_1 = (-2/5)Q$.

8. **(A)** Since Q cannot change and C is increased (because of the dielectric), $\Delta V = Q/C$ must decrease. Also, since $U_E = Q^2/(2C)$, an increase in C with no change in Q implies a decrease in U_E.

9. **(B)** By definition, $W_E = -q\Delta V$, which gives

$$W_E = -q(V_B - V_A) = -(-0.05 \text{ C})(100 \text{ V} - 200 \text{ V}) = -5 \text{ J}$$

Notice that neither the length of the segment AB nor that of the curved path from A to B is relevant.

10. **(D)**

Capacitors 1 and 2 are in series, so their equivalent capacitance is $C_{1\text{-}2} = C/2$. (This is obtained from the equation $1/C_{1\text{-}2} = 1/C_1 + 1/C_2 = 1/C + 1/C = 2/C$.) Capacitors 4 and 5 are also in series, so their equivalent capacitance is $C_{4\text{-}5} = C/2$. The capacitances $C_{1\text{-}2}$, C_3, and $C_{4\text{-}5}$ are in parallel, so the overall equivalent capacitance is $(C/2) + C + (C/2) = 2C$.

SECTION II: FREE RESPONSE

1. (a) Labeling the four charges as given in the diagram, we get

$$U_E = \frac{1}{4\pi\varepsilon_0} \sum_{i<j} \frac{q_i q_j}{r_{ij}}$$

$$= \frac{1}{4\pi\varepsilon_0} \left(\frac{q_1 q_2}{r_{12}} + \frac{q_1 q_3}{r_{13}} + \frac{q_1 q_4}{r_{14}} + \frac{q_2 q_3}{r_{23}} + \frac{q_2 q_4}{r_{24}} + \frac{q_3 q_4}{r_{34}} \right)$$

$$= \frac{1}{4\pi\varepsilon_0} \left(\frac{Q^2}{s} + \frac{-Q^2}{s\sqrt{2}} + \frac{-Q^2}{s} + \frac{-Q^2}{s} + \frac{-Q^2}{s\sqrt{2}} + \frac{Q^2}{s} \right)$$

$$= \frac{1}{4\pi\varepsilon_0} \frac{-2Q^2}{s\sqrt{2}}$$

$$= -\frac{\sqrt{2}}{4\pi\varepsilon_0} \frac{Q^2}{s}$$

(b) Let $\mathbf{E}_i$ denote the electric field at the center of the square due to Charge i. Then by symmetry, $\mathbf{E}_1 = \mathbf{E}_3$, $\mathbf{E}_2 = \mathbf{E}_4$, and $E_1 = E_2 = E_3 = E_4$. The horizontal components of the four individual field vectors cancel, leaving only a downward-pointing electric field of magnitude $E_{total} = 4E_1 \cos 45°$:

$$E_{total} = 4E_1 \cos 45°$$

$$= 4 \frac{1}{4\pi\varepsilon_0} \frac{Q}{\left(\frac{1}{2}s\sqrt{2}\right)^2} \cdot \frac{\sqrt{2}}{2}$$

$$= \frac{\sqrt{2}}{\pi\varepsilon_0} \frac{Q}{s^2}$$

(c) The potential at the center of the square is zero:

$$V = \frac{1}{4\pi\varepsilon_0} \sum_i \frac{q_i}{r_i}$$

$$= \frac{1}{4\pi\varepsilon_0} \left(\frac{q_1}{r_1} + \frac{q_2}{r_2} + \frac{q_3}{r_3} + \frac{q_4}{r_4} \right)$$

$$= \frac{1}{4\pi\varepsilon_0} \left(\frac{Q}{\frac{1}{2}s\sqrt{2}} + \frac{Q}{\frac{1}{2}s\sqrt{2}} + \frac{-Q}{\frac{1}{2}s\sqrt{2}} + \frac{-Q}{\frac{1}{2}s\sqrt{2}} \right)$$

$$= 0$$

(d) At every point on the center horizontal line shown, $r_1 = r_4$ and $r_2 = r_3$, so V will equal zero (just as it does as the center of the square):

$$V = \frac{1}{4\pi\varepsilon_0} \sum_i \frac{q_i}{r_i}$$

$$= \frac{1}{4\pi\varepsilon_0} \left(\frac{q_1}{r_1} + \frac{q_2}{r_2} + \frac{q_3}{r_3} + \frac{q_4}{r_4} \right)$$

$$= \frac{1}{4\pi\varepsilon_0} \left(\frac{Q}{r_1} + \frac{Q}{r_2} + \frac{-Q}{r_3} + \frac{-Q}{r_4} \right)$$

$$= 0$$

(e) The work done by the electric force as q is displaced from Point A to Point B is given by the equation $W_E = -q\,\Delta V_{A \to B} = -q(V_B - V_A) = -qV_B$ (since $V_A = 0$).

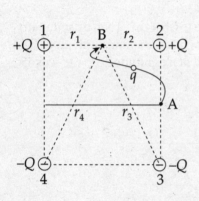

$$W_E = -qV_B = -q\left[\frac{1}{4\pi\varepsilon_0} \sum_i \frac{q_i}{r_{i \to B}} \right]$$

$$= \frac{-q}{4\pi\varepsilon_0} \left(\frac{q_1}{r_{1 \to B}} + \frac{q_2}{r_{2 \to B}} + \frac{q_3}{r_{3 \to B}} + \frac{q_4}{r_{4 \to B}} \right)$$

$$= \frac{-q}{4\pi\varepsilon_0} \left(\frac{Q}{\frac{1}{2}s} + \frac{Q}{\frac{1}{2}s} + \frac{-Q}{\sqrt{s^2 + (\frac{1}{2}s)^2}} + \frac{-Q}{\sqrt{s^2 + (\frac{1}{2}s)^2}} \right)$$

$$= \frac{-q}{4\pi\varepsilon_0} \left(\frac{4Q}{s} + \frac{-2Q}{\frac{\sqrt{5}}{2}s} \right)$$

$$= \frac{-qQ}{\pi\varepsilon_0 s} \left(1 - \frac{1}{\sqrt{5}} \right)$$

2. (a) The capacitance is $C = \varepsilon_0 A/d$. Since the plates are rectangular, the area A is equal to Lw, so $C = \varepsilon_0 Lw/d$.

(b) and (c) Since the electron is attracted upward, the top plate must be the positive plate:

(d) The acceleration of the electron is $a = F_E/m = qE/m = eE/m$, vertically upward. Therefore, applying Big Five #3 for vertical motion, $\Delta y = v_{0y}t + \frac{1}{2}a_y t^2$, we get

$$\Delta y = \frac{1}{2}\frac{eE}{m}t^2 \quad (1)$$

To find t, notice that $v_{0x} = v_0$ remains constant (because there is no horizontal acceleration). Therefore, the time necessary for the electron to travel the horizontal distance L is $t = L/v_0$. In this time, Δy is $d/2$, so Equation (1) becomes

$$\frac{d}{2} = \frac{1}{2}\frac{eE}{m}\left(\frac{L}{v_0}\right)^2 \quad \Rightarrow \quad E = \frac{dmv_0^2}{eL^2}$$

(e) Substituting the result of part (d) into the equation $\Delta V = Ed$ gives

$$\Delta V = \frac{d^2 mv_0^2}{eL^2}$$

Since $Q = C\Delta V$ (by definition), the result of part (a) now gives

$$Q = \frac{\varepsilon_0 Lw}{d} \cdot \frac{d^2 mv_0^2}{eL^2} = \frac{\varepsilon_0 wdmv_0^2}{eL}$$

(f) Applying the equation $U_E = \frac{1}{2}C(\Delta V)^2$, we get

$$U_E = \frac{1}{2} \cdot \frac{\varepsilon_0 Lw}{d} \cdot \left(\frac{d^2 mv_0^2}{eL^2}\right)^2 = \frac{\varepsilon_0 wd^3 m^2 v_0^4}{2e^2 L^3}$$

3. (a) Outside the sphere, the sphere behaves as if all the charge were concentrated at the center. Inside the sphere, the electrostatic field is zero:

$$E(r) = \begin{cases} 0 & (r < a) \\ \dfrac{1}{4\pi\varepsilon_0}\dfrac{Q}{r^2} & (r > a) \end{cases}$$

(b) On the surface and outside the sphere, the electric potential is $(1/4\pi\varepsilon_0)(Q/r)$. Within the sphere, V is constant (because $E = 0$) and equal to the value on the surface. Therefore,

$$V(r) = \begin{cases} \dfrac{1}{4\pi\varepsilon_0}\dfrac{Q}{a} & (r \le a) \\ \dfrac{1}{4\pi\varepsilon_0}\dfrac{Q}{r} & (r > a) \end{cases}$$

(c) See diagrams:

4. (a) To find the electric field inside the sphere, construct a spherical Gaussian surface of radius $R < a$. We need to determine the charge enclosed by this sphere. Therefore, consider a thin spherical shell of radius r and thickness dr. The charge within this shell is $dQ = \rho \, dV = \rho \, (4\pi r^2 \, dr)$, so the total charge within a sphere of radius R is

$$Q_{\text{within } R} = \int dQ$$

$$= \int_{r=0}^{r=R} \rho_0 \left(\frac{r}{a}\right)^3 \cdot 4\pi r^2 \, dr \qquad (1)$$

$$= \frac{4\pi\rho_0}{a^3} \int_0^R r^5 \, dr$$

$$= \frac{2\pi\rho_0 R^6}{3a^3}$$

For the Gaussian surface, Gauss's Law then gives

$$\Phi_E = \frac{1}{\varepsilon_0} Q_{enclosed}$$

$$E(4\pi R^2) = \frac{1}{\varepsilon_0} \frac{2\pi\rho_0 R^6}{3a^3}$$

$$E = \frac{\rho_0}{6\varepsilon_0 a^3} R^4$$

Now, to find the electric field outside the sphere, we first determine the sphere's total charge. Replacing $r = R$ in Equation (1) by $r = a$ gives

$$\text{total } Q = \int_{r=0}^{r=a} \rho_0 \left(\frac{r}{a}\right)^3 \cdot 4\pi r^2 \, dr$$

$$= \frac{4\pi\rho_0}{a^3} \int_0^a r^5 \, dr$$

$$= \frac{2\pi\rho_0 a^3}{3}$$

Thus, for points outside the sphere, the electric field is

$$E = \frac{1}{4\pi\varepsilon_0} \frac{Q}{r^2} = \frac{1}{4\pi\varepsilon_0} \frac{2\pi\rho_0 a^3}{3r^2} = \frac{\rho_0 a^3}{6\varepsilon_0 r^2}$$

In summary, then,

$$E(r) = \begin{cases} \dfrac{\rho_0}{6\varepsilon_0 a^3} r^4 & (r < a) \\[2ex] \dfrac{\rho_0 a^3}{6\varepsilon_0 r^2} & (r \geq a) \end{cases}$$

(b) We follow the same procedure used in Example 11.14: The potential at some distance, let's call it r_0, from the center is equal to the negative of the work done by the electric field as a charge q is brought to r_0 from infinity, divided by q. (By definition, $V = U_E/q = -W_E/q$, where we take $V = 0$ at infinity.) So our first step (the big one) is to compute the work done by the electric field in bringing a charge q in from infinity to a point inside the sphere at a distance of $r_0 < a$ from the center:

$$W_E = W_{E,\,\infty \text{ to } a} + W_{E,\,a \text{ to } r_0}$$

$$= \int_\infty^a q \cdot \frac{\rho_0 a^3}{6\varepsilon_0 r^2}\, dr + \int_a^{r_0} q \cdot \frac{\rho_0}{6\varepsilon_0 a^3} r^4\, dr$$

$$= \frac{q\rho_0 a^3}{6\varepsilon_0} \int_\infty^a \frac{1}{r^2}\, dr + \frac{q\rho_0}{6\varepsilon_0 a^3} \int_a^{r_0} r^4\, dr$$

$$= \frac{q\rho_0 a^3}{6\varepsilon_0} \left[-\frac{1}{r} \right]_\infty^a + \frac{q\rho_0}{6\varepsilon_0 a^3} \left[\frac{r^5}{5} \right]_a^{r_0}$$

$$= -\frac{q\rho_0 a^2}{6\varepsilon_0} + \frac{q\rho_0}{30\varepsilon_0 a^3} (r_0^5 - a^5)$$

$$= \frac{q\rho_0}{30\varepsilon_0} \left(\frac{r_0^5}{a^3} - 6a^2 \right)$$

Taking the negative of this result, dividing by q, and replacing r_0 by r gives our answer:

$$V = \frac{-W_E}{q} = \frac{\rho_0}{30\varepsilon_0} \left(6a^2 - \frac{r^5}{a^3} \right) \qquad (r < a)$$

On the surface and outside the sphere, the potential is

$$V = \frac{1}{4\pi\varepsilon_0} \frac{Q_{\text{total}}}{r} = \frac{1}{4\pi\varepsilon_0} \frac{2\pi\rho_0 a^3}{3r} = \frac{\rho_0 a^3}{6\varepsilon_0 r} \qquad (r \geq a)$$

In summary,

$$V(r) = \begin{cases} \dfrac{\rho_0}{30\varepsilon_0} \left(6a^2 - \dfrac{r^5}{a^3} \right) & (r < a) \\[4mm] \dfrac{\rho_0 a^3}{6\varepsilon_0 r} & (r \geq a) \end{cases}$$

As a check on these formulas, we notice first that the function $V(r)$ is continuous (as it must always be); the only question about continuity is at $r = a$. But continuity here is assured because substituting $r = a$ into either of the expressions for $V(r)$ gives the same result:

$$\frac{\rho_0}{30\varepsilon_0} \left(6a^2 - \frac{r^5}{a^3} \right) \bigg|_{r=a} = \frac{\rho_0}{30\varepsilon_0} (6a^2 - a^2) = \frac{\rho_0 a^2}{6\varepsilon_0}$$

$$\frac{\rho_0 a^3}{6\varepsilon_0 r} \bigg|_{r=a} = \frac{\rho_0 a^2}{6\varepsilon_0}$$

Second, we can verify that $E = -dV/dr$:

$$-\frac{dV}{dr} = \begin{cases} -\dfrac{d}{dr}\left[\dfrac{\rho_0}{30\varepsilon_0}\left(6a^2 - \dfrac{r^5}{a^3}\right)\right] & (r < a) \\[4mm] -\dfrac{d}{dr}\left[\dfrac{\rho_0 a^3}{6\varepsilon_0 r}\right] & (r \geq a) \end{cases}$$

$$= \begin{cases} \dfrac{\rho_0}{6\varepsilon_0 a^3}r^4 & (r < a) \\[4mm] \dfrac{\rho_0 a^3}{6\varepsilon_0 r^2} & (r \geq a) \end{cases}$$

$$= E(r)$$

(c) See the diagrams:

CHAPTER 12 REVIEW QUESTIONS

SECTION I: MULTIPLE CHOICE

1. **(A)** Let ρ_s denote the resistivity of silver and let A_s denote the cross-sectional area of the silver wire. Then

$$R_B = \frac{\rho_B L}{A_B} = \frac{(5\rho_S)L}{4^2 A_S} = \frac{5}{16}\frac{\rho_S L}{A_S} = \frac{5}{16}R_S$$

2. **(D)** The equation $I = V/R$ implies that increasing V by a factor of 2 will cause I to increase by a factor of 2.

3. **(C)** Use the equation $P = V^2/R$:

$$P = \frac{V^2}{R} \quad \Rightarrow \quad R = \frac{V^2}{P} = \frac{(120 \text{ V})^2}{60 \text{ W}} = 240 \ \Omega$$

4. **(B)** The current through the circuit is

$$I = \frac{\mathcal{E}}{r+R} = \frac{40 \text{ V}}{(5 \ \Omega)+(15 \ \Omega)} = 2 \text{ A}$$

Therefore, the voltage drop across R is $V = IR = (2 \text{ A})(15 \ \Omega) = 30$ V.

5. **(E)** The 12 Ω and 4 Ω resistors are in parallel and are equivalent to single 3 Ω resistor, because $1/(12 \ \Omega) + 1/(4 \ \Omega) = 1/(3 \ \Omega)$. This 3 Ω resistor is in series with the top 3 Ω resistor, giving a equivalent resistance in the top branch of $3 + 3 = 6 \ \Omega$. Finally, this 6 Ω resistor is in parallel with the bottom 3 Ω resistor, giving an overall equivalent resistance of 2 Ω, because $1/(6 \ \Omega) + 1/(3 \ \Omega) = 1/(2 \ \Omega)$.

6. **(D)** If each of the identical bulbs has resistance R, then the current through each bulb is $\mathcal{E}/R$. This is unchanged if the middle branch is taken out of the parallel circuit. (What *will* change is the total amount of current provided by the battery.)

7. **(B)** The three parallel resistors are equivalent to a single 2 Ω resistor, because $1/(8 \ \Omega) + 1/(4 \ \Omega) + 1/(8 \ \Omega) = 1/(2 \ \Omega)$. This 2 Ω resistance is in series with the given 2 Ω resistor, so their equivalent resistance is $2 + 2 = 4 \ \Omega$. Therefore, three times as much current will flow through this equivalent 4 Ω resistance in the top branch as through the parallel 12 Ω resistor in the bottom branch, which implies that the current through the bottom branch is 3 A, and the current through the top branch is 9 A. The voltage drop across the 12 Ω resistor is therefore $V = IR = (3 \text{ A})(12 \ \Omega) = 36$ V.

8. **(E)** Since points a and b are grounded, they're at the same potential (call it zero).

Traveling from b to a across the battery, the potential increases by 24 V, so it must decrease by 24 V across the 8 Ω resistor as we reach point a. Thus, $I = V/R = (24\ \text{V})/(8\ \Omega) = 3$ A.

9. **(D)** The equation $P = I^2R$ gives

$$P = (0.5\ \text{A})^2(100\ \Omega) = 25\ \text{W} = 25\ \text{J/s}$$

Therefore, in 20 s, the energy dissipated as heat is

$$E = Pt = (25\ \text{J/s})(20\ \text{s}) = 500\ \text{J}$$

10. **(D)** The equivalent resistance is $R = 50 + 200 = 250\ \Omega$, so the time constant is

$$\tau = RC = (250\ \Omega)(200\ \mu\text{F}) = 0.05\ \text{s}$$

SECTION II: FREE RESPONSE

1. (a) The two parallel branches, the one containing the 40 Ω resistor and the other a total of 120 Ω, is equivalent to a single 30 Ω resistance. This 30 Ω resistance is in series with the three 10 Ω resistors, giving an overall equivalent circuit resistance of $10 + 10 + 30 + 10 = 60\ \Omega$. Therefore, the current supplied by the battery is $I = V/R = (120\ \text{V})/(60\ \Omega) = 2$ A, so it must supply energy at a rate of $P = IV = (2\ \text{A})(120\ \text{V}) = 240$ W.

(b) Since three times as much current will flow through the 40 Ω resistor as through the branch containing 120 Ω of resistance, the current through the 40 Ω resistor must be 1.5 A.

(c) (i) $V_a - V_b = IR_{20} + IR_{100} = (0.5\ \text{A})(20\ \Omega) + (0.5\ \text{A})(100\ \Omega) = 60$ V.

(ii) Point a is at the higher potential (current flows from high to low potential).

(d) Because energy is equal to power multiplied by time, we get

$$E = Pt = I^2Rt = (0.5\ \text{A})^2(100\ \Omega)(10\ \text{s}) = 250\ \text{J}$$

(e) Using the equation $R = \rho L/A$, with $A = \pi r^2$, we find

$$R = \frac{\rho L}{\pi r^2} \quad \Rightarrow \quad r = \sqrt{\frac{\rho L}{\pi R}} = \sqrt{\frac{(0.45 \; \Omega \cdot m)(0.04 \; m)}{\pi (100 \; \Omega)}} \doteq 0.0076 \; m = 7.6 \; mm$$

2. (a) The initial current, I_0, is $\mathcal{E}/r$.

   (b) Apply the equation $Q(t) = Q_f(1 - e^{-t/RC})$. We want $1 - e^{-t/RC}$ to equal 1/2, so

   $$1 - e^{-t/RC} = \tfrac{1}{2} \quad \Rightarrow \quad e^{-t/RC} = \tfrac{1}{2} \quad \Rightarrow \quad -\frac{t}{RC} = \ln \tfrac{1}{2} = -\ln 2 \quad \Rightarrow \quad t = (\ln 2)RC$$

   (c) Because it is connected to the positive terminal of the battery, the top plate will become positively charged.

   (d) When the current through r is zero, the capacitor is fully charged, with the voltage across its plates matching the emf of the battery. Therefore,

   $$U_E = \tfrac{1}{2}CV^2 = \tfrac{1}{2}C\mathcal{E}^2$$

   (e) The current established by the discharging capacitor decreases exponentially according to the equation $I(t) = I_0 e^{-t/t} = (\mathcal{E}/R)e^{-t/RC}$.

   (f) The power dissipated is given by the joule heating law, $P = I^2 R$:

   $$P(t) = [I(t)]^2 R = \left(\frac{\mathcal{E}}{R}e^{-t/RC}\right)^2 R = \frac{\mathcal{E}^2}{R}e^{-2t/RC}$$

   (g) We give two solutions. First, the total energy dissipated by the resistor will equal the integral of $P(t)$ from $t = 0$ to $t = \infty$:

   $$
   \begin{aligned}
   E &= \int_0^\infty P(t)\,dt \\
   &= \int_0^\infty \frac{\mathcal{E}^2}{R}e^{-2t/RC}\,dt \\
   &= \frac{\mathcal{E}^2}{R}\left[-\frac{RC}{2}e^{-2t/RC}\right]_0^\infty \\
   &= \frac{C\mathcal{E}^2}{2}
   \end{aligned}
   $$

   Alternatively, simply notice that all the energy stored in the capacitor will be dissipated as heat by the resistor R. But from part (d), we know that the initial energy stored in the capacitor (before discharging) was $\tfrac{1}{2}C\mathcal{E}^2$.

CHAPTER 13 REVIEW QUESTIONS

SECTION I: MULTIPLE CHOICE

1. **(D)** Statement I is false: The magnetic field lines due to a current-carrying wire encircle the wire in closed loops. Statement II is also false: Since the magnetic force is always perpendicular to the charged particle's velocity vector, it can do work on the charged particle; therefore, it cannot change the particle's kinetic energy. Statement III, however, is true: If the charged particle's velocity is parallel (or antiparallel) to the magnetic field lines, then the particle will feel no magnetic force.

2. **(C)** The magnitude of the magnetic force is $F_B = qvB$, so the acceleration of the particle has magnitude

$$a = \frac{F_B}{m} = \frac{qvB}{m} = \frac{(4.0 \times 10^{-9} \text{ C})(3 \times 10^4 \text{ m/s})(0.1 \text{ T})}{2 \times 10^{-4} \text{ kg}} = 0.06 \text{ m/s}^2$$

3. **(D)** By the right-hand rule, the direction of $\mathbf{v} \times \mathbf{B}$ is into the plane of the page. Since the particle carries a negative charge, the magnetic force it feels will be out of the page.

4. **(D)** Since $\mathbf{F}_B$ is always perpendicular to $\mathbf{v}$, $\mathbf{v}$ cannot be upward or downward in the plane of the page; this eliminates choices B and C. The velocity vector also cannot be to the right (choice A), since then $\mathbf{v}$ would be antiparallel to $\mathbf{B}$, and $\mathbf{F}_B$ would be zero. Because the charge is positive, the direction of $\mathbf{F}_B$ will be the same as the direction of $\mathbf{v} \times \mathbf{B}$. In order for $\mathbf{v} \times \mathbf{B}$ to be downward in the plane of the page, the right-hand rule implies that $\mathbf{v}$ must be out of the plane of the page.

5. **(A)** The magnetic force provides the centripetal force on the charged particle. Therefore,

$$qvB = \frac{mv^2}{r} \quad \Rightarrow \quad qB = \frac{mv}{r} \quad \Rightarrow \quad mv = qBr \quad \Rightarrow \quad p = qBr$$

6. **(D)** The strength of the magnetic field at a distance r from a long, straight wire carrying a current I is given by the equation $B = (\mu_0/2\pi)(I/r)$. Therefore,

$$\frac{\mu_0}{2\pi} \frac{I}{r} = \frac{(4\pi \times 10^{-7} \text{ T·m/A})}{2\pi} \frac{10 \text{ A}}{0.02 \text{ m}} = 1 \times 10^{-4} \text{ T}$$

7. **(D)** By Newton's Third Law, neither choice A nor choice B can be correct. Also, as we learned in Example 13.9, if two parallel wires carry current in the same direction, the magnetic force between them is attractive; this eliminates choices C and E. Therefore, the answer must be D. The strength of the magnetic field at a distance r from a long, straight wire carrying a current I_1 is given by the equation $B_1 = (\pi_0/2\pi)(I_1/r)$. The magnetic force on a wire of length ℓ carrying a current I through a magnetic field $\mathbf{B}$ is $I(\ell \times \mathbf{B})$, so the force on Wire #2 (F_{B2}) due to the magnetic field of Wire #1 (B_1) is

$$F_{B2} = I_2 \ell B_1 = I_2 \ell \frac{\mu_0}{2\pi} \frac{I_1}{r}$$

which implies

$$\frac{F_{B2}}{\ell} = \frac{\mu_0}{2\pi} \frac{I_1 I_2}{r} = \frac{(4\pi \times 10^{-7} \text{ N}/\text{A}^2)}{2\pi} \frac{(5 \text{ A})(10 \text{ A})}{0.01 \text{ m}} = 0.001 \text{ N}/\text{m}$$

8. **(E)** The strength of the magnetic field at a distance r from a long, straight wire carrying a current I is given by the equation $B = (\mu_0/2\pi)(I/r)$. Therefore, the strength of the magnetic field at point P due to either wire is $B = (\mu_0/2\pi)(I/\frac{1}{2}d)$. By the right-hand rule, the direction of the magnetic field at P due to the top wire is into the plane of the page and the direction of the magnetic field at P due to the bottom wire is out of the plane of the page. Since the two magnetic field vectors at P have the same magnitude and opposite directions, the net magnetic field at point P is zero.

9. **(B)** The strength of the magnetic field within a hollow, ideal solenoid is given by the equation $B = \mu_0 nI$, where n denotes the number of turns per unit length and I is the current in the solenoid. Therefore,

$$B = \mu_0 nI = \mu_0 \frac{N}{\ell} I \quad \Rightarrow \quad N = \frac{\ell B}{\mu_0 I}$$

This gives

$$N = \frac{\ell B}{\mu_0 I} = \frac{(0.80 \text{ m})(0.2 \text{ T})}{(4\pi \times 10^{-7} \text{ T} \cdot \text{m}/\text{A})(20 \text{ A})} = 6400$$

10. **(E)** By Ampere's Law, $\oint_{\text{loop}} \mathbf{B} \cdot d\mathbf{s} = \mu_0 I_{\text{through loop}}$. Therefore,

$$I_{\text{through loop}} = \frac{\oint_{\text{loop}} \mathbf{B} \cdot d\mathbf{s}}{\mu_0} = \frac{6.28 \times 10^{-6} \text{ T} \cdot \text{m}}{4\pi \times 10^{-7} \text{ T} \cdot \text{m}/\text{A}} = 5 \text{ A}$$

SECTION II: FREE RESPONSE

1. (a) The acceleration of an ion of charge q is equal to F_E/m. The electric force is equal to qE, where $E = V/d$. Therefore, $a = qV/(dm)$.

   (b) Using $a = qV/(dm)$ and the equation $v^2 = v_0^2 + 2ad = 2ad$, we get

   $$v^2 = 2\frac{qV}{dm}d \quad \Rightarrow \quad v = \sqrt{\frac{2qV}{m}}$$

   As an alternate solution, notice that the change in the electrical potential energy of the ion from the source S to the entrance to the magnetic-field region is equal to qV; this is equal to the gain in the particle's kinetic energy. Therefore,

   $$qV = \tfrac{1}{2}mv^2 \quad \Rightarrow \quad v = \sqrt{\frac{2qV}{m}}$$

(c) (i) and (ii) Use the right-hand rule. Since **v** points to the right and **B** is into the plane of the page, the direction of **v** × **B** is upward. Therefore, the magnetic force on a positively-charged particle (cation) will be upward, and the magnetic force on a negatively-charged particle (anion) will be downward. The magnetic force provides the centripetal force that causes the ion to travel in a circular path. Therefore, a cation would follow Path 1 and an anion would follow Path 2.

(d) Since the magnetic force on the ion provides the centripetal force,

$$qvB = \frac{mv^2}{r} \quad \Rightarrow \quad qvB = \frac{mv^2}{\frac{1}{2}y} \quad \Rightarrow \quad m = \frac{qBy}{2v}$$

Now, by the result of part (b),

$$m = \frac{qBy}{2\sqrt{\dfrac{2qV}{m}}} \quad \Rightarrow \quad m^2 = \frac{q^2B^2y^2}{\dfrac{8qV}{m}} \quad \Rightarrow \quad m^2 = \frac{mq^2B^2y^2}{8qV} \quad \Rightarrow \quad m = \frac{qB^2y^2}{8V}$$

(e) Since the magnetic force cannot change the speed of a charged particle, the time required for the ion to hit the photographic plate is equal to the distance traveled (the length of the semicircle) divided by the speed computed in part (b):

$$t = \frac{s}{v} = \frac{\pi \cdot \frac{1}{2}y}{\sqrt{\dfrac{2qV}{m}}} = \frac{1}{2}\pi y\sqrt{\frac{m}{2qV}}$$

(f) Since the magnetic force **F**$_B$ is always perpendicular to a charged particle's velocity vector **v**, it can do no work on the particle. Thus, the answer is zero.

2. (a) The current in the rectangular loop is equal to V divided by the resistance of the rectangular loop. Using the equation $R = \rho \ell / A$, we have

$$R = \frac{\rho\ell}{A} = \frac{\rho \cdot 2(a+b)}{\pi(\frac{1}{2}d)^2} = \frac{8\rho(a+b)}{\pi d^2}$$

Therefore, the current in the rectangular loop is

$$I_{\text{loop}} = \frac{V}{R} = \frac{\pi d^2 V}{8\rho(a+b)}$$

(b) We use the equation $\mathbf{F}_B = I(\boldsymbol{\ell} \times \mathbf{B})$ to find the magnetic force on each side of the rectangular loop. By symmetry, the magnetic forces on the sides of length a have the same magnitude but opposite direction, so they cancel. The total magnetic force on the loop is equal to the sum of the magnetic forces on the sides of length b. Current in the rectangle is directed clockwise, so the current in the bottom wire of length b (the one closer to the wire) is directed to the left and the current in the top wire of length b is directed to the right. Currents that are parallel feel an attractive force, while currents that are antiparallel feel a repulsive force. Since the strength of the magnetic field at a distance r from a long, straight wire carrying a current I is given by the equation $B = (\mu_0/2\pi)(I/r)$, we find that

magnetic force on bottom wire:

$$\mathbf{F}_{B1} = I_{\text{loop}} b \cdot \frac{\mu_0 I}{\pi c}, \text{ upward (away from the long wire)}$$

magnetic force on top wire:

$$\mathbf{F}_{B2} = I_{\text{loop}} b \cdot \frac{\mu_0 I}{\pi(c+a)}, \text{ downward (toward the long wire)}$$

Since $\mathbf{F}_{B1}$ has a greater magnitude than $\mathbf{F}_{B2}$, and the forces point in opposite directions (with the direction of the net force equaling the direction of $\mathbf{F}_{B1}$), the magnitude of the total magnetic force on the loop is equal to the difference between the magnitudes of $\mathbf{F}_{B1}$ and $\mathbf{F}_{B2}$. Therefore,

$$\mathbf{F}_B = \mathbf{F}_{B1} + \mathbf{F}_{B2} = I_{\text{loop}} b \cdot \frac{\mu_0 I}{\pi c} - I_{\text{loop}} b \cdot \frac{\mu_0 I}{\pi(c+a)}, \text{ upward}$$

$$= \frac{\mu_0 I \cdot I_{\text{loop}} b}{\pi}\left(\frac{1}{c} - \frac{1}{c+a}\right), \text{ upward}$$

$$= \frac{\mu_0 I \cdot I_{\text{loop}} b}{\pi}\frac{a}{c(c+a)}, \text{ upward}$$

Substituting the result of part (a) for I_{loop} gives

$$\mathbf{F}_B = \frac{\mu_0 I \cdot \dfrac{\pi d^2 V}{8\rho(a+b)} b}{\pi}\frac{a}{c(c+a)}, \text{ upward}$$

$$= \frac{\mu_0 I \cdot d^2 V a b}{8\rho(a+b)(a+c)c}, \text{ upward (away from long wire)}$$

(c) The circumference of the circle will be equal to the perimeter of the rectangle; thus,

$$2\pi r = 2(a+b) \quad \Rightarrow \quad r = \frac{a+b}{\pi}$$

(d) If the long straight wire passes through the center of the circular loop, then the magnetic field line of the straight wire would coincide with the current in the loop. Whether the current in the loop is parallel or antiparallel to the direction of the magnetic field line makes no difference; the magnetic force on the current-carrying loop would be zero (because $\ell \times \mathbf{B}$ would be $\mathbf{0}$).

(e) The current in the sliding wire is directed to the right, and the magnetic field is into the plane of the page, so the right-hand rule tells us that the direction of $\ell \times \mathbf{B}$ [and, therefore, of $\mathbf{F_B} = I(\ell \times \mathbf{B})$, the magnetic force on the sliding wire] will be upward. If this upward force is to balance the downward gravitational force, then, because $\ell = x$,

$$IxB = mg \quad \Rightarrow \quad I = \frac{mg}{xB}$$

3. (a) Neither of the straight portions of the wire contribute to the magnetic field at point C; this is because $\hat{\mathbf{r}}$ is parallel (or antiparallel) to ℓ, so the cross product $\ell \times \hat{\mathbf{r}}$, which appears in the Biot–Savart Law, would be zero. Therefore, only the curved portion of the wire generates a magnetic field at C. Refer to the diagram below:

By the Biot–Savart Law, the magnetic field at C due to a length $d\ell$ of the curved has magnitude

$$dB = \frac{\mu_0}{4\pi} \frac{I \cdot d\ell}{r^2} = \frac{\mu_0}{4\pi} \frac{I \cdot (x\,d\theta)}{x^2} = \frac{\mu_0 I}{4\pi x} d\theta$$

Integrating this from $\theta = 0$ to $\theta = \phi$ gives

$$B = \int dB = \frac{\mu_0 I}{4\pi x} \int_0^\phi d\theta = \frac{\mu_0 I \phi}{4\pi x}$$

By the right-hand rule, the direction of $\mathbf{B}$ at C is into the plane of the page. (Either curl the fingers of your right hand in the direction of the current in the curve and notice that your thumb points into the page, or apply the right hand rule to $d\ell \times \hat{\mathbf{r}}$.)

(b) If the charged particle is placed at rest at point C, then it would feel no magnetic force. Only particles that move through magnetic fields feel a magnetic force.

(c) Since the current in the straight wire is antiparallel to the magnetic field at C, it will experience zero magnetic force ($\ell \times \mathbf{B} = 0$).

4. (a) The current in the rod is equal to the current density times the cross-sectional area of the rod: $I = JA = J(\pi R^2)$.

(b) (i) We apply Ampere's Law to a circular loop of radius $r < R$. The magnetic field lines will be circles centered on the central axis of the rod (thus coinciding with the position of the Amperian loop drawn below):

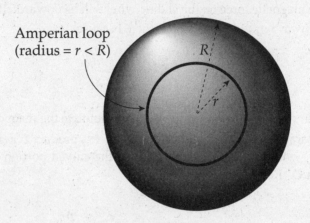

Amperian loop
(radius = $r < R$)

R

r

$$\oint_{\text{loop}} \mathbf{B} \cdot d\mathbf{s} = \mu_0 I_{\text{through loop}}$$
$$B(2\pi r) = \mu_0 \cdot JA_{\text{enclosed by loop}}$$
$$= \mu_0 \cdot J(\pi r^2)$$
$$B = \tfrac{1}{2}\mu_0 \cdot Jr$$

To write this result in terms of I, we simply note from part (a) that $J = I/(\pi R^2)$, so

$$B = \tfrac{1}{2}\mu_0 \cdot Jr = \tfrac{1}{2}\mu_0 \cdot \frac{I}{\pi R^2} \cdot r = \frac{\mu_0}{2\pi}\frac{I}{R^2} r$$

(b) (ii) Applying Ampere's Law to an Amperian loop of radius $r > R$,

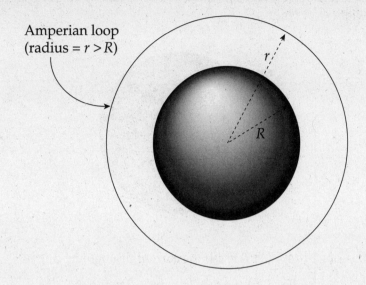

Amperian loop
(radius = $r > R$)

r

R

we get

$$\oint_{\text{loop}} \mathbf{B} \cdot d\mathbf{s} = \mu_0 I_{\text{through loop}}$$

$$B(2\pi r) = \mu_0 \cdot J A_{\text{enclosed by loop}}$$

$$= \mu_0 \cdot J(\pi R^2)$$

$$B = \tfrac{1}{2} \mu_0 J \frac{R^2}{r}$$

To write this result in terms of I, we once again use $J = I/(\pi R^2)$, giving

$$B = \tfrac{1}{2} \mu_0 J \frac{R^2}{r} = \tfrac{1}{2} \mu_0 \cdot \frac{I}{\pi R^2} \cdot \frac{R^2}{r} = \frac{\mu_0}{2\pi} \frac{I}{r}$$

which is certainly a familiar result!

(c) Since current density is current per unit area, the units of J are A/m^2. Therefore,

$$J = \sigma r \quad \Rightarrow \quad [J] = [\sigma][r] \quad \Rightarrow \quad [\sigma] = \frac{[J]}{[r]} = \frac{\text{A}/\text{m}^2}{\text{m}} = \frac{\text{A}}{\text{m}^3}$$

(d) Since the current density varies with the radial distance from the rod's center, construct a thin ring of width dr at radius r:

The area of this ring is $dA = (2\pi r)\,dr$, so the current through the ring is

$$dI = J\,dA = (\sigma r)(2\pi r\,dr) = 2\pi\sigma\,r^2\,dr$$

Therefore, the total current through the rod is

$$I = \int dI = \int_{r=0}^{r=R}(2\pi\sigma \cdot r^2\,dr) = 2\pi\sigma\int_0^R r^2\,dr = \tfrac{2}{3}\pi\sigma R^3 \qquad (1)$$

(e) (i) As in part (b), construct an Amperian loop of radius $r < R$. The current through such a loop is given by the result of Equation (1) above with r replacing R. Therefore,

$$\oint_{\text{loop}} \mathbf{B}\cdot d\mathbf{s} = \mu_0 I_{\text{through loop}}$$
$$B(2\pi r) = \mu_0 \cdot (\tfrac{2}{3}\pi\sigma r^3)$$
$$B = \tfrac{1}{3}\mu_0\sigma r^2$$

To write this result in terms of I, we simply note from part (a) that $\sigma = I/\tfrac{2}{3}\pi R^3$, so

$$B = \tfrac{1}{3}\mu_0\sigma r^2 = \tfrac{1}{3}\mu_0 \cdot \frac{I}{\tfrac{2}{3}\pi R^3} \cdot r^2 - \frac{\mu_0}{2\pi}\frac{I}{R^3}r^2$$

(e) (ii) We can either follow the same procedure as in (b) (ii)—and use the results of (d) and (e) (i)—or we can simply notice that outside the wire, the full current I would pass through our circular Amperian loop of radius $r > R$, so the magnetic field at such points must be given once again by the familiar formula

$$B = \frac{\mu_0}{2\pi}\frac{I}{r}$$

CHAPTER 14 REVIEW QUESTIONS

SECTION I: MULTIPLE CHOICE

1. **(E)** Since **v** is upward and **B** is out of the page, the direction of $\mathbf{v} \times \mathbf{B}$ is to the right. Therefore, free electrons in the wire will be pushed to the left, leaving an excess of positive charge at the right. Therefore, the potential at point b will be higher than at point a, by $\mathcal{E} = vBL$ (motional emf).

2. **(C)** Consider a small radial segment of length dr as shown:

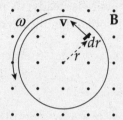

Its velocity is $v = \omega r$, so the motional emf in this little piece is $d\mathcal{E} = (\omega r)B\,dr$. Integrating from $r = 0$ to $r = a$ gives the induced emf between the center and the rim:

$$\mathcal{E} = \int d\mathcal{E} = \int_{r=0}^{r=a} \omega r B\,dr = \omega B \int_0^a r\,dr = \tfrac{1}{2}\omega B a^2$$

3. **(D)** Since the loop is so small, we can assume that the magnetic field due to the wire is uniform throughout the loop's enclosed area and equal to its value at the loop's center. The magnetic field due to the wire is given by $B = (\mu_0/2\pi)(I/r)$, so as the loop is moved, the magnetic field and the magnetic flux through the loop change:

$$\left|\mathcal{E}_{avg}\right| = \left|\frac{\Delta\Phi_B}{\Delta t}\right| = \left|\frac{\Delta(BA)}{\Delta t}\right| = \left|A\frac{\Delta B}{\Delta t}\right| = \left|\frac{\pi r^2}{t}\left(\frac{\mu_0 I}{2\pi x_1} - \frac{\mu_0 I}{2\pi x_2}\right)\right| = \frac{\mu_0 I r^2}{2t}\left(\frac{1}{x_1} - \frac{1}{x_2}\right) = \frac{\mu_0 I r^2 (x_2 - x_1)}{2t x_1 x_2}$$

Therefore, the current induced in the loop will be

$$I = \frac{\left|\mathcal{E}_{avg}\right|}{R} = \frac{\mu_0 I r^2 (x_2 - x_1)}{2t x_1 x_2 R}$$

Since the flux is into the page and increasing, Lenz's law says that the induced current will be counterclockwise, to oppose the increasing into-the-page flux.

4. **(A)** The magnetic field through the loop is $B = \mu_0 nI$. Since its area is $A = \pi r^2$, the magnetic flux through the loop is $\Phi_B = BA = (\mu_0 nI)(\pi r^2)$. If the current changes (with $\Delta I/\Delta t = -a$), then the magnetic flux through the loop changes, which, by Faraday's Law, implies that an emf (and a current) will be induced. We get

$$\mathcal{E} = -\frac{\Delta\Phi_B}{\Delta t} = -\frac{\Delta(\mu_0 nI \cdot \pi r^2)}{\Delta t} = -(\mu_0 n\pi r^2)\frac{\Delta I}{\Delta t} = -\mu_0 \pi n r^2 (-a) = \mu_0 \pi n r^2 a$$

Since the magnetic flux into the page is decreasing, the direction of the induced current will be clockwise (opposing a *decreasing into-the-page flux* means that the induced current will create more into-the-page flux).

5. **(C)** By definition, magnetic field lines emerge from the north pole and enter at the south pole. Therefore, as the north pole is moved upward through the loop, the upward magnetic flux increases. To oppose an increasing upward flux, the direction of the induced current will be clockwise (as seen from above) to generate some downward magnetic flux. Now, as the south pole moves away from the center of the loop, there is a decreasing upward magnetic flux, so the direction of the induced current will be counterclockwise.

6. **(E)** Since the current in the straight wire is steady, there is no change in the magnetic field, no change in magnetic flux, and, therefore, no induced current.

7. **(A)** Use the equation $I(t) = I_{max}(1 - e^{-t/\tau_L})$. In order for $I(t)$ to equal $\frac{3}{4}I_{max}$, we must have $e^{-t/\tau_L} = \frac{1}{4}$. Therefore,

$$-t/\tau_L = \ln\tfrac{1}{4} = -\ln 4 \;\Rightarrow\; t = (\ln 4)\tau_L = (\ln 4)\frac{L}{R}$$

8. **(D)** The value of I_{max} is $\mathcal{E}/R$. Since the magnetic energy stored in an inductor is given by $U_B = \frac{1}{2}LI^2$, we have

$$U_B = \tfrac{1}{2}L\left(\frac{\mathcal{E}}{R}\right)^2 = \frac{L\mathcal{E}^2}{2R^2}$$

9. **(B)** By definition of self-inductance, $L = N\Phi_B/I$. The total magnetic flux through all the windings of the solenoid is $N\Phi_B$, which is equal to LI. Since $I = \mathcal{E}/R$, we have

$$\Phi_{B,total} = L(\mathcal{E}/R)$$

10. **(D)** Faraday's Law shows how a changing B-field generates an E-field. The Ampere–Maxwell Law shows the reverse: how a changing E-field generates a B-field.

SECTION II: FREE RESPONSE

1. (a) Consider a small section of length dx of the rod at a distance x from the nonrotating end:

The velocity of this small piece is $v = \omega x$, so the motional emf induced between its ends is $d\mathcal{E} = vB\,dx = \omega xB\,dx$. Integrating this from $x = 0$ to $x = \ell$ gives

$$\mathcal{E} = \int d\mathcal{E} = \int_{x=0}^{x=\ell} \omega xB\,dx = \omega B \int_0^\ell x\,dx = \tfrac{1}{2}\omega B\ell^2$$

(b) Refer to the view from above of the rod:

By the right-hand rule, the direction of $\mathbf{v} \times \mathbf{B}$ is to the right, so the magnetic force on free electrons will be to the left, leaving excess *positive* charge at the right (rotating) end.

(c) Consider a small section of length dy at a distance y from the straight wire:

Since the magnetic field at the position of this section is $(\mu_0/2\pi)(I/y)$, the motional emf induced between its ends is $d\mathcal{E} = vB\,dy = v(\mu_0/2\pi)(I/y)\,dy$. Integrating this from $y = a$ to $y = a + \ell$ gives

$$\mathcal{E} = \int d\mathcal{E} = \int_{y=a}^{y=a+\ell} \frac{\mu_0}{2\pi}\frac{I}{y} v\,dy = \frac{\mu_0 Iv}{2\pi} \int_a^{a+\ell} \frac{dy}{y} = \frac{\mu_0 Iv}{2\pi}\ln\frac{a+\ell}{a}$$

(d) The magnetic field above the wire (where the rod is sliding) is out of the plane of the page, so the direction of $\mathbf{v} \times \mathbf{B}$ is downward.

Therefore, free electrons in the rod will be pushed upward to the far end of the rod, causing it to become negatively charged.

2. (a) As the loop rotates, the angle that the normal to the loop's enclosed area makes with $\mathbf{B}$ changes according to the equation $\theta = \omega t$. Therefore, the magnetic flux through the loop is

$$\Phi_B(t) = BA \cos\theta = BA \cos\omega t = abB \cos\omega t$$

(b) According to Faraday's Law, the induced emf is equal to the rate of change of magnetic flux through the loop (with a minus sign included to conform to Lenz's Law). Therefore,

$$\varepsilon = -\frac{d\Phi_B}{dt} = -\frac{d}{dt}(abB\cos\omega t) = -[abB\omega(-\sin\omega t)] = ab\omega B \sin\omega t$$

(c) Using the result of part (b) with the equation $I = \varepsilon/R$, we find that the induced current is a function of time given by

$$I(t) = \frac{\varepsilon}{R} = \frac{ab\omega B \sin\omega t}{R}$$

(d) As the loop rotates from $\theta = 0$ to $\theta = \pi/2$, the magnetic flux (to the right, the $+x$ direction) through the loop decreases from $BA = abB$ to zero. To oppose this decreasing flux to the right, the current will be induced in a direction to generate a magnetic field with a component in the $+x$ direction. The current will be flowing from point 3 to 4 to 1 to 2 to 3.

(e) The rate at which energy is dissipated as heat in the loop is given by the equation $P = I^2R = (\varepsilon/R)^2R = \varepsilon^2/R$, so

$$P = \frac{\varepsilon^2}{R} = \frac{(ab\omega B \sin\omega t)^2}{R} = \frac{a^2b^2\omega^2B^2}{R}\sin^2\omega t$$

In one revolution, ωt increases from 0 to 2π, so the energy dissipated is

$$E = \int P\,dt = \int_{t=0}^{t=2\pi/\omega} \frac{a^2 b^2 \omega^2 B^2}{R} \sin^2 \omega t\,dt$$

$$= \frac{a^2 b^2 \omega^2 B^2}{R} \int_{t=0}^{t=2\pi/\omega} \sin^2 \omega t\,dt$$

$$= \frac{a^2 b^2 \omega^2 B^2}{R} \int_{t=0}^{t=2\pi/\omega} \tfrac{1}{2}(1 - \cos 2\omega t)\,dt$$

$$= \frac{a^2 b^2 \omega^2 B^2}{R} \left[\tfrac{1}{2}t - \tfrac{1}{4\omega} \sin 2\omega t \right]_{t=0}^{t=2\pi/\omega}$$

$$= \frac{a^2 b^2 \omega^2 B^2}{R} \cdot \frac{\pi}{\omega}$$

$$= \frac{\pi a^2 b^2 \omega B^2}{R}$$

(f) The work done by the externally-provided torque is transformed into the heat lost in the loop. Equivalently, the rate at which the torque does work is equal to the rate at which heat energy is dissipated in the wires of the loop. Since the power associated with the external torque is $P = \tau\omega$, the result of part (e) gives

$$\tau\omega = \frac{a^2 b^2 \omega^2 B^2}{R} \sin^2 \omega t \quad \Rightarrow \quad \tau = \frac{a^2 b^2 \omega B^2}{R} \sin^2 \omega t$$

3. (a) Construct an Amperian loop of radius R whose center coincides with the center of the toroid. Then only the current in the inner set of N windings pierces through the area bounded by the loop, so Ampere's Law becomes

$$\oint_{\text{loop}} \mathbf{B} \cdot d\mathbf{s} = \mu_0 I_{\text{through loop}}$$

$$B(2\pi R) = \mu_0 (NI)$$

$$B = \frac{\mu_0}{2\pi} \frac{NI}{R}$$

(b) Because there is no magnetic field outside the toroid, the magnetic flux through the loop is equal to B times the cross-sectional area of the toroid (which is πa^2). Therefore, by Faraday's Law,

$$\mathcal{E} = -\frac{d\Phi_B}{dt} = -\frac{d}{dt}(B \cdot \pi a^2)$$

$$= -\frac{d}{dt}\left(\frac{\mu_0 NI}{2\pi R} \cdot \pi a^2\right)$$

$$= -\frac{\mu_0 Na^2}{2R}\frac{dI}{dt}$$

$$= -\frac{\mu_0 Na^2}{2R} \cdot \frac{d}{dt}(I_0 \sin\omega t)$$

$$= -\frac{\mu_0 I_0 Na^2 \omega}{2R}\cos\omega t$$

(c) Writing Faraday's Law in the form

$$\oint_{\text{loop}} \mathbf{E} \cdot d\mathbf{s} = -\frac{d\Phi_B}{dt}$$

and applying it to the circular loop of radius $2a$, we find that

$$\oint_{\text{loop}} \mathbf{E} \cdot d\mathbf{s} = -\frac{d\Phi_B}{dt}$$

$$E(2\pi \cdot r_{\text{loop}}) = -\frac{d\Phi_B}{dt}$$

$$E(2\pi \cdot 2a) = -\frac{\mu_0 I_0 Na^2 \omega}{2R}\cos\omega t$$

$$E = -\frac{\mu_0 I_0 Na\omega}{8\pi R}\cos\omega t$$

(d) By definition, the self-inductance, L, is equal to $N\Phi_B/I$. Since

$$\Phi_B = B \cdot \pi a^2 = \frac{\mu_0 NI}{2\pi R} \cdot \pi a^2 = \frac{\mu_0 NIa^2}{2R}$$

as we calculated in the solution to part (b), we find that

$$L = \frac{N\Phi_B}{I} = \frac{N}{I} \cdot \frac{\mu_0 NIa^2}{2R} = \frac{\mu_0 N^2 a^2}{2R}$$

CHAPTER 15 REVIEW QUESTIONS

SECTION I: MULTIPLE CHOICE

1. **(D)** From the equation $\lambda f = v$, we find that

$$\lambda = \frac{v}{f} = \frac{10 \text{ m/s}}{5 \text{ Hz}} = 2 \text{ m}$$

2. **(C)** The speed of a transverse traveling wave on a stretched rope is given by the equation $v = \sqrt{F_T / \mu}$. Therefore,

$$v = \sqrt{\frac{F_T}{m/L}} = \sqrt{\frac{80 \text{ N}}{(1 \text{ kg})/(5 \text{ m})}} = \sqrt{400 \text{ m}^2/\text{s}^2} = 20 \text{ m/s}$$

3. **(D)** The time interval from a point moving from its maximum displacement above $y = 0$ (equilibrium) to its maximum displacement below equilibrium is equal to one-half the period of the wave. In this case,

$$T = \frac{1}{f} = \frac{\lambda}{v} = \frac{8 \text{ m}}{2 \text{ m/s}} = 4 \text{ s}$$

so the desired time is $\frac{1}{2}(4 \text{ s}) = 2 \text{ s}$.

4. **(D)** The standard equation for a transverse traveling wave has the form $y = A \sin(\omega t \pm \kappa x)$, where ω is the angular frequency and κ is the angular wave number. Here, $\kappa = \frac{1}{2}\pi \text{ cm}^{-1}$. Since, by definition, $\kappa = 2\pi/\lambda$, we have

$$\lambda = \frac{2\pi}{\kappa} = \frac{2\pi}{\frac{1}{2}\pi \text{ cm}^{-1}} = 4 \text{ cm}$$

5. **(E)** The distance between successive nodes is always equal to $\frac{1}{2}\lambda$. If a standing wave on a string fixed at both ends has a total of 4 nodes, the string must have a length L equal to $3(\frac{1}{2}\lambda)$. If $L = 6$ m, then λ must equal 4 m.

6. **(B)** We found in the previous question that $\lambda = 4$ m. Since $v = 40$ m/s, the frequency of this standing wave must be

$$f = \frac{v}{\lambda} = \frac{40 \text{ m/s}}{4 \text{ m}} = 10 \text{ Hz}$$

7. **(A)** In general, sound travels faster through solids than through gases. Therefore, when the wave enters the air from the metal rod, its speed will decrease. The frequency, however, will not change. Since $v = \lambda f$ must always be satisfied, a decrease in v implies a decrease in λ.

8. **(A)** The distance from S_2 to P is 5 m (it's the hypotenuse of 3-4-5 triangle), and the distance from S_1 to P is 4 m. The difference between the path lengths to point P is 1 m, which is half the

wavelength. Therefore, the sound waves are always exactly out of phase when they reach point P from the two speakers, causing destructive interference there. By contrast, since point Q is equidistant from the two speakers, the sound waves will always arrive in phase at Q, interfering constructively. Since there's destructive interference at P and constructive interference at Q, the amplitude at P will be less than at Q.

9. (E) The intensity (power per unit area) is proportional to $1/r^2$, where r is the distance between the source and the detector. If r increases by a factor of 10, the intensity decreases by a factor of 100. Because the decibel scale is logarithmic, if the intensity decreases by a factor of $100 = 10^2$, the decibel level decreases by $10 \log (10^2) = 20$ dB.

10. (B) An air column (such as an organ pipe) with one closed end resonates at frequencies given by the equation $f_n = nv/(4L)$ for odd integers n. The fundamental frequency corresponds, by definition, to $n = 1$. Therefore,

$$f_1 = \frac{v}{4L} = \frac{340 \text{ m/s}}{4(0.17 \text{ m})} = 500 \text{ Hz}$$

11. (B) The speed of the chirp is

$$v = \lambda f = (8.75 \times 10^{-3} \text{ m})(40 \times 10^3 \text{ Hz}) = 350 \text{ m/s}$$

If the distance from the bat to the tree is d, then the wave travels a total distance of $d + d = 2d$ (round-trip distance). If T is the time for this round-trip, then

$$2d = vT \quad \Rightarrow \quad d = \frac{vT}{2} = \frac{(350 \text{ m/s})(0.4 \text{ s})}{2} = 70 \text{ m}$$

12. (A) Since the car is traveling away from the stationary detector, the observed frequency will be lower than the source frequency. This eliminates choices B and C. Using the Doppler Effect equation, we find that

$$f_D = \frac{v}{v + v_S} \cdot f_S = \frac{340 \text{ m/s}}{(340 + 20) \text{ m/s}} \cdot (600 \text{ Hz}) = \frac{34}{36}(600 \text{ Hz})$$

SECTION II: FREE RESPONSE

1. (a) The speed of a transverse traveling wave on a stretched rope is given by the equation $v = \sqrt{F_T / \mu}$. Therefore,

$$v^2 = \frac{F_T}{\mu} \quad \Rightarrow \quad F_T = \mu v^2 = (0.4 \text{ kg/m})(12 \text{ m/s})^2 = 58 \text{ N}$$

(b) Use the fundamental equation $\lambda f = v$:

$$f = \frac{v}{\lambda} = \frac{12 \text{ m/s}}{2 \text{ m}} = 6 \text{ Hz}$$

(c) (i) Because higher harmonic numbers correspond to shorter wavelengths, the harmonic number of the 3.2 m standing wave must be higher than that of the 4 m standing wave. We're told that these harmonic numbers are consecutive integers, so if n is the harmonic number of the 4 m standing wave, then $n + 1$ is the harmonic number of the 3.2 m wave. Therefore,

$$\frac{2L}{n} = 4 \text{ m} \qquad \text{and} \qquad \frac{2L}{n+1} = 3.2 \text{ m}$$

The first equation says that $2L = 4n$, and the second one says that $2L = 3.2(n + 1)$. Therefore, $4n$ must equal $3.2(n + 1)$; solving this equation gives $n = 4$. Substituting this into either one of the displayed equations then gives $L = 8$ m.

(ii) Because $\mu = 0.4$ kg/m, the mass of the rope must be

$$m = \mu L = (0.4 \text{ kg/m})(8 \text{ m}) = 3.2 \text{ kg}$$

(d) We determined this in the solution to part (c) (i). The 4 m standing wave has harmonic number $n = 4$.

(e)

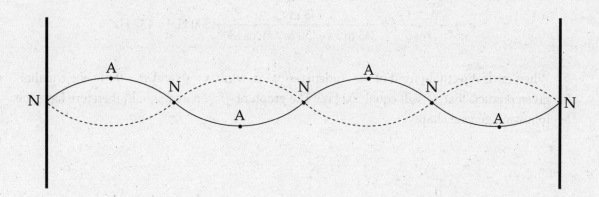

2. (a) For a stationary observer and a source moving away, the Doppler Effect equation predicts that

$$f_D = \frac{v}{v + v_C} \cdot f_C = \frac{345 \text{ m/s}}{(345 + 50) \text{ m/s}} (500 \text{ Hz}) = 437 \text{ Hz}$$

(b) Yes. If the source is stationary and the observer moves away, the Doppler Effect equation now gives

$$f_D = \frac{v - v_D}{v} \cdot f_C = \frac{(345 - 50) \text{ m/s}}{345 \text{ m/s}} (500 \text{ Hz}) = 428 \text{ Hz}$$

(c) With $\theta = 60°$, the given equation becomes

$$f' = \frac{v}{v - v_C \cos\theta} \cdot f = \frac{345 \text{ m/s}}{345 \text{ m/s} - (50 \text{ m/s})\cos 60°} (500 \text{ Hz}) = 539 \text{ Hz}$$

Notice that the observed frequency is higher than the source frequency, which we expect since the car is traveling toward the students.

(d) With $\theta = 120°$, the given equation becomes

$$f' = \frac{v}{v - v_C \cos\theta} \cdot f = \frac{345 \text{ m/s}}{345 \text{ m/s} - (50 \text{ m/s})\cos 120°}(500 \text{ Hz}) = 466 \text{ Hz}$$

Notice that the observed frequency is now lower than the source frequency, which we expect since the car is traveling away from the students.

(e) When the car is far to the left of the students' position, θ is very small (approaches 0°). Therefore, for large negative x, the observed frequency should approach

$$f' = \frac{v}{v - v_C \cos\theta} \cdot f = \frac{345 \text{ m/s}}{345 \text{ m/s} - (50 \text{ m/s})\cos 0°}(500 \text{ Hz}) = 585 \text{ Hz}$$

When the car is far to the right of the students' position, θ approaches 180°. Therefore, for large positive x, the observed frequency should approach

$$f' = \frac{v}{v - v_C \cos\theta} \cdot f = \frac{345 \text{ m/s}}{345 \text{ m/s} - (50 \text{ m/s})\cos 180°}(500 \text{ Hz}) = 437 \text{ Hz}$$

When car is directly in front of the students—that is, when $x = 0$ (and $\theta = 90°$)—the equation given predicts that f' will equal 500 Hz. The graph of f' versus x should therefore have the following general shape:

CHAPTER 16 REVIEW QUESTIONS

SECTION I: MULTIPLE CHOICE

1. **(B)** From the equation $\lambda f = c$, we find that

$$\lambda = \frac{c}{f} = \frac{3.0 \times 10^8 \text{ m/s}}{1.0 \times 10^{18} \text{ Hz}} = 3.0 \times 10^{-10} \text{ m}$$

2. **(D)** Since the fringe is bright, the waves must interfere constructively. This implies that the difference in path lengths must be a whole number times the wavelength, eliminating choices B, C, and E. The central maximum is equidistant from the two slits, so $\Delta \ell = 0$ there. At the first bright fringe above the central maximum, we have $\Delta \ell = \lambda$.

3. **(C)** First, eliminate choices A and B: The index of refraction is never smaller than 1. Refer to the following diagram:

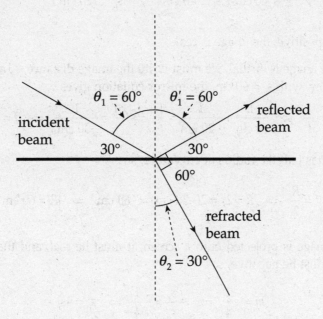

Since the reflected and refracted beams are perpendicular to each other, we have $\theta_2 = 30°$. Snell's Law then becomes

$$n_1 \sin \theta_1 = n_2 \sin \theta_2$$
$$1 \cdot \sin 60° = n_2 \sin 30°$$
$$\tfrac{1}{2}\sqrt{3} = n_2 \cdot \tfrac{1}{2}$$
$$\sqrt{3} = n_2$$

4. **(A)** The frequency is unchanged, but because the speed of light in diamond is less than in air, the wavelength of the light in diamond is shorter than its wavelength in air:

$$\lambda_{\text{in diamond}} = \frac{1}{f} v_{\text{in diamond}} = \frac{1}{f} \frac{c}{n_{\text{diamond}}} = \frac{1}{n_{\text{diamond}}} \lambda_{\text{in air}} = \frac{500 \text{ nm}}{2.4} = 208 \text{ nm}$$

5. **(A)** If the speed of light is less in Medium 2 than in Medium 1, then Medium 2 must have the higher index of refraction; that is, $n_2 > n_1$. Snell's Law then implies that $\theta_2 < \theta_1$: The beam will refract toward the normal upon transmission into Medium 2.

6. **(A)** The critical angle for total internal reflection is computed as follows:

$$\sin \theta_c = \frac{n_2}{n_1} = \frac{1.45}{2.90} = \frac{1}{2} \quad \Rightarrow \quad \theta_c = 30°$$

Total internal reflection can happen only if the incident beam originates in the medium with the higher index of refraction and strikes the interface of the other medium at an angle of incidence greater than the critical angle.

7. **(D)** If $s_o = 60$ cm and $f = 40$ cm, the mirror equation tells us that

$$\frac{1}{s_o} + \frac{1}{s_i} = \frac{1}{f} \quad \Rightarrow \quad \frac{1}{60 \text{ cm}} + \frac{1}{s_i} = \frac{1}{40 \text{ cm}} \quad \Rightarrow \quad \frac{1}{s_i} = \frac{1}{120 \text{ cm}} \quad \Rightarrow \quad s_i = 120 \text{ cm}$$

And, since s_i is positive, the image is real.

8. **(D)** Because the image is virtual, we must write the image distance, s_i, as a negative quantity: $s_i = -20$ cm. Now, with $s_o = 60$ cm, the mirror equation gives

$$\frac{1}{s_o} + \frac{1}{s_i} = \frac{1}{f} \quad \Rightarrow \quad \frac{1}{60 \text{ cm}} + \frac{1}{-20 \text{ cm}} = \frac{1}{f} \quad \Rightarrow \quad \frac{1}{f} = \frac{1}{-30 \text{ cm}} \quad \Rightarrow \quad f = -30 \text{ cm}$$

The focal length is half the radius of curvature, so

$$f = \frac{R}{2} \quad \Rightarrow \quad R = 2f = 2(-30 \text{ cm}) = -60 \text{ cm} \quad \Rightarrow \quad |R| = 60 \text{ cm}$$

9. **(C)** Since the image is projected onto a screen, it must be real, and therefore inverted. The magnification must be negative, so

$$m = -\frac{1}{4} \quad \Rightarrow \quad -\frac{s_i}{s_o} = -\frac{1}{4} \quad \Rightarrow \quad s_o = 4s_i$$

Because $s_i = 60$ cm, the object distance, s_o, must be 240 cm. Therefore,

$$\frac{1}{s_o} + \frac{1}{s_i} = \frac{1}{f} \quad \Rightarrow \quad \frac{1}{240 \text{ cm}} + \frac{1}{60 \text{ cm}} = \frac{1}{f} \quad \Rightarrow \quad \frac{1}{f} = \frac{1}{48 \text{ cm}} \quad \Rightarrow \quad f = 48 \text{ cm}$$

10. **(B)** A bi-concave lens is a diverging lens. Diverging lenses (like convex mirrors) have negative focal lengths and therefore cannot form real images. (Notice that statement D is false; diverging lenses and convex mirrors always form diminished, virtual images, as you can verify using the mirror and magnification equations.)

SECTION II: FREE RESPONSE

1. (a) Interference effects can be observed only if the light is coherent. Using two independent light sources at the slits in Barrier 2 would generate incoherent light waves. The set-up shown guarantees that the light reaching the two slits will be coherent.

(b) Maxima are located at positions given by the equation $y_m = m\lambda L/d$, where m is an integer ($y_0 = 0$ is the central maximum). The first-order maximum for red light occurs at

$$y_{1,\,red} = \frac{1 \cdot \lambda_{red} L}{d} = \frac{1 \cdot (750 \times 10^{-9}\ \text{m})(4.0\ \text{m})}{0.50 \times 10^{-3}\ \text{m}} = 0.006\ \text{m} = 6.0\ \text{mm}$$

and the first-order maximum for violet light occurs at

$$y_{1,\,violet} = \frac{1 \cdot \lambda_{violet} L}{d} = \frac{1 \cdot (400 \times 10^{-9}\ \text{m})(4.0\ \text{m})}{0.50 \times 10^{-3}\ \text{m}} = 0.0032\ \text{m} = 3.2\ \text{mm}$$

Therefore, the vertical separation of these maxima on the screen is $\Delta y = 6.0\ \text{mm} - 3.2\ \text{mm} = 2.8\ \text{mm}$.

(c) Maxima are located at positions given by the equation $y_m = m\lambda L/d$, where m is an integer. We therefore want to solve the equation

$$y_{m,\,violet} = y_{n,\,orange\text{-}yellow}$$

$$\frac{m\lambda_{violet} L}{d} = \frac{n\lambda_{orange\text{-}yellow} L}{d}$$

$$m\lambda_{violet} = n\lambda_{orange\text{-}yellow}$$

$$m(400\ \text{nm}) = n(600\ \text{nm})$$

The smallest integers that satisfy this equation are $m = 3$ and $n = 2$. That is, the third-order maximum for violet light coincides with the third-order maximum for orange-yellow light. The position on the screen (relative to the central maximum at $y = 0$) of these maxima is

$$y_{3,\,violet} = \frac{m\lambda_{violet} L}{d} = \frac{3(400 \times 10^{-9}\ \text{m})(4.0\ \text{m})}{0.50 \times 10^{-3}\ \text{m}} = 0.0096\ \text{m} = 9.6\ \text{mm}$$

(d) Within the glass, the wavelength is reduced by a factor of $n = 1.5$ from the wavelength in air. Therefore, the difference in path lengths, $d \sin\theta$, must be equal to $m(\lambda/n)$ in order for constructive interference to occur. This implies that the maxima are located at positions given by $y_m = m\lambda L/(nd)$. The distance between adjacent bright fringes is therefore

$$y_{m+1} - y_m = \frac{(m+1)\lambda L}{nd} - \frac{m\lambda L}{nd} = \frac{\lambda L}{nd} = \frac{(500 \times 10^{-9}\ \text{m})(4.0\ \text{m})}{1.5(0.50 \times 10^{-3}\ \text{m})} = 0.0027\ \text{m} = 2.7\ \text{mm}$$

2. (a) Beam 1 undergoes a 180° phase change when it reflects off the soap film. The refracted portion of the incident beam does not undergo a phase change upon reflection at the film/air boundary, because it strikes the boundary to a medium whose index is lower; therefore, Beam 2 does not suffer a 180° phase change.

(b) We're told that the criterion for destructive interference in this case is $\Delta \ell = 2T = m(\lambda/n)$, where n is the refractive index of the soap film and m is a whole number. Therefore, the criterion for *constructive* interference must be

$$\Delta \ell = 2T = (m + \tfrac{1}{2})\frac{\lambda}{n}$$

(c) Using the criterion for constructive interference from part (c), we solve for λ:

$$\lambda = \frac{2Tn}{m + \tfrac{1}{2}} = \frac{2(462 \text{ nm})(1.38)}{m + \tfrac{1}{2}} = \frac{1275 \text{ nm}}{m + \tfrac{1}{2}}$$

Now, we try various values of m:

$m = 0$ $\qquad \lambda_{m=0} = \dfrac{1275 \text{ nm}}{0 + \tfrac{1}{2}} = 2550 \text{ nm}$ $\qquad$ not visible (infrared)

$m = 1$ $\qquad \lambda_{m=1} = \dfrac{1275 \text{ nm}}{1 + \tfrac{1}{2}} = 850 \text{ nm}$ $\qquad$ not visible (infrared)

$m = 2$ $\qquad \lambda_{m=2} = \dfrac{1275 \text{ nm}}{2 + \tfrac{1}{2}} = 510 \text{ nm}$ $\qquad$ visible (green)

$m = 3$ $\qquad \lambda_{m=3} = \dfrac{1275 \text{ nm}}{3 + \tfrac{1}{2}} = 364 \text{ nm}$ $\qquad$ not visible (ultraviolet)

Therefore, the visible wavelength that the film will reflect most strongly is $\lambda = 510$ nm (green), so the film will appear this color when viewed upon reflection.

(d) In this case, *both* beams suffer a 180° phase change upon reflection, because each beam reflects off a boundary beyond which the refractive index is higher. Therefore, relative to each other, there is no phase difference, and destructive interference occurs when the difference in path lengths, $\Delta \ell \approx 2T$, is equal to a whole number plus one-half a wavelength:

$$\text{destructive interference: } 2T = (m + \tfrac{1}{2})\frac{\lambda}{n}$$

where n is the refractive index of the coating (and λ is the wavelength in air). To cause yellow-green light of wavelength 570 nm to destructively interfere (to suppress its reflection from the lens), the coating thickness must satisfy

$$T = (m + \tfrac{1}{2})\frac{\lambda}{2n}$$

The smallest value for T (the thinnest coating) occurs when $m = 0$:

$$T_{\text{min}} = (0 + \tfrac{1}{2})\frac{\lambda}{2n} = \frac{570 \text{ nm}}{4(1.42)} = 100 \text{ nm}$$

3. (a) Since the image is formed behind the mirror, it is virtual.

    (b) Virtual images are upright.

    (c) Writing $s_i = -72$ cm (negative because the image is virtual), the magnification is

    $$m = -\frac{s_i}{s_o} = -\frac{-72 \text{ cm}}{40 \text{ cm}} = 1.8$$

    so the height of the image is $h_i = |m| \cdot h_o = 1.8(5 \text{ cm}) = 9 \text{ cm}$.

    (d) The mirror equation can be used to solve for the mirror's focal length:

    $$\frac{1}{s_o} + \frac{1}{s_i} = \frac{1}{f} \;\Rightarrow\; \frac{1}{40 \text{ cm}} + \frac{1}{-72 \text{ cm}} = \frac{1}{f} \;\Rightarrow\; \frac{1}{90 \text{ cm}} = \frac{1}{f} \;\Rightarrow\; f = 90 \text{ cm}$$

    Therefore, the mirror's radius of curvature is $R = 2f = 2(90 \text{ cm}) = 180 \text{ cm}$.

    (e)

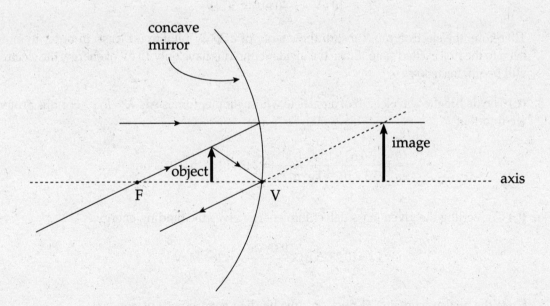

CHAPTER 17 REVIEW QUESTIONS

SECTION I: MULTIPLE CHOICE

1. **(B)** Combining the equation $E = hf$ with $f = c/\lambda$ gives us

$$E = \frac{hc}{\lambda} = \frac{(4.14 \times 10^{-15} \text{ eV} \cdot \text{s})(3.00 \times 10^{8} \text{ m}/\text{s})}{2.07 \times 10^{-9} \text{ m}} = 600 \text{ eV}$$

2. **(D)** The energy of the incident photons is

$$E = hf = (4.14 \times 10^{-15} \text{ eV} \cdot \text{s})(7.2 \times 10^{15} \text{ Hz}) = 30 \text{ eV}$$

   Since $E > \phi$, photoelectrons will be produced, with maximum kinetic energy

$$K_{max} = E - \phi = 30 \text{ eV} - 6 \text{ eV} = 24 \text{ eV}$$

3. **(A)** If the atom's ionization energy is 25 eV, then the electron's ground-state energy must be –25 eV. Making a transition from the –16 eV energy level to the ground state will cause the emission of a photon of energy

$$\Delta E = (-16 \text{ eV}) - 25 \text{ eV} = 9 \text{ eV}$$

4. **(E)** The gap between the ground-state and the first excited state is

$$-10 \text{ eV} - (-40 \text{ eV}) = 30 \text{ eV}$$

   Therefore, the electron must absorb the energy of a 30 eV photon (at least) in order to move even to the first excited state. Since the incident photons have only 15 eV of energy, the electron will be unaffected.

5. **(C)** The de Broglie wavelength of a particle whose momentum is p is $\lambda = h/p$. For this proton, we find that

$$\lambda = \frac{h}{p} = \frac{6.63 \times 10^{-34} \text{ J} \cdot \text{s}}{3.3 \times 10^{-23} \text{ kg} \cdot \text{m}/\text{s}} = 2.0 \times 10^{-11} \text{ m} = 0.02 \text{ nm}$$

6. **(C)** Converting the given mass defect into energy gives the binding energy:

$$E_{B} = (0.2825 \text{ u}) \times \frac{931 \text{ MeV}}{1 \text{ u}} = 263 \text{ MeV}$$

   Since the nucleus contains 31 nucleons, the binding energy per nucleon is

$$\frac{263 \text{ MeV}}{31 \text{ nucleons}} = 8.5 \text{ MeV}/\text{nucleon}$$

Note: Choices D and E are impossible. The maximum binding energy of any stable nucleus is about 8.8 MeV/nucleon, and choices A and B are too low for a nucleus containing 31 nucleons. Only small nuclei ($A < 12$) have binding energy per nucleon values less than 7.5 MeV/nucleon.

7. **(A)** In β^- decay, a neutron is transformed into a proton and an electron. Therefore, the total nucleon number (mass number) doesn't change, but the number of protons (the atomic number) increases by one.

8. **(A)** Since the mass number decreased by 4 and the atomic number decreased by 2, this is an alpha decay.

9. **(B)** After 3 half-lives, the activity will drop to $(1/2)^3 = 1/8$ its initial value, and after 4 half-lives, it will drop to $(1/2)^4 = 1/16$ its initial value. Since $1/10$ is between $1/8$ and $1/16$, the time interval in this case is between 3 and 4 half-lives, that is, between $3(2.5 \text{ h}) = 7.5$ h and $4(2.5 \text{ h})$ = 10 h. Only choice C is in this range.

10. **(B)** In order to balance the mass number (the superscripts), we must have $2 + 63 = 64 + A$, so $A = 1$. In order to balance the charge (the subscripts), we need $1 + 29 = 30 + Z$, so $Z = 0$. A particle with a mass number of 1 and no charge is a neutron, $_0^1 n$.

11. **(E)** In order to balance the mass number (the superscripts), we must have $196 + 1 = 197 + A$, so $A = 0$. In order to balance the charge (the subscripts), we need $78 + 0 = 78 + Z$, so $Z = 0$. The only particle listed that has zero mass number and zero charge is a gamma-ray photon, $_0^0 \gamma$.

SECTION II: FREE RESPONSE

1. (a) If ionizing lithium twice leaves the atom with just one electron, then it must have originally had three electrons. Since neutral atoms have the same number of protons as electrons, Z must be 3 for lithium.

(b) First, use the formula given for E_n to determine the values of the first few electron energy levels:

$$E_1 = \frac{3^2}{1^2}(-13.6 \text{ eV}) = -122.4 \text{ eV}$$

$$E_2 = \frac{3^2}{2^2}(-13.6 \text{ eV}) = -30.6 \text{ eV}$$

$$E_3 = \frac{3^2}{3^2}(-13.6 \text{ eV}) = -13.6 \text{ eV}$$

$$E_4 = \frac{3^2}{4^2}(-13.6 \text{ eV}) = -7.65 \text{ eV}$$

Differences between electron energy levels equal the energies of the emitted photons. Since $E = hf = hc/\lambda$, we have $\lambda = hc/E$. Since the E's are in electronvolts and the wavelengths in nanometers, it is particularly helpful to notice that

$$hc = (4.14 \times 10^{-15} \text{ eV} \cdot \text{s})(3.00 \times 10^8 \times 10^9 \text{ nm/s}) = 1240 \text{ eV} \cdot \text{nm}$$

The goal here is to match the energy-level differences with the given wavelengths, using the equation $\lambda = (1240 \text{ eV·nm})/E$.

Using this diagram, the four wavelengths given correspond to the following photon energies and energy-level transitions:

$$\lambda = 11.4 \text{ nm} \quad \leftrightarrow \quad E = \frac{hc}{\lambda} = \frac{1240 \text{ eV·nm}}{11.4 \text{ nm}} = 109 \text{ eV} \quad \leftrightarrow \quad (3 \rightarrow 1 \text{ transition})$$

$$\lambda = 13.5 \text{ nm} \quad \leftrightarrow \quad E = \frac{hc}{\lambda} = \frac{1240 \text{ eV·nm}}{13.5 \text{ nm}} = 92 \text{ eV} \quad \leftrightarrow \quad (2 \rightarrow 1 \text{ transition})$$

$$\lambda = 54.0 \text{ nm} \quad \leftrightarrow \quad E = \frac{hc}{\lambda} = \frac{1240 \text{ eV·nm}}{54.0 \text{ nm}} = 23 \text{ eV} \quad \leftrightarrow \quad (4 \rightarrow 2 \text{ transition})$$

$$\lambda = 72.9 \text{ nm} \quad \leftrightarrow \quad E = \frac{hc}{\lambda} = \frac{1240 \text{ eV·nm}}{72.9 \text{ nm}} = 17 \text{ eV} \quad \leftrightarrow \quad (3 \rightarrow 2 \text{ transition})$$

(c) No. In order for a spectral line to have a wavelength between 54.0 nm and 72.9 nm, there must be any energy-level transition with an energy between 17 eV and 23 eV. As the diagram above shows, no such intermediate transition is possible.

(d) The 11.4 nm line corresponds to a photon energy of 109 eV. Therefore, the next shortest wavelength must correspond to the next highest possible photon energy. According to the diagram, the next highest available transition energy after 109 eV is 115 eV. This wavelength of the photon emitted in this $(4 \rightarrow 1)$ transition is

$$\lambda = \frac{hc}{E} = \frac{1240 \text{ eV·nm}}{115 \text{ eV}} = 10.8 \text{ nm}$$

2. (a) According to the table given, the atomic number of thorium is 90. Therefore, the nucleus contains 90 protons and 229 – 90 = 139 neutrons.

(b) The daughter nucleus is radium-225 (atomic number = 88, mass number = 225):

$$^{229}_{90}\text{Th} \rightarrow {}^{4}_{2}\alpha + {}^{225}_{88}\text{Ra}$$

(c) The disintegration energy, Q, is the energy equivalent of the mass that is lost in the decay. Since

$$\Delta m = m_{\text{Th}} - (m_{\alpha} + m_{\text{Ra}})$$
$$= (229.03 \text{ u}) - (4.0015 \text{ u} + 225.02 \text{ u})$$
$$= 0.0085 \text{ u}$$

the value of Q is

$$Q = 0.0085 \text{ u} \times \frac{931 \text{ MeV}}{1 \text{ u}} = 7.9 \text{ MeV}$$

(d) If radium-225 undergoes β^- decay, its daughter is actinium-225:

$$^{225}_{88}\text{Ra} \rightarrow {}^{225}_{89}\text{Ac} + {}^{0}_{-1}\text{e} + \bar{\nu}_e$$

(e) Before the disintegration, the linear momentum of the ^{229}Th nucleus is zero, so the total linear momentum of the daughter nucleus and the ejected alpha particle must also be zero after the decay. Therefore, $m_{\alpha}\mathbf{v} + M\mathbf{V} = \mathbf{0}$ (by conservation of linear momentum), so

$$V = \frac{m_{\alpha}v}{M}$$

(f) The statement of the question says that $\frac{1}{2}m_{\alpha}v^2 + \frac{1}{2}MV^2 = Q$. Substituting the result of part (e), we can solve for v:

$$\frac{1}{2}m_{\alpha}v^2 + \frac{1}{2}M\left(\frac{m_{\alpha}v}{M}\right)^2 = Q$$

$$\frac{1}{2}m_{\alpha}v^2\left(1 + \frac{m_{\alpha}}{M}\right) = Q$$

$$v = \sqrt{\frac{2Q}{m_{\alpha}\left(1 + \frac{m_{\alpha}}{M}\right)}}$$

$$= \sqrt{\frac{2\left(7.9 \times 10^6 \text{ eV} \cdot \frac{1.6 \times 10^{-19} \text{ J}}{1 \text{ eV}}\right)}{\left(4.0015 \text{ u} \cdot \frac{1.66 \times 10^{-27} \text{ kg}}{1 \text{ u}}\right)\left(1 + \frac{4.0015 \text{ u}}{225.02 \text{ u}}\right)}}$$

$$= 1.9 \times 10^7 \text{ m/s}$$

We can now find V:

$$V = \frac{m_\alpha v}{M} = \frac{(4.0015 \text{ u})(1.9 \times 10^7 \text{ m/s})}{225.02 \text{ u}} = 3.4 \times 10^5 \text{ m/s}$$

(g) (i) Since we're told in part (d) that the daughter has a half-life of 15 days, a time interval of 30 days is equal to 2 half-lives, so the mass of the sample will decrease to $(1/2)^2 = 1/4 = 25\%$ its initial amount.

(ii) To calculate the fraction remaining after 40 days (which is not a whole number times the half-life), we use the exponential decay formula:

$$m = m_0 \left(\tfrac{1}{2}\right)^{t/T_{1/2}} = m_0 \left(\tfrac{1}{2}\right)^{40 \text{ d}/15 \text{ d}} = m_0 \left(\tfrac{1}{2}\right)^{2.67} = m_0 (0.16)$$

Therefore, 16% of the sample will remain after 40 days.

19

THE PRINCETON REVIEW
AP PHYSICS B
DIAGNOSTIC EXAM

PHYSICS B

You must take the entire B Exam as follows:

1st 90 minutes	Section I—Multiple Choice
	70 Questions
	Percent of Total Grade—50
2nd 90 minutes	Section II—Free Response
	6 Questions
	Percent of Total Grade—50

Each question in a section has equal weight. Calculators are NOT permitted on Section I of the exam but are allowed on Section II. However, calculators cannot be shared with other students and calculators with typewriter-style (QWERTY) keyboards will not be permitted. A table of information that may be helpful is found on the following page.

Use a separate sheet of paper to record your answers.

TABLE OF INFORMATION

CONSTANTS AND CONVERSION FACTORS

1 unified atomic mass unit.	$1\ u = 1.66 \times 10^{-27}\ kg$
	$= 931\ MeV/c^2$
Proton mass,	$m_p = 1.67 \times 10^{-27}\ kg$
Neutron mass,	$m_n = 1.67 \times 10^{-27}\ kg$
Electron mass,	$m_e = 9.11 \times 10^{-31}\ kg$
Magnitude of electron charge,	$e = 1.60 \times 10^{-19}\ C$
Avogadro's number,	$N_0 = 6.02 \times 10^{23}\ mol^{-1}$
Universal gas constant,	$R = 8.31\ J/(mol \cdot K)$
Boltzmann's constant,	$k_B = 1.38 \times 10^{-23}\ J/K$
Speed of light,	$c = 3.00 \times 10^{8}\ m/s$
Planck's constant,	$h = 6.63 \times 10^{-34}\ J \cdot s$
	$= 4.14 \times 10^{-15}\ eV \cdot s$
	$hc = 1.99 \times 10^{-25}\ J \cdot m$
	$= 1.24 \times 10^{3}\ eV \cdot nm$
Vacuum permittivity,	$\varepsilon_0 = 8.85 \times 10^{-12}\ C^2/N \cdot m^2$
Coulomb's law constant	$k = 1/4\pi\varepsilon_0 = 9.0 \times 10^{9}\ N \cdot m^2/C^2$
Vacuum permeability,	$\mu_0 = 4\pi \times 10^{-7}\ Wb/(A \cdot m)$
Magnetic constant,	$k' = \mu_0/4\pi = 10^{-7}\ Wb/(A \cdot m)$
Universal gravitational constant,	$G = 6.67 \times 10^{-11}\ m^3/kg \cdot s^2$
Acceleration due to gravity at the Earth's surface,	$g = 9.8\ m/s^2$
1 atmosphere pressure,	$1\ atm = 1.0 \times 10^{5}\ N/m^2$
	$= 1.0 \times 10^{5}\ Pa$
1 electron volt,	$1\ eV = 1.60 \times 10^{-19}\ J$
1 angstrom,	$1\ Å = 1 \times 10^{-10}\ m$

UNITS

Name	Symbol
meter	m
kilogram	kg
second	s
ampere	A
kelvin	K
mole	mol
hertz	Hz
newton	N
pascal	Pa
joule	J
watt	W
coulomb	C
volt	V
ohm	Ω
henry	H
farad	F
weber	Wb
tesla	T
degree Celsius	°C
electron-volt	eV

PREFIXES

Factor	Prefix	Symbol
10^{9}	giga	G
10^{6}	mega	M
10^{3}	kilo	k
10^{-2}	centi	c
10^{-3}	milli	m
10^{-6}	micro	μ
10^{-9}	nano	n
10^{-12}	pico	p

VALUES OF TRIGONOMETRIC FUNCTIONS FOR COMMON ANGLES

Angle	Sin	Cos	Tan
0°	0	1	0
30°	1/2	$\sqrt{3}/2$	$\sqrt{3}/3$
37°	3/5	4/5	3/4
45°	$\sqrt{2}/2$	$\sqrt{2}/2$	1
53°	4/5	3/5	4/3
60°	$\sqrt{3}/2$	1/2	$\sqrt{3}$
90°	1	0	∞

The following conventions are used in this examination.

I.   Unless otherwise stated, the frame of reference of any problem is assumed to be inertial.

II. The direction of any electric current is the direction of flow of positive charge (conventional current).

III. For any isolated electric charge, the electric potential is defined as zero at an infinite distance from the charge.

IV. The work done by a thermodynamic system is defined as a positive quantity.

Directions: Each of the questions or incomplete statements below is followed by five suggested answers or completions. Select the one that is best in each case and mark it on the your sheet.

1. If the acceleration of an object is not zero, then all of the following could be constant EXCEPT the object's

   I. speed.
   II. linear momentum.
   III. kinetic energy.

   (A) I only
   (B) I and II only
   (C) I and III only
   (D) II only
   (E) II and III only

2. A rock is dropped off a cliff and falls the first half of the distance to the ground in 2.0 seconds. How long will it take to fall the second half? (Ignore air resistance.)

   (A) 0.8 s
   (B) 1.0 s
   (C) 1.4 s
   (D) 2.0 s
   (E) 2.4 s

3. A particle travels in a circular path of radius 0.2 m with a constant kinetic energy of 4 J. What is the net force on the particle?

   (A) 4 N
   (B) 16 N
   (C) 20 N
   (D) 40 N
   (E) Cannot be determined from the information given

4. Which of the following is NOT a vector quantity?

   (A) Displacement
   (B) Velocity
   (C) Acceleration
   (D) Linear momentum
   (E) Potential energy

Questions 5–7 refer to the following figure:

5. If the surface of the incline is frictionless, how long will it take the block to reach the bottom if it was released from rest at the top?

   (A) 0.7 s
   (B) 1.4 s
   (C) 2.0 s
   (D) 2.8 s
   (E) 4.0 s

6. If the surface of the incline is frictionless, with what speed will the block reach the bottom if it was released from rest at the top?

   (A) 8 m/s
   (B) 10 m/s
   (C) 14 m/s
   (D) 18 m/s
   (E) 20 m/s

7. If the coefficient of kinetic friction between the block and the incline is 0.4, how much work is done by the normal force on the block as it slides down the full length of the incline?

   (A) 0 J
   (B) 2.0 J
   (C) 4.0 J
   (D) 4.9 J
   (E) 9.8 J

GO ON TO THE NEXT PAGE

8. Two satellites are in circular orbit around the earth. The distance from Satellite 1 to the earth's center is r_1, and the distance from Satellite 2 to the earth's center is r_2. If the speed of Satellite 1 is v_1, what is the speed of Satellite 2?

(A) $v_1\sqrt{r_2/r_1}$

(B) $v_1\sqrt{r_1/r_2}$

(C) $v_1(r_2/r_1)$

(D) $v_1(r_2/r_1)^2$

(E) $v_1(r_1/r_2)^2$

9. Which of the following would increase the capacitance of a parallel-plate capacitor?

(A) Using smaller plates
(B) Replacing the dielectric material between the plates with one that had a smaller dielectric constant
(C) Moving the plates closer together
(D) Increasing the voltage between the plates
(E) Decreasing the voltage between the plates

10. A simple harmonic oscillator has a frequency of 2.5 Hz and an amplitude of 0.05 m. What is the period of the oscillations?

(A) 0.4 s
(B) 0.2 s
(C) 8 s
(D) 20 s
(E) 50 s

11. What happens to the image formed by a concave mirror as the object is moved toward the focal point?

(A) The image moves away from the mirror and gets shorter.
(B) The image moves away from the mirror and gets taller.
(C) The image moves toward the mirror and gets shorter.
(D) The image moves toward the mirror and gets taller.
(E) None of the above

12. The diagram above (not drawn to scale) gives the first few electron energy levels within a single-electron atom. Which of the following gives the energy of a photon that could NOT be emitted by this atom during an electron transition?

(A) 17 eV
(B) 42 eV
(C) 64 eV
(D) 255 eV
(E) 302 eV

13. During an isothermal expansion, a confined ideal gas does 150 J of work against its surroundings. Which of the following describes the heat transfer during this process?

(A) 150 J of heat was added to the gas.
(B) 150 J of heat was removed from the gas.
(C) 300 J of heat was added to the gas.
(D) 300 J of heat was removed from the gas.
(E) No heat was transferred because the process was isothermal.

14. Sound waves travel at 350 m/s through warm air and at 3500 m/s through brass. What happens to the wavelength of a 700 Hz acoustic wave as it enters brass from warm air?

(A) It decreases by a factor of 20.
(B) It decreases by a factor of 10.
(C) It increases by a factor of 10.
(D) It increases by a factor of 20.
(E) The wavelength remains unchanged.

GO ON TO THE NEXT PAGE

15. In the figure above, the coefficient of sliding friction between the small block and the tabletop is 0.2. If the pulley is frictionless and massless, what will be the acceleration of the blocks once they are released from rest?

   (A) $(0.5)g$
   (B) $(0.6)g$
   (C) $(0.7)g$
   (D) $(0.8)g$
   (E) $(0.9)g$

16. Two people, one of mass 100 kg and the other of mass 50 kg, stand facing each other on an ice-covered (essentially frictionless) pond. If the heavier person pushes on the lighter one with a force **F**, then

   (A) the force felt by the heavier person is $-\frac{1}{2}\mathbf{F}$.
   (B) the force felt by the heavier person is $-2\mathbf{F}$.
   (C) the magnitude of the acceleration of the
        lighter person will be $\frac{1}{2}$ of the magnitude
        of the acceleration of the heavier person.
   (D) the magnitude of the acceleration of the
        lighter person will be twice the magnitude
        of the acceleration of the heavier person.
   (E) None of the above

17. Francium-212 is radioactive with a half-life of 20 minutes. A laboratory technician carefully monitored the decay of a sample of this radioisotope and records the activity throughout the day. It is recorded that the sample's activity is 20 decays per second at 4:00 PM. At what time is it recorded that the sample's activity is 320 decays per second?

   (A) 2:20 PM
   (B) 2:40 PM
   (C) 3:00 PM
   (D) 3:20 PM
   (E) 5:20 PM

18. The figure above shows two positively-charged particles. The $+Q$ charge is fixed in position, and the $+q$ charge is brought close to $+Q$ and released from rest. Which of the following graphs best depicts the acceleration of the $+q$ charge as a function of its distance r from $+Q$?

19. A spring of force constant 800 N/m is hung from a ceiling. A block of mass 4.0 kg is hung from its lower end and allowed to come to rest. How far will the block stretch the spring?

   (A) 0.49 cm
   (B) 0.98 cm
   (C) 3.2 cm
   (D) 4.9 cm
   (E) 9.8 cm

GO ON TO THE NEXT PAGE

20. A crane lifts a shipping crate that weighs 5000 N at a constant speed of 4 m/s. At what rate is this crane doing work on the crate?

(A) 1,250 W
(B) 2,000 W
(C) 4,000 W
(D) 10,000 W
(E) 20,000 W

21. Each of the following particles is projected with the same speed into a uniform magnetic field **B** such that the particle's initial velocity is perpendicular to **B**. Which one would move in a circular path with the largest radius?

(A) Proton
(B) Beta particle
(C) Alpha particle
(D) Electron
(E) Positron

22. An astronaut lands on a planet whose mass and radius are each twice that of Earth. If the astronaut weighs 800 N on Earth, how much will he weigh on this planet?

(A) 200 N
(B) 400 N
(C) 800 N
(D) 1600 N
(E) 3200 N

23. An object of mass 5 kg is acted upon by exactly four forces, each of magnitude 10 N. Which of the following could NOT be the resulting acceleration of the object?

(A) 0 m/s^2
(B) 2 m/s^2
(C) 4 m/s^2
(D) 8 m/s^2
(E) 10 m/s^2

24. What is the maximum efficiency of an engine operating between a heat source at 127°C and a heat reservoir (sink) at 27°C?

(A) 25%
(B) 33%
(C) 50%
(D) 67%
(E) 79%

25. A rope stretched between two fixed points can support transverse standing waves. What is the ratio of the sixth harmonic frequency to the third harmonic frequency?

(A) 1/2
(B) $1/\sqrt{2}$
(C) 2
(D) $2\sqrt{2}$
(E) 4

26. How much current does a 60 W light bulb draw if it operates at a voltage of 120 V?

(A) 0.25 A
(B) 0.5 A
(C) 2 A
(D) 4 A
(E) 30 A

GO ON TO THE NEXT PAGE

Questions 27–28 refer to the following figure:

27. How much work is done by the electric field created by the stationary charge $+Q = +2.0$ C to move a charge of $+1.0 \times 10^{-9}$ C from position X to position Y?

(A) 150 J
(B) 300 J
(C) 560 J
(D) 1000 J
(E) 3000 J

28. If E_Y is the electric field strength at position Y and E_Z is the electric field strength at position Z, what is the value of E_Z/E_Y?

(A) $\sqrt{3/4}$
(B) $\sqrt{4/3}$
(C) 4/3
(D) 9/16
(E) 16/9

29. A 50 g block of marble (specific heat = 0.9 kJ/kg·°C) at 150°C is placed in an insulated beaker containing 200 g of ammonia (specific heat = 4.7 kJ/kg·°C) at 20°C. What will be the common temperature of the marble and ammonia when they reach thermal equilibrium?

(A) 26°C
(B) 41°C
(C) 58°C
(D) 77°C
(E) 94°C

30. A beam of monochromatic light entering a glass window pane from the air will experience a change in

(A) frequency and wavelength.
(B) frequency and speed.
(C) speed and wavelength.
(D) speed only.
(E) wavelength only.

31. A metal loop of wire shown above is situated in a magnetic field **B** pointing out of the plane of the page. If **B** decreases uniformly in strength, the induced electric current within the loop is

(A) clockwise and decreasing.
(B) clockwise and increasing.
(C) counterclockwise and decreasing.
(D) counterclockwise and constant.
(E) counterclockwise and increasing.

32. How does λ_e, the de Broglie wavelength of an electron (mass = m_e), compare with λ_p, the de Broglie wavelength of a proton (mass = m_p) moving with the same kinetic energy as the electron?

(A) $\lambda_e = \lambda_p \sqrt{m_p / m_e}$
(B) $\lambda_e = \lambda_p \sqrt{m_e / m_p}$
(C) $\lambda_e = \lambda_p (m_p / m_e)^2$
(D) $\lambda_e = \lambda_p (m_e / m_p)^2$
(E) $\lambda_e = \lambda_p$, because the electron and proton have the same magnitude of charge

GO ON TO THE NEXT PAGE

string

rod

θ

33. If the rod in the figure above is uniform and has mass m, what is the tension in the supporting string?

(A) $\frac{1}{2}mg \sin \theta$

(B) $mg \sin \theta$

(C) $\frac{1}{2}mg \cos \theta$

(D) $\frac{1}{2}mg$

(E) mg

34. Which of the following statements is true concerning phase changes?

(A) When a liquid freezes, it releases thermal energy into its immediate environment.
(B) When a solid melts, it releases thermal energy into its immediate environment.
(C) For most substances, the latent heat of fusion is greater than the latent heat of vaporization.
(D) As a solid melts, its temperature increases.
(E) As a liquid freezes, its temperature decreases.

35. Which of the following changes to a double-slit interference experiment would increase the widths of the fringes in the diffraction pattern that appears on the screen?

(A) Use light of a shorter wavelength.
(B) Move the screen closer to the slits.
(C) Move the slits closer together.
(D) Use light with a lower wave speed.
(E) Increase the intensity of the light.

$${}^{13}_{6}C + (?) \rightarrow {}^{13}_{7}N + n$$

36. Identify the missing particle in the nuclear reaction given above.

(A) Electron
(B) Proton
(C) Deuteron
(D) Positron
(E) Gamma-ray photon

Questions 37–38 refer to the circuit shown below:

37. If each of the resistors in the circuit has a resistance of $3\,\Omega$, what must be the emf of the battery if the circuit draws a total current of 3 A?

(A) $\frac{3}{10}$ V

(B) $\frac{10}{3}$ V

(C) 10 V
(D) 30 V
(E) 54 V

38. Which of the following relates P_b, the rate at which energy is dissipated by Resistor b, and P_e, the rate at which energy is dissipated by Resistor e?

(A) $P_b = 3P_e$
(B) $P_b = 9P_e$
(C) $P_b = P_e$
(D) $P_e = 3P_b$
(E) $P_e = 9P_b$

GO ON TO THE NEXT PAGE

39. In which of the following situations involving a source of sound and a detector of the sound is it possible that there is NO perceived Doppler shift?

   (A) The source travels toward the stationary detector.
   (B) The detector travels toward the stationary source.
   (C) Both the source and detector travel in the same direction.
   (D) Both the source and detector travel in opposite directions, with the source and detector moving away from each other.
   (E) Both the source and detector travel in opposite directions, with the source and detector moving toward each other.

40. If L, M, and T denote the dimensions of length, mass, and time, respectively, what are the dimensions of power?

   (A) ML/T^2
   (B) L^2M/T^2
   (C) M^2L/T^2
   (D) L^2M/T^3
   (E) M^2L/T^3

41. Consider two adjacent transparent media. The speed of light in Medium 1 is v_1, and the speed of light in Medium 2 is v_2. If $v_1 < v_2$, then total internal reflection will occur at the interface between these media if a beam of light is

   (A) incident in Medium 1 and strikes the interface at an angle of incidence greater than $\sin^{-1}(v_1/v_2)$.
   (B) incident in Medium 1 and strikes the interface at an angle of incidence greater than $\sin^{-1}(v_2/v_1)$.
   (C) incident in Medium 2 and strikes the interface at an angle of incidence greater than $\sin^{-1}(v_1/v_2)$.
   (D) incident in Medium 2 and strikes the interface at an angle of incidence greater than $\sin^{-1}(v_2/v_1)$.
   (E) Total internal reflection is impossible in the situation described.

42. An object (mass = m) above the surface of the Moon (mass = M) is dropped from an altitude h equal to the Moon's radius (R). What is the object's impact speed?

   (A) $\sqrt{GM/R}$
   (B) $\sqrt{GM/(2R)}$
   (C) $\sqrt{2GM/R}$
   (D) $\sqrt{2GMm/R}$
   (E) $\sqrt{GMm/(2R)}$

43. Traveling at an initial speed of 1.5×10^6 m/s, a proton enters a region of constant magnetic field of magnitude 1.5 T. If the proton's initial velocity vector makes an angle of 30° with the magnetic field, compute the proton's speed 4 s after entering the magnetic field.

   (A) 5.0×10^5 m/s
   (B) 7.5×10^5 m/s
   (C) 1.5×10^6 m/s
   (D) 3.0×10^6 m/s
   (E) 6.0×10^6 m/s

44. At a distance of 20 m from a source of sound, the sound level is 40 dB. If the observer backs up to a distance of 40 m from the source, what will the sound level be?

   (A) 10 dB
   (B) 14 dB
   (C) 20 dB
   (D) 28 dB
   (E) 34 dB

45. An electric dipole consists of a pair of equal but opposite point charges of magnitude 4.0 nC separated by a distance of 2.0 cm. What is the electric field strength at the point midway between the charges?

   (A) 0
   (B) 9.0×10^4 N/C
   (C) 1.8×10^5 N/C
   (D) 3.6×10^5 N/C
   (E) 7.2×10^5 N/C

GO ON TO THE NEXT PAGE

46. A lightweight toy car crashes head-on into a heavier toy truck. Which of the following statements is true as a result of the collision?

    I.   The car will experience a greater impulse than the truck.
   II. The car will experience a greater change in momentum than the truck.
  III. The magnitude of the acceleration experiences by the car will be greater than that experienced by the truck.

(A) I and II only
(B) II only
(C) III only
(D) II and III only
(E) I, II, and III

47. A projectile is launched with an initial velocity of magnitude a at an angle β to the horizontal. Find its maximum vertical displacement, ignoring effects due to the air.

(A) $(a^2 \sin 2\beta)/(2g)$
(B) $(a^2 \sin^2 \beta)/(2g)$
(C) $(a^2 \sin 2\beta)/g$
(D) $(a^2 \sin^2 \beta)/g$
(E) $(a \sin \beta \cos \beta)/g$

48. A simple pendulum executes simple harmonic motion as it swings through small angles of oscillation. If θ_{max} denotes the amplitude of the oscillations, which of the following statements is true?

(A) When $\theta = 0$, the tangential acceleration is 0.
(B) When $\theta = \theta_{max}$, the tangential acceleration is 0.
(C) When $\theta = 0$, the speed is 0.
(D) When $\theta = 0$, the restoring force is maximized.
(E) When $\theta = \theta_{max}$, the speed is maximized.

49. Assume that the Moon (mass = m) orbits Earth (mass = M) in a circular path of radius R. What is the Moon's orbital angular momentum with respect to Earth's center?

(A) $\sqrt{GmM/R}$
(B) $\sqrt{GmMR}$
(C) $m\sqrt{GM/R}$
(D) $m\sqrt{GMR}$
(E) $m\sqrt{GM/R^2}$

50. In an experiment designed to study the photoelectric effect, it is observed that low-intensity visible light of wavelength 550 nm produced no photoelectrons. Which of the following best describes what would occur if the intensity of this light were increased dramatically?

(A) Almost immediately, photoelectrons would be produced with a kinetic energy equal to the energy of the incident photons.
(B) Almost immediately, photoelectrons would be produced with a kinetic energy equal to the energy of the incident photons minus the work function of the metal.
(C) After several seconds, necessary for the electrons to absorb sufficient energy from the incident light, photoelectrons would be produced with a kinetic energy equal to the energy of the incident photons.
(D) After several seconds, necessary for the electrons to absorb sufficient energy from the incident light, photoelectrons would be produced with a kinetic energy equal to the energy of the incident photons minus the work function of the metal.
(E) Nothing would happen.

GO ON TO THE NEXT PAGE

I

a

I

51. Electric current is established in each of two long parallel wires, as shown in the figure above. Describe the force per unit length on each wire.

(A) Attractive, strength $= (\mu_0/2\pi)I^2/a^2$
(B) Repulsive, strength $= (\mu_0/2\pi)I^2/a^2$
(C) Attractive, strength $= (\mu_0/2\pi)I^2/a$
(D) Repulsive, strength $= (\mu_0/2\pi)I^2/a$
(E) Attractive, strength $= (\mu_0/2\pi)I^2/(\frac{1}{2}a)^2$

52. An object is placed 100 cm from a plane mirror. How far is the image from the object?

(A) 50 cm
(B) 100 cm
(C) 150 cm
(D) 200 cm
(E) 300 cm

53. What happens to the pressure, P, of an ideal gas if the temperature is increased by a factor of 2 and the volume is increased by a factor of 8?

(A) P decreases by a factor of 16.
(B) P decreases by a factor of 4.
(C) P decreases by a factor of 2.
(D) P increases by a factor of 4.
(E) P increases by a factor of 16.

54. Two nuclides that have the same excess number of neutrons over protons are called *isodiapheres*. Which of the following is an isodiaphere of $^{68}_{30}\text{Zn}$?

(A) $^{67}_{31}\text{Ga}$
(B) $^{74}_{32}\text{Ge}$
(C) $^{75}_{33}\text{As}$
(D) $^{72}_{34}\text{Se}$
(E) $^{78}_{35}\text{Br}$

55. The plates of a capacitor are charged to a potential difference of 5 V. If the capacitance is 2 mF, what is the charge on the positive plate?

(A) 0.005 C
(B) 0.01 C
(C) 0.02 C
(D) 0.5 C
(E) 0.1 C

56. An object of mass 2 kg increases in speed from 2 m/s to 4 m/s in 3 s. Calculate the total work performed on the object during this time interval.

(A) 4 J
(B) 6 J
(C) 12 J
(D) 36 J
(E) Cannot be determined from the information given

57. A confined ideal gas undergoes a cyclical process in three steps—an isobaric step, followed by an isochoric step, followed by an isothermal step. Which of the following must be true?

(A) The change in internal energy of the gas is equal to the work done during the isobaric step.
(B) The change in internal energy of the gas is equal to the work done during the isobaric step minus the work done during the isothermal step.
(C) The work done during the isothermal step is equal but opposite to the work done during the isochoric step.
(D) The total work done during the cycle is equal in magnitude, but opposite in sign, to the area enclosed by the cycle in a $P–V$ diagram.
(E) The total work done during the cycle is equal to the net amount of heat transferred.

GO ON TO THE NEXT PAGE

58. How much force is required to lift a 49-newton object with an acceleration of 9.8 m/s²?

  (A) 9.8 N
  (B) 49 N
  (C) 98 N
  (D) 147 N
  (E) 196 N

59. Why do baseball catchers wear a mitt rather than just using their bare hands to catch a pitched baseball?

  (A) The impulse delivered to the catcher's hand is reduced due to the presence of the mitt.
  (B) The force on the catcher's hand is reduced because of the increased area provided by the mitt.
  (C) The baseball's change in momentum is reduced due to the presence of the mitt.
  (D) The force on the catcher's hand is reduced because the mitt increases the time of impact.
  (E) The force on the catcher's hand is reduced because the mitt decreases the time of impact.

60. What did Rutherford's experiments on alpha particle scattering indicate about the structure of the atom?

  (A) Atoms are roughly spherical with a radius of about 10^{-10} m.
  (B) The electrons occupy quantized energy levels, absorbing or emitting energy only when they make a quantum jump between these levels.
  (C) The density of positive charge within an atom is not uniform throughout the atom's volume.
  (D) Allowed electron orbits must have a circumference equal to a whole number times the electron's de Broglie wavelength.
  (E) Alpha particles are positively charged.

61. A bi-convex lens has a radius of curvature of magnitude 20 cm. Which of the following best describes the image formed of an object of height 2 cm placed 30 cm from the lens?

  (A) Real, inverted, height = 1 cm
  (B) Virtual, upright, height = 0.25 cm
  (C) Real, upright, height = 1 cm
  (D) Virtual, inverted, height = 0.25 cm
  (E) Real, inverted, height = 4 cm

62. Lenz's law concerning induced emf can be viewed most directly as a result of which of the following principles?

  (A) Gauss's law
  (B) Ampere's law
  (C) Biot–Savart law
  (D) Conservation of charge
  (E) Conservation of energy

copper sphere (with cavity)

plastic ball

insulating stand

63. The figure above shows a solid copper sphere carrying a charge of +1 mC that contains a hollow cavity. Which of the following best describes what will occur when a plastic ball carrying a charge of +1 mC is placed inside the cavity?

  (A) A charge of +1 mC will appear on the wall of the cavity, leaving zero net charge on the outer surface of the sphere.
  (B) A charge of +1 mC will appear on the wall of the cavity, leaving a charge of –2 mC on the outer surface of the sphere.
  (C) A charge of –1 mC will appear on the wall of the cavity, leaving a charge of –2 mC on the outer surface of the sphere.
  (D) A charge of –1 mC will appear on the wall of the cavity, leaving a charge of +2 mC on the outer surface of the sphere.
  (E) Nothing will happen.

GO ON TO THE NEXT PAGE

$$^7_3\text{Li} + \text{d} \rightarrow {}^8_4\text{Be} + \text{n}$$

64. In the nuclear reaction given above, the total mass of the reactants is 9.028 u, and the total mass of the products is 9.012 u. Which of the following is true?

(A) A particle of matter is missing from the right-hand side of the reaction as given.
(B) The reaction releases about 5 MeV of energy.
(C) The reactant particles must absorb about 5 MeV of energy to initiate the reaction.
(D) The reaction releases about 15 MeV of energy.
(E) The reactant particles must absorb about 15 MeV of energy to initiate the reaction.

65. How much work is required to charge a 10 μF capacitor to a potential difference of 100 V?

(A) 0.005 J
(B) 0.01 J
(C) 0.05 J
(D) 0.1 J
(E) 0.5 J

66. The figure shown above is a solid block of asphalt containing a small spherical hole near the center of the block. If the block is heated until each side increases in length by 4%, what will happen to the radius of the hole?

(A) It will decrease by 16%.
(B) It will decrease by 12%.
(C) It will decrease by 4%.
(D) It will increase by 4%.
(E) It will increase by 12%.

67. In the figure shown above, a loop of metal wire containing a tiny light bulb is attached to an insulating handle and placed over a coil of wire in which a current can be established by a source of emf and controlled by a variable resistor. The plane of the top loop is parallel to the plane of the bottom coil. Which of the following could NOT cause the bulb to light?

(A) Rotating the handle 90° while keeping the plane of the top loop parallel to the plane of the bottom coil.
(B) Raising the handle up and away from the coil.
(C) Lowering the handle down toward the coil.
(D) Decreasing the resistance of the coil.
(E) Increasing the resistance of the coil.

GO ON TO THE NEXT PAGE

68. Which of the following types of electromagnetic radiation has the longest wavelength?

    (A) Gamma rays
    (B) Ultraviolet
    (C) Blue light
    (D) X-rays
    (E) Orange light

69. Two traveling waves of equal frequency, one of amplitude 4 cm and the other of amplitude 6 cm, superimpose in a single medium. Which of the following best describes the displacement, D, of the resultant wave?

    (A) $2 \text{ cm} \leq D \leq 10 \text{ cm}$
    (B) $D = 5 \text{ cm}$
    (C) $D = 10 \text{ cm}$
    (D) $10 \text{ cm} \leq D \leq 12 \text{ cm}$
    (E) $12 \text{ cm} \leq D \leq 24 \text{ cm}$

70. A uniform bar is lying on a flat table. Besides the gravitational and normal forces (which cancel), the bar is acted upon by exactly two other forces, F_1 and F_2, which are parallel to the surface of the table. If the net force on the rod is zero, then which one of the following is true?

    (A) the net torque on the bar must also be zero.
    (B) the bar can accelerate translationally if F_1 and F_2 are not applied at the same point.
    (C) the net torque will be zero if F_1 and F_2 are applied at the same point.
    (D) the bar cannot accelerate translationally or rotationally.
    (E) None of the above

STOP

END OF SECTION I

IF YOU FINISH BEFORE TIME IS CALLED, YOU MAY
CHECK YOUR WORK ON THIS SECTION.

DO NOT GO ON TO SECTION II UNTIL YOU ARE TOLD TO DO SO.

PHYSICS B
SECTION II
Free-Response Questions
Time—90 minutes
6 required questions of equal weight
Percent of total grade—50

<u>General Instructions</u>

Use a seperate piece of paper to answer these questions.

Show your work. Be sure to write CLEARLY and LEGIBLY. If you make an error, you may save time by crossing it out rather than trying to erase it.

ADVANCED PLACEMENT PHYSICS B EQUATIONS

NEWTONIAN MECHANICS

$v = v_0 + at$

$s = s_0 + v_0 t + \frac{1}{2} at^2$

$v^2 = v_0{}^2 + 2a(s - s_0)$

$\sum \mathbf{F} = \mathbf{F}_{net} = m\mathbf{a}$

$F_f \le \mu N$

$a_c = \dfrac{v^2}{r}$

$\tau = rF \sin \theta$

$\mathbf{p} = m\mathbf{v}$

$\mathbf{J} = \mathbf{F}\Delta t = \Delta \mathbf{p}$

$K = \frac{1}{2} mv^2$

$\Delta U_g = mgh$

$W = \mathbf{F} \cdot \mathbf{s} = Fs \cos \theta$

$P_{avg} = \dfrac{W}{\Delta t}$

$p = Fv$

$\mathbf{F}_s = -k\mathbf{x}$

$U_s = \frac{1}{2} kx^2$

$T_s = 2\pi \sqrt{\dfrac{m}{k}}$

$T_p = 2\pi \sqrt{\dfrac{\ell}{g}}$

$T = \dfrac{1}{f}$

$F_G = -\dfrac{Gm_1 m_2}{r^2}$

$U_G = -\dfrac{Gm_1 m_2}{r}$

- a = acceleration
- F = force
- f = frequency
- h = height
- J = impulse
- K = kinetic energy
- k = spring constant
- ℓ = length
- N = normal force
- m = mass
- P = power
- p = momentum
- r = distance
- s = displacement
- T = period
- t = time
- U = potential energy
- v = velocity or speed
- W = work
- x = displacement
- μ = coefficient of friction
- θ = angle
- τ = torque

ELECTRICITY AND MAGNETISM

$F = \dfrac{1}{4\pi\varepsilon_0} \dfrac{q_1 q_2}{r^2}$

$\mathbf{E} = \dfrac{\mathbf{F}}{q}$

$U_E = qV = \dfrac{1}{4\pi\varepsilon_0} \dfrac{q_1 q_2}{r}$

$E_{avg} = -\dfrac{V}{d}$

$V = \dfrac{1}{4\pi\varepsilon_0} \sum \dfrac{q}{r}$

$C = \dfrac{Q}{V}$

$C = \dfrac{\varepsilon_0 A}{d}$

$U_c = \frac{1}{2} QV = \frac{1}{2} CV^2$

$I_{avg} = \dfrac{\Delta Q}{\Delta t}$

$R = \dfrac{\rho \ell}{A}$

$V = IR$

$P = IV$

$C_p = \sum_i C_i$

$\dfrac{1}{C_s} = \sum_i \dfrac{1}{C_i}$

$R_s = \sum_i R_i$

$\dfrac{1}{R_p} = \sum_i \dfrac{1}{R_i}$

$F_B = qvB \sin \theta$

$F_B = BI\ell \sin \theta$

$B = \dfrac{\mu_0}{2\pi} \dfrac{I}{r}$

$\phi_m = \mathbf{B} \cdot \mathbf{A} = BA \cos \theta$

$\varepsilon_{avg} = -\dfrac{\Delta \phi_m}{\Delta t}$

$\varepsilon = B\ell v$

- A = area
- B = magnetic field strength
- C = capacitance
- d = distance
- ε = emf
- F = force
- I = current
- ℓ = length
- P = power
- Q = charge
- q = point charge
- R = resistance
- r = distance
- t = time
- U = potential (stored) energy
- V = electric potential or potential difference
- v = velocity or speed
- ρ = resistivity
- ϕ = magnetic flux

ADVANCED PLACEMENT PHYSICS B EQUATIONS

HEAT, KINETIC THEORY, AND THERMODYNAMICS

$\Delta \ell = \alpha \ell \Delta T$

$Q = mL$

$Q = mc\Delta T$

$pV = nRT$

$K_{avg} = \frac{3}{2} k_B T$

$v_{rms} = \sqrt{\dfrac{3RT}{M}} = \sqrt{\dfrac{3k_B T}{\mu}}$

$W = p\Delta V$

$\Delta U = Q - W$

$\Delta U = nc_V \Delta T$

$e = \dfrac{W}{Q_H} = \dfrac{Q_H - Q_c}{Q_H}$

$e_c = \dfrac{T_H - T_C}{T_H}$

c = specific heat or molar specific heat
e = efficiency
K_{avg} = average molecular kinetic energy
L = heat of transformation
ℓ = lenght
M = molecular mass
m = mass of sample
n = number of moles
p = pressure
Q = heat
T = temperature
U = internal energy
V = volume
v_{rms} = root-mean-square velocity
W = work done by system
α = coefficient of linear expansion
μ = mass of molecule

MODERN PHYSICS

$E = h\nu = pc$

$K_{max} = h\nu - \phi$

$\lambda = \dfrac{h}{p}$

$E_0 = m_0 c^2$

E = energy
K = kinetic energy
m_0 = (rest) mass
p = momentum
λ = wavelength
ν = frequency
ϕ = work function

GEOMETRY AND TRIGONOMETRY

Rectangle
$A = bh$

Triangle
$A = \frac{1}{2} bh$

Circle
$A = \pi r^2$
$C = 2\pi r$

Parallelepiped
$V = \ell w h$

Circle
$V = \pi r^2 \ell$
$V = 2\pi r \ell + 2\pi r^2$

Sphere
$V = \dfrac{4}{3}\pi r^3$
$V = 4\pi r^2$

Right Triangle
$a^2 + b^2 = c^2$

$\sin \theta = \dfrac{a}{c}$

$\cos \theta = \dfrac{b}{c}$

$\tan \theta = \dfrac{a}{b}$

A = area
C = circumference
V = volume
S = surface area
b = base
h = height
ℓ = length
w = width
r = radius

WAVES AND OPTICS

$v = \nu \lambda$

$n = \dfrac{c}{v}$

$n_1 \sin \theta_1 = n_2 \sin \theta_2$

$\sin \theta_c = \dfrac{n_2}{n_1}$

$\dfrac{1}{s_i} + \dfrac{1}{s_o} = \dfrac{1}{f}$

$M = \dfrac{h_i}{h_o} = -\dfrac{s_i}{s_o}$

$f = \dfrac{R}{2}$

$d \sin \theta = m\lambda$

$x_m = \dfrac{m\lambda L}{d}$

d = separation
f = focal length
h = height
L = distance
M = magnification
m = an integer
n = index of refraction
R = radius of curvature
s = distance
v = speed
x = distance
λ = wavelength
ν = frequency
θ = angle

Directions: Answer all six questions. The suggested time is about 15 minutes per question for answering each of the questions, which are worth 15 points each. The parts within a question may not have equal weight.

1.   (15 points)

A light spring of natural length 10 cm with force constant $k = 500$ N/m is embedded vertically in the ground. A ball of mass $m = 0.15$ kg is placed on top of the spring, which is compressed 8.0 cm; when released, the spring pushes the ball. When the ball reaches ground level, it leaves its light supporting platform and continues vertically upward. When it reaches the top of its path, a batter strikes the ball at an angle θ_0 to the horizontal. Ignore air resistance.

(a)   Find the height h at which the batter strikes the ball.

(b)   If the batter gives the ball an initial velocity of 30 m/s with $\theta_0 = 0$ by striking the ball with an impact time of 4 ms, determine:
   (i)   the average force exerted on the ball by the bat;
   (ii)   how long the ball is in flight after it's been hit;
   (iii)   how far the ball travels horizontally.

(c)   If the ball failed to release from the platform, with what frequency would it oscillate?

GO ON TO THE NEXT PAGE

2.   (15 points)

The figure below shows an electric circuit containing a source of emf, $\mathcal{E}$, a variable resistor (r) and a resistor of fixed resistance R. The resistor R is immersed in a sealed beaker containing a mass m of water, currently at temperature T_i. When the switch S is closed, current through the circuit causes the resistor in the water to dissipate heat, which is absorbed by the water. A stirrer at the bottom of the beaker simply ensures that the temperature is uniform throughout the water at any given moment. The apparatus is well-insulated (insulation not shown), and it may be assumed that no heat is lost to the walls or lid of the beaker or to the stirrer.

(a)   Determine the current in the circuit once S is closed. Write your answer in terms of $\mathcal{E}$, r, and R.

(b)   How much heat is dissipated by the resistor R in time t?

(c)   (i)   Give an equation that expresses T, the temperature of the water as a function of time t since turning on the circuit. Write your answer in terms of $\mathcal{E}$, r, R, T_i, m, and c (the specific heat of water).

[question continues next page]

GO ON TO THE NEXT PAGE

(ii) On the axes below, provide a sketch of T vs. t. Be sure to mark $T = T_i$ at $t = 0$.

(d) Explain briefly how the temperature of the water can be increased more rapidly by adjusting the rotation rate of the stirrer.

(e) Given that the specific heat of water is $c = 4.186$ kJ/kg·°C and the heat of vaporization of water is $L = 2260$ kJ/kg, will it take longer for this apparatus to heat the water to the boiling point (100°C) or to convert the water to steam?

GO ON TO THE NEXT PAGE

3. (15 points)

Rainbows are formed by a combination of total internal reflection and dispersion of sunlight through water droplets. Assume that the water droplets have a radius of 0.5 mm and a density of 1.0 g/cm³. The index of refraction for water is 1.333 for light of wavelength 589 nm (yellow), but varies slightly across the visible spectrum from a low of 1.317 to a high of 1.345, with higher frequencies of light having higher refractive indices. The figure below shows a water droplet and an incident beam of sunlight. The beams drawn inside the droplet do not take dispersion into account.

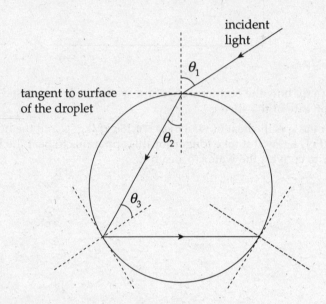

(a) How much does the water droplet weigh?

(b) If $\theta_1 = 60°$, determine θ_2 (ignore dispersion here; simply use $n = 1.333$).

(c) (i) How fast does red light travel through the droplet?

     (ii) Estimate how long a beam of light spends within the droplet.

(d) What must be true about the size of θ_3 in order for total internal reflection to occur?

(e) On the diagram above, provide a sketch of a ray of red light and a ray of violet light emerging from the droplet.

(f) In order to see a rainbow, does the incident light need to come from in front of you, arrive from behind you, or does it matter? Explain briefly.

GO ON TO THE NEXT PAGE

4. (15 points)

A *cyclotron* is a device used to accelerate charged particles to high speeds. It consists of two hollow containers—called *dees* because of their shape—facing each other and separated by a small gap. They are immersed in a uniform magnetic field, **B**, and are attached to a source of alternating voltage. A charged particle is projected from the center of the cyclotron into Dee #1, and the magnetic force causes it to turn in a circle. When it completes its semicircular path within one dee, the polarity of the voltage is reversed, and the particle is accelerated across the gap into the adjacent dee. This process continues, and the particle spirals outward at faster and faster speeds, until it emerges from Dee #2. Notice that the voltage must be alternated twice during each revolution of the particle. The figure below shows a view—looking down from above—of a cyclotron.

(a) Explain why the electric field in the gap must be used to increase the speed of the particle.

Assume that the charged particle to be accelerated by the cyclotron is a proton.

(b) Should the magnetic field point into the plane of the page or out of the plane of the page in order to cause the particle to rotate clockwise as shown in the figure?

For each of the following, write your answer in terms of the magnetic field strength B, the proton's charge $(+e)$ and mass (m), and fundamental constants.

(c) Show that the time to complete one revolution does not depend on the speed of the proton, and determine this orbital period.

(d) How many revolutions does the proton make per second?

(e) What must be the frequency (in Hz) of the alternating voltage?

(f) If the maximum radius of the proton's orbit is R, what is its maximum kinetic energy upon exiting? (Your answer should also include R.)

GO ON TO THE NEXT PAGE

5. (15 points)

The figure below shows two boxes attached by a light cord that runs over a frictionless peg. The mass of the block on the 60° incline is $M = 8$ kg, and the mass of the block on the 45° incline is $m = 2$ kg.

Assume that both inclined surfaces are frictionless for parts (a), (b), and (c).

(a) Find the acceleration of the blocks once they are released from rest.

(b) What is the total force exerted by the cord on the peg?

(c) If block M is released from rest at a height of $H = 1.5$ m above the bottom of the triangle, find its speed when it reaches the bottom.

(d) Answer the question posed in part (a) assuming that the coefficient of sliding friction between the blocks and the inclined surfaces is 0.2.

6.　(15 points)

The figure below is a view from above of two clay balls moving toward each other on a frictionless surface. They collide completely inelastically at the indicated point and are observed to then move in the direction indicated by the post-collision velocity vector, $\mathbf{v'}$. The masses are $m_1 = 200$ g and $m_2 = 100$ g, and the speed of m_1 just before impact is $v_1 = 6.0$ m/s.

(a)　What is v_2?

(b)　What is v', the common speed of the clay balls immediately after the collision?

(c)　If the specific heat of clay is 1.5 kJ/kg·°C, determine the temperature increase of the balls as a result of the collision. (Assume that both clay balls were at the same temperature before colliding.)

END OF EXAMINATION

STOP
IF YOU FINISH BEFORE TIME IS CALLED,
YOU MAY CHECK YOUR WORK
ON THIS SECTION.

DO NOT GO ON
UNTIL YOU ARE TOLD TO DO SO.

20

ANSWERS AND
EXPLANATIONS

SECTION I

1. **(D)** If the acceleration is not zero, then the velocity is changing. Since linear momentum (Item II) is the product of mass and velocity, it cannot remain constant if the velocity is changing. However, the object's speed (Item I) could be constant (consider, for example, uniform circular motion), so its kinetic energy (Item III), the scalar $K = \frac{1}{2}mv^2$, could be constant as well.

2. **(A)** For an object released from rest and in free fall, the distance covered in t seconds is given by the equation $y = \frac{1}{2}gt^2$. With $g = 10$ m/s^2 and $t = 2$ s, this gives $y = \frac{1}{2}(10$ m/s$^2)(2$ s$)^2 = 20$ m. If this is half the distance, then the total distance is $Y = 2y = 40$ m. How long will it take the object to fall the total distance of 40 m? Using $Y = \frac{1}{2}gT^2$, we find that

$$T = \sqrt{\frac{2Y}{g}} = \sqrt{\frac{2(40 \text{ m})}{10 \text{ m/s}^2}} = 2.8 \text{ s}$$

Therefore, the time necessary to fall the second half of the distance is $T - t = 2.8$ s $- 2$ s $= 0.8$ s.

3. **(D)** Since the particle travels in a circular path with constant kinetic energy (which implies constant speed), the net force on the particle is the centripetal force:

$$F = \frac{mv^2}{r} = \frac{2(\frac{1}{2}mv^2)}{r} = \frac{2K}{r} = \frac{2(4 \text{ J})}{0.2 \text{ m}} = 40 \text{ N}$$

4. **(E)** Energy is a scalar, not a vector, quantity. Displacement, velocity, acceleration, and linear momentum (the product of mass and velocity) are all vector quantities.

5. **(D)** The acceleration of the block is $a = g \sin \theta$, where θ is the incline angle, and the distance it must travel—the length of the incline—is $h/\sin \theta = h/\sin 30° = 2h$. Using the equation $s = \frac{1}{2}at^2$, we find that

$$t = \sqrt{\frac{2s}{a}} = \sqrt{\frac{2(2h)}{g \sin \theta}} = \sqrt{\frac{4(10 \text{ m})}{(10 \text{ m/s}^2)\sin 30°}} = 2.8 \text{ s}$$

6. **(C)** The easiest way to answer this question is to use conservation of energy:

$$mgh = \frac{1}{2}mv^2 \implies v = \sqrt{2gh} = \sqrt{2(10 \text{ m/s}^2)(10 \text{ m})} = 14 \text{ m/s}$$

7. **(A)** Since the normal force is perpendicular to the object's displacement, it does no work.

8. **(B)** The gravitational force provides the centripetal force on each satellite, so

$$\frac{GMm}{r^2} = \frac{mv^2}{r} \implies v = \sqrt{\frac{GM}{r}}$$

Therefore,

$$\frac{v_2}{v_1} = \frac{\sqrt{GM/r_2}}{\sqrt{GM/r_1}} = \sqrt{\frac{r_1}{r_2}} \implies v_2 = v_1\sqrt{\frac{r_1}{r_2}}$$

9. **(C)** The capacitance of a parallel-plate capacitor is $C = \kappa e_0 A/d$, where κ is the dielectric constant, A is the area of each plate, and d is their separation distance. Decreasing d will cause C to increase.

10. **(A)** The period is the reciprocal of the frequency: $T = 1/f = 1/(2.5 \text{ Hz}) = 0.4$ s.

11. **(B)** One way to answer this question is to invent some numbers that satisfy the conditions of the question and observe what happens. Let's choose $f = 1$ m, and take $s_{o1} = 3$ m and $s_{o2} = 2$ m (notice that $f < s_{o2} < s_{o1}$, which means that the object is moving closer to the focal point). Using the mirror equation, we find that

$$\frac{1}{s_{o1}} + \frac{1}{s_{i1}} = \frac{1}{f} \implies \frac{1}{3 \text{ m}} + \frac{1}{s_{i1}} = \frac{1}{1 \text{ m}} \implies s_{i1} = \frac{3}{2} \text{ m}$$

$$\frac{1}{s_{o2}} + \frac{1}{s_{i2}} = \frac{1}{f} \implies \frac{1}{2 \text{ m}} + \frac{1}{s_{i2}} = \frac{1}{1 \text{ m}} \implies s_{i2} = 2 \text{ m}$$

Since $s_{i2} > s_{i1}$, the image is moving away from the mirror (eliminating choices C and D). Now for the magnifications:

$$m_1 = -\frac{s_{i1}}{s_{o1}} = -\frac{\frac{3}{2} \text{ m}}{3 \text{ m}} = -\frac{1}{2}$$

$$m_2 = -\frac{s_{i2}}{s_{o2}} = -\frac{2 \text{ m}}{2 \text{ m}} = -1$$

Since $|m_2| > |m_1|$, the image gets taller. (You can also use ray diagrams.)

12. **(B)** The energies emitted during electron transitions are equal to the differences between the allowed energy levels. Choice A, 17 eV, is equal to the energy emitted when an electron drops from the –21 eV level to the –38 eV level. Choice C, 64 eV, is equal to the energy emitted when an electron drops from the –21 eV level to the –85 eV level. Choice D, 255 eV, is equal to the energy emitted when an electron drops from the –85 eV level to the –340 eV level. And choice E, 302 eV, is equal to the energy emitted when an electron drops from the –38 eV level to the –340 eV level. However, no electron transition in this atom could give rise to a 42 eV photon.

13. **(A)** Because the expansion is isothermal, no change in temperature occurs, which implies that no change in the internal energy of the gas takes place. Since $\Delta U = Q - W$ (the first law of thermodynamics), the fact that $\Delta U = 0$ implies that $Q = W$. Since $W = +150$ J, it must be true that $Q = +150$ J also.

14. **(C)** The frequency does not change, so the wavelength must (because the wave speed changes):

$$\lambda_{\text{in brass}} = \frac{v_{\text{in brass}}}{f} = \frac{10 v_{\text{in air}}}{f} = 10 \lambda_{\text{in air}}$$

15. **(C)** The net force on the two-block system is $3mg - F_f$, where F_f is the magnitude of the frictional force acting on the small block. Since $F_f = \mu mg$, we find that

$$a = \frac{F_{net}}{\text{total mass}} = \frac{3mg - (0.2)mg}{m + 3m} = \frac{(2.8)mg}{4m} = (0.7)g$$

16. **(D)** By Newton's Third Law, the force on the heavier person is equal but opposite to the force on the lighter person, eliminating choices A and B. Since the lighter person has $\frac{1}{2}$ the mass of the heavier person and acceleration is inversely proportional to mass, the magnitude of the lighter person's acceleration will be twice that of the heavier person.

17. **(B)** An activity of 20 decays per second—recorded at 4:00 PM—is $\frac{1}{16}$ of the value 320 decays per second, which had to be recorded earlier (eliminating choice E). If the activity drops to $\frac{1}{16}$ its previous value, the sample must have gone through 4 half-lives—because $\frac{1}{16} = \left(\frac{1}{2}\right)^4$—which is 4(20 min) = 80 min. Eighty minutes before 4:00 PM was 2:40 PM.

18. **(A)** If the mass of the $+q$ charge is m, then its acceleration is

$$a = \frac{F_E}{m} = \frac{1}{4\pi\varepsilon_0}\frac{Qq}{mr^2}$$

The graph in (A) best depicts an inverse-square relationship between a and r.

19. **(D)** When the block comes to rest, the spring force, kx, balances the gravitational force, mg. Therefore,

$$kx = mg \implies x = \frac{mg}{k} = \frac{(4.0 \text{ kg})(9.8 \text{ N}/\text{kg})}{800 \text{ N}/\text{m}} = 0.049 \text{ m} = 4.9 \text{ cm}$$

20. **(E)** Since the crate is being lifted with constant velocity, the magnitude of the force exerted by the crane must also be constant and equal to the magnitude of the gravitational force on the crate. Power can then be found from the equation

$$P = Fv = (5000 \text{ N})(4 \text{ m/s}) = 20,000 \text{ W}$$

21. **(C)** When the particle enters the magnetic field, the magnetic force provides the centripetal force to cause the particle to execute uniform circular motion:

$$|q|vB = \frac{mv^2}{r} \implies r = \frac{mv}{|q|B}$$

Since v and B are the same for all the particles, the largest r is found by maximizing the ratio $m/|q|$. The value of $m/|q|$ for an alpha particle is about twice that for a proton and thousands of times greater than that of an electron or positron.

22. **(B)** The value of g near the surface of a planet depends on the planet's mass and radius:

$$mg = \frac{GMm}{r^2} \quad \Rightarrow \quad g = \frac{GM}{r^2}$$

Therefore, calling this Planet X, we find that

$$g_X = \frac{GM_X}{r_X^2} = \frac{G(2M_{Earth})}{(2r_{Earth})^2} = \frac{1}{2}\frac{GM_{Earth}}{r_{Earth}^2} = \frac{1}{2}g_{Earth}$$

Since g is half as much on the planet as it is on Earth, the astronaut's weight (mg) will be half as much as well.

23. **(E)** The maximum net force on the object occurs when all four forces act in the same direction, giving $F_{net} = 4F = 4(10\text{ N}) = 40\text{ N}$, and a resulting acceleration of $a = F_{net}/m = (40\text{ N})/(5\text{ kg}) = 8$ m/s². These four forces could not give the object an acceleration greater than this.

24. **(A)** The Carnot efficiency is equal to $(T_H - T_C)/T_H$, where the temperatures are expressed in *kelvins*. Since 127°C = 127 + 273 = 400 K and 27°C = 27 + 273 = 300 K, we get

$$e = \frac{T_H - T_C}{T_H} = \frac{400\text{ K} - 300\text{ K}}{400\text{ K}} = \frac{1}{4} = 25\%$$

25. **(C)** The nth harmonic frequency is equal to n times the fundamental frequency, f_1. Therefore,

$$\frac{f_6}{f_3} = \frac{6f_1}{3f_1} = 2$$

26. **(B)** We use the equation for the power dissipated by a resistor, $P = IV$:

$$I = \frac{P}{V} = \frac{60\text{ W}}{120\text{ V}} = 0.5\text{ A}$$

27. **(A)** The work done by the electric field is equal and opposite to the change in the electrical potential energy, $\Delta U = q\,\Delta\phi = qV$:

$$
\begin{aligned}
W_{X\to Y} &= -\Delta U_{X\to Y} = -qV_{X\to Y} \\
&= -q\left[kQ\left(\frac{1}{r_Y} - \frac{1}{r_X}\right)\right] \\
&= -(1.0\times10^{-9}\text{ C})\left[(9\times10^9\text{ N}\cdot\text{m}^2/\text{C}^2)(2.0\text{ C})\left(\frac{1}{0.04\text{ m}} - \frac{1}{0.03\text{ m}}\right)\right] \\
&= -(18\text{ N}\cdot\text{m}^2)(25\text{ m}^{-1} - 33\tfrac{1}{3}\text{ m}^{-1}) \\
&= 150\text{ J}
\end{aligned}
$$

28. **(E)** The electric field strength is given by $E = kQ/r^2$. Therefore,

$$\frac{E_Z}{E_Y} = \frac{kQ/r_Z^2}{kQ/r_Y^2} = \frac{r_Y^2}{r_Z^2} = \frac{(4 \text{ cm})^2}{(3 \text{ cm})^2} = \frac{16}{9}$$

29. **(A)** The heat lost by the marble is $Q = -m_{marble}c_{marble}\Delta T_{marble}$, which is equal to the heat gained by the ammonia, $Q = m_{ammonia}c_{ammonia}\Delta T_{ammonia}$. Therefore,

$$-m_{marble}c_{marble}(T_f - 150°C) = m_{ammonia}c_{ammonia}(T_f - 20°C)$$
$$-(0.050 \text{ kg})(0.9 \text{ kJ / kg} \cdot °C)(T_f - 150°C) = (0.200 \text{ kg})(4.7 \text{ kJ / kg} \cdot °C)(T_f - 20°C)$$
$$-45(T_f - 150) = 940(T_f - 20)$$
$$-985T_f = -25550$$
$$T_f = 26$$

30. **(C)** When a wave enters a new medium, its frequency does not change, but its wave speed does. Since $\lambda f = v$, the change in wave speed implies a change in wavelength also.

31. **(D)** Since the magnetic flux out of the page is decreasing, the induced current will oppose this change (as always), attempting to create more magnetic flux out of the page. In order to do this, the current must circulate in the counterclockwise direction (remember the right-hand rule). As B decreases uniformly (that is, while $\Delta B / \Delta t$ is negative and constant), the induced emf,

$$\mathcal{E} = -\frac{\Delta \Phi_B}{\Delta t} = -A \frac{\Delta B}{\Delta t}$$

is nonzero and constant, which implies that the induced current, $I = \mathcal{E}/R$, is also nonzero and constant.

32. **(A)** The de Broglie wavelength of a particle moving with linear momentum of magnitude $p = mv$ is given by the equation $\lambda = h/p$, where h is Planck's constant. Because

$$p = mv = \sqrt{m(mv^2)} = \sqrt{2m(\tfrac{1}{2}mv^2)} = \sqrt{2mK}$$

we find that

$$\frac{\lambda_e}{\lambda_p} = \frac{h/\sqrt{2m_e K}}{h/\sqrt{2m_p K}} = \frac{\sqrt{2m_p K}}{\sqrt{2m_e K}} = \sqrt{\frac{m_p}{m_e}} \quad \Rightarrow \quad \lambda_e = \lambda_p \sqrt{\frac{m_p}{m_e}}$$

33. **(D)** With respect to the point at which the rod is attached to the vertical wall, the tension in the string exerts a counterclockwise (CCW) torque, and the gravitational force—which acts at the rod's center of mass—exerts a clockwise (CW) torque. If the rod is in equilibrium, these torques must balance. Letting L denote the length of the rod, this gives

$$\tau_{CCW} = \tau_{CW}$$
$$F_T L \sin\theta = (\tfrac{1}{2}L)(mg)\sin\theta$$
$$F_T = \tfrac{1}{2}mg$$

34. **(A)** Statement B is false, because a solid must *absorb* thermal energy in order to melt. Statement C is false since it generally requires much more energy to break the intermolecular bonds of a liquid to change its state to vapor than to loosen the intermolecular bonds of a solid to change its state to liquid. And statements D and E are false: While a substance undergoes a phase change, its temperature remains constant. The only true statement is A.

35. **(C)** Relative to the central maximum, the locations of the bright fringes on the screen are given by the expression $m(\lambda L/d)$, where λ is the wavelength of the light used, L is the distance to the screen, d is the separation of the slits, and m is an integer. The width of a fringe is therefore $(m + 1)(\lambda L/d) - m(\lambda L/d) = \lambda L/d$. One way to increase $\lambda L/d$ is to decrease d.

36. **(B)** Nuclear reactions must conserve mass number and charge, so the missing particle must be a proton:

$$^{13}_{6}C + ^{1}_{1}p \rightarrow ^{13}_{7}N + ^{1}_{0}n$$

37. **(D)** Resistors b, c, and d are equivalent to a single 1 Ω resistor, since

$$\frac{1}{3\,\Omega} + \frac{1}{3\,\Omega} + \frac{1}{3\,\Omega} = \frac{1}{1\,\Omega}$$

Therefore, the total resistance in the circuit is (3 Ω) + (1 Ω) + (3 Ω) + (3 Ω) = 10 Ω. From $V = IR$, we find that $V = (3\ A)(10\ \Omega) = 30$ V.

38. **(E)** The power dissipated by a resistor is I^2R. Since the current through Resistor b is $\frac{1}{3}$ of the current through Resistor e, we find that

$$\frac{P_b}{P_e} = \frac{I_b^2 R}{I_e^2 R} = \frac{I_b^2}{I_e^2} = \frac{\left(\frac{1}{3}I_e\right)^2}{I_e^2} = \frac{1}{9} \Rightarrow P_e = 9P_b$$

39. **(C)** If both the source and detector travel in the same direction and at the same speed, there will be no relative motion and hence no Doppler shift.

40. **(D)** The SI unit for power, P, is the watt, where 1 watt = 1 joule per second. One joule is equal to 1 newton·meter, and 1 newton = 1 kg·m/s². Therefore,

$$[P] = \frac{J}{s} = \frac{N \cdot m}{s} = \frac{\frac{kg \cdot m}{s^2} \cdot m}{s} = \frac{kg \cdot m^2}{s^3} \Rightarrow [P] = \frac{ML^2}{T^3}$$

41. **(A)** In order for total internal reflection to occur, the beam must be incident in the medium with the higher index of refraction and strike the interface at an angle of incidence greater than the critical angle. Since $v_1 < v_2$, the refractive index of Medium 1, $n_1 = c/v_1$, must be *greater* than the index of Medium 2 ($n_2 = c/v_2$), and the critical angle is $\theta_c = \sin^{-1}(n_2/n_1) = \sin^{-1}(v_1/v_2)$.

42. **(A)** Because the initial height of the object is comparable to the radius of the Moon, we cannot simply use mgh for its initial potential energy. Instead, we must use the more general expression $U = -GMm/r$, where r is the distance from the center of the Moon. Notice that since $h = R$, the object's initial distance from the Moon's center is $h + R = R + R = 2R$. Conservation of Energy then gives

$$K_i + U_i = K_f + U_f$$
$$0 - \frac{GMm}{2R} = \frac{1}{2}mv^2 - \frac{GMm}{R}$$
$$\frac{GMm}{2R} = \frac{1}{2}mv^2$$
$$v = \sqrt{\frac{GM}{R}}$$

43. **(C)** Since the magnetic force is always perpendicular to the object's velocity, it does zero work on any charged particle. Zero work means zero change in kinetic energy, so the speed remains the same. Remember: The magnetic force can only change the direction of a charged particle's velocity, not its speed.

44. **(E)** The intensity of a wave is equal to the power delivered per unit area. By increasing the distance from the source by a factor of 2, the area is increased by a factor of $2^2 = 4$. Since the intensity decreases by a factor that is less than 10, the sound level (in decibels) drops by an amount that is less than 10. The answer must be E.

45. **(E)** By definition, an electric dipole consists of a pair of charges that are equal in magnitude but opposite in sign. The electric field at the point midway between the charges is equal to the sum of the electric fields due to each charge alone:

Because the individual electric field vectors point in the same direction, their magnitudes add to give the total electric field:

$$E_{\text{total}} = 2E = 2\frac{kQ}{r^2} = 2\frac{kQ}{\left(\frac{1}{2}d\right)^2} = 8\frac{kQ}{d^2} = 8 \cdot \frac{(9 \times 10^9 \text{ N} \cdot \text{m}^2/\text{C}^2)(4.0 \times 10^{-9} \text{ C})}{(2.0 \times 10^{-2} \text{ m})^2}$$
$$= 7.2 \times 10^5 \text{ N/C}$$

46. **(C)** By Newton's Third Law, both vehicles experience the same magnitude of force and, therefore, the same impulse; so Statement I is false. Invoking Newton's Second Law, in the form *impulse = change in momentum*, we see that Statement II is therefore also false. However, since the car has a smaller mass than the truck, its acceleration will be greater in magnitude than that of the truck, so Statement III is true.

47. **(B)** The projectile reaches its maximum height when its vertical velocity drops to zero. Since $v_y = v_{0y} - gt$, this occurs at time $t = v_{0y}/g$ after launch. The vertical displacement at this time is

$$\Delta y = v_{0y}t - \tfrac{1}{2}gt^2 = v_{0y}\frac{v_{0y}}{g} - \tfrac{1}{2}g\left(\frac{v_{0y}}{g}\right)^2 = \frac{v_{0y}^2}{2g} = \frac{(a\sin\beta)^2}{2g}$$

48. **(A)** At the instant a simple harmonic oscillator passes through equilibrium, the restoring force is zero. Therefore, the tangential acceleration of the pendulum bob is also zero.

49. **(D)** The angular momentum, L, of a particle is equal to rmv, so we must first determine v. Since the earth's gravitational pull provides the centripetal force on the Moon,

$$\frac{GMm}{R^2} = \frac{mv^2}{R} \quad \Rightarrow \quad v = \sqrt{\frac{GM}{R}}$$

Therefore,

$$L = rmv = Rm\sqrt{\frac{GM}{R}} = m\sqrt{GMR}$$

50. **(E)** If the photons of the incident light have insufficient energy to liberate electrons from the metal's surface, then simply increasing the number of these weak photons (that is, increasing the intensity of the light) will do nothing. In order to produce photoelectrons, each photon of the incident light must have an energy at least as great as the work function of the metal.

51. **(D)** The force per unit length on each wire is $(\mu_0/2\pi)I_1I_2/r$, where r is the separation distance. Since $I_1 = I_2 = I$ and $r = a$, the force per unit length on each wire is $(\mu_0/2\pi)I^2/a$. And remember that when the currents are in opposite directions, the force between the wires is repulsive.

52. **(D)** The distance from the mirror to the image is equal to the distance from the mirror to the object. Therefore, the distance from the object to the image is 100 cm + 100 cm = 200 cm.

53. **(B)** Use the Ideal Gas Law:

$$P' = \frac{nRT'}{V'} = \frac{nR(2T)}{8V} = \frac{1}{4}\frac{nRT}{V} = \frac{1}{4}P$$

54. **(E)** The nuclide $^{68}_{30}\text{Zn}$ has 30 protons and 68 − 30 = 38 neutrons, so the excess number of neutrons over protons is 38 − 30 = 8. Of the choices given, only the nuclide $^{78}_{35}\text{Br}$ shares this property; it has 35 protons and 78 − 35 = 43 neutrons, giving an excess of neutrons over protons of 43 − 35 = 8.

55. **(B)** The charge on each plate has magnitude $Q = CV = (2 \times 10^{-3}\,\text{F})(5\,\text{V}) = 0.01\,\text{C}$.

56. **(C)** Use the work–energy theorem:

$$W = \Delta K = \tfrac{1}{2}m(v_f^2 - v_i^2) = \tfrac{1}{2}(2\,\text{kg})[(4\,\text{m/s})^2 - (2\,\text{m/s})^2] = 12\,\text{J}$$

57. **(E)** Since the process is cyclic, $\Delta U = 0$, so neither choice A nor B can be true. Since the work done during an isochoric step is always zero (because there is no change in volume), choice C is incorrect also. Choice D is not always true; in some cases, the total work done is equal to the area enclosed by the cycle (no change in sign necessary). But choice E must be true; since $\Delta U = 0$, the first law of thermodynamics says that $W = Q$.

58. **(C)** Draw a free-body diagram:

"up" is the positive direction

The net force on the object is $F - F_W$, so

$$F - F_W = ma$$

$$F = F_W + ma$$

$$= F_W + \frac{F_W}{g}a$$

$$= (49\ \text{N}) + \frac{49\ \text{N}}{9.8\ \text{m/s}^2}(9.8\ \text{m/s}^2)$$

$$= 98\ \text{N}$$

59. **(D)** The impulse delivered to the ball is equal to the ball's change in momentum, and the presence of the mitt does not change this; choices A and C are eliminated. The extra area decreases the *pressure* on the catcher's hand, but not the force (eliminating choice B). The padding of the mitt causes the time during which the ball comes to a stop to increase, which decreases the magnitude of the ball's acceleration (since $a = \Delta v/\Delta t$). A decrease in the magnitude of the acceleration means a decrease in the magnitude of the force (since $a = F/m$).

60. **(C)** Statements A and E were known before Rutherford conducted this series of experiments, and statements B and D concerning the electrons were proposed later by Bohr. What Rutherford discovered with these experiments was that an atom's positive charge was not uniformly distributed throughout the entire atom but was instead concentrated into a very small volume at the atom's center.

61. **(A)** A bi-convex lens is a converging lens, so it has a positive focal length. Since $f = R/2$, we have $f = (20\ \text{cm})/2 = 10\ \text{cm}$. The lens equation then gives

$$\frac{1}{s_o} + \frac{1}{s_i} = \frac{1}{f} \quad \Rightarrow \quad \frac{1}{30\ \text{cm}} + \frac{1}{s_i} = \frac{1}{10\ \text{cm}} \quad \Rightarrow \quad s_i = 15\ \text{cm}$$

Because s_i is positive, the image is real, and real images are inverted. This eliminates choices B, C, and D. The magnification is

$$m = -\frac{s_i}{s_o} = -\frac{15 \text{ cm}}{30 \text{ cm}} = -\frac{1}{2}$$

so the height of the image is

$$h_i = |m| \cdot h_o = \frac{1}{2}(2 \text{ cm}) = 1 \text{ cm}$$

62. **(E)** If Lenz's law were violated, then energy conservation would also be violated. The other principles listed as choices are unrelated to Lenz's law.

63. **(E)** Because no electrostatic field can exist within the body of a conductor, a charge of –1 mC will appear on the wall of the cavity to "guard" the +1 mC charge of the plastic ball. Since the sphere has a charge of +1 mC, a net charge of (+1 mC) – (–1 mC) = +2 mC will appear on the outer surface of the copper sphere.

64. **(D)** Since the mass of the products is less than the mass of the reactants, some mass has been converted to energy in this exothermic reaction. Because the difference in mass is 9.028 u – 9.012 u = +0.016 u, and 1 u is equivalent to 931 MeV of energy, the reaction's disintegration energy is

$$Q = (+0.016 \text{ u}) \times \frac{931 \text{ MeV}}{1 \text{ u}} = +15 \text{ MeV}$$

65. **(C)** The work required to charge the capacitor is equal to the resulting increase in the stored electrical potential energy:

$$U = \frac{1}{2}CV^2 = \frac{1}{2}(10 \times 10^{-6} \text{ F})(100 \text{ V})^2 = 0.05 \text{ J}$$

66. **(D)** All linear dimensions within the block—including the radius of the hole—will increase by the same amount during thermal expansion. (To see that the hole does indeed get bigger, imagine that it were filled with a spherical ball of asphalt. This ball would get bigger as the block expanded, so if the ball were removed, it would leave behind a bigger hole.)

67. **(A)** Choices B, C, D, and E all change the magnetic flux through the loop containing the light bulb, thus inducing an emf and a current. However, just swinging the handle over as described in choice A changes neither the area presented to the magnetic field lines from the bottom coil nor the density of the field lines at the position of the loop. No change in magnetic flux means no induced emf and no induced current.

68. **(E)** Gamma rays and X-rays are very high-energy, short-wavelength radiations. Ultraviolet light has a higher energy and shorter wavelength than visible. Within the visible spectrum, the colors are—in order of increasing frequency—ROYGBV, so orange light has a lower frequency (and thus longer wavelength) than blue light.

69. **(A)** If these waves interfere completely destructively, the displacement of the resultant wave will be 6 cm – 4 cm = 2 cm. If they interfere completely constructively, then the displacement of the resultant wave will be 6 cm + 4 cm = 10 cm. In general, then, the displacement of the resultant wave will be no less than 2 cm and no greater than 10 cm.

70. **(C)** Since $\mathbf{F}_{net} = \mathbf{F}_1 + \mathbf{F}_2 = \mathbf{0}$, the bar cannot accelerate translationally, so B is false. The net torque does *not* need to be zero, as the following diagram shows (eliminating choices A and D):

However, since $\mathbf{F}_2 = -\mathbf{F}_1$, choice C is true; one possible illustration of this is given below:

SECTION II

1. (a) The elastic potential energy of the spring turns into kinetic energy of the ball which then becomes gravitational potential energy of the ball. Let the zero for gravitational potential energy be the initial position of the ball on the compressed spring (i.e., 8 cm below ground level). Then

$$K_i + U_i = K_f + U_f$$
$$0 + (0 + \tfrac{1}{2}kx^2) = 0 + [mg(h + 0.08 \text{ m}) + 0]$$
$$h = \frac{\tfrac{1}{2}kx^2}{mg} - 0.08 \text{ m}$$
$$= \frac{\tfrac{1}{2}(500 \text{ N}/\text{m})(0.08 \text{ m})^2}{(0.15 \text{ kg})(9.8 \text{ N}/\text{kg})} - 0.08 \text{ m}$$
$$= 1.0 \text{ m}$$

(b) (i) Use the impulse–momentum theorem (Newton's Second Law):

$$J = \Delta p$$

$$F_{avg}\Delta t = m\Delta v$$

$$F_{avg} = m\frac{\Delta v}{\Delta t}$$

$$= (0.15 \text{ kg})\frac{30 \text{ m/s}}{0.004 \text{ s}}$$

$$= 1100 \text{ N}$$

(b) (ii) The ball is in flight until its vertical displacement is $-h$ (calling *up* the positive direction). Therefore,

$$\Delta y = v_{0y}t - \tfrac{1}{2}gt^2 = -\tfrac{1}{2}gt^2 \implies t = \sqrt{\frac{-2\Delta y}{g}} = \sqrt{\frac{2h}{g}} = \sqrt{\frac{2(1.0 \text{ m})}{9.8 \text{ m/s}^2}} = 0.45 \text{ s}$$

(b) (iii) The ball's horizontal displacement is $v_{0x}t$, where t is the time calculated in part (b) (ii):
$$\Delta x = v_{0x}t = (30 \text{ m/s})(0.45 \text{ s}) = 13.5 \text{ m}$$

(c) The frequency of this simple harmonic oscillator is

$$f = \frac{1}{2\pi}\sqrt{\frac{k}{m}} = \frac{1}{2\pi}\sqrt{\frac{500 \text{ N/m}}{0.15 \text{ kg}}} = 9.2 \text{ Hz}$$

2. (a) Since the total resistance in the circuit is $r + R$, Ohm's law gives

$$I = \frac{\varepsilon}{r + R}$$

(b) The power dissipated as heat by resistor R is $P = I^2R$; multiplying this by the time, t, gives Q, the heat dissipated:

$$Q = Pt = I^2Rt = \frac{\varepsilon^2 Rt}{(r+R)^2}$$

(c) (i) Use the equation $Q = mc\,\Delta T$ with Q as given in part (b):

$$Q = mc\Delta T$$

$$\frac{\varepsilon^2 Rt}{(r+R)^2} = mc(T - T_i)$$

$$T = \frac{\varepsilon^2 R}{(r+R)^2 mc}t + T_i$$

(c) (ii) The graph of T vs. t is a straight line with slope $\mathcal{E}^2 R/[(r+R)^2 mc]$:

(d) The movement of the blades of the stirrer through the water transfers mechanical work to thermal energy. The faster the stirrer rotates (i.e., the more rotational kinetic energy it has), the more heat will be transferred to the water and the faster the temperature will rise. [In fact, given enough time, the rotating stirrer could bring the water to boil all by itself (assuming that heat losses to the beaker, the lid, etc. could be kept low).]

(e) The heat necessary to bring the water to a boil is $Q_1 = mc(100°C - T_i)$, and the additional heat necessary to completely vaporize it is $Q_2 = mL$. Since the water is in liquid form, the lowest T_i could be is 0°C, so the maximum value of Q_1 is

$$Q_{1, max} = mc(100°C) = m(418.6 \text{ kJ/kg})$$

But $Q_2 = m(2260 \text{ kJ/kg})$, so we see that that $Q_2 > Q_1$. Since the resistor supplies heat at a steady rate, it will take much longer to vaporize the water to steam than to bring it to the boiling point.

3. (a) The weight of the water droplet is mg, where $m = \rho V$ (density times volume):

$$w = mg = \rho V g = \rho \cdot \tfrac{4}{3}\pi r^3 \cdot g$$

$$= \frac{1.0 \times 10^{-3} \text{ kg}}{\text{cm}^3} \cdot \tfrac{4}{3}\pi(0.05 \text{ cm})^3 \cdot (9.8 \text{ N/kg})$$

$$= 5.1 \times 10^{-6} \text{ N}$$

(b) Use Snell's Law:

$$n_1 \sin\theta_1 = n_2 \sin\theta_2$$

$$1 \cdot \sin 60° = 1.333 \sin\theta_2$$

$$\sin\theta_2 = 0.6497$$

$$\theta_2 = 41°$$

(c) (i) Since red light has the lowest frequency in the visible spectrum, the index of refraction for red light in water must be 1.317 (according to the information given in the description of the problem). Therefore,

$$v_{red} = \frac{c}{n_{red}} = \frac{3.00 \times 10^8 \text{ m/s}}{1.317} = 2.28 \times 10^8 \text{ m/s}$$

(c) (ii) The total distance traveled within the droplet is roughly equal to two diameters, so a reasonable estimate for the travel time is

$$t = \frac{2d}{v} = \frac{2(2r)}{c/n} = \frac{4rn}{c} = \frac{4(0.5 \times 10^{-3} \text{ m})(1.33)}{3.00 \times 10^8 \text{ m/s}} = 8.9 \times 10^{-12} \text{ s}$$

(d) For total internal reflection to occur, the angle θ_3 must be greater than θ_c, the critical angle. Using $n = 1.333$ for the refractive index, we find that

$$\theta_c = \sin^{-1} \frac{n_2}{n_1} = \sin^{-1} \frac{1}{1.333} = 49°$$

(e) The beam will bend away from the normal upon exiting the droplet into the air, but since $n'_{violet} > n'_{red}$, the angle of refraction for violet will be (slightly) smaller than for red (with the other colors in between):

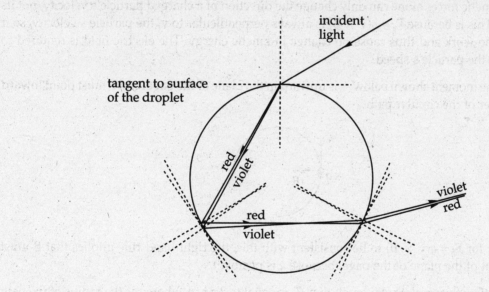

(f) From the figure, it is clear that the light must originate behind us, reflect off the back of the water droplet and then refract toward our eyes.

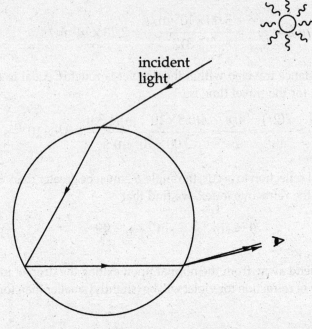

4. (a) Magnetic forces alone can only change the direction of a charged particle's velocity, not its speed. This is because $\mathbf{F}_B = q(\mathbf{v} \times \mathbf{B})$ is always perpendicular to $\mathbf{v}$, the particle's velocity, so it can do no work and thus cause no change in kinetic energy. The electric field is required to increase the particle's speed.

(b) At the moment shown below, $\mathbf{v}$ is upward in the plane of the page, and $\mathbf{F}$ must point toward the center of the circular path.

In order for $\mathbf{F}_B = q(\mathbf{v} \times \mathbf{B})$ to be consistent with this, the right-hand rule implies that $\mathbf{B}$ must point out of the plane of the page (because q is positive).

(c) The time to complete one revolution, T, is equal to $2\pi r/v$, where r is the radius of the path and v is the speed. Since the magnetic force provides the centripetal force,

$$qvB = \frac{mv^2}{r} \quad \Rightarrow \quad qB = \frac{mv}{r} \quad \Rightarrow \quad \frac{r}{v} = \frac{m}{qB} \quad \Rightarrow \quad T = \frac{2\pi r}{v} = \frac{2\pi m}{qB} = \frac{2\pi m}{eB}$$

Therefore, T depends only on e, m, and B.

(d) Since T is the time for one revolution, the number of revolutions per unit time is the reciprocal of T,

$$eB/(2\pi m)$$

(e) The description given with the problem states that "the voltage must be alternated twice during each revolution of the particle." Therefore, the frequency of the alternating voltage must be twice the value found in part (d),

$$2eB/(2\pi m) = eB/(\pi m)$$

(f) From part (c), we know that

$$evB = \frac{mv^2}{r} \quad \Rightarrow \quad v = \frac{eBr}{m}$$

Therefore,

$$K_{max} = \tfrac{1}{2}mv_{max}^2 = \tfrac{1}{2}m\left(\frac{eBr_{max}}{m}\right)^2 = \tfrac{1}{2}m\left(\frac{eBR}{m}\right)^2 = \frac{e^2B^2R^2}{2m}$$

5. (a) First draw free-body diagrams for the blocks:

Now apply Newton's Second Law:

$$Mg\sin 60° - F_T = Ma$$

add equations $\Bigg\{\;\dfrac{F_T - mg\sin 45° = ma}{Mg\sin 60° - mg\sin 45° = Ma + ma}$

$$a = \frac{M\sin 60° - m\sin 45°}{M + m}g$$

$$= \frac{(8\ \text{kg})\sin 60° - (2\ \text{kg})\sin 45°}{8\ \text{kg} + 2\ \text{kg}}(9.8\ \text{m/s}^2)$$

$$= 5.4\ \text{m/s}^2$$

(b) Using the value for a determined above, find F_T; we can use either of the two original equations from part (a):

$$F_T = mg\sin 45° + ma$$

$$= (2\text{ kg})(9.8\text{ m/s}^2)\sin 45° + (2\text{ kg})(5.4\text{ m/s}^2)$$

$$= 24.7\text{ N}$$

From the following diagram,

we see that the total force exerted by the cord on the peg is

$$\mathbf{F} = [(-F_T\sin 30°)\hat{\mathbf{i}} + (F_T\sin 45°)\hat{\mathbf{i}}] + [(-F_T\cos 30°)\hat{\mathbf{j}} + (-F_T\cos 45°)\hat{\mathbf{j}}]$$

$$= F_T[(-\sin 30° + \sin 45°)\hat{\mathbf{i}} + (-\cos 30° - \cos 45°)\hat{\mathbf{j}}]$$

so

$$F = F_T\sqrt{(-\sin 30° + \sin 45°)^2 + (-\cos 30° - \cos 45°)^2}$$

$$= (24.7\text{ N})\sqrt{2.518}$$

$$= 39\text{ N}$$

(c) Refer to the following diagram:

Using Conservation of Energy, we find that

$$K_i + U_i = K_f + U_f$$

$$0 + (MgH + mgh) = (\tfrac{1}{2}Mv^2 + \tfrac{1}{2}mv^2) + mg(h + \ell\sin 45°)$$

$$MgH = \tfrac{1}{2}v^2(M + m) + mg\ell\sin 45°$$

$$= \tfrac{1}{2}v^2(M + m) + mg\frac{H}{\sin 60°}\sin 45°$$

$$v = \sqrt{\frac{MgH\left(1 - \frac{\sin 45°}{\sin 60°}\right)}{\tfrac{1}{2}(M + m)}}$$

$$= \sqrt{\frac{(8\text{ kg})(9.8\text{ m/s}^2)(1.5\text{ m})\left(1 - \frac{\sin 45°}{\sin 60°}\right)}{\tfrac{1}{2}(8\text{ kg} + 2\text{ kg})}}$$

$$= 2.1\text{ m/s}$$

(d) First draw free-body diagrams for the blocks:

Now apply Newton's Second Law:

$$Mg\sin 60° - F_T - \mu Mg\cos 60° = Ma$$

add equations ⎰ $F_T - mg\sin 45° - \mu mg\cos 45° = ma$

$$\overline{Mg\sin 60° - mg\sin 45° - \mu Mg\cos 60° - \mu mg\cos 45° = Ma + ma}$$

This gives

$$a = \frac{M(\sin 60° - \mu \cos 60°) - m(\sin 45° + \mu \cos 45°)}{M+m} g$$

$$= \frac{(8 \text{ kg})(\sin 60° - 0.2 \cos 60°) - (2 \text{ kg})(\sin 45° + 0.2 \cos 45°)}{8 \text{ kg} + 2 \text{ kg}}(9.8 \text{ m/s}^2)$$

$$= 4.3 \text{ m/s}^2$$

6. (a) The diagram given with the question shows that after the clay balls collide, they move in the $-y$ direction, which means that the horizontal components of their linear momenta canceled. In other words, $\mathbf{p}_{1x} + \mathbf{p}_{2x} = \mathbf{0}$:

$$m_1 \mathbf{v}_{1x} + m_2 \mathbf{v}_{2x} = \mathbf{0}$$

$$(m_1 v_1 \sin 45°)\hat{\mathbf{i}} + (m_2 v_2 \sin 60°)(-\hat{\mathbf{i}}) = \mathbf{0}$$

$$v_2 = \frac{m_1 v_1 \sin 45°}{m_2 \sin 60°}$$

$$= \frac{(200 \text{ g})(6.0 \text{ m/s}) \sin 45°}{(100 \text{ g}) \sin 60°}$$

$$= 9.8 \text{ m/s}$$

(b) Apply conservation of linear momentum in the y direction:

$$m_1 \mathbf{v}_{1y} + m_2 \mathbf{v}_{2y} = (m_1 + m_2)\mathbf{v}'_y$$

$$(m_1 v_1 \cos 45°)(-\hat{\mathbf{j}}) + (m_2 v_2 \cos 60°)(-\hat{\mathbf{j}}) = (m_1 + m_2)\mathbf{v}'_y$$

$$v'_y = \frac{m_1 v_1 \cos 45° + m_2 v_2 \cos 60°}{m_1 + m_2}$$

$$= \frac{(200 \text{ g})(6.0 \text{ m/s}) \cos 45° + (100 \text{ g})(9.8 \text{ m/s}) \cos 60°}{200 \text{ g} + 100 \text{ g}}$$

$$= 4.5 \text{ m/s}$$

(c) The total kinetic energy before the collision was

$$K = \tfrac{1}{2}m_1v_1^2 + \tfrac{1}{2}m_2v_2^2$$

$$= \tfrac{1}{2}(0.200 \text{ kg})(6.0 \text{ m/s})^2 + \tfrac{1}{2}(0.100 \text{ kg})(9.8 \text{ m/s})^2$$

$$= 8.4 \text{ J}$$

The kinetic energy after the collision is

$$K' = \tfrac{1}{2}(m_1 + m_2)v'^2$$

$$= \tfrac{1}{2}(0.200 \text{ kg} + 0.100 \text{ kg})(4.5 \text{ m/s})^2$$

$$= 3.0 \text{ J}$$

If we assume that all of the difference, $K' - K = 8.4 \text{ J} - 3.0 \text{ J} = 5.4 \text{ J}$, was transformed to thermal energy, Q, then

$$\Delta T = \frac{Q}{(m_1 + m_2)c} = \frac{5.4 \text{ J}}{(0.300 \text{ kg})(1.5 \times 10^3 \text{ J/kg} \cdot {}^\circ\text{C})} = 0.012^\circ\text{C}$$

21

THE PRINCETON REVIEW
AP PHYSICS C
DIAGNOSTIC EXAM

PHYSICS C

You may take the entire C Exam or Mechanics only or Electricity and Magnetism only as follows:

	Entire C Exam Both Mech. and Elect. & Mag.	Mechanics only	Electricity & Magnetism only
1st 45 min.	Sec. I, Mech. 35 questions	Sec. I, Mech. 35 questions	Sec. I, Elect. & Mag. 35 questions
2nd 45 min.	Sec. I, Elect. & Mag. 35 questions	Sec. II Mech. 3 questions	Sec. II, Elect. & Mag. 3 questions
3rd 45min.	Sec. II Mech. 3 questions		
4th 45 min.	Sec. II, Elect. & Mag. 3 questions		

Separate grades are reported for Mechanics and for Electricity and Magnetism. Each section of each examination is 50 percent of the total grade; each question in a section has equal weight. Calculators are NOT permitted on Section I of the exam but are allowed on Section II. However, calculators cannot be shared with other students and calculators with typewriter-style (QWERTY) keyboards will not be permitted. A table of information that may be helpful is found on the following page.

The Physics C Examination contains a total of 70 multiple-choice questions. If you are taking
— *Mechanics only*, **please be careful to answer numbers 1–35,**
— *Electricity and magnetism only*, **please be careful to answer numbers 36–70,**
— *the entire examination* (Mechanics *and* Electricity and Magnetism), **answer numbers 1–70 on your answer sheet.**

TABLE OF INFORMATION

CONSTANTS AND CONVERSION FACTORS

1 unified atomic mass unit.	$1\ u = 1.66 \times 10^{-27}\ \text{kg}$
	$= 931\ \text{MeV}/c^2$
Proton mass,	$m_p = 1.67 \times 10^{-27}\ \text{kg}$
Neutron mass,	$m_n = 1.67 \times 10^{-27}\ \text{kg}$
Electron mass,	$m_e = 9.11 \times 10^{-31}\ \text{kg}$
Magnitude of electron charge,	$e = 1.60 \times 10^{-19}\ \text{C}$
Avogadro's number,	$N_0 = 6.02 \times 10^{23}\ \text{mol}^{-1}$
Universal gas constant,	$R = 8.31\ \text{J}/(\text{mol} \cdot \text{K})$
Boltzmann's constant,	$k_B = 1.38 \times 10^{-23}\ \text{J/K}$
Speed of light,	$c = 3.00 \times 10^8\ \text{m/s}$
Planck's constant,	$h = 6.63 \times 10^{-34}\ \text{J} \cdot \text{s}$
	$= 4.14 \times 10^{-15}\ \text{eV} \cdot \text{s}$
	$hc = 1.99 \times 10^{-25}\ \text{J} \cdot \text{m}$
	$= 1.24 \times 10^3\ \text{eV} \cdot \text{nm}$
Vacuum permittivity,	$\varepsilon_0 = 8.85 \times 10^{-12}\ \text{C}^2/\text{N} \cdot \text{m}^2$
Coulomb's law constant,	$k = 1/4\pi\varepsilon_0 = 9.0 \times 10^9\ \text{N} \cdot \text{m}^2/\text{C}^2$
Vacuum permeability,	$\mu_0 = 4\pi \times 10^{-7}\ \text{Wb}/(\text{A} \cdot \text{m})$
Magnetic constant,	$k' = \mu_0/4\pi = 10^{-7}\ \text{Wb}/(\text{A} \cdot \text{m})$
Universal gravitational constant,	$G = 6.67 \times 10^{-11}\ \text{m}^3/\text{kg} \cdot \text{s}^2$
Acceleration due to gravity at the Earth's surface,	$g = 9.8\ \text{m/s}^2$
1 atmosphere pressure,	$1\ \text{atm} = 1.0 \times 10^5\ \text{N/m}^2$
	$= 1.0 \times 10^5\ \text{Pa}$
1 electron volt,	$1\ \text{eV} = 1.60 \times 10^{-19}\ \text{J}$
1 angstrom,	$1\ \text{Å} = 1 \times 10^{-10}\ \text{m}$

UNITS

Name	Symbol
meter	m
kilogram	kg
second	s
ampere	A
kelvin	K
mole	mol
hertz	Hz
newton	N
pascal	Pa
joule	J
watt	W
coulomb	C
volt	V
ohm	Ω
henry	H
farad	F
weber	Wb
tesla	T
degree Celsius	°C
electron-volt	eV

PREFIXES

Factor	Prefix	Symbol
10^9	giga	G
10^6	mega	M
10^3	kilo	k
10^{-2}	centi	c
10^{-3}	milli	m
10^{-6}	micro	μ
10^{-9}	nano	n
10^{-12}	pico	p

VALUES OF TRIGONOMETRIC FUNCTIONS FOR COMMON ANGLES

Angle	Sin	Cos	Tan
0°	0	1	0
30°	1/2	$\sqrt{3}/2$	$\sqrt{3}/3$
37°	3/5	4/5	3/4
45°	$\sqrt{2}/2$	$\sqrt{2}/2$	1
53°	4/5	3/5	4/3
60°	$\sqrt{3}/2$	1/2	$\sqrt{3}$
90°	1	0	∞

The following conventions are used in this examination.

I. Unless otherwise stated, the frame of reference of any problem is assumed to be inertial.

II. The direction of any electric current is the direction of flow of positive charge (conventional current).

III. For any isolated electric charge, the electric potential is defined as zero at an infinite distance from the charge.

Directions: Each of the questions or incomplete statements below is followed by five suggested answers or completions. Select the one that is best in each case and then mark it on your answer sheet.

1. A rock is dropped off a cliff and falls the first half of the distance to the ground in t_1 seconds. If it falls the second half of the distance in t_2 seconds, what is the value of t_2/t_1? (Ignore air resistance.)

   (A) $1/2\sqrt{2}$
   (B) $1/\sqrt{2}$
   (C) $1/2$
   (D) $1 - (1/\sqrt{2})$
   (E) $\sqrt{2} - 1$

2. A box of mass m slides on a horizontal surface with initial speed v_0. It feels no forces other than gravity and the force from the surface. If the coefficient of kinetic friction between the box and the surface is μ, how far does the box slide before coming to rest?

   (A) $v_0^2/(2\mu g)$
   (B) $v_0^2/(\mu g)$
   (C) $2v_0^2/(\mu g)$
   (D) $mv_0^2/(\mu g)$
   (E) $2mv_0^2/(\mu g)$

3. An object initially at rest experiences a time-varying acceleration given by $a = (2 \text{ m/s}^3)t$ for $t \geq 0$. How far does the object travel in the first 3 seconds?

   (A) 9 m
   (B) 12 m
   (C) 18 m
   (D) 24 m
   (E) 27 m

4. Which of the following conditions will ensure that angular momentum is conserved?

   I. Conservation of linear momentum
   II. Zero net external force
   III. Zero net external torque

   (A) I and II only
   (B) I and III only
   (C) II and III only
   (D) II only
   (E) III only

5. In the figure shown, a tension force $\mathbf{F}_T$ causes a particle of mass m to move with constant angular speed ω in a circular path (perpendicular to the page) of radius R. Which of the following expressions gives the magnitude of $\mathbf{F}_T$?

   (A) $m\omega^2 R$
   (B) $m\sqrt{\omega^4 R^2 - g^2}$
   (C) $m\sqrt{\omega^4 R^2 + g^2}$
   (D) $m(\omega^2 R - g)$
   (E) $m(\omega^2 R + g)$

GO ON TO THE NEXT PAGE

6. An object (mass = m) above the surface of the Moon (mass = M) is dropped from an altitude h equal to the Moon's radius (R). With what speed will the object strike the lunar surface?

(A) $\sqrt{GM/R}$

(B) $\sqrt{GM/(2R)}$

(C) $\sqrt{2GM/R}$

(D) $\sqrt{2GMm/R}$

(E) $\sqrt{GMm/(2R)}$

7. The figure above shows a linear spring anchored to the ceiling. If the mass of the block hanging from its lower end is doubled, what effect will this change have on the block's equilibrium position and oscillation period?

(A) Equilibrium position: Lowered by a factor of $\sqrt{2}$
Oscillation period: Decreased by a factor of $\sqrt{2}$

(B) Equilibrium position: Lowered by a factor of $\sqrt{2}$
Oscillation period: Increased by a factor of $\sqrt{2}$

(C) Equilibrium position: Lowered by a factor of $\sqrt{2}$
Oscillation period: Increased by a factor of 2

(D) Equilibrium position: Lowered by a factor of 2
Oscillation period: Decreased by a factor of $\sqrt{2}$

(E) Equilibrium position: Lowered by a factor of 2
Oscillation period: Increased by a factor of $\sqrt{2}$

8. A uniform cylinder of mass m and radius r unrolls without slipping from two strings tied to a vertical support. If the rotational inertia of the cylinder is $\frac{1}{2}mr^2$, find the acceleration of its center of mass.

(A) $\frac{1}{4}g$

(B) $\frac{1}{2}g$

(C) $\frac{1}{3}g$

(D) $\frac{2}{3}g$

(E) $\frac{3}{4}g$

9. A uniform cylinder, initially at rest on a frictionless, horizontal surface, is pulled by a constant force $\mathbf{F}$ from time $t = 0$ to time $t = T$. From time $t = T$ on, this force is removed. Which of the following graphs best illustrates the speed, v, of the cylinder's center of mass from $t = 0$ to $t = 2T$?

(A)

(B)

(C)

(D)

(E)

GO ON TO THE NEXT PAGE

10. An engine provides 10 kW of power to lift a heavy load at constant velocity a distance of 20 m in 5 s. What is the mass of the object being lifted?

   (A) 100 kg
   (B) 150 kg
   (C) 200 kg
   (D) 250 kg
   (E) 500 kg

11. A satellite is in circular orbit around the earth. If the work required to lift the satellite to its orbit height is equal to the satellite's kinetic energy while in this orbit, how high above the surface of the earth (radius = R) is the satellite?

   (A) $\frac{1}{2}R$
   (B) $\frac{2}{3}R$
   (C) R
   (D) $\frac{3}{2}R$
   (E) $2R$

12. The figure above shows a uniform bar of mass M resting on two supports. A block of mass $\frac{1}{2}M$ is placed on the bar twice as far from Support 2 as from Support 1. If $\mathbf{F}_1$ and $\mathbf{F}_2$ denote the downward forces on Support 1 and Support 2, respectively, what is the value of F_2/F_1?

   (A) 1/2
   (B) 2/3
   (C) 3/4
   (D) 4/5
   (E) 5/6

13. A rubber ball (mass = 0.08 kg) is dropped from a height of 2 m, and after bouncing off the floor, rises almost to its original height. If the impact time with the floor is measured to be 0.04 s, what average force did the floor exert on the ball?

   (A) 0.16 N
   (B) 16 N
   (C) 25 N
   (D) 36 N
   (E) 64 N

14. A disk of radius 0.1 m initially at rest undergoes an angular acceleration of 2.0 rad/s². If the disk only rotates, find the total distance traveled by a point on the rim of the disk in 4.0 s.

   (A) 0.4 m
   (B) 0.8 m
   (C) 1.2 m
   (D) 1.6 m
   (E) 2.0 m

15. In the figure above, a small ball slides down a frictionless quarter-circular slide of radius R. If the ball starts from rest at a height equal to $2R$ above a horizontal surface, find its horizontal displacement, x, at the moment it strikes the surface.

   (A) $2R$
   (B) $\frac{5}{2}R$
   (C) $3R$
   (D) $\frac{7}{2}R$
   (E) $4R$

GO ON TO THE NEXT PAGE

16. The figure above shows a particle executing uniform circular motion in a circle of radius R. Light sources (not shown) cause shadows of the particle to be projected onto two mutually perpendicular screens. The positive directions for x and y along the screens are denoted by the arrows. When the shadow on Screen 1 is at position $x = -(0.5)R$ and moving in the $+x$ direction, what is true about the position and velocity of the shadow on Screen 2 at that same instant?

(A) $y = -(0.866)R$; velocity in $-y$ direction
(B) $y = -(0.866)R$; velocity in $+y$ direction
(C) $y = -(0.5)R$; velocity in $-y$ direction
(D) $y = +(0.866)R$; velocity in $-y$ direction
(E) $y = +(0.866)R$; velocity in $+y$ direction

17. The figure shows a view from above of two objects attached to the end of a rigid massless rod at rest on a frictionless table. When a force **F** is applied as shown, the resulting rotational acceleration of the rod about its center of mass is $kF/(mL)$. What is k?

(A) $\frac{3}{8}$
(B) $\frac{1}{2}$
(C) $\frac{5}{8}$
(D) $\frac{3}{4}$
(E) $\frac{5}{6}$

18. A lightweight toy car crashes head-on into a heavier toy truck. Which of the following statements is true as a result of the collision?

   I. The car will experience a greater impulse than the truck.

   II. The car will experience a greater change in momentum than the truck.

   III. The magnitude of the acceleration experienced by the car will be greater than that experienced by the truck.

(A) I and II only
(B) II only
(C) III only
(D) II and III only
(E) I, II, and III

19. A homogeneous bar is lying on a flat table. Besides the gravitational and normal forces (which cancel), the bar is acted upon by exactly two other external forces, $\mathbf{F}_1$ and $\mathbf{F}_2$, which are parallel to the surface of the table. If the net force on the rod is zero, which one of the following is also true?

(A) The net torque on the bar must also be zero.
(B) The bar cannot accelerate translationally or rotationally.
(C) The bar can accelerate translationally if $\mathbf{F}_1$ and $\mathbf{F}_2$ are not applied at the same point.
(D) The net torque will be zero if $\mathbf{F}_1$ and $\mathbf{F}_2$ are applied at the same point.
(E) None of the above

20. An astronaut lands on a planet whose mass and radius are each twice that of Earth. If the astronaut weighs 800 N on Earth, how much will he weigh on this planet?

(A) 200 N
(B) 400 N
(C) 800 N
(D) 1600 N
(E) 3200 N

GO ON TO THE NEXT PAGE

21. A particle of mass $m = 1.0$ kg is acted upon by a variable force, $F(x)$, whose strength is given by the graph given above. If the particle's speed was zero at $x = 0$, what is its speed at $x = 4$ m?

(A) 5.0 m/s
(B) 8.7 m/s
(C) 10 m/s
(D) 14 m/s
(E) 20 m/s

22. The radius of a collapsing spinning star (assumed to be a uniform sphere) decreases to $\frac{1}{16}$ its initial value. What is the ratio of the final rotational kinetic energy to the initial rotational kinetic energy?

(A) 4
(B) 16
(C) 16^2
(D) 16^3
(E) 16^4

23. An object is projected with an initial velocity of magnitude $v_0 = 40$ m/s toward a vertical wall as shown in the figure above. The object will hit the wall closest to which point?

(A) A
(B) B
(C) C
(D) D
(E) E

24. If L, M, and T denote the dimensions of length, mass, and time, respectively, what are the dimensions of impulse?

(A) LM/T^3
(B) LM/T^2
(C) LM/T
(D) L^2M/T^2
(E) M^2L/T

25. The figure shown is a view from above of two clay balls moving toward each other on a frictionless surface. They collide perfectly inelastically at the indicated point and are observed to then move in the direction indicated by the post-collision velocity vector, $\mathbf{v}'$. If $m_1 = 2m_2$ what is v_2?

(A) $v_1(\sin 45°)/(2 \sin 60°)$
(B) $v_1(\cos 45°)/(2 \cos 60°)$
(C) $v_1(2 \cos 45°)/(\cos 60°)$
(D) $v_1(2 \sin 45°)/(\sin 60°)$
(E) $v_1(\cos 45°)/(2 \sin 60°)$

GO ON TO THE NEXT PAGE

26. In the figure above, the coefficient of static friction between the two blocks is 0.80. If the blocks oscillate with a frequency of 2.0 Hz, what is the maximum amplitude of the oscillations if the small block is not to slip on the large block?

   (A) 3.1 cm
   (B) 5.0 cm
   (C) 6.2 cm
   (D) 7.5 cm
   (E) 9.4 cm

27. When two objects collide, the ratio of the relative speed after the collision to the relative speed before the collision is called the *coefficient of restitution, e.* If a ball is dropped from height H_1 onto a stationary floor, and the ball rebounds to height H_2, what is the coefficient of restitution of the collision?

   (A) H_2/H_1

   (B) $\sqrt{H_1/H_2}$

   (C) $\sqrt{H_2/H_1}$

   (D) $(H_1/H_2)^2$

   (E) $(H_2/H_1)^2$

28. The figure above shows a square metal plate of side length 40 cm and uniform density, lying flat on a table. A force **F** of magnitude 10 N is applied at one of the corners, as shown. Determine the torque produced by **F** relative to the center of rotation.

   (A) 0 N·m
   (B) 1.0 N·m
   (C) 1.4 N·m
   (D) 2.0 N·m
   (E) 4.0 N·m

29. A small block of mass $m = 2.0$ kg is pushed from the initial point $(x_i, z_i) = (0\ m, 0\ m)$ upward to the final point $(x_f, z_f) = (3\ m, 3\ m)$ along the path indicated. Path 1 is a portion of the parabola $z = x^2$, and Path 2 is a quarter circle whose equation is $(x - 2)^2 + (z - 2)^2 = 2$. How much work is done by gravity during this displacement?

   (A) −59 J
   (B) −77 J
   (C) −86 J
   (D) −103 J
   (E) −126 J

30. If the figure shown, the block (mass = m) is at rest at $x = A$. As it moves back toward the wall due to the force exerted by the stretched spring, it is also acted upon by a frictional force whose strength is given by the expression bx, where b is a positive constant. What is the block's speed when it first passes through the equilibrium position ($x = 0$)?

   (A) $A\sqrt{(k+b)/m}$

   (B) $A\sqrt{(k-b)/m}$

   (C) $A\sqrt{(\frac{1}{2}k+b)/m}$

   (D) $A\sqrt{(\frac{1}{2}k-b)/m}$

   (E) $A\sqrt{\frac{1}{2}(k-b)/m}$

GO ON TO THE NEXT PAGE

$x = 0$ $x = L$

31. The rod shown above can pivot about the point $x = 0$ and rotates in a plane perpendicular to the page. Its linear density, λ, increases with x such that $\lambda(x) = kx$, where k is a positive constant. Determine the rod's moment of inertia in terms of its length, L, and its total mass, M.

    (A) $\frac{1}{6}ML^2$
    (B) $\frac{1}{4}ML^2$
    (C) $\frac{1}{3}ML^2$
    (D) $\frac{1}{2}ML^2$
    (E) $2ML^2$

32. A particle is subjected to a conservative force whose potential energy function is

$$U(x) = (x - 2)^3 - 12x$$

    where U is given in joules when x is measured in meters. Which of the following represents a position of stable equilibrium?

    (A) $x = -4$
    (B) $x = -2$
    (C) $x = 0$
    (D) $x = 2$
    (E) $x = 4$

33. At what angle to the horizontal should an ideal projectile be launched so that its horizontal displacement (the range) is equal to its maximum vertical displacement?

    (A) $\sin^{-1}(1/g)$
    (B) $\cos^{-1}(1/g)$
    (C) $45°$
    (D) $\tan^{-1} 2$
    (E) $\tan^{-1} 4$

34. A particle's kinetic energy is changing at a rate of -6.0 J/s when its speed is 3.0 m/s. What is the magnitude of the force on the particle at this moment?

    (A) 0.5 N
    (B) 2.0 N
    (C) 4.5 N
    (D) 9.0 N
    (E) 18 N

35. An object of mass 2 kg is acted upon by three external forces, each of magnitude 4 N. Which of the following could NOT be the resulting acceleration of the object?

    (A) 0 m/s^2
    (B) 2 m/s^2
    (C) 4 m/s^2
    (D) 6 m/s^2
    (E) 8 m/s^2

STOP

END OF SECTION I, MECHANICS

IF YOU FINISH BEFORE TIME IS CALLED, YOU MAY CHECK YOUR WORK
ON SECTION I, MECHANICS, ONLY

DO NOT TURN TO ANY OTHER TEST MATERIALS.

PHYSICS C
SECTION I, ELECTRICITY AND MAGNETISM
Time—45 minutes
35 Questions

Directions: Each of the questions or incomplete statements below is followed by five suggested answers or completions. Select the one that is best in each case and mark it on your answer sheet.

36. A nonconducting sphere is given a nonzero net electric charge, $+Q$, and then brought close to a neutral conducting sphere of the same radius. Which of the following will be true?

(A) An electric field will be induced within the conducting sphere.
(B) The conducting sphere will develop a net electric charge of $-Q$.
(C) The spheres will experience an electrostatic attraction.
(D) The spheres will experience an electrostatic repulsion.
(E) The spheres will experience no electrostatic interaction.

37. Which of the following would increase the capacitance of a parallel-plate capacitor?

(A) Using smaller plates
(B) Replacing the dielectric material between the plates with one that has a smaller dielectric constant
(C) Decreasing the voltage between the plates
(D) Increasing the voltage between the plates
(E) Moving the plates closer together

38. Each of the following particles is projected with the same speed into a uniform magnetic field **B** such that the particle's initial velocity is perpendicular to **B**. Which one would move in a circular path with the largest radius?

(A) Proton
(B) Beta particle
(C) Alpha particle
(D) Electron
(E) Positron

GO ON TO THE NEXT PAGE

39. An ellipsoid-shaped conductor is negatively charged. Which one of the following diagrams best illustrates the charge distribution and electric field lines?

(A)

(B)

(C)

(D)

(E)

A ——————

B ————————————

C ████████

D ████████████████

40. The four wires shown above are each made of aluminum. Which wire will have the greatest resistance?

(A) Wire A
(B) Wire B
(C) Wire C
(D) Wire D
(E) All the wires have the same resistance, because they're all composed of the same material.

41. Which of the following is NOT equal to one tesla?

(A) $1 \text{ J}/(\text{A·m}^2)$
(B) $1 \text{ kg}/(\text{C·s})$
(C) $1 \text{ N}/(\text{A·m})$
(D) $1 \text{ V·s}/\text{m}^2$
(E) $1 \text{ A·N}/\text{V}$

42. The figure above shows two Gaussian surfaces: a cube with side length d and a sphere with diameter d. The net electric charge enclosed within each surface is the same, $+Q$. If Φ_C denotes the total electric flux through the cubical surface, and Φ_S denotes the total electric flux through the spherical surface, then which of the following is true?

(A) $\Phi_C = (\pi/6)\,\Phi_S$
(B) $\Phi_C = (\pi/3)\,\Phi_S$
(C) $\Phi_C = \Phi_S$
(D) $\Phi_C = (3/\pi)\,\Phi_S$
(E) $\Phi_C = (6/\pi)\,\Phi_S$

43. The figure above shows two vertical conducting plates that carry equal but opposite charges. A ball of mass m and charge $-q$ is suspended from a light string in the region between the plates. If the voltage between the plates is V, which of the following gives the angle θ?

(A) $\cos^{-1}(qV/mgx)$
(B) $\sin^{-1}(qV/mgx)$
(C) $\tan^{-1}(qV/mgx)$
(D) $\cos^{-1}(qV/x)$
(E) $\sin^{-1}(qV/x)$

44. An object carries a charge of -1 C. How many excess electrons does it contain?

(A) 6.25×10^{18}
(B) 8.00×10^{18}
(C) 1.60×10^{19}
(D) 3.20×10^{19}
(E) 6.25×10^{19}

GO ON TO THE NEXT PAGE

Each of the resistors shown in the circuit below has a resistance of 200 Ω. The emf of the ideal battery is 24 V.

45. How much current is provided by the source?

   (A) 30 mA
   (B) 48 mA
   (C) 64 mA
   (D) 72 mA
   (E) 90 mA

46. What is the ratio of the power dissipated by R_1 to the power dissipated by R_4?

   (A) 1/9
   (B) 1/4
   (C) 1
   (D) 4
   (E) 9

47. What is the value of the following product?

   $$20 \ \mu F \times 500 \ \Omega$$

   (A) 0.01 henry
   (B) 0.01 ampere per coulomb
   (C) 0.01 weber
   (D) 0.01 second
   (E) 0.01 volt per ampere

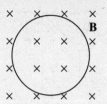

48. A copper wire in the shape of a circle of radius 1 m, lying in the plane of the page, is immersed in a magnetic field, **B**, that points into the plane of the page. The strength of **B** varies with time, t, according to the equation

   $$B(t) = 2t(1 - t)$$

   where B is given in teslas when t is measured in seconds. What is the magnitude of the induced electric field in the wire at time $t = 1$ s?

   (A) $(1/\pi)$ N/C
   (B) 1 N/C
   (C) 2 N/C
   (D) π N/C
   (E) 2π N/C

GO ON TO THE NEXT PAGE

49. In the figure above, the top half of a rectangular loop of wire, x meters by y meters, hangs vertically in a uniform magnetic field, **B**. Describe the magnitude and direction of the current in the loop necessary for the magnetic force to balance the weight of the mass m supported by the loop.

(A) $I = mg/xB$, clockwise

(B) $I = mg/xB$, counterclockwise

(C) $I = mg/\left(x + \frac{1}{2}y\right)B$, clockwise

(D) $I = mg/\left(x + \frac{1}{2}y\right)B$, counterclockwise

(E) $I = mg/(x + y)B$, clockwise

51. The figure above shows a pair of long, straight current-carrying wires and four marked points. At which of these points is the net magnetic field zero?

(A) Point 1 only

(B) Points 1 and 2 only

(C) Point 2 only

(D) Points 3 and 4 only

(E) Point 3 only

50. A solid nonconducting cylinder of radius R and length L contains a volume charge density given by the equation $\rho(r) = (+3 \text{ C/m}^4)r$, where r is the radial distance from the cylinder's central axis. This means that the total charge contained within a concentric cylinder of radius $r < R$ and length $\ell < L$ is equal to $2\pi\ell r^3$. Find an expression for the strength of the electric field inside this cylinder.

(A) $1/\varepsilon_0 r^2$

(B) $r/2\varepsilon_0$

(C) $2r/\varepsilon_0$

(D) r^2/ε_0

(E) $r^2/2\varepsilon_0$

GO ON TO THE NEXT PAGE

fixed in
position

52. The figure above shows two positively-charged
particles. The $+Q$ charge is fixed in position, and
the $+q$ charge is brought close to $+Q$ and released
from rest. Which of the following graphs best
depicts the acceleration of the $+q$ charge as a
function of its distance r from $+Q$?

(A)

(B)

(C)

(D)

(E)

$Q_1 = 24 \ \mu C$
$C_1 = 3 \ \mu F$

S

$Q_2 = 12 \ \mu C$
$C_2 = 6 \ \mu F$

53. Once the switch S in the figure above is closed
and electrostatic equilibrium is regained, how
much charge will be stored on the positive plate
of the 6 μF capacitor?

(A) 9 μC
(B) 18 μC
(C) 24 μC
(D) 27 μC
(E) 36 μC

GO ON TO THE NEXT PAGE

insulating
support

54. A metal bar of length L is pulled with velocity **v** through a uniform magnetic field, **B**, as shown above. What is the voltage produced between the ends of the bar?

(A) vB, with Point X at a higher potential than Point Y

(B) vB, with Point Y at a higher potential than Point X

(C) vBL, with Point X at a higher potential than Point Y

(D) vBL, with Point Y at a higher potential than Point X

(E) None of the above

55. An electric dipole consists of a pair of equal but opposite point charges of magnitude 4.0 nC separated by a distance of 2.0 cm. What is the electric field strength at the point midway between the charges?

(A) 0

(B) 9.0×10^4 V/m

(C) 1.8×10^5 V/m

(D) 3.6×10^5 V/m

(E) 7.2×10^5 V/m

56. The figure above shows a cross-section of two concentric spherical metal shells of radii R and $2R$, respectively. Find the capacitance.

(A) $1/(8\pi\varepsilon_0 R)$

(B) $1/(4\pi\varepsilon_0 R)$

(C) $2\pi\varepsilon_0 R$

(D) $4\pi\varepsilon_0 R$

(E) $8\pi\varepsilon_0 R$

57. Traveling at an initial speed of 1.5×10^6 m/s, a proton enters a region of constant magnetic field, **B**, of magnitude 1.0 T. If the proton's initial velocity vector makes an angle of 30° with the direction of **B**, compute the proton's speed 4 s after entering the magnetic field.

(A) 5.0×10^5 m/s

(B) 7.5×10^5 m/s

(C) 1.5×10^6 m/s

(D) 3.0×10^6 m/s

(E) 6.0×10^6 m/s

GO ON TO THE NEXT PAGE

There is initially no current through any circuit element in the following diagram.

58. What is the current through r immediately after the switch S is closed?

(A) 0

(B) $\dfrac{\mathcal{E}}{r + R_1}$

(C) $\dfrac{\mathcal{E}}{r + R_2}$

(D) $\dfrac{\mathcal{E}(r + R_1)}{rR_1}$

(E) $\dfrac{\mathcal{E}(R_1 + R_2)}{r(R_1 + R_2) + R_1 R_2}$

59. After the switch has been kept closed for a long time, how much energy is stored in the inductor?

(A) $\dfrac{L\mathcal{E}^2}{2(r + R_1)^2}$

(B) $\dfrac{L\mathcal{E}^2}{2(r + R_2)^2}$

(C) $\dfrac{L(\mathcal{E}R_1)^2}{2[r(R_1 + R_2) + R_1 R_2]^2}$

(D) $\dfrac{L(\mathcal{E}R_2)^2}{2[r(R_1 + R_2) + R_1 R_2]^2}$

(E) $\dfrac{L[\mathcal{E}(R_1 + R_2)]^2}{2[r(R_1 + R_2) + R_1 R_2]^2}$

60. After having been closed for a long time, the switch is suddenly opened. What is the current through r immediately after S is opened?

(A) 0

(B) $\dfrac{\mathcal{E}}{r + R_1}$

(C) $\dfrac{\mathcal{E}}{r + R_2}$

(D) $\dfrac{\mathcal{E}(r + R_1)}{rR_1}$

(E) $\dfrac{\mathcal{E}(R_1 + R_2)}{r(R_1 + R_2) + R_1 R_2}$

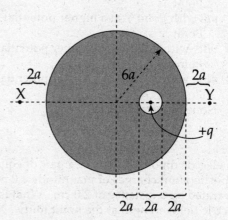

61. A solid, neutral metal sphere of radius $6a$ contains a small cavity, a spherical hole of radius a as shown above. Within this cavity is a charge, $+q$. If E_X and E_Y denote the strength of the electric field at points X and Y respectively, which of the following is true?

(A) $E_Y = 4E_X$
(B) $E_Y = 16E_X$
(C) $E_Y = E_X$
(D) $E_Y = (11/5)E_X$
(E) $E_Y = (11/5)^2 E_X$

GO ON TO THE NEXT PAGE

62. In the figure above, seven point charges are fixed in position at the corners of a cube of side length x. How much work will the electric field created by these seven charges perform on an eighth charge, $-Q$, as it is moved from very far away and placed at the vacant corner of the cube?

(A) $\dfrac{Q^2}{4\pi\varepsilon_0 x}\left(1 - \frac{1}{\sqrt{2}} + \frac{1}{\sqrt{3}}\right)$

(B) $\dfrac{Q^2}{4\pi\varepsilon_0 x}\left(-1 + \frac{1}{\sqrt{2}} - \frac{1}{\sqrt{3}}\right)$

(C) $\dfrac{Q^2}{4\pi\varepsilon_0 x}\left(1 + \frac{2}{\sqrt{2}} - \frac{1}{\sqrt{3}}\right)$

(D) $\dfrac{Q^2}{4\pi\varepsilon_0 x}\left(2 - \sqrt{2} + \frac{1}{\sqrt{3}}\right)$

(E) $\dfrac{Q^2}{4\pi\varepsilon_0 x}\left(-2 + \sqrt{2} - \frac{1}{\sqrt{3}}\right)$

63. A battery is connected in series with a switch, a resistor of resistance R, and an inductor of inductance L. Initially, there is no current in the circuit. Once the switch is closed and the circuit is completed, how long will it take for the current to reach 99% of its maximum value?

(A) $(\ln\frac{99}{100})RL$

(B) $(\ln 100)RL$

(C) $(\ln\frac{1}{100})L/R$

(D) $L/R(\ln\frac{100}{99})$

(E) $(\ln 100)L/R$

64. The resistance of the variable resistor R in the circuit above is adjusted until the power it dissipates is maximized. Which of the following expressions gives its maximum power dissipation?

(A) $\mathcal{E}^2/8r$

(B) $\mathcal{E}^2/4r$

(C) $\mathcal{E}^2/2r$

(D) $\mathcal{E}^2/r$

(E) None of the above

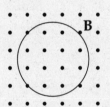

65. The metal loop of wire shown above is situated in a magnetic field **B** pointing out of the plane of the page. If **B** decreases uniformly in strength, the induced electric current within the loop is

(A) clockwise and decreasing.
(B) clockwise and increasing.
(C) counterclockwise and decreasing.
(D) counterclockwise and constant.
(E) counterclockwise and increasing.

GO ON TO THE NEXT PAGE

area = A

vacuum

d dielectric slab } z

vacuum

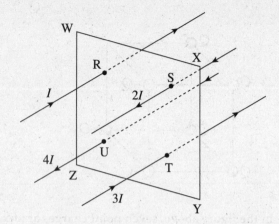

66. A dielectric of thickness z is placed between the plates of a parallel-plate capacitor, as shown above. If K is the dielectric constant of the slab, what is the capacitance?

(A) $\dfrac{\varepsilon_0 A}{d - z(1 - K)}$

(B) $\dfrac{\varepsilon_0 A}{d + z(K - 1)}$

(C) $\dfrac{\varepsilon_0 A}{d - z(K - 1)}$

(D) $\dfrac{\varepsilon_0 A}{d - z\left(1 - \frac{1}{K}\right)}$

(E) $\dfrac{\varepsilon_0 A}{d + z\left(1 - \frac{1}{K}\right)}$

$+Q$ ●   ○ $-Q$

67. Consider the two source charges shown above. At how many points in the plane of the page are the electric field and the electric potential both equal to zero?

(A) 0
(B) 1
(C) 2
(D) 3
(E) 4

68. The figure above shows four current-carrying wires passing perpendicularly through the interior of a square whose vertices are W, X, Y, and Z. The points where the wires pierce the plane of the square (namely, R, S, T, and U) themselves form the vertices of a square each side of which has half the length of each side of WXYZ. If the currents are as labeled in the figure, what is the absolute value of

$$\oint \mathbf{B} \cdot d\boldsymbol{\ell}$$

where the integral is taken around WXYZ?

(A) $\frac{1}{2}\mu_0 I$
(B) $\mu_0 I$
(C) $\sqrt{2}\,\mu_0 I$
(D) $2\mu_0 I$
(E) $5\mu_0 I$

GO ON TO THE NEXT PAGE

69. The positions of two isolated point charges, $+Q$ and $-Q$, are fixed as shown in the figure above. Which of the following statements is/are true?

    I. A charge $+q$ moving along line ℓ would experience no change in electrical potential energy.

    II. There is exactly one point on line ℓ where the total electrostatic force on $+q$ is equal to zero.

    III. At any point P on line ℓ, the intersection of the equipotential surface containing P with the plane of the figure is an ellipse with the charges $+Q$ and $-Q$ at the foci.

(A) I only
(B) I and II only
(C) II only
(D) I and III only
(E) II and III only

70. Two point charges, each $+Q$, are fixed a distance L apart. A particle of charge $-q$ and mass m is placed as shown in the figure above. What is this particle's initial acceleration when released from rest?

(A) $\dfrac{\sqrt{2}Qq}{2\pi\varepsilon_0 L^2 m}$

(B) $\dfrac{\sqrt{2}Qq}{\pi\varepsilon_0 L^2 m}$

(C) $\dfrac{2Qq}{\pi\varepsilon_0 L^2 m}$

(D) $\dfrac{2\sqrt{2}Qq}{\pi\varepsilon_0 L^2 m}$

(E) $\dfrac{4Qq}{\pi\varepsilon_0 L^2 m}$

STOP

END OF SECTION I, ELECTRICITY AND MAGNETISM

IF YOU FINISH BEFORE TIME IS CALLED, YOU MAY
CHECK YOUR WORK ON THIS SECTION.

DO NOT GO ON TO SECTION II UNTIL YOU ARE TOLD TO DO SO.

PHYSICS C

SECTION II

Free-Response Questions

Mechanics	45 minutes	3 required questions of equal weight
Electricity and Magnetism	45 minutes	3 required questions of equal weight

Section II is 50 percent of the total grade for each of the two examinations.
Mark one of the boxes below to indicate which questions you are answering.

☐ Mechanics only

☐ Electricity and Magnetism only

☐ Both Mechanics and Electricity and Magnetism

GO ON TO THE NEXT PAGE

PHYSICS C
SECTION II, MECHANICS
Time—45 minutes
3 Questions

Directions: Answer all three questions. The suggested time is about 15 minutes per question for answering each of the questions, which are worth 15 points each. The parts within a question may not have equal weight.

Mech 1.   A massless, frictionless pulley is suspended from a rigid rod attached to the roof of an elevator car. Two masses, m and M (with $M > m$), are suspended on either side of the pulley by a light, inextendable cord. The distance from the top of the elevator car to the center of mass of the pulley, y_p, is fixed.

(a)   Assume that the elevator car is descending at constant velocity. For each of the following, write your answer in terms of m, M, and g.

    (i)   Determine the accelerations of the masses.

    (ii)   Find the tension in the cord.

(b)   Now assume that the elevator car is descending with a nonzero (but constant) acceleration, b.

    (i)   State why the coordinate system which uses the center of the pulley as its origin is not an inertial reference system.

For parts (ii) and (iii), use the top of the elevator shaft as a reference. Write your answers in terms of m, M, g, and b.

    (ii)   Find the acceleration of the masses.

    (iii)   Determine the tension in the cord.

    (iv)   For what value of b would the answer to part (iii) be zero?

GO ON TO THE NEXT PAGE

Mech 2.   A narrow tunnel is drilled through the earth (mass = M, radius = R), connecting points P and Q, as shown in the diagram on the left below. The perpendicular distance from the earth's center, C, to the tunnel is x. A package (mass = m) is dropped from Point P into the tunnel; its distance from P is denoted y and its distance from C is denoted r. See the diagram on the right.

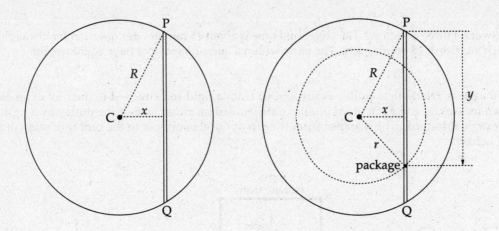

(a)   Assuming that the earth is a homogenous sphere, use the fact that the gravitational force F on the package is due to m and the mass contained within the sphere of radius $r < R$ to show that

$$F = -\frac{GMm}{R^3}r$$

(b)   Use the equation $F(r) = -dU/dr$ to find an expression for the change in gravitational potential energy of the package as it moves from Point P to a point where its distance from the earth's center is r. Write your answer in terms of G, M, m, R, and r.

(c)   Apply conservation of energy to determine the speed of the package in terms of G, M, R, x, and y. (Ignore friction.)

(d)   (i)   At what point in the tunnel—that is, for what value of y—will the speed of the package be maximized?

        (ii)   What is this maximum speed? (Write your answer in terms of G, M, R, and x.)

GO ON TO THE NEXT PAGE

Mech 3.   The diagram below is a view from above of three hockey pucks on a frictionless horizontal surface. The pucks with masses m and $2m$ are connected by a massless rigid rod of length L and are initially at rest. The puck of mass $3m$ is moving with velocity **v** directly toward puck m. When puck $3m$ strikes puck m, the collision is perfectly inelastic.

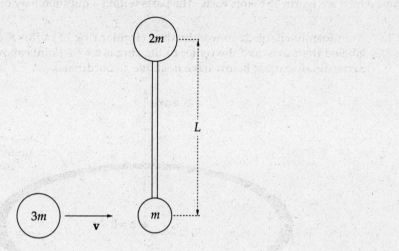

(a)   Immediately after the collision,

   (i)   where is the center of mass of the system?

   (ii)   what is the speed of the center of mass? (Write your answer in terms of **v**.)

   (iii)   what is the angular speed of the system? (Write your answer in terms of v and L.)

(b)   What fraction of the system's initial kinetic energy is lost as a result of the collision?

STOP

END OF SECTION II, MECHANICS

IF YOU FINISH BEFORE TIME IS CALLED, YOU MAY CHECK YOUR WORK ON SECTION II, MECHANICS, ONLY. DO NOT TURN TO ANY OTHER TEST MATERIALS.

Directions: Answer all three questions. The suggested time is about 15 minutes per question for answering each of the questions, which are worth 15 points each. The parts within a question may not have equal weight.

E & M 1.   A uniformly-charged, nonconducting, circular ring of radius R carries a charge $+Q$. Its central axis is labeled the z axis, and the center of the ring is $z = 0$. Points above the ring on the z axis have positive z coordinates; those below have negative z coordinates.

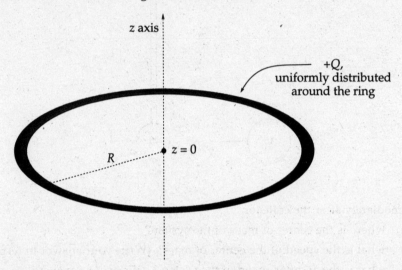

    (a)   Calculate the electric potential at an arbitrary point on the z axis. Write your answer in terms of Q, z, R, and fundamental constants.

    (b)   (i)   At what point(s) on the z axis will the potential have its greatest value?

            (ii)   What is this maximum potential value?

    (c)   Find an expression for the electric field (magnitude and direction) at an arbitrary point on the z axis. Write your answer in terms of Q, z, R, and fundamental constants.

    (d)   (i)   At what point(s) on the z axis will the electric field strength have its greatest value?

            (ii)   What is this maximum electric field strength?

A particle of charge $-q$ and mass m is released from rest at $z = +A$ (where $A \ll R$).

    (e)   What is its speed as it passes through $z = 0$? Give an answer that has been derived by applying the approximation $(1 + x)^{-n} \approx 1 - nx$ if $x \ll 1$. Your answer should be written in terms of Q, q, m, A, R, and fundamental constants.

    (f)   The particle will execute (approximately) simple harmonic motion. Derive [from your answer to part (e) or otherwise] an expression for its frequency of oscillation.

GO ON TO THE NEXT PAGE

E & M 2.   In the circuit shown below, the capacitor is uncharged and there is no current in any circuit element.

In each of the following, k is a number greater than 1; write each of your answers in terms of $\mathcal{E}, r, R,$ $C, k,$ and fundamental constants.

(a)   At $t = 0$, the switch S is moved to position 1.

   (i)   At what time t is the current through R equal to $\frac{1}{k}$ of its initial value?

   (ii)   At what time t is the charge on the capacitor equal to $\frac{1}{k}$ of its maximum value?

   (iii)   At what time t is the energy stored in the capacitor equal to $\frac{1}{k}$ of its maximum value?

(b)   After the switch has been at position 1 for a very long time, it is then moved to position 2. Let this redefine $t = 0$ for purposes of the following questions.

   (i)   How long will it take for the current through R to equal $\frac{1}{k}$ of its initial value?

   (ii)   At what time t is the charge on the capacitor equal to $\frac{1}{k}$ of its initial value?

GO ON TO THE NEXT PAGE

E & M 3.   The diagram below shows two parallel conducting rails connected by a third rail of length L, raised to an angle of θ with the horizontal (supported by a pair of insulating columns). A metal strip of length L, mass m, and resistance R is free to slide without friction down the rails. The apparatus is immersed in a vertical, uniform magnetic field, **B**. The resistance of the stationary rails may be neglected.

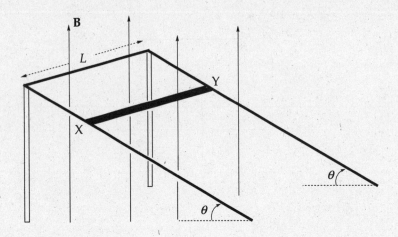

(a)   As the strip slides down the rails with instantaneous speed v, determine

　　(i)   the induced emf. (Write your answer in terms of L, B, v, and θ.)

　　(ii)   the direction of the induced current in the strip (X to Y, or Y to X?).

　　(iii)   the value of the induced current. (Write your answer in terms of L, B, R, v, and θ.)

(b)   The strip XY will eventually slide down the rails at a constant velocity. Derive an expression for this velocity in terms of L, B, R, m, g, and θ.

(c)   When the strip is sliding with the constant velocity determined in part (b), show that the power dissipation in the strip is equal to the rate at which gravity is doing work on the strip.

STOP

END OF SECTION II, ELECTRICITY AND MAGNETISM

IF YOU FINISH BEFORE TIME IS CALLED, YOU MAY CHECK YOUR WORK ON SECTION II, MECHANICS, ONLY. DO NOT TURN TO ANY OTHER TEST MATERIALS.

22

ANSWERS AND
EXPLANATIONS

SECTION I, MECHANICS

1. **(E)** Let y denote the total distance that the rock falls and let T denote the total time of the fall. Then $\frac{1}{2}y = \frac{1}{2}gt_1^2$ and $y = \frac{1}{2}gT^2$, so

$$\frac{t_2}{t_1} = \frac{T-t_1}{t_1} = \frac{T}{t_1} - 1 = \frac{\sqrt{2y/g}}{\sqrt{y/g}} - 1 = \sqrt{2} - 1$$

2. **(A)** The work–energy theorem says that the work done by friction is equal to the change in kinetic energy of the box. Therefore,

$$-\mu mgd = -\tfrac{1}{2}mv_0^2 \quad \Rightarrow \quad d = \frac{v_0^2}{2\mu g}$$

3. **(A)** Integrating $a(t)$ gives $v(t)$:

$$v(t) = \int a(t)\,dt = \int 2t\,dt = t^2 + v_0$$

Since $v_0 = 0$, we have $v(t) = t^2$. Now integrating $v(t)$ from $t = 0$ to $t = 3$ s gives the object's displacement during this time interval:

$$s = \int_0^3 v(t)\,dt = \int_0^3 t^2\,dt = \tfrac{1}{3}t^3\Big|_0^3 = 9 \text{ m}$$

4. **(E)** Angular momentum is conserved when no net external torque is applied (Item III). However, a body can experience a net nonzero torque even when the net external force is zero (which is the condition that guarantees conservation of linear momentum), so neither Item I nor Item II necessarily ensure conservation of angular momentum.

5. **(C)** The figure below shows that $F_T \sin\theta = mg$ and $F_T \cos\theta = mv^2/R = m\omega^2 R$:

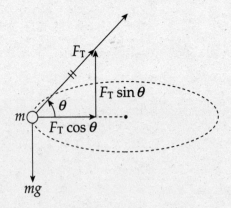

We can eliminate θ from these equations by remembering that $\sin^2\theta + \cos^2\theta$ is always equal to 1:

$$\left(\frac{mg}{F_T}\right)^2 + \left(\frac{m\omega^2 R}{F_T}\right)^2 = 1 \quad \Rightarrow \quad \frac{m^2g^2 + m^2\omega^4 R^2}{F_T^2} = 1 \quad \Rightarrow \quad F_T = m\sqrt{\omega^4 R^2 + g^2}$$

6. **(A)** Because the initial height of the object is comparable to the radius of the Moon, we cannot simply use mgh for its initial potential energy. Instead, we must use the more general expression $U = -GMm/r$, where r is the distance from the center of the Moon. Notice that since $h = R$, the object's initial distance from the Moon's center is $h + R = R + R = 2R$. Conservation of energy then gives

$$K_i + U_i = K_f + U_f$$

$$0 - \frac{GMm}{2R} = \tfrac{1}{2}mv^2 - \frac{GMm}{R}$$

$$\frac{GMm}{2R} = \tfrac{1}{2}mv^2$$

$$v = \sqrt{\frac{GM}{R}}$$

7. **(E)** At equilibrium, the net force on the block is zero (by definition), so $ky = mg$, which gives $y = mg/k$. If m doubles, then so does y. This eliminates choices A, B, and C. Since $T = 2\pi\sqrt{m/k}$, T is proportional to $\sqrt{m}$. Therefore, if m increases by a factor of 2, then T increases by a factor of $\sqrt{2}$.

8. **(D)** Let F_T be the tension in each string. Then $F_{net} = ma$ becomes $mg - 2F_T = ma$. Also, the total torque exerted by the tension forces on the cylinder is $2rF_T$, so $\tau_{net} = I\alpha$ becomes $2rF_T = (\tfrac{1}{2}mr^2)\alpha$. Because the cylinder doesn't slip, $\alpha = a/r$, so $2F_T = \tfrac{1}{2}ma$. These equations can be combined to give $mg - \tfrac{1}{2}ma = ma$, which implies $mg = \tfrac{3}{2}ma$. Therefore, $a = \tfrac{2}{3}g$.

9. **(B)** The cylinder slides across the surface with acceleration $a = F/m$ until time $t = T$, when a drops to zero (because F becomes zero). Therefore, from time $t = 0$ to $t = T$, the velocity is steadily increasing (because the acceleration is a positive constant), but, at $t = T$, the velocity remains constant. This is illustrated in graph (B). (Note: The cylinder cannot roll because the surface is frictionless.)

10. **(D)** The speed of the object being lifted is $v = (20 \text{ m})/(5 \text{ s}) = 4 \text{ m/s}$. Since $P = Fv$, we find that $F = P/v = 10 \text{ kW}/(4 \text{ m/s}) = 2.5 \text{ kN} = 2500 \text{ N}$. Since the object is being lifted with constant velocity, the net force on it must be zero, so F must be equal to the object's weight, mg. This gives $m = F/g = 2500 \text{ N}/(10 \text{ N/kg}) = 250 \text{ kg}$.

11. **(A)** Let m and M denote the mass of the satellite and the earth, respectively. The work required to lift the satellite to height h above the surface of the earth is

$$W = \Delta U = -\frac{GMm}{R+h} - \left(-\frac{GMm}{R}\right) = \frac{GMmh}{R(R+h)}$$

The earth's gravitational pull provides the necessary centripetal force on the satellite, so

$$\frac{GMm}{(R+h)^2} = \frac{mv^2}{R+h} \quad \Rightarrow \quad mv^2 = \frac{GMm}{R+h} \quad \Rightarrow \quad K = \frac{GMm}{2(R+h)}$$

Because we're told that $W = K$, we find that

$$\frac{GMmh}{R(R+h)} = \frac{GMm}{2(R+h)} \Rightarrow \frac{h}{R} = \frac{1}{2} \Rightarrow h = \frac{R}{2}$$

12. **(D)** First note that if L is the total length of the bar, then the distance of the block from Support 1 is $\frac{1}{3}L$ and its distance from Support 2 is $\frac{2}{3}L$. Let P_1 denote the point at which Support 1 touches the bar. With respect to P_1, the upward force exerted by Support 1, F_1, produces no torque, but the upward force exerted by Support 2, F_2, does. Since the net torque must be zero if the system is in static equilibrium, the counterclockwise torque of F_2 must balance the total clockwise torque produced by the weight of the block and of the bar (which acts at the bar's midpoint):

$$L \cdot F_2 = \tfrac{1}{3}L \cdot \tfrac{1}{2}Mg + \tfrac{1}{2}L \cdot Mg \Rightarrow F_2 = \tfrac{2}{3}Mg$$

Now with respect to P_2, the point at which Support 2 touches the bar,

$$L \cdot F_1 = \tfrac{2}{3}L \cdot \tfrac{1}{2}Mg + \tfrac{1}{2}L \cdot Mg \Rightarrow F_1 = \tfrac{5}{6}Mg$$

These results give $F_2/F_1 = \tfrac{2}{3}Mg / \tfrac{5}{6}Mg = \tfrac{4}{5}$.

13. **(C)** Because the ball rebounded to the same height from which it was dropped, its takeoff speed from the floor must be the same as the impact speed. Calling *up* the positive direction, the change in linear momentum of the ball is $p_f - p_i = mv - (-mv) = 2mv$, where $v = \sqrt{2gh}$ (this last equation comes from the equation $\frac{1}{2}mv^2 = mgh$). The impulse–momentum theorem, $J = \Delta p$, now gives

$$F_{avg}\Delta t = 2m\sqrt{2gh} \Rightarrow F_{avg} = \frac{2m\sqrt{2gh}}{\Delta t} = \frac{2(0.08 \text{ kg})\sqrt{2(10 \text{ m}/\text{s}^2)(2 \text{ m})}}{0.04 \text{ s}} = 25 \text{ N}$$

14. **(D)** Using the Big Five equation $\Delta\theta = \omega_0 t + \frac{1}{2}\alpha t^2$, we find that

$$\Delta\theta = \tfrac{1}{2}(2 \text{ rad}/\text{s}^2)(4.0 \text{ s})^2 = 16 \text{ rad}$$

Therefore, $\Delta s = r\Delta\theta = (0.1 \text{ m})(16 \text{ rad}) = 1.6 \text{ m}$.

15. **(C)** The ball's initial velocity from the slide is horizontal, so $v_{0y} = 0$, which implies that $\Delta y = -\frac{1}{2}gt^2$. Since $\Delta y = -R$,

$$-R = -\tfrac{1}{2}gt^2 \Rightarrow t = \sqrt{\frac{2R}{g}}$$

The (horizontal) speed with which the ball leaves the slide is found from the equation $mgR = \frac{1}{2}mv^2$, which gives $v = \sqrt{2gR}$. Therefore,

$$\Delta x = v_{0x}t = \sqrt{2gR} \cdot \sqrt{\frac{2R}{g}} = 2R$$

Since the ball travels a horizontal distance of 2R from the end of the slide, the total horizontal distance from the ball's starting point is R + 2R = 3R.

16. **(A)** From the diagram below,

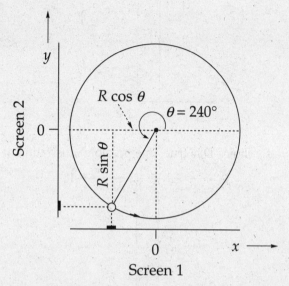

if $R \cos \theta = -(0.5)R$, then $\theta = 240°$. Therefore, $y = R \sin \theta = R \sin 240° = -(0.866)R$. Also, it is clear that the particle's subsequent motion will cause the shadow on Screen 2 to continue moving in the $-y$ direction.

17. **(C)** The center of mass of the system is at a distance of

$$y_{cm} = \frac{(m)(0) + (2m)(L)}{m + 2m} = \tfrac{2}{3}L$$

below the mass m. With respect to this point, the clockwise torque produced by the force **F** has magnitude

$$\tau = rF = \left(\tfrac{2}{3}L - \tfrac{1}{4}L\right)F = \tfrac{5}{12}LF$$

Since the rotational inertia of the system about its center of mass is

$$I = \sum m_i r_i^2 = m\left(\tfrac{2}{3}L\right)^2 + (2m)\left(\tfrac{1}{3}L\right)^2 = \tfrac{2}{3}mL^2$$

the equation $\tau = I\alpha$ becomes

$$\tfrac{5}{12}LF = \left(\tfrac{2}{3}mL^2\right)\alpha \quad \Rightarrow \quad \alpha = \frac{\tfrac{5}{8}F}{mL}$$

18. **(C)** By Newton's Third Law, both vehicles experience the same magnitude of force and, therefore, the same impulse; so Statement I is false. Invoking Newton's Second Law, in the form *impulse = change in momentum*, we see that Statement II is therefore also false. However, since the car has a smaller mass than the truck, its acceleration will be greater in magnitude than that of the truck, so Statement III is true.

19. **(D)** Since $\mathbf{F}_{net} = \mathbf{F}_1 + \mathbf{F}_2 = 0$, the bar cannot accelerate translationally, so C is false. The net torque does *not* need to be zero, as the following diagram shows (eliminating choices A and B):

However, since $\mathbf{F}_2 = -\mathbf{F}_1$, choice D is true; one possible illustration of this is given below:

20. **(B)** The value of g near the surface of a planet depends on the planet's mass and radius:

$$mg = \frac{GMm}{r^2} \quad \Rightarrow \quad g = \frac{GM}{r^2}$$

Therefore, calling this Planet X, we find that

$$g_X = \frac{GM_X}{r_X^2} = \frac{G(2M_{Earth})}{(2r_{Earth})^2} = \frac{1}{2}\frac{GM_{Earth}}{r_{Earth}^2} = \frac{1}{2}g_{Earth}$$

Since g is half as much on the planet as it is on Earth, the astronaut's weight (mg) will be half as much as well.

21. **(C)** The work done by the force $F(x)$ is equal to the area under the given curve. The region under the graph can be broken into two triangles and a rectangle, and it is then easy to figure out that the total area is 50 N·m. Since work is equal to change in kinetic energy (and $v_i = 0$),

$$W = \Delta K = \tfrac{1}{2}m(v_f^2 - v_i^2) \quad \Rightarrow \quad v_f = \sqrt{\frac{2W}{m}} = \sqrt{\frac{2(50 \text{ N·m})}{1.0 \text{ kg}}} = 10 \text{ m/s}$$

22. **(C)** Since no external torques act on the star as it collapses (just like a skater when she pulls in her arms), angular momentum, $I\omega$, is conserved, and the star's rotational speed increases. The moment of inertia of a sphere of mass m and radius r is given by the equation $I = kmr^2$ (with $k = \tfrac{2}{5}$, but the actual value is irrelevant), so we have

$$\omega_f = \frac{I_i}{I_f}\omega_i = \frac{kmr_i^2}{kmr_f^2}\omega_i = \frac{r_i^2}{r_f^2}\omega_i = \frac{r_i^2}{\left(\frac{1}{16}r_i\right)^2}\omega_i = 16^2\omega_i$$

Therefore,

$$\frac{K_f}{K_i} = \frac{\frac{1}{2}I_f\omega_f^2}{\frac{1}{2}I_i\omega_i^2} = \frac{\frac{1}{2}kmr_f^2\omega_f^2}{\frac{1}{2}kmr_i^2\omega_i^2} = \frac{r_f^2\omega_f^2}{r_i^2\omega_i^2} = \frac{\left(\frac{1}{16}r_i\right)^2(16^2\omega_i)^2}{r_i^2\omega_i^2} = 16^2$$

23. **(B)** The projectile's horizontal speed is $v_0\cos 60° = \frac{1}{2}v_0 = 20$ m / s, so it reaches the wall in 1 s. In this time, the projectile's vertical displacement is

$$\Delta y = (v_0\sin\theta_0)t - \frac{1}{2}gt^2 = [(40\text{ m / s})\sin 60°](1\text{ s}) - \frac{1}{2}(10\text{ m / s}^2)(1\text{ s})^2 \approx 30\text{ m}$$

Since the projectile's initial height is 1 m, it strikes the wall at a height of about 31 m.

24. **(C)** Impulse, J, is defined to be force × time, so

$$[J] = [F][t] = \text{N} \cdot \text{s} = \frac{\text{kg} \cdot \text{m}}{\text{s}^2} \cdot \text{s} = \frac{\text{kg} \cdot \text{m}}{\text{s}} = \frac{\text{ML}}{\text{T}}$$

25. **(D)** The diagram given with the question shows that after the clay balls collide, they move in the −y direction, which means that the horizontal components of their linear momenta canceled. In other words, $\mathbf{p}_{1x} + \mathbf{p}_{2x} = \mathbf{0}$:

$$m_1\mathbf{v}_{1x} + m_2\mathbf{v}_{2x} = \mathbf{0}$$
$$(m_1v_1\sin 45°)\hat{\mathbf{i}} + (m_2v_2\sin 60°)(-\hat{\mathbf{i}}) = \mathbf{0}$$
$$v_2 = \frac{m_1v_1\sin 45°}{m_2\sin 60°}$$
$$= \frac{2\sin 45°}{\sin 60°}v_1$$

26. **(B)** The horizontal position of the blocks can be given by the equation

$$x = A\sin(\omega t + \phi_0)$$

where A is the amplitude, ω is the angular frequency, and ϕ_0 is the initial phase. Differentiating this twice gives the acceleration:

$$a = \frac{d^2x}{dt^2} = -A\omega^2\sin(\omega t + \phi_0) \implies a_{max} = A\omega^2$$

This means that the maximum force on block m is $F_{max} = ma_{max} = mA\omega^2$. The static friction force must be able to provide this much force; otherwise, the block will slip. Therefore,

$$F_{static,\ max} \geq mA\omega^2$$

$$\mu mg \geq mA\omega^2$$

$$A \leq \frac{\mu mg}{m\omega^2} = \frac{\mu g}{(2\pi f)^2} = \frac{(0.80)(10 \text{ m}/\text{s}^2)}{4\pi^2(2.0 \text{ Hz})^2} \approx 0.05 \text{ m}$$

27. **(C)** The ball strikes the floor with speed $v_1 = \sqrt{2gH_1}$, and it leaves the floor with speed $v_2 = \sqrt{2gH_2}$. Therefore,

$$e = \frac{v_2}{v_1} = \frac{\sqrt{2gH_2}}{\sqrt{2gH_1}} = \sqrt{\frac{H_2}{H_1}}$$

28. **(D)** The center of rotation is the center of mass of the plate, which is at the geometric center of the square because the plate is homogeneous. Since the line of action of the force coincides with one of the sides of the square, the lever arm of the force, ℓ, is simply equal to $\frac{1}{2}s$. Therefore,

$$\tau = \ell F = \tfrac{1}{2}sF = (0.20 \text{ m})(10 \text{ N}) = 2.0 \text{ N·m}$$

29. **(A)** Since gravity is a conservative force, the actual path taken is irrelevant. If the block rises a vertical distance of $z = 3$ m, then the work done by gravity is

$$W = -mgz = -(2.0 \text{ kg})(9.8 \text{ N}/\text{kg})(3 \text{ m}) = -59 \text{ J}$$

30. **(B)** The work done by the friction force as the block slides from $x = A$ to $x = 0$ is

$$W_{friction} = \int_A^0 bx\,dx = \tfrac{1}{2}bx^2\Big|_A^0 = -\tfrac{1}{2}bA^2$$

Now use conservation of energy, using $U(x) = \frac{1}{2}kx^2$:

$$K_i + U_i + W_{friction} = K_f + U_f$$

$$0 + \tfrac{1}{2}kA^2 - \tfrac{1}{2}bA^2 = \tfrac{1}{2}mv^2 + 0$$

$$v = A\sqrt{\frac{k-b}{m}}$$

31. **(D)** Consider an infinitesimal slice of width dx at position x; its mass is $dm = \lambda\,dx = kx\,dx$. Then, by definition of rotational inertia,

$$I = \int r^2\,dm = \int_0^L x^2(kx\,dx) = \tfrac{1}{4}kx^4\Big|_0^L = \tfrac{1}{4}kL^4$$

Because the total mass of the rod is

$$M = \int dm = \int_0^L kx\,dx = \tfrac{1}{2}kx^2 \Big|_0^L = \tfrac{1}{2}kL^2$$

we see that $I = \tfrac{1}{2}ML^2$.

32. **(E)** Points of equilibrium occur when dU/dx is equal to zero:

$$\frac{dU}{dx} = 0 \;\Rightarrow\; 3(x-2)^2 - 12 = 0 \;\Rightarrow\; (x-2)^2 = 4 \;\Rightarrow\; x = 0,\ 4$$

Points of *stable* equilibrium occur when $dU/dx = 0$ and d^2U/dx^2 is positive (because then the equilibrium point is a relative minimum). Since

$$\frac{d^2U}{dx^2} = 6(x-2)$$

the point $x = 4$ is a point of stable equilibrium ($x = 0$ is unstable).

33. **(D)** The range of a projectile is given by the equation

$$R = \frac{2v_0^2 \sin\theta_0 \cos\theta_0}{g}$$

and the maximum height attained by the projectile is

$$H = \frac{v_0^2 \sin^2\theta_0}{2g}$$

In order for R to equal H, it must be true that

$$\frac{2v_0^2 \sin\theta_0 \cos\theta_0}{g} = \frac{v_0^2 \sin^2\theta_0}{2g} \;\Rightarrow\; 2\cos\theta_0 = \frac{\sin\theta_0}{2} \;\Rightarrow\; \tan\theta_0 = 4 \;\Rightarrow\; \theta_0 = \tan^{-1}4$$

34. **(B)** Differentiate the equation $K = \tfrac{1}{2}mv^2$ with respect to time:

$$\frac{dK}{dt} = \tfrac{1}{2}m \cdot 2v\frac{dv}{dt} = mv\frac{dv}{dt} = v \cdot m\frac{dv}{dt} = v \cdot ma = vF$$

This tells us that

$$F = \frac{dK/dt}{v} = \frac{-6.0\ \text{J/s}}{3.0\ \text{m/s}} = -2\ \text{N}$$

35. **(E)** The maximum net force on the object occurs when all three forces act in the same direction, giving $F_{net} = 3F = 3(4\ \text{N}) = 12\ \text{N}$, and a resulting acceleration of $a = F_{net}/m = (12\ \text{N})/(2\ \text{kg}) = 6$ m/s^2. These three forces could not give the object an acceleration greater than this.

SECTION I, ELECTRICITY AND MAGNETISM

36. **(C)** The proximity of the charged sphere will induce negative charge to move to the side of the uncharged sphere closer to the charged sphere. Since the induced negative charge is closer than the induced positive charge to the charged sphere, there will be a net electrostatic attraction between the spheres.

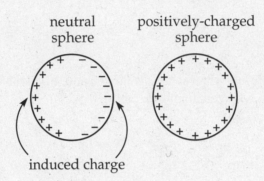

37. **(E)** The capacitance of a parallel-plate capacitor is $C = K\varepsilon_0 A/d$, where K is the dielectric constant, A is the area of each plate, and d is their separation distance. Decreasing d will cause C to increase.

38. **(C)** When the particle enters the magnetic field, the magnetic force provides the centripetal force to cause the particle to execute uniform circular motion:

$$|q|vB = \frac{mv^2}{r} \quad \Rightarrow \quad r = \frac{mv}{|q|B}$$

Since v and B are the same for all the particles, the largest r is found by maximizing the ratio $m/|q|$. The value of $m/|q|$ for an alpha particle is about twice that for a proton and thousands of times greater than that of an electron or positron.

39. **(A)** Electric field lines are always perpendicular to the surface of a conductor, eliminating choices B and E. Excess charge on a conductor always resides on the surface (eliminating choice D), and there is a greater density of charge at points where the radius of curvature is smaller (eliminating choice C).

40. **(B)** The resistance of a wire made of a material with resistivity ρ and with length L and cross-sectional area A is given by the equation $R = \rho L/A$. Since Wire B has the greatest length and smallest cross-sectional area, it has the greatest resistance.

41. **(E)** From the equation $F = qvB$, we see that 1 tesla is equal to 1 N·s/(C·m). Since

$$\frac{1\,\text{N·s}}{\text{C·m}} = \frac{1\,\text{N}}{\text{A·m}} = \frac{1\,\text{J}}{\text{A·m}^2}$$

choices A and C are eliminated. Furthermore,

$$\frac{1\,\text{N}\cdot\text{s}}{\text{C}\cdot\text{m}} = \frac{1\,\text{kg}\cdot\text{m}/\text{s}}{\text{C}\cdot\text{m}} = \frac{1\,\text{kg}}{\text{C}\cdot\text{s}}$$

eliminating choice B. Finally, since

$$\frac{1\,\text{J}}{\text{A}\cdot\text{m}^2} = \frac{1\,\text{C}\cdot\text{V}}{(\text{C}/\text{s})\cdot\text{m}^2} = \frac{1\,\text{V}\cdot\text{s}}{\text{m}^2}$$

choice D is also eliminated.

42. **(C)** Gauss's Law states that the total electric flux through a closed surface is equal to $(1/\varepsilon_0)$ times the net charge enclosed by the surface. Both the cube and the sphere contain the same net charge, so Φ_C must be equal to Φ_S.

43. **(C)** The electric field between the plates is uniform and equal to V/x, so the magnitude of the electric force on the charge is $F_E = qE = qV/x$. From the following free-body diagram

we see that

$$F_T \sin\theta = F_E = qE = \frac{qV}{x} \quad \text{and} \quad F_T \cos\theta = mg$$

Dividing the first equation by the second one, we find that

$$\frac{F_T \sin\theta}{F_T \cos\theta} = \frac{qV/x}{mg} \quad\Rightarrow\quad \tan\theta = \frac{qV}{mgx} \quad\Rightarrow\quad \theta = \tan^{-1}\frac{qV}{mgx}$$

44. **(A)** Because charge is quantized, a negatively-charged object must have a charge q, equal to whole number, n, times the elementary charge, $-e$. Therefore,

$$q = n(-e) \quad\Rightarrow\quad n = \frac{q}{-e} = \frac{-1\,\text{C}}{-1.60\times10^{-19}\,\text{C}} = \frac{1}{1.60}\times10^{19} = 6.25\times10^{18}$$

45. **(E)** Resistors R_2, R_3, and R_4 are in parallel, so their equivalent resistance, $R_{2\text{-}3\text{-}4}$, satisfies

$$\frac{1}{R_{2\text{-}3\text{-}4}} = \frac{1}{R_2} + \frac{1}{R_3} + \frac{1}{R_4} = \frac{3}{200\ \Omega} \quad \Rightarrow \quad R_{2\text{-}3\text{-}4} = \tfrac{200}{3}\ \Omega$$

Since this is in series with R_1, the total resistance in the circuit is

$$R = R_1 + R_{2\text{-}3\text{-}4} = \tfrac{800}{3}\ \Omega$$

The current provided by the source must therefore be

$$I = \frac{\mathcal{E}}{R} = \frac{24\ \text{V}}{\tfrac{800}{3}\ \Omega} = \tfrac{9}{100}\ \text{A} = \tfrac{90}{1000}\ \text{A} = 90\ \text{mA}$$

46. **(E)** The current through R_4 is $\frac{1}{3}$ the current through R_1 and $R_4 = R_1$, so

$$\frac{P_1}{P_4} = \frac{I_1^2 R_1}{I_4^2 R_4} = \frac{I_1^2 R_1}{\left(\frac{1}{3} I_1\right)^2 R_1} = 9$$

47. **(D)** Because the time constant for an R–C circuit is equal to the product of resistance and capacitance, $\tau = RC$, this product has the dimensions of time.

48. **(B)** Apply Faraday's Law of Electromagnetic Induction:

$$\oint \mathbf{E} \cdot d\boldsymbol{\ell} = -\frac{d\Phi_B}{dt}$$

$$E(2\pi r) = -\frac{d}{dt}(BA)$$

$$= -A \frac{dB}{dt}$$

$$= -\pi r^2 \cdot \frac{d}{dt}(2t - 2t^2)$$

$$= -\pi r^2 (2 - 4t)$$

$$E = -r(1 - 2t)$$

Since $r = 1$ m, the value of E at $t = 1$ s is $E = 1$ N/C.

49. **(A)** The magnetic force, $\mathbf{F}_B$, on the top horizontal wire of the loop must be directed upward and have magnitude mg. (The magnetic forces on the vertical portions of the wire will cancel.) By the right-hand rule, the current in the top horizontal wire must be directed to the right—because $\mathbf{B}$ is directed into the plane of the page—in order for $\mathbf{F}_B$ to be directed upward; therefore, the current in the loop must be clockwise (eliminating choices B and D). Since $F_B = IxB$, we must have

$$IxB = mg \quad \Rightarrow \quad I = \frac{mg}{xB}$$

50. **(D)** Construct a cylindrical Gaussian surface of radius $r < R$ and length $\ell < L$ within the given cylinder. By symmetry, the electric field must be radial, so the electric flux through the lids of the Gaussian cylinder is zero. The lateral surface area of the Gaussian cylinder is $2\pi r\ell$, so by Gauss's Law,

$$\Phi_E = \frac{Q_{enclosed}}{\varepsilon_0} \quad \Rightarrow \quad E(2\pi r\ell) = \frac{2\pi \ell r^3}{\varepsilon_0} \quad \Rightarrow \quad E = \frac{r^2}{\varepsilon_0}$$

51. **(A)** Call the top wire (the one carrying a current I to the right) Wire 1, and call the bottom wire (carrying a current $2I$ to the left) Wire 2. Then in the region between the wires, the individual magnetic field vectors due to the wires are both directed into the plane of the page, so they could not cancel in this region. Therefore, the total magnetic field could not be zero at either Point 2 or Point 3. This eliminates choices B, C, D, and E, so the answer must be A. Since the magnetic field created by a current-carrying wire is proportional to the current and inversely proportional to the distance from the wire, the fact that Point 1 is in a region where the individual magnetic field vectors created by the wires point in opposite directions and that Point 1 twice as far from Wire 2 as from Wire 1 implies that the total magnetic field there will be zero.

52. **(A)** If the mass of the $+q$ charge is m, then its acceleration is

$$a = \frac{F_E}{m} = \frac{1}{4\pi\varepsilon_0}\frac{Qq}{mr^2}$$

The graph in A best depicts an inverse-square relationship between a and r.

53. **(C)** Once the switch is closed, the capacitors are in parallel, which means the voltage across C_1 must equal the voltage across C_2. Since $V = Q/C$,

$$\frac{Q_2'}{C_2} = \frac{Q_1'}{C_1} \quad \Rightarrow \quad Q_2' = \frac{C_2}{C_1}Q_1' = \frac{6\ \mu F}{3\ \mu F}Q_1' = 2Q_1'$$

The total charge, $24\ \mu C + 12\ \mu C = 36\ \mu C$, must be redistributed so that $Q_2' = 2Q_1'$. Therefore, we see that $Q_2' = 24\ \mu C$ (and $Q_1' = 12\ \mu C$).

54. **(E)** Because **v** is parallel to **B**, the charges in the bar feel no magnetic force, so there will be no movement of charge in the bar and no motional emf.

55. **(E)** Along the line joining the two charges of an electric dipole, the individual electric field vectors point in the same direction, so they add constructively. At the point equidistant from both charges, the total electric field vector has magnitude

$$E_+ + E_- = 2E = 2\frac{kQ}{\left(\frac{1}{2}d\right)^2} = \frac{8kQ}{d^2}$$

$$= \frac{8(9\times10^9\ \text{N}\cdot\text{m}^2/\text{C}^2)(4.0\times10^{-9}\ \text{C})}{(2.0\times10^{-2}\ \text{m})^2}$$

$$= 72\times10^4\ \text{N/C}$$

$$= 7.2\times10^5\ \text{N/C}\ \ (\text{or V/m})$$

56. **(E)** Imagine placing equal but opposite charges on the spheres, say, $+Q$ on the inner sphere and $-Q$ on the outer sphere. Then the electric field between the spheres is radial and depends only on $+Q$, and its strength is

$$E = \frac{1}{4\pi\varepsilon_0} \frac{Q}{r^2}$$

Therefore, the potential difference between the spheres is

$$V = \int_R^{2R} \mathbf{E} \cdot d\mathbf{r} = \frac{Q}{4\pi\varepsilon_0} \int_R^{2R} \frac{1}{r^2} dr = \frac{Q}{4\pi\varepsilon_0} \left[-\frac{1}{r} \right]_R^{2R} = \frac{Q}{4\pi\varepsilon_0} \left(\frac{1}{R} - \frac{1}{2R} \right) = \frac{Q}{8\pi\varepsilon_0 R}$$

Now, by definition, $C = Q/V$, so

$$C = \frac{Q}{V} = Q \cdot \frac{1}{V} = Q \cdot \frac{8\pi\varepsilon_0 R}{Q} = 8\pi\varepsilon_0 R$$

57. **(C)** Since the magnetic force is always perpendicular to the object's velocity, it does zero work on any charged particle. Zero work means zero change in kinetic energy, so the speed remains the same. Remember: The magnetic force can only change the direction of a charged particle's velocity, not its speed.

58. **(B)** The presence of the inductor in the branch containing R_2 effectively removes R_2 from the circuit at time $t = 0$ (the inductor produces a large back emf when the switch is closed and the current jumps abruptly). Initially, then, current only flows in the loop containing the resistors r and R_1. Since their total resistance is $r + R_1$, the initial current is $\mathcal{E}/(r + R_1)$.

59. **(C)** After a long time, the current through the branch containing the inductor and R_2 increases to its maximum value. With all three resistors in play, the total resistance is

$$R = r + \frac{R_1 R_2}{R_1 + R_2} = \frac{r(R_1 + R_2) + R_1 R_2}{R_1 + R_2}$$

The current provided by the source, $\mathcal{E}/R$, splits at the junction leading to the parallel combination containing R_1 and R_2. The amount which flows through R_2 (and the inductor) is

$$I_2 = \frac{R_1}{R_1 + R_2} \cdot \frac{\mathcal{E}}{R}$$

so the energy stored in the inductor is

$$U_B = \frac{LI_2^2}{2} = \frac{L}{2} \left[\frac{R_1}{R_1 + R_2} \cdot \frac{\mathcal{E}(R_1 + R_2)}{r(R_1 + R_2) + R_1 R_2} \right]^2 = \frac{L(\mathcal{E}R_1)^2}{2[r(R_1 + R_2) + R_1 R_2]^2}$$

60. **(A)** Once the switch is opened, the resistor r is cut off from the circuit, so no current passes through it. (Current *will* flow around the loop containing R_1 and R_2, gradually decreasing until the energy stored in the inductor is exhausted.)

61. **(C)** If a conducting sphere contains a charge of $+q$ within an inner cavity, a charge of $-q$ will move to the wall of the cavity to "guard" the interior of the sphere from an electrostatic field, regardless of the size, shape, or location of the cavity. As a result, a charge of $+q$ is left on the exterior of the sphere (and it will be uniform). So at points outside the sphere, the sphere behaves as if this charge $+q$ were concentrated at its center, so the electric field outside is simply kQ/r^2. Since points X and Y are at the same distance from the center of the sphere, the electric field strength at Y will be the same as at X.

62. **(A)** The work done by the electric field on the eighth charge is equal and opposite to the change in electrical potential energy of this charge as it is brought into place; that is, $W_E = -\Delta U_E$. We find ΔU_E from the equation $\Delta U_E = qV$, where V is the potential at the final location of the eighth charge (remember that we take $V = 0$ at ∞). The potential at the vacant corner is equal to the sum $\Sigma_i\, kQ_i/r_i$, where Q_i is the charge at corner i and r_i is the distance from corner i to the vacant corner. If we number the corners as in the diagram below,

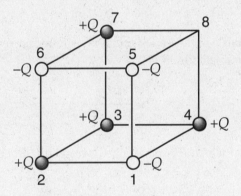

then corners 4, 5, and 7 are each at distance x from corner 8; corners 1, 3, and 6 are each at distance $x\sqrt{2}$; and corner 2 is at distance $x\sqrt{3}$. Notice that the terms involving r_4 and r_5 cancel, and those involving r_1 and r_3 cancel in the sum:

$$V_8 = k\sum_i \frac{Q_i}{r_i}$$

$$= k\left(\frac{-Q}{r_1} + \frac{Q}{r_2} + \frac{Q}{r_3} + \frac{Q}{r_4} + \frac{-Q}{r_5} + \frac{-Q}{r_6} + \frac{Q}{r_7}\right)$$

$$= k\left(\frac{Q}{r_2} + \frac{-Q}{r_6} + \frac{Q}{r_7}\right)$$

$$= \frac{kQ}{x}\left(\frac{1}{\sqrt{3}} - \frac{1}{\sqrt{2}} + 1\right)$$

$$= \frac{Q}{4\pi\varepsilon_0 x}\left(1 - \frac{1}{\sqrt{2}} + \frac{1}{\sqrt{3}}\right)$$

Therefore,

$$W_E = -qV = -(-Q)V = \frac{Q^2}{4\pi\varepsilon_0 x}\left(1 - \frac{1}{\sqrt{2}} + \frac{1}{\sqrt{3}}\right)$$

63. **(E)** The current in an L–R series circuit—in which initially no current flows—increases with time t according to the equation

$$I(t) = I_{max}(1 - e^{-t/\tau})$$

where $I_{max} = \mathcal{E}/R$ and τ is the inductive time constant, L/R. The time t at which $I = (99\%)I_{max}$ is found as follows:

$$1 - e^{-t/\tau} = \frac{99}{100}$$
$$e^{-t/\tau} = \frac{1}{100}$$
$$-t/\tau = \ln\frac{1}{100}$$
$$t = (-\ln\frac{1}{100})\tau = (\ln 100)\tau = (\ln 100)L/R$$

64. **(B)** Since the total resistance in this series circuit is $r + R$, the current through R is $I = \mathcal{E}/(r + R)$. Therefore, the power dissipated by R is

$$P = \frac{\mathcal{E}^2 R}{(r + R)^2}$$

To find the value of R at which P is maximized, we set dP/dR equal to zero and solve:

$$\frac{dP}{dR} = \frac{(r+R)^2\mathcal{E}^2 - \mathcal{E}^2 R \cdot 2(r+R)}{(r+R)^4} = 0$$
$$(r+R)^2\mathcal{E}^2 - \mathcal{E}^2 R \cdot 2(r+R) = 0$$
$$\mathcal{E}^2(r+R)[(r+R) - 2R] = 0$$
$$R = r$$

Therefore, maximum power dissipation occurs when R equals r. For this value of R, the power dissipated by R is

$$P_{max} = \frac{\mathcal{E}^2 r}{(r+r)^2} = \frac{\mathcal{E}^2}{4r}$$

65. **(D)** Since the magnetic flux out of the page is decreasing, the induced current will oppose this change (as always), attempting to create more magnetic flux out of the page. In order to do this, the current must circulate in the counterclockwise direction (remember the right-hand rule). As B decreases *uniformly* (that is, while dB/dt is negative and *constant*), the induced emf,

$$\mathcal{E} = -\frac{\Delta\Phi_B}{\Delta t} = -A\frac{\Delta B}{\Delta t}$$

is nonzero and constant, which implies that the induced current, $I = \mathcal{E}/R$, is also nonzero and constant.

66. **(D)** The easiest way to answer this question is to notice that if $z = d$, then the expression for the capacitance must be equal to $K\varepsilon_0 A/d$. Only the expression in choice D satisfies this.

To obtain the result directly, one way to proceed is to treat the given configuration as three capacitors stacked on top of each other in series. The top capacitor has capacitance $C_1 = \varepsilon_0 A/z_1$ (where z_1 is the thickness of the top "slab" of vacuum), the middle capacitor has capacitance $C_2 = K\varepsilon_0 A/z$, and the bottom capacitor has capacitance $C_3 = \varepsilon_0 A/z_2$ (where z_2 is the thickness of the bottom "slab" of vacuum). Notice that $z_1 + z_2 = d - z$. The total capacitance, C, satisfies

$$\frac{1}{C} = \frac{1}{C_1} + \frac{1}{C_2} + \frac{1}{C_3}$$

$$= \frac{z_1}{\varepsilon_0 A} + \frac{z}{K\varepsilon_0 A} + \frac{z_2}{\varepsilon_0 A}$$

$$= \frac{1}{\varepsilon_0 A}\left(z_1 + \frac{z}{K} + z_2\right)$$

$$= \frac{1}{\varepsilon_0 A}\left(d - z + \frac{z}{K}\right)$$

$$= \frac{d - z\left(1 - \frac{1}{K}\right)}{\varepsilon_0 A}$$

$$C = \frac{\varepsilon_0 A}{d - z\left(1 - \frac{1}{K}\right)}$$

67. **(A)** The potential is zero at the point midway between the charges, but nowhere is the electric field equal to zero.

68. **(D)** Ampere's Law states that

$$\oint \mathbf{B} \cdot d\boldsymbol{\ell} = \mu_0 I_{\text{net through loop}}$$

Because a total current of $2I + 4I = 6I$ passes through the interior of the loop in one direction, and a total current of $I + 3I = 4I$ passes through in the opposite direction, the net current passing through the loop is $6I - 4I = 2I$. Therefore, the absolute value of the integral of **B** around the loop WXYZ is equal to $\mu_0(2I)$.

69. **(A)** Statement I is true: Since the line ℓ is the perpendicular bisector of the line segment joining the two charges, every point on ℓ is equidistant from the two charges. Therefore, the electric potential at *any* point on this line is

$$k(+Q)/r + k(-Q)/r = 0$$

so ℓ is an equipotential. By definition, then, a charge moving along ℓ would experience no change in electrical potential energy. Statement II is false: The individual field vectors created by each source charge do not point in opposite directions at any point on ℓ, so at no point on

ℓ would the total electric field be zero, immediately implying that at no point on ℓ would the electrostatic force on a charge be zero. Statement III is also false: The equipotentials in the plane of the page are not ellipses with the source charges as foci. In fact, as we showed in the discussion of Statement I, the line ℓ itself is an equipotential (and it's not an ellipse!).

70. **(A)** First notice that the distance between $-q$ and each charge $+Q$ is $\frac{1}{\sqrt{2}}L$. Now refer to the following diagram, where we've invoked Coulomb's Law to determine the two electrostatic forces:

We find that

The magnitude of **F** is

$$F = \frac{kQq}{(\frac{1}{\sqrt{2}}L)^2}\sqrt{1^2+1^2} = k\frac{2\sqrt{2}\cdot Qq}{L^2} = \frac{1}{4\pi\varepsilon_0}\frac{2\sqrt{2}\cdot Qq}{L^2} = \frac{\sqrt{2}\cdot Qq}{2\pi\varepsilon_0 L^2}$$

so dividing this by m gives the initial acceleration of the charge $-q$.

SECTION II, MECHANICS

1. **(a)** Since the pulley is not accelerating, it can serve as the origin of an inertial reference frame. Applying Newton's Second Law to the masses using the following free-body diagrams,

gives

$$F_T - mg = ma \quad \text{and} \quad Mg - F_T = Ma$$

Adding these equations eliminates F_T, and we find that

$$Mg - mg = (m + M)a \quad \Rightarrow \quad a = \frac{M - m}{M + m}g$$

The acceleration of block m is $(M - m)g/(M + m)$ upward, and the acceleration of block M is this value, $(M - m)g/(M + m)$, downward.

(a) (ii) Substitute the value for a into either one of the equations containing F_T:

$$F_T = mg + ma = mg + m \cdot \frac{M - m}{M + m}g = \frac{2Mmg}{M + m}$$

(b) (i) Because the center of the pulley is accelerating, it cannot serve as an inertial reference frame. Inertial frames are non-accelerating.

(b) (ii) Refer to the following diagram:

Since the second time derivative of displacement is acceleration,

$$F_T - mg = m\ddot{Y}_m$$
$$Mg - F_T = M\ddot{Y}_M$$

Now since $Y_m = z + y_m$ and $Y_M = z + y_M$, it is also true that

$$\ddot{Y}_m = \ddot{z} + \ddot{y}_m \quad \text{and} \quad \ddot{Y}_M = \ddot{z} + \ddot{y}_M$$

Because our positive direction is *up* for m and *down* for M, and $\ddot{z}$ is equal to b downward,

$$\ddot{Y}_m = -b + \ddot{y}_m \qquad \text{and} \qquad \ddot{Y}_M = b + \ddot{y}_M$$

Therefore,

$$F_T - mg = m(-b + \ddot{y}_m) \quad \Rightarrow \quad F_T - m(g-b) = m\ddot{y}_m$$
$$Mg - F_T = M(b + \ddot{y}_M) \quad \Rightarrow \quad M(g-b) - F_T = M\ddot{y}_M$$

Adding these equations (and remembering that $\ddot{y}_m = \ddot{y}_M$), we find that

$$M(g-b) - m(g-b) = (M+m)\ddot{y}$$
$$\ddot{y} = a = \frac{M-m}{M+m}(g-b)$$

(b) (iii) Substitute the value for a into either one of the equations containing F_T:

$$F_T - m(g-b) = m\left[\frac{M-m}{M+m}(g-b)\right]$$
$$F_T = m(g-b)\left[1 + \frac{M-m}{M+m}\right]$$
$$= \frac{2Mm}{M+m}(g-b)$$

(b) (iv) F_T will equal zero if $b = g$.

2. **(a)** The mass contained in a sphere of radius $r < R$ is

$$M_{\text{within } r} = \rho V_{\text{within } r} = \frac{M}{\frac{4}{3}\pi R^3}\left(\tfrac{4}{3}\pi r^3\right) = \frac{r^3}{R^3}M$$

so

$$F = -\frac{Gm}{r^2}\left(\frac{r^3}{R^3}M\right) = -\frac{GMm}{R^3}r$$

(b) Since $dU = -F(r)\,dr$,

$$\Delta U\big|_R^r = \int_R^r dU = \int_R^r -F(r)\,dr = \int_R^r \frac{GMm}{R^3}r\,dr = \frac{GMm}{R^3}\left[\tfrac{1}{2}r^2\right]_R^r = \frac{GMm}{2R^3}(r^2 - R^2)$$

(c) Conservation of energy, $K_i + U_i = K_f + U_f$, can be written in the form $\Delta K = -\Delta U$, which gives

$$\tfrac{1}{2}mv^2 = -\frac{GMm}{2R^3}(r^2 - R^2)$$

$$v = \sqrt{\frac{GM}{R^3}(R^2 - r^2)}$$

By applying the Pythagorean theorem to the two right triangles in the figure,

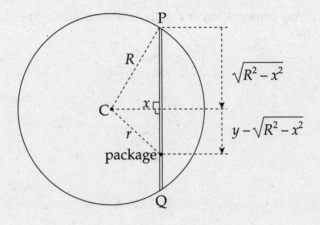

we see that

$$r^2 = x^2 + \left(y - \sqrt{R^2 - x^2}\right)^2$$

so the expression given above for v can be rewritten in the form

$$v = \sqrt{\frac{GM}{R^3}\left[R^2 - x^2 - \left(y - \sqrt{R^2 - x^2}\right)^2\right]} \quad (*)$$

$$= \sqrt{\frac{GM}{R^3}\left[2y\sqrt{R^2 - x^2} - y^2\right]}$$

(d) (i) From expression (*) given in part (c) above, we can see that the value of y which will maximize v is

$$y = \sqrt{R^2 - x^2}$$

This is the midpoint of the tunnel.

(d) (ii) The maximum value for v is

$$v_{max} = \sqrt{\frac{GM}{R^3}\left[R^2 - x^2\right]}$$

3. **(a) (i)** Once the $3m$ puck sticks to the m puck, the center of mass of the system is

$$y_{cm} = \frac{(m+3m)(0)+(2m)(L)}{(m+3m)+2m} = \tfrac{1}{3}L$$

above the bottom pucks on the rod.

(a) (ii) Applying conservation of linear momentum, we find that

$$(3m)\mathbf{v} = (3m+m+2m)\mathbf{v}'_{cm} \quad \Rightarrow \quad \mathbf{v}'_{cm} = \tfrac{1}{2}\mathbf{v}$$

(a) (iii) Now applying conservation of angular momentum, we find that

$$L_i = L_f$$
$$L_i = I_f \omega_f$$
$$\omega_f = \frac{L_i}{I_f}$$
$$= \frac{(\tfrac{1}{3}L)(3m)v}{\left[(m+3m)(\tfrac{1}{3}L)^2 + (2m)(\tfrac{2}{3}L)^2\right]}$$
$$= \frac{3v}{4L} \text{ (clockwise)}$$

(b) The kinetic energy before the collision was the initial translational kinetic energy of the $3m$ puck:

$$K_i = \tfrac{1}{2}(3m)v^2$$

After the collision, the total kinetic energy is the sum of the system's translational kinetic energy and its rotational kinetic energy:

$$K' = K'_{translational} + K'_{rotational}$$
$$= \tfrac{1}{2}Mv_{cm}^2 + \tfrac{1}{2}I\omega^2$$
$$= \tfrac{1}{2}(3m+m+2m)(\tfrac{1}{2}v)^2 + \tfrac{1}{2}\left[(3m+m)(\tfrac{1}{3}L)^2 + (2m)(\tfrac{2}{3}L)^2\right]\left(\tfrac{3v}{4L}\right)^2$$
$$= \tfrac{9}{8}mv^2$$

Therefore, the fraction of the initial kinetic energy that is lost due to the collision is

$$\frac{K-K'}{K} = \frac{\tfrac{3}{2}mv^2 - \tfrac{9}{8}mv^2}{\tfrac{3}{2}mv^2} = \tfrac{1}{4}$$

SECTION II, ELECTRICITY AND MAGNETISM

1. (a) Consider a small arc on the ring, subtended by an angle $d\theta$. The length of the arc is $ds = R\,d\theta$, so the charge it carries is $dQ = (Q/2\pi R)(R\,d\theta) = (Q/2\pi)\,d\theta$, since $\lambda = Q/(2\pi R)$ is the linear charge density.

The distance from this arc to an arbitrary point P on the z axis is $(z^2 + R^2)^{1/2}$, so the contribution to the electric potential at P due to this arc is

$$dV = \frac{1}{4\pi\varepsilon_0}\frac{dQ}{r} = \frac{Q\,d\theta}{8\pi^2\varepsilon_0(z^2 + R^2)^{1/2}}$$

Integrating this from $\theta = 0$ to $\theta = 2\pi$ (i.e., all the way around the ring), we find that

$$V = \int_0^{2\pi}\frac{Q\,d\theta}{8\pi^2\varepsilon_0(z^2 + R^2)^{1/2}} = \frac{Q}{8\pi^2\varepsilon_0(z^2 + R^2)^{1/2}}\cdot 2\pi = \frac{Q}{4\pi\varepsilon_0(z^2 + R^2)^{1/2}}$$

(b) (i) From the expression derived in part (a), we see that V will be maximized when $z = 0$. That is, the point on the z axis where the potential due to the ring is greatest is at the center of the ring.

(b) (ii) Putting $z = 0$ into the expression from part (a), we find that

$$V_{max} = \frac{Q}{4\pi\varepsilon_0(0^2 + R^2)^{1/2}} = \frac{Q}{4\pi\varepsilon_0 R}$$

(c) The easiest way to obtain an expression for the electric field is to use the relationship $E(z) = -dV/dz$:

$$E = -\frac{dV}{dz} = -\frac{d}{dz}\left[\frac{Q}{4\pi\varepsilon_0(z^2 + R^2)^{1/2}}\right]$$

$$= -\frac{Q}{4\pi\varepsilon_0} \cdot \frac{d}{dz}(z^2 + R^2)^{-1/2}$$

$$= -\frac{Q}{4\pi\varepsilon_0}\left[-\tfrac{1}{2}(z^2 + R^2)^{-3/2} \cdot 2z\right]$$

$$= \frac{Qz}{4\pi\varepsilon_0(z^2 + R^2)^{3/2}}$$

To include the direction—and thereby find **E**—let's use $\hat{\mathbf{k}}$ to denote the unit vector that defines the positive direction along the z axis. Then

$$\mathbf{E} = \frac{Qz}{4\pi\varepsilon_0(z^2 + R^2)^{3/2}}\hat{\mathbf{k}}$$

(d) (i) To maximize E, we set dE/dz equal to zero and solve for z:

$$\frac{dE}{dz} = \frac{Q}{4\pi\varepsilon_0} \cdot \frac{d}{dz}\left[\frac{z}{(z^2 + R^2)^{3/2}}\right] = \frac{Q}{4\pi\varepsilon_0} \cdot \frac{(z^2 + R^2)^{3/2} - z \cdot \frac{3}{2}(z^2 + R^2)^{1/2} \cdot 2z}{(z^2 + R^2)^3} \overset{\text{set}}{=} 0$$

This gives

$$(z^2 + R^2)^{3/2} - z \cdot \tfrac{3}{2}(z^2 + R^2)^{1/2} \cdot 2z = 0$$
$$(z^2 + R^2)^{1/2}[(z^2 + R^2) - 3z^2] = 0$$
$$(z^2 + R^2) - 3z^2 = 0$$
$$z = \pm\frac{1}{\sqrt{2}}R$$

[Note: To verify that these values of z do indeed maximize E, we could check that the value of d^2E/dz^2 is negative at these points, or simply notice that on physical grounds, any extremum must be a maximum because $E = 0$ at $z = 0$ and $z = \pm\infty$, so $E(z)$ must rise then fall back to zero.]

(d) (ii) At either of the two points found above, the value of E is

$$E_{\text{max}} = \frac{Q \cdot \frac{1}{\sqrt{2}}R}{4\pi\varepsilon_0\left[(\frac{1}{\sqrt{2}}R)^2 + R^2\right]^{3/2}} = \frac{Q}{4\pi\varepsilon_0} \cdot \frac{\frac{1}{\sqrt{2}}R}{(\frac{3}{2})^{3/2}R^3} = \frac{Q}{6\sqrt{3}\pi\varepsilon_0 R^2}$$

(e) The change in kinetic energy of the particle is equal to the work done by the electric field, which is equal to $(-q)\Delta V$. Using the expression for V derived in part (a), we find that

$$\tfrac{1}{2}mv^2 = (-q)\Delta V$$

$$= (-q)\left[\frac{Q}{4\pi\varepsilon_0(A^2+R^2)^{1/2}} - \frac{Q}{4\pi\varepsilon_0(0^2+R^2)^{1/2}}\right]$$

$$= \frac{qQ}{4\pi\varepsilon_0}\left[\frac{1}{R} - \frac{1}{(A^2+R^2)^{1/2}}\right]$$

$$= \frac{qQ}{4\pi\varepsilon_0}\left[\frac{1}{R} - \frac{1}{\left[R^2\left(1+\frac{A^2}{R^2}\right)\right]^{1/2}}\right]$$

$$= \frac{qQ}{4\pi\varepsilon_0 R}\left[1 - \left(1+\frac{A^2}{R^2}\right)^{-1/2}\right]$$

$$\approx \frac{qQ}{4\pi\varepsilon_0 R}\left[1 - \left(1-\frac{A^2}{2R^2}\right)\right]$$

$$= \frac{qQA^2}{8\pi\varepsilon_0 R^3}$$

$$v = A\sqrt{\frac{qQ}{4\pi\varepsilon_0 R^3 m}}$$

(f) In simple harmonic motion, the position of an oscillator with amplitude A is given by the equation $z = A\sin(t\omega + \phi_0)$, where ω is the angular frequency. Differentiating $z(t)$ with respect to time, we get the velocity: $v = A\omega\cos(\omega t + \phi_0)$, which implies that the maximum speed is $A\omega$. The speed computed in part (e) is the maximum speed of the oscillator as it passes through the equilibrium position ($z = 0$, where $F = 0$), so

$$A\omega = v_{max}$$

$$= A\sqrt{\frac{qQ}{4\pi\varepsilon_0 R^3 m}}$$

$$\omega = \sqrt{\frac{qQ}{4\pi\varepsilon_0 R^3 m}}$$

$$f = \frac{1}{2\pi}\sqrt{\frac{qQ}{4\pi\varepsilon_0 R^3 m}}$$

2. (a) (i) The current decays exponentially according to the equation

$$I(t) = \frac{\varepsilon}{r+R}e^{-t/(r+R)C}$$

where the initial cu rrent, $I(0)$, is equal to $\mathcal{E}/(r+R)$. To find the time t at which $I(t) = I(0)/k$, we solve the following equation:

$$\frac{\mathcal{E}}{r+R}e^{-t/(r+R)C} = \frac{1}{k} \cdot \frac{\mathcal{E}}{r+R}$$

$$e^{-t/(r+R)C} = \frac{1}{k}$$

$$-\frac{t}{(r+R)C} = \ln\frac{1}{k}$$

$$-\frac{t}{(r+R)C} = -\ln k$$

$$t = (\ln k)(r+R)C$$

(a) (ii) The charge on the capacitor increases according to the equation

$$Q(t) = C\mathcal{E}\left[1 - e^{-t/(r+R)C}\right]$$

The maximum value is $C\mathcal{E}$ (when the capacitor is fully charged). To find the time t at which $Q(t) = C\mathcal{E}/k$, we solve the following equation:

$$C\mathcal{E}\left[1 - e^{-t/(r+R)C}\right] = \frac{1}{k}C\mathcal{E}$$

$$1 - e^{-t/(r+R)C} = \frac{1}{k}$$

$$e^{-t/(r+R)C} = 1 - \frac{1}{k}$$

$$-\frac{t}{(r+R)C} = \ln\frac{k-1}{k}$$

$$\frac{t}{(r+R)C} = \ln\frac{k}{k-1}$$

$$t = (\ln\frac{k}{k-1})(r+R)C$$

(a) (iii) The field energy stored in the capacitor can be written in the form $U_E(t) = [Q(t)]^2/(2C)$, where $Q(t)$ is the function of time given in part (ii) above. We are asked to find the time t at which

$$U(t) = \frac{1}{k}U_{max}$$

$$\frac{[Q(t)]^2}{2C} = \frac{1}{k} \cdot \frac{(C\mathcal{E})^2}{2C}$$

$$\left\{C\mathcal{E}\left[1 - e^{-t/(r+R)C}\right]\right\}^2 = \frac{1}{k}(C\mathcal{E})^2$$

$$1 - e^{-t/(r+R)C} = \frac{1}{\sqrt{k}}$$

$$e^{-t/(r+R)C} = 1 - \frac{1}{\sqrt{k}}$$

$$-\frac{t}{(r+R)C} = \ln\frac{\sqrt{k}-1}{\sqrt{k}}$$

$$\frac{t}{(r+R)C} = \ln\frac{\sqrt{k}}{\sqrt{k}-1}$$

$$t = \left(\ln\frac{\sqrt{k}}{\sqrt{k}-1}\right)(r+R)C$$

(b) (i) Once the switch is turned to position 2, the capacitor discharges through resistor R (only). Since the capacitor is fully charged (to $V = \mathcal{E}$) when the switch is moved to position 2, the current will decrease exponentially according to the equation

$$I(t) = I_0 e^{-t/RC}$$

where $I_0 = I_{max} = \mathcal{E}/R$. To find the time at which I is equal to I_0/k, we solve the following equation:

$$I_0 e^{-t/RC} = \tfrac{1}{k} I_0$$
$$e^{-t/RC} = \tfrac{1}{k}$$
$$-\frac{t}{RC} = \ln \tfrac{1}{k}$$
$$\frac{t}{RC} = \ln k$$
$$t = (\ln k)RC$$

(b) (ii) Since the charge on the capacitor obeys the same equation as the current—as given in (b) (i) above, simply replacing I by Q—the time t at which the charge drops to $1/k$ its initial value is the same as the time t at which the current drops to $1/k$ times its initial value: $t = (\ln k)RC$.

3. **(a) (i)** As the strip XY slides down the rails, the magnetic flux through the rectangular region bounded by the strip increases. This change in magnetic flux induces an emf. If ℓ denotes the distance the strip has slid down the rails, then the magnetic flux through the rectangular region is

$$\Phi_B = BA \cos \theta = BL\ell \cos \theta$$

The rate of change of Φ_B is

$$\frac{d\Phi_B}{dt} = \frac{d}{dt}(BL\ell \cos \theta) = BL \cos \theta \frac{d\ell}{dt} = BL \cos \theta \cdot v$$

where $v = d\ell/dt$ is the speed with which the strip slides. By Faraday's Law, this is the (magnitude of the) induced emf.

(a) (ii) As the strip slides down, the area increases, so the magnetic flux upward increases. To oppose this change (in accordance with Lenz's Law), the induced current must flow in such a way as to create some magnetic flux downward. By the right-hand rule, then, current must flow from Y to X.

(a) (iii) The induced current depends on the speed of the sliding strip and is equal to

$$I = \frac{\mathcal{E}}{R} = \frac{BL \cos \theta \cdot v}{R}$$

(b) In order for the strip to slide with constant velocity, the net force on it must be zero. The force it feels parallel to the rails and downward is $F_w \sin \theta = mg \sin \theta$. The following diagram

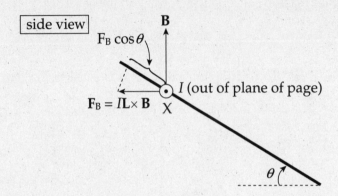

which is a side view of the apparatus looking at the X end of the strip, shows that the force the strip feels parallel to the rails and upward is

$$F_B \cos\theta = ILB\cos\theta = \frac{BL\cos\theta \cdot v}{R} LB\cos\theta = \frac{B^2 L^2 v \cos^2\theta}{R}$$

The net force on the strip is zero when these two opposing forces balance; the speed at which this occurs will be denoted v_f:

$$\frac{B^2 L^2 v_f \cos^2\theta}{R} = mg\sin\theta$$

$$v_f = \frac{mgR\sin\theta}{B^2 L^2 \cos^2\theta}$$

(c) The rate at which thermal energy is produced in the strip is $I^2 R$. When $v = v_f$, this is equal to

$$
\begin{aligned}
P_{\text{dissipated by strip}} &= I^2 R \\
&= \left(\frac{BL\cos\theta}{R} \cdot v_f \right)^2 R \\
&= \left(\frac{BL\cos\theta}{R} \cdot \frac{mgR\sin\theta}{B^2 L^2 \cos^2\theta} \right)^2 R \\
&= \frac{m^2 g^2 R \sin^2\theta}{B^2 L^2 \cos^2\theta} \\
&= \frac{mgR\sin\theta}{B^2 L^2 \cos^2\theta} \cdot mg\sin\theta \\
&= v_f \cdot mg\sin\theta \\
&= v_f \cdot (F_w \sin\theta) \\
&= \text{rate at which gravity does work on strip}
\end{aligned}
$$

where the last equality follows from the formula $P = Fv$ for the power produced by a constant force **F** acting on an object whose velocity, **v**, is parallel to **F**.

ABOUT THE AUTHOR

Steve Leduc has been teaching at the university level since the age of 19, earned his Sc.B. in Theoretical Mathematics from MIT at 20 and his M.A. in Mathematics from UCSD at 22. After his graduate studies, Steve co-founded Hyperlearning, Inc., an educational services company that provided supplemental courses in undergraduate math and science for students from the University of California, where he lectured on seventeen different courses in mathematics and physics. He's published two math books, *Differential Equations* in 1995 and *Linear Algebra* in 1996. Through Hyperlearning, he has directed the creation and administration of the most successful preparation course for the medical school entrance exam (the MCAT) in California, where he has taught physics to thousands of pre-meds. Hyperlearning merged with The Princeton Review in 1996, and Steve now holds the position of National Director of Research & Development for Hyperlearning, the Medical Division of The Princeton Review. He currently owns six to the fourth power CDs and has seen *Monty Python and The Holy Grail*, *Star Trek II: The Wrath of Khan*, and *Blade Runner* about six to the fourth power times.

—*Paul Kanarek*

www.review.com

Expert Advice

Talk About It

www.review.com

Pop Surveys

Paying for it

www.review.com

THE
PRINCETON
REVIEW

www.review.com

Getting in

Word du Jour

www.review.com

Find-O-Rama School & Career Search

www.review.com

Best Schools

Finding it

www.review.com

FIND US...

International

Hong Kong
4/F Sun Hung Kai Centre
30 Harbour Road, Wan Chai,
Hong Kong
Tel: (011)85-2-517-3016

Japan
Fuji Building 40, 15-14
Sakuragaokacho, Shibuya Ku,
Tokyo 150, Japan
Tel: (011)81-3-3463-1343

Korea
Tae Young Bldg, 944-24,
Daechi- Dong, Kangnam-Ku
The Princeton Review- ANC
Seoul, Korea 135-280,
South Korea
Tel: (011)82-2-554-7763

Mexico City
PR Mex S De RL De Cv
Guanajuato 228 Col. Roma
06700 Mexico D.F., Mexico
Tel: 525-564-9468

Montreal
666 Sherbrooke St.
West, Suite 202
Montreal, QC H3A 1E7 Canada
Tel: (514) 499-0870

Pakistan
1 Bawa Park - 90 Upper Mall
Lahore, Pakistan
Tel: (011)92-42-571-2315

Spain
Pza. Castilla, 3 - 5º A, 28046
Madrid, Spain
Tel: (011)341-323-4212

Taiwan
155 Chung Hsiao East Road
Section 4 - 4th Floor,
Taipei R.O.C., Taiwan
Tel: (011)886-2-751-1243

Thailand
Building One, 99 Wireless Road
Bangkok, Thailand 10330
Tel: (662) 256-7080

Toronto
1240 Bay Street, Suite 300
Toronto M5R 2A7 Canada
Tel: (800) 495-7737
Tel: (716) 839-4391

Vancouver
4212 University Way NE,
Suite 204
Seattle, WA 98105
Tel: (206) 548-1100

locations

National (U.S.)

We have over 60 offices around the U.S. and run courses in over 400 sites. For courses and locations within the U.S. call 1 (800) 2/Review and you will be routed to the nearest office.